THE FINAL ASSASSINATIONS REPORT

REPORT OF THE SELECT COMMITTEE ON ASSASSINATIONS U.S. HOUSE OF REPRESENTATIVES

Foreword by Tom Wicker
Associate Editor of
THE NEW YORK TIMES

Introduction by G. Robert Blakey
Chief Counsel and Staff Director

THE FINAL ASSASSINATIONS REPORT
REPORT OF THE SELECT COMMITTEE ON ASSASSINATIONS
U. S. HOUSE OF REPRESENTATIVES
A Bantam Book / July 1979

Bantam Books are published by Bantam Books, Inc. Its trade-
mark, consisting of the words "Bantam Books" and the por-
trayal of a bantam, is Registered in U.S. Patent and Trademark
Office and in other countries. Marca Registrada. Bantam
Books, Inc., 666 Fifth Avenue, New York, New York 10019.

NOW,
AFTER FIFTEEN YEARS
OF PUBLIC DOUBT,
PUBLIC CONTROVERSY
AND PUBLIC CLAMOR,
THE GOVERNMENT HAS RESPONDED.

The assassination of John F. Kennedy on November 22, 1963, has been the single most shattering event of our recent lifetimes; its reverberations are still with us. Fifteen years after the publication of the Warren Commission Report (which was Bantam's first venture into instant publishing), a large portion of the American public still questions the judgment that President Kennedy was killed by a single assassin who acted alone. Because of this public doubt, a special House select committee spent 2½ years and over $5 million investigating the deaths of JFK and Martin Luther King, Jr. The task of the committee was to conduct two murder investigations, to present both cases to a public "jury" in a responsible trial atmosphere and, finally, to make recommendations. This book contains its main report. We think the committee's work is of great significance; we are pleased to publish it now as our 66th Bantam Extra and, in response to the public interest, to make it immediately available together with a 64-page insert illustrating key committee exhibits, many never before publicly released, and exclusive introductory material by Tom Wicker of the *New York Times* and by the committee's chief counsel, G. Robert Blakey.

The Publisher

CONTENTS

FOREWORD

I was in the press bus following President Kennedy's car when he was shot to death in Dallas on November 22, 1963. But we were far back in the motorcade—not the best place to learn what had happened. Most reporters on the scene that day had to piece things together from sketchy reports, hasty medical briefings, and what little they might have seen for themselves.

But even in such uncertain circumstances, from the moment the president's car sped out of Dealey Plaza through the Triple Underpass to Parkland Hospital, the possibility of conspiracy arose in every mind. The new president, Lyndon B. Johnson, was said to have insisted on being sworn in while still in Dallas, on the chance that the assassination might have been the work of a foreign nation intent on launching war during the resulting confusion.

Two days later, Jack Ruby—a man with underworld connections—silenced Lee Harvey Oswald forever, and conspiracy theories bloomed like evil flowers. Until it was learned that Oswald had a vaguely leftist background, the most frequent assumption was that Kennedy had been murdered by the "right wing," of which Dallas, at the time, was the acknowledged capital.

Adlai Stevenson, only shortly before, had received rough treatment from a Dallas crowd; Johnson and his wife had been pushed around and spit on during a campaign appearance there in 1960. Kennedy had been urged by some of his associates not to visit Dallas, but he took the attitude that an American president could not refuse to go to any American city for fear of violence.

Oswald's political coloration shifted most speculation toward some kind of "Communist conspiracy." European reporters, arriving in Dallas in droves, brought with them all kinds of historically conditioned assumptions that the murder must have had political origins. Nor was it hard to detect an undercurrent of suspicion that Lyndon Johnson himself, or maybe the Texas millionaires who were assumed to control him, had been responsible. The deed had been done in Dallas, after all, and who stood to gain the most from it?

It was to lay such doubts to rest and get the true story (or, some said then and still think, *any* plausible explanation that exonerated him) published before the 1964 elections, if possible, that Johnson created the Warren Commission and personally bluffed and browbeat a reluctant Chief Justice Earl Warren into heading it.

The Warren Commission's thesis that Oswald had acted alone—hence, no conspiracy—was widely greeted with relief and praise. But it did not for a moment silence the conspiracy theorists, who almost immediately began pointing to discrepancies in the Commission's evidence and conclusion. The Commission had scarcely taken itself out of existence before hot-eyed assassination buffs began to consider *it* part of the conspiracy, or at least part of the cover-up of the conspiracy.

Over the ensuing years, conspiracy theories have continued to flourish, supported by investigators ranging from the bizarre to the scholarly. Perhaps the most persistent suggestions have been that Castro ordered "the hit"—or else that anti-Castro Cubans did. Others believe the CIA was involved. The Mafia, the FBI, Vietnamese avenging the death of Ngo Dinh Diem—all have come under suspicion. Recent poll figures show that an astonishing 80 percent of the American people believe some form of conspiracy was responsible for Kennedy's murder.

Even I found myself at one point considered a conspirator. Writing in *Times Talk,* the house organ of the *New York Times,* about the experience of covering the assassination, I recalled that the first thing amiss I had personally noticed on November 22, 1963, was a policeman riding his motorcycle up an embankment near the Triple Underpass. But in writing my account of the day's events for the *Times* of November 23, I had not included this minor detail—as I considered it. I was astonished to find this omission later cited as evidence that I had tried that day to conceal the truth from the public!

This unpleasant experience may have tinged my view; but even before that, virtually from the hour of Oswald's arrest, I had been among those who rejected the idea of conspiracy. So I have remained through the years, enduring a good deal of scorn from the most persistent theorists, a breed all too likely to believe that anyone who disagrees with them must be a conspirator himself.

So I was dismayed in 1978 when the House Select Committee on Assassinations said in a preliminary report that John Kennedy was "probably assassinated as a result of a conspiracy." Acoustical evidence from a police motorcycle radio tape, long available but newly analyzed, had convinced a majority of the committee that a second gunman had fired at, although he had not hit, the president; and a second gunman almost certainly meant a conspiracy.

It was less surprising that the committee also found "a likelihood" that a conspiracy had existed in its second area of investigation—the killing in 1968 of the Reverend Dr. Martin Luther King. In that case it concluded that James Earl Ray, acting alone, had committed the murder, as found by the original FBI investigation, but had probably been in touch with people who wanted King dead.

The Kennedy finding obviously is the more sensational, contravening the Warren Commission as it does. My first reaction was that the House committee's acoustical evidence was flimsy stuff that would set off a whole new round of conspiracy theories and witchhunts.

Now that I have the full report in hand and have had a chance to study—if only briefly—its evidence and conclusions on the Kennedy murder, I consider the report reassuring as well as troubling. I am no more persuaded by its central conclusion—the existence of a second gunman—than conspiracy theorists were by the Warren Commission Report; nor was the committee itself anywhere near unanimous on this point. But its painstaking review of the evidence, including some the Warren Commission never saw or discounted if it did, actually puts to rest most of the wilder speculations of the years since 1963.

Thus, the committee reports that, "on the basis of the evidence available to it," the Soviet Union was not involved in the assassination of President Kennedy. On the same basis, neither was the government of Fidel Castro, neither were "anti-Castro Cuban groups, as groups," and neither was "the national syndicate of organized crime, as a group." And there is no hedge at all in the committee's flat declaration that the Secret Service, the FBI, and the CIA "were not involved" in the Kennedy assassination.

That blows away virtually every conspiracy theory of any real consequence, although the committee carefully left open the possibility that evidence not now available to it might someday emerge. The committee also refused to rule out the possibility that *individual* anti-Castro Cubans or participants in organized crime might have been involved. The latter seem to be the preferred, but not proven, culprits, in the majority of view—although in the fine print, they include a discussion of the possibility, again not ruled out, that the conspiracy may have been among Oswald and only one or two left-wing acquaintances. That, the committee concludes, "would not have been fundamentally different from an assassination by Oswald alone."

So what the House select committee gives us with one hand—a second gunman and a conspiracy—it tends to take away with the other. And its report makes a rather convincing case that even if there was a conspiracy, it was almost certainly among small-timers who happened to pull off the biggest hit of all.

All that of course, only focuses more attention on the real question raised by the committee report. *Did* a second gunman fire at Kennedy on that sunlit day in Dallas when for so many Americans their world of certainties began to come apart?

Aside from a certain distaste for persons who try to persuade me that, say, two such different men as Richard Russell of Georgia and Earl Warren were part of a conspiracy to cover up the murder of a president, I have had two strongly held reasons for believing the Warren Commission's theory about John Kennedy's death.

I took the first from a well-known attorney. Shortly after the Commission report appeared, he explained to me that in any criminal case, both the prosecutor and the defense counsel might try to present to the jury a theory of what happened. They weave evidence and testimony into a coherent account they hope a jury will believe. If the prosecutor presents the more believable theory, backed by the most impressive evidence, he is likely to get a conviction. If the defense counsel convinces the jury—or in his case some members of it—that *his* version is more plausible, the defendant probably wins acquittal.

The Warren Commission, the attorney said, had presented what he considered a highly plausible theory of what happened in Dallas on November 22, 1963. Then, in volume after volume, it had presented credible and overwhelming evidence to support its theory. The Commission, in short, had explained what happened and backed up its explanation.

This did not mean, he continued, that the Warren Commission's case was airtight. There were holes in it, discrepancies here and there, a few implausibilities (John Connally, then governor of Texas, still cannot believe that a bullet that struck him had already passed through Kennedy's body), and the more the evidence was studied, the more the experts might be able to raise questions here, doubts there. But *overall*, the Warren Commission had presented the only believable explanation of what had happened on the day of the murder, and of why it had happened.

For his part, the attorney said, as one among the vast jury of the American public, he accepted the Commission's explanation and would until someone gave him *a more believable account*, supported with equally or more impressive evidence. It would not be enough for someone to cite discrepancies in the Commission's case, unless they conclusively destroyed that case; and even then he would require *a plausible alternative explanation* of what had happened.

Such a plausible alternative has never been supplied—certainly not by the zealots, and not in my judgment by the reputable scholars and journalists who have pored so purposefully over ballistics tests, the Zapruder film, the medical reports, and all the other arcana of the Kennedy assassination.

Now the House committee, despite 2½ years of Herculean effort and $5.4 million expended, fails also to offer what I consider the necessary alternative to the Warren Commission thesis. Its evidence suggested to the majority of the committee a "high probability" of a second gunman —of course, a vital difference from the Commission's findings—and therefore a conspiracy. But that evidence could not enable the majority to take the next, crucial, step; it could not "identify the other gunman or the extent of the conspiracy." It could not tell us what happened that day in Dallas, and why, if there was indeed a second gunman.

Even the "evidence" suggesting that gunman's presence—as I read it—rests rather dubiously on an admittedly ingenious series of acoustical reconstructions, the results of which are highly problematical. I do not suggest that these tests were not soundly conceived and honestly performed and evaluated; but they seem to me too heavily dependent on assumptions and interpretations, any one of which, if wrong, might have thrown off the whole. Indeed, Rep. Robert W. Edgar of Pennsylvania, writing in dissent, quotes legal and scientific experts who rejected the acoustical findings *as evidence,* without questioning their value as experiments.

Rep. Richardson Preyer of North Carolina, one of the most respected men in the House and chairman of the committee's Kennedy assassination subcommittee, defended the acoustical evidence at a news conference; he said it was "convincing as a new set of fingerprints on a second rifle." He originally had been skeptical, he said, but in the course of the investigation he concluded that there was "no way to dismiss" the acoustical findings. But Rep. Harold Sawyer of Michigan, another dissenter, said that if the evidence on which the conspiracy finding rests were presented to him for prosecution, "I'd file it in the circular file." He termed the acoustical information "the ultimate in bootstrap evidence."

The acoustical tests were based on a police motorcycle radio tape fifteen years old, the source of which the committee never did finally establish. In order for the tape to have any validity, the report concedes, it would have to have been taken from the radio of a motorcycle that was in Dealey Plaza when the shots rang out. Other sounds on the tape—of sirens and chimes—can hardly be reconciled with that location. Rep. Sawyer said the full committee had never met to resolve the conflicts presented by the sounds of sirens and chimes on the tape.

The testimony of Dallas police officer H. B. McLain, from whose motorcycle radio the committee believed the tape had been taken, contradicted that belief on a crucial point concerning the sound of sirens. The report resolves this contradiction by saying that "the committee believed McLain was in error"—just the sort of thing for which, elsewhere it properly criticizes the Warren Commission.

The committee also attempted to support its acoustical findings by photographic and testimonial evidence. But no photographs of the "grassy knoll" sustain or preclude the idea of a second gunman there. And of 178 persons interviewed who were in Dealey Plaza at the time of the assassination, *only four* claimed to have heard shots from both the grassy knoll and the School Book Depository; yet it is the House committee majority's thesis that three shots were fired from the depository and one from the knoll. Only 11.8 percent of these people believed the shots came from the knoll; 27.5 percent said they came from the depository—testimony, again, that hardly proves anything either way.

In fact, on December 13, 1978, a first draft of the committee report stated that "the available scientific evidence is insufficient to find that there was a conspiracy to assassinate President Kennedy." That was after the committee's first acoustical expert had testified that the evidence of the radio tape offered only a 50 percent chance that a second gunman had fired a shot from the grassy knoll. By December 29, a second team of experts, after further acoustical sleuthing, had told the committee that there was a 95 percent probability that a second gunman had fired his shot and missed.

As a consequence, the 12-member committee switched to the second-gunman and conspiracy theses, only a few days before the committee went out of existence, and with four members—Edgar, Sawyer, Rep. Samuel L. Devine of Ohio, and Rep. Charles Thone of Nebraska—dissenting from these important conclusions. (Rep. Christopher J. Dodd dissented too, but not from the second-gunman thesis.) Both the last-minute turnabout and the divided committee, I think, argue that these major conclusions, however honestly reached, were both hasty and risky. The acoustical evidence might better have been presented as a possibility worth further investigation, without putting the committee's imprimatur on a conspiracy theory, and a unanimous committee would have been a more credible committee.

The House committee had found, moreover, that most of the Warren Commission's major conclusions were unassailable. Perhaps the most consistently disputed by conspiracy theorists has been the Commission finding that a single bullet fired by Oswald struck Kennedy in the back, exited through his throat, passed through John Connally's torso, hit his wrist, and lodged in his thigh. This bullet later was found on a stretcher on which Connally was carried into Parkland Hospital.

The House committee's panel of pathologists, who between them had conducted more than 100,000 autopsies, concluded with only one dissenting voice that this much-disputed "single-bullet theory" was correct. Altogether, the Warren Commission reported three shots were fired—the one that hit both men, one that missed both, and one that struck Kennedy in the back of his skull and killed him. The House committee's pathologists agreed again and corroborated also the Commission's other crucial finding— that all three shots were fired from *behind*.

It may well be wondered then, why the House committee was willing to assert so confidently, on the basis of acoustical speculations alone, that a fourth shot, missing both men, was fired from the grassy knoll by a second gunman—particularly when the committee concedes that there is no physical evidence (such as a spent shell) that such a shot was fired. Nor does the committee profess to know who fired that fourth shot, from what kind of weapon, for what purpose, in collusion with whom—much less what happened to him or her after allegedly firing.

One underpinning the committee sought to give its theory was the assertion that Oswald and Jack Ruby had connections with underworld characters, particularly in New Orleans, who could have masterminded the murder. A considerable web of allegations to that effect is woven. I will leave the reader to weigh these allegations, together with the frequent use of "might have" and "could have" in the text describing them; but I would be willing to take them much more seriously as a cause if more and better evidence had been adduced as to the supposed effect—two gunmen in a conspiracy to murder John Kennedy.

The House committee is severe, and properly so, with the Warren Commission, the FBI, the Secret Service, and the CIA for the original flawed investigations of the Kennedy and King murders. But it cannot be merely assumed that if these agencies had been more effective, they would have discovered a conspiracy; they might have, but they might just as easily have eliminated many of the loopholes and inconsistencies that over the years have fed the conspiracy theorists and shaken public confidence—particularly in the Kennedy case.

As to Martin Luther King, the House committee is less sensational and appears to me to be on sounder ground (although, again, some members dissented from the finding of conspiracy). In particular, the committee makes a devastating case that the FBI, in its reprehensible COINTELPRO campaign to discredit King, may have helped create a climate of hatred that brought about his murder. As Rep. Dodd put it, in a partial dissent from the King conspiracy findings, "The FBI's conduct toward Dr. King not only dishonors that agency, but dishonors each and every one of us."

The most avid public attention, however, will inevitably be centered on the House committee's startling contention that a second gunman was in Dealey Plaza, indicating a conspiracy to kill President Kennedy. In the absence of any explanation whatever of his or her supposed presence and actions, or of what the committee majority believes happened in Dallas, on November 22, 1963, and owing to the considerable doubts I have about the acoustical findings, I decline to accept this latest of so many conspiracy theories.

I do so not least because of the second reason I have always thought that Oswald acted alone when he killed Kennedy (call it a stubborn refusal to face facts, if you insist); its obverse, I believe, is why so many Americans seem to *want* a conspiracy to have been responsible. A lonely, unstable young man, fiercely desiring recognition, bitterly angry at a world that denied it to him; a sudden opportunity to strike at that world by striking at another young man unfairly (as Oswald thought) granted immense recognition, immense power—I believe that is the way things happen. Ours is a world not so much of plans and conspiracies but of chance, circumstance, and individuality, against which not even presidents can be always immune.

But most Americans, it has seemed to me after discussing the Kennedy assassination with many an audience, do not want to believe that. They want John Kennedy to have died for some *reason* of state or politics. They want an explanation that gives more than ordinary meaning to his murder, that equates it somehow with the office he held and the power he dispensed. For many Americans, it is simply not sufficient to the case to be told that a disgruntled loser like Lee Harvey Oswald could strike at a president, particularly at one so shining as John Kennedy.

Presidents, we want to think, are spared such mean deaths, such common fate. But no one can be, when chance and circumstance—more deadly by far than leaders and planners—conspire against them.

Tom Wicker
July 1979

INTRODUCTION

Reports of the assassinations of President John F. Kennedy and Dr. Martin Luther King, Jr. are no less dreadful when read fifteen and ten years later.

From Dallas, at 1:30 P.M. on November 22, 1963, the UPI teletyped:

> Kennedy . . . wounded; perhaps seriously; perhaps fatally; by assassin's bullet.

A *Washington Post* writer captured the reaction of a bereaved nation:

> . . . disbelief; then, as the news sank in . . . shock. Partisan feelings, petty differences disappeared in common grief.

Late in the afternoon of April 4, 1968, Dr. King was struck down by a sniper's bullet.

The *Washington Star* of April 5 headlined:

AMERICANS, BLACK AND WHITE, SHOCKED

The *New York Times* added:

> Dismay, shame, anger and foreboding marked the nation's reaction.

Few of us over the age of twenty have forgotten where we were when we learned of President Kennedy's death. My memory of that sad day is vivid. As a young lawyer with the Department of Justice in Washington, D.C., I had spent the morning in a meeting with Attorney General Robert F. Kennedy discussing investigations in Chicago, where I was going to work in a strike force in the Department's drive on organized crime. We broke for lunch.

While preparing to go out for a sandwich, I learned of the president's death. The meeting was never reconvened, and I never made it to Chicago. When the organized crime program faltered after the assassination, I left the department to teach at Notre Dame Law School.

If our ability to recall the moment that we heard about Dr. King's death is less precise, it is probably because not all of us were as intimately involved in his work as we should have been. It may also be because the civil rights leader, a man of peace, had lived so long under the threat of violence; in fact, his call for an end to racism, war, and economic injustice, in the context of the turbulent 1960s, almost seemed to invite attack. His death, coming after Kennedy's, was not so shocking; it was almost expected. On the last night of his life, Dr. King himself seemed to anticipate what was going to happen to him. He told an audience at Mason Temple Church in Memphis:

> Like anybody, I'd like to live a long life. Longevity has its place, but I'm not concerned about that now. I just want to do God's will, and He's allowed me to go up to the mountain. And I've looked over. And I've seen the Promised Land.

The parallel between these two tragic events of a trying decade in our history are striking—a dynamic leader, in his prime, shot down by a sniper who was promptly determined to have been a lone assassin. That Lee Harvey Oswald and James Earl Ray had acted without accomplices were the conclusions of official investigations that immediately followed—by the Warren Commission in the case of Oswald in September 1964; by the FBI in the case of Ray, who concurred, at least momentarily, by pleading guilty on March 10, 1969.

In the aftermath of each assassination, there came, too, a questioning of the official findings, stated by critical authors, some of whom reflected an honest concern for the sufficiency and accuracy of the investigations, while others were apparently more motivated by the profit—financial and otherwise—that they could hope to extract from the emotions of a dispirited American people.

EVOLUTION OF SKEPTICISM

The effort of President Johnson and senior officials of his administration to assure the people that the Kennedy assassination was an isolated act had already been seriously undermined when Jack Ruby killed Oswald on November 24, 1963. A *New York Times* reporter wrote:

> . . . it is difficult for people to believe that the assassination was the work of a single demented person.

And a *Washington Star* columnist was prophetic:

> Unless evidence against Lee Harvey Oswald, complete with corroborating testimony, is conclusive beyond any reasonable doubt, the most sinister doubts will continue to be expressed throughout the world.

Nevertheless, the Warren Commission did much to still those doubts—at least for a time. Lord Devlin, one of Britain's most distinguished jurists, wrote in *The Atlantic* of the Commission's report:

> Each fact is to be found in its proper place to sustain each conclusion. The minor conclusions support the major, and on the major, the verdict rests.

There remained, however, a body of dissenting opinion. On October 19, 1964, The *Washington Post* reported on a survey by Louis Harris: 31 percent of the American people still thought that Oswald had not been alone.

By 1968 the doubters would more than double in number, thanks in large part to the work of assassination critics in books and articles. Four of the most prominent authors who made a distinct impression on the public attitude were:

—Mark Lane, a young New York attorney who was retained by Oswald's mother to defend her son before the Warren Commission. When he was not given an official role in the proceedings, Lane presented his brief for the defense in *Rush to Judgment,* a bestseller published in 1966. The book catalogued a variety of so-called investigative and analytical errors in the work of the Commission, calling particular attention, for example, to the so-called single-bullet theory: the hypothesis that one bullet struck both President Kennedy and Governor John B. Connally of Texas. (See Report p. 35 and following for the committee's discussion of the single-bullet theory.)

—Edward Jay Epstein, who began his first book,

Inquest: The Warren Commission and the Establishment of Truth, as a master's thesis at Cornell. The publication of *Inquest* in 1966 was the high-water mark of an intellectual assault on the unwisdom of establishing a blue-ribbon commission to look into the death of a president.

—Josiah Thompson, an authority on the Danish philosopher Kierkegaard, who took leave from his position as a professor at Haverford College to research and write *Six Seconds in Dallas,* published in 1967. Thompson went beyond a negative denunciation of the Warren inquiry, proposing that there were actually three shooter locations and that Governor Connally was hit by a bullet fired later than the one that struck the president in the back.

—Sylvia Meagher, who published a *Subject Index to the Warren Report and Hearings and Exhibits* in 1966 and *Accessories after the Fact* in 1967. *Accessories* was an attempt to survey and critically appraise all the questions raised in the Kennedy assassination and how the Warren Commission resolved or arguably failed to resolve them.

By 1966 the popular press had also picked up the beat. In July *Look* featured an article titled, "The Warren Commission Report on the Assassination Is Struck by a Wave of Doubts." In November *Life* published "A Matter of Reasonable Doubt," a critical evaluation of the single-bullet hypothesis based on testimony by Governor Connally after examining a film of the assassination by Abraham Zapruder.

Finally, the investigation by New Orleans District Attorney Jim Garrison seemed for a time to lend official sanction to the hunt for conspirators. But Garrison's bizarre tactics, which received national attention in the 1969 "show" trial of a New Orleans businessman, strained the patience of thinking people. There was a lesson to be learned from the reaction to Garrison's antics—dissent had to be able to withstand the same sort of hard analysis that the critics had applied to the work of the Warren Commission. There was irony, too, as it turned out. Some of what Garrison suggested in a manner that made mockery of due process did, in fact, deserve more serious attention than it received at the time.

The substance of the criticism of the work of the Warren Commission hinged on three general points:

1. The evidence that Oswald fired the shots—scientific tests and witness testimony—was open to question.

2. Whether or not Oswald fired the shots, the assassination was the result of a conspiracy.

3. The federal government, if not actually involved in the conspiracy, undertook to cover up vital evidence of the plot.

It can be said today—with the advantage of the congressional investigation—that the alternative theories of the critics to the single-assassin hypothesis ranged from ridiculous to reasonable. Some can be dismissed as pure fancy—the idea, for example, that a man holding an umbrella in Dealey Plaza at the moment of the assassination was flashing a sinister signal.* Similarly, the notion is pure fancy that there were two Oswalds, one who defected to the Soviet Union in 1959, and another, a disguised KGB assassin, who returned to the United States in 1962. But other suspicions that there may have been more than one gunman turned out to be not so farfetched.

Conspiracy theories in the assassination of Dr. King did not so readily find their way into print, nor did they attract the widespread public attention accorded to putative plots to kill the president. Clearly, the best reason for this difference between the two assassinations is that James Earl Ray lived to stand trial, plead guilty, and be sentenced to ninety-nine years in the Tennessee state penitentiary. Nevertheless, it was Ray himself who, at the time of his plea, put forth the initial hints that he had not been alone and that he had been an unwitting dupe in a wider conspiracy.

Ray himself realized that one of the most intriguing puzzles of the case was his source of income over the period leading up to the assassination and during his flight abroad. He offered the mysterious "Raoul" as his benefactor, claiming that Raoul had been the mastermind of the assassination. (See Report p. 402 and following for the Committee's conclusion about Raoul.)

Authors of books about Ray and the murder of Dr. King generally reject the idea of conspiracy:

---

*The "umbrella man," in testimony before the committee, explained he was protesting U.S. foreign policy, using the umbrella to serve as a symbolic reminder of the appeasement policies of Neville Chamberlain, Great Britain's prime minister in the years leading to World War II.

—William Bradford Huie started out as a believer in a conspiracy, which was implied in an account he wrote for *Look*. But in *He Slew the Dreamer*, published in 1968, Huie attributed the slaying to Ray's hatred of blacks and his craving for notoriety.

—Gerold Frank, author of *An American Death*, published in 1972, never seemed to have doubted that Ray acted alone. He was so unimpressed with the Raoul story that he dispatched it as a fabrication in just two pages.

—George McMillan, in *The Making of an Assassin*, published in 1976, offered a psychological study of Ray, assuming his guilt as a fact.

One writer who espoused a theory of conspiracy in Dr. King's death was Mark Lane, who in 1977 collaborated with entertainer-activist Dick Gregory to produce *Code Name "Zorro,"* which argued a case for Ray's defense. Lane also represented Ray when he appeared before the committee. In addition, Lane and Gregory submitted several points in behalf of their theory that Dr. King was the victim of a plot—possibly official in character. (See Report p. 557, for the committee's assessment of Lane's principal allegations and his conduct during the committee investigation.)

GENESIS OF THE COMMITTEE INVESTIGATION

The House Select Committee on Assassinations was established in September 1976 by House Resolution 1540, which authorized a full and complete investigation of the circumstances surrounding the deaths of President Kennedy and Dr. King.* Although the critics had lobbied diligently for congressional action, the principal impetus for the overwhelming support of HR 1540 (it passed the House by a vote of 280 to 65) came from another source —the Final Report of the Senate Select Committee on Governmental Operations with Respect to Intelligence Activities. In its report, dated April 1976, the Senate commit-

---

*The committee expired as the term of the 94th Congress ended on January 3, 1977. On February 2, 1977, the House passed HR 222, again authorizing the committee and directing it not only to investigate the deaths of President Kennedy and Dr. King, but also to determine whether existing laws that cover assassination are adequate and to see if there had been a full sharing of information by federal agencies during the course of prior investigations. HR 222 extended the committee for only two months. Another resolution—HR 433—was passed on March 30, 1977, constituting the committee until January 3, 1979.

tee published revelations that raised in the minds of many the serious possibility of government complicity in both assassinations.

Two astonishing facts had been developed in the Senate investigation:

—The CIA, as part of an assassination of foreign leaders (executive action) program, had enlisted the cooperation of top underworld figures in the United States in an effort to assassinate Fidel Castro of Cuba. In addition, word of the CIA-Mafia plots had been withheld by the Agency from the Warren Commission.

—The FBI, in its counterintelligence program (CO-INTELPRO), had targeted Dr. King in an attempt to tarnish his reputation and destroy his effectiveness as a national leader.

As it turned out, the House Select Committee found no evidence of complicity of the CIA, FBI, or any government agency in either assassination. (See Final Report, Section I C 2, p. 116 and following, for an analysis of the CIA-Mafia plots; Section II E 1, p. 566 and following, for an assessment of COINTELPRO.)

NATURE AND SCOPE OF THE INVESTIGATION

In its early days, the House Select Committee on Assassinations had some rough sailing. It could well be that the committee inherited from the critics a tendency to disagree among themselves. But there is little I can say about the internal strife of early 1977, since I only know what I read in the newspapers. The upshot was well publicized— a chairman submitted his resignation, and a chief counsel departed soon thereafter. What I do know is that a decent, honorable, and able man (an experienced trial lawyer), Louis Stokes of Ohio, was named chairman in March 1977, and I was appointed chief counsel and staff director in June. Neither of us came to our jobs with fixed intentions or presuppositions about either case. But each of us was determined to do a professional job, uphold the dignity of the House of Representatives, and not exploit the deaths of either President Kennedy or Dr. King for any partisan or personal advantage. Under the leadership of Chairman Stokes, it was resolved, then and there, that the committee would conduct its investigation in private until it was appropriate to hold public hearings, and it would do its best to remain immune from the fever of assassination demonology.

The mandate of the committee, as it had been stipulated in HR 222, prescribed four issues for the investigation:

1. Who assassinated President Kennedy and Dr. King?
2. Did the assassin or assassins in either case have assistance—was there a conspiracy?
3. Did the responsible federal agencies perform adequately in sharing information prior to each assassination, in protecting President Kennedy and Dr. King, and in conducting their investigations of the assassinations?
4. Was there a need for new legislation or for amending existing legislation with respect to assassination?

It was quickly apparent that the first two issues posed potential dangers for a congressional committee, since they entailed an examination of the conduct of individuals that might well be criminal and that might, in view of the heinous nature of the crimes, arouse a public outcry of moral indignation. Our concern was not limited to the reputations of individuals who might become "subjects" of the investigation, that is, possible suspects. We also had to consider the rights of "innocent associates" of any subject.

Obviously, no fine or imprisonment could be imposed as a direct result of our investigation, for it was not a criminal investigation; it was a legislative inquiry by a committee of the House of Representatives. Nevertheless, the risk of injury to someone's reputation demanded that we act with care. That is one reason, for example, that the committee rigidly adhered to a rule of the House by first taking testimony that might defame, degrade, or incriminate a person in executive session. That way, we could avoid publicly presenting baseless and harmful allegations.

Still, there were dangers inherent in the nature of a congressional investigation and the procedures employed by a House committee. These procedures are markedly different from those followed when individual conduct is examined by either the executive or judicial branch of government. An understanding of this report depends on an awareness of these procedures and their contrasts to a criminal inquiry.

The Constitution assigns to Congress the power and responsibility to legislate. And while Congress was not granted by the Constitution express authority to investigate, the Supreme Court has ruled that "the power of inquiry—with process to enforce it—is an essential and appropriate auxiliary to the legislative function."

Congressional investigations differ sharply from judicial trials in several respects. There is no impartial judge presiding over a congressional hearing. Should a witness object to a question, he must seek a ruling from the chairman, who may himself have asked it. If the chairman overrules the objection and directs the witness to answer, he must do so or run the risk of being in contempt of Congress. Consequently, a witness in a congressional proceeding is under considerable pressure to answer questions.

Another difference between a congressional hearing and a trial is that an individual in a congressional proceeding can be compelled by a grant of immunity to testify despite his Fifth Amendment right to claim self-incrimination. In a trial, of course, a defendant cannot be forced to take the stand. In addition, there are no legal constraints on what committee members may say publicly prior to the appearance of a witness, who may also be subject of the investigation; a prosecutor in a criminal case must refrain from public comment in advance of a trial.

A witness before a congressional committee cannot object to the admission of evidence; even hearsay is admissible. Moreover, a "subject" of a congressional investigation has no right, as does the defendant in a trial, to cross-examine witnesses who have testified against him, to have subpoenas issued for witnesses, or to make a statement on his own behalf.

Finally, with respect to the rights of a witness, there is no constitutional provision for him to be represented by an attorney. A rule of the House does provide that witnesses may be accompanied by their lawyers, but it is only "for the purpose of advising them concerning their constitutional rights."

Out of a deep concern for civil liberties, the select committee adopted certain rules of its own in an attempt to offset the risk inherent in conducting an assassination investigation in a congressional context. Public comment about the proceedings was, for example, tightly restricted. The chairman did not sit in the chair when he asked more than routine questions. In the event a witness was unable for financial or other reasons to obtain counsel, it was provided. A lawyer for a witness could submit questions to be asked of a client, and a witness or his lawyer could make a concluding statement to explain or amplify his testimony.

There are other even more important differences between a congressional hearing and a trial. The requirements, for example, that govern the outcome are radically dissimilar.

A congressional committee votes on its findings, as does a jury, but rather than unanimity, a simple majority will carry, as the dissents to this report illustrate. In addition, a congressional committee need not establish facts beyond a reasonable doubt—it may base recommendations or its legislation on facts it finds "probable" or even just "likely." This has ominous implications for a "suspect," who may be denied the opportunity for the vindication that would be associated with a judicial verdict of not guilty under a different standard.

It may be forcefully argued that when evidence of criminal conduct is introduced before a congressional committee—evidence that in the end falls short of clear and convincing persuasion—the responsible course of action for the committee might be to refrain from making the evidence public. We weighed this option by evaluating the importance of public knowledge about each of the four issues of our mandate in light of the risk to the reputations and rights of persons being investigated. Ultimately, we determined that a complete analysis of all four issues and public disclosure of that analysis were necessary, if the committee was going to fulfill its legislative responsibilities and its constitutional duty of informing the American public.

Beyond its duty to legislate and oversee executive agencies, the committee was constitutionally obligated, we believed, to make public the facts it had learned about the assassinations. This obligation was increased by the degree of public doubt about the earlier investigations. At the time the committee was established, according to the Gallup Poll, 80 percent of the American people believed President Kennedy had been the victim of conspiracy, and 70 percent thought that the murder of Dr. King was likewise the result of a conspiracy.

Implicit in the informing function of Congress was the imperative that we respond to public concern over the performance of the federal agencies. The doubts that had stirred the public extended to serious suspicions that the agencies—principally the CIA and FBI—had engaged in a coverup, extending to complicity in the assassinations themselves. With the integrity of the government at stake, the committee believed it would not suffice to respond simply by issuing its conclusions on government culpability. Conclusions without supporting facts would in the committee's view, a view that I shared, merely have served to increase the suspicions. We had a responsibility, therefore, to state our conclusions as to who might have participated in the assassinations and to supply a factual basis for those conclusions.

The third issue of our mandate was based on another traditional responsibility of Congress—to oversee the performance of agencies of the executive branch. As Woodrow Wilson observed, "Quite as important as legislating is vigilant oversight of administration." The committee considered its evaluation of such agencies as the CIA, FBI, and Secret Service as essential, and we realized that our evaluation would also depend on our own independent determination of the facts in each assassination. It would have been irresponsible for us to have passed judgment on, say, the FBI finding that Oswald had acted alone without first coming to our own conclusion on that crucial issue.

The fourth issue of the mandate—whether new laws should be enacted or existing laws amended—was the most appropriate in terms of the committee's legislative responsibility. To make such a determination, however, the committee was also first required to assess the prior investigations themselves and to perform an independent and objective analysis of the facts in each assassination.

STRUCTURE OF THE INVESTIGATION

In planning the investigation, we had to realize we had a time deadline and limited resources. In thirty months, the committee spent about $5.5 million, which may sound like a lot, but it should be contrasted with the fact that the Warren Commission spent the equivalent in 1977 dollars of over 10 million in ten months. At any rate, it was mandatory that we establish priorities among the issues and concentrate on those where we thought we had the best chance of learning the truth and settling public doubts.

The actual investigation—that is, the period of rigorous factfinding—lasted only six months, from January to July 1978. But it was intense and wide ranging. Trips were made to foreign countries, including Mexico, Canada, Portugal, England, and Cuba. In all, there were 562 trips to 1,463 points for over a total of 4,758 days in the field;

335 witnesses were heard, either in public or executive session; a total of more than 4,924 interviews were conducted; 524 subpoenas were issued; and immunity orders were obtained for 165 witnesses.

Up until December 1977, we were largely consumed by exploratory work—rebuilding a staff, mastering the critical literature on both cases, preparing an investigative plan, and devising procedures for obtaining facts and presenting them effectively, both in public hearings during the latter half of 1978 and in this report.

We were acutely aware of the need for strict security precautions, not only because of the classified nature of much of the material we were to review, but also because the investigation could have been seriously compromised by premature disclosure of its results. Further, we realized that a person's reputation might be unjustly injured by publication of unverified information. Accordingly, each member of the staff was required to meet the requirements for a top-secret clearance. And strict discipline characterized our work.

In order that we could review the materials of a government agency, such as the CIA or FBI, much of which is classified, we entered into an agreement that was formalized in a memorandum of understanding, a document that established how the materials would be handled. The agreement with the CIA provided for access to unsanitized information, meaning nothing removed, not even "sources and methods" data. Such access was unprecedented in congressional dealings with an intelligence agency.

The information developed in the investigation fell under three general categories: scientific evidence, the results of analysis in the fields of forensic pathology, ballistics, photography, acoustics, photography, fingerprinting, and so on; documentation, in the form of official government files; and the testimony of witnesses. We knew that the scientific evidence would be of the highest reliability; that official files could be of substantial value in certain areas of the investigation; and that witness testimony would have to be sharply qualified by the limits of human memory, bias, and possibly a motive to lie. We knew, too, that the trail was cold; that witnesses had died; and that we lacked the legal tools to conduct a criminal-type investigation. But we were determined to do what we could.

In the public hearing phase of the investigation, we held more than thirty-five days of evidentiary hearings and two days of public policy sessions. Hearings testimony is published in separate volumes that supplement this report, as are reports by the Committee staff and our scientific panels. In all, the committee's published materials, in addition to this report, fill 27 volumes.

THE REPORT

The committee's last official act, in December 1978, was to approve its findings and recommendations, which were published in January 1979. This report is a commentary on those findings and recommendations; it summarized the evidence on which they were based and presents the committee's analysis of that evidence.

The final line in both assassinations is conspiracy. It is ironic in light of the suspicions that caused the committee to be created that we did not find government agency complicity, not even a coverup by the favorite targets of the critics, the CIA and FBI. What we did find was not so much "coverup" as a "failure to uncover" by those agencies and others in government that conspiracies were responsible for the deaths of President Kennedy and Dr. King. To put it bluntly, the official findings on the conspiracy question in both cases were wrong.

In stating its conclusions about the assassinations in this report, the committee, for good reason, speaks with muted tongue. As I have noted, we were deeply concerned about the inherent risk of a legislative investigation into criminal conduct. We decided, therefore, that our language ought to be moderate and that we ought not state a finding beyond what is absolutely indicated by the evidence.

The committee realized further that ultimately individual responsibility in the conspiracies had to be determined, under our system of government, in a court of law. When it became apparent that follow-up investigation was necessary, we became more aware than ever that we must make our findings with moderation and limit them to the crucial facts in each case. It was a sobering experience for me to discover failures by our government to the degree that we set out in this report. The failures were so sobering that some members of the committee were not willing to carry the conclusions out to the full force of the evidence. Realizing that there would be an opportunity for others to fill in the details—that there might be indictments and trials as a result of future investigation—we decided to present an understated case. We chose a cautious approach.

Yes, there are still unanswered questions. It would have

been neat and tidy if we simply could have put our stamp of approval on the official findings of 1964 and 1968. But they turn out to be inadequate and wrong, and we were left to ask, but not able to answer with assurance, questions like these:

Why did Yuri Nosenko, the KGB defector, lie about his knowledge of Oswald?

Was Fidel Castro told in 1963 that Oswald had threatened the president when he visited the Cuban consulate in September 1963?

Did anti-Castro Cuban exiles put Oswald up to killing the president?

Was the Kennedy assassination a sophisticated organized crime "hit"?

Was "Raoul" in reality a brother of James Earl Ray?

Did the St. Louis contract supply the motive for Dr. King's murder?

FUTURE ACTION

Down Pennsylvania Avenue, not far from the Capitol, there is a department of government, called in Washington simply, "Justice." The Attorney General and his deputies may feel there are matters of greater urgency than knowing the truth about the deaths of President Kennedy and Dr. King, that their limited time and resources might well be better spent on "current cases," or that if these two cases were actively reopened, the department might fail in its efforts to solve them. If they do, they are overlooking something that has always seemed clear to me. The American people are willing to accept failure when there has been an honest effort to succeed. What they will not accept from our government—or anyone else—is a refusal to make that effort.

The committee, I believe, has done its job. By that I mean it has fully answered the questions posed in its mandate for its legislative purposes. It has assessed the performance of government agencies and found it to have been flawed. It has made recommendations for administrative and legislative reform.

As for issue one, the committee was satisfied with the identification of the killers of President Kennedy and Dr. King. But, on the issue of conspiracy, we have, I believe, drastically altered the verdict of history.

For reasons I have listed, we stopped short of that climactic point in mystery novels when the murderer is named. I do not apologize. I believe the committee fulfilled its mandate to the letter, given the restrictions that are appropriate in a legislative proceeding. We did what we could and what it was proper for us to do.

But where *do* we go from here?

It is up to the government—the executive branch, specifically that department called "Justice." In his recent national policy reconsideration at Camp David, President Carter is reported to have marked the Kennedy assassination as the beginning of the period of decline of public trust in the institutions of government. I agree. A frank recognition of the failures of the past and a courageous effort to rectify them now could make the beginning of a restoration of that public confidence. The place to begin is with the Kennedy assassination. The committee has provided a roadmap that indicates the points of departure for subsequent investigation that need not be limited as congressional investigations are—New Orleans, in the case of the Kennedy assassination; St. Louis, in the case of the King assassination. The government, to live up to the meaning of justice, can do no less than to pursue the course the committee has charted.

Why? Because statutes of limitation do not apply to murder, certainly not the murders of men like John F. Kennedy and Martin Luther King, Jr.

Justice demands no less.

G. Robert Blakey
Cornell Law School
July 1979

I

FINDINGS OF THE SELECT COMMITTEE ON ASSASSINATIONS IN THE ASSASSINATION OF PRESIDENT JOHN F. KENNEDY IN DALLAS, TEX., NOVEMBER 22, 1963

INTRODUCTION: THE KENNEDY PRESIDENCY IN PERSPECTIVE

John Fitzgerald Kennedy, the 35th President of the United States, was shot to death on November 22, 1963, while riding in a motorcade in Dallas, Tex. Kennedy had represented for many the dawn of a new era of hope. In his account of the Kennedy administration, "A Thousand Days," historian and Kennedy staff member Arthur M. Schlesinger, Jr., wrote:

> * * * [T]here can be no doubt that Kennedy's magic was not alone that of wealth and power and good looks, or even of these things joined to intelligence and will. It was, more than this, the hope that he could redeem American politics by releasing American life from its various bondages to orthodoxy. [1]†

When the young President died, much of the world grieved. West Berlin Mayor Willy Brandt's words reflected the sense of loss: "A flame went out for all those who had hoped for a just peace and a better world." [2] A stunned nation felt deeply the loss of a promising leader. The assassination, wrote historian Christopher Lasch, "helped to dispel the illusion that the United States was somehow exempt from history, a nation uniquely favored and destined * * * to be spared the turmoil and conflict which had always characterized the politics of other countries." [3]

†Numerals in square brackets in the middle or at the end of sentence are for references which are at the end of the report.

1

John Fitzgerald Kennedy was the fourth victim of Presidential assassination, preceded by Abraham Lincoln in 1865, James A. Garfield in 1881, and William McKinley in 1901.

The first Presidential assassination occurred within 1 week of the end of the Civil War. President Lincoln was shot by John Wilkes Booth on April 14, 1865, while watching a British comedy, "Our American Cousin," at Ford's Theater in Washington, D.C. He died the following morning. Booth, an actor and Confederate sympathizer, fled Washington immediately after the crime. He reportedly was trapped in a burning barn by Federal troops on April 26, 1865, where he died of a gunshot wound to the head.

A military commission established to try persons accused of complicity in the assassination of President Lincoln found that the murder was part of a conspiracy to kill Lincoln, Vice President Andrew Johnson and Secretary of State William H. Seward. Having lost heart, George A. Atzerodt did not attack Johnson as planned, but Seward was seriously wounded by Lewis Payne, a former Confederate soldier. As a result of the investigation by the Office of the Judge Advocate General of the U.S. Army, several defendants were accused of conspiring with Confederate President Jefferson Davis and a group of Confederate Commissioners in Canada to murder Lincoln. The accused were Confederate courier John T. Surratt, his mother, Mary E. Surratt, David Herold, a half-wit Confederate sympathizer, and Confederate veterans Samuel Arnold and Michael O'Laughlin. Edward Spangler, a stagehand to Ford's Theater, and Dr. Samuel A. Mudd, a physician who set the leg Booth injured in his esape from the theater, were accused of aiding the assassin's escape. Mrs. Surratt, Herold, Payne, and Atzerodt were found guilty and hanged on July 19, 1865. Three others received life sentences. John Surratt initially fled to Canada and then to Italy, where he joined the Papal Zouaves in Rome under an assumed name. He was captured in November 1866 and returned to the United States to stand trial on charges of complicity in the assassination. He was freed when the trial ended with a hung jury.

Several conspiracy theories emerged after the Lincoln

assassination. Surratt's flight to Italy, coupled with the fact that many of Booth's co-conspirators were Roman Catholic, stirred the anti-Catholic sentiments of the "Know-Nothing Movement," which charged that the assassination was part of a Papist plot. Although the military commission ultimately dismissed the contention that the conspirators were in league with Jacob Thompson, head of the Confederate Commission to Canada, under the supervision of Confederate President Jefferson Davis, that theory also persisted. Another contention was advanced by those who opposed the execution of Mrs. Surratt. Suspicious of those in charge of her arrest and prosecution, they believed that Secretary of War Edwin M. Stanton was the real mastermind of the assassination.

In 1866 and 1867, the House of Representatives authorized two separate investigations into the death of President Lincoln. [5] Neither finally laid to rest the suspicions around the death of President Lincoln.

President James A. Garfield was shot in the back by Charles J. Guiteau on July 2, 1881 in Washington, D.C. Guiteau, a religious fanatic and would-be officeholder, had been denied access to the White House after he had asked to be appointed U.S. Ambassador to Austria. When Garfield appointed James A. Blaine as Secretary of State, an incensed Guiteau apparently believed that the President had betrayed a faction of the Republican Party.

In the ensuing murder trial, there was no suggestion that the defendant was involved in any conspiracy. Guiteau maintained that he had acted as an agent of God in a political emergency and therefore was not guilty of wrongdoing. Despite a history of mental illness in Guiteau's family, the insanity defense presented by his counsel failed. Guiteau was declared sane, found guilty and hanged before a large crowd. Contrary to events following the Lincoln assassination, no theories of possible conspiracy surfaced in the wake of Garfield's slaying.

While attending the Pan-American Exposition at Buffalo, N.Y., on September 6, 1901, President William McKinley was shot. He died 8 days later, the victim of assassin Leon F. Czolgosz, a factory worker and anarchist. Although an anarchist group had published a warning about Czolgosz 5 days before McKinley was shot and Czolgosz insisted he had acted alone, many believed that the assassination was the result of an anarchist plot.

Czolgosz refused to testify at his own trial which was held 4 days after McKinley's funeral. After 34 minutes of deliberation, the jury found him guilty of murder. Czolgosz did not appeal the verdict, and he was executed in the electric chair.

McKinley's assassination came after a wave of anarchist terrorism in Europe. Between 1894 and 1900, anarchist assassins had killed M. F. Sadi Carnot, President of France; Elizabeth, Empress of Austria; and Humbert I, King of Italy. Following McKinley's death, vigilantes in the United States attacked anarchist communities. Anarchist leaders such as Emma Goldman were arrested. Responding to a plea by the new President, Theodore Roosevelt, Congress passed a series of restrictive measures that limited the activities of anarchists and added alien anarchists to the list of excluded immigrants. Despite a spate of frenzied charges of an anarchist conspiracy, no plot was ever proven, and the theories appeared to collapse shortly after the execution of Czolgosz.

Three Presidents who preceded John F. Kennedy were the targets of attempted assassinations. On January 30, 1835, Richard Lawrence tried to kill President Andrew Jackson on the steps of the U.S. Capitol, but both pistols he carried misfired, and Jackson was not injured. Following the attempt, some of Jackson's supporters charged a Whig conspiracy, but this allegation was never substantiated. Lawrence was found not guilty by reason of insanity and spent the rest of his life in mental institutions.

On February 15, 1933, in Miami, Fla., President-elect Franklin D. Roosevelt was fired upon by Guiseppe Zangara, an unemployed Italian immigrant bricklayer. Zangara missed Roosevelt, but mortally wounded Chicago Mayor Anton Cermak. Zangara was tried, found guilty of murder and executed. No conspiracy was charged in the shooting.

Two Puerto Rican nationalists attacked Blair House, the temporary residence of President Harry S. Truman in Washington, D.C., on November 1, 1950, with the apparent intention of assassinating the President. A White House guard and one of the nationalists, Griselio Torresola, were killed in the ensuing gun battle. The surviving nationalist, Oscar Collazo, explained that the action against Truman had been sparked by news of a revolt in Puerto Rico. He believed the assassination would call the attention of the American people to the appalling economic conditions in his country. The two would-be assassins were acting in league with P. Albuzio Campos, president of the Nationalist Party of Puerto Rico. Truman was not harmed during the assault. Collazo was tried and sentenced to death, but President Truman commuted the sentence to life imprisonment.

A NEW PRESIDENT

In an era when the United States was confronted with intractable, often dangerous, international and domestic issues, the Kennedy administration was inevitably surrounded by controversy as it made policies to deal with the problems it faced. Although a popular President, John F. Kennedy was reviled by some, an enmity inextricably related to his policies. The possibility of nuclear holocaust overshadowed the administration's reshaping of cold war foreign policy as it grappled with Cuba, Berlin, Laos, Vietnam, relations in the Third World and Western Europe, and U.S. military strength. At home, an emerging Black protest movement, persistent unemployment, poverty and urban blight, governmental disorganization, congressional resistance to the President's New Frontier program, and the menace of organized crime were among the problems Kennedy faced. He relied on the counsel of some of the foremost thinkers of his age as he pursued new approaches in leading the country.

In the summer of 1960, Senator John F. Kennedy won the Democratic Party's nomination for President. In his acceptance speech, he emphasized the challenges of the 1960's and declared that "we stand today on the edge of a 'New Frontier,'" a phrase that later became attached to his program. Two days before his election in November, Kennedy pledged, "I am not promising action in the first 100 days alone. I am promising you 1,000 days of exacting Presidential leadership." With the slogan "Let's get this country moving again," he pledged to combat unemployment, the sluggish economy, what he called a missile gap, and the Communist government in Havana. Kennedy defeated the Republican candidate, Richard M. Nixon, by a slim margin of 118,450 out of nearly 69 million votes cast. He was the first Roman Catholic and, at age 43, the youngest man ever elected President.

On a cold January morning in 1961, the new President stood before the nation that elected him and voiced these memorable words:

> Let every nation know, whether it wishes us well or ill, that we shall pay any price, bear any burden, meet any hardship, support any friend, oppose any foe, to assure the survival and the success of liberty.

No words could have portrayed more aptly the determination of John F. Kennedy as he assumed office as the spokesman for "a new generation of Americans." His mettle yet to be tested, an articulate, confident new President confronted the issues that put him in conflict with forces at home and abroad.

Despite his narrow election victory, Kennedy's popularity was high at the time he took office. The Gallup Poll showed a 69 percent favorable rating. During his term, that popularity fluctuated, and, in the autumn of 1963, it appeared to be in decline. It was concern over that slump and the implications for the 1964 Presidential contest that led, in large part, to Kennedy's decision to make the ill-fated Texas trip in November 1963.

FOREIGN AFFAIRS: A FRAGILE PEACE

The cold war was President Kennedy's foremost concern, as the United States and the Soviet Union stood poised to obliterate each other or to coexist. Kennedy, who emphasized the need for a strong military during his campaign, tacked an additional $4 billion to the defense budget approved by President Dwight D. Eisenhower. To demonstrate that the United States would not retreat from its treaty commitments, his military build-up was the largest in the peacetime history of the country. John Foster Dulles, Secretary of State under Eisenhower, had relied almost exclusively on a rigid foreign policy based on nuclear power and military pacts. Rejecting "massive retaliation" with nuclear arms, Kennedy urged the strengthening of conventional forces and emphasized the need for a flexible, diversified military that would counter the threat posed by Communist guerrilla armies. Nonetheless, he was committed to negotiation and steadfastly pursued a nuclear arms limitation treaty, despite Soviet threats in Cuba, Berlin, Southeast Asia, and elsewhere. Some critics were confused by his call for a strong military while pursuing a nuclear treaty, but Kennedy saw military preparedness as the foundation for achieving peaceful solutions.

Kennedy's first move in United States-Soviet relations was to reply to Soviet Premier Nikita Khrushchev's January 1961 congratulatory note:

> We are ready and anxious to cooperate with all who are prepared to join in genuine dedication to the assurance of a peaceful and more fruitful life for mankind.

The Cuban threat

With Premier Fidel Castro's increasing ties to the Soviet Union, Communist Cuba, just 90 miles from the United States, became an early focal point of Kennedy administration concern. In February 1961, Soviet Deputy Prime Minister Andrei Gromyko visited Cuba to arrange large-scale economic and military assistance. The United States ended formal diplomatic contacts with Cuba shortly after Gromyko's trip.

Soon after taking office, Kennedy learned that since the spring of 1960, the U.S. Government had been training a guerrilla force of anti-Castro Cuban exiles in Florida and Guatemala with the ultimate objective of invading Cuba and overthrowing Castro. Kennedy sanctioned the training and reluctantly allowed the invasion to proceed, but he limited U.S. participation and support.

On April 17, 1961, a force of anti-Castro Cuban refugees attempted to establish a beachhead in Cuba at the Bay of Pigs. The United States had grossly underestimated the popular support for the Castro regime. An anticipated internal uprising never occurred, and Castro's forces defeated the invaders within a few days. President Kennedy accepted "sole responsibility" for the debacle when the United States could no longer disavow its role in the ill-fated expedition. Privately, however, he blamed the CIA and reportedly vowed to "splinter the agency into a thousand pieces."

The Cuban Revolutionary Council, a group of anti-Castro exiles that was to have become the provisional government after Castro's overthrow, was particularly bitter about the Bay of Pigs. Its principal leaders—An-

7

tonio Maceo, Justo Carillo, Carlos Heria, Antonio de Varona, Manuel Ray, and José Miró Cardona—had formed the Council with the CIA's sanction and had been promised recognition by the U.S. Government. They were outraged by the failure of the United States to support the invasion force. At a meeting with President Kennedy shortly after the invasion, the angry leaders blamed his military advisers for the defeat, but Kennedy replied that he alone was responsible. On the other hand, Kennedy attempted to reassure them, promising that the United States was committed to returning Cuban refugees to their homeland.

A stunning setback for the new administration, the Bay of Pigs defeat resulted in worldwide criticism of the United States, both for its role in the invasion and for its reluctance to back the refugees with sufficient force to allow the expedition to succeed. It also gave Khrushchev the occasion to lecture the new President on international morality and raised questions about Kennedy as a coolheaded leader. While anti-Castro Cuban exiles in the United States believed they had been betrayed by Kennedy and accused him of being a weak leader who was soft on communism, the administration was criticized from the left as a reactionary return to barbarism.

Kennedy traveled to Europe in June and met with Soviet Premier Khrushchev for 12 hours in Vienna, Austria. Nuclear testing, disarmament, and Berlin were discussed, but the leaders reached no agreement. Khrushchev threatened to end four-power control of Berlin by signing a treaty with East Germany that would give it control over access routes to West Berlin. In late June, he told the allies to get out of the city by the end of the year, charging that the air corridors were being used to import spies and saboteurs into East Germany.

On his return to the United States, Kennedy said:

> I made it clear to Mr. Khrushchev that the security of Western Europe, and therefore our own security, are deeply involved in our presence and our access rights to West Berlin; that those rights are based on law and not on sufferance; and that we are determined to maintain those rights at any risk and thus meet our obligation to the people of West Berlin, and their right to choose their own future.

Kennedy responded to Khrushchev's threat with a call for 217,000 more men in uniform. He ordered the draft doubled, tripled if necessary, and requested authority to activate Reserve and National Guard units. With the Soviet determination to eliminate West Berlin and the U.S. commitment to preserve it, the prospect of a third world war was greater than ever. The crisis intensified with the August 1961 construction of a wall that prevented eastern European refugees from entering West Berlin. The United States responded by sending troops and tanks to West Berlin. Western rights remained intact, and the crisis subsided with Khrushchev's decision in late 1961 not to sign a treaty with East Germany. U.S. armored units in Berlin were pulled back in January 1962.

Combating communism in Latin America

Meanwhile, to encourage progressive democracy in the underdeveloped world, the administration embarked on programs of assistance. Peace Corps volunteers brought technical and educational expertise to emerging areas. Promising to "transform the American continent into a vast crucible of revolutionary ideas and efforts," Kennedy determined to wipe out the seedbed of communism in Latin America and contain Communist Cuba by raising the living standards with his Alliance for Progress. He proposed that the Latin American Republics join the United States in a 10-year plan for developing the Americas to satisfy the basic needs of housing, employment, land, health care, and education, thus relieving the economic distress that made the countries vulnerable to Castro-style revolutions. Formed in August 1961, the Alliance for Progress received the enthusiastic support of many Latin Americans, which was evident in the acclaim for Kennedy when he visited Colombia and Venezuela in 1961 and Mexico in 1962. At the Inter-American Conference in January 1962, he said, "I think communism has been isolated in this hemisphere and I think the hemisphere can move toward progress."

The arms race

An escalating arms race and the harmful effects of radioactive contamination from nuclear tests deeply troubled the Kennedy administration. Despite an earlier promise by Khrushchev to join the United States in a no-test policy, the Soviets resumed nuclear tests on August 30, 1961, and exploded 50 devices that fall. Kennedy urged Khrushchev to join with the United States and Great Britain in an agreement banning atmospheric tests. When the Soviet Premier refused, Kennedy ordered resumption of underground tests. In March 1962, after studying Soviet advances, Kennedy reluctantly renewed atmospheric tests with a series of blasts over Christmas Island in the central Pacific. He told a writer it was his fate to "take arms against a sea of troubles and, by opposing, end them."

The missile crisis

Acting on his pledge to defend the Western Hemisphere if it was threatened by Soviet aggression, Kennedy faced the greatest crisis of his brief Presidency in Cuba in October 1962. It was the closest the world had ever come to nuclear war. On October 16, aerial reconnaissance photographs of Cuba appeared to show installation of offensive nuclear missiles. This initial discovery was verified, and on October 20, Kennedy returned abruptly to Washington from a political trip to Chicago on the pretext of a sudden cold. On Monday, October 22, he revealed that the United States had discovered from aerial photographs that the Soviet Union had deployed ballistic missiles and Ilyushin–28 bombers in Cuba. He announced that he had ordered an air-sea quarantine on all offensive weapons bound for Cuba and promised more drastic action if the missiles and bombers were not removed. President Kennedy grimly stated that the United States would intercept any Soviet vessel with arms and that the United States would retaliate if the Soviets attacked any nation in the Western Hemisphere. The U.S. Armed Forces were at combat readiness, on "maximum alert." After a tense 6 days, Khrushchev announced his decision to dismantle and withdraw offensive weapons from Cuba in return for Kennedy's agreement not to invade Cuba and to lift the blockade. Kennedy received widespread international support during the missile crisis and was later credited with having achieved a turning point in the cold war favorable to the West.

Among anti-Castro Cuban exiles and some rightwing

factions in this country, however, there was outrage over Kennedy's decision. Despite his reassurances that the Cubans would be returned to their homeland, he had promised not to invade Cuba. Militant rightwing extremists argued that the United States should have invaded Cuba, removed the Russians and their arms, and toppled Castro.

On December 29, 1962, President Kennedy greeted over 1,000 Cubans who had been captured at the Bay of Pigs and ransomed from Castro's jails by the United States. In a ceremony at the Orange Bowl in Miami, he accepted the brigade's invasion flag and addressed their concerns about the future. The President declared, "I can assure you that this flag will be returned to this brigade in a free Cuba."

Southeast Asia

Abandoning the Eisenhower administration's mistrust of neutral nations, Kennedy pursued a cautious approach in Laos where Communists had captured many of the northern provinces in 1961. In July 1962, the United States was able to get all parties in Laos to agree to a tripartite coalition government and withdrawal of all foreign troops.

In South Vietnam, however, the administration decided to take a stand against Communist-inspired "wars of liberation." U.S. involvement dated back to 1956, when the Eisenhower administration backed the decision of the South Vietnamese Government to postpone elections there because Communist victory appeared imminent. The United States was pledged to support the pro-American regime of Ngo Dinh Diem in the fear that if one Southeast Asian nation fell to the Communists, others would soon follow. Kennedy continued that policy, although with growing reluctance by 1963.

In 1961, Viet Cong guerrillas backed by Ho Chi Minh of North Vietnam attacked South Vietnamese troops, murdered officials, and placed the Diem regime in jeopardy. Kennedy responded initially by sending more than 4,000 military advisers to South Vietnam and, over the following months, U.S. participation grew steadily. In his move away from the "all or nothing" nuclear arsenal strategy of the 1950's, Kennedy emphasized a varied military capability to meet the jungle war-

11

fare tactics of the enemy in countries such as Vietnam. He also directed economic aid to Southeast Asia to meet the Communist threat there. In November 1962, Secretary of Defense Robert McNamara announced that the United States was winning the war in South Vietnam.

When the Chinese invaded northern India in 1962, Kennedy authorized an airlift of arms to halt the Chinese Communist advance.

Pledge to defend Europe

To some critics, Kennedy's foreign policy, combining military bluster with negotiation, appeared vacillating and self-defeating. Their misgivings seemed to be confirmed by actions of some traditional allies of the United States. President Charles de Gaulle of France, for example, insisted on a defense capability independent of the United States and refused to sign any nuclear arms limitation treaty, thus threatening the cohesiveness of the North Atlantic Treaty Organization. In addition, Kennedy's acceptance of the principle of neutrality, manifested by the Laos agreement, was criticized by some who believed countries were either American friends or enemies.

Kennedy reasserted his pledge to defend Western Europe during a trip there in June 1963. "The United States will risk its cities to defend yours," he assured the West Germans, who feared a pullout of U.S. troops. In a speech to an enthusiastic West Berlin crowd, Kennedy described himself as a "Berliner," saying that "all free men, wherever they may live, are citizens of Berlin."

Cold war thaw

Uneasiness over Cuba continued in 1963. The Soviet presence was symbolized by an attack of a Cuban Air Force MIG fighter on an American shrimp boat in March 1963. Some 17,000 Russian troops still occupied the island nation, and 500 antiaircraft missiles plus a large supply of other Soviet armaments were emplaced there.

Yet, with Kennedy's foreign policy emphasis on gradual progress, a thaw in the cold war was perceptible. In a major policy address on June 10, 1963, at American University in Washington, D.C., Kennedy proposed a "strategy of peace" to lead the United States and

12

Soviet Union out of the "vicious and dangerous cycles" of the cold war.

Let us focus on a peace based not on a sudden revolution in human nature but on a gradual evolution of human institutions.

He announced that the United States, Great Britain, and the Soviet Union would begin work on a treaty to outlaw nuclear tests.

A major accomplishment of the Kennedy administration, the nuclear test ban treaty, was signed in Moscow on August 5, 1963, and ratified by the U.S. Senate in September. This limited treaty, prohibiting atmospheric testing of nuclear weapons, represented the first limitation of arms expansion since the beginning of the cold war in 1945. The administration had hoped, however, for a more comprehensive agreement. Underground testing was not covered because of Soviet resistance to onsite inspection, and China and France refused to sign the treaty.

Although praised by many as a step toward peace, the treaty had its detractors. Air Force Gen. Thomas D. White described it as "next to unilateral disarmament," while scientist Edward Teller called for resumption of atmospheric testing to maintain American nuclear supremacy.

In October, the United States, Great Britain, and the Soviet Union agreed to refrain from using nuclear weapons in outer space.

Growing involvement in Vietnam

The Vietnam conflict intensified and U.S. involvement expanded steadily, although Kennedy refused to make any major increases in support. By October 1963, the United States had 16,000 troops in South Vietnam. As U.S. helicopters flew combat support missions and U.S. planes strafed enemy lines, U.S. advisers radically altered life there with the strategic hamlet resettlement program, an effort to concentrate the population in various areas. Some Americans criticized this involvement in support of the Diem dictatorship. At the insistence of his brother, Ngo Dinh Nhu, the Roman Catholic Diem had instituted a number of repressive measures against the country's Buddhists, who made up 70 percent of the population. His troops attacked pagodas, and Buddhists were jailed. The self-immolation of protesting Buddhist monks dramatically called into question the American role in Vietnam.

By threatening withdrawal of economic support, the United States sought to persuade the Diem government to change its brutal policies. Diem resisted, denying that the Buddhists were being persecuted and charging that, in fact, they were aiding the Communists by demanding a change of government. U.S. advisers warned that Diem's unpopular regime imperiled the battle against the Viet Cong.

On November 1, 1963, Diem and his brother, Nhu, were killed in a military coup. The United States quickly recognized the new government.

Détente

Kennedy's willingness to negotiate with the Russians, combined with a Sino-Soviet split, eased East-West tension and sparked optimism about the prospects for world peace. Other moves indicating Soviet-American détente and peaceful coexistence included installation of a "hot line" emergency telephone system from Washington to Moscow in the summer of 1963, approval of the sale of 4 million tons of surplus wheat to the Soviet Union, and initiation of cultural exchange programs. Kennedy also made overtures to Castro concerning normalization of relations, a move that enraged anti-Castro exiles in the United States. His steps away from dangerous nuclear diplomacy were praised by many, but some doubted that Kennedy's policy would contain communism and insure the strength of the United States.

AT HOME: A TROUBLED LAND

President Kennedy's New Frontier domestic program was not readily accepted. The administration's relations with Congress, dominated as it was by a conservative bloc of Republicans and southern Democrats, were difficult. Kennedy's major proposals—aid to education, medical care for the elderly and the creation of a Department of Urban Affairs—were rejected. Although measures were adopted to increase Federal aid to depressed areas, to increase and expand the minimum wage, and to increase social security benefits, the administration failed to persuade Congress to enact the widespread social legislation it sought.

Civil rights progress

The administration's most dramatic accomplishments were in the area of civil rights, though the President did not live to see the passage of the comprehensive legislation he proposed, the most far-reaching since Reconstruction. Kennedy appointed Blacks to high administration posts and to Federal judgeships. He gave Attorney General Robert F. Kennedy his sanction for vigorous enforcement of civil rights laws to extend voting rights, end segregation, and fight racial discrimination. Attorney General Kennedy expanded the Civil Rights Division of the Department of Justice, and President Kennedy issued a strongly worded Executive order against discrimination in employment that established a Committee on Equal Employment Opportunity headed by Vice President Johnson. Kennedy's civil rights program, however, increasingly alienated southerners and conservatives.

Violence erupted soon after Kennedy took office. In May 1961, the Congress of Racial Equality staged a series of freedom rides in Alabama in an effort to integrate buses and terminals. One bus was burned by a mob in Anniston, Ala. An angry segregationist crowd attacked demonstrators in Montgomery, Ala., and several persons were injured. Attorney General Kennedy ordered several hundred U.S. marshals to Montgomery to protect the demonstrators. National Guardsmen with fixed bayonets scattered a mob that tried to overwhelm the marshals, who were protecting a mass meeting at a Black church where civil rights leader Martin Luther King, Jr., was speaking.

Sparked by the vicious treatment of the nonviolent demonstrators, protests continued in Mississippi. The Attorney General petitioned the Interstate Commerce Commission, and in September 1961, the ICC adopted rules banning segregation on interstate buses and in terminals.

Trouble exploded again in 1962 when James Meredith, a 29-year-old Black Air Force veteran, gained admission to the all-white University of Mississippi. Meredith had been refused admission, despite Federal court orders requiring that he be enrolled. The Kennedy administration supported an effort to force compliance by the State, but Governor Ross Barnett was equally determined to defy the orders. In his fourth attempt to enroll at the university, Meredith arrived in Oxford on September 30, escorted by 300 U.S. marshals. He was met by a mob of 2,500 students and segregationist extremists who howled, "Two-four-one-three, we hate Kennedy." The hecklers attacked the marshals with bricks and bottles. The marshals responded with tear gas. A bloody night-long riot that left two dead and scores injured was quelled only after Federal troops had been dispatched by President Kennedy. Meredith registered the next day and began classes with the protection of marshals, who remained with him until his graduation in August 1963.

Urging the need for legislation in a February 28, 1963, address to Congress on civil rights, President Kennedy attacked the scourge of racial discrimination:

Race discrimination hampers our economic growth by preventing the maximum development and utilization of our manpower. It hampers our world leadership by contradicting at home the message we preach abroad. It mars the atmosphere of a united and classless society in which this Nation rose to greatness. It increases the costs of public welfare, crime, delinquency, and disorder. Above all, it is wrong. Therefore, let it be clear, in our own hearts and minds, that it is not merely because of the economic waste of discrimination. that we are committed to achieving true equality of opportunity. The basic reason is because it is right.

Although the administration's civil rights policies generated the dogged opposition of segregationists in the South, Black leaders criticized the President for not pursuing change even more forcefully. Dr. King said:

16

This administration has outstepped all previous ones in the breadth of its civil rights activity. Yet the movement, instead of breaking out into the open plains of progress, remans constricted and confined. A sweeping revolutionary force is pressed into a narrow tunnel.[7]

Blacks continued demonstrations for equal rights in the spring of 1963. In April and May, Dr. King led an attack on what he called "the most segregated city in the United States," Birmingham, Ala. Demonstrators were met by police dogs, electric cattle prods, and fire hoses. The brutal response to the nonviolent protestors led to worldwide outrage. Black leaders and Birmingham community leaders ultimately reached a compromise agreement to integrate public facilities. Birmingham became a rallying cry for the civil rights movement across the Nation. Over 700 demonstrations swept the South that summer, and northern public opinion increasingly supported the protestors.

In June 1963, Alabama Governor George Wallace, in defiance of a Federal court order, stood on the steps of the University of Alabama to prevent the admission of two Black students. Wallace bowed, however, to National Guard troops that had been federalized by the President. The Black students entered the university. In the same month, Medgar Evers, the NAACP field secretary for Mississippi, was shot to death in front of his home in Jackson, Miss.

The turbulence sparked President Kennedy's special message to Congress in June 1963, in which he asked the legislators to help end "rancor, violence, disunity and national shame" by pushing what was described as the most sweeping civil rights legislation since Reconstruction. The bill would, among other things, guarantee access to public accommodations and the right to vote. "We are confronted primarily with the moral issue," Kennedy said. He warned that Federal inaction would mean continued racial strife, declaring, "The fires of frustration and discord will burn in every city, North and South, where legal remedies are not at hand."

On August 28, 1963, an interracial group of more than 200,000 persons joined "The March for Jobs and

17

Freedom" in Washington, D.C., to urge the Congress to pass the comprehensive civil rights legislation the Kennedy administration envisioned. Violence shattered the hopeful mood in the wake of the Washington march when a bomb exploded on September 17 at the Sixteenth Street Baptist Church in Birmingham, Ala. during a Sunday School session. Four young Black girls were killed and 23 other persons were injured. Despite the national unrest, Congress did not rush to pass the civil rights bill.

Economic policies

Kennedy's Keynesian, New Deal economic policies brought him into conflict with business. For example, he advocated deficit spending at a time of economic growth in an attempt to overcome persistent high unemployment. He also proposed costly welfare programs to improve the plight of the Nation's poor and issued voluntary wage-price guidelines that he was determined to enforce.

As the Kennedy administration grappled with thorny economic issues—persistent unemployment, recession—a steel price hike set the stage for the most dramatic economic crisis of Kennedy's term. In March 1962, the administration persuaded the United Steel Workers Union to accept a contract he called "noninflationary" in the belief that such an agreement would ameliorate the recession by preventing a rise in prices. A few days later, however, the U.S. Steel Corp. announced an increase of 3.5 percent, or $6 per ton, and most other steel companies followed suit. Kennedy commented, "My father always told me all businessmen are sons-of-bitches, but I never believed it until now." [8] In the 3 days that followed the increase, four antitrust investigations of the steel industry were initiated, a bill to roll back the price increase was considered, wage and price controls were discussed and the Department of Defense began to divert purchases away from U.S. Steel. Kennedy denounced the increase as "wholly unjustifiable and irresponsible defiance of the public interest," and said the steel industry had shown its "utter contempt for their fellow citizens." U.S. Steel finally rescinded the price increase when several other steel companies said they would hold the price line. Despite the President's assurance after the steel crisis subsided that "this administration harbors no ill will against any individual, any industry, corporation, or segment of the American economy," business leaders complained about Government interference and hostility.

Government reform

Kennedy was also concerned about the autonomy of federal agencies and reorganization of the Federal bureaucracy. He saw a need for greater control over the Central Intelligence Agency after the Bay of Pigs fiasco. Its independent role in the Southeast Asian conflict and in Cuba particularly troubled him. The CIA's budget was twice that of the State Department, its staff had doubled in the 1950's, and, it was said by its critics, in some Embassies it had more personnel than the State Department. Kennedy replaced Director Allen Dulles with John McCone, cut the Agency's budget, and assigned Robert Kennedy as Agency watchdog.

Kennedy's relations with Federal Bureau of Investigation Director J. Edgar Hoover were cool. In an attempt to bridle the independent Hoover, the administration insisted that the facts reflect the law that the FBI was under the Department of Justice and that the Department was led by the Attorney General. Attorney General Robert Kennedy also compelled a reluctant Hoover to investigate civil rights and organized crime cases.

War on organized crime

The Kennedy administration made an unprecedented effort to fight the insidious menace of organized crime. The President had first encountered the problem when he became a member of the Senate Select Committee on Labor Racketeering. Robert Kennedy was chief counsel of the committee, and later, as Attorney General, he became the President's surrogate in a campaign against the underworld.

Dramatic developments in the war on organized crime had occurred just before Kennedy came to the White House. A roundup of hoodlums in Apalachin, N.Y., in 1957, followed by an abortive prosecution of many of the leaders, demonstrated the impotence of Federal enforcement. The Senate testimony of Mafia member Joseph Valachi in 1963 became the catalyst for a renewed effort to strengthen Federal criminal laws that could be used to control the threat of organized crime.

The zeal of the Kennedy brothers signified the roughest period for organized crime in Department of Justice history. Historian Arthur Schlesinger, Jr., wrote in "Robert Kennedy and His Times" that, as a result of the Attorney General's pressure, "the national Government took on organized crime as it had never done before." [9] Schlesinger observed:

In New York, Robert Morgenthau, the Federal attorney, successfully prosecuted one syndicate leader after another. The Patriarca gang in Rhode Island and the De Cavalcante gang in New Jersey were smashed. Convictions of racketeers by the Organized Crime Section and the Tax Division steadily increased—96 in 1961, 101 in 1962, 373 in 1963. So long as John Kennedy sat in the White House, giving his Attorney General absolute backing, the underworld knew that the heat was on. [10]

The Attorney General focused on targets he had become acquainted with as counsel for the Rackets Committee. He was particularly concerned about the alliance of the top labor leaders and racketeers as personified by Teamster President James R. Hoffa. Schlesinger wrote that "the pursuit of Hoffa was an aspect of the war against organized crime." [11] He added:

The relations between the Teamsters and the syndicates continued to grow. The FBI electronic microphone, planted from 1961 to 1964 in the office of Anthony Giacalone, a Detroit hood, revealed Hoffa's deep if wary involvement with the local mob. For national purposes a meeting place was the Rancho La Costa Country Club near San Clemente, Calif., built with $7 million in loans from the Teamsters' pension fund; its proprietor, Morris B. Dalitz, had emerged from the Detroit [sic. Cleveland] underworld to become a Las Vegas and Havana gambling figure. Here the Teamsters and the mob golfed and drank together. Here they no doubt reflected that,

20

as long as John Kennedy was President, Robert Kennedy would be unassailable. [12]

As with the Civil Rights Division, Robert Kennedy expanded the Organized Crime Division at Justice. As a result of information collected by the FBI, syndicate operations were seriously disrupted in some cases, and leading organized crime figures were concerned about the future.

Opposition from the far right

As the policies of the Kennedy administration broke new ground, political extremists in the United States seemed increasingly willing to resort to violence to achieve their goals. In an address at the University of Washington in Seattle on November 16, 1961, President Kennedy discussed the age of extremism: two groups of frustrated citizens, one urging surrender and the other urging war. He said:

It is a curious fact that each of these extreme opposites resembles the other. Each believes that we have only two choices: appeasement or war, suicide or surrender, humiliation or holocaust, or be either Red or dead.

The radical right condemned Kennedy for his "big Government" policies, as well as his concern with social welfare and civil rights progress. The ultra-conservative John Birch Society, Christian Anti-Communist Crusade led by Fred C. Schwarz, and the Christian Crusade led by Rev. Billy James Hargis attracted an anti-Kennedy following. The right wing was incensed by Kennedy's transfer of Gen. Edwin A. Walker from his command in West Germany to Hawaii for distributing right-wing literature to his troops. The paramilitary Minutemen condemned the administration as "soft on communism" and adopted guerrilla warfare tactics to prepare for the fight against the Communist foe. At the other extreme, the left labeled Kennedy a reactionary disappointment, a tool of the "power elite."

President Kennedy saw the danger of a politically

21

polarized society and spoke against extremist solutions, urging reason in an ordered society. In the text of the speech he had planned to deliver in Dallas on November 22, 1963, he wrote:

Today * * * voices are heard in the land—voices preaching doctrines wholly unrelated to reality, wholly unsuited to the sixties, doctrines which apparently assume that words will suffice without weapons, that vituperation is as good as victory and that peace is a sign of weakness.

NOVEMBER 1963: A TRIP TO TEXAS [13]

At the beginning, John F. Kennedy had been an extremely popular President. His ratings, ironically, were highest in the aftermath of the April 1961 Bay of Pigs invasion, when he received a remarkable 83 percent approval rating in the Gallup Poll. But by the fall of 1963, he had slipped to 59 percent, and he became concerned about the political implications. In October, Newsweek magazine reported that the civil rights issue alone had cost Kennedy 3.5 million votes, adding that no Democrat in the White House had ever been so disliked in the South. In Georgia, the marquee of a movie theater showing PT 109 read, "See how the Japs almost got Kennedy." [14]

An inveterate traveler, Kennedy interspersed his diplomatic missions abroad with trips around the country. He made 83 trips in 1963. In June he visited Germany, Ireland and Italy; later in the summer he toured the western United States—North Dakota, Wyoming, Montana, Washington, Utah, Oregon, Nevada, and California—to gain support for his legislative program.

Not only did Kennedy enjoy traveling, but he almost recklessly resisted the protective measures the Secret Service urged him to adopt. He would not allow blaring sirens, and only once—in Chicago in November 1963—did he permit his limousine to be flanked by motorcycle police officers. He told the special agent in charge of the White House detail that he did not want agents to ride on the rear of his car.

Kennedy was philosophical about danger. According to Arthur M. Schlesinger, "A Thousand Days," Kennedy believed assassination was a risk inherent in a democratic society. In 1953, Schlesinger recounted, then-Senator Kennedy read his favorite poem to his new bride, Jacqueline Bouvier Kennedy. It was "I have a Rendezvous with Death," by Alan Seeger. [15]

> It may be he shall take my hand
> And lead me into his dark land
> And close my eyes and quench my breath ...
>
> But I've a rendezvous with Death
> At midnight in some flaming town,
> When Spring trips north again this year,
> And I to my pledged word am true,
> I shall not fail that rendezvous.

During the November 1963 Texas trip he told a special White House assistant:

> * * * if anybody really wanted to shoot the President * * * it was not a very difficult job—all one had to do was get on a high building someday with a telescopic rifle, and there was nothing anybody could do to defend against such an attempt.

Kennedy had decided to visit the South to bolster his image in that region. He chose to visit Florida because it had voted Republican in 1960, and Texas because it only had been saved by Lyndon Johnson by an extremely slim margin. According to Texas Governor John B. Connally, Kennedy first mentioned a political trip to Texas in the summer of 1962 when Connally, a former Secretary of the Navy, was running for Governor. Kennedy broached the idea to Connally again the following summer.

Despite some obvious political reasons for a Texas visit, some members of Kennedy's staff opposed it because the State was not favorably disposed to the President. From 1961 to 1962, the Secret Service had received 34 threats on the President's life from Texas. Political embarrassment seemed a certainty. The decision to travel to Dallas was even more puzzling. Many perceived Dallas as a violent, hysterical center of right-wing fanaticism. There, in 1960, then-Texas Senator Lyndon B. Johnson had been heckled and spat upon. In October 1963, just a month before the President's scheduled visit,

Ambassador to the United Nations Adlai Stevenson was jeered, hit with a placard and spat upon. Byron Skelton, the National Democratic Committeeman from Texas, wrote Attorney General Robert Kennedy about his concern for President Kennedy's safety and urged him to dissuade his brother from going to Texas.

There are several probable explanations for the decision to visit Dallas. Kennedy was to visit four other cities—San Antonio, Houston, Austin, and Fort Worth—and it was feared that ignoring Dallas would harm his image in Texas. Kennedy also was anxious to win over business, and Dallas was the place to address business leaders in Texas. As a result of his economic policies, particularly the rollback of steel prices, Kennedy believed he was perceived as hostile to business. Before the November Texas trip, he shared his concern with Governor Connally:

If these people are silly enough to think that I am going to dismantle this free enterprise system, they are crazy.

All the other trips that summer and fall, including the visit to Florida, had been successful. In his testimony before this committee, Governor Connally explained that he believed that Texas was a State crucial to a Kennedy victory in 1964, and contended that Kennedy came to Texas for two reason: to raise money and to enhance his own political prospects in Texas.

Word of the trip to Texas first appeared in the Dallas papers on September 13, and Kennedy's itinerary for Texas was announced by Governor Connally on November 1. The President was scheduled to address a luncheon of business leaders at the Trade Mart in Dallas on November 22. He decided to travel into the city in a motorcade that was to follow the normal Dallas parade route. Kennedy liked motorcades, for they afforded an opportunity to get close to the people, and he made a special point of arranging one in Dallas because he believed it would be his one chance that day to greet workers and minorities. The final motorcade route through Dealey Plaza in downtown Dallas was selected on November 1.

In 1963, the Secret Service had identified six categories of persons who posed a threat to the President: right-wing extremists, left-wing extremists, Cubans, Puerto Ricans, Black militants, and a miscellaneous category that included mental patients. It identified two cities as particularly threatening—Miami and Chicago. Dallas was considered a potential source of political embarrassment. Prior to the trip to Dallas, the Secret Service had not uncovered any serious threats there, and no extensive investigation was conducted in the city.

Beginning a week before the trip, defamatory posters and leaflets excoriating the President appeared throughout Dallas. Some carried Kennedy's picture with the caption, "Wanted for Treason: This Man Is Wanted for Treasonous Activities Against the United States." It was suggested the President's Dallas parade route should not be published, but at the urging of Kennedy's staff, it appeared in the Dallas newspapers on November 18 and 19.

The President and Mrs. Kennedy traveled to Texas on November 21. That day, Kennedy visited San Antonio and Houston, where he was warmly greeted by enthusiastic crowds. He flew to Fort Worth that evening.

One of the President's first acts on the morning of November 22 was to call the woman who had arranged the accommodations that he and the First Lady occupied at Fort Worth's Texas Hotel. She had hung the walls with original paintings by modern masters such as Vincent Van Gogh and Claude Monet, and the special effort of the citizens of Forth Worth greatly impressed the Kennedys. That rainy morning, the President addressed the Forth Worth Chamber of Commerce. The speech was well received and, as Governor Connally recounted, it was laced with fun. Later in the morning, after a query from Dallas, the President said that if the weather was clear, he did not want the protective bubble used on the Presidential limousine.

The President and his entourage took off for Dallas at approximately 11:20 a.m. While the Presidential plane, Air Force One, was airborne, the President looked out the window and remarked to the Governor with a smile, "Our luck is holding. It looks as if we'll get sunshine." A clear sky, brilliant sunshine, 68-degree temperature—a marvelous autumn day—provided the backdrop for the President and Mrs. Kennedy as they arrived at Love Field in Dallas. The First Lady was presented with a bouquet of roses, and the couple attended a reception held in their honor at the airport by the community leaders of Dallas. After greeting them, the President moved to shake hands with the enthusiastic crowd which, according to some estimates, may have numbered 4.000 persons. For a few minutes, the President and the First Lady walked along the security barrier, greeting people. Then they joined Governor and Mrs. Connally in the Presidential limousine. Two Secret Service agents. one the driver, sat in front. The President and his wife sat in the rear seat, with the President on the right, in keeping with military protocol. as Commander in Chief of the Armed Forces. Governor Connally sat on a jump seat directly in front of the President. with his back to Kennedy, and Mrs. Connally occupied the left jump seat. Two cars with members of the Dallas Police Department, including Chief Jesse Curry, and Secret Service agents, preceded the Presidential limousine. Behind, a followup car carried Secret Service agents and members of the White House staff. To the rear of that car, the Vice President and Mrs. Johnson and Senator Ralph Yarborough rode in another limousine. Next came the Vice President's followup car, and then a long line of limousines, trucks and various vehicles containing Members of Congress and other dignitaries, photographers, the President's physician, and members of the White House staff and the press.

The motorcade left Love Field at about 11:50 a.m. Governor Connally recalled he was worried, not about violence, but about the possibility that some incident might occur that would embarrass the President and disrupt the atmosphere of confidence that had been building throughout the trip. That morning. a hostile full-page advertisement, sponsored by the "American-thinking Citizens of Dallas," had appeared in the pages of the Dallas Morning News. It charged, among other things, that Kennedy had ignored the Constitution. scrapped the Monroe Doctrine in favor of the "Spirit of Moscow," and had been "soft on Communists, fellow-travelers, and ultra-leftists in America." The Governor was apprehensive that there might be unfriendly demonstrations during the motorcade or that the crowd's mood would be indifferent or even sullen.

The Governor's concern subsided as the motorcade passed through the outskirts of Dallas and neared the center of the city. The crowds grew larger and they were unmistakably friendly, with people smiling, waving, and calling the President's name. In Connally's words,

The further we got toward town, the denser became the crowds, and when we got down on Main Street, the crowds were extremly thick. They were pushed off of curbs; they were out in the street, and they were backed all the way up against the walls of the buildings. They were just as thick as they could be. I don't know how many. But, there were at least a quarter of a million people on the parade route that day and everywhere the reception was good.

Governor Connally noticed that Mrs. Kennedy, who had appeared apprehensive the previous day, was more relaxed and enjoyed the Dallas crowd. The only hostile act he remembered was a heckler with a placard that read "Kennedy Go Home." The President noticed the sign, and asked Governor and Mrs. Connally if they had seen it. Connally said, "Yes, but we were hoping you didn't."

"Well, I saw it. Don't you imagine he's a nice fellow?" Kennedy asked.

The Governor said, "Yes, I imagine he's a nice fellow."

Connally's fear of an embarrassing incident seemed to be unfounded. He recalled:

The crowds were larger than I had anticipated. They were more enthusiastic than I could ever have hoped for.

This enthusiasm was apparent in a number of incidents. A little girl held up a sign with the request, "President Kennedy, will you shake hands with me?" The President noticed the sign, had the car stopped and shook hands with the little girl. The car was mobbed by an admiring crowd that was only separated from the Presidential limousine by Secret Service agents. At another stop, as the motorcade approached downtown Dallas, the President caught sight of a Roman Catholic nun with a group of schoolchildren. He stopped and spoke with the group. Several times enthusiastic onlookers broke away from the curbside throng and attempted to reach the limousine. Secret Service agents cleared the admirers from the street.

The crowds grew thicker as the Presidential parade approached downtown. The motorcade followed the traditional Dallas parade route into the downtown business district, turning onto Main Street, which brought it through the center of the Dallas commerical district. It moved westward along Main toward Dealey Plaza. People crowded the sidewalks, surged into the street, and waved from office building windows. The motorcade tunneled through the throng. The Governor later remarked that the business community, the group Kennedy sought to impress, would have to be affected by this remarkable reception. Connally said "* * * the trip had been absolutely wonderful, and we were heaving a sigh of relief because once we got through the motorcade at Dallas and through the Dallas luncheon, then everything else was pretty much routine."

President Kennedy was clearly delighted by his Dallas welcome.

At the corner of Main and Houston, the motorcade made a sharp 90-degree turn to the right and headed north for one block, toward the Texas School Book Depository. As the limousine approached Houston and Elm, Mrs. Connally, elated by the reception, said, "Mr. President, you can't say Dallas doesn't love you." "That's obvious," the President replied.

At Elm Street, the limousine made a hairpin turn to the left and headed west, passing the book depository.

At about 12:30 p.m., as the President waved to the crowds, shots rang out.

Mrs. Connally heard a noise, turned to her right, and saw the President clutch his neck with both hands, then slump down in the seat. Governor Connally immediately thought the noise was a rifle shot. He turned from his straight-backed jump seat in an attempt to catch sight of the President because he feared an assassination attempt. The Governor described the scene:

I never looked. I never made the full turn. About the time I turned back where I was facing more or less straight ahead, the way the car was moving, I was hit. I was knocked over, just doubled over by the force of the bullet. It went in my back and came out my chest about 2 inches below and to the left of my right nipple. The force of the bullet drove my body over almost double, and when I looked, immediately I could see I was drenched with blood. So, I knew I had been badly hit and I more or less straightened up. At about this time, Nellie [Mrs. Connally] reached over and pulled me down into her lap.

I was in her lap facing forward when another shot was fired * * * I did not hear the shot that hit me. I wasn't conscious of it. I am sure I heard it, but I was not conscious of it at all. I heard another shot. I heard it hit. It hit with a very pronounced impact * * * it made a very, very strong sound.

Immediately, I could see blood and brain tissue all over the interior of the car and all over our clothes. We were both covered with brain tissue, and there were pieces of brain tissue as big as your little finger * * *

* * * * * * * * * *

When I was hit, or shortly before I was hit—no, I guess it was after I was hit—I said first, just almost in despair, I said, "no, no, no," just thinking how tragic it was that we had gone through this 24 hours, it had all been so wonderful and so beautifully executed.

The President had been so marvelously received and then here, at the last moment, this great tragedy. I just said, "no, no, no, no." Then I said right after I was hit, I said, "My God, they are going to kill us all."

Mrs. Connally initially thought the Governor was dead as he fell into her lap. She did not look back after her husband was hit, but heard Mrs. Kennedy say, "They have shot my husband." After one shot, Mrs. Connally recalled, the President's wife said, "They have killed my husband. I have his brains in my hand."

Roy Kellerman, the Secret Service agent in the right front seat said, "Let's get out of here fast." Bill Geer, the driver, accelerated tremendously. "So we pulled out of the motorcade," Mrs. Connally recalled "and we must have been a horrible sight flying down the freeway with those dying men in our arms."

She added, "There was no screaming in that horrible car. It was just a silent, terrible drive."

The wounded President and Governor were rushed to Parkland Hospital.

At 1 p.m., the President of the United States was pronounced dead, 1,037 days after his term had begun.

A. LEE HARVEY OSWALD FIRED THREE SHOTS AT PRESIDENT JOHN F. KENNEDY; THE SECOND AND THIRD SHOTS HE FIRED STRUCK THE PRESIDENT; THE THIRD SHOT HE FIRED KILLED THE PRESIDENT

1. PRESIDENT KENNEDY WAS STRUCK BY TWO RIFLE SHOTS FIRED FROM BEHIND HIM

The President's Commission on the Assassination of President Kennedy (Warren Commission) concluded that President Kennedy was struck by two bullets that were fired from above and behind him. [1] According to the Commission, one bullet hit the President near the base of the back of the neck, slightly to the right of the spine, and exited from the front of the neck. The other entered the right rear of the President's head and exited from the right side of the head, causing a large wound. [2]

The Commission based its finding primarily upon the testimony of the doctors who had treated the President at Parkland Memorial Hospital in Dallas and the doctors who performed the autopsy on the President at the Naval Medical Center in Bethesda, Md. [3]

In forming this conclusion, neither the members of the Warren Commission, nor its staff, nor the doctors who had performed the autopsy, took advantage of the X-rays and photographs of the President that were taken during the course of the autopsy. [4] The reason for the failure of the Warren Commission to examine these primary materials is that there was a commitment to make public all evidence examined by the Commission. [5] The Commission was concerned that publication of the autopsy X-rays and photographs would be an invasion of the privacy of the Kennedy family. [6] The Commission's decision to rely solely on the testimony of the doctors precluded the possibiliy that the Commission might make use of a review of the autopsy evidence by independent medical experts to determine if they concurred with the findings of the doctors at Parkland and Bethesda.

A determination of the number and location of the

President's wounds was critical to resolving the question of whether there was more than one assassin. The secrecy that surrounded the autopsy proceedings, therefore, has led to considerable skepticism toward the Commission's findings. Concern has been expressed that authorities were less than candid, since the Navy doctor in charge of the autopsy conducted at Bethesda Naval Hospital destroyed his notes, and the Warren Commission decided to forego an opportunity to view the X-rays and photographs or to permit anyone else to inspect them.

The skepticism has been reinforced by a film taken of the Presidential motorcade at the moment of the assassination by an amateur movie photographer, Abraham Zapruder. In the Zapruder film, the President's head is apparently thrown backward as the front right side of the skull appears to explode, suggesting to critics of the Warren Commission's findings that the President was struck by a bullet that entered the front of the head. [7] Such a bullet, it has been argued, was fired by a gunman positioned on the grassy knoll, a parklike area to the right and to the front of where the moving limousine was located at the instant of the fatal shot. [8]

Since the Warren Commission completed its investigation, two other Government panels have subjected the X-rays and photographs taken during the autopsy on President Kennedy to examination by independent medical experts. A team of forensic pathologists appointed by Attorney General Ramsey Clark in 1968, [9] and a panel retained by the Commission on CIA Activities Within the United States (Rockefeller Commission) in 1975, [10] reached the same basic conclusion: the President was struck by two bullets from behind. But neither panel published the X-rays and photographs, nor did either explain the basis of its conclusions in a public hearing. Consequently, neither panel was able to relieve significantly doubts that have persisted over the years about the nature and location of the President's wounds.

(a) Reliance on scientific analysis

The committee believed from the beginning of its investigation that the most reliable evidence upon which it could base determinations as to what happened in Dealey Plaza on November 22, 1963, was an analysis of hard scientific data. Accordingly, the committee contracted with leading independent experts in the fields of forensic pathology, ballistics, photography, acoustics, neutron activation analysis, and other disciplines. The reports submitted by these experts were fully considered by the committee in formulating its findings.

(1) *The medical evidence.*—The committee's forensic pathology panel was composed of nine members, eight of whom were chief medical examiners in major local jurisdictions in the United States. [11] As a group, they had been responsible for more than 100,000 autopsies, [12] an accumulation of experience the committee deemed invaluable in the evaluation of the medical evidence—including the autopsy X-rays and photographs—to determine the cause of death of the President and the nature and location of his wounds. The panel was also asked to recommend guidelines in the event of a future assassination of a President or other high Federal official. [12]

The committee also employed experts to authenticate the autopsy materials. Neither the Clark Panel nor the Rockefeller Commission undertook to determine if the X-rays and photographs were, in fact, authentic. The committee, in light of the numerous issues that had arisen over the years with respect to autopsy X-rays and photographs, believed authentication to be a crucial step in the investigation. [14]

The authentication of the autopsy X-rays and photographs was accomplished by the committee with the assistance of its photographic evidence panel as well as forensic dentists, forensic anthropologists, and radiologists working for the committee. [15] Two questions were put to these experts:

Could the photographs and X-rays stored in the National Archives be positively identified as being of President Kennedy?

Was there any evidence that any of these photographs or X-rays had been altered in any manner?

To determine if the photographs of the autopsy subject were in fact of the President, forensic anthropologists compared the autopsy photographs with antemortem pictures of the President. This comparison was done on the basis of both metric and morphological features. The metric analysis relied upon a series of facial measurements taken from the photographs, while the morphological analysis was focused on consistency of physical features, particularly those that could be considered distinctive (shape of the nose, patterns of facial lines, et cetera). Once unique characteristics were identified, posterior and anterior autopsy photographs were compared to verify that they, in fact, depicted the same person.

The anthropologists studied the autopsy X-rays in conjunction with premortem X-rays of the President. A sufficient number of unique anatomic characteristics were present in X-rays taken before and after the President's death to conclude that the autopsy X-rays were of President Kennedy. This conclusion was consistent with the findings of a forensic dentist employed by the committee. [16] Since many of the X-rays taken during the course of the autopsy included the President's teeth, it was possible to determine, using the President's dental records, that the X-rays were of the President.

Once the forensic dentist and anthropologists had determined that the autopsy photographs and X-rays were of the President, photographic scientists and radiologists examined the original autopsy photographs, negatives, transparencies, and X-rays for signs of alteration. They concluded there was no evidence of the photographic or radiographic materials having been altered. [17] Consequently, the committee determined that the autopsy X-rays and photographs were a valid basis for the conclusions of the committee's forensic pathology panel.

While the examination of the autopsy X-rays and photographs was the principal basis of its analysis, the forensic pathology panel also had access to all relevant witness testimony. In addition, all tests and evidence analyses requested by the panel were performed. [18] It was only after considering all of this evidence that the panel reached its conclusions.

The forensic pathology panel concluded that President Kennedy was struck by two, and only two, bullets, each of which entered from the rear.[1] The panel further concluded that the President was struck by one bullet that entered in the upper right of the back and exited from the front of the throat, and one bullet that entered in the right rear of the head near the cowlick area and exited from

---

[1]In many of its conclusions, the forensic pathology panel voted 8 to 1, with the dissenting vote being consistently that of Cyril H. Wecht, M.D., coroner of Allegheny County, Pa. In all references to conclusions of the panel, unless it is specifically stated that it was unanimous, it should be assumed that Dr. Wecht dissented.

the right side of the head, toward the front. This second bullet caused a massive wound to the President's head upon exit. There is no medical evidence that the President was struck by a bullet entering the front of the head, [19] and the possibility that a bullet could have struck the President and yet left no evidence is extremely remote. Because this conclusion appears to be inconsistent with the backward motion of the President's head in the Zapruder film, the committee consulted a wound ballistics expert to determine what relationship, if any, exists between the direction from which a bullet strikes the head and subsequent head movement. [20] The expert concluded that nerve damage from a bullet entering the President's head could have caused his back muscles to tighten which, in turn, could have caused his head to move toward the rear. [21] He demonstrated the phenomenon in a filmed experiment which involved the shooting of goats. [22] Thus, the committee determined that the rearward movement of the President's head would not be fundamentally inconsistent with a bullet striking from the rear. [23]

The forensic pathology panel determined that Governor Connally was struck by a bullet from the rear, one that entered just below the right armpit and exited below the right nipple of the chest. It then shattered the radius bone of the Governor's right wrist and caused a superficial wound to the left thigh. [24] Based on its examination of the nature and alinement of the Governor's wounds, the panel concluded that they were all caused by a single bullet that came from the rear. It concluded further that, having caused the Governor's wounds, the bullet was dislodged from his left thigh.

The panel determined that the nature of the wounds of President Kennedy and Governor Connally was consistent with the possibility that one bullet entered the upper right back of President Kennedy and, after emerging from the front of the neck, caused all of the Governor's wounds. [25] A factor that influenced the panel significantly was the ovoid shape of the wound in the Governor's back, indicating that the bullet had begun to tumble or yaw before entering. [26] An ovoid wound is characteristic of one caused by a bullet that has passed through or glanced off an intervening object. [27] Based on the evidence available to it, the panel concluded that a single bullet passing through both President Kennedy and

Governor Connally would support a fundamental conclusion that the President was struck by two, and only two, bullets, each fired from behind. [28] Thus, the forensic pathology panel's conclusions were consistent with the so-called single bullet theory advanced by the Warren Commission. [29]

(2) *Reaction times and alinement.*—The hypothesis that both the President and the Governor were struck by a single bullet had originally been based on the Warren Commission's examination of the Zapruder film and test firings of the assassination rifle. The time between the observable reactions of the President and of the Governor was too short to have allowed, according to the Commission's test firings, two shots to have been fired from the same rifle. [30] FBI marksmen who test-fired the rifle for the Commission employed the telescopic sight on the rifle, and the minimum firing time between shots was approximately 2.25 to 2.3 seconds. [31] The time between the observable reactions of the President and the Governor, according to the Commission, was less than two seconds.[2]

The Commission determined that its hypothesis that the same bullet struck both the President and the Governor was supported by visual observations of the relative alinement of the two men in the limousine, by a trajectory analysis, and by wound ballistics tests. The Commission said, however, that a determination of which shot hit the Governor was "not necessary to any essential findings." [32]

(3) *Neutron activation analysis.*—In addition to the conclusion reached by the committee's forensic pathology panel, the single bullet theory was substantiated by the findings of a neutron activation analysis performed for the committee. [33] The bullet alleged to have caused the injuries to the Governor and the President was found on a stretcher at Parkland Hospital. [34] Numerous critics have alleged that this bullet, labeled "pristine" because it appeared to have been only slightly damaged, could not have caused the injuries to both the Governor (particularly his shattered wrist) and the President. Some have even suggested the possibility that the bullet wounded neither

---

[2]In its report, the committee's photographic evidence panel suggested that Governor Connally reacted to his wounds approximately one second after President Kennedy. This interval might have been even less, but a sign obstructing Zapruder's field of view made it impossible to study the Governor immediately after the President first appeared to be reacting to having been shot.

Connally nor Kennedy, that it was planted on the stretcher. [35] Neutron activation analysis, however, established that it was highly likely that the injuries to the Governor's wrist were caused by the bullet found on the stretcher in Parkland Hospital. [36] Further, the committee's wound ballistics expert concluded that the bullet found on the stretcher—Warren Commission exhibit 399 (CE 399)—is of a type that could have caused the wounds to President Kennedy and Governor Connally without showing any more deformity than it does. [37]

In determining whether the deformity of CE 399 was consistent with its having passed through both the President and Governor, the committee considered the fact that it is a relatively long, stable, fully jacketed bullet, typical of ammunition often used by the military. Such ammunition tends to pass through body tissue more easily than soft nose hunting bullets. [38] Committee consultants with knowledge in forensic pathology and wound ballistics concluded that it would not have been unusual for such a fully jacketed bullet to have passed through the President and the Governor and to have been only minimally deformed. [39]

The neutron activation analysis further supported the single bullet theory by indicating that there was evidence of only two bullets among the fragments recovered from the limousine and its occupants. [40] The consultant who conducted the analysis concluded that it was "highly likely" that CE 399 and the fragments removed from Governor Connally's wrist were from one bullet; that one of the two fragments recovered from the floor of the limousine and the fragment removed from the President's brain during the autopsy were from a second bullet.[3] [41] Neutron activation analysis showed no evidence of a third bullet among those fragments large enough to be tested.

(4) *Photographic evidence.*—The committee also considered photographic evidence in its analysis of the shots. The Zapruder film, the only continuous chronological visual record of the assassination, is the best available photographic evidence of the number and timing of the shots that struck the occupants of the Presidential limousine.

The committee's panel of photographic experts examined specially enhanced and stablized versions of the Zapruder

_____

[3]The other large fragment recovered from the floor of the limousine had no lead in it, and therefore was not subjected to neutron activation analysis.

film for two purposes: (1) to try to draw conclusions about the timing of the shots from visual reactions of the victims; and (2) to determine whether the alinement of the President and the Governor was consistent with the single bullet theory. The panel also examined still photographs.

Several conclusions with respect to the validity of the single bullet theory were reached. [42] The panel concluded there is clear photographic evidence that two shots, spaced approximately 6 seconds apart, struck the occupants of the limousine. By Zapruder frame 207, when President Kennedy is seen going behind a sign that obstructed Zapruder's view, he appears to be reacting to a severe external stimulus. This reaction is first indicated in the vicinity of frame 200 of the Zapruder film. The President's right hand freezes in the midst of a waving motion, followed by a rapid leftward movement of his head. [43] There is, therefore, photographic evidence of a shot striking the President by this time.

Governor Connally shows no indication of distress before he disappears behind the sign at Zapruder frame 207, but as he emerges from behind the sign after frame 222, he seems to be reacting to some severe external stimulus. [44] By frame 226, when all of the limousine occupants have reappeared in Zapruder's field of view, the panel found indications in observable physical attitude and changes of facial expression to indicate that both the President and the Governor were reacting to their wounds. The President's reactions were obvious—he leans forward and clutches his throat. The Governor displays a pronounced rigid posture and change in facial expression.[4] [45]

To study the relative alinement of the President and Governor Connally within the limousine, the photographic panel paid particular attenton to the Zapruder frames just before the President and the Governor were obstructed by the sign, employing a stereoscopic (depth) analysis of frames 187 and 193 and still photographs taken at about the same time from the south side of Elm Street. The panel

---

[4] There is no scientific method for determining the elapsed time between when a shot hits and when a person visibly reacts. Different people have different reaction times; moreover, a person's reaction time often depends on where he has been hit.

found that the alinement of the President and the Governor during this period was consistent with the single bullet hypothesis. [46]

The photographic evidence panel determined, further, that the explosive effect of the second shot to strike President Kennedy, the fatal head shot, is depicted in Zapruder frame 313. By frame 313, the President's head is seen exploding, leading the panel to conclude that the actual moment of impact was approximately frame 312. [47]

(5) *Acoustical evidence and blur analysis.*—The committee performed two other scientific tests that addressed the question of the direction and timing of the bullets that struck the President. First, it contracted with acoustical consultants for an analysis of a tape recording of a radio transmission made at the time of the assassination. The experts decided there were four shots on the recording. [48] The first, second and fourth came from the Texas School Book Depository behind the President, the third came from the grassy knoll to the right front of the President. Taking the shot to the President's head at frame 312 as the last of the four shots, and thus as a possible base point,[5] it was possible to correlate the other sounds identified as probable gunfire with the Zapruder film. [49] Since the acoustical consultants concluded that the two earliest shots came from the depository, the shots (or at least their shock waves) would have reached the limousine at between frames 157 and 161 and frames 188 and 191. When coupled with the photographic evidence showing a reaction by President Kennedy beginning in the vicinity of frame 200, it appeared that he was first struck by a bullet at approximately frame 190.[6]

Second, the photographic evidence panel also studied the blurs on the Zapruder film that were caused by Zapruder's panning errors, that is, the effect of a lack of smooth motion as Zapruder moved from left to right with his camera. This was done in an effort to determine whether the blurs resulted from Zapruder's possible reac-

[5]The committee considered using frame 328 as a possible base point. In this analysis, the head shot occurring at frame 312 would, according to the acoustics results, have originated from the grassy knoll. This alternative, however, was rejected.

[6]A more detailed description of the reasoning leading to this conclusion is set forth in section I B, infra.

tion to the sound of gunshots. [50] This analysis indicated that blurs occurring at frames 189–197 and 312–334 may reasonably be attributed to Zapruder's startle reactions to gunshots. The time interval of the shots associated with these blurs was determined to be approximately 6 to 7 seconds. The possibility that other blurs on the film might be attributable to Zapruder's reactions to gunshots could not be confirmed or dismissed without additional data.

Taken together with other evidence, the photographic and acoustical evidence led the committee to conclude that President Kenndy and Governor Connally were struck, by one bullet at approximately Zapruder frame 190, and that the President was struck by another bullet at frame 312.

Thus, from the results of the analyses by its experts in the fields of forensic pathology, photography, acoustics, wound ballistics and neutron activation analysis, the committee concluded that President Kennedy was struck by two shots fired from behind.

2. THE SHOTS THAT STRUCK PRESIDENT KENNEDY FROM BEHIND WERE FIRED FROM THE SIXTH FLOOR WINDOW OF THE SOUTHEAST CORNER OF THE TEXAS SCHOOL BOOK DEPOSITORY BUILDING

The Warren Commission concluded that the shots that killed President and wounded Governor Connally "* * * were fired from the sixth floor window at the southeast corner of the Texas School Book Depository." [51] It based its conclusion on eyewitness testimony, physical evidence found on the sixth floor of the depository, medical evidence and the absence of "* * * credible evidence that the shots were fired from * * * any other location." [52]

(a) Scientific analysis

In investigating this aspect of the case, the committee relied heavily on the scientific analysis of physical evidence, and again the conclusions of the forensic pathology panel were relevant. The panel concluded that the two bullets that struck the President came from behind and that the fatal head shot was moving in a downward direction when it struck the President.[7] [53] Thus, forensic pathology provided reliable evidence as to the origin of the shots: The gunman who fired the shot that hit President Kennedy and Governor Connally at approximately frame 190 of the Zapruder film fired from behind, and the gunman who fired the shot that hit the President in the head at frame 312 was positioned above and to the rear of the Presidential limousine.

(1) *Trajectory analysis.*—Another project pertaining to the origin of the shots involved the trajectory of the bullets that hit the President. Although the Warren Commission also studied trajectory, its analysis consisted of proving that a bullet fired from the southeast corner of the sixth floor of the book depository could have hit the President and then hit the Governor and that another bullet fired from that location could have caused the wound to the President's head. Basically, the purpose of the Commission's trajectory analysis was to prove that it was possible for the prime suspect. Lee Harvey Oswald, to have hit both the President and the Governor from the sixth floor of the depository.

The committee approached the problem without making prior assumptions as to the origin of the shots. It was an interdisciplinary effort, drawing from the expertise of forensic pathologists, acoustical and photographic analysts, and an engineer from the staff of the National Aeronautics and Space Administration, who plotted the trajectories. [54]

The trajectory analysis was based on three types of data. From the acoustical analysis of the radio transmission, the time of the shots was obtained. From the photographic analysis of the Zapruder film and the acoustical analysis, it was possible to know with relative precision when each of the shots struck—at approximately Zapruder frame 190, for the shot that struck the President in the back of the neck, and at Zapruder frame 312, for the fatal shot to the President's head. Through an

---

[7]The panel used both the location of the wounds and Zapruder frame 312 to determine the "downward" slope of the fatal head shot. It did not attempt to determine the slope of the bullet that struck the President's back because the moment of impact was not thought to be visible in the film. This decision by the forensic pathology panel was made well before the photographic panel reached its conclusion regarding the President's and Governor Connally's reactions as shown in the Zapruder film.

41

analysis of those frames and still photographs taken at approximately the same time from the south side of Elm Street, it was possible to determine the location of the limousine in the plaza, the sitting positions of President Kennedy and Governor Connally and their alinement to one another. [55]

By then coordinating this data with the forensic pathology panel's analysis of the exit and entry wounds sustained by President Kennedy, it was possible to plot the path of the bullets out to their source. Separate direction and slope trajectories were developed for two bullets—the one that caused the President's back and neck wounds, and the one that caused his fatal head wound. [56] A third trajectory analysis was conducted to test the hypothesis that the first bullet also caused the wounds to Governor Connally, using for this analysis the exit wounds to the President's neck and the entry wound to the Governor's back. [57]

All three trajectories intercepted the southeast face of the Texas School Book Depository building.[58] While the trajectories could not be plotted with sufficient precision to determine the exact point from which the shots were fired, they each were calculated with a margin of error reflecting the precision of the underlying data. The margins of error were indicated as circles within which the shots originated. The southeast corner window of the depository was inside each of the circles.[59]

(2) *Photographic evidence.*—The photographic evidence panel examined evidence possibly relevant to the question of the origin of the shots, as follows:

The panel examined a motion picture of the southeast corner window of the depository taken a short time prior to the shots.[60] While there is an impression of motion in the film, the panel could not attribute it to the movement of a person or an object and instead attributed the motion to photographic artifacts.[61] The panel's findings were the same with respect to apparent motion in adjacent windows shown in the film.[62]

The panel studied two photographs taken within minutes of the assassination. [63] While no human face or form could be detected in the sixth floor southeast window, the panel was able to conclude that a stack of boxes in the window had been rearranged during the interval of the taking of the two photographs. [64]

There is evidence, a motion picture film made by Charles L. Bronson, that some independent researchers believe shows a figure or figures in the sixth floor depository window several minutes before the shooting. The film came to the attention of the committee toward the end of its investigation. Some members of the committee's photographic evidence panel did conduct a preliminary review (without enhancement) of the film. While motion was detected in the window, it was considered more likely to be a random photographic artifact than human movement. Nevertheless, the limited review was not sufficient to determine definitively if the film contained evidence of motion made by human figures.[65] Because of its high quality, it was recommended that the Bronson film be analyzed further.

(b) Witness testimony

While the committee relied primarily on scientific analysis of physical evidence as to the origin of the shots, it also considered the testimony of witnesses. The procedure used to analyze their statements was as follows:

First, all available prior statements were read by the committee and studied for consistency. The objective was to identify inconsistencies either between the words of one witness and another or between the various words of a witness whose story had changed. The statements were obtained from the files of the Dallas Police Department, Dallas Sheriff's Office, the FBI, Secret Service, and Warren Commission.

Second, an attempt was made to locate the witnesses and to show them the statements they made in the course of the original investigation. Each witness was asked to read his statements and to indicate whether they were complete and accurate. If statements were inaccurate, or if a witness was aware of information that was not included, he was asked to make corrections or provide additional information. In addition, where relevant questions had not been asked, the committee asked them.[66]

There are inherent limitations in such a process. Any information provided by a witness in 1978—15 years after the assassination—must be viewed in light of the passage of time that causes memories to fade and honest accounts to become distorted. Certainly, it cannot be considered with the same reliability as information provided in 1963–64. To the extent that they are based on witness testimony, the conclusions of the committee were vitally affected by the quality of the original investigation. The inconsistencies in the statements—the questions not asked, the witnesses not interviewed—all created problems that defied resolution 15 years after the events in Dallas.

Nevertheless, the committee considered all of the witness statements and determined to what extent they corroborated or independently substantiated, or contradicted, the conclusions indicated by the scientific evidence.

An example of such witness testimony is that relating to the discovery of the rifle and shell casings in the Texas School Book Depository. (Because detailed versions of witness testimony taken in the original investigation are a matter of public record, only brief résumés are included here.)

Deputy Sheiriff Luke Mooney testified to the Warren Commission that at approximately 1 p.m. on November 22, 1963, he discovered three spent rifle shells on the sixth floor of the Texas School Book Depository. [67] He stated that he was in the southeast corner of the building when he noticed boxes stacked high in the vicinity of the window. [68] He then squeezed in between a space in the boxes and saw three spent rifle shells in the vicinity of the window. [69] Mooney also told of seeing boxes stacked up as though they were a prop or rest for a weapon. [70]

Deputy Sheriff Eugene Boone told the Warren Commission that he arrived on the sixth floor of the depository subsequent to the discovery of the three spent rifle shells. [71] He said he went to the east end of the floor and began working his way across to the west end, looking in under and around boxes and pallets. [72] At the wall near a row of windows, he noticed a small space between some of the boxes. When he squeezed through the opening, he saw a rifle between two rows of boxes. The time was 1:22 p.m.[73]

(c) Firearms evidence

The rifle Boone found, a 6.5 millimeter Mannlicher-Carcano, was analyzed by the FBI in 1963–64 and by the committee's firearms panel in 1978, as was the other firearms evidence that was recovered. It was determined in both investigations that the bullet found on a stretcher at Parkland Hospital had been from the rifle found in the depository, as were two fragments recovered from the Presidential limousine. [74] Further, the three cartridge cases found on the sixth floor of the depository were determined to have been fired in the Mannlicher-Carcano.[8] [75]

Through neutron activation analysis, the committee found that the firearms evidence could be even more directly linked to the wounds suffered by the President and Governor Connally. It is highly likely that the bullet found on the stretcher was the one that passed through Governor Connally's wrist, leaving tiny particles behind, and the fragments retrieved from the limousine came from the same bullet as the fragments taken from President Kennedy's brain. [76]

Over the years, skepticism has arisen as to whether the rifle found in the depository by Boone is the same rifle that was delivered to the Warren Commission and is presently stored in the National Archives. The suspicion has been based to some extent on allegations that police officers who first discovered the rifle identified it as a 7.5 millimeter German Mauser. [77] The controversy was intensified by the allegation that various photographs of the rifle, taken at different times, portray inconsistencies with respect to the proportions of the various component parts.[78]

To resolve the controversy, the committee assembled a wide range of photographs of the rifle: a police photograph taken where it was found in the depository; a motion picture film taken by a television station showing the rifle when it was found by the police; a series of photographs of a police officer carrying the rifle from the depository; photographs taken as the rifle was carried through the halls of Dallas Police Department; and photographs taken later by the FBI and Dallas Police Department.[79]

The examination by committee photographic consultants

---

[8]The committee firearms panel determined that the evidence stored in the National Archives ballistically matched the bullets fired by the FBI in 1964 tests from the Mannlicher-Carcano found by Boone. Since the rifle had been test-fired numerous times since 1963, its barrel had been altered by wear, and bullets the panel fired from the rifle did not match either the FBI test cartridges or those found on the sixth floor of depository or that found on the stretcher.

determined that all photographs were of the same rifle. Both a study of proportions and a comparison of identifying marks indicated that only one rifle was involved.[80]

(d) Summary of the evidence

In the final analysis, the committee based its finding that the shots that struck President Kennedy were fired from the Texas School Book Depository on the quantity and quality of the evidence, to wit:

> The findings of forensic pathologists that the shots that hit the President came from behind;
>
> The results of the trajectory analysis that traced the bullets to the vicinity of sixth floor window of the depository;
>
> The conclusion of acoustics experts that the shots came from the vicinity of the sixth floor window of the depository;
>
> The positive identification by firearms experts that the rifle found on the sixth floor of the depository was the one that fired the bullet found on a stretcher at Parkland Hospital and fragments retrieved from the Presidential limousine;
>
> The results of neutron activation analysis indicating that it was highly likely that the bullet found on the stretcher at Parkland Hospital was the one that passed through Governor Connally's wrist, and that the fragments found in the limousine were from the bullet that struck the President in the head;
>
> The conclusion of photographic experts that the rifle found in the depository was the same one that was repeatedly photographed in November 1963 and that is presently stored at the National Archives.

The committee also weighed the firsthand testimony of witnesses but with caution, because of the problem of the passage of time. Besides the statements of law officers on the scene immediately after the assassination, it considered the accounts of bystanders in Dealey Plaza, bearing in mind that these were recollections of fleeting moments when emotions were running high. The committee noted, however, that a number of the Dealey Plaza witnesses said they saw either a rifle or a man with a rifle in the vicinity of the sixth floor southeast corner window of the book depository.

3. LEE HARVEY OSWALD OWNED THE RIFLE THAT WAS USED TO FIRE THE SHOTS FROM THE SIXTH FLOOR WINDOW OF THE SOUTHEAST CORNER OF THE TEXAS SCHOOL BOOK DEPOSITORY BUILDING

The Warren Commission concluded that Lee Harvey Oswald owned the rifle found on the sixth floor of the Texas School Book Depository. Since the Commission further concluded that Oswald was the assassin of the President, his background is relevant.

(a) Biography of Lee Harvey Oswald

Oswald was born in New Orleans, La., on October 18, 1939, two months after the death of his father. His mother remarried, and, from 1945 until 1952, the family lived in a number of cities in Texas and Lousiana. This marriage ended in divorce when Oswald was nine.

In 1952, Oswald and his mother moved to New York City. His school record was marked by chronic truancy, and a psychiatric examination suggested that he was emotionally disturbed. Oswald and his mother returned to New Orleans in 1954.

After finishing the ninth grade, the 16-year-old Oswald dropped out of school. The following year, he joined the U.S. Marine Corps. Asserting the ill health and distressing financial situation of his mother, Oswald obtained a release from the Marines in 1959. Following his discharge, he spent 3 days with his mother in Fort Worth, Tex., and then went to New Orleans. From there, he traveled to the Soviet Union where he tried to become a Soviet citizen.

In April 1961, Oswald married a 19-year-old Russian woman, Marina Nikolaevna Prusakova, whom he had met while working in Minsk. Having become disillusioned with Soviet life, he returned to the United States with his wife and baby daughter the following year. The Oswalds arrived in Fort Worth, Tex., on June 14, 1962, and soon became acquainted with a number of people in the Dallas-Fort Worth Russian-speaking community. Oswald moved to Dallas in October 1962, where he found a job with a graphic arts company. Marina followed in November, but their marriage was plagued by intermittent feuding.

In March 1963, according to the Warren Commission, Oswald purchased a Mannlicher-Carcano rifle and telescopic sight from a Chicago mail order house. He also ordered a .38 caliber Smith and Wesson pistol from a Los Angeles firm. According to Marina Oswald, he probably used the rifle in an attempt in April to kill Edwin A. Walker, a retired Army general who had been relieved from his post in West Germany for distributing right-wing literature to his troops. Walker was not harmed.

In April 1963, Oswald went to New Orleans. Meanwhile, Marina and the baby moved to the home of a friend, Ruth Paine, in Irving, Tex., in late April. In May, she joined Oswald in New Orleans. On July 19, Oswald was dismissed from his job for inefficiency. In May and June, Oswald had expressed an interest in the Fair Play for Cuba Committee. In August, he distributed pro-Castro leaflets and also made two radio broadcasts on behalf of the Castro regime. Marina Oswald and her baby returned to Texas to stay with Ruth Paine in Irving on September 22.

Oswald went to Mexico City in the latter part of September. He visited the Russian Embassy and Consulate and the Cuban Consulate there, but he failed to get permission to travel to either country. He returned to Dallas on October 3, 1963. He visited Marina in Irving on several occasions but continued to try to find a place to live in Dallas. On October 14, Oswald moved into a roominghouse on North Beckley Avenue in Dallas. He began work at the Texas School Book Depository 2 days later. On October 20, Marina gave birth to their second daughter. She returned to the Paine home in Irving where Oswald visited on November 1, and from November 8 until November 11. Oswald next visited Marina and his children in Irving on the evening of November 21. He returned to Dallas the following morning.

Shortly after the assassination of President Kennedy on November 22, 1963, Dallas Patrolman J. D. Tippit was shot and killed. At approximately 2 p.m., Lee Harvey Oswald was arrested in the Texas Theatre. He was subsequently charged in the murder of Tippit and named as a suspect in the Kennedy assassination.

On November 24, 1963, while he was being escorted through the basement of Dallas police headquarters in preparation for being transferred to the Dallas County Sheriff's office, Oswald was fatally wounded by a single shot fired from a pistol by Jack Ruby, a Dallas nightclub operator.

As noted, the Warren Commission had traced the chain of possession of the alleged assassination rifle and determined that the name on the money order and purchase form used to buy the rifle was "A. Hidell," which it determined to be an alias used by Oswald.[81] It also determined that the rifle was sent to a Dallas post office box rented on October 9, 1962 by Oswald. [82] Through handwriting analysis, the Commission determined that Oswald had filled out and signed the documents relative to the purchase and receipt of the rifle. [83] Moreover, the Commission received testimony that Oswald owned a rifle and that it was not in its usual storage place at the residence of Michael and Ruth Paine in Irving, Tex., when police searched the residence on the afternoon of November 22, 1963. [84]

Photographs of Oswald holding a rifle were also recovered from among his personal possessions, and the Commission concluded that the rifle in the photograph was the one found on the sixth floor of the book depository. [85] A palmprint taken from the barrel of the rifle was identified as a latent palmprint of Oswald.[86] Finally, the Commission treated as significant evidence a brown paper sack on which was identified a latent palmprint of Oswald. [87] It contained fibers that were determined to be identical to certain fibers of a blanket in which Oswald had allegedly wrapped the rifle.[88]

The committee concluded that the rifle found on the sixth floor of the book depository was the murder weapon. This determination, coupled with Warren Commission evidence of Oswald's ownership of the rifle, if accepted, proved conclusively that Oswald was the owner of the murder weapon.

Nevertheless, doubt has been cast on the evidence that Oswald owned the rifle in question. Critics of the Warren Commission have asserted that the chain of possession is meaningless, because more than one Mannlicher-Carcano was issued with the serial number C2766. [89] They have also argued that the photograph of Oswald holding the rifle is a fake and that his palmprint was planted on the barrel.[90]

[b] The committee's approach

The committee decided that one way to determine whether Oswald did, in fact, own the murder weapon was to test the reliability of the evidence used by the Warren Commission to establish ownership and to subject the available evidence to further scientific analysis.

The committee posed these questions:

> Could the handwriting on the money order used to purchase the rifle and the application for the post office box be established with confidence as that of Lee Harvey Oswald?[9]

> Are the photographs of Oswald holding the rifle authentic, and is that rifle the one that was found in the book depository after the assassination?

(1) *Handwriting analysis.*—With respect to the first issue, the committee's questioned documents panel, composed of three experts with approximately 90 years of combined experience in the field of questioned document examination, was provided with approximately 50 documents allegedly containing Oswald's handwriting.[91] The panel was asked to determine whether all of the documents were written by the same person. Among the documents provided to the panel was the money order sent to Klein's Sporting Goods Co. of Chicago to pay for a Mannlicher-Carcano, serial number C2766, the application for the post office box to which the rifle was subsequently mailed, and two fingerprints cards signed by Oswald.[92] One of the cards was signed at the time of his enlistment in the Marine Corps on October 24, 1956; the other, dated August 9, 1963, was signed by Oswald at the time he was arrested in New Orleans for disturbing the peace. (Although Oswald was fingerprinted when he was arrested in Dallas on November 22, 1963, he refused to sign the card.)[10]

The questioned documents panel determined that the money order and the post office box application were filled out and signed by the same person and that the handwriting on them was identical to the handwriting on the two fingerprint cards signed by Oswald.[94] On the basis of this analysis, the committee determined that Oswald bought the weapon in question from Klein's Sporting Goods Co.

(2) *The backyard photographs.*—The photographs of

---

[9]The committee also attempted to have its handwriting experts analyze other documents, such as the order for the rifle and the envelope in which it was mailed. The originals had, however, been destroyed, and microfilm copies that existed were not suitable for conclusive tests.

[10]The fingerprints on all three cards were examined by the committee's fingerprint expert and determined to be those of the same person. [93]

Oswald holding the rifle, with a pistol strapped to his waist and also holding copies of "The Militant" and "The Worker," were taken by his wife in the backyard of Oswald's home on Neeley Street in Dallas in March or April 1963, according to the testimony of Oswald's widow, Marina, given to the Warren Commission and the Committee.[11][95] There had been considerable controversy about the photographs. While in the custody of the Dallas police from November 22 to November 24, 1963, Oswald claimed that he did not own a rifle and that the photographs were composites, with his head superimposed over someone's else's body.[96] The Warren Commission, however, concluded that the photographs were authentic. [97] Critics of the Commission have questioned their authenticity for reasons generally based on alleged shadow inconsistencies, an indication of a grafting line between the mouth and chin, inconsistent body proportions and a disparate square-shaped chin.[98]

To determine if evidence of fakery was present in these photographs, the photographic evidence panel first sought to determine if they could be established as having been taken with Oswald's Imperial Reflex camera. This was done by studying the photographs (and the single available original negative) for unique identifying characteristics that would have been imparted by that camera. Once this was successfully done, the objects imaged in the photographs, as well as their shadows, were analyzed photogrammetrically. Finally, the materials were visually scrutinized, using magnification, stereoscopic analysis, and digital image processing.[99]

In its analyses, the photographic evidence panel worked with the original negative and first-generation prints of the photographs.[100] Only such materials contain the necessary and reliable photographic information. In contrast, some of the critics who claimed the photographs were faked relied on poor quality copies for their analyses.

---

[11]Marina Oswald, because of her testimony, played a central but troubling role in the investigation of the Warren Commission. A great deal of what the Commission sought to show about Oswald rested on her testimony, yet she gave incomplete and inconsistent statements at various times to the Secret Service, FBI, and the Commission. Marina's role in the committee's investigation was less central, since the committee's examination of what happened in Dallas rested primarily on the results of scientific analysis. The committee found no evidence that would indicate that Marina had foreknowledge of the assassination or that she helped her husband in any way in his efforts to assassinate the President. In its investigation of conspiracy, the committee's undertaking was not furthered by Marina's testimony, since she professed to know little of Oswald's associates in New Orleans or Dallas.

[101] Copies tend to lose detail and include defects that impair accurate representation of the photographic image.

After subjecting these original photographic materials and the camera alleged to have taken the pictures to sophisticated analytical techniques, the photographic evidence panel concluded that it could find no evidence of fakery.[102]

Of equal significance, a detailed scientific photographic analysis was conducted by the panel to determine whether the rifle held by Oswald in the backyard photographs was, in fact, the rifle stored at the National Archives. The panel found a unique identifying mark present on the weapon in the Archives that correlated with a mark visible on the rifle in the Oswald backyard photographs, as well as on the alleged assassination rifle as it appeared in photographs taken after the assassination in 1963.[103] Because this mark was considered to be a unique random pattern (i.e., caused by wear and tear through use), it was considered sufficient to warrant the making of a positive identification.

In addition, the relative lengths of component parts of the alleged assassination rifle at the National Archives were compared to component parts of the rifle that appeared in various 1963 photographs, including the backyard photographs.[104] They were found to be entirely consistent, component part for component part, with each other.[12] Upon completion of its analysis, the photographic evidence panel concluded that the rifle depicted in the backyard photographs is the one that was found in the book depository after the assassination and that was stored at the National Archives.[105]

In addition to the photographic analysis, the committee was able to employ handwriting analysis to aid in the determination of whether the photograph was authentic. During the course of the committee's investigation, George de Mohrenschildt, who had been a friend of Oswald, committed suicide. The committee, pursuant to ¬a subpoena, obtained de Mohrenschildt's personal papers, which included another copy of the Oswald backyard photograph. This copy, unlike any of those previous recovered, had an inscription on the back: "To my dear friend George, from

---

[12]Previous studies analyzing the relative lengths of the component parts of rifles shown in various postassassination photograps that questioned the identification of the rifle failed to consider the effect of perspective on the way that an object is imaged in a photograph.

Lee." It was dated April 1963 and signed "Lee Harvey Oswald."[106]

In an unpublished manuscript, de Mohrenschildt referred to this copy of the photograph and stated that after his return from Haiti, where he had been at the time of the assassination, he discovered the photograph among personal possessions that he had previously stored in a warehouse.[107] The committee examined the photograph to determine its authenticity and examined the handwriting to determine if Oswald had actually written the inscription and signed it. If Oswald did sign the photograph, his claim that he did not own the rifle and that the photograph was a fake could be discounted.

The photographic panel found no evidence of fakery in the backyard photographs, including the one found in de Mohrenschildt's effects.[108] The handwriting on the back of the de Mohrenschildt copy was determined by the questioned documents panel to be identical to all the other documents signed by Oswald, including the fingerprint cards.[109]

Thus, after submitting the backyard photographs to the photographic and handwriting panels, the committee concluded that there was no evidence of fakery in the photographs and that the rifle in the photographs was identical to the rifle found on the sixth floor of the depository on November 22, 1963. Having resolved these issues, the committee concluded that Lee Harvey Oswald owned the rifle from which the shots that killed President Kennedy were fired.

4. LEE HARVEY OSWALD, SHORTLY BEFORE THE ASSASSINA-
TION, HAD ACCESS TO AND WAS PRESENT ON THE SIXTH
FLOOR OF THE TEXAS SCHOOL BOOK DEPOSITORY BUILDING

The Warren Commission found that Lee Harvey Oswald worked principally on the first and sixth floors of the Texas School Book Depository, gathering books listed on orders and delivering them to the shipping room on the first floor.[110] He had, therefore, ready access to the sixth floor and to the southeast corner window from which the shots were fired. The Commission reached this conclusion by interviewing Oswald's supervisors and fellow employees.[111]

(a) Testimony of school book depository employees

In its investigation, the committee also considered the statements and testimony of employees of the Texas

School Book Depository who worked with and supervised Oswald. Roy Truly, superintendent of the depository, had stated to the Warren Commission that Oswald "had occasion to go to the sixth floor quite a number of times every day, each day, after books."[112] Truly and others testified that Oswald normally had access to the sixth floor of the depository, and a number of them said that they saw and heard Oswald in the vicinity of the sixth floor throughout the morning of November 22, 1963.[113]

(b) Physical evidence of Oswald's presence

In determining whether Oswald was actually present on the sixth floor of the depository, the committee paid primary attention to scientific analysis of physical evidence. Materials were examined for fingerprints, including a long, rectangular paper sack that was discovered near the southeast corner window and cartons that were found stacked adjacent to the window. The paper sack, which was suitable for containing a rifle, showed a latent palmprint and fingerprint of Oswald; one of the cartons showed both a palmprint and fingerprint identified as belonging to Oswald, and the other showed just his palmprint. The determination that Oswald's prints were on the sack and cartons was originally made in the investigation that immediately followed the assassination. It was confirmed by a fingerprint expert retained by the committee.[114]

The committee was aware that Oswald's access to the sixth floor during the normal course of his duties would have provided the opportunity to handle these items at any time before the assassination. Nevertheless, the committee believed that the way the boxes were stacked at the window and the proximity of the paper sack to the window from which the shots were fired must be considered as evidence indicating that he handled the boxes in the process of preparing the so-called sniper's nest and that he had used the paper sack to carry the rifle into the depository.

(c) Oswald's whereabouts

As for Oswald's presence on the sixth floor shortly before the assassination, the committee considered the testimony of Oswald's fellow employees at the depository. Although a number of them placed him on the fifth or sixth floor just before noon, a half hour before the assassination, one recalled he was on the first floor at that same time.[115]

The committee decided not to try to reconcile the testimony of these witnesses. Whether Oswald was on the first, fifth or sixth floor at noon, he could have still been on the sixth floor at 12:30. There was no witness who said he saw Oswald anywhere at the time of the assassination, and there was no witness who claimed to have been on the sixth floor and therefore in a position to have seen Oswald, had he been there.

(1) *Lovelady or Oswald?*—It has been alleged that a photograph taken of the President's limousine at the time of the first shot shows Oswald standing in the doorway of the depository.[116] Obviously, if Oswald was the man in the doorway, he could not have been on the sixth floor shooting at the President.

The Warren Commission determined that the man in the doorway was not Oswald, it was Billy Lovelady, another depository employee.[117] Critics have challenged that conclusion, charging that Commission members did not personally question Lovelady to determine if he was in fact that man in the photograph. In addition, they argue that no photograph of Lovelady was published in any of the volumes issued by the Warren Commission.[118]

The committee asked its photographic evidence panel to determine whether the man in the doorway was Oswald, Lovelady or someone else. Forensic anthropologists working with the panel compared the photograph with pictures of Oswald and Lovelady, and a photoanalyst studied the pattern of the shirt worn by the man in the doorway and compared it to the shirts worn by the two men that day.[119] Based on an assessment of the facial features, the anthropologists determined that the man in the doorway bore a much stronger resemblance to Lovelady than to Oswald. In addition, the photographic analysis of the shirt in the photograph established that it corresponded more closely with the shirt worn that day by Lovelady. Based on these analyses, the committee concluded that it was highly improbable that the man in the doorway was Oswald and highly probable that he was Lovelady.

The committee's belief that the man in the doorway was

Lovelady was also supported by an interview with Lovelady in which he affirmed to committee investigators that he was the man in the photograph.[120]

(2) *Witness testimony.*—The committee also considered witness testimony as to Oswald's whereabouts immediately following the assassination. Three witnesses were particularly significant. Depository Superintendent Roy Truly and Dallas Police Officer M. L. Baker both entered the depository right after the shots were fired. They encountered Oswald on the second floor, and in testimony to the Warren Commission, they gave the time as 2 to 3 minutes after the shots.[121] A witness who personally knew Oswald, Mrs. Robert A. Reid, also a depository employee, testified to the Warren Commission that she also saw him on the second floor approximately 2 minutes after the assassination.[122]

The testimony of these three witnesses was mutually corroborating. Since all were outside the depository when the shots were fired, their statements that it took them about 2 minutes to get to the second floor were reasonable.[123] It appeared equally reasonable that in those same 2 minutes Oswald could have walked from the sixth floor window to the rear stairway and down four flights of stairs to the second floor.

The conclusion with respect to this evidence alone was not that Lee Harvey Oswald was the assassin, but merely that the testimony of these witnesses appeared credible and was probative on the question of Oswald's whereabouts at the time of the assassination.

5. LEE HARVEY OSWALD'S OTHER ACTIONS TEND TO SUPPORT THE CONCLUSION THAT HE ASSASSINATED PRESIDENT KENNEDY

The Warren Commission concluded that shortly after the assassination, Oswald boarded a bus, but when the bus got caught in a traffic jam, he disembarked and took a taxicab to his roominghouse.[124] The Commission also found that Oswald changed clothes at the roominghouse and walked about nine-tenths of a mile away from it before he encountered Dallas Police Officer J. D. Tippit. [125] After being stopped by Tippit, the Commission concluded, Oswald drew a revolver and shot Tippit four times, killing him. He then ran from the scene.[126] He was apprehended at approximately 1:50 p.m. in a nearby movie house, the Texas Theatre.[127]

The committee found that while most of the depository

employees were outside of the building at the time of the assassination and returned inside afterwards, Oswald did the reverse; he was inside before the assassination, and afterward he went outside. That Oswald left the building within minutes of the assassination was significant. Every other depository employee either had an alibi for the time of the assassination or returned to the building immediately thereafter. Oswald alone neither remained nor had an alibi.

(a) The Tippit murder

The committee investigated the murder of Officer Tippit primarily for its implications concerning the assassination of the President. The committee relied primarily on scientific evidence. The committee's firearms panel determined positively that all four cartridge cases found at the scene of the Tippit murder were fired from the pistol that was found in Lee Harvey Oswald's possession when he was apprehended in the Texas Theatre 35 minutes after the murder.[13][128]

In addition, the committee's investigators interviewed witnesses present at the scene of the Tippit murder.[129] Based on Oswald's possession of the murder weapon a short time after the murder and the eyewitness identifications of Oswald as the gunman, the committee concluded that Oswald shot and killed Officer Tippit. The committee further concluded that this crime, committed while fleeing the scene of the assassination, was consistent with a finding that Oswald assassinated the President.

The Warren Commission had investigated the possibility that Oswald and Tippit were associated prior to the assassination, but it failed to find a connection.[130] Similarly, the committee's investigation uncovered no direct evidence of such a relationship, nor did it attribute any activity or association to Officer Tippit that could be deemed suspicious. The committee, however, did find and interview one witness who had not been interviewed by the Warren Commission or FBI in 1963–64. His name is Jack Ray Tatum, and he reported witnessing the final moments of the shooting of Officer Tippit.[131] Oswald,

---

[13]Since Oswald's revolver had been partially modified to shoot different ammunition than the type it was manufactured to shoot, it was not possible for the panel to determine whether the bullets that killed Tippit were fired from it. The panel did determine that the characteristics of the bullets were consistent with their having been fired from Oswald's revolver.

according to Tatum, after initially shooting Tippit from his position on the sidewalk, walked around the patrol car to where Tippit lay in the street and stood over him while he shot him at point blank range in the head. This action, which is often encountered in gangland murders and is commonly described as a coup de grace, is more indicative of an execution that an act of defense intended to allow escape or prevent apprehension. Absent further evidence—which the committee did not develop—the meaning of this evidence must remain uncertain.[14]

(b) Oswald: A capacity for violence?

The committee also considered the question of whether Oswald's words or actions indicated that he possessed a "capacity for violence." The presence of such a trait would not, in and of itself, prove much. Nevertheless, the absence of any words or actions by Oswald that indicated a capacity for violence would be inconsistent with the conclusion that Oswald assassinated the President and would be of some significance.

In this regard, the committee noted that Oswald had on more than one occasion exhibited such behavior. The most blatant example is the shooting of Officer Tippit. The man who shot Tippit shot him four times at close range and in areas that were certain to cause death. There can be no doubt that the man who murdered officer Tippit intended to kill him, and, as discussed above, the committee concluded that Oswald was that man.

Another example of such behavior occurred in the Texas Theatre at the time of Oswald's arrest. All of the police officers present—and Oswald himself—stated that Oswald physically attempted to resist arrest.[132] The incident is particularly significant, if, as some of the officers testified, Oswald attempted, albeit unsuccessfully, to fire his revolver during the course of the struggle.

Another incident considered by the committee in evaluating Oswald's capacity for violence was the attempted murder of Maj. Gen. Edwin A. Walker on April 10, 1963. The Warren Commission concluded that Oswald shot at Walker and that this demonstrated "his propensity

---

[14]The committee did verify from the Tippit autopsy report that there was one wound in the body that slanted upward from front to back. Though previously unexplained, it would be consistent with the observations of Jack Ray Tatum.

to act dramatically and, in this instance violently, in furtherance of his beliefs."[133] Many critics of the Commission, however, dispute the conclusion that Oswald was the shooter in the Walker case.[134]

The committee turned to scientific analysis to cast light on the issue. As discussed earlier, the evidence is conclusive that Oswald owned a Mannlicher-Carcano rifle. The committee's firearms panel examined the bullet fragment that was removed from the wall in the home of General Walker and found that it had characteristics similar to bullets fired from Oswald's Mannlicher-Carcano rifle.[135] In addition, neutron activation analysis of this fragment confirmed that it was probably a Mannlicher-Carcano bullet.[136]

In addition, the committee considered the testimony of Marina Oswald, who stated, among other things, that Lee Harvey Oswald told her that he had shot at Walker. [137] Further, the committee's handwriting experts determined that a handwritten note that, according to Marina Oswald's testimony, was written to her by Oswald prior to the Walker shooting, was written by Oswald. [138] This undated note, although it did not mention General Walker, clearly indicated that Oswald was about to attempt an act during the course of which he might be killed or taken into custody.[139].[15]

The committee concluded that the evidence strongly suggested that Oswald attempted to murder General Walker and that he possessed a capacity for violence. Such evidence is supportive of the committee's conclusion that Oswald assassinated President Kennedy.

(c) The motive

Finding a possible motive for Oswald's having assassinated President Kennedy was one of the most difficult issues that the Warren Commission addressed. The Commission stated that "many factors were undoubtedly in-

---

[15]With respect to the Walker shooting, reports of the Dallas Police Department, made at the time of the shooting and referred to in the Warren Report, reflected that there was one witness who stated he saw more than one person leaving the scene after the shooting. Another witness, according to police reports, stated he saw two men, two nights before the shooting, driving in the vicinity of the Walker house in a suspicious manner. These statements were never substantiated, and the case remains unsolved. Nevertheless, if they are true, a possible implication is that Oswald had associates who would engage in a conspiracy to commit murder. The committee conducted a limited investigation to see if leads could be developed that might assist in identifying these possible associates. No leads were developed, and this line of inquiry was abandoned.

volved in Oswald's motivation for the assassination, and the Commission does not believe that it can ascribe to him any one motive or group of motives."[140] The Commission noted Oswald's overriding hostility to his environment, his seeking a role in history as a great man, his commitment to Marxism, and his capacity to act decisively without regard to the consequences when such action would further his aims of the moment.[141]

The committee agreed that each of the factors listed by the Warren Commission accurately characterized various aspects of Oswald's political beliefs, that those beliefs were a dominant factor in his life and that in the absence of other more compelling evidence, it concluded that they offered a reasonable explanation of his motive to kill the President.

It is the committee's judgment that in the last 5 years of his life, Oswald was preoccupied with political ideology. The first clear manifestation of this preoccupation was his defection to the Soviet Union in the fall of 1959 at the age of 20.[142] This action, in and of itself, was an indication of the depth of his political commitment. The words that accompanied the act went even further. Oswald stated to officials at the American Embassy in Moscow that he wanted to renounce his citizenship and that he intended to give the Russians any information concerning the Marine Corps and radar operations that he possessed.[143] In letters written to his brother Robert, Oswald made it clear that in the event of war he would not hesitate to fight on the side of the Russians against his family or former country.[144] The paramount importance of his political commitment was indicated in one letter in which he informed his family that he did not desire to have any futher communications with them as he was starting a new life in Russia. It was also reflected in his attempt to commit suicide when he was informed he would not be allowed to remain in the Soviet Union.[145] In considering which were the dominant forces in Oswald's life, the committee, therefore, relied on Oswald's willingness to renounce his citizenship, to betray military secrets, to take arms against his own family, and to give up his own life, if necessary, for his political beliefs.

Upon Oswald's return to the United States from the Soviet Union in 1962, although his fervor for that country might have diminished, his words and actions still re-volved around ideological causes. Oswald made no attempt to hide or tone down his deep-seated feelings. He expounded them to those with whom he associated, even when they could be expected to be opposed. He subscribed to Marxist and Communist publications such as "The Worker" and "The Militant," and he openly corresponded with the American Communist Party and the Socialist Worker's Party.[146] His devotion to his political beliefs was cogently symbolized by the photograph, authenticated by the committee's photographic and handwriting panels, in which he is defiantly holding copies of "The Worker" and "The Militant" and his rifle, with a handgun strapped to his waist.[147]

His involvement in the Fair Play for Cuba Committee was another example of Oswald's affinity for political action.[148] This organization was highly critical of U.S. policy toward the Cuban government of Fidel Castro. Oswald not only professed to be a member of the organization, but he characteristically chose to become a highly visible spokesman. He corresponded with the national office, distributed handbills on the streets of New Orleans and twice appeared on a local radio program representing himself as a spokesman for the organization.

The committee fully recognized that during the course of Oswald's activities in New Orleans, he apparently became involved with certain anti-Castro elements, although such activities on Oswald's part have never been fully explained.[149] Considering the depth of his political commitment, it would not have been uncharacteristic for Oswald to have attempted to infiltrate anti-Castro Cuban organizations.[150] But the significant point is that regardless of his purpose for joining, it is another example of the dominance of political activity in Oswald's life.

A short time before the assassination of the President, Oswald traveled to Mexico City, where he went to the Cuban Consulate and indicated an intense desire to travel to Cuba and Russia.[151] Once again, it appears that Oswald was ready to leave his family and his country to fulfill a political goal. Precisely why Oswald wanted to go to Cuba or Russia is not known, but it was certainly of significance that he chose those particular countries, both of which are Marxist.

Finally, in considering the extent to which Oswald acted on behalf of his political beliefs, the Walker shooting also was relevant. As discussed above, the committee concluded that Oswald attempted to murder Major General Walker in April 1963. In the city of Dallas, no one figure so epitomized anticommunism as General Walker. Considering the various activities to which Oswald devoted his time, his efforts and his very existence, General Walker could be readily seen as "an ultimate enemy." It is known that Oswald was willing to risk death for his beliefs, so it is certainly not unreasonable to find that he might attempt to kill Walker, a man who was intensely opposed to his ideology.

In analyzing Oswald's possible political motive, the committee considered the fact that as one's position in the politcal spectrum moves far enough to the left or right, what may otherwise be recognized as strikingly dissimilar viewpoints on the spectrum may be viewed as ideologically related. President Kennedy and General Walker hardly shared a common political ideology. As seen in terms of American political thinking, Walker was a staunch conservative while the President was a liberal. It can be argued, however, that from a Marxist's perspective, they could be regarded as occupying similar positions. Where Walker was stridently anti-Communist, Kennedy was the leader of the free world in its fight against communism. Walker was a militarist. Kennedy had ordered the invasion of Cuba and had moved to within a hairsbreadth of nuclear war during the Cuban missile crisis. Consequently, it may be argued that Oswald could have seen Walker and Kennedy in the same ideological light.

The depth and direction of Oswald's ideological commitment is, therefore, clear. Politics was the dominant force in his life right down to the last days when, upon being arrested for the assassination, he requested to be represented by a lawyer prominent for representing Communists. Although no one specific ideological goal that Oswald might have hoped to achieve by the assassination of President Kennedy can be shown with confidence, it appeared to the committee that his dominant motivation, consistent with his known activities and beliefs, must have been a desire to take political action. It seems reasonable to conclude that the best single explanation for the assassination was his conception of political action, rooted in his twisted ideological view of himself and the world around him.

B. Scientific Acoustical Evidence Establishes a High Probability That Two Gunmen Fired at President John F. Kennedy; Other Scientific Evidence Does Not Preclude the Possibility of Two Gunmen Firing at the President; Scientific Evidence Negates Some Specific Conspiracy Allegations

The committee tried to take optimum advantage of scientific analysis in exploring issues concerning the assassination. In many cases, it was believed that scientific information would be the most reliable information available, since some witnesses had died and the passage of time had caused the memories of remaining witnesses to fail and caused other problems affecting the trustworthiness of their testimony.

As noted in the preceding section of this report, the committee turned to science as a major source of evidence for its conclusion that Lee Harvey Oswald fired three shots from the Texas School Book Depository, two of which hit President Kennedy. The evidence that was most relied upon was developed by committee panels specializing in the fields of forensic pathology, ballistics, neutron activation, analysis, handwriting identification, photography and acoustics. Of these, acoustics—a science that involves analysis of the nature and origin of sound impulses—indicated that the shots from the book depository were not the only ones fired at President Kennedy.

(a) Warren Commission analysis of a tape

The Warren Commission had also employed scientific analysis in its investigation and had recognized that acoustics might be used to resolve some questions about the shots fired at the Prseident. It had obtained a tape recording, an alleged on-the-scene account of the assassination made by Sam Pate, a Dallas radio newsman, but an FBI examination of the tape "failed to indicate the presence of any sounds which could be interpreted as gunshots."[1] The FBI also informed the Commission that the newsman had stated that most of the tape was not recorded in Dealey Plaza at the time of the assassination, but was recorded in a studio several days later after he had been dismissed by his station, KBOX.[2]

The Commission independently submitted the tape for analysis to Dr. Lawrence Kersta of Bell Telephone Acoustics & Speech Research Laboratory. As reported in a letter from Kersta to the Commission on July 17, 1964,[3] spectograms (visual representations of tonal qualities in the sounds) were made of a key 8-second portion of the tape. The spectograms indicated there were six nonvoiced noises—one nonvoiced "spike" (a scientific term for a graphic display of a noise) followed by three other nonvoiced spikes of different acoustical characteristics occurring .86 seconds, 1.035 seconds and 1.385 seconds after the first. These, in turn, were followed by two events apparently caused by sound and believed to have been related to the previous ones. Dr. Kersta did not indicate in his letter that he had found shots, and the results of his tests were not mentioned in the Warren Report.

The committee was unable to locate the Kersta spectographs in the National Archives until late 1978 (they had been misfiled), but it did obtain the tape recording made on November 22, 1963, by KBOX reporter Sam Pate. On May 11, 1978, the committee submitted the tape to an acoustical consultant for analysis, with these results:[4]

> While a portion of the tape was recorded on November 22, 1963, in the vicinity of Dealey Plaza, it was thought not to be contemporaneous with the assassination. Other portions of the tape, moreover, seemed to have been recorded, at least in large part, in a studio, since appropriate background noise was not present.
>
> And even if the tape had been made during the firing of the shots and had recorded them, Kersta's spectographic analysis would not have found them. The committee's consultant advised that spectographic analysis is appropriate only for detecting tonal, or harmonic, sound. To identify a gunshot, the analysis must be able to portray a waveform on an oscilloscope or similar such device.

(b) Dallas Police Department recordings

To resolve questions concerning the number, timing, and origin of the shots fired in Dealey Plaza, the committee asked its acoustical consultant to examine recordings not analyzed acoustically by the Warren Commission, specifically, Dallas Police Department dispatch transmissions for November 22, 1963.[1]

These transmissions, received over the police radio network from officers in the field, were recorded at Dallas police headquarters. Two recording systems were in use at the time—a Dictabelt for channel 1, and a Gray Audograph disc recording for channel 2.[2][5]

The committee held 2 days of public hearings—on September 11, 1978 and December 29, 1978—in which it attempted to present the essential evidence from the acoustical analysis. Because of time limitations, it was not possible to present all the evidence in the hearings.

(1) *Analysis by Bolt Beranek and Newman.*—In order to identify the nature and origin of sound impulses in a recording, acoustical analysis may include, among other means of examination, a delineation and study of the shape of its electrical waveforms and a precise measurement and study of the timing of impulses on the recording. In May 1978, the committee contracted with Bolt Beranek and Newman Inc. (BBN) of Cambridge, Mass., to perform this sort of analysis. The study was supervised by Dr. James E. Barger, the firm's chief scientist.

Bolt Beranek and Newman specializes in acoustical analysis and performs such work as locating submarines by analyzing underwater sound impulses. It pioneered the technique of using sound recordings to determine the timing and direction of gunfire in an analysis of a tape that was recorded during the shootings at Kent State University in 1970. In a criminal case brought against members of the National Guard by the Department of Justice, the analysis of the tape by BBN, combined with

---

[1]Transcripts of the Dallas dispatch transmissions had been provided to the Warren Commission by the FBI and the Dallas Police Department. They were used to resolve issues not related to the number, timing or origin of the shots fired in Dealey Plaza. It did not appear that an acoustical analysis of these tapes or Dictabelts was performed for the Commission by the FBI or any other agency or private organization.

[2]Channel 1 transmissions were a continuous record of Dallas police activity; channel 2 transmissions were voice activated, and therefore an intermittent record of communications, for the most part those of Dallas Police Chief Jesse E. Curry and the headquarters dispatcher.

photographs taken at the time of the shootings, were used by the prosecution in its presentation to a grand jury to help establish which guardsmen were the first to fire shots. The firm was also selected by Judge John J. Sirica to serve on a panel of technical experts that examined the Watergate tapes in 1973.

The Dallas police dispatch materials given to BBN to analyze in May 1978 were as follows:

> The original Dictabelt recordings made on November 22, 1963, of transmissions over channel 1;
>
> A tape recording of channel 1 Dictabelts;
>
> A tape recording of transmissions over channel 2.[7][3]

These materials were obtained by a committee investigator in March 1978, from Paul McCaghren, who in 1963 was a Dallas police lieutenant who had submitted investigative reports and materials on the assassination to Chief Curry.[8] In 1969, a newly appointed chief of police had ordered that a locked cabinet outside his office be opened. It contained reports and materials concerning the assassination that had been submitted to Curry; among the items were the Dictabelt recordings and tapes of the November 22, 1963, dispatch transmissions. McCaghren, who in 1969 was director of the Intelligence Division, had then taken custody of the materials and retained them until he gave them to the committee's investigator in 1978. [9] There was no evidence that any of the materials had been tampered with while in the police department's or McCaghren's possession.

To the human ear, the tapes and Dictabelts contain no discernible sounds of gunfire. The dispatcher's voice notations of the time of day indicate that channel 2 apparently was not in use during the period when the shots were fired. Channel 1 transmissions, however, were inadvertently being recorded from a motorcycle or other police vehicle whose radio transmission switch was stuck in the "on" position.[10]

BBN was asked to examine the channel 1 Dictabelts and the tape that was made of them to see if it could determine: (1) if they were, in fact, recorded transmissions from a motorcycle with a microphone stuck in the "on"

---

[3]Prior to the BBN analysis of the original Dictabelt and tapes, the firm was given a tape that had been supplied to the committee by a Warren Commission critic in the belief that it was an original. BBN determined that this tape was a second generation copy of the original. Because it was an imperfect copy, it was not used in the BBN work. [6]

position in Dealey Plaza; (2) if the sounds of shots had been, in fact, recorded; (3) the number of shots; (4) the time interval between the shots; (5) the location of the weapon or weapons used to fire the shots; and (6) the type of weapon or weapons used.

BBN converted the sounds on the tape into digitized waveforms and produced a visual representation of the waveforms. [11] By employing sophisticated electronic filters, BBN filtered out "repetitive noise," such as repeated firings of the pistons of a motorcycle engine.[12] It then examined the tape for "sequences of impulses" that might be significant. (A "sequence of impulses" might be caused by a loud noise—such as gunfire—followed by the echoes from that loud noise.) Six sequences of impulses that could have been caused by a noise such as gunfire were initially identified as having been transmitted over channel 1.[13] Thus, they warranted further analysis.

These six sequences of impulses, or impulse patterns, were subjected to preliminary screening tests to determine if any could be conclusively determined not to have been caused by gunfire during the assassination. The screening tests were designed to answer the following questions:[14]

Do the impulse patterns, in fact, occur during the period of the assassination?

Are the impulse patterns unique to the period of the assassination?

Does the span of time of the impulse patterns approximate the duration of the assassination as indicated by a preliminary analysis of the Zapruder film? (Are there at least 5.6 seconds between the first and last impulse?[4])

Does the shape of the impulse patterns resemble the shape of impulse patterns produced when the sound of gunfire is recorded through a radio transmission system comparable to the one used for the Dallas police dispatch network?

Are the amplitudes of the impulse patterns similar to those produced when the sound of gunfire is recorded through a transmission system comparable to the one used for the Dallas police dispatch network?

---

[4]The 5.6-second standard was based on a preliminary examination of the Zapruder film that showed evidence of Kennedy and Connally reacting to their wounds. The difference between approximate impact moments was calculated using the 18.3 frame per second rate of the Zapruder camera. This 5.6-second standard was derived before the photographic evidence panel had reported the results of its observations of the Zapruder film.

All six impulse patterns passed the preliminary screening tests.[1]

BBN next recommended that the committee conduct an acoustical reconstruction of the assassination in Dealey Plaza to determine if any of the six impulse patterns on the dispatch tape were caused by shots and, if so, if the shots were fired from the Texas School Book Depository or the grassy knoll. [16] The reconstruction would entail firing from two locations in Dealey Plaza the depository and the knoll—at particular target locations and recording the sounds through numerous microphones. The purpose was to determine if the sequences of impulses recorded during the reconstruction would match any of those on the dispatch tape. If so, it would be possible to determine if the impulse patterns on the dispatch tape were caused by shots fired during the assassination from shooter locations in the depository and on the knoll.[17]

The theoretical rationale for the reconstruction was as follows:

The sequence of impulses from a gunshot is caused by the noise of the shot, followed by several echoes. Each combination of shooter location, target location and microphone location produces a sequence of uniquely spaced impulses. At a given microphone location, there would be a unique sequence of impulses, depending on the location of the noise source (gunfire) and the target, and the urban environment of the surrounding area (echo-producing structures in and surrounding Dealey Plaza). The time of arrival of the echoes would be the significant aspect of the sequence of impulses that would be used to compare the 1963 dispatch tape with the sounds recorded during the 1978 reconstruction.[18]

The echo patterns in a complex environment such as Dealey Plaza are unique, so by conducting the reconstruction, the committee could obtain unique "acoustical fingerprints" of various combinations of shooter, target and microphone locations. The fingerprint's identifying characteristic would be the unique time-spacing between the echoes. If any of the acoustical fingerprints produced in the 1978 reconstruction matched those on the 1963 Dallas police dispatch tape, it would be a strong indication that the sounds on the 1963 Dallas police dispatch tape were caused by gunfire recorded by a police microphone in Dealey Plaza. [19]

At the time of the reconstruction in August 1978, the committee was extremely conscious of the significance of Barger's preliminary work, realizing, as it did, that his analysis indicated that there possibly were too many shots, spaced too closely together,[5] for Lee Harvey Oswald to have fired all of them, and that one of the shots came from the grassy knoll, not the Texas School Book Despository.

The committee's awareness that it might have evidence that Oswald was not a lone assassin affected the manner in which it conducted the subsequent phase of the investigation. For example, it was deemed judicious to seek an independent review of Barger's analysis before proceeding with the acoustical reconstruction. So, in July 1978, the committee contacted the Acoustical Society of America to solicit recommendations for persons qualified to review the BBN analysis and the proposed Dallas reconstruction. The society recommended a number of individuals, and the committee selected Prof. Mark Weiss of Queens College of the City University of New York and his research associate, Ernest Aschkenasy. Professor Weiss had worked on numerous acoustical projects. He had served, for example, on the panel of technical experts appointed by Judge John J. Sirica to examine the White House tape recordings in conjunction with the Watergate grand jury investigation. Aschkenasy had specialized in developing computer programs for analyzing large volumes of acoustical data.

Weiss and Aschkenasy reviewed Barger's analysis and conclusions and concurred with them. In addition, they agreed that the acoustical reconstruction was necessary, [20] and they approved Barger's plan for conducting it.

The committee authorized an acoustical reconstruction, to be conducted on August 20, 1978. Four target locations were selected, based on: [21]

> The estimated positions of the Presidential limousine according to a correlation of the channel 1 transmissions with the Zapruder film, indicating that the first shot was fired between Zapruder frames 160 and 170 and that the second shot was fired between Zapruder frames 190 and 200;[6]

---

[5]For example, the time between two of the impulse patterns that might represent gunfire was less than a second, too brief an interval to have permitted Oswald to fire two shots.

[6]The committee ultimately determined that the shots were fired a few Zapruder frames earlier than it believed to be the case in August 1978.

The position of the President at the time of the fatal head shot (Zapruder frame 312); and

Evidence that a curb in Dealey Plaza may have been struck by a bullet during the assassination.

Two shooter locations were selected for the reconstruction:[22]

The sixth floor southeast corner window of the Texas School Book Depository, since substantial physical evidence and witness testimony indicated shots were fired from this location; and

The area behind a picket fence atop the grassy knoll, since there was considerable witness testimony suggesting shots were fired from there.[7]

A Mannlicher-Carcano rifle was fired from the depository, since it was the type of weapon found on the sixth floor on November 22, 1963. [23] Both a Mannlicher-Carcano (chosen mainly because it fires a medium velocity supersonic bullet) and a pistol, which fires a subsonic bullet, were fired from the grassy knoll, since there was no evidence in August 1978 as to what type of weapon, if any, may have been fired from there on November 22, 1963.[8] [24] Microphones to record the test shots were placed every 18 feet in 36 different locations along the motorcade route where a motorcycle could have been transmitting during the assassination. [25]

A recording was made of the sounds received at each microphone location during each test shot, making a total of 432 recordings of impulse sequences (36 microphone locations times 12 shots), or "acoustical fingerprints," for various target-shooter-microphone combinations. Each recorded acoustical fingerprint was then compared with each of the six impulse patterns on the channel 1 dispatch tape to see if and how well the significant points in each impulse pattern matched up. The process required a total of 2,592 comparisons (432 recordings of impulse sequences times six impulse patterns), an extensive effort that was not completed until 4 days before Barger was to testify at a committee public hearing on September 11, 1978. [26]

The time of the arrival of the impulses, or echoes, in each sequence of impulses was the characteristic being

---

[7]The committee noted the absence of physical evidence of shots from the grassy knoll.
[8]As is discussed *infra*, there are important differences between the impulse patterns caused by a subsonic bullet, as opposed to a supersonic bullet.

compared, not the shape, amplitude or any other characteristic of the impulses or sequence.[27] If a point (representing time of arrival of an echo) in a sequence of the 1963 dispatch tape could be correlated within 6/1,000 of a second to a point in a sequence of the reconstruction, it was considered a match.[28]

A ±6/1,000 of a second "window" was chosen, because the exact location of the motorcycle was not known. Since the microphones were placed 18 feet apart in the 1978 reconstruction, no microphone was expected to be in the exact location of the motorcycle microphone during the assassination in 1963. Since the location was not apt to be exactly the same, and the time of arrival of the echo is unique at each spot, the ±6/1,000 of a second "window" would allow for the contingency that the motorcycle was near, but not exactly at, one of the microphone locations selected for the reconstruction.[29]

Those sequences of impulses that had a sufficiently high number of points that matched (a "score" or correlation coefficient of .6 or higher) were considered significant.[30] The "score" or correlation coefficient was set at this level to insure finding all sequences that might represent a true indication that the 1963 dispatch tape contained gunfire. Setting it at this level, however, also allowed a sequence of impulses on the dispatch tape that might have been caused by random noise or other factors to be considered a match and therefore significant.[31] Such a match, since it did not in fact represent a true indication of gunfire on the 1963 dispatch tape, would be considered an "invalid match."[32]

Of the 2,592 comparisons between the six sequences of impulses on the 1963 police dispatch tape and the sequences obtained during the acoustical reconstruction in August 1978, 15 had a sufficient number of matching points (a correlation coefficient of .6 or higher) to be considered significant.[33] The first and sixth sequence of impulses on the dispatch tape had no matches with a correlation coefficient over .5. The second sequences of impulses on the dispatch tape had four significant matches, the third sequence had five, the fourth sequence had three, and the fifth sequence had three.[34] Accordingly, impulses one and six on the dispatch tape did not pass the most rigorous acoustical test and were deemed not to have been caused by gunfire from the Texas School Book Depository or grassy knoll.

[35] Additional analysis of the remaining four impulse sequences was still necessary before any of them could be considered as probably representing gunfire from the Texas School Book Depository or the grassy knoll.

The locations of the microphones that recorded the dispatches in the 1978 reconstruction were plotted on a graph that depicted time and distance. It was observed that the location of the microphones at which matches were recorded tended to cluster around a line on the graph that was, in fact, consistent with the approximate speed of the motorcade (11 mph), as estimated from the Zapruder film.[36] For example, of the 36 microphones placed along the motorcade route, the one that recorded the sequence of impulses that matched the third impulse on the 1963 dispatch tape was farther along the route than the one that recorded the impulses that matched the second impulse on the dispatch tape. The location of the microphones was such, it was further observed, that a motorcycle traveling at approximately 11 miles per hour would cover the distance between two microphones in the elapsed time between impulses on the dispatch tape. This relationship between the location of the microphones and the time between impulses was consistent for the four impulses on the dispatch tape, a very strong indication, the committee found, that the impulses on the 1963 dispatch tape were picked up by a transmitter on a motorcycle or other vehicle as it proceeded along the motorcade route. Applying a statistical formula, Barger estimated that since the microphones clustered around a line representing the speed of the motorcade, there was a 99 percent probability that the Dallas police dispatch tape did, in fact, contain impulses transmitted by a microphone in the motorcade in Dealey Plaza during the assassination.[37]

Some of the matches found between the 1978 reconstruction and the dispatch tape were, however, thought to be clearly "invalid," that is, they did not represent a true indication of gunfire from the Texas School Book Depository or the grassy knoll. In one case, for example, there was a match for a shot in the reconstruction that had been aimed at a target located in a different direction from where the Presidential limousine was located at the moment, the limousine's location having been established by a correlation of the dispatch tape and the Zapruder film. [38] Only an unlikely misfire could explain why an assassin would fire in the opposite direction. By applying similar principles of logic, six matches were ruled out. This left three matches for impulse pattern one, three for impulse pattern two, one for impulse pattern three and two for impulse pattern four.[39] The remaining matches for impulse patterns one, two and four on the dispatch tape were for rifle firings from the Texas School Book Depository in the 1978 reconstruction, while the match for impulse pattern three was for a rifle firing from the grassy knoll.

These matches did not, however, prove conclusively that the impulses on the 1963 dispatch tape did, in fact, represent gunfire from the book depository or grassy knoll. There still was a chance that random or other noise could have produced the pattern on the dispatch tape that matched the pattern obtained in the reconstruction, therefore being invalid as well. Based on statistical probabilities, including the observation that the locations of the microphones that picked up the matching impulse patterns tended to cluster along a line on the graph that approximated the speed of the motorcycle, Barger estimated there was a 50 percent chance that any one of the matches was invalid.[40] Consequently, Barger testified before the committee in September 1978 that the probability of there having been a shot from the grassy knoll was only 50 percent.[41] He based this estimate on there being only one match for impulse three, combined with his conclusion that there was a 50–50 chance that any one match, including the one for impulse pattern three, had been caused by random noise and was invalid.[42] (Barger was also saying, however, that if the match for impulse pattern three was valid, it meant that a shot was fired at President Kennedy from the grassy knoll.)[9]

(2) *Weiss-Aschkenasy analysis.*—In mid-September 1978, the committee asked Weiss and Aschkenasy, the acoustical analysts who had reviewed Barger's work, if they could go beyond what Barber had done to determine with greater certainty if there had been a shot from the grassy knoll. Weiss and Aschkenasy conceived an analytical

---

[9]With respect to the other shots. Barger estimated there was an 88 percent chance that impulse pattern one represented a shot from the book depository (based on three matches), 88 percent again for impulse pattern two (three matches) and a 75 percent chance that impulse pattern four represented a shot from the depository (two matchs). [43] At the time of his testimony in September 1978, Barger estimated that the probability of all four impulses actually representing gunshots was only 29 percent. [44]

extension of Barger's work that might enable them to refine the probability estimate.[45] They studied Dealey Plaza to determine which structures were most apt to have caused the echoes received by the microphone in the 1978 acoustical reconstruction that had recorded the match to the shot from the grassy knoll. They verified and refined their identifications of echo-generating structures by examining the results of the reconstruction. And like BBN, since they were analyzing the arrival time of echoes, they made allowances for the temperature differential, because air temperature affects the speed of sound.[46] Barger then reviewed and verified the identification of echo-generating sources by Weiss and Aschkenasy.[47]

Once they had identified the echo-generating sources for a shot from the vicinity of the grassy knoll and a microphone located near the point indicated by Barger's tests, it was possible for Weiss and Aschkenasy to predict precisely what impulse sequences (sound fingerprints) would have been created by various specific shooter and microphone locations in 1963.[48] (The major structures in Dealey Plaza in 1978 were located as they had been in 1963.) Weiss and Aschkenasy determined the time of sound travel for a series of sound triangles whose three points were shooter location, microphone location and echo-generating structure location. While the locaton of the structures would remain constant, the different combinations of shooter and microphone locations would each produce a unique sound travel pattern, or sound fingerprint.[49] Using this procedure, Weiss and Aschkenasy could compare acoustical fingerprints for numerous precise points in the grassy knoll area with the segment identified by Barger on the dispatch tape as possibly reflecting a shot fired from the knoll.[50][10]

Because Weiss and Aschkenasy could analytically construct what the impulse sequences would be at numerous specific shooter and microphone locations, they decided to look for a match to the 1963 police dispatch to tape that correlated to within $\pm 1/1,000$ of a second, as opposed to $\pm 6/1,000$ of a second, as Barger had done.[51] By looking for a match with such precision, they considerably reduced the possibility that any match they found

---

[10]Weiss and Aschkenasy examined only the impulse sequence that Barger indicated had come from the grassy knoll. Due to time constraints, they did not analyze the three impulse sequences indicating shots fired from the Texas School Book Depository.

could have been caused by random or other noise.[52] thus substantially reducing the percentage probability of an invalid match.

Weiss and Aschkenasy initially pinpointed a combination of shooter-microphone locations for which the early impulses in pattern three matched those on the dispatch tape quite well, although later impulses in the pattern did not. Similarly, they found other microphone locations for which later impulses matched those on the dispatch tape, while the earlier ones did not. They then realized that a microphone mounted on a motorcycle or other vehicle would not have remained stationary during the period it was receiving the echoes. They computed that the entire impulse pattern or sequence of echoes they were analyzing on the dispatch tape occurred over approximately three-tenths of a second, during which time the motorcycle or other vehicle would have, at 11 miles per hour, traveled about five feet. By taking into account the movement of the vehicle, Weiss and Aschkenasy were able to find a sequence of impulses representing a shot from the grassy knoll in the reconstruction that matched both the early and late impulses on the dispatch tape.[53]

Approximately 10 feet from the point on the grassy knoll that was picked as the shooter location in the 1978 reconstruction and four feet from a microphone location which, Barger found, recorded a shot that matched the dispatch tape within ±6/1,000 of a second, Weiss and Aschkenasy found a combination of shooter and microphone locations they needed to solve the problem. It represented the initial position of a microphone that would have received a series of impulses matching those on the dispatch tape to within ±1/1.000 of a second. The microphone would have been mounted on a vehicle that was moving along the motorcade route at 11 miles per hour.[54]

Weiss and Aschkenasy also considered the distortion that a windshield might cause to the sound impulses received by a motorcycle microphone. They reasoned that the noise from the initial muzzle blast of a shot would be somewhat muted on the tape if it traveled through the windshield to the microphone. Test firing conducted under the auspices of the New York City Police Department confirmed this hypothesis. Further, an examination of the dispatch tape reflected similar distortions on shots one, two, and three, when the indicated positions of the motorcycle would have placed the windshield between the shooter and the microphone.[11] On shot four, Weiss and Aschkenasy found no such distortion.[55] The analysts' ability to predict the effect of the windshield on the impulses found on the dispatch tape, and having their predictions confirmed by the tape, indicated further that the microphone was mounted on a motorcycle in Dealey Plaza and that it had transmitted the sounds of the shots fired during the assassination.

Since Weiss and Aschkenasy were able to obtain a match to within $\pm 1/1,000$ of a second, the probability that such a match could occur by random chance was slight. Specifically, they mathematically computed that, with a certainty factor of 95 percent or better, there was a shot fired at the Presidential limousine from the grassy knoll. [56]

Barger independently reviewed the analysis performed by Weiss and Aschkenasy and concluded that their analytical procedures were correct. [57] Barger and the staff at BBN also confirmed that there was a 95 percent chance that at the time of the assassination a noise as loud as a rifle shot was produced at the grassy knoll. When questioned about what could cause such a noise if it were not a shot, Barger noted it had to be something capable of causing a very loud noise—greater than a single firecracker. [58] Further, given the echo patterns obtained, the noise had to have originated at the very spot behind the picket fence on the grassy knoll that had been identified, [59] indicating that it could not have been a backfire from a motorcycle in the motorcade.[60]

In addition, Barger emphasized, the first part of the sequence of impulses identified as a shot from the grassy knoll was marked by an N–wave, a characteristic impulse caused by a supersonic bullet. [61] The N–wave, also referred to as a supersonic shock wave, travels faster than the noise of the muzzle blast of a gun and therefore arrives at a listening device such as a microphone ahead of the noise of a muzzle blast. The presence of the N–wave was, therefore, a significant additional indication that the

---

[11]The motorcycle was traveling 120 feet behind the Presidential limousine when the shots were fired. This put shots one and two from the book depository, as well as shot three from the grassy knoll, in front of the motorcycle windshield.

third impulse on the police dispatch tape represented gunfire, and, in particular, a supersonic bullet.[62] The weapon may well have been a rifle, since most pistols—except for some, such as a .44 magnum—fire subsonic bullets.

The N–wave was further substantiation for a finding that the third impulse represented a shot fired in the direction of the President. Had the gun been discharged when aimed straight up or down, or away from the motorcade, no N–wave would have appeared.[63] Of the impulse patterns on the dispatch tape that indicated shots from the book depository, those that would be expected to contain an N–wave, given the location of the vehicle's microphone, did so, further corroborating the conclusion that these impulses did represent supersonic bullets.[64]

When questioned about the probability of the entire third impulse pattern representing a supersonic bullet being fired at the President from the grassy knoll, Barger estimated there was a 20 percent chance that the N–wave, as opposed to the sequence of impulses following it, was actually caused by random noise.[65] Accordingly, the mathematical probability of the entire sequence of impulses actually representing a supersonic bullet was 76 percent, the product of a 95 percent chance that the impulse pattern represented noise as loud as a rifle shot from the grassy knoll times an 80 percent chance that the N–wave was caused by a supersonic bullet.[66]

The committee found no evidence or indication of any other cause of noise as loud as a rifle shot coming from the grassy knoll at the time the impulse sequence was recorded on the dispatch tape, and therefore concluded that the cause was probably a gunshot fired at the motorcade.

(3) *Search for a motorcycle.*—As the work of Weiss and Aschkenasy produced strong indications of a shot from the grassy knoll, the committee began a search of documentary and photographic evidence to determine if a motorcycle or other vehicle had been in the locations indicated by the acoustical tests.

Earlier in its investigation, the committee had interviewed many Dallas police officers who had ridden in the Presidential motorcade, although the purpose of the interviews was not to determine the location of a motorcycle that might have had its radio transmitting switch stuck in the "on" position. Among the officers who were interviewed, one who subsequently testified in a public hearing was H. B. McLain. In his interview on September 26, 1977, McLain said that he had been riding to the left rear of Vice President Johnson's car and that just as he was completing his turn from Main onto Houston Street, he heard what he believed to have been two shots.[67] Sergeant Jimmy Wayne Courson was also interviewed on September 26, 1977. He stated that his assignment in the motorcade was in front of the press bus, approximately six or seven cars to the rear of the Presidential limousine, and that when he turned onto Houston Street, he heard three shots about a second apart.[68] Neither officer was asked specifically whether his radio was on channel one or two, or whether his microphone switch might have been stuck in the transmit position.

The committee obtained Dallas Police Department assignment records confirming that McLain and Courson had both been assigned to the left side of the motorcade,[69] and it discovered photographic evidence[70] that Courson was riding to the rear of McLain, and, as Courson recalled, [71] he was in the vicinity of the press bus. The available films revealed that throughout the motorcade the spacing of the motorcycles varied, but McLain was generally several car lengths ahead of Courson and therefore much closer to the Presidential and Vice Presidential limousines. [72] No photographs of the precise location of the two officers at the moment of the assassination were, at that time, found. Photographs taken shortly before the assassination, however, did indicate that McLain was on Houston Street heading toward Elm as the Presidential limousine was turning onto Elm in front of the Texas School Book Depository.[12][73] At the time of the assassination, therefore, he would have been in the approximate position of the transmitting microphone, as indicated by the acoustical analysis.

The committee reviewed transcripts of the Dallas police dispatch tapes for both channel one and channel two. It did not find any voice transmissions from McLain on either

---

[12]Subsequent to the committee's final vote on its findings, additional photographic evidence of the actions of Officer McLain was received by the committee from Robert Groden, a consultant to the committee. [74] It supported the committee's conclusion with respect to McLain's testimony, but since it was not received until after the vote, it was not relied upon in this report.

channel on November 22, 1963. (As noted, it was determined that the shots fired during the assassination were recorded over channel one. If it could have been established that McLain was transmitting over channel two, then the gunfire transmissions could not have come from his motorcycle radio.)

McLain was asked by the committee to come to Washington to testify. He was shown all of the photographic evidence that the committee had assembled, as well as the Dallas police records of the motorcade assignments. McLain testified before the committee on December 29, 1978, that he was assigned to ride on the left side of the motorcade; that since he would slow down at corners, often stopping momentarily, and then speed up during straight stretches, his exact position in the motorcade varied; and that he was the first motorcycle to the rear of the Vice Presidential limousine. [75]

He further stated that he was the officer in the photographs taken of the motorcade on Main and Houston Streets, and that at the time of the assassination he would have been in the approximate position of the open microphone near the corner of Houston and Elm, indicated by the acoustical analysis.[76] He did not recall using his radio during the motorcade nor what channel it was tuned to on that day.[77] He stated it usually was tuned to channel one.[78] The button on his transmitter receiver, he acknowledged, often got stuck in the "on" position when he was unaware of it, but he did not know if it was stuck during the motorcade.[79]

McLain testified before the committee that he recalled hearing only one shot and that he thereafter heard Chief Curry say to go to the hospital.[80] McLain testified it was possible that he heard the broadcast of Chief Curry (which would have been on channel two) over the speaker of his own radio, or over the speaker of the radio of another motorcycle.[81]

Following the hearing, the committee secured a copy of the daily assignment sheet for motorcycles from the Dallas Police Department and found that McLain had been assigned motorcycle number 352 and call sign 155 on November 22, 1963.[82] Preliminary photographic enhancement of the films taken on Houston and Main Streets indicated that the number on the rear of the motorcycle previously identified as having been ridden by McLain was, in fact, 352.[83][13]

The committee recognized that its acoustical analysis first established and then relied on the fact that a Dictabelt had recorded transmissions from a radio with a stuck microphone switch located in Dealey Plaza The committee realized that the authenticity of the tape and the location of the stuck microphone were both of great importance to the acoustical analysis. Consequently, it sought to verify that the tape in fact contained a broadcast from an open motorcycle mircrophone in Dealey Plaza during the assassination.

The findings of the acoustics experts may be challenged by raising a variety of questions, questions prompted, for example, by the sound of sirens on the tape, [84] by statements by Officer McLain subsequent to his hearing testimony in which he denied that it was his radio that was transmitting, [85] by what appears to be the sound of a carillon bell on the tape, [86] and by the apparent absence of crowd noise. The committee carefully considered these questions as they bore on the authenticity of the tape and the location of the stuck microphone.

Approximately 2 minutes after the impulse sequences that, according to the acoustical analysis, represent gunfire, the dispatch tape contains the sound of sirens for approximately 40 seconds. The sirens appear to rise and then recede in intensity, suggesting that the position of the microphone might have been moving closer to and then farther away from the sirens, or that the sirens were approaching the microphone and then moving away from it.[87]

If the sirens were approaching the microphone and then

---

[19]During his public testimony, McLain also identified photographs of motorcycles on Elm Street (JFK Exhibit F–675), and at Parkland Hospital (JFK Exhibits 674, 676, 677, and 678) as possibly portraying his motorcycle. One of the pictures at Parkland Hospital (JFK Exhibit F–674) apparently indicates that the microphone button was turned to channel one. With respect to the photograph on Elm Street, McLain stated that the other motorcycle in the picture appeared to be ridden by Sergeant Courson. At that time, counsel cautioned that the photographs were being introduced for a limited purpose, since they had not been analyzed by any photographic experts; it was unclear if the cycle in each photograph was that of McLain; and the channel selector, even if it was on channel one, could have been switched after the shots were fired. Preliminary photographic analysis of those pictures conducted by one expert in the time available after the hearing cast doubt upon the accuracy of at least McLain's identification of Courson in Exhibit F–675, and indicated that the channel selector on the motorcycle in Exhibit F–674 may have been on channel two instead of one. Because the committee was unable to conduct comprehensive and thorough analyses of those photographs, it did not rely on Exhibits F–674, F–675, F–676, F–677 or F–678 in forming any conclusions.

moving away from it, it could be suggested that the motor-cycle with the stuck transmitter was stationary on the Stemmons Freeway and not in Dealey Plaza. The sirens would appear to increase and then decrease as some vehicles in the motorcade, with their sirens turned on, drove along the freeway on the way to Parkland Hospital, approaching and then passing by the motorcycle with the stuck microphone. According to a transcript of channel two transmissions, approximately 3½ minutes after the assassination Dallas Police Department dispatcher Gerald D. Henslee stated that an unknown motorcycle on Stemmons Freeway appeared to have its microphone switch stuck open on channel one.[88] The committee interviewed Henslee on August 12, 1978. He told the committee he had assumed the motorcycle was on the freeway from the noise of the sirens. [89] Other Dallas police officers have also speculated that the motorcycle may have been standing near the Trade Mart.

Officer McLain's acknowledged actions subsequent to the assassination might explain the sound of sirens on the tape. McLain was in fact probably on Stemmons Freeway at the time Henslee noted that an unknown motorcycle appeared to have its microphone switch stuck open. McLain himself testified that following the assassination, he sped up to catch the front cars of the motorcade that had entered Stemmons Freeway en route to Parkland Hospital.[90] In any event, it is certain he left the plaza shortly after the assassination. The cars in the motorcade had their sirens on, and this could account for the sound of the sirens increasing as McLain drew closer to them, whether he left Dealey Plaza immediately or shortly after the assassination.[14] A variety of other actions might also account for the sound appearing to recede. Officer McLain might have fallen back after catching the cars, he might have passed by the cars, or he might have arrived at the hospital shortly after catching up, at a time when the sirens were being turned down as the cars approached the hospital.

Subsequent to his hearing testimony, McLain stated that he believed he turned on his siren as soon as he heard Curry's order to proceed to Parkland Hospital. He said that everyone near him had their sirens on immediately. [91]

---

[14]McLain's microphone was so constructed that it would pick up only the siren of the motorcycle on which it was mounted or one of a motorcycle or other vehicle that was no more than 300 feet away.

Should his memory be reliable, the broadcast of the shots during the assassination would not have been over his radio, because the sound of sirens on the tape does not come until approximately 2 minutes later. The committee believed that McLain was in error on the point of his use of his siren. Since those riding in the motorcade near Chief Curry had their sirens on, there may have been no particular need for McLain to turn his on, too. The acoustical analysis pinpointing the location of the microphone, the confirmation of the location of the motorcycle by photographs, his own testimony as to his location, and his slowing his motorcycle as it rounded the corner of Houston and Elm (as had been previously indicated by the acoustical analysis), [92] and the likelihood that McLain did not leave the plaza immediately, but lagged behind momentarily after the assassination, led the committee to conclude it was Officer McLain whose radio microphone switch was stuck open.

Further, the committee noted, it would have been highly improbable for a motorcycle on Stemmons Freeway to have received the echo patterns for the four impulses that appear on the dispatch tape. As noted in more detail below, to contend that the microphone was elsewhere carries with it the burden of explaining all that appears on the tape. To be sure, those who argue the microphone was in Dealey Plaza must explain the sounds that argue it was not. Similarly, those who contend it was not in Dealey Plaza must explain the sounds that indicate it was. As Aschkenasy testified, the echo patterns on the tape would only have been received by a microphone located in a physical environment with the same acoustical characteristics as Dealey Plaza.[93] It is extremely unlikely that the echo patterns on the tape, if received from elsewhere, would so closely parallel the echo patterns characteristic of Dealey Plaza.

The tape contains the faint sound of a carillon-like bell about 7 seconds after the last impulse believed to have been a shot, but no such bell was known to have been in the vicinity of Dealey Plaza. Accordingly, the possibility that the motorcycle with the stuck radio transmitter might not have been in Dealey Plaza was considered. The committee found that the radio system used by the Dallas Police Department permitted more than one transmitter to operate at the same time, and this frequently occurred.[94] The motorcycle whose radio transmitted the sound of a bell was apparently not positioned in Dealey Plaza, but this did not mean that the transmissions of gunshots were also from a radio not in Dealey Plaza. The logical explanation was that the dispatch tape contains the transmissions of two or more radios.[95[

The absence of identifiable crowd noise on the tape also might raise questions as to whether the motorcycle with the stuck transmitter was in Dealey Plaza. The lack of recognizable crowd noise, however, may be explained by the transmission characteristics of the microphone. Dallas police motorcycle radios were equipped with a directional microphone and were designed to transmit only very loud sounds. A human voice would transmit only if it originated very close to the front of the mike. The chief objective of this characteristic was to allow a police officer, when speaking directly into the microphone, to be heard over the sound of his motorcycle engine. Background noise, such as that of a crowd, would not exceed the noise level from the much closer motorcycle engine, and it would not be identifiable on a tape of the radio transmission. The sound of a rifle shot is so pronounced, however, that it would be picked up even if it originated considerably farther away from the microphone than other less intense noise sources, such as a crowd.[96]

(c) Other evidence with respect to the shots

To address further the question of whether the dispatch tape contained sounds from a microphone in Dealey Plaza with a stuck transmitting switch, the committee reviewed independent evidence. It reasoned that if the timing, number and location of the shooters, as shown on the tape, were corroborated or independently substantiated in whole or in part by other scientific or physical evidence— that is, the Zapruder film, findings of the forensic pathology and firearms panels, the neutron activation analysis and the trajectory analysis—the validity of the acoustical analysis and the authenticity of the tape could be established. Conversely, any fundamental inconsistency in the evidence would undermine the analysis and the authenticity of the tape.

The tape and acoustical analysis indicated that, in addition to the shot from the knoll, there were three shots fired at President Kennedy from the Texas School Book Depository. This aspect of the analysis was corrobated or independently substantiated by three cartridge cases found on the sixth floor of the Texas School Book Depository on November 22, 1963, cartridge cases that had been fired in Oswald's rifle,[97] along with other evidence related to the number of shots fired from Oswald's rifle. This corroboration was considered significant by the committee, since it tended to prove that the tape did indeed record the sounds of shots during the assassination.

Further corroboration or substantiation was sought by correlating the Zapruder film to the acoustical tape. The Zapruder film contains visual evidence that two shots struck the occupants of the Presidential limousine.[98] The committee attempted to correlate the observable reactions of President Kennedy and Governor Connally in the film to the time spacing of the four impulses found in the recording of the channel one transmission. The correlation between the film and the recording, however, could only be approximate because it was based on the estimated real-time characteristics of the recording (calculated from the frequent time annotations made by the dispatcher) [99] and the average running time of the film (between 18.0 and 18.5, or an average of 18.3 frames per second.[15]

The committee correlated the film to the tape in two ways. The first assumed the fourth shot was the fatal head shot to the President and occurred at frame 312. Its results are as follows: [101]

	Channel time	Bullet reached limousine at Zapruder frame No.	Acoustical determination of source of impulse
Impulse pattern I	12:30:47.0	157–161	TSBD.
Impulse pattern II	12:30:48.6	188–191	TSBD.
Impulse pattern III	12:30:54.6	295–296	Grassy knoll.
Impulse pattern IV	12:30:55.3	312	TSBD.

[15] The 18.3 frame per second rate of the Zapruder film was an average of the 18.0 to 18.5 frame per second rate determined in 1964 by the FBI under laboratory conditions in which the camera was set and run in the manner that Zapruder said he had operated it at the time of the assassination. [100] Given the 18.0 to 18.5 frame per second average running speed of the film, a differential of four frames is a differential of less than a quarter of a second. For this reason, an absolute correlation between events in the recording and the observable reactions on the film was not expected. If there were no reasonable correlation between the tape and film, however, substantial questions concerning the authenticity of the tape could be raised. (A more detailed explanation of the calculation of Zapruder frames based on the running speeds of the camera is set forth in vol. V of the HSCA–JFK hearings, at pp. 722–724.)

The committee believed that the fourth impulse pattern probably represented that fatal head shot to the President that hit at Zapruder frame 312. Nevertheless, the possibility of frame 312 representing the shot fired from the grassy knoll, with the fourth shot consequently occurring at frame 328, was also considered. The problem with this possibility is that it appeared to be inconsistent with other scientific evidence that established that all the shots that struck the President and the Governor came from the Texas School Book Depository.

The forensic pathology panel concluded that there was no evidence that the President or Governor was hit by a bullet fired from the grassy knoll and that only two bullets, each fired from behind, struck them. [102] Further, neutron activation analysis indicated that the bullet fragments removed from Governor Connally's wrist during surgery, those removed from the President's brain during the autopsy, and those found in the limousine were all very likely fragments from Mannlicher-Carcano bullets. [103] It was also found that there was evidence of only two bullets among all the specimens tested—the fragments removed from Governor Connally's wrist during surgery were very likely from the almost whole bullet found on the stretcher at Parkland Hospital, and the fragments removed from the President's brain during the autopsy very likely matched bullet fragments found in the limousine. [104] The neutron activation analysis findings, when combined with the finding of the committee that the almost whole bullet found on the stretcher at Parkland Hospial as well as the larger fragment found in the limousine were fired from Oswald's Mannlicher-Carcano rifle, [105] established that only two bullets struck the President and the Governor, and each was fired from the rifle found on the sixth floor of the Texas School Book Depository and owned by Oswald.

The committee considered whether proper synchronization of the tape to the film should assume that the shot from the grassy knoll hit the President at Zapruder frame 312. It did so because Dr. Michael Baden, chairman of the committee's forensic pathology panel, acknowledged there was a possibility, although highly remote, that the head wound depicted in Zapruder frame 312 could have been caused by a shot from the grassy knoll, and that medical evidence of it had been destroyed by a shot from the rear a fraction of a second later. [106][16] The significance of this, the committee reasoned, was the realization that it could mean that the President's fatal head wound was caused by the shooter from the grassy knoll, not Oswald.

Since the medical, ballistics and neutron activation analysis evidence, taken together, established that the President was struck by two bullets fired from Oswald's rifle found on the sixth floor of the Texas School Book Depository, the committee sought to determine if such shots could have struck the President, given the known position of his body, even if the grassy knoll shot struck him at Zapruder frame 312. The results of correlating the acoustical tape to the film, assuming the shot from the knoll was at Zapruder frame 312, are as follows:[107]

	Zapruder frame	Acoustical determination of origin
Impulse pattern I	173–177	TSBD.
Impulse pattern II	205–208	TSBD.
Impulse pattern III	312	Grassy knoll.
Impulse pattern IV	328–329	TSBD.

It was determined by medical, ballistics and neutron activation evidence that the President was struck in the head by a bullet fired from a rifle found on the sixth floor of the Texas School Book Depository. For that bullet to have destroyed the medical evidence of the President being hit at Zapruder frame 312, it would have had to have struck at Zapruder frame 328–329. But a preliminary trajectory analysis, based on the President's location and body position at frame 328–329 failed to track to a shooter in the sixth floor southeast corner window of the depository within a minimum margin of error radius, [108] thus indicating it was highly unlikely the President was struck in the head at Zapruder frame 328 by a shot fired from the sixth floor southeast corner window of the depository. Further, there is no visual evidence in the Zapruder film of the President being struck in the head

[16]In addition, the blur analysis conducted by the photographic evidence panel appeared to be more consistent with the grassy knoll shot striking the President. The analysis reflected no significant panning errors by Zapruder after frame 296. Such errors would have been expected if the third (grassy knoll) shot occurred 0.7 second before the fatal head shot. Assuming the head shot was the grassy knoll shot, Zapruder made significant panning errors after both the third and fourth shots. (See Blur Analysis. Appendix to the HSCA–JFK hearings, vol. VI, par. 81ff.)

at Zapruder fames 173–177 or 205–208, the frames at which shots one and two would have been fired if the shot from the knoll was a hit to the head at frame 312. Accordingly, if the shot from the grassy knoll occurred at frame 312, no shot fired from the Texas School Book Depository would have struck the President in the head at any time. Such a finding is contrary to the weight of the scientific evidence. The committee concluded, therefore, that the shot fired from the grassy knoll was not the shot visually represented at Zapruder frame 312; that the shot from the grassy knoll missed President Kennedy;[17] and that the most accurate synchronization of the tape and the film would be one based on a correlation of impulse pattern four on the tape with the fatal head shot to the President at frame 312 of the Zapruder film. When the tape and film are so synchronized, the sequence on the film corroborated or substantiated the timing of the shots indicated on the 1963 tape.

According to the more logical synchronization, the first shot would have occurred at approximately Zapruder frame 160. This would also be consistent with the testimony of Governor Connally, who stated that he heard the first shot and began to turn in response to it. [109] His reactions, as shown in Zapruder frames 162–167, reflect the start of a rapid head movement from left to right.[110]

The photographic evidence panel's observations were also relevant to the acoustics data that indicated that the second shot hit the limousine's occupants at about Zapruder frames 188–191. The panel noted that at approximately Zapruder frame 200 the President's movements suddenly freeze, as his right hand seemed to stop abruptly in the midst of a waving motion. Then, during frames 200–202, his head moves rapidly from right to left. The sudden interruption of the President's hand-waving motion, coupled with his rapid head movements, was considered by the photographic panel as evidence of President Kennedy's reaction to some "severe external stimulus."[111]

Finally, the panel observed that Governor Connally's actions during frames 222–226, as he is seen emerging from behind the sign that obstructed Zapruder's view, in-

---

[17] The committee noted there was no physical evidence of where a shot from the grassy knoll might have hit. Since a shot from the Texas School Book Depository hit the President in the head less than one second after the shot from the knoll, there would have been little apparent reason for a gunman on the knoll to fire a second shot.

dicated he was also reacting to some "severe external stimulus."[18] [112] Based upon this observation and upon the positions of President Kennedy and Governor Connally within the limousine, the panel concluded that the relative alinement of the two men was consistent with the theory that they had been struck by the same bullet.[113]

The forensic pathology panel, with one member in dissent, stated that the medical evidence was consistent with the hypothesis that a single bullet caused the wounds to the Governor and the President.[114]

The committee conducted a trajectory analysis for the shot that it ultimately concluded struck both the Governor and the President. It was based on the location of the limousine and the body positions of President Kennedy and Governor Connally at Zapruder frame 190 and the bullet's course as it could be determined from their wounds.[19] When President Kennedy's entry and exit wounds were used as reference points for the trajectory line, it intersected the Texas School Book Depository within a 13-foot radius of a point approximately 14 feet west of the building's southeast corner and approximately 2 feet below the sixth floor window sills. [115] When President Kennedy's exit wound and Governor Connally's entrance wound were used as the reference points for the trajectory line, it intersected the Texas School Book Depository within a 7-foot radius of a point approximately 2 feet west of the southeast corner and 9 feet above the sixth floor window sills.[116]

The committee's examination of the synchronization of the tape to the Zapruder film, therefore, demonstrated that the timing of the impulses on the tape matched the timing of events seen in the film. Further, the other scientific evidence available to the committee was consistent with the reactions viewed the film and the timing of the shots indicated by the acoustical analysis. The synchronization of the 1963 dispatch tape with the film, based on a fatal hit to the President's head at frame 312 having

[18]The panel reached no conclusion concerning Governor Connally's reactions, if any, from Zapruder frame 207 to frame 221, since during this .82-second interval he was behind the sign that obstructed Zapruder's field of view. Connally could conceivably have started his reaction at frames 200–206, but too little of his body is visible during these frames to permit such a finding.

[19]Because the committee concluded that the shot from the grassy knoll did not hit the President at Zapruder frame 312, it did not undertake a trajectory analysis for the second shot from the depository, one that would have occurred in the area of Zapruder frames 205–208 if the shot from the grassy knoll had hit the President at Zapruder frame 312.

88

been fired from the Texas School Book Depository, along with related evidence, corroborated or independently substantiated that the tape is one of transmissions from a microphone that recorded the assassination in Dealey Plaza on November 22, 1963.

Despite the existence of adequate corroboration or substantiation of the tape's authenticity, the committee realized that other questions were posed by the timing sequence of the impulses on the tape. The acoustical analysis had indicated both the first and second impulse patterns were shots from the vicinity of Texas School Book Depository, but that there were only 1.66 seconds between the onset of each of these impulse patterns. The committee recognized that 1.66 seconds is too brief a period for both shots to have been fired from Oswald's rifle, given the results of tests performed for the Warren Commission that found that the average minimum firing time between shots was 2.3 seconds.[117]

The tests for the Warren Commission, however, were based on an assumption that Oswald used the telescopic sight on the rifle. [118] The committee's panel of firearms experts, on the other hand, testified that given the distance and angle from the sixth floor window to the location of the President's limousine, it would have been easier to use the open iron sights.[119] During the acoustical reconstruction performed for the committee in August, the Dallas Police Department marksmen in fact used iron sights and had no difficulty hitting the targets.

The committee test fired a Mannlicher-Carcano rifle using the open iron sights. It found that it was possible for two shots to be fired within 1.66 seconds.[120] One gunman, therefore, could have fired the shots that caused both impulse pattern 1 and impulse pattern 2 on the dispatch tape. The strongest evidence that one gunman did, in fact, fire the shots that caused both impulse patterns was that all three cartridge cases found on the sixth floor of the Texas School Book Depository came from Oswald's rifle. [121] In addition, the fragments from the two bullets that were found were identified as having been fired from Oswald's rifle.[122] Accordingly, the 1.66 seconds between the onset of the first and second impulse patterns on the tape are not too brief a period of time for both of these patterns to represent gunfire, and for Oswald to have been the person responsible for firing both shots.

To explore further whether the tape contained sounds

transmitted from a microphone in Dealey Plaza, the committee reviewed evidence produced by its photographic evidence panel. The panel conducted a "jiggle analysis" of the Zapruder film on the theory that Zapruder's panning errors, which would be apparent as a blur in the film, might have been caused by his reaction to the sound of gunfire. An original jiggle analysis, performed without knowledge of the results of the acoustical analysis, showed strong indications of shots occurring at about frame 190 and at about frame 310. [123] The photographic evidence panel also noted some correlation between the acoustics results and a panning error reaction to the apparent sound of gunfire at about frame 160. Little evidence of another shot was found in the jiggle analysis,[20] but the expert who performed it testified that since the third and fourth shots occurred within less than a second of each other, it might be difficult to differentiate between them.[124]

In summary, the various scientific projects indicated that there was a high probability that two gunmen were firing at the President. Scientifically, the existence of the second gunman was established only by the acoustical study, but its basic validity was corroborated or independently substantiated by the various other scientific projects.

The committee had its photographic evidence panel examine evidence that might also reveal that there was in fact more than one gunman shooting at the President. Each item of relevant photographic evidence available to the committee was evaluated to determine whether image enhancement techniques (digital image processing, photo-optical/chemical enhancement, and autoradiographic enhancement) might show additional gunmen.[125] As the use of nonoriginal photographic materials frequently introduces image distortion that precludes accurate photointerpretation, only original photographic materials were subjected to image enchancement techniques.[126] Similarly, since opaque film, such as photographic print paper, does not have the dynamic range (of brightness) of properly processed transparent film, it was not as suitable for enhancement.[127]

There was considerable witness testimony, as well as a large body of critical literature, that had indicated the grassy knoll as a source of gunshots. Accordingly, this

---

[20]Indication of a shot from the grassy knoll might have been expected in the jiggle analysis at about frame 295.

area received particular emphasis in the photographic interpretation analysis. The panel directed its attention to that portion of the knoll that extended from the retaining wall situated by the pergola to the stockade fence to the west of the wall. This analysis included enhancement of photographs taken by Mary Moorman, Philip Willis and Orville Nix, as well as Zapruder.

Mary Moorman, a bystander, had taken a Polaroid photograph of the grassy knoll at approximately the time of Zapruder frame 313. [128] As far as the committee knew, it was the one photograph taken at the moment of the fatal head shot that showed the area that the acoustical analysis indicated was the location of the second gunman. Viewing the photograph with the naked eye, one could detect images that might be constructed as something significant behind the stockade fence. These images may, however, only represent parts of a tree, or they may be photographic artifacts. Due to the poor quality of the photograph and its deterioration over the years, it was not possible to determine the nature of the images with the naked eye. The photograph, because of this poor quality and because it was taken on opaque film that is less suitable for photographic enhancement, was considered by the photographic evidence panel to be of limited usefulness.[129] Prior to the acoustical analysis, it was the subject of only limited clarification efforts, none of which involved computer technology.[130] Enhancement attempts in the region of the retaining wall produced no significant increase in detail and no evidence of any human form.[131] Because the stockade fence region of the photograph was of even poorer quality than the retaining wall area, no enhancement attempts were recommended.[132] Subsequent to the acoustical analysis, the author of the section of the photographic evidence panel's report that addressed the question of whether there were other gunmen in Dealey Plaza indicated that the likelihood of successfully enhancing this print was extremely remote.[133]

The significance of the Moorman film may, therefore, be largely negative. It was not possible to draw anything positive from the film 15 years after it was taken. Nevertheless, if the film did not contain images that might be construed to be a figure behind the fence, it would be a troubling lack of corroboration for the acoustical analysis. At the same time, the committee noted, the Department of

Justice might consider further enhancement, if it is deemed to be feasible.

Zapruder frame 41, showing a bush situated between Zapruder and the Presidential limousine, was also analyzed by the photographic evidence panel. Image enhancement techniques successfully established the presence of a human head visible among the leaves of the bush in Zapruder's field of view.[134] Photogrammetric analysis determined that this so-called gunman in the bush was actually located on the other side of the bush from Zapruder.[135] It is probably one of the men who can be seen in other photographs standing in the middle of the sidewalk that runs from the top of the grassy knoll down to Elm Street. Consequently, he was not, as had been alleged, in a position to have been a hidden gunman. Further, the linear feature associated with this person, alleged by Warren Commission critics to be a rifle, is actually in front of the leaves on the same side of the bush as Zapruder.[163] Analytical photogrammetry and image enhancement with special color analysis attributed this linear feature to natural surroundings. The narrow portion of the linear feature (the alleged rifle barrel) was established to be one of a number of twigs in the bush. [137] All of them were characterized by the same general direction and spacing, consistent with the natural growth patterns of the bush. [138] The thicker part of the linear feature (the alleged rifle "stock") was a hole in the bushes through which a portion of the Presidential limousine was visible.[139]

Willis photograph No. 5 was the third knoll photograph enhanced and evaluated by the panel. The relevant area of analysis was the retaining wall situated approximately 41 feet to the east of the point of the stockade fence that, according to the acoustics analysis, was the source of gunfire. A fleshtone comparison performed by analyzing measurements of color values on an object located behind the west end of the retaining wall confirmed that the image perceived was actually a human being.[140] The panel did perceive "a very distinct straight-line feature" near the region of this person's hands, but it was unable to deblur the image sufficiently to reach any conclusion as to whether the feature was, in fact, a weapon.[141]

Photographic enhancement of selected portions of a film taken by Orville Nix was also performed by the panel. One object in the vicinity of the retaining wall near the pergola was carefully studied, but the panel could not identify it as a human being and decided that the image was more likely the result of light and shadow patterns.[142]

The Nix frames analyzed included those that purportedly depict a gunman in a "classic" firing stance. This "individual" is located by the southwest corner of the pergola beyond the retaining wall, approximately 41 feet north of the point of the stockade fence that, according to the acoustics study, was the source of gunfire. The panel was able to conclude that this image was not, in fact, a human being. Its conclusion was based on both a shadow analysis and its inability to attribute fleshtones or motion to the alleged gunman.[143]

None of the photographs of the grassy knoll that were analyzed by the photographic evidence panel revealed any evidence of a puff of smoke or flash of light,[144] as reported by several people in the crowd.

The committee's analysis of available photographic evidence, therefore, did not confirm or preclude the presence of a gunman firing at the President from behind the stockade fence on the grassy knoll. In addition to photographs of the knoll area, the committee enhanced photographic materials of the Texas School Book Depository taken by Robert Hughes, Tom Dillard, and James Powell. These were examined for any evidence with respect to the source of the shots fired from the depository, as well as any evidence of conspiratorial activity before or after the assassination. (The committee was not aware of the existence of any photographs of the sixth floor southeast corner window of the depository at the actual moment of the assassination.) The Hughes film, taken moments before the first shot was fired at the President, was enhanced for the purpose of determining whether any motion could be discerned in the sixth floor southeast corner window where Oswald was alleged to have been positioned. Although motion in this window was noted, the panel concluded that it was only apparent rather than real.[145] This conclusion was based on the rapidity of the perceived motion, its lack of consistent direction, and the fact that the object disappears from view during a two-frame (approximately one-ninth of a second) sequence.[146] Accordingly, the motion was attributed to photographic artifact.[147] An appearance of motion in an adjacent set of windows was also attributed to a photographic artifact.[148]

The question of motion in both sets of windows is similarly raised by the film taken by Charles L. Bronson several minutes before the assassination. Because this film was not made avilable to the committee until December 2, 1978, it was not reviewed by the full panel. In a preliminary examination of the film by several members of the panel, it was observed that the characteristics of the Bronson film were similar to those of the Hughes film that were examined by the entire panel. The apparent motion in the window seemed to be random and therefore not likely to be caused by human motion.[149] Because of the high quality of the Bronson film, the panel members recommended it be subjected to computer analysis.[150] The committee recommended, in turn, that the Bronson film be subjected to analysis by the Department of Justice.

Enhancement efforts with respect to the Dillard and Powell photographs, taken shortly after the assassination, successfully generated considerable detail within the depository window.[151] Based upon its review of these materials, the panel was able to conclude that at the time these photographs were taken, no human forms were present in the sixth floor southeast corner window of the depository.[152]

No photographs of the sixth floor southeast corner window of the Texas School Book Depository were taken at the time of the assassination, and photographic evidence did not confirm or preclude a firing by an assassin from the window. Photographs of the sixth floor window taken shortly before and after the assassination did not reveal evidence of human forms. Allegations that these photographs contain evidence of there having been more than one gunman on the sixth floor were not supported by the enhancement efforts. In summary, the photographic evidence with respect to the grassy knoll and the Texas School Book Depository did not confirm or preclude that a gunman fired at the President from either location.

None of the scientific evidence available to the committee—photography, forensic pathology, ballistics, neutron activation analysis—was inconsistent with the acoustical evidence that established a high probability that two gunmen fired at the President.

(d) *Witness testimony on the shots.*—The committee, in conjunction with its scientific projects, had a consultant retained by Bolt Beranek and Newman analyze the testimony of witnesses in Dealey Plaza on November 22, 1963, to advise the committee what weight, if any, it should give such testimony, and to relate the testimony to the acoustics evidence the committee had obtained.

The statements of 178 persons who were in Dealey Plaza, all of whom were available to the Warren Commission, were analyzed:[153] 49 (27.5 percent) believed the shots had come from the Texas School Book Depository; 21 (11.8 percent) believed the shots had come from the grassy knoll; 30 (16.9 percent) believed the shots had originated elsewhere; and 78 (43.8 percent) were unable to tell which direction the shots were fired from. Only four individuals believed shots had originated from more than one location.[154]

Some comment on these statistics is called for. The committee noted that a significant number of witnesses reported that shots originated from the grassy knoll. The small number of those who thought shots originated from both the book depository and grassy knoll might be explained by the fact that the third and fourth shots were only seven-tenths of a second apart. Such a brief interval might have made it difficult for witnesses to differentiate between the two shots, or to distinguish their direction. While recognizing the substantial number of people who reported shots originating from the knoll, the committee also believed the process of collecting witness testimony was such that it would be unwise to place substantial reliance upon it. The witness were interviewed over a substantial period of time, some of them several days, even weeks, after the assassination. By that time, numerous accounts of the number and direction of the shots had been published. The committee believed that the witnesses' memories and testimony on the number, direction, and timing of the shots may have been substantially influenced by the intervening publicity concerning the events of November 22, 1963.[155] Consequently, standing alone, the statistics are an unreliable foundation upon which to rely with great confidence for any specific finding. It was of obvious importance, however, that some witness testimony would corroborate the acoustical finding of a shot from the grassy knoll. If no testimony indicated shots from the knoll, there would have been a troubling lack of corroboration for the acoustical analysis.

The Warren Commission had available to it the same testimony concerning shots from the knoll, but it believed it should not be credited because of "the difficulty of accurate perception."[156] The Commission stated, "*** the physical and other evidence" only compelled the conclusion that at least two shots were fired.[157] The Commission noted, however, that the three cartridge cases that were found, when taken together with the witness testimony, amounted to a preponderance of evidence that three shots were fired.[158] Nevertheless, the Commission held, "*** there is no credible evidence to indicate shots were fired from other than the Texas School took Depository." [159] It therefore discounted the testimony of shots from the grassy knoll.

While recognizing that the Commission was correct in acknowledging the difficulty of accurate witness perception, the committee obtained independent acoustical evidence to support it. Consequently, it was in a position where it had to regard the witness testimony in a different light.

The committee assembled for the purpose of illustration the substance of the testimony of some of the witnesses who believed the shots may have come from somewhere in addition to the depository. A Dallas police officer, Bobby W. Hargis, was riding a motorcycle to the left and slightly to the rear of the limousine. Hargis described the direction of the shots in a deposition given to the Warren Commission on April 8, 1964:

> Well, at the time it sounded like the shots were right next to me. There wasn't any way in the world I could tell where they were coming from, but at the time there was something in my head that said that they probably could have been coming from the railroad overpass, because I thought since I had got splattered * * * I had a feeling that it might have been from the Texas School Book Depository, and these two places was (sic) the primary place that could have been shot from.[160]

Hargis stated that after the shooting he saw a man fall to the ground at the base of the incline and cover his child. He also saw other people running. Hargis himself stopped his motorcycle and ran up the incline.[161]

The man Officer Hargis saw lying on the ground was probably William Eugene Newman. Newman and his wife and child were observing the motorcade from the curb near the west end of the concrete standard on Elm Street. Newman gave this description of their actions after hearing the shots of the sheriff's department on November 22, 1963:

> Then we fell down on the grass as it seemed that we were in direct path of fire . . . I thought the shots had come from the garden directly behind me, that was on an elevation from where I was as I was right on the curb. I do not recall looking toward the Texas School Book Depository. I looked back in the vicinity of the garden.[162]

Abraham Zapruder, since deceased, was standing on a concrete abutment on the grassy knoll, just beyond the Stemmons' freeway sign, aiming his 8 millimeter camera at the motorcade. He testified in a deposition given to the Commission on July 22, 1964, that he thought a shot may have come from behind him, but then acknowledged in response to questions from Commission counsel that it could have come from anywhere. He did, however, differentiate among the effects the shots had on him. One shot, he noted, caused reverberations all around him and was much more pronounced than the others. [163] Such a difference, the committee noted, would be consistent with the differing effects Zapruder might notice from a shot from the knoll, as opposed to the Texas School Book Depository.

A Secret Service agent, Paul E. Landis, Jr., wrote a statement on the shooting, dated November 30, 1963. Landis was in the follow-up car, behind the Presidential limousine, on the outside running board on the right. He indicated that the first shot "sounded like the report of a high powered rifle from behind me, over my right shoulder." [164] According to his statement, the shot he identified as number two might have come from a different direction. He said:

> I still was not certain from which direction the second shot came, but my reaction at this time was that the shot came from somewhere towards the front, right-hand side of the road.[165]

Another witness, S. M. Holland, since deceased, also noted signs of a shot coming from a group of trees on the knoll. Holland was standing on top of the railroad overpass above Elm Street. Testifying in a deposition to the Warren Commission on April 8, 1964, he indicated he heard four shots. After the first, he said, he saw Governor Connally turned around.[166] Then there was another report. The first two sounded as if they came from "the upper part of the street." The third was not as loud as the others. Holland said:

There was a shot, a report. I don't know whether it was a shot. I can't say that. And a puff of smoke came out about 6 or 8 feet above the ground right out from under those trees. And at just about this location from where I was standing, you could see that puff of smoke, like someone had thrown a firecracker, or something out, and that is just about the way it sounded. It wasn't as loud as the previous reports or shots.[167]

When counsel for the Warren Commission asked Holland if he had any doubts about the four shots, he said:

I have no doubt about it. I have no doubt about seeing that puff of smoke come out from those trees either.[168]

These witnesses are illustrative of those present in Dealey Plaza on November 22, 1963, who believed a shot came from the grassy knoll.

(1) *Analysis of the reliability of witness testimony.*— The committee also conducted, as part of the acoustical reenactment in Dealey Plaza in August 1978, a test of the capacity of witnesses to locate the direction of shots, hoping the experiment might give the committee an independent basis with which to evaluate what weight, if any, to assign to witness testimony. Two expert witnesses were asked to locate the direction of shots during the test,[169] and Dr. David Green, the BBN consultant, supervised the test and prepared a report on the reactions of the expert witnesses. Green concluded in the report, "* * * it is difficult to draw any firm conclusions relative to the reports of witnesses in the plaza as to the possible locus of any assassin." [170] Nevertheless, he stated that "it is hard to believe a rifle was fired from the knoll" during the assassination, since such a shot would be easy to "localize." Green cited as support for his conclusion the fact that only four of the 178 Dealey Plaza witnesses pointed to more than one location as the origin of the shots.[171]

In its evaluation of Green's conclusions, the committee considered the different circumstances affecting the expert witnesses in the test and the actual witnesses to the assassination. The expert witnesses in August 1978 were expecting the shooting and knew in advance that guns would be fired only from the Texas School Book Depository and the grassy knoll, and they had been told their assignment was to determine the direction of the shots. Further, there was no test in which shots were fired within seven-tenths of a second of each other, so no reliable conclusion could be reached with respect to the possibility that such a brief interval would cause confusion. Dr. Green's report also reflects that even though the two trained observers correctly identified the origin of 90 percent of the shots, their own notes indicated something short of certainty.[172] Their comments were phrased with equivocation: "Knoll?;" "Over my head. Not really on knoll or even behind me;" "Knoll/underpass;" and "Knoll? Not really confident." Their comments, in short, frequently reflected ambiguity as to the origin of the shots, indicating that the gunfire from the grassy knoll often did not sound very different from shots fired from the book depository.

An analysis by the committee of the statements of witnesses in Dealey Plaza on November 22, 1963, moreover, showed that about 44 percent were not able to form an opinion about the origin of the shots,[173] attesting to the ambiguity showed in the August 1978 experiment. Seventy percent of the witnesses in 1963 who had an opinion as to origin said it was either the book depository or the grassy knoll.[21][174] Those witnesses who thought the shots originated from the grassy knoll represented 30 percent of those who chose between the knoll and the book depository and 21 percent of those who made a decision as to origin. Since most of the shots fired on November 22, 1963 (three out of four, the committee determined) came from the book depository, the fact that so many witnesses thought they heard shots from the knoll lent additional weight to a conclusion that a shot came from there.

The committee, therefore, concluded that the testimony of witnesses in Dealey Plaza on November 22, 1963 sup-

[21]The interviews of witnesses to the assassination may have reflected a tendency to make a "forced choice" between the two locations, caused by the actions of police and other spectators in Dealey Plaza indicating the knoll and the depository were the two shooters locations, an attitude that was substantiated by press reports of shooter locations that, in some instances, preceded interviews with witnesses.

ported the finding of the acoustical analysis that there was a high probability that a shot was fired at the President from the grassy knoll. There were also witness reports of suspicious activity in the vicinity of the knoll.[175].

(e) Certain conspiracy allegations

While the committee recognized, as discussed in section C, that a finding that two gunmen fired at the President did not in itself establish that President Kennedy was assassinated as a result of a conspiracy, it did establish, in the context of common experience, the probability that a conspiracy did exist that day. Consequently, the committee sought to employ scientific analysis to examine some conspiracy theories about the assassination. The scientific analysis that could be applied to these conspiracy allegations refuted each one of them.

The committee had its photographic evidence panel investigate allegations concerning certain specific individuals who had been linked to the assassination and were allegedly present in Dealey Plaza. Forensic anthropologists were asked to compare photographs of these known subjects with those of unidentified persons photographed in Dealey Plaza on the day of the assassination. The anthropological studies involved comparison of morphological traits (wrinkles, scars, and shape of ears, nose, et cetera) and facial dimensions and statural measurements to the extent that these could be derived from the photographs examined and other related documents available to the committee.[176]

The first photograph examined contained an individual appearing in a press photograph of motorcade spectators on Houston Street.[177] Some critics had contended the individual appeared to be Joseph A. Milteer, a militant conservative who had been secretly recorded on tape by a police informant 2 weeks prior to the assassination as he described a plan to assassinate the President.[22] The anthropologists concluded, however, that based on available photographs and records of Milteer's height, the individual in the photograph could not have been Milteer.[178]

Press photographs of three "tramps" apprehended by the Dallas police near Dealey Plaza shortly after the as-

---

[22]The committee's analysis of the response by the Secret Service to the threat posed by Milteer's alleged plan is described in section D1 of this report.

sassination were analyzed and compared with photographs of a number of persons, including E. Howard Hunt,[23] Frank Sturgis, Thomas Vallee, Daniel Carswell, and Fred Lee Chrisman, each of whom had been alleged by critics to be linked to the assassination. Of all the subjects compared, only Fred Lee Chrisman, a conservative active in New Orleans at the time of the assassination, was found to have a facial measurements consistent with any of the tramps. [180] Anthropologists could not make a positive identification of Chrisman, [181] however. The committee could not establish any link between Chrisman and the assassination. In addition, the committee independently determined that Chrisman was not in Dealey Plaza on the day of the assassination.[182]

The committee sought, by employing scientific analysis, to explore other allegations of conspiratorial activity. Establishing the authenticity of the autopsy photographs and X-rays was of fundamental importance, not only because these evidentiary materials were a primary basis for the committee's findings concerning the nature and causes of the President's head wounds, but because allegations that they had been altered raised implications of a wide-based conspiracy operating at high levels of the U.S. Government. As it has been noted, the committee found that the X-rays and photographs had not been altered.

Another conspiratorial theory that implied there was an extensive and sophisticated conspiracy rested on the allegation that the photographs of Oswald in his backyard holding a rifle were composites. Similar conspiratorial implications were raised by the allegation that the rifle currently in the National Archives was a different rifle than that seen in the backyard photographs of Oswald with the rifle, as well as other photographs of the rifle taken on November 22 and November 23, 1963. As discussed in section A3, scientific analysis performed by the committee refuted each of these allegations.[183]

The final conspiratorial theory the committee investigated by scientific analysis was the so-called "two Oswald theory." This was an assertion by some critics that the Lee

---

[23]During the course of the committee's investigation, a rumor was circulating that the comittee had uncovered a memorandum in CIA files indicating Hunt was in Dallas on November 22, 1963. The rumor was not founded on fact. In addition, Hunt gave the committee a sworn deposition [179] in which he denied the allegation, and the committee found no evidence that contradicted Hunt's deposition.

Harvey Oswald who returned from Russia in 1962 was a different person than the Lee Harvey Oswald who defected to Russia in 1959. [184] Forensic anthropologists analyzed and compared a number of photos of Oswald taken at different times during his life for any indication that they were not photographs of one and the same individual. Based on an analysis of facial dimensions, they found all the photographs consistent with those of a single individual.[185]

In addition, the photographic evidence panel conducted height and proportion studies of various Oswald photographs, utilizing test photographs of subjects against a height chart. [186] The panel noted that significant variations can arise from this type of measurement due to differences in orientation and distance of the subject from the camera. [187] The panel explained, "* * * unless the subject photographed is standing directly with his back against the height chart at a correct distance from a properly positioned camera equipped with an appropriate lens, it is unreasonable to assume that the resulting picture is ever a precisely accurate indicator of both his height and head size." [188] The panel noted that because of these impediments to accuracy, the use of height charts in pictures is no longer a common practice in law enforcement or industrial security work.[189]

The committee also engaged the services of three handwriting experts to explore the "two Oswald theory." These experts viewed documents purported to have been written by Lee Harvey Oswald. They examined documents from the years 1956 to 1963 to determine if the handwriting of the man who joined the Marines in 1956 was the same as that of the man who had applied for a passport in 1959, tried to revoke his American citizenship in 1959, returned to the United States in 1962, journeyed to Mexico in late September 1963, and ordered the rifle which was found on the sixth floor of the Texas School Book Depository on November 22, 1963. A careful examination of these documents demonstrated that the man who signed those items was the same man throughout the entire 7-year period.[190] Accordingly, on the basis of the committee's scientific analysis, there was no evidence to support the allegation that the Lee Harvey Oswald who returned from Russia in 1962 was a different person than the Lee Harvey Oswald who defected to Russia in 1959.

(f) *Summary of the evidence*

Where it was available, the committee extensively employed scientific analysis to assist it in the resolution of numerous issues. The committee considered all the other evidence available to evaluate the scientific analysis. In conclusion, the committee found that the scientific acoustical evidence established a high probability that two gunmen fired at President John F. Kennedy. Other scientific evidence did not preclude the possibility of two gunmen firing at the President, but it did negate some specific conspiracy allegations.

C. The Committee Believes, on the Evidence Available to It, That President John F. Kennedy Was Probably Assassinated as a Result of a Conspiracy. The Committee is Unable to Identify the Other Gunman or the Extent of the Conspiracy

Supreme Court Justice Oliver Wendell Holmes once simply defined conspiracy as "a partnership in criminal purposes."[1] That definition is adequate. Nevertheless, it may be helpful to set out a more precise definition. If two or more individuals agreed to take action to kill President Kennedy, and at least one of them took action in furtherance of the plan, and it resulted in President Kennedy's death, the President would have been assassinated as a result of a conspiracy.

The committee recognizes, of course, that while the word "conspiracy" technically denotes only a "partnership in criminal purposes," it also, in fact, connotes widely varying meanings to many people, and its use has vastly differing societal implications depending upon the sophistication, extent and ultimate purpose of the partnership. For example, a conspiracy to assassinate a President might be a complex plot orchestrated by foreign political powers; it might be the scheme of a group of American citizens dissatisfied with particular governmental policies; it also might be the plan of two largely isolated individuals with no readily discernible motive.

Conspiracies may easily range, therefore, from those with important implications for social or governmental institutions to those with no major societal significance. As the evidence concerning the probability that President Kennedy was assassinated as a result of a "conspiracy" is analyzed, these various connotations of the word "conspiracy" and distinctions between them ought to be constantly borne in mind. Here, as elesewhere, words must be used carefully, lest people be misled.[1]

---

[1] It might be suggested that because of the widely varying meanings attached to the word "conspiracy," it ought to be avoided. Such a suggestion, however, raises another objection—the search for euphemistic variations

A conspiracy cannot be said to have existed in Dealey Plaza unless evidence exists from which, in Justice Holmes' words, a "partnership in criminal purposes" may be inferred. The Warren Commission's conclusion that Lee Harvey Oswald was not involved in a conspiracy to assassinate the President was, for example, largely based on its findings of the absence of evidence of significant association [2] between Oswald and other possible conspirators and no physical evidence of conspiracy.[3] The Commission reasoned, quite rightly, that in the absence of association or physical evidence, there was no conspiracy.

Even without physical evidence of conspiracy at the scene of the assassination, there would, of course, be a conspiracy if others assisted Oswald in his efforts. Accordingly, an examination of Oswald's associates is necessary. The Warren Commission recognized that a first premise in a finding of conspiracy may be a finding of association. Because the Commission did not find any significant Oswald associates, it was not compelled to face the difficult questions posed by such a finding. More than association is required to establish conspiracy. There must be at least knowing assistance or a manifestation of agreement to the criminal purpose by the associate.

It is important to realize, too, that the term "associate" may connote widely varying meanings to different people. A person's associate may be his next door neighbor and vacation companion, or it may be an individual he has met only once for the purpose of discussing a contract for a murder. The Warren Commission examined Oswald's past and concluded he was essentially a loner. [4] It reasoned, therefore, that since Oswald had no significant associations with persons who could have been involved with him in the assassination, there could not have been a conspiracy.[5]

With respect to Jack Ruby,[2] the Warren Commission

---

can lead to a lack of candor. There is virtue in seeing something for what it is, even if the plain truth causes discomfort.

[2] The Warren Commission devoted its Appendix XVI to a biography of Jack Ruby in which his family background, psychological makeup, education and business activities were considered. While the evidence was sometimes contradictory, the Commission found that Ruby grew up in Chicago, the son of Jewish immigrants; that he lived in a home disrupted by domestic strife; [6] that he was troubled psychologically as a youth and not educated beyond high school; and that descriptions of his temperament ranged from "mild mannered" to "violent." [7] In 1963, Ruby was 52 and unmarried. He ran a Dallas nightclub but was not particularly successful in business. His acquaintances included a number of Dallas police officers who frequented his nightclub, as well as other types of people who comprised his clientele.

similarly found no significant associations, either between Ruby and Oswald or between Ruby and others who might have been conspirators with him.[8] In particular, it found no connections between Ruby and organized crime, and it reasoned that absent such associations, there was no conspiracy to kill Oswald or the President.[9]

The committee conducted a three-pronged investigation of conspiracy in the Kennedy assassination. On the basis of extensive scientific analysis and an analysis of the testimony of Dealey Plaza witnesses, the committee found there was a high probability that two gunmen fired at President Kennedy.

Second, the committee explored Oswald's and Ruby's contacts for any evidence of significant associations. Unlike the Warren Commission, it found certain of these contacts to be of investigative significance. The Commission apparently had looked for evidence of conspiratorial association. Finding none on the face of the assocations it investigated, it did not go further. The committee, however, conducted a wider ranging investigation. Notwithstanding the possibility of a benign reason for contact between Oswald or Ruby and one of their associates, the committee examined the very fact of the contact to see if it contained investigative significance. Unlike the Warren Commission, the committee took a close look at the associates to determine whether conspiratorial activity in the assassination could have been possible, given what the committee could learn about the associates, and whether the apparent nature of the contact should, therefore, be examined more closely.[3]

Third, the committee examined groups—political organizations, national governments and so on—that might have had the motive, opportunity and means to assassinate the President.

The committee, therefore, directly introduced the hypothesis of conspiracy and investigated it with reference to known facts to determine if it had any bearing on the assassination.

The committee examined a series of major groups or organizations that have been alleged to have been involved in a conspiracy to assassinate the President. If any of these

---

[9]The committee found associations of both Ruby and Oswald that were unknown to the Warren Commission.

groups or organizations, as a group, had been involved in the assassination, the conspiracy to assassinate President Kennedy would have been one of major significance.

As will be detailed in succeeding sections of this report, the committee did not find sufficient evidence that any of these groups or organizations were involved in a conspiracy in the Kennedy assassination. Accordingly, the committee concluded, on the basis of the evidence available to it, that the Soviet government, the Cuban government, anti-Castro Cuban groups, and the national syndicate of organized crime were not involved in the assassination. Further, the committee found that the Secret Service, the Federal Bureau of Investigation, and the Central Intelligence Agency were not involved in the assassination.

Based on the evidence available to it, the committee could not preclude the possibility that individual members of anti-Castro Cuban groups or the national syndicate of organized crime were involved in the assassination. There was insufficient evidence, however, to support a finding that any individual members were involved. The ramifications of a conspiracy involving such individuals would be significant, although of perhaps less import than would be the case if a group itself, the national syndicate, for example, had been involved.

The committee recognized that a finding that two gunmen fired simultaneously at the President did not, by itself, establish that there was a conspiracy to assassinate the President. It is theoretically possible that the gunmen were acting independently, each totally unaware of the other. It was the committee's opinion, however, that such a theoretical possibility is extremely remote. The more logical and probable inference to be drawn from two gunmen firing at the same person at the same time and in the same place is that they were acting in concert, that is, as a result of a conspiracy.

The committee found that, to be precise and loyal to the facts it established, it was compelled to find that President Kennedy was probably killed as a result of a conspiracy. The committee's finding that President Kennedy was probably assassinated as a result of a conspiracy was premised on four factors:

(1) Since the Warren Commission's and FBI's investigation into the possibility of a conspiracy was

seriously flawed, their failure to develop evidence
of a conspiracy could not be given independent
weight.

The Warren Commission was, in fact, incorrect in concluding that Oswald and Ruby had no significant associations, and therefore its finding of no
conspiracy was not reliable.

(3) While it cannot be inferred from the significant associations of Oswald and Ruby that any of
the major groups examined by the committee were
involved in the assassination, a more limited conspiracy could not be ruled out.

(4) There was a high probability that a second
gunman, in fact, fired at the President.

At the same time, the committee candidly stated, in
expressing its finding of conspiracy in the Kennedy assassination, that it was "unable to identify the other gunman or the extent of the conspiracy." The photographic
and other scientific evidence available to the committee
was insufficient to permit the committee to answer these
questions. In addition, the committee's other investigative
efforts did not develop evidence from which Oswald's conspirator or conspirators could be firmly identified. It is
possible, of course, that the extent of the conspiracy was
so limited that it involved only Oswald and the second
gunman. The committee was not able to reach such a
conclusion, for it would have been based on speculation,
not evidence. Aspects of the investigation did suggest that
the conspiracy may have been relatively limited, but to
state with precision exactly how small was not possible.
Other aspects of the committee's investigation did suggest, however, that while the conspiracy may not have
involved a major group, it may not have been limited to
only two people. These aspects of the committee's investigation are discussed elsewhere.

If the conspiracy to assassinate President Kennedy was
limited to Oswald and a second gunman, its main societal
significance may be in the realization that agencies of the
U.S. Government inadequately investigated the possibility
of such a conspiracy. In terms of its implications for
government and society, an assassination as a consequence
of a conspiracy composed solely of Oswald and a small
number of persons, possibly only one, and possibly a
person akin to Oswald in temperament and ideology, would

not have been fundamentally different from an assassination by Oswald alone.[4]

1. **THE COMMITTEE BELIEVES, ON THE BASIS OF THE EVIDENCE AVAILABLE TO IT, THAT THE SOVIET GOVERNMENT WAS NOT INVOLVED IN THE ASSASSINATION OF PRESIDENT KENNEDY**

With the arrest of Lee Harvey Oswald in the assassination of President Kennedy, speculation arose over the sig-

---

[4]If the conspiracy was, in fact, limited to Oswald, the second gunman, and perhaps one or two others, the committee believes it was possible they shared Oswald's left-wing political disposition. A consistent pattern in Oswald's life (see section A 5) was a propensity for actions with political overtones. It is quite likely that an assassination conspiracy limited to Oswald and a few associates was in keeping with that pattern.

Further, it is possible that associates of Oswald in the Kennedy assassination had been involved with him in earlier activities. Two possibilities: the attempt on the life of Gen. Edwin A. Walker in April 1963 and the distribution of Fair Play for Cuba Committee literature in August 1963. With respect to the Walker incident, there was substantial evidence that Oswald did the shooting (section A 5), although at the time of the shooting it was not sufficient to implicate Oswald or anyone else. It was not until after the Kennedy assassination that Oswald became a suspect in the Walker attack, based on the testimony of his widow Marina. Marina's characterization of Oswald is more consistent with his having shot at Walker alone than his having assistance, although at the time of the shooting there was testimony that tended to indicate more than one person was involved. Further, it is not necessary to believe all of what Marina said about the incident or to believe that Oswald told her all there was to know, since either of them might have been concealing the involvement of others.

According to a general offense report of the Dallas police, Walker reported at approximately 9:10 p.m. on April 10, 1963, that a bullet had been fired through a first floor window of his home at 4011 Turtle Creek Boulevard, Dallas. Detectives subsequently found that a bullet had first shattered a window, then gone through a wall and had landed on a stack of papers in an adjoining room. In their report the detectives described the bullet as steel-jacketed, of unknown caliber.

Police located a 14-year-old boy in Walker's neighborhood who said that after hearing the shot, he climbed a fence and looked into an alley to the rear of Walker's home. The boy said he then saw some men speeding down the alley in a light green or light blue Ford, either a 1959 or 1960 model. He said he also saw another car, a 1958 Chevrolet, black and white down the side, in a church parking lot adjacent to Walker's house. The car door was open, and a man was bending over the back seat, as though he was placing something on the floor of the car.

On the night of the incident, police interviewed Robert Surrey, an aide to Walker. Surrey said that on Saturday, April 6, at about 9 p.m., he had seen two men sitting in a dark purple or brown 1963 Ford at the rear of Walker's house. Surrey also said the two men got out of the car and walked around the house. Surrey said he was suspicious and followed the car, noting that it carried no license plate.

If it could be shown that Oswald had associates in the attempt on General Walker, they would be likely candidates as the grassy knoll gunman. The committee recognized, however, that this is speculation, since the existence, much less identity, of an Oswald associate in the Walker shooting was hardly established. Further, the committee failed in its effort to develop productive leads in the Walker shooting.

With respect to the Cuba literature incident, Oswald was photographed with two associates distributing pro-Castro pamphlets in August 1963. As a result of a fight with anti-Castro Cubans, Oswald was arrested, but his associates were not. Of the two associates, only one was identified in the Warren Commission investigation (Warren Report. p. 292). Although the second associate was clearly portrayed in photographs (see Pizzo Exhibits 453–A and 453–B. Warren Commission Report, Vol. XXI, p. 139), the Commission was unable to identify him, as was the case with the committee.

nificance of Oswald's defection to the Soviet Union from October 1959 to June 1962 and his activities while living in that country. Specifically, these troubling questions were asked:

Had Oswald been enlisted by the KGB, the Soviet secret police?

Could the assassination have been the result of a KGB plot?[1]

(a) United States-Soviet relations

To put these concerns in context, it is necessary to look at Soviet-American relations in the 1960's. United States-Soviet relations had, in fact, been turbulent during the Kennedy presidency. There had been major confrontations: over Berlin, where the wall had come to symbolize the barrier between the two superpowers; and over Cuba, where the emplacement of Soviet missiles had nearly started World War III.[2]

A nuclear test-ban treaty in August 1963 seemed to signal détente, but in November, tension was building again, as the Soviets harassed American troop movements to and from West Berlin.[3] And Cuba was as much an issue as ever. In Miami, on November 18, President Kennedy vowed the United States would not countenance the establishment of another Cuba in the Western hemisphere.[4]

(b) The Warren Commission investigation

The Warren Commission considered the possibility of Soviet complicity in the assassination, but it concluded there was no evidence of it.[5] In its report, the Commission noted that the same conclusion had been reached by Secretary of State Dean Rusk and Secretary of Defense Robert McNamara, among others.[6] Rusk testified before the Commission on June 10, 1964:

> I have seen no evidence that would indicate to me that the Soviet Union considered that it had any interest in the removal of President Kennedy * * * I can't see how it could be to the interest of the Soviet Union to make any such effort.

(c) The committee's investigation

The committee, in analyzing Oswald's relationship to Russian intelligence, considered:

Statements of both Oswald and his wife, Marina, about their life in the Soviet Union; [7]

Documents provided by the Soviet Government to the Warren Commission concerning Oswald's residence in the Soviet Union;[8]

Statements by Soviet experts in the employ, current or past, of the Central Intelligence Agency;[9]

Files on other defectors to the Soviet Union;[10] and

Statements by defectors from the Soviet Union to the United States.[11]

(1) *Oswald in the U.S.S.R.*—The committee reviewed the documents Oswald wrote about his life in the Soviet Union, including his diary and letters to his mother, Marguerite, and brother, Robert.[12] They paralleled, to a great extent, the information in documents provided to the Warren Commission by the Soviet Government after the assassination.[13] These documents were provided to the Commission in response to its request that the Soviet Government give the Commission any "available information concerning the activities of Lee Harvey Oswald during his residence from 1959 to 1962 in the Soviet Union, in particular, copies of any official records concerning him."[14]

Two sets of documents, totaling approximately 140 pages, were turned over to the Commission by the Soviets in November 1963 and in May 1964.[15] They were routine, official papers. None of them appeared to have come from KGB files, and there were no records of interviews of Oswald by the KGB, nor were there any surveillance reports. Unfortunately, the authenitcity of the documents could not be established. The signatures of Soviet officials, for example, were illegible.[16]

Nevertheless, the Soviet documents and Oswald's own statements give this account of Oswald's stay in the Soviet Union:

He lived there from October 1959 to June 1962.

He attempted suicide on learning he would not be permitted to remain in the U.S.S.R.

111

He worked in a radio plant in Minsk.

He met and married Marina.

He was originally issued a residence visa for stateless persons and later issued a residence visa for foreigners.

He obtained exit visas for himself and his family before departing the Soviet Union.

Neither the documents nor Oswald's own statements indicate that he was debriefed or put under surveillance by the KGB.

The committee interviewed U.S. officials who specialize in Soviet intelligence, asking them what treatment they would have expected Oswald to have received during his defection.[17] For the most part, they suspected that Oswald would have routinely been debriefed by the KGB and that many persons who came in contact with Oswald in the U.S.S.R. would have been connected with the KGB.[18]

(2) *Treatment of defectors by the Soviet Government.*—The committee examined the CIA and FBI files on others who had defected in the same period as Oswald and who had eventually returned to the United States. [19] The purpose was to determine the frequency of KGB contact and whether the treatment of Oswald appeared to be significantly different from the norm. The defectors studied by the committee were selected because their backgrounds and other characteristics were similar to Oswald's, on the theory that their treatment by the KGB could be expected to parallel that of Oswald, if he was not a special case, a recruited assassin, for example.

The examination of the defector files were inconclusive, principally because the case of nearly every defector was unique.[20] In addition, the files available on the experiences of the defectors were often not adequate to extract meaningful data for the purpose of this investigation, since they were compiled for other reasons.[21] As to contacts with the KGB, the experiences of American defectors appeared to have varied greatly. Some reported daily contact with Soviet intelligence agents, while others did not mention ever having been contacted or debriefed.[22]

(3) *Yuri Nosenko*—Of all the areas investigated by the committee with respect to possible Soviet involvement in the assassination, none seemed as potentially rewarding as an examination of statements made by KGB officers who had defected to the United States. In determining how the

KGB treats American defectors, an ex-KGB officer would certainly be of greatest interest. In this regard, the committee had access to three such men, one of whom, Yuri Nosenko, claimed to possess far more than general information about American defectors.

In January 1964,[5] Nosenko, identifying himself as a KGB officer, sought asylum in the United States.[23] He claimed to have worked in the KGB Second Chief Directorate whose functions, in many respects, are similar to those of the FBI.[24] According to Nosenko, while working in 1959 in a KGB department dealing with American tourists, he learned of a young American who sought to defect to the Soviet Union. The American was Lee Harvey Oswald.[25]

Nosenko stated he had worked extensively on the Oswald case, and he provided the FBI and CIA with data pertaining to Oswald's request to defect and remain in the Soviet Union, the initial rejection of that request by the KGB, Oswald's suicide attempt and a subsequent decision to permit him to remain in Russia.[26] Although the KGB, according to Nosenko, was well aware of Oswald, it made no attempt to debrief or interview him.[27] Never was any consideration given by the KGB to enlist Oswald into the Soviet intelligence service.[28]

The committee was most interested in Nosenko's claim that in 1963, after Oswald was arrested in the assassination, he had an opportunity to see the KGB file on the suspected assassin. As a result, Nosenko said, he was able to state categorically that Oswald was not a Soviet agent and that no officer of the KGB had ever interviewed or debriefed him.[29]

Nosenko's testimony, however, did not settle the question of Soviet complicity in the assassination. From the time of his defection, some U.S. intelligence officers suspected Nosenko was on a disinformation mission to mislead the American Government. Since other CIA officials believed Nosenko was a bona fide defector, a serious disagreement at the top level of the Agency resulted.[30]

The Warren Commission found itself in the middle of the Nosenko controversy—and in a quandary of its own, since the issue of Nosenko's reliability bore significantly on the assassination investigation.[31] If he was telling the truth, the Commission could possibly write off Soviet involve-

---

[5] Nosenko had first contacted the U.S. Government in June 1962.

ment in a conspiracy.[6] If, on the other hand, Nosenko was lying, the Commission would be faced with a dilemma. While a deceitful Nosenko would not necessarily point to complicity, it would leave the issue in limbo. The Warren Commission chose not to call Nosenko as a witness or to mention him in its report, apparently because it could not resolve the issue of his reliability.[32]

The committee, on the other hand, reviewed all available statements and files pertaining to Nosenko.[33] It questioned Nosenko in detail about Oswald, finding significant inconsistencies in statements he had given the FBI, CIA and the committee.[34] For example, Nosenko told the committee that the KGB had Oswald under extensive survelliance, including mail interception, wiretap and physical observation. Yet, in 1964, he told the CIA and FBI there had been no such surveillance of Oswald.[35] Similarly, in 1964, Nosenko indicated there had been no psychiatric examination of Oswald subsequent to his suicide attempt, while in 1978 he detailed for the committee the reports he had read about psychiatric examination of Oswald.[36]

The committee also found that the CIA had literally put Nosenko in solitary confinement from 1964 to 1968.[37] Strangely, while he was interrogated during this period, he was questioned very little about Oswald.[38] The Agency did not seem to realize Nosenko's importance to an investigation of the assassination. While Richard Helms, then the CIA's Deputy Director for Plans, did tell Chief Justice Warren about Nosenko, the Agency's interest in him seemed to be largely limited to its own intelligence-gathering problem: did the KGB send Nosenko to the United States to deceive the CIA on many matters, only one of them perhaps related to the assassination?[39]

In the end, the committee, too, was unable to resolve the Nosenko matter. The fashion in which Nosenko was treated by the Agency—his interrogation and confinement —virtually ruined him as a valid source of information on the assassination. Nevertheless, the committee was certain Nosenko lied about Oswald—whether it was to the FBI and CIA in 1964, or to the committee in 1978, or perhaps to both.[40] The reasons he would lie about Oswald range

---

[6]The Commission as well as the committee recognized that Nosenko could have been candid and that the connection between Oswald and the KGB could have been compartmentalized, that is, known only to a select few people, not including Nosenko.

from the possibility that he merely wanted to exaggerate his own importance to the disinformation hypothesis with its sinister implications.

Lacking sufficient evidence to distinguish among alternatives,[7] the committee decided to limit its conclusion to a characterization of Nosenko as an unreliable source of information about the assassination, or, more specifically, as to whether Oswald was ever contacted, or placed under surveillance, by the KGB.

(4) *Opinions of other defectors.*—In addition to interviewing Nosenko, the committee questioned two other former KGB officers who had defected to the United States. While neither could base an opinion on any personal experience with that part of the KGB in which Nosenko said he had served, both said that Oswald would have been of interest to the Soviet intelligence agency, that he would have been debriefed and that he may have been kept under surveillance.[41]

(5) *Marina Oswald.*—The committee not only considered a possible connection between Oswald and the KGB, it also looked into charges that his widow, Marina, was an agent of the KGB, or that she at least influenced her husband's actions in the assassination on orders from Soviet officials. The committee examined Government files on Marina, it questioned experts on Soviet affairs and former KGB officers, and it took testimony from Marina herself.[42] The committee could find no evidence to substantiate the allegations about Marina Oswald Porter.

Mrs. Porter testified before the committee that Oswald had never been contacted directly by the KGB, though she assumed that he and she alike had been under KGB surveillance when they lived in the Soviet Union.

(6) *Response of the Soviet Government.*—Finally, the committee attempted to obtain from the Soviet Government any information on Oswald that it had not provided to the Warren Commission. In response to a committee request relayed by the State Department, the Soviet Government informed the committee that all the information it had on Oswald had been forwarded to the Warren Commission.[43]

---

[7]Beyond those reasons for falsification that can be attributed to Nosenko himself, there has been speculation that the Soviet Government, while not involved in the assassination, sent Nosenko on a mission to allay American fears. Hence, while his story about no connection between Oswald and the KGB might be false, his claim of no Soviet involvement in the assassination would be truthful.

The committee concluded, however, that it is highly probable that the Soviet Government possessed information on Oswald that it has not provided to the U.S. Government. It would be the extensive information that most likely was gathered by a KGB surveillance of Oswald and Marina while they were living in Russia. It is also quite likely that the Soviet Government withheld files on a KGB interview with Oswald.[8]

(d) Summary of the evidence

Its suspicions notwithstanding, the committee was led to believe, on the basis of the available evidence, that the Soviet Government was not involved in the assassination. In the last analysis, the committee agreed with the testimony of former Secretary of State Dean Rusk. To wit, there is no evidence that the Soviet Government had any interest in removing President Kennedy, nor is there any evidence that it planned to take advantage of the President's death before it happened or attempted to capitalize on it after it occurred. In fact, the reaction of the Soviet Government as well as the Soviet people seemed to be one of genuine shock and sincere grief. The committee believed, therefore, on the basis of the evidence available to it, that the Soviet Government was not involved in the assassination.

2. THE COMMITTEE BELIEVES, ON THE BASIS OF THE EVIDENCE AVAILABLE TO IT, THAT THE CUBAN GOVERNMENT WAS NOT INVOLVED IN THE ASSASSINATION OF PRESIDENT KENNEDY

When the leader of a great nation is assassinated, those initially suspected always include his adversaries. When President John F. Kennedy was struck down by rifle fire in Dallas in November 1963, many people suspected Cuba and its leader, Fidel Castro Ruz, of involvement in the assassination, particularly after it was learned that Lee Harvey Oswald, the alleged assassin, had sought to travel to

---

[8]The committee concluded that it should not necessarily be inferred from the failure of the Soviet Government to cooperate with the committee that it was involved in the assassination. Just as agencies of the U.S. intelligence community are reluctant to share their confidential files, a similar response might be expected to come from the KGB. The Soviet Government, it could be argued, would have little to gain and much to lose by turning over its files. While the committee recognized the logic of this argument, it regretted that the Soviet Government, in the interest of historical truth, did not cooperate.

Cuba in September 1963.[1] To evaluate those suspicions properly, it is necessary to look at Cuban-American relations in the years immediately before and after President Kennedy took office.

(a) United States-Cuban relations

The triumphant arrival of Fidel Castro in Havana on January 1, 1959, marking a victorious climax of the revolution he had led, was initially heralded in the United States as well as in Cuba. Castro was hailed as a champion of the people, a man who would lead a free and democratic Cuba. While some suspected that Castro had Communist leanings, the majority of the American public supported him.[2] The appointment of Philip Bonsal as U.S. Ambassador to Cuba, replacing Earl E. T. Smith, who was personally wary of Castro, was a clear signal that the United States was interested in amicable relations with the revolutionary government. On appointing Bonsal, President Eisenhower expressed the hope for an "ever closer relationship between Cuba and the United States."[3]

By the end of 1959, however, United States-Cuban relations had deteriorated to the point that there was open hostility between the two countries.[4] President Kennedy was to inherit the problem in 1961, and by the time of his assassination on November 22, 1963, the antagonism had developed into a serious international crisis.

To begin with, the United States deplored the mass executions of officials of the Batista government that Castro had deposed.[5] In reply, Castro charged that the United States had never voiced objections to killing and torture by Batista. He said the trials and sentences would continue. [6] In his revolutionary economic policies, Castro took steps that severely challenged the traditional role of the United States. In March 1959, the Cuban Government took over the United States-owned Cuban Telephone Co.: in May, U.S. companies were among those expropriated in the Cuban Government's first large-scale nationalization action; also in May, the agrarian reform law resulted in the expropriation of large landholdings, many of them U.S.-owned.[7]

Vice President Nixon met with Castro in Washington in April, Castro left the meeting convinced that Nixon was hostile. For his part, Nixon recommended to President

117

Eisenhower that the United States take measures to quash the Cuban revolution.[8]

Disillusionment with Castro also spread to significant elements of the Cuban populace. In June, the chief of the Cuban Air Force, Maj. Pedro Diaz Lanz, fled to the United States, charging there was Communist influence in the armed forces and the Government of Cuba.[9] A few weeks later, Manuel Urrutria Lleo, the President of Cuba, stated on Cuban national television that communism was not concerned with the welfare of the people and that it constituted a threat to the revolution. In the succeeding flurry of events, President Urrutria resigned after Castro accused him of "actions bordering on treason."[10]

By the summer of 1960, Castro had seized more than $700 million in U.S. property; the Eisenhower administration had canceled the Cuban sugar quota; Castro was cementing his relations with the Soviet Union, having sent his brother Raul on a visit to Moscow; Ernesto "Che" Guevara, a top Castro lieutenant, had proclaimed publicly that the revolution was on a course set by Marx; and CIA Director Allen Dulles had said in a speech that communism had pervaded Castro's revolution.[11] On March 17, 1960, President Eisenhower quietly authorized the CIA to organize, train, and equip Cuban refugees as a guerrilla force to overthrow Castro.[12]

On January 2, 1961, the United States broke diplomatic relations with Cuba.[13] A period of increased tension followed. It was marked by an exchange of bitter statements by the new U.S. President, John F. Kennedy, and the Cuban Premier. Castro charged CIA complicity in counterrevolutionary activity against his Government and publicly predicted an imminent U.S. invasion.[14] In his State of the Union address on January 30, Kennedy said:

> In Latin America, Communist agents seeking to exploit that region's peaceful revolution of hope have established a base on Cuba, only 90 miles from our shores. Our objection with Cuba is not over the people's drive for a better life. Our objection is to their domination by foreign and domestic tyrannies * * *.

President Kennedy said further that "* * * Communist domination in this hemisphere can never be negotiated." [15]

118

(1) *Bay of Pigs.*—After much deliberation, President Kennedy gave the go-ahead for a landing of anti-Castro Cubans, with U.S. support, at the Bay of Pigs on the southern coast of Las Villas Province. It was launched on April 17, 1961, but it was thwarted by Cuban troops, said to have been commanded by Castro himself.[16]

On President Kennedy's orders, no U.S. military personnel actually fought on Cuban soil, but U.S. sponsorship of the landing was readily apparent. President Kennedy publicly acknowledged "sole responsibility" for the U.S. role in the abortive invasion.[17]

After the Bay of Pigs debacle, the tension continued to escalate. As early as April 20, President Kennedy reaffirmed in a speech to the American Society of Newspaper Editors, that the United States was resolved not to abandon Cuba to communism.[18] On May 1, Secretary of State Dean Rusk told the Senate Foreign Relations Subcommittee on Latin American Affairs that if the Castro regime engaged in acts of aggression, the United States would "defend itself."[19] On May 17, the House of Representatives passed a resolution declaring Cuba to be "a clear and present danger" to the Western Hemisphere.[20]

Throughout 1961 and 1962, U.S. policy was to subject Cuba to economic isolation and to support stepped-up raids by anti-Castro guerrillas, many of which were planned with the assassination of Castro and other Cuban officials as a probable conseqence, if not a specific objective.[21] The Cuban Government, in turn, assumed—often correctly—that the raids were instigated and directed by the U.S. Government.[22] In preparation for another large-scale attack, the Castro regime sought and received increased military support from the Soviet Union.[23]

(2) *Cuban missile crisis.*—All-out war between the United States and the U.S.S.R. was narrowly averted in the Cuban missile crisis in the fall of 1962. On October 22, President Kennedy announced that U.S. photographic reconnaissance flights had discovered that work was underway in Cuba on offensive missile sites with a nuclear strike capability. [24] On October 23, the President issued a proclamation imposing a quarantine on the delivery of offensive weapons to Cuba, to be enforced by a U.S. naval blockade.[125]

Negotiations conducted between the United States and the Soviet Union resulted in an end to the immediate crisis on November 20, 1962.[26] To most observers, President Kennedy had won the confrontation with Castro and Soviet leader Nikita Khrushchev.[9] War had been averted, however narrowly. Russian IL–28 bombers were to be withdrawn from Cuba, and progress was being made on the removal of offensive missiles and other weapons.[27] The Soviets and the Cubans gained a "no invasion" pledge that was conditional upon a United Nations inspection to verify that Soviet offensive weapons had been removed from Cuba.[28] Because Castro never allowed the inspection, the United States never officially made the reciprocal pledge not to invade Cuba.[29]

There is evidence that by the fall of 1963, informal overtures for better United States-Cuban relations had been authorized by President Kennedy.[30] Talks between United States and Cuban officials at the United Nations were under consideration. In addition, the United States had attempted in the period after the missile crisis to stem the anti-Castro raids by, at least publicly, refusing to sanction them.[31] But covert action by the United States had neither ceased nor escaped Castro's notice, and the rhetoric indicated that the crisis could explode anew at any time.[32]

On September 7, 1963, in an interview with Associated Press reporter Daniel Harker, Castro warned against the United States "aiding terrorist plans to eliminate Cuban leaders," and added that U.S. leaders would be in danger if they promoted any attempt to eliminate the leaders of Cuba.[33] On November 18, in Miami, Fla., just 4 days before his assassination, President Kennedy stated:

> * * * what now divides Cuba from my country
> * * * is the fact that a small band of conspirators
> has stripped the Cuban people of their freedom and
> handed over the independence and sovereignty of
> the Cuban nation to forces beyond this hemisphere.
> They have made Cuba a victim of foreign imperial-
> ism, an instrument of the policy of others, a weapon
> in an effort dictated by external powers to subvert
> the other American Republics. This, and this alone,
> divides us.[34]

---

[9]When it became known to anti-Castro Cuban exiles that Kennedy had agreed to stop the raids on Cuba, the exiles considered the Kennedy-Khrushchev deal anything but a victory. To them, it was another betrayal (see section C 3 for details).

(b) Earlier investigations of Cuban complicity

When President Kennedy was assassinated on November 22, 1963, the basic outlines of the recent history of United States-Cuban relations, if not the specific details, were known to every American who even occasionally read a newspaper. Thus, when speculation arose as to the possibility of conspiracy, Fidel Castro and his Communist government were natural suspects. While rationality may have precluded any involvement of the Cuban Government, the recognition that Castro had been among the late President's most prominent enemies compelled such speculation.

(1) *The Warren Commission investigation.*—Investigative efforts into the background of Lee Harvey Oswald led to an early awareness of his Communist and pro-Castro sympathies, his activities in support of the Fair Play for Cuba Committee, and a trip he made in September 1963 to Mexico City where he visited the Soviet Embassy and the Cuban consulate.[35]

All of this information had been gathered prior to the beginning of the Warren Commission's investigation, and it was sufficient to alert the Commission to the need to investigate the possibility of a conspiracy initiated or influenced by Castro. The report of the Warren Commission reflects that it was indeed considered, especially with respect to the implications of Oswald's Mexico City trip. [36] In addition, the Warren Commission reviewed various specific allegations of activity that suggested Cuban involvement, concluding, however, that there had been no such conspiracy.[37] For the next few years, suspicions of Cuban involvement in the assassination were neither widespread nor vocal. Nevertheless, beginning with a 1967 column by Drew Pearson and Jack Anderson, press reports that suggested Castro's involvement in the assassination began to circulate once again.[38] Specifically, they posed the theory that President Kennedy might have been assassinated in retaliation for CIA plots against the life of the Cuban leader.

(2) *The U.S. Senate investigation.*—Thereafter, the Senate Select Committee to Study Governmental Operations with Respect to Intelligence Activities was formed to investigate the performance of the CIA and other U.S. intelligence agencies.[39] The Senate committee detailed

two general types of operations that the CIA had directed against Castro. One, referred to as the AMLASH operation, involved the CIA's relationship with an important Cuban figure (code-named AMLASH) who,[40] while he was trusted by Castro, professed to the CIA that he would be willing to organize a coup against the Cuban leader. The CIA was in contact with AMLASH from March 1961 until June 1965.[41] A second plot documented by the Senate committee was a joint effort by the CIA and organized crime in America. It was initiated in 1960 in a conversation between the agency's Deputy Director for Plans, Richard Bissell, and the Director of Security, Col. Sheffield Edwards. According to the Senate committee, this operation lasted until Februay 1963.[42]

The Senate committee concluded from its review of the joint operations of the CIA and organized crime that "* * * Castro probably would not have been certain that the CIA was behind the underworld attempts."[43] Nor, in the view of the Senate committee, would Castro have distinguished between the CIA-underworld plots and the numerous other plots by Cuban exiles which were not affiliated in any way with the CIA.[44] By emphasizing these two conclusions, the Senate committee apparently intended to suggest that the efforts by the CIA and organized crime to eliminate Castro would not have resulted in any retaliation against officials of the United States.[45]

The Senate committee identified the AMLASH operation as being "clearly different" from the CIA-underworld plots. [46] It was still in progress at the time of the assassination, and it could clearly be traced to the CIA, since AMLASH's proposed coup had been endorsed by the CIA, with the realization that the assassination of Castro might be a consequence.[47] Nevertheless, the Senate committee found "* * * no evidence that Fidel Castro or others in the Cuban Government plotted President Kennedy's assassination in retaliation for U.S. operations against Cuba."[48] The Senate committee left the door open, however, stating, "* * * the investigation should continue in certain areas, and for that reason [the committee] does not reach any final conclusions."[49]

(3) *The CIA's response to the Senate.*—In response to publication of the report of the Senate committee, a special internal CIA task force was assigned in 1977 to investigate and evaluate the critical questions that had been

raised. The task force first considered the retaliation thesis. It advanced the position that the Senate committee had essentially ignored the history of adversarial relations between the United States and Cuba which, if provocation were the issue, provided adequate grounds to support a theory of possible retaliation without the necessity of reaching for specific Agency programs such as the Mafia and AMLASH plots.[50] In essence, the task force report suggests, those plots were only one aspect of a large picture and in themselves were not sufficient to have provoked retaliation.[51].

The 1977 CIA task force then specifically responded to the Senate committee with respect to the AMLASH operation:

> Whatever the relationship with AMLASH, following the death of President Kennedy, there is every indication that during President Kennedy's life AMLASH had no basis for believing that he had CIA support for much of anything. Were he a provocateur reporting to Castro, or if he was merely careless and leaked what he knew, he had no factual basis for leaking or reporting any actual CIA plot directed against Castro.[52]

With respect to the CIA-sponsored organized crime operations, the CIA task force noted:

> It is possible that the CIA simply found itself involved in providing additional resources for independent operations that the syndicate already had underway * * * [I]n a sense CIA may have been piggy-backing on the syndicate and in addition to its material contributions was also providing an aura of official sanction.[53]

The task force argued, therefore, that the plots should have been seen as Mafia, not CIA, endeavors.

A conclusion of the Senate committee had been that further investigation was warranted, based in part on its findings that the CIA had responded inadequately to the Warren Commission's request for all possible relevant information. The CIA had not told the Commission of the plots.[54] In response, the 1977 CIA task force observed:

123

While one can understand today why the Warren Commission limited its inquiry to normal avenues of investigation, it would have served to reinforce the credibility of its effort had it taken a broader view of the matter. CIA, too, could have considered in specific terms what most saw in general terms—the possibility of Soviet or Cuban involvement in the JFK assassination because of the tensions of the time * * * The Agency should have taken broader initiatives, then, as well. That CIA employees at the time felt—as they obviously did—that the activities about which they knew had no relevance to the Warren Commission inquiry does not take the place of a record of conscious review.[55]

(c) The committee's analysis of the CIA task force report

The committee believed its mandate compelled it to take a new look at the question of Cuban complicity in the assassination.

The Warren Commission had expressed its view, as follows:

> * * * the investigation of the Commission has thus produced no evidence that Oswald's trip to Mexico was in any way connected with the assassination of President Kennedy, nor has it uncovered evidence that the Cuban Government had any involvement in the assassination.[56]

There are two ways that this statement may be read:

> The Warren Commission's investigation was such that had a conspiracy existed, it would have been discovered, and since it was not, there was no conspiracy.

> The Warren Commission's investigation, limited as it was, simply did not find a conspiracy.

Although the Commission inferred that the first interpretation was the proper one, the committee investigated the possibility that the second was closer to the truth.

Similarly, the committee investigated to see if there was a factual basis for a finding made by the Senate Select Committee that the CIA plots to assassinate Castro could have given rise to crucial leads that could have been pursued in 1963 and 1964, or, at a minimum, would have provided critical additional impetus to the Commission's investigation.[57]

As previously noted, although the 1977 CIA Task Force Report at least nominally recognized that the Agency, in 1962–64, "* * * could have considered in specific terms what most saw then in general terms—the possibility of Soviet or Cuban involvement in the assassination because of the tensions of the time," and that the Agency "should have taken broader initiatives then," the remainder of the Task Force Report failed to specify what those broader initiatives should have been or what they might have produced. It did, however, enumerate four areas for review of its 1963–64 performance:

Oswald's travel to and from the U.S.S.R.;

Oswald's Mexico visit in September–October 1963;

The CIA's general extraterritorial intelligence collection requirements; and

Miscellaneous leads that the Senate committee alleged the Agency had failed to pursue.[58]

The 1977 Task Force Report reviewed the question of Agency operations directed at Cuba, including, in particular, the Mafia and AMLASH plots.[59] In each area, the report concluded that the Agency's 1963–64 investigation was adequate and could not be faulted, even with the benefit of hindsight.[60] The task force uncritically accepted the Senate committee's conclusions where they were favorable to the Agency,[10] and it critically rejected the Senate committee's conclusions (as in the case of AMLASH) wherever some possible investigative oversight was suggested.[62]

The 1977 Task Force Report, in sum, did little more than suggest that any theoretically "broader initiatives" the Agency could have taken in 1963–64 would have uncovered nothing. They would only have served to head off outside criticism. That conclusion is illustrated in the following passage of the report:

* * * [our] findings are essentially negative. However, it must be recognized that CIA cannot be as confident of a cold trail in 1977 as it could have been in 1964; this apparent fact will be noted by the critics

---

[10]For example, with respect to the Agency's investigation of Oswald's trip to Russia, the report summarily concluded, "Book V of the SSC Final Report, in not criticizing the Agency's performance in this aspect of the investigation, seems to have accepted it as adequate, and it will not be detailed here." [61]

of the Agency, and by those who have found a career in the questions already asked and yet to be asked about the assassination of President Kennedy.[63]

The committee, of course, realized that the CIA's 1977 review might be correct, that broader initiatives might only have been window dressing and would have produced nothing of substance. But the 1977 report failed to document that fact, if it were a fact. For example, it provided no detailed résumé of the backgrounds of those CIA case officers, Cubans and Mafia figures who plotted together to kill Castro. There is nothing in the report on the activities of the anti-Castro plotters during the last half of 1963. If the Agency had been truly interested in determining the possible investigative significance to the Kennedy assassination of such CIA-Cuban-Mafia associations, the committee asumed it would have directed its immediate attention to such activities in that period.

The task force report also noted that even without its taking broader initiatives, the CIA still sent general directives to overseas stations and cited, as an example, a cable which read:

> Tragic death of President Kennedy requires all of us to look sharp for any unusual intelligence development. Although we have no reason to expect anything of a particular military nature, all hands should be on the quick alert for the next few days while the new President takes over the reins.[64]

The report reasoned that the CIA's tasking of its stations was "necessarily general," since little was known at the time about which it could be specific. [65]

The CIA task force further noted that 4 days after this general cable was sent, a follow-up request for any available information was sent to 10 specific stations. The task force argued, in any event, that such general requirements for intelligence-gathering would have been adequate, since "relevant information on the subject" would have been reported anyway. [66]

Conspicuously absent from such self-exculpatory analysis was any detailed discussion of what specific efforts the Agency's stations actually made to secure "relevant information" about the assassination. For example, it became generally known that in 1963 the CIA had a station in Florida through which it monitored the activities of most of the anti-Castro Cuban groups operating in the United States. While the Florida station was mentioned, the task force report failed to make a comprehensive analysis of what requirements were placed on the station and the station's response. It might have been expected that the station would have been required to contact and debrief all of its Cuban sources. In addition, the station should have been asked to use all of its possible sources to determine if any operatives in the anti-Castro Cuban community had information about possible Cuban Government involvement or about any association between Oswald and possible Cuban Government agents. Further, the station, or possibly other units of the CIA, should have been tasked to attempt to reconstruct the details of the travels and activities of known pro-Castro Cuban operatives in the United States for 60 or 90 days prior to the assassination. (Such undertakings might have been made without specific cables or memoranda requiring them. The Task Force Report implied such efforts were taken by the stations "on their own initiative." [67] But the Task Force Report failed to document or even discuss the details of such efforts or the responses of the stations to CIA headquarters.)

The committee found that the CIA's 1977 Task Force Report was little more than an attempted rebuttal of the Senate Select Committee's criticisms, and not a responsible effort to evaluate objectively its own 1963–64 investigation or its anti-Castro activities during the early 1960's or to assess their significance vis-a-vis the assassination.

The committee made an effort to evaluate these questions through its own independent investigation. In investigating the implications of the CIA plots and the Warren Commission's ignorance of them, the committee conducted interviews, depositions and hearings for the purpose of taking testimony from pertinent individuals, conducted interviews in Mexico and Cuba, and reviewed extensive files at the CIA and FBI.[68]

(1) *AMLASH.*—Turning first to the AMLASH operation, the committee received conflicting testimony as to whether, prior to the Kennedy assassination, it was considered to be an assassination plot. Former CIA Director Richard M. Helms, in his testimony before the committee, stated that the AMLASH operation was not designed to be an assassination plot.[69] And, as already indicated, the

1977 Task Force Report concluded that AMLASH had "no factual basis for leaking or reporting any actual Central Intelligence Agency plot directed against Castro" during the President Kennedy's life.[70]

The committee, however, noted that such characterizations were probably both self-serving and irrelevant. The committee found that the evidence confirmed the Senate committee's report that AMLASH himself envisioned assassination as an essential first step in any overthrow of Castro.[71] It also noted that it was Castro's point of view, not the Agency's, that would have counted.

The CIA's files reflect that as early as August 1962, AMLASH spoke to his CIA case officer about being interested in the "* * * sabotage of an oil refinery and the execution of a top ranking Castro subordinate, of the Soviet Ambassador and of Castro himself."[72] The case officer, in his report, while stating he made no commitments to AMLASH, acknowledged that he did tell AMLASH "* * * schemes like he envisioned certainly had their place, but that a lot of coordination, planning, information-collection, et cetera, were necessary prerequisities to insure the value and success of such plans."[73] Further, cables between the case officer and CIA headquarters reflected that the Agency decided not to give AMLASH a "physical elimination mission as [a] requirement," but that it was something "he could or might try to carry out on his own initiative."[74] Thus, the CIA's relationship with AMLASH at least left him free to employ assassination in the coup he was contemplating. That relationship could also have been viewed by Castro as one involving the CIA in his planned assassination.

Ultimately, the CIA also provided AMLASH with the means of assassination and assurances that the U.S. Government would back him in the event his coup was successful.[75] CIA files reflect that AMLASH returned to Cuba shortly after the August 1962 meetings.[76] He next left Cuba and met with a CIA officer in September 1963. At that time, the CIA learned that AMLASH had not abandoned his intentions and that he now wanted to know what the U.S. "plan of action" was.[77] On October 11, the case officer cabled headquarters that AMLASH was determined to make the attempt on Castro with or without U.S. support.[78] On October, 21, he reported that AMLASH wanted assurance that the United States would support him if his effort was successful.[79]

On October 29, Desmond FitzGerald, chief of the Special Affairs Staff, met with AMLASH, representing himself as a spokesman for Attorney General Robert Kennedy. Fitz-Gerald gave AMLASH the assurance he had asked for, [80] although the CIA has argued that the support did not specifically include assassination.

At the end of the meeting, according to the case officer's memorandum, AMLASH asked for "technical support" which, according to FitzGerald's memory, was described by AMLASH as being a high-powered rifle, or other weapon, to kill Castro.[81] Although the CIA files reflect that AMLASH did not receive the assurances of pre-assassination "technical support" he had asked for on October 29, the matter was further discussed, at least within the Agency, and on November 20 AMLASH was told that the meeting he "had requested" had been granted. [82] The technical support, as the Senate committee reported, was actually offered to AMLASH on November 22, 1963, the day President Kennedy was assassinated.[83]

Whether CIA officials chose to characterize their activity as an assassination plot, it is reasonable to infer that had Castro learned about the meetings between AMLASH and the CIA, he could also have learned of AMLASH's intentions, including the fact that his assassination would be a natural and probable consequence of the plot. In a deposition to the committee, Joseph Langosch, in 1963 the Chief of Counterintelligence for the CIA's Special Affairs Staff,[84] recalled that, as of 1962, it was highly possible that Cuban intelligence was aware of AMLASH and his association with the CIA.[85] (SAS was responsible for CIA operations against the Government of Cuba and as such was in charge of the AMLASH operation.[86])

The committee was unable to determine if that possibility was a reality. The Cuban Government informed the committee that it had come to believe that AMLASH was in fact Rolando Cubela (based upon its construction of a profile from biographic information on AMLASH made public by the Senate committee). [87] It stated it did not know of Cubela's intentions until 1966.[88]

The committee was unable to confirm or deny the validity of that Cuban Government's belief that AMLASH was Cubela. Nevertheless, the committee considered the statement that, if Cubela were AMLASH, the Cuban Government did not know of his intentions until 1966. On this point, the committee was unable to accept or reject the Cuban Government's claim with confidence. The committee merely noted that the statement was corroborated by other information known about the dates of Cubela's arrest and trial in Cuba and the charges against him. The Cuban Government's position must, however, be recognized as potentially self-serving, since it must be assumed the Cuban Government would be inclined not to reveal any knowledge it may have had about AMLASH's assassination plans and the CIA prior to November 22, 1963. If it had indicated it knew, it would have contributed to the credibility of the Senate's theories about possible Cuban involvement in the assassination as a retaliatory act.[89]

The committee, while in Cuba, spoke to Rolando Cubela, who was serving a life sentence for acts against the Cuban Government. He confirmed the statements of the Cuban Government to the committee[90] that he did not give the Cuban Government any information that would have led it to believe that the CIA was involved in a plot on Castro's life in 1963. In considering Cubela's testimony, the committee took into account the possible influence of his confinement.

After reviewing all the available evidence, the committee concluded that Castro may well have known about the AMLASH plot by November 22, 1963, and, if so, he could have either documented or assumed it was backed by the United States and that it was directed at his life. The committee believed that the details of the AMLASH operation should have been provided to the Warren Commission, since the Commission might have been able to develop leads to participants in the Kennedy assassination. At a minimum, the existence of the plot, if it had been brought to the Commission's attention, would have served as a stimulus in the 1963–64 investigation.

In conclusion, the committee believed a description of the activities of participants in the AMLASH plot should have been provided to the Warren Commission. It based this not only on the possibility that the plots could have increased Castro's motivation to conspire to assassinate President Kennedy (assuming he, in fact, was privy to the plot prior to November 22, 1963), but also because knowledge of the AMLASH plot might have increased the interest of the CIA, FBI, and Warren Commission in a more thorough investigation of the question of Cuban conspiracy. In stating this view, the committee did not reject the suggestion in the CIA's 1977 Task Force Report that Castro already had significant motivation to assassinate President Kennedy, even if he were not aware of the AMLASH plot. The committee noted, however, that to the extent that that thesis was true, it did not negate the conclusion that the AMLASH plot was relevant and that information about it should have been supplied to the Warren Commission. If it had been made available, it might have affected the course of the investigation.

(2) *CIA-Mafia Plots.*—Turning next to the CIA-Mafia plots, the committee found in its investigation that organized crime probably was active in attempts to assassinate Castro, independent of any activity it engaged in with the CIA, as the 1977 Task Force Report had suggested. [91] The committee found that during the initial stages of the joint operation, organized crime decided to assist the CIA for two reasons: CIA sponsorship would mean official sanction and logistical support for a Castro assassination; and a relationship with the CIA in the assassination of a foreign leader could be used by organized crime as leverage to prevent prosecution for unrelated offenses.[92]

During the latter stages of the CIA-Mafia operation, from early 1962 to early 1963, however, organized crime may no longer have been interested in assassinating Castro.[93] The Soviet influence in Cuba had rendered the prospect of regaining the old Havana territory less likely, and there were fortunes to be made in the Bahamas and elsewhere.[94] There is reason to speculate that the Mafia continued to appear to participate in the plots just to keep the CIA interested, in hopes of preventing prosecution of organized crime figures and others involved in the plots.[95]

This theory is supported by the actions of Robert Maheu, an FBI agent turned private investigator who had acted as a CIA-organized crime go-between, and John Roselli, a Mafia principal in the plots.[96] Maheu, for example, was the subject of an FBI wiretap investigation in Las Vegas in the spring of 1962. He had installed a telephone wiretap, which he claimed was done as a favor to Mafia chieftain Sam Giancana, who was also involved in the anti-Castro plots.[97] Maheu's explanation to the FBI was that the tap was placed as part of a CIA effort to obtain Cuban intelligence information through organized crime contacts. The CIA corroborated Maheu's story, and the case was not prosecuted.[98] In addition, in 1966, Maheu used his contacts with the CIA to avoid testifying before a Senate committee that was conducting hearings into invasion of privacy.[99]

As for Roselli, the committee considered it significant that public relations about the plots corresponded with his efforts to avoid deportation in 1966 and 1971 and to escape prosecution for illegal gambling activities in 1967. [100] It was Roselli who managed the release of information about the plots and who proposed the so-called turnaround theory of the Kennedy assassination (Cuban exiles hired by the Mafia as hit men, captured by Castro, were forced to "turn around" and murder President Kennedy).[101] The committee found it quite plausible that Roselli would have manipulated public perception of the facts of the plots, then tried to get the CIA to intervene in his legal problems as the price for his agreeing to make no further disclosures.

The allegation that President Kennedy was killed as a result of a Mafia-CIA plot that was turned around by Castro was passed to Drew Pearson and Jack Anderson by Washington attorney Edward P. Morgan; its ultimate source was Roselli.[102] The committee found little credibility in such an explanation for the President's death because, if for no other reason, it would have been unnecessarily risky. The committee determined from CIA files that, in 1963, the Cuban Government had agents of its own in nearly every country of the Western Hemisphere, including the United States, who undoubtedly would have been more dependable for such an assignment. Even if Castro had wanted to minimize the chance of detection by hiring non-Cuban killers, it appeared unlikely to the committee that he would have tried to force Mafia members or their Cuban exile confederates to engage in the assassination of an American head of state.

The committee found it more difficult to dismiss the possibility that the Mafia, while it was not turned around by Castro, might have voluntarily turned around with him. By late 1962 and 1963, when the underworld leaders involved with the CIA in the plots had perhaps lost their motivation to assassinate Castro, they had been given sufficient reason by the organized crime program of the

Department of Justice to eliminate President Kennedy.

The committee's investigation revealed that Mafia figures are rational, pragmatic "businessmen" who often realine their associations and form partnerships, with ex-enemies when it is expedient.[103] While Castro, by 1963, was an old enemy of organized crime, it was more important that both Castro and the Mafia were ailing financially, chiefly as a result of pressures applied by the Kennedy administration.[104] Thus, they had a common motive that might have made an alliance more attractive than a split based on mutal animosity.

By 1963 also, Cuban exiles bitterly opposed to Castro were being frustrated by the Kennedy administration. [105] Many of them had come to conclude that the U.S. President was an obstacle requiring elimination even more urgently than the Cuban dictator.[106] The Mafia had been enlisted by the CIA because of its access to anti-Castro Cuban operatives both in and out of Cuba. [107] In its attempt to determine if the Mafia plot associations could have led to the assassination, the committee, therefore, recognized that Cuban antagonism toward President Kennedy did not depend on whether the Cubans were pro- or anti-Castro.

The committee found that the CIA-Mafia-Cuban plots had all the elements necessary for a successful assassination conspiracy—people, motive and means, and the evidence indicated that the participants might well have considered using the resources at their disposal to increase their power and alleviate their problems by assassinating the President. Nevertheless, the committee was ultimately frustrated in its attempt to determine details of those activities that might have led to the assassination—identification of participants, associations, timing of events and so on. Many of the key figures of the Castro plots had, for example, since died, or, as in the case of both Giancana and Roselli, had been murdered.

The committee was also unable to confirm in its investigation the findings of the Senate committee and the CIA that there were reasons to discount the dangers to President Kennedy that may have resulted from CIA associations with the Mafia in anti-Castro activities. The committee did not agree with the Senate committee that Castro would not have blamed President Kennedy for the CIA-Mafia plots against his life. They were formulated in the United States, and the history of United States-Cuban relations shows that when Castro erred in his assumptions, it was in the direction of attributing more, not less, responsibility for attempts to depose him to U.S. Government actions than might have been merited.

In its 1977 Task Force Report, the CIA commented on this reality:

> The United States provided a haven and base for Cuban exiles, who conducted their independent operations against the Castro government. Some of these exiles had the support of CIA, as well as from other elements of the U.S. Government, and still others had support from private sources. With or without official U.S. support these exiles spoke in forceful Latin terms about what they hoped to do. The Cuban intelligence services had agents in the exile community in America and it is likely that what they reported back to Havana assigned to CIA responsibility for many of the activities under consideration, whether CIA was involved or not.[108]

From its investigation of documents and from the testimony of officials and others, the committee decided that the Senate committee was probably mistaken in its conclusion that the CIA-Mafia plots were less significant than the AMLASH plot. In the judgment of the committee, the CIA-Mafia plots, like the AMLASH plot, should have been aggressively explored as part of the 1963–64 investigation of the assassination of President Kennedy. At that time, it might still have been possible to determine precise dates of trips, meetings, telephone communications, and financial transactions, and the participants in these potentially pertinent transactions could have been questioned. At least in this one respect, the committee must concur with a sentiment expressed in the 1977 CIA Task Force Report:

> Today the knowledge of the persons involved directly in the various Cuban operations in the period preceding President Kennedy's death cannot be recaptured in the form that it existed then. These persons are scattered, their memories are blurred by time, and some are dead.[109]

The committee, moreover, was unable to accept the conclusion of the CIA and the Senate committee that the CIA-Mafia plots were irrelevant because they had been terminated in February 1963, several months before the assassination. The record is clear that the relationships created by the plots did not terminate, nor had the threat to Castro abated by that time. There is insufficient evidence to conclude that the inherently sinister relationships had become benign by November 22, 1963.

In June 1963, according to the interim report of the Senate committee, Roselli had dinner with William Harvey, chief of the CIA's Cuban Task Force.[110] CIA files show that Roselli continued to maintain direct contact with Harvey at least until 1967, and he was in touch, at least indirectly, with the Agency's Chief of the Operational Support Branch, Office of Security, as late as 1971.[111] The Task Force Report itself alluded to information that, as late as June 1964, gangster elements in Miami were offering $150,000 for Castro's life, "an amount mentioned to the syndicate representatives by CIA case officers at an earlier date."[112]

In the absence of documentation of the activities of Mafia plot participants between February 1963 and November 22, 1963—which had not been obtained in earlier investigations, and the committee was able to do no better—the committee found it difficult to dismiss the CIA-Mafia plots, even assuming they had been terminated in February 1963, as of no consequence to the events in Dallas on November 22, 1963. The plots, in short, should have been made known to the Warren Commission. If they had been investigated in 1964, they might have provided insights into what happened in Dallas and resolved questions that have persisted.

(3) *Summary of the evidence.*—By its conclusions about the AMLASH operation and the CIA-Mafia plots—that they were of possible consequence to the assassination investigation and therefore should have been revealed to the Warren Commission—the committee did not intend to imply it had discovered a link to the assassination. To the contrary, the committee was not able to develop evidence that President Kennedy was murdered in retaliation for U.S. activities against Castro. What the committee did determine, however, was that there was no basis, in terms of relevance to the assassination, for the CIA to decide that the AMLASH operation and the CIA-Mafia plots were of

no significance to the Warren Commission's investigation. On the other hand, the possibility that President Kennedy was assassinated in retaliation for anti-Castro activities of the CIA should have been considered quite pertinent, especially in light of specific allegations of conspiracy possibly involving supporters of the Cuban leader.

(d) Cubana Airlines flight allegation

The committee considered specific allegations of conspiracy involving supporters of Castro.

One such charge, referred to in book V of the Senate select committee's report, concerns a Cubana Airlines flight from Mexico City to Havana on the evening of November 23, 1963.[113] It had been alleged that the flight was delayed hours, awaiting the arrival at 9:30 p.m. of a private twin-engined aircraft.[114] The aircraft was supposed to have deposited an unidentified passenger who boarded the Cubana flight without clearing customs and traveled to Havana in the pilot's cabin.[115]

The Senate committee reported that the Cubana flight departed at 10 p.m. This committee checked the times of key events that night by reviewing extensive investigative agency documents. It found the following facts:

The Cubana flight was on the ground in Mexico City for a total of only about 4 hours and 10 minutes and thus could not have been delayed five hours.[116]

The Cubana flight had departed for Havana at 8:30 p.m., about an hour before the arrival of the private aircraft reportedly carrying a mysterious passenger, so he could not have taken the flight.[117]

The committee found that extensive records of flight arrivals and departures at the Mexico City airport were available and deemed it doubtful that the alleged transfer of a passenger from a private aircraft to the Cubana flight could have gone unnoticed, had it occurred.[118] The committee concluded, therefore, that the transfer did not occur.

(e) Gilberto Policarpo Lopez allegation

More troubling to the committee was another specific allegation discussed by the Senate committee. It concerned a Cuban-American named Gilberto Policarpo Lopez.[119] According to the account, Lopez obtained a tourist card in

Tampa, Fla., on November 20, 1963, entered Mexico at Nuevo Laredo on November 23, and flew from Mexico City to Havana on November 27.[120] Further, Lopez was alleged to have attended a meeting of the Tampa chapter of the Fair Play for Cuba Committee on November 1, 1963, and at a December meeting of the chapter, Lopez was reported to be in Cuba.[121]

The committee first examined the CIA files on Policarpo Lopez.[122] They reflect that in early December 1963, CIA headquarters received a classified message stating that a source had requested "urgent traces on U.S. citizen Gilberto P. Lopez."[123] According to the source, Lopez had arrived in Mexico on November 23 en route to Havana and had disappeared with no record of his trip to Havana. The message added that Lopez had obtained tourist card No. 24553 in Tampa on November 20, that he had left Mexico for Havana November 27 on Cubana Airlines, and that his U.S. passport number was 310162.[124]

In another classified message of the same date, it was reported that the FBI had been advised that Lopez entered Mexico on November 27 at Nuevo Laredo.[125]

Two days later these details were added: Lopez had crossed the border at Laredo, Tex., on November 23; registered at the Roosevelt Hotel in Mexico City on November 25; and departed Mexico on November 27 on a Cubana flight for Havana.[126] Another dispatch noted that Lopez was the only passenger on Cubana flight 465 on November 27 to Havana.[127] It said he used a U.S. passport and Cuban courtesy visa. It noted, too: "Source states the timing and circumstances surrounding subject's travel through Mexico and departure for Havana are suspicious." It was this dispatch that alerted headquarters to the source's "urgent" request for all available data on Lopez. [128]

The same day as the dispatch, headquarters sent a cable identifying the Cuban-American as Gilberto Policarpo Lopez, born January 26, 1940. It added that Lopez was not identical with a Gilberto Lopez who had been active in pro-Castro groups in Los Angeles.[129]

Headquarters was also told that there existed a "good" photograph of Lopez, showing him wearing dark glasses. A copy of the photograph with "27 November 1963" stamped on the back was found in his CIA file by committee investigators in 1978.[130]

In March 1964, CIA headquarters received a classified

message: a source had reported in late February that an American citizen named Giberto Lopes[11] had been involved in the Kennedy assassination; that Lopes had entered Mexico on foot from Laredo, Tex., on November 13 carrying U.S. passport 319962, which had been issued July 13, 1960; that he had been issued Mexican travel form B24553 in Nuevo Laredo; that Lopes had proceeded by bus to Mexico City "where he entered the Cuban Embassy"; and that he left the Cuban Embassy on November 27 and was the only passenger on flight 465 for Cuba.[132]

The following day, a classified message was sent to headquarters stating that the information "jibes fully with that provided station by [source] in early December 1963." [133]

A file had been opened on Lopez at headquarters on December 16, 1963.[134] It contained a "Review of [material omitted] file on U.S. Citizen" by an operations officer of the responsible component of the agency. In the review, the file was classified as a "counterintelligence case, (that is, involving a foreign intelligence or security service)." The date of entry of that category in the agency's records is indicated as January 22, 1975.[135]

The committee also reviewed an FBI investigation of Gilberto Policarpo Lopez in Key West, Fla., contained in a report dated August 26, 1964.[136]

In an interview, Lopez' cousin, Guillermo Serpa Rodriguez, had said that Lopez had come to the United States soon after Castro came to power, stayed about a year and returned to Cuba because he was homesick. He returned to the United States in 1960 and 1961, fearing he would be drafted into the Cuban militia.[137]

The FBI also interviewed an American woman Lopez

---

[11]The committee noted the discrepancies in this message, as follows: the spelling of Lopes, for Lopez; the November 13 date and passport number 319962, issued July 13, 1960; and Lopez entering Mexico on foot. In its 1977 Task Force Report, the CIA cited the several "inaccuracies," as they had been repeated in the report of the Senate Select Committee, as reason to refute the report itself. The TFR pointed out that Lopez' name had been misspelled "Lopes," that it had Lopez entering Mexico on foot, when the CIA had information that he had traveled by automobile; that it listed incorrect digits for Lopez' passport number: that it stated that Lopez' Mexican tourist visa had been issued in Nuevo Laredo. not Tampa; and it reported that he had stayed at the Cuban Embassy. Based on these inaccuracies, the TFR concluded, "the source was patently and extensively misinformed." The TFR therefore discounted the March cable that held that the information "jibed" with what the CIA's source had earlier reported. [131]

The discrepancies pointed out in the TFR were apparently intended to explain why the CIA had not taken more aggressive investigative steps to determine whether there had been a connection between Lopez and the assassination.

had married in Key West. She listed companies where he had been employed, including a construction firm in Tampa. She also said he began suffering from epileptic attacks, was confined for a time at Jackson Memorial Hospital in Miami in early 1963, and was treated by doctors in Coral Gables and Key West. She said she believed the epilepsy was brought on by concern for his family in Cuba.[138]

Lopez' wife said she received a letter from him in about November 1963, saying he had returned to Cuba once more. She said she had been surprised, although he had mentioned returning to Cuba before he left for Tampa in November 1963. In a later letter, Lopez told his wife he had received financial assistance for his trip to Cuba from an organization in Tampa. His wife explained that he would not have been able to pay for the trip without help. She said, however, he had not had earlier contacts with Cuban refugee organizations.[139]

Rodriguez said Lopez left Key West in late 1963 for Tampa with the hope of being able to return to Cuba, explaining he was afraid he would be drafted into the U.S. military. Rodriguez said Lopez had not been involved in pro-Castro activity in Key West, but that he was definitely pro-Castro, and he had once gotten into a fistfight over his Castro sympathies.[140]

The FBI had previously documented that Lopez had actually been in contact with the Fair Play for Cuba Committee and had attended a meeting in Tampa on November 20, 1963. In a March 1964 report, it recounted that at a November 17 meeting of the Tampa FPCC, Lopez had said he had not been granted permission to return to Cuba but that he was awaiting a phone call about his return to his homeland. In that March report, a Tampa FPCC member was quoted as saying she called a friend in Cuba on December 8, 1963, and was told that Lopez had arrived safely. She also said that the Tampa chapter of the FPCC had given Lopez about $190 for the trip to Cuba and that he had gone to Cuba by way of Mexico because he did not have a passport.[141]

The March 1964 FBI report stated that Lopez did have a U.S. passport—it had been issued in January 1960 and was numbered 310162. His Mexican tourist card was numbered M8–24553 and was issued November 20, 1963 in Tampa. The report also confirmed that Lopez entered Mexico via Laredo, Tex., by automobile on November 23, and he departed for Havana on November 27, the only passenger on a Cubana flight. He was carrying a Cuban courtesy visa. [142]

Lopez' FBI file contained a memorandum from the Tampa office. Dated October 26, 1964, it read:

It is felt that information developed regarding the subject is not sufficient to merit consideration for the Security Index.[143]

The only information transmitted by the FBI to the Warren Commission, the committee determined, concerned a passport check on Lopez. Information sent to the Commission by the FBI on the Tampa chapter of the FPCC did not contain information on Lopez' activities. The CIA apparently did not provide any information to the Warren Commission on Lopez.[144] The committee concurred with the Senate select committee that this omission was egregious, since sources had reported within a few days of the assassination that the circumstances surrounding Lopez' travel to Cuba seemed "suspicious." Moreover, in March 1964, when the Warren Commission's investigation was in its most active stage, there were reports circulating that Lopez had been involved in the assassination.

In its 1977 Task Force Report, the CIA responded to the charges of the Senate committee. It claimed that the agency had carried its investigation of Lopez as far as it could, having questioned a Cuban defector about him.[145] The committee found that the absence of access to additional sources of information was not an adequate explanation for the agency's failure to consider more seriously the suspicions of its sources or to report what information it did have to the Warren Commission. Attempts in the Task Force Report to denigrate the information that was provided on Lopez were not an adequate substitute for enabling the Warren Commission itself to pursue the leads more aggressively.

From the information gathered by the FBI, there appeared to be plausible reasons both for Lopez' desire to return to Cuba and for his solicitation of financial aid from the Tampa FPCC chapter. Lopez' contacts in Florida appeared to have been innocent and not connected with the assassination, and while there was a suggestion in the Senate committee's report that Lee Harvey Oswald also was in contact with the Tampa FPCC chapter, the committee could find no evidence of it. Nor could the committee find any evidence that Oswald was in the contact with Lopez.

Lopez' association with the Fair Play for Cuba Committee, however, coupled with the act that the dates of his travel to Mexico via Texas coincided with the assassination, plus the reports in Mexico that Lopez' activities were "suspicious," all amount to a troublesome circumstance that the committee was unable to resolve with confidence.

(f) Other allegations

The committee also pursued allegations of Cuban complicity that were not suggested by the investigation of the Senate committee. For example, it looked into an allegation by one Autulio Ramirez Ortiz, who hijacked an aircraft to Cuba in 1961. Ramirez claimed that while being held by the Cuban Government, he worked in an intelligence facility where he found a dossier on Lee Harvey Oswald. [146] It was labeled the "Osvaldo-Kennedy" file and contained a photograph of "Kennedy's future assassin."[147] In the Spanish language manuscript of a book he wrote, Ramirez claimed the Oswald file read, in part, "* * * The KGB has recommended this individual * * * He is a North American, married to an agent of the Soviet organism who has orders to go and reside in the United States. Oswald is an adventurer. Our Embassy in Mexico has orders to get in contact with him. Be very careful."[148]

The committee, in executive session, questioned Ramirez, who had been returned to the United States to serve a 20-year Federal sentence for hijacking.[149] He testified he was unable to describe the photograph he had allegedly seen and that the writing in the file was in Russian, a language he does not speak.[150]

The committee sought from the FBI and CIA independent evidence of the accuracy of Ramirez' allegations, but there was no corroboration of the existence of an "Osvaldo-Kennedy" file to be found. On the other hand, in every instance where there was independent evidence of allegations made by Ramirez (the identities of Cuban officials named by him, for example) Ramirez' statements were found to be accurate.[151]

In the end, however, the committee was forced to dismiss Ramirez' story about the "Osvaldo-Kennedy" file. The decisive factor was the committee's belief that the Cuban intelligence system in the 1961–63 period was too sophisticated to have been infiltrated by Ramirez in the manner he had described. While some details of his story could be corroborated, the essential aspects of his allegation were incredible.

The committee also considered the allegation that appeared in an article in a 1967 issue of the National Enquirer, written by a British freelancer named Comer Clark. [152] Purportedly based on an exclusive interview with Castro, it quoted the Cuban President as admitting to having heard of threats by Oswald to assassinate President Kennedy. According to Clark, Castro told him that while at the Cuban consulate in Mexico City in September 1963, Oswald vowed he would kill the President.[153]

On a trip to Havana in April 1978, the committee met with President Castro and asked him about the charge. Castro denied there had ever been an interview with Clark.[154] He also suggested that had such a threat been overheard by Cuban officials, they and he would have been morally obligated to transmit it to the U.S. authorities. [155]

The committee did not agree that the Cuban Government would have been obligated to report the threat. Nothing in the evidence indicated that the threat should have been taken seriously, if it had occurred, since Oswald had behaved in an argumentative and obnoxious fashion during his visit to the consulate.[156] Cuban officials would have been justified, the committee reasoned, to have considered the threat an idle boast, deserving no serious attention.

The accuracy of Clark's account was also undermined by the committee's investigation of his background. Clark had been the author of articles with such sensational titles as "British Girls as Nazi Sex Slaves," "I Was Hitler's Secret Love" and "German Plans to Kidnap the Royal Family." The committee was unable to question Clark himself, as he had since died.[157]

Despite the committee's doubts about the Clark interview with Castro, it was informed that the substance of it had been independently reported to the U.S. Government. A highly confidential but reliable source reported that Oswald had indeed vowed in the presence of Cuban consulate officials to assassinate the President.[158]

This information prompted the committee to pursue the report further in file reviews and interviews. The files that were further included records of conversations of relevant people at appropriate times and places. Only one of them provided any possible corroboration. It was the record of a reported conversation by an employee of the Cuban Embassy named Luisa Calderon.[159] The absence of other corroboration must be considered significant.

A blind memorandum[12] provided by the CIA to the committee contained Calderon's pertinent remarks:

1. A reliable source reported that on November 22, 1963, several hours after the assassination of President John F. Kennedy, Luisa Calderon Carralero, a Cuban employee of the Cuban Embassy in Mexico City, and believed to be a member of the Cuban Directorate General of Intelligence (DGI), discussed news of the assassination with an acquaintance. Initially, when asked if she had heard the latest news, Calderon replied, in what appeared to be a joking manner, "Yes, of course, I knew almost before Kennedy."

2. After further discussion of the news accounts about the assassination, the acquaintance asked Calderon what else she had learned. Calderon replied that they [assumed to refer to personnel of the Cuban Embassy] learned about it a little while ago.[160]

Luisa Calderon's statements on the day of the assassination could be construed as either an indication of foreknowledge or mere braggadocio. The preponderance of the evidence led the committee to find that it was braggadocio. While the committee attempted to interview Calderon in Cuba, it was unable to, since she was ill.[161] Nevertheless, it forwarded interrogatories to her, which she responded to denying foreknowledge of the assassination. [162] The committee also interviewed other employees of the Cuban consulate in Mexico City in 1963, all of whom denied the allegation.[163] While it may be argued that they had a reason to do so because of Castro's view that the Cuban Government would have had a moral obligation to report the threat had it occurred, these officials, in the committee's judgment, indicated by their demeanor that they were testifying truthfully.

The committee also made a judgment about the risk that would have been incurred by Cubans had they testified falsely on this issue or by those who might have orches-

---

[12]There is no indication on a blind memorandum of either origin or destination.

trated their false testimony. Based on newspaper reporting alone, the Cuban Government might reasonably have believed that the committee had access to extensive information about conversations in the Cuban consulate in Mexico City and that such information might have provided convincing evidence of a coverup. To have been caught in a lie in public testimony in the United States[13] would have been a major embarrassment for the Cuban Government, one that might have implied more than moral responsibility for failing to report a threat against President Kennedy in advance of the assassination.

On balance, the committee did not believe that Oswald voiced a threat to Cuban officials. However reliable the confidential source may be, the committee found it to be in error in this instance.

The committee investigated other aspects of Oswald's trip to Mexico City in September 1963 to see if it could develop information that bore on the question of a Cuban conspiracy. It considered the claim by the Cuban consul in Mexico City in 1963, Eusebio Azcue, that a man posing as Oswald applied for a Cuban visa.[14] It also investigated two plausible, though unsubstantiated, allegations of activities that had not previously been publicly revealed:

> That of a Mexican author, Elena Garro de Paz, who claimed that Oswald and two companions had attended a "twist" party at the home of Ruben Duran, brother-in-law of Silvia Duran, the secretary of Cuban consul Azcue who dealt with Oswald when he applied at the consulate for a Cuban visa.[164]

> That of a Mexican named Oscar Contreras who, in 1967, claimed he had met Oswald on the campus of the National Autonomous University of Mexico. [165]

The committee conducted extensive interviews with respect to these allegations.[166]

The significance of the Elena Garro allegation, aside from its pointing to Oswald associations in Mexico City that the Warren Commission did not investigate, lay in her description of one of the companions as gaunt and blond-

---

[13]In addition to a tape-recorded interview with President Castro in Havana, the committee heard testimony in public hearing from two former Cuban consuls in Mexico City, Eusebio Azcue and Alfredo Mirabal, and it tape-recorded an interview with Silvia Duran, a secretary at the Cuban Consulate in Mexico City in 1963 who had had one or more encounters with Oswald.
[14]Details of the issue of an alleged Oswald imposter are presented in section I D 4.

haired.[167] These are characteristics that both Azcue and Silvia Duran attributed to the visitor to the Cuban consulate who identified himself as Lee Harvey Oswald.[168] Even though "gaunt and blond-haired" did not describe Oswald, Duran said that the American visitor was the man later arrested in the assassination of the President.[169] Azcue, on the other hand, insisted that the visitor was not the individual whose published photograph was that of Oswald. [170]

The committee was unable to obtain corroboration for the Elena Garro allegation, although Silvia Duran did confirm that there was a "twist" party at her brother-in-law's home in the fall of 1963 and that Elena Garro was there. [171] She denied, however, that Oswald was there, insisting that she never saw Oswald outside of the Cuban consulate. [172] The committee was unable to check the story with official U.S. investigative agencies because they failed to pursue it, even though they were aware of it in 1964.[15]

The committee's investigation was sufficient, however, to develop a conclusion that the Elena Garro allegation had warranted investigation when it was first received by the CIA in October 1964. Even in the late 1960's, at a time when Garro and others were available for questioning, there was still the potential for sufficient corroboration[16] to make the allegation worth pursuing. Further, while the allegation did not specifically show a Cuban conspiracy, it did indicate significant Oswald associations that were not known to the Warren Commission.

The other Oswald association in Mexico City that might have proven significant, had it been pursued, was the one

---

[15]The committee's investigation in Mexico City was further inhibited by the refusal of the CIA to make available its sources on the Elena Garro allegation, and, as a committee of the U.S. Congress in a foreign country, it was bound by a decision of the Mexican Government to permit its citizens to decide individually if they wished to meet with committee representatives [173]

The CIA, moreover, had failed to pursue the Elena Garro allegation adequately in 1964. A review of the CIA file indicated that the allegation was treated skeptically because Agency officials apparently considered Elena Garro to be other than totally rational. Inquiries of sources were ordered, but the files do not indicate that any responses were actively solicited or, in fact, received. The Agency files on this aspect of the case are devoid of any substance that would suggest an active CIA investigation.

The committee did ultimately locate Elena Garro in Europe, but attempts by telephone to persuade her to come to the United States to testify did not succeeed. [174]

[16]Elena Garro maintained that after the assassination she wanted to report her story to authorities but that she was warned of possible danger by a man named Manuel Calvillo. Elena Garro alleged that Calvillo placed her in the Hotel Vermont in Mexico City where she remained for several days. In 1967, the CIA did in fact receive confirmation of Elena Garro's stay at the Hotel Vermont immediately after the assassination.

alleged by Oscar Contreras, a student at the National Autonomous University of Mexico. The committee made an effort to investigate this allegation. Silvia Duran, for example, admitted to the committee that she had advised Oswald he might obtain a Cuban visa if he could get a letter of recommendation from a Mexican in good standing with the Cuban revolutionary hierarchy.[175] The committee also learned that the chairman of the philosophy department at the National Autonomous University, Ricardo Guerra, held seminars from time to time at the Duran home on Kant, Hegel, and Marx.[176] The committee speculated that these circumstances might explain why Oswald contacted Contreras, who reported to Mexican authorities that Oswald approached him in September 1963 following a roundtable discussion at the school of philosophy.[17]

The committee's attempts to contact Contreras were frustrated. On two occasions, the Mexican Government said he would be available for an interview, but neither materialized. The committee also was unable to contact Guerra, who in 1978 was Mexico's Ambassador to East Germany.[177] The significance of the Contreras allegation, therefore, remains largely indeterminate.

The committee also pondered what deductions might be drawn from Azcue's conviction that the man who applied for a Cuban visa was not Oswald. One possibility considered, although ultimately rejected by the committee, was that there was a sinister association between Oswald and the Castro regime that Azcue was attempting to conceal.

The committee weighed the evidence on both sides of the Oswald-at-the-Cuban-consulate issue:

That it was Oswald was indicated by the testimony of Silvia Duran and Alfredo Mirabal, who was in the

---

[17]The Contreras story, as in the case of the Elena Garro allegation, was not adequately pursued when it first came to the attention of the CIA in 1967. At that time, the Agency was informed by the U.S. Consul in Tampico, Mexico, that Contreras had passed the information to him. An Agency employee later discussed the matter in more detail with the Consul and then met with Contreras himself. The CIA confirmed that Contreras had been a student in 1963 and was politically a strong supporter of Fidel Castro. The Contreras story was considered, according to Agency files, to be the first significant development in the investigation of the Kennedy assassination after 1965. Nevertheless, no attempt was made to determine who Contreras' associates were or how Oswald might have contacted him. Instead, the case was simply reported to the FBI. According to FBI files, no follow-up investigation was conducted.

process of succeeding Azcue as Cuban consul when the visit occurred in late September 1963. They both identified Oswald from post-assassination photographs as the man who applied for a Cuban visa.

That it was not Oswald was a possibility raised by the committee's inability to secure a photograph of him entering or leaving the Soviet Embassy or the Cuban consulate. The committee obtained evidence from the Cuban Government that such photographs were being taken routinely in 1963. Further, the committee found that Oswald paid at least five visits to the Soviet Embassy or the Cuban consulate.[18][178]

The committee also sought to understand the significance of a Secret Service investigation of threats against President Kennedy by pro-Castro Cubans. In April 1961, for example, when the President and Mrs. Kennedy were scheduled to address a special meeting of the Council of the Organization of American States, the State Department reported that Cuba would be represented by one Quentin Pino Machado. Machado, a Cuban diplomat, described as a character of ill repute, armed and dangerous, ultimately did not attend the meeting.[179]

On November 27, 1963, a Miami Secret Service informant told Special Agent Ernest Aragon that if the assassination involved an international plot in which Castro had participated, then Castro's agent in the plot would have been Machado, a well-known terrorist. There were rumors in the Miami Cuban community at the time that Machado had been assigned to escort Oswald from Texas to Cuba after the assassination. The plan went awry, the report continued, because Oswald had not been wearing clothing of a prearranged color and because of the shooting of Dallas Patrolman J. D. Tippit.[180]

The reports on Machado, along with other suspicions of Castro complicity in the assassination, were forwarded only in brief summary form by the Secret Service to the Warren Commission. The committee could find no rec-

---

[18]The committee believed that photographs of Oswald might have been taken and subsequently lost or destroyed. The committee did obtain a photograph of a man whose description seemed to match that given by Azcue and Duran of the "gaunt and blond-haired" visitor to the Cuban consulate. They each stated, however, that he was not the man they had described as the one who, in the name of Lee Harevy Oswald, had applied for a visa to Cuba.

ord of follow-up action.[181] The committee's investigation of actions by the Secret Service subsequent to the assassination, however, revealed the most extensive work of the Agency to have been in response to reports of pro-Castro Cuban involvement.[182]

(g) The committee's trip to Cuba

The committee took its investigation to Cuba in the spring and summer of 1978. It sought information on numerous allegations, such as those mentioned above, and it put to President Castro the question of Cuban involvement in the assassination. The committee found the Cuban Government to be cooperative, both in supplying written reports and documents in response to questions and by making a number of its citizens available for interviews.[183] While the committee was unable to interview Luisa Calderon personally, the Cuban Government did permit its former consuls in Mexico City, Eusebio Azcue and Alfredo Mirabal, to come to Washington to testify in a public hearing of the committee.[184]

In response to the question of Cuban complicity in the assassination, Castro replied:

> That [the Cuban Government might have been involved in the President's death] was insane. From the ideological point of view it was insane. And from the political point of view, it was tremendous insanity. I am going to tell you here that nobody, nobody ever had the idea of such things. What would it do? We just tried to defend our folks here, within our territory. Anyone who subscribed to that idea would have been judged insane * * * absolutely sick. Never, in 20 years of revolution, I never heard anyone suggest nor even speculate about a measure of that sort, because who could think of the idea of organizing the death of the President of the United States. That would have been the most perfect pretext for the United States to invade our country which is what I have tried to prevent for all these years, in every possible sense. Since the United States is much more powerful than we are, what could we gain from a war with the United States? The United States would lose nothing. The destruction would have been here.[185]

Castro added:

> I want to tell you that the death of the leader does not change the system. It has never done that. [186]

In the interview, Castro also commented on his speech of September 7, 1963, which on its face might have been viewed as an indication that Castro may have been prompted to retaliate for a CIA-inspired attempt on his life:

> So, I said something like those plots start to set a very bad precedent, a very serious one—that could become a boomerang against the authors of those actions * * * but I did not mean to threaten by that. I did not mean even that * * * not in the least * * * but rather, like a warning that we knew; that we had news about it; and that to set those precedents of plotting the assassination of leaders of other countries would be a very bad precedent * * * something very negative. And, if at present, the same would happen under the same circumstances, I would have no doubt in saying the same as I said [then] because I didn't mean a threat by that. I didn't say it as a threat. I did not mean by that that we were going to take measures—similar measures—like a retaliation for that. We never meant that because we knew that there were plots. For 3 years, we had known there were plots against us. So the conversation came about very casually, you know; but I would say that all these plots or attempts were part of the everyday life.[187]

Finally, President Castro noted that although relations between the United States and Cuba were strained during the Kennedy administration, by 1963 there were definite hopes for reconciliation.[188] The committee confirmed from the historical record that, in 1963, the Cuban Government made several overtures. While, for the most part, Kennedy did not respond favorably, he did, in November, direct that the possibility of holding talks be explored by United Nations Delegate William Atwood with Cuban United Nations Ambassador Carlos Lechuga. There was also reason to believe that French journalist Jean Daniel was asked by Kennedy to relay a peace message to Castro.[190] At least, that was how Castro interpreted it when he met with Daniel on November 20, 1963.[191]

In his interview with the committee, Castro referred to these two developments toward rapprochement, as he viewed them, suggesting that he would not have had a motive to eliminate President Kennedy. Instead, it would have been to his advantage, Castro insisted, to have pursued the prospect for better relations that had been portended.[192]

(h) Deficiencies of the 1963–64 investigation

In attempting to resolve the question of possible Cuban conspiracy, the committee concluded that a definitive answer had to come, if at all, largely from the investigation conducted in 1963–64 by the Warren Commission and the FBI and CIA. What the committee was able to do 15 years later could fill in important details, but it could not make up for basic insufficiencies. Unfortunately, the committee found that there were in fact significant deficiencies in the earlier investigation. The Warren Commission knew far less than it professed to know about Oswald's trip to Mexico and his possible association with pro-Castro agents in Mexico and elsewhere. This was true, in part, because the Commission had demanded less of the FBI and CIA than called for in its mandate.[193]

For its part, the FBI mechanically ran out thousands of leads, but it failed to make effective use of its Cuban Section of the Domestic Intelligence Division or to develop and systematically pursue investigative hypotheses of possible Cuban complicity. It must be said that the FBI generally exhausted its resources in confirming the case against Lee Harvey Oswald as the lone assassin, a case that Director J. Edgar Hoover, at least, seemed determined to make within 24 hours of the assassination. [194]

With respect to the CIA, the committee determined that it could have been better equipped to investigate the question of Cuban complicity.[19] The CIA had, at the time,

[19]With respect to the incident at the home of Sylvia Odio in Dallas (see sec. C 3), the CIA had developed since 1963 the ability to identify from physical descriptions possible intelligence agents who may have been involved. In fact, at the committee's request, the CIA attempted to identify Odio's visitors, and it determined that they may have been members of Cuban intelligence. [195] The committee showed photographs supplied by the CIA to Odio who stated they did not appear to be the visitors in

only limited access to Cuban intelligence defectors, and most of its information sources inside Cuba were better equipped to report on economic developments and troop movements than on political decisions, especially sensitive ones, such as those involving political assassination.[198]

As the CIA admitted in its 1977 Task Force Report, it could have taken "broader initiatives" in pursuing the investigation. The committee found that such initiatives could have included more comprehensive instructions on debriefing Cuban sources and more explicit tasking of stations for specific investigative efforts.

With respect to the CIA's investigation of possible Cuban complicity, however, the committee found that the Agency's shortcomings were not attributable to any improper motive. The committee found that the CIA did generally gather and analyze the information that came to its attention regarding possible Cuban involvement, at least until the Warren Commission made its report in 1964. Indeed, the committee noted that the Agency acted not only out of dedication, but out of a specific motivation related to Cuba. The officers, agents and employees in the Cuba-related divisions had devoted their careers to the overthrow of Castro, and evidence of his participation in the assassination, if it had existed and could have been brought to light, would have vindicated their long-frustrated efforts, if not, in fact, led directly a U.S. invasion of Cuba and destruction of the Castro regime.

That being said, the committee did not ignore the possibility that certain CIA officials who were aware that close scrutiny of U.S.-Cuban relations in the early 1960's could have inadvertently exposed the CIA-Mafia plots against Castro, might have attempted to prevent the CIA's assassination investigation or that of the Warren Commission from delving deeply into the question of Cuban complicity. The committee determined, however, that only CIA Deputy Director Richard Helms would have been in a position to have had both the requisite knowledge and the power to accomplish such a coverup, and it was satis-

---

question. [196] The committee came to the conclusion that had she been shown photographs in 1963, when the event was clearer in her mind, she might have been able to make an identification. It is also regrettable that the CIA did not make use of a defector from Cuba who had worked in intelligence and who might have been able to identify the Odio visitors. [197]

fied, on the basis of its investigation, that it was highly unlikely he in fact did so.[199]

While noting the deficiencies in the CIA assassination investigation, the committee was impressed with certain overseas capabilities of the CIA in 1963. The Agency had, for example, comprehensive coverage of anti-Castro Cuban groups that, in turn, had extensive information sources in and out of Cuba.[200] Thus, while it was flawed in certain specific respects, the committee concluded that the CIA assassination investigation could, in fact, be relied on—with only limited reservations—as a general indicator of possible Cuban involvement. That investigation found no evidence of Cuban complicity.

(i) Summary of the findings

While the committee did not take Castro's denials at face value, it found persuasive reasons to conclude that the Cuban Government was not involved in the Kennedy assassination. First, by 1963 there were prospects for repairing the hostility that had marked relations between the two countries since Castro had come to power. Second, the risk of retaliation that Cuba would have incurred by conspiring in the assassination of an American President must have canceled out other considerations that might have argued for that act. President Castro's description of the idea as "insane" is appropriate. And there was no evidence indicating an insane or grossly reckless lack of judgment on the part of the Cuban Government. Third, the CIA had both the motive to develop evidence of Cuban involvement and access to at least substantial, if incomplete, information bearing on relevant aspects of it, had such involvement existed. Its absence, therefore, must be weighed in the balance. Finally, the Cuban Government's cooperation with this committee in the investigation must be a factor in any judgment. In conclusion, the committee found, on the basis of the evidence available to it, that the Cuban Government was not involved in the assassination of President Kennedy.

3. THE COMMITTEE BELIEVES, ON THE BASIS OF THE EVIDENCE AVAILABLE TO IT, THAT ANTI-CASTRO CUBAN GROUPS, AS GROUPS, WERE NOT INVOLVED IN THE ASSASSINATION OF PRESIDENT KENNEDY, BUT THAT THE AVAILABLE EVIDENCE DOES NOT PRECLUDE THE POSSIBILITY THAT INDIVIDUAL MEMBERS MAY HAVE BEEN INVOLVED

The committee investigated possible involvement in the assassination by a number of anti-Castro Cuban groups and individual activists for two primary reasons:

First, they had the motive, based on what they considered President Kennedy's betrayal of their cause, the liberation of Cuba from the Castro regime; the means, since they were trained and practiced in violent acts, the result of the guerrilla warfare they were waging against Castro; and the opportunity, whenever the President, as he did from time to time, appeared at public gatherings, as in Dallas on November 22, 1963.

Second, the committee's investigation revealed that certain associations of Lee Harvey Oswald were or may have been with anti-Castro activists.

The committee, therefore, paid close attention to the activities of anti-Castro Cubans—in Miami, where most of them were concentrated and their organizations were headquartered,[1] and in New Orleans and Dallas, where Oswald, while living in these cities in the months preceding the assassination, reportedly was in contact with anti-Castro activists.[2]

The Warren Commission did not, of course, ignore Oswald's ties to anti-Castroites. From the evidence that was available in 1964, two Warren Commission staff attorneys, W. David Slawson and William Coleman, went so far as to speculate that Oswald, despite his public posture as a Castro sympathizer, might actually have been an agent of anti-Castro exiles.[3] Indeed, pressing for further investigation of the possibility, they wrote a memorandum which read in part:

The evidence here could lead to an anti-Castro involvement in the assassination on some sort of basis as this: Oswald could have become known to the Cubans as being strongly pro-Castro. He made no secret of his sympathies, so the anti-Castro Cubans must have realized that law enforcement authorities were also aware of Oswald's feelings and that, therefore,

153

if he got into trouble, the public would also learn of them * * * Second, someone in the anti-Castro organization might have been keen enough to sense that Oswald had a penchant for violence * * * On these facts, it is possible that some sort of deception was used to encourage Oswald to kill the President when he came to Dallas * * * The motive of this would, of course, be the expectation that after the President was killed, Oswald would be caught or at least his identity ascertained, the law enforcement authorities and the public would blame the assassination on the Castro government and a call for its forceful overthrow would be irresistible * * *.[4]

While it is seemingly in contradiction of Oswald's personal character and known public posture, the committee seriously considered, therefore, the possibility of an anti-Castro conspiracy in the assassination (perhaps with Oswald unaware of its true nature). It is appropriate to begin that consideration with an examination of the history of United States-Cuban relations from the perspective of the anti-Castro movement, beginning with the victorious end of the revolution on January 1, 1959.[5]

(a) The anti-Castro Cuban perspective

The anti-Castro movement began not long after Fidel Castro assumed control of Cuba.[6] At first, the Cuban people cheered the revolution and its leader for the defeat of the dictatorial Batista regime, but it was not long before many former supporters found reason to condemn the new premier's policies and politics.[7] Many Cubans were deeply disillusioned when it became apparent that the Castro government was renouncing the country's long affiliaton with the United States and moving closer to the Soviet Union.[8] As Castro's preference for Marxism became evident, underground opposition movements were born.[9] They survived for a time within Cuba, but as the effectiveness of Castro's militia system was recognized, they retreated to the exile communities of Miami and other cities in the United States.[10]

The U.S. Government was responsive to the efforts of exiles to remove a Communist threat from the Caribbean, only 90 miles from the Florida coast, and to recapture business investments lost to the nationalization of industry in Cuba.[11] An official, yet covert, program to train and equip exiles determined to overthrow Castro was sanctioned by President Eisenhower and his successor, President Kennedy, and carried out by the American intelligence agencies, particularly the Central Intelligence Agency.[12] The Cuban exiles, dependent on the United States for arms and logistical support, had little choice but to put their trust in Washington.[13]

Their trust collapsed, however, at the Bay of Pigs on April 17, 1961, when an exile invasion of Cuba was annihilated by Castro's troops.[14] The failure of American airpower to support the landing shattered the confidence of the anti-Castro Cubans in the U.S. Government.[15] They blamed President Kennedy, and he publicly accepted responsibility for the defeat.[16]

President Kennedy's readiness to take the blame for the Bay of Pigs served to intensify the anger of the exiles.[17] In executive session before the committee, Manuel Antonio Varona, who in 1961 was the head of the united exile organization, the Revolutionary Democratic Front, told of a tense and emotional encounter with the President at the White House, as hope for the invasion was fading.[18] "We were not charging Mr. Kennedy with anything," Varona testified.[19] "We knew he was not in charge of the military efforts directly. Nevertheless, President Kennedy told us he was the one—the only one responsible." [20]

A noted Cuban attorney, Mario Lazo, summed up Cuban feeling toward President Kennedy in his book, "Dagger in the Heart":

The Bay of Pigs was wholly self-inflicted in Washington. Kennedy told the truth when he publicly accepted responsibility * * * The heroism of the beleaguered Cuban Brigade had been rewarded by betrayal, defeat, death for many of them, long and cruel imprisonment for the rest. The Cuban people * * * had always admired the United States as strong, rich, generous—but where was its sense of honor and the capacity of its leaders?[21]

President Kennedy was well aware of the bitter legacy of the Bay of Pigs debacle. Far from abandoning the

Cuban exiles, he set out to convince them of his loyalty to their cause. One of the most emotionally charged events of his relationship with the Cuban exiles occurred on December 29, 1962, at the Orange Bowl in Miami.[22] He had come to welcome the survivors of the invasion force, Brigade 2506, the 1,200 men who had been ransomed from Cuba after almost 20 months in prison. [23] The President was presented with the brigade flag in a dramatic and tumultuous scene.[24]

The euphoria was false and misleading. Although the Cuban exiles cheered President Kennedy that day, there also coursed through the crowd a bitter resentment among some who felt they were witnessing a display of political hypocrisy. Later, it would be claimed that the brigade feeling against President Kennedy was so strong that the presentation nearly did not take place, and it would be alleged (incorrectly, as it turned out) that the brigade flag given to Kennedy was actually a replica.[25].

It is not possible to know fully how the Bay of Pigs defeat changed President Kennedy's attitude toward Cuba, but when journalists Taylor Branch and George Crile wrote in Harper's Magazine about a massive infusion of U.S. aid to clandestine anti-Castro operations in the wake of the Bay of Pigs, they titled their article, "The Kennedy Vendetta." [26] What is known is that the period between the Bay of Pigs and the Cuban missile crisis in October 1962 can be characterized as the high point of anti-Castro activity. [27] Miami, the center of the exile community, became a busy staging ground for armed infiltrations of Cuba.[29] While not every raid was supported or even known about in advance by Government agencies, the United States played a key role in monitoring, directing and supporting the anti-Castro Cubans.[29] Although this effort was cloaked in secrecy, most Cubans in the exile community knew what was happening and who was supporting the operations.[30]

(1) *The missile crisis and its aftermath.*—At the time of the missile crisis in October 1962, the Cuban exiles were initially elated at the prospect of U.S. military action that might topple the Castro regime.[31] In the end, it seemed to the world that President Kennedy had the best of the confrontation with Castro and Soviet leader Nikita Khrushchev by demanding, and getting, the withdrawal of offensive missiles and bombers from Cuba. From the exiles'

perspective, however, they had been compromised, since as part of the bargain, President Kennedy made a pledge not to invade Cuba.[20][32]

Anti-Castro forces in the United States were all the more embittered in the spring of 1963 when the Federal Government closed down many of their training camps and guerrilla bases.[34] In cases where government raids intercepted the illegal arms transfers, weapons were confiscated and arrests were made.[35] Some anti-Castro operations did continue, however, right up to the time of the assassination, though the committee found that U.S. backing had by that time been reduced.[36]

(2) *Attitude of anti-Castro Cubans toward Kennedy.*—President Kennedy's popularity among the Cuban exiles had plunged deeply by 1963. Their bitterness is illustrated in a tape recording a meeting of anti-Castro Cubans and right-wing Americans in the Dallas suburb of Farmer's Branch on October , 1963.[37] In it, a Cuban identified as Nestor Castellanos vehemently criticized the United States and blamed President Kennedy for the U.S. Government's policy of "noninterference" with respect to the Cuban issue.[38] Holding a copy of the September 26 edition of the Dallas Morning News, featuring a front-page account of the President's planned trip to Texas in November, Castellanos vented his hostility without restraint:

CASTELLANOS. * * * we're waiting for Kennedy the 22d, buddy. We're going to see him in one way or the other. We're going to give him the works when he gets in Dallas. Mr. good ol' Kennedy. I wouldn't even call him President Kennedy. He stinks.

QUESTION. Are you insinuating that since this downfall came through the leader there [Castro in Cuba] that this might come to us * * *?

CASTELLANOS. Yes ma'am, your present leader. He's the one who is doing everything right now to help the United States to become Communist.[21] [39]

---

[20]The United States never actually signed the pledge, since it was conditioned on United Nations inspection of the weapons withdrawal that Castro would not honor. The fine point of signing the pledge was of little importance to the Cuban exiles, however, who could point out later that no invasion did, in fact, occur. [33]

[21]The committee uncovered no evidence that linked Castellanos to the assassination. His speech is quoted to illustrate the depth of feeling that existed in the Cuban exile community in 1963.

157

(b) The committee investigation

The committee initiated its investigation by identifying the most violent and frustrated anti-Castro groups and their leaders from among the more than 100 Cuban exile organizations in existence in November 1963.[40] These groups included Alpha 66, the Cuban Revolutionary Junta (JURE), Commandos L, the Directorio Revolucionario Estudiantil (DRE), the Cuban Revolutionary Council (CRC) which included the Frente Revolucionario Democratico (FRD), the Junta del Gobierno de Cuba en el Exilio (JGCE), the 30th of November, the International Penetration Forces (InterPen), the Revolutionary Recovery Movement (MRR), and the Ejercito Invasor Cubano (EIC).[41] Their selection evolved both from the committee's independent field investigation and the examination of the files and records maintained by the Federal and local agencies then monitoring Cuban exile activity. These agencies included local police departments, the FBI, the CIA, the Bureau of Narcotics and Dangerous Drugs (now the Drug Enforcement Administration, or DEA), the Customs Service, the Immigration and Naturalization Service and the Department of Defense.[42]

The groups that received the committee's attention were "action groups"—those most involved in military actions and propaganda campaigns. Unlike most others, they did not merely talk about anti-Castro operations, they actually carried out infiltrations into Cuba, planned, and sometimes attempted, Castro's assassination, and shipped arms into Cuba. These were also the groups whose leaders felt most betrayed by U.S. policy toward Cuba and by the President; they were also those whose operations were frustrated by American law enforcement efforts after the missile crisis.

(1) *Homer S. Echevarria.*—For the most part the committee found that the anti-Castro Cuban leaders were more vociferous than potentially violent in their tirades against the President. Nevertheless, it was unable to conclude with certainty that all of the threats were benign. For example, one that the committee found particularly disturbing—especially so, since it was not thoroughly looked into in the 1963–64 investigation—came to the attention of the Secret Service within days of the President's death, prompting the Acting Special Agent-in-Charge of the Chicago field office to write an urgent

memorandum indicating he had received reliable information of "a group in the Chicago area who [sic] may have a connection with the J. F. K. assassination." [43] The memorandum was based on a tip from an informant who reported a conversation on November 21, 1963, with a Cuban activist named Homer S. Echevarria.[44] They were discussing an illegal arms sale, and Echevarria was quoted as saying his group now had "plenty of money" and that his backers would proceed "as soon as we take care of Kennedy." [45]

Following the initial memorandum, the Secret Service instructed its informant to continue his association with Echevarria and notified the Chicago FBI office.[46] It learned that Echevarria might have been a member of the 30th of November anti-Castro organization, that he was associated with Juan Francisco Blanco-Fernandez, military director of the DRE, and that the arms deal was being financed through one Paulino Sierra Martinez by hoodlum elements in Chicago and elsewhere.[47]

Although the Secret Service recommended further investigation, the FBI initially took the position that the Echevarria case "was primarily a protection matter and that the continued investigation would be left to the U.S. Secret Service," [48] and that the Cuban group in question was probably not involved in illegal activities.[49] The Secret Service initially was reluctant to accept this position, since it had developed evidence that illegal acts were, in fact, involved.[50] Then, on November 29, 1963, President Johnson created the Warren Commission and gave the FBI primary investigative responsibility in the assassination.[51] Based on its initial understanding that the President's order meant primary, not exclusive, investigative responsibility, the Secret Service continued its efforts;[52] but when the FBI made clear that it wanted the Secret Service to terminate its investigation,[53] it did so, turning over its files to the FBI.[54] The FBI, in turn, did not pursue the Echevarria case.[55]

While it was unable to substantiate the content of the informant's alleged conversations with Echevarria or any connection to the events in Dallas, the committee did establish that the original judgment of the Secret Service was correct, that the Echevarria case did warrant a thorough investigation. It found, for example, that the 30th of November group was backed financially by the Junta del Gobierno de Cuba en el Exilio (JGCE), a

Chicago-based organization run by Paulino Sierra Martinez. [56] JGCE was a coalition of many of the more active anti-Castro groups that had been founded in April 1963; it was dissolved soon after the assassination.[22][57] Its purpose was to back the activities of the more militant groups, including Alpha 66 and the Student Directorate, or DRE, both of which had reportedly been in contact with Lee Harvey Oswald.[58] Much of JGCE's financial support, moreover, allegedly came from individuals connected to organized crime.[59]

As it surveyed the various anti-Castro organizations, the committee focused its interest on reported contacts with Oswald. Unless an association with the President's assassin could be established, it is doubtful that it could be shown that the anti-Castro groups were involved in the assassination. The Warren Commission, discounting the recommendations of Slawson and Coleman, had either regarded these contacts as insignificant or as probably not having been made or else was not aware of them.[60] The committee could not so easily dismiss them.

(2) *Antonio Veciana Blanch.*—The committee devoted a significant portion of its anti-Castro Cuban investigation to an alleged contact with Oswald that had been reported by Antonio Veciana Blanch, the founder of Alpha 66 which, throughout 1962 and most of 1963, was one of the most militant of the exile groups.[61] Its repeated hit-and-run attacks had drawn public criticism from President Kennedy in the spring of 1963, to which Veciana replied, "We are going to attack again and again."

Veciana claimed to have had the active support of the CIA, and in 1976 he reported to a Senate investigator that from 1960 to 1973 his adviser, whom he believed to be a representative of the CIA, was known to him as Maurice Bishop.[62] Veciana stated that over their 13-year association, he and Bishop met on over 100 occasions and that Bishop actually planned many Alpha 66 operations.[63] He also said that he knew the man only as Maurice Bishop and that all of their contacts were initiated by Bishop.[64]

Veciana said that Bishop had guided him in planning assassination attempts of Castro in Havana in 1961 and in

---

[22]The committee established—though it could make no judgment about there having been a connection—that many of the anti-Castro Cuban groups ceased their operations at about the time of President Kennedy's assassination. The Echevarria allegation is also discussed in section I D (1) (b) *infra*.

Chile in 1971; that Bishop had directed him to organize Alpha 66 in 1962; and that Bishop, on ending their relationship in 1973, had paid him $253.000 in cash for his services over the years.[65] Veciana also revealed that at one meeting with Bishop in Dallas in late August or early September 1963, a third party at their meeting was a man he later recognized as Lee Harvey Oswald.[66]

Veciana also indicated to the committee that subsequent to the assassination, he had been contacted by Bishop, who was aware that Veciana had a relative in Cuban intelligence in Mexico.[67] Bishop, according to Veciana, offered to pay Veciana's relative a large sum of money if he would say that it was he and his wife who had met with Oswald in Mexico City.[68] Veciana said he had agreed to contact his relative, but he had been unable to do so.

The committee pursued the details of Veciana's story, particularly the alleged meeting with Oswald. It conducted numerous file reviews and interviews with associates and former associates of Veciana, to try to confirm the existence of a Maurice Bishop or otherwise assess Veciana's credibility. On a trip to Cuba, the committee interviewed Veciana's relative, the Cuban intelligence agent.

While the committee was unable to find corroboration for the contacts with Bishop, it did substantiate other statements by Veciana. For example, he did organize an attempted assassination of Castro in Havana in 1961,[70] and he probably did participate in another plot against Castro in Chile in 1971.[71] That Veciana was the principal organizer of the militant Alpha 66 organization was a matter of record.[72]

The committee went to great lengths in its unsuccessful effort to substantiate the existence of Bishop and his alleged relationship with Oswald. It reviewed CIA files, but they showed no record of such an agent or employee. It circulated a sketch via the national news media, but no one responded with an identification.[73] It pursued a lead originating with the Senate investigation that a former chief of the CIA's Western Hemisphere Division of the Directorate of Operations bore a resemblance to the Bishop sketch.[74] The committee arranged for a chance meeting between Veciana and the CIA officer, who had since retired.[75] Veciana said he was not Bishop.[76] In an executive session of the committee, the retired officer testified under oath that he had never used the name

Bishop, had never known anyone by that name and had never known Veciana.[77] Veciana, also before a committee executive session, testified the officer was not Bishop, although he bore a "physical similarity." [23][78]

A former Director of the CIA, John McCone, and an agent who had participated in covert Cuban operations, each told the committee they recalled that a Maurice Bishop had been associated with the Agency, though neither could supply additional details.[80] Subsequently, McCone was interviewed by CIA personnel, and he told them that his original testimony to the committee had been in error.[81] The agent did confirm, however, even after a CIA reinterview, that he had seen the man known to him as Maurice Bishop three or four times at CIA headquarters in the early 1960's.[82] He did not know his organizational responsibilities, and he had not known him personally.[83] The agent also testified that he had been acquainted with the retired officer who had been chief of the Western Hemisphere Division and that he was not Bishop.[84]

The committee also requested files on Bishop from the FBI and Department of Defense, with negative results. [85] It did discover, however, that Army intelligence had an operational interest in Veciana as a source of information on Alpha 66 activities, and that Veciana complied, hoping to be supplied in return with funds and weapons. [86] Veciana acknowledged his contacts with the Army, but he stated that the only relationship those contacts had to Bishop was that he kept Bishop informed of them.[87]

The CIA's files reflected that the Agency had been in contact with Veciana three times during the early 1960's, but the Agency maintained it offered him no encouragement.[88] (The committee could discover only one piece of arguably contradictory evidence—a record of $500 in operational expenses, given to Veciana by a person

---

[23]The committee suspected that Veciana was lying when he denied that the retired CIA officer was Bishop. The committee recognized that Veciana had an interest in renewing his anti-Castro operations that might have led him to protect the officer from exposure as Bishop so they could work together again. For his part, the retired officer aroused the committee's suspicion when he told the committee he did not recognize Veciana as the founder of Alpha 66, especially since the officer had once been deeply involved in Agency anti-Castro operations. Further, a former CIA case officer who was assigned from September 1960 to November 1962 to the JM/WAVE station in Miami told the committee that the retired officer had in fact used the alias, Maurice Bishop. The committee also interviewed a former assistant of the retired officer but he could not recall his former superior ever having used the name or having been referred to as Bishop. [79]

162

with whom the CIA had maintained a longstanding operational relationship.[89] The CIA further insisted that it did not at any time assign a case officer to Veciana.[24] [90]

The committee was left with the task of evaluating Veciana's story, both with respect to the existence of Maurice Bishop and the alleged meeting with Oswald, by assessing Veciana's credibility. It found several reasons to believe that Veciana had been less than candid:

First, Veciana waited more than 10 years after the assassination to reveal his story.

Second, Veciana would not supply proof of the $253,000 payment from Bishop, claiming fear of the Internal Revenue Service.

Third, Veciana could not point to a single witness to his meetings with Bishop, much less with Oswald.

Fourth, Veciana did little to help the committee identify Bishop.

In the absence of corroboration or independent substantiation, the committee could not, therefore, credit Veciana's story of having met with Lee Harvey Oswald.

(3) *Silvia Odio.*—The incident of reported contact between Oswald and anti-Castro Cubans that has gained the most attention over the years involved Silvia Odio, a member of the Cuban Revolutionary Junta, or JURE.[91] Mrs. Odio had not volunteered her information to the FBI. [92] The FBI initially contacted Mrs. Odio after hearing of a conversation she had had with her neighbor in which she described an encounter with Lee Harvey Oswald. [93] Subsequently, in testimony before the Warren Commission, she said that in late September 1963, three men came to her home in Dallas to ask for help in preparing a fundraising letter for JURE.[94] She stated that two of the men appeared to be Cubans, although they also had characteristics that she associated with Mexicans.[95] The two individuals, she remembered, indicated that their "war" names were "Leopoldo" and "Angelo."[96] The third man, an American, was introduced to her as "Leon Oswald,"

<hr>

[24]The committee found it probable that some agency of the United States assigned a case officer to Veciana, since he was the dominant figure in an extremely active anti-Castro organization. The committee established that the CIA assigned case officers to Cuban revolutionaries of less importance than Veciana, though it could not draw from that alone an inference of CIA deception of the committee concerning Veciana, since Bishop could well have been in the employ of one of the military intelligence agencies or even perhaps of some foreign power.

and she was told that he was very much interested in the anti-Castro Cuban cause.[97]

Mrs. Odio stated that the men told her that they had just come from New Orleans and that they were then about to leave on a trip.[98] The next day, one of the Cubans called her on the telephone and told her that it had been his idea to introduce the American into the underground "* * * because he is great, he is kind of nuts." [99] The Cuban also said that the American had been in the Marine Corps and was an excellent shot, and that the American had said that Cubans "* * * don't have any guts * * * because President Kennedy should have been assassinated after the Bay of Pigs, and some Cubans should have done that, because he was the one that was holding the freedom of Cuba actually. [100] Mrs. Odio claimed the American was Lee Harvey Oswald.[101]

Mrs. Odio's sister, who was in the apartment at the time of the visit by the three men and who stated that she saw them briefly in the hallway when answering the door, also believed that the American was Lee Harvey Oswald. [102] Mrs. Odio fixed the date of the alleged visit as being September 26 or 27.[103] She was positive that the visit occurred prior to October 1.[104]

The Warren Commission was persuaded that Oswald could not have been in Dallas on the dates given by Mrs. Odio.[105] Nevertheless, it requested the FBI to conduct further investigation into her allegation, and it acknowledged that the FBI had not completed its Odio investigation at the time its report was published in September 1964.[106]

How the Warren Commission treated the Odio incident is instructive. In the summer of 1964, the FBI was pressed to dig more deeply into the Odio allegation.[107] On July 24, chief counsel J. Lee Rankin, in a letter to FBI Director J. Edgar Hoover, noted, ". . . the Commission already possesses firm evidence that Lee Harvey Oswald was on a bus traveling from Houston, Tex., to Mexico City, Mexico, on virtually the entire day of September 26." [108] J. Wesley Liebeler, the Warren Commission assistant counsel who had taken Mrs. Odio's deposition, disagreed, however, that there was firm evidence of Oswald's bus trip to Mexico City.[109] In a memorandum to another Commission attorney, Howard Willens, on September 14, 1964, Liebeler objected to a section of the Warren Report in which it was stated there was strong evidence that Oswald was on a bus to Mexico on the date in question.[110] Liebeler argued, "There really is no evidence at all that [Oswald] left Houston on that bus." [111] Liebeler also argued that the conclusion that there was "persuasive" evidence that Oswald was not in Dallas on September 24, 1963, a day for which his travel was unaccounted, was "too strong."[112] Liebeler urged Willens to tone down the language of the report,[113] contending in his memorandum: "There are problems. Odio may well be right. The Commission will look bad if it turns out that she is."[114]

On August 23, 1964, Rankin again wrote to Hoover to say, "It is a matter of some importance to the Commission that Mrs. Odio's allegation either be proved or disproved."[115] Rankin asked that the FBI attempt to learn the identities of the three visitors by contacting members of anti-Castro groups active in the Dallas area, as well as leaders of the JURE organization.[116] He asked the FBI to check the possibility that Oswald had spent the night of September 24, in a hotel in New Orleans, after vacating his apartment.[117] Portions of this investigation, which were inconclusive in supporting the Warren Commission's contention that Mrs. Odio was mistaken, were not sent to Rankin until November 9, [118] at which time the final report already had been completed.[119]

The FBI did attempt to alleviate the "problems." In a report dated September 26, it reported the interview of Loran Eugene Hall who claimed he had been in Dallas in September 1963, accompanied by two men fitting the general description given by Silvia Odio, and that it was they who had visited her.[120] Oswald, Hall said, was not one of the men.[121] Within a week of Hall's statement, the other two men Hall said had accompanied him, Lawrence Howard and William Seymour, were interviewed. [122] They denied ever having met Silvia Odio.[123] Later, Hall himself retracted his statement about meeting with Mrs. Odio.[124]

Even though the Commission could not show conclusively that Oswald was not at the Odio apartment, and even though Loran Hall's story was an admitted fabrication, the Warren report published this explanation of the Odio incident:

While the FBI had not yet completed its investigation into this matter at the time the report went to press, the Commission has concluded that Lee Harvey Oswald was not at Mrs. Odio's apartment in September 1963.[125]

Not satisfied with that conclusion, the committee conducted interviews with and took depositions from the principals—Silvia Odio,[126] members of her family,[127] and Dr. Burton Einspruch,[128] her psychiatrist. (Mrs. Odio had contacted Dr. Einspruch for consultation about problems that could not be construed to affect her perception or credibility.) [129] The committee also set up a conference telephone call between Dr. Einspruch in Dallas and Silvia Odio in Miami, during which she related to him the visit of the three men. [130] Mrs. Odio and Dr. Einspruch concurred that she had told him of the nighttime meeting shortly after its occurrence, but prior to the President's assassination.[131]

Loran Hall testified before the committee in executive session on October 5, 1977; Howard and Seymour were interviewed.[132] The FBI agent who wrote up the Hall story also testified before the committee.[133] From a review of FBI files, the committee secured a list of persons who belonged to the Dallas chapter of JURE, and the committee attempted to locate and interview these individuals. Additionally, staff investigators interviewed the leader of JURE, Manolo Ray, who was residing in Puerto Rico.[134]

Further, the committee secured photographs of scores of pro-Castro and anti-Castro activists who might have fit the descriptions of the two individuals who, Mrs. Odio said, had visited her with Oswald.[135] The committee also used the resources of the CIA which conducted a check on all individuals who used the "war" names of "Leopoldo" and "Angelo," and the name "Leon," or had similar names. [136] An extensive search produced the names and photographs of three men who might possibly have been in Dallas in September 1963.[137] These photographs were shown to Mrs. Odio, but she was unable to identify them as the men she had seen.[138]

The committee was inclined to believe Silvia Odio. From the evidence provided in the sworn testimony of the witnesses, it appeared that three men did visit her apartment in Dallas prior to the Kennedy assassination and identified themselves as members of an anti-Castro organization. Based on a judgment of the credibility of Silvia and Annie

Odio, one of these men at least looked like Lee Harvey Oswald and was introduced to Mrs. Odio as Leon Oswald.

The committee did not agree with the Warren Commission's conclusion that Oswald could not have been in Dallas at the requisite time. Nevertheless, the committee itself could reach no definite conclusion on the specific date of the visit. It could have been as early as September 24, the morning of which Oswald was seen in New Orleans, [139] but it was more likely on the 25th, 26th or 27th of September. If it was on these dates, then Oswald had to have had access to private transportation to have traveled through Dallas and still reached Mexico City when he did, judging from other evidence developed by both the Warren Commission and the committee.[140]

(c) Oswald and anti-Castro Cubans

The committee recognized that an association by Oswald with anti-Castro Cubans would pose problems for its evaluation of the assassin and what might have motivated him. In reviewing Oswald's life, the committee found his actions and values to have been those of a self-proclaimed Marxist who would be bound to favor the Castro regime in Cuba, or at least not advocate its overthrow. For this reason, it did not seem likely to the committee that Oswald would have allied himself with an anti-Castro group or individual activist for the sole purpose of furthering the anti-Castro cause. The committee recognized the possibility that Oswald might have established contacts with such groups or persons to implicate the anti-Castro movement in the assassination. Such an implication might have protected the Castro regime and other left-wing suspects, while resulting in an intensive investigation and possible neutralization of the opponents of Castro. It is also possible, despite his alleged remark about killing Kennedy, that Oswald had not yet contemplated the President's assassination at the time of the Odio incident, or if he did, that his assassination plan had no relation to his anti-Castro contacts, and that he was associating with anti-Castro activists for some other unrelated reason. A variety of speculations are possible, but the committee was forced to acknowledge frankly that, despite its efforts, it was unable to reach firm conclusions as to the meaning or significance of the Odio incident to the President's assassination.

(1) *Oswald in New Orleans.*—Another contact by Lee

Harvey Oswald with anti-Castro Cuban activists that was not only documented, but also publicized at the time in the news media, occurred when he was living in New Orleans in the summer of 1963, an especially puzzling period in Oswald's life. His actions were blatantly pro-Castro, as he carried a one-man Fair Play for Cuba Committee crusade into the streets of a city whose Cuban population was predominantly anti-Castro. Yet Oswald's known and alleged associations even at this time included Cubans who were of an anti-Castro persuasion and their anti-Communist American supporters.

New Orleans was Oswald's home town; he was born there on October 18, 1939.[141] In April 1963, shortly after the Walker shooting, he moved back, having lived in Fort Worth and Dallas since his return from the Soviet Union the previous June.[142] He spent the first 2 weeks job hunting, staying with the Murrets, Lillian and Charles, or "Dutz," as he was called, the sister and brother-in-law of Oswald's mother, Marguerite.[143] After being hired by the Reily Coffee Co. as a maintenance man, he sent for his wife Marina and their baby daughter, who were still in Dallas, and they moved into an apartment on Magazine Street. [144]

In May, Oswald wrote to Vincent T. Lee, national director of the Fair Play for Cuba Committee, expressing a desire to open an FPCC chapter in New Orleans and requesting literature to distribute.[145] He also had handouts printed, some of which were stamped "L. H. Oswald, 4907 Magazine Street," others with the alias, "A. J. Hidell, P.O. Box 30016," still others listing the FPCC address as 544 Camp Street.[146]

In letters written earlier that summer and spring to the FPCC headquarters in New York, Oswald had indicated that he intended to rent an office.[147] In one letter he mentioned that he had acquired a space but had been told to vacate 3 days later because the building was to be remodeled. The Warren Commission failed to discover any record of Oswald's having rented an office at 544 Camp and concluded he had fabricated the story.[149]

In investigating Oswald after the assassination, the Secret Service learned that the New Orleans chapter of the Cuban Revolutionary Council (CRC), an anti-Castro organization, had occupied an office at 544 Camp Street for about 6 months during 1961–62.[150] At that time, Sergio Arcacha Smith was the official CRC delegate for the New

Orleans area.[151] Since the CRC had vacated the building 15 months before Oswald arrived in New Orleans, the Warren Commission concluded that there was no connection with Oswald.[152] Nevertheless, the riddle of 544 Camp Street persisted over the years.

Oswald lost his job at the Reily Coffee Co. in July, and his efforts to find another were futile.[153] Through the rest of the summer, he filed claims at the unemployment office.[154]

On August 5, Oswald initiated contact with Carlos Bringuier, a delegate of the Directorio Revolucionario Estudiantil (DRE).[155] According to his testimony before the Warren Commission, Bringuier was the only registered member of the group in New Orleans.[156] Bringuier also said he had two friends at the time, Celso Hernandez and Miguel Cruz, who were also active in the anti-Castro cause.[157] Oswald reportedly told Bringuier that he wished to join the DRE, offering money and assistance to train guerrillas.[158] Bringuier, fearful of an infiltration attempt by Castro sympathizers or the FBI, told Oswald to deal directly with DRE headquarters in Miami.[159] The next day, Oswald returned to Bringuier's store and left a copy of a Marine training manual with Rolando Pelaez, Bringuier's brother-in-law.[160]

On August 9, Bringuier learned that a man was carrying a pro-Castro sign and handing out literature on Canal Street. [161] Carrying his own anti-Castro sign, Bringuier, along with Hernandez and Cruz, set out to demonstrate against the pro-Castro sympathizer.[162] Bringuier recognized Oswald and began shouting that he was a traitor and a Communist.[163] A scuffle ensued, and police arrested all participants.[164] Oswald spent the night in jail. [165] On August 12, he pleaded guilty to disturbing the peace and was fined $10.[166] The anti-Castro Cubans were not charged.[167]

During the incident with Bringuier, Oswald also encountered Frank Bartes, the New Orleans delegate of the CRC from 1962–64.[168] After Bringuier and Oswald were arrested in the street scuffle, Bartes appeared in court with Bringuier.[169] According to Bartes, the news media surrounded Oswald for a statement after the hearing. [170] Bartes then engaged in an argument with the media and Oswald because the Cubans were not being given an opportunity to present their anti-Castro views.[171]

On August 16, Oswald was again seen distributing pro-

Castro literature.[172] A friend of Bringuier, Carlos Quiroga, brought one of Oswald's leaflets to Bringuier, and volunteered to visit Oswald and feign interest in the FPCC in order to determine Oswald's motives.[173[Quiroga met with Oswald for about an hour.[174] He learned that Oswald had a Russian wife and spoke Russian himself. Oswald gave Quiroga an application for membership in the FPCC chapter, but Quiroga noted he did not seem intent on actually enlisting members.[175]

Oswald's campaign received newspaper, television, and radio coverage.[176] William Stuckey, a reporter for radio station WDSU who had been following the FPCC, interviewed Oswald on August 17 and proposed a television debate between Oswald and Bringuier, to be held on August 21. [177] Bringuier issued a press release immediately after the debate, urging the citizens of New Orleans to write their Congressman demanding a congressional investigation of Lee Harvey Oswald.[178]

Oswald largely passed out of sight from August 21 until September 17, the day he applied for a tourist card to Mexico.[179] He is known to have written letters to left-wing political organizations, and he and Marina visited the Murrets on Labor Day.[180] Marina said her husband spent his free time reading books and practicing with his rifle.[181

(2) *Oswald in Clinton, La.*—While reports of some Oswald contacts with anti-Castro Cubans were known at the time of the 1964 investigation, allegations of additional Cuba-related associations surfaced in subsequent years. As an example, Oswald reportedly appeared in August–September 1963 in Clinton, La., where a voting rights demonstration was in progress. The reports of Oswald in Clinton were not, as far as the committee could determine, available to the Warren Commission, although one witness said he notified the FBI when he recognized Oswald from news photographs right after the assassination.[25][182] In fact, the Clinton sightings did not publicly surface until 1967, when they were introduced as evidence in the assassination investigation being conducted by New Orleans District Attorney Jim Garrison.[184] In that investigation, one suspect, David W. Ferrie, a staunch anti-Castro par-

[25]Reeves Morgan, a member of the Louisiana Legislature, testified he was called back by the FBI a few days later and asked what Oswald had been wearing. He said he was not contacted again. The FBI had no record of Morgan's call. [183]

tisan, died within days of having been named by Garrison; the other, Clay L. Shaw, was acquitted in 1969.[185] Aware that Garrison had been fairly criticized for questionable tactics, the committee proceeded cautiously, making sure to determine on its own the credibility of information coming from his probe. The committee found that the Clinton witnesses were credible and significant. They each were interviewed or deposed, or appeared before the committee in executive session. While there were points that could be raised to call into question their credibility, it was the judgment of the committee that they were telling the truth as they knew it.

There were six Clinton witnesses, among them a State representative, a deputy sheriff and a registrar of voters. [186] By synthesizing the testimony of all of them, since they each contributed to the overall account, the committee was able to piece together the following sequence of events.

Clinton, La., about 130 miles from New Orleans, is the county seat of East Feliciana Parish. In the late summer of 1963 it was targeted by the Congress of Racial Equality for a voting rights campaign.[187] Oswald first showed up in nearby Jackson, La., seeking employment at East Louisiana State Hospital, a mental institution.[188] Apparently on advice that his job would depend on his becoming a registered voter, Oswald went to Clinton for that purpose (although the committee could find no record that he was successful.[189]

In addition to the physical descriptions they gave that matched that of Oswald, other observations of the witnesses tended to substantiate their belief that he was, in fact, he man they saw. For example, he referred to himself as "Oswald," and he produced his Marine Corps discharge papers as identification.[190] Some of the witnesses said that Oswald was accompanied by two older men whom they identified as Ferrie and Shaw.[191] If the witnesses were not only truthful but accurate as well in their accounts, they established an association of an undetermined nature between Ferrie, Shaw and Oswald less than 3 months before the assassination.

(3) *David Ferrie.*—The Clinton witnesses were not the only ones who linked Oswald to Ferrie. On November 23, the day after the assassination, Jack S. Martin, a part-time private detective and police informant, told the office of the New Orleans District Attorney that a former Eastern Air-

lines pilot named David Ferrie might have aided Oswald in the assassination.[192] Martin had known Ferrie for over 2 years, beginning when he and Ferrie had performed some investigative work on a case involving an illegitimate religious order in Louisville, Ky. [193] Martin advised Assistant New Orleans District Attorney Herman Kohlman that he suspected Ferrie might have known Oswald for some time and that Ferrie might have once been Oswald's superior officer in a New Orleans unit of the Civil Air Patrol.[194] Martin made further allegations to the FBI on November 25.[195] He indicated he thought he saw a photograph of Oswald and other CAP members when he visited Ferrie's home and that Ferrie might have assisted Oswald in purchasing a foreign firearm.[196] Martin also informed the FBI that Ferrie had a history of arrests and that Ferrie was an amateur hypnotist, possibly capable of hypnotizing Oswald.[197]

The committee reviewed Ferrie's background. He had been fired by Eastern Airlines,[198] and in litigation over the dismissal, which continued through August 1963, he was counseled by a New Orleans attorney named G. Wray Gill.[199] Ferrie later stated that in March 1962, he and Gill made an agreement whereby Gill would represent Ferrie in his dismissal dispute in return for Ferrie's work as an investigator on other cases.[200] One of these cases involved deportation proceedings against Carlos Marcello, the head of the organized crime network in Louisiana and a client of Gill.[26][201] Ferrie also said he had entered into a similar agreement with Guy Banister, a former FBI agent (Special Agent-in-Charge in Chicago) who had opened a private detective agency in New Orleans.[203]

(4) *544 Camp Street*.—Banister's firm occupied an office in 1963 in the Newman Building at 531 Lafayette Street. [204] Another entrance to the building was at 544 Camp Street, the address Oswald had stamped on his Fair Play for Cuba Committee handouts.[205] During the summer of 1963, Ferrie frequented 544 Camp Street regu-

---

[26]The committee learned that Ferrie's associations with Marcello might have begun earlier. An unconfirmed U.S. Border Patrol report indicated that in February 1962, Ferrie piloted an airplane that returned Marcello to the United States following his ouster from the country by Federal agents in April 1961, as part of the Kennedy administration's crackdown on organized crime. Marcello denied to the committee in executive session that Ferrie flew him out of Latin America, saying that he flew commercial airlines. Records do not exist that can confirm or refute this contention. [202]

larly as a result of his working relationship with Banister.
[206]

Another occupant of the Newman Building was the Cuban Revolutionary Council, whose chief New Orleans delegate until 1962 was Sergio Arcacha Smith.[207] He was replaced by Luis Rabel who, in turn, was succeeded by Frank Bartes.[208] The committee interviewed or deposed all three CRC New Orleans delegates.[209] Arcacha said he never encountered Oswald and that he left New Orleans when he was relieved of his CRC position in early 1962. [210] Rabal said he held the post from January to October 1962, but that he likewise never knew or saw Oswald and that the only time he went to the Newman Building was to remove some office materials that Arcacha had left there. [211] Bartes said the only time he was in contact with Oswald was in their courtroom confrontation, that he ran the CRC chapter from an office in his home and that he never visited an office at either 544 Camp Street or 531 Lafayette Street.[212]

The committee, on the other hand, developed information that, in 1961, Banister, Ferrie, and Arcacha were working together in the anti-Castro cause. Banister, a fervent anti-Communist, was helping to establish Friends of Democratic Cuba as an adjunct to the New Orleans CRC chapter run by Arcacha in an office in the Newman Building.[213] Banister was also conducting background investigations of CRC members for Arcacha.[214] Ferrie, also strongly anti-Communist and anti-Castro, was associated with Arcacha (and probably Banister) in anti-Castro activism.[215]

On November 22, 1963, Ferrie had been in a Federal courtroom in New Orleans in connection with legal proceedings against Carlos Marcello.[27][216] That night he drove with two young friends, to Houston, Tex., then to Galveston on Saturday, November 23, and back to New Orleans on Sunday.[218] Before reaching New Orleans, he learned from a telephone conversation with G. Wray Gill that Martin had implicated him in the assassination.[219] Gill also told Ferrie about the rumors that he and Oswald had served together in the CAP and that Oswald supposedly had Ferrie's library card in his possession when he was arrested in Dallas.[220] When he got to his residence, Fer-

---

[27]With Ferrie's employer, G. Wray Gill, as his counsel, Marcello was successfully resisting an attempt by the Government to have him legally deported or convicted of a crime. [217]

rie did not go in, but sent in his place one of his companions on the trip, Alvin Beauboeuf.[221] Beauboeuf and Ferrie's roommate, Layton Martens, were detained by officers from the district attorney's office.[222] Ferrie drove to Hammond, La., and spent the night with a friend.[223]

On Monday, November 25, Ferrie turned himself in to the district attorney's office where he was arrested on suspicion of being involved in the assassination.[224] In subsequent interviews with New Orleans authorities, the FBI and the Secret Service, Ferrie denied ever having known Oswald or having ever been involved in the assassination. [225] He stated that in the days preceding November 22, he had been working intensively for Gill on the Marcello case.[226] Ferrie said he was in New Orleans on the morning of November 22, at which time Marcello was acquitted in Federal court of citizenship falsification.[227] He stated that he took the weekend trip to Texas for relaxation.[228] Ferrie acknowledged knowing Jack Martin, stating that Martin resented him for forcibly removing him from Gill's office earlier that year.[229]

The FBI and Secret Service investigation into the possibility that Ferrie and Oswald had been associated ended a few days later.[230] A Secret Service report concluded that the information provided by Jack Martin that Ferrie had been associated with Oswald and had trained him to fire a rifle was "without foundation."[231] The Secret Service report went on to state that on November 26, 1963, the FBI had informed the Secret Service that Martin had admitted that his information was a "figment of his imagination."[28][232] The investigation of Ferrie was subsequently closed for lack of evidence against him.[234]

(5) *A committee analysis of Oswald in New Orleans.*— The Warren commission had attempted to reconstruct a daily chronology of Oswald's activities in New Orleans during the summer of 1963, and the committee used it, as well as information arising from critics and the Garrison investigation, to select events and contacts that merited closer analysis. Among these were Oswald's confrontation with Carlos Bringuier and with Frank Bartes, his reported activities in Clinton, La., and his ties, if any, to Guy

---

[28]It appeared to the committee that the FBI overstated Martin's recantation in its information to the Secret Service. Martin had cautioned the FBI that he had no evidence to support his suspicions but that he believed they merited investigation. [233]

Banister, David Ferrie, Sergio Arcacha Smith and others who frequented the office building at 544 Camp Street.

The committee deposed Carlos Bringuier and interviewed or deposed several of his associates.[235.] It concluded that there had been no relationship between Oswald and Bringuier and the DRE with the exception of the confrontation over Oswald's distribution of pro-Castro literature. The committee was not able to determine why Oswald approached the anti-Castro Cubans, but it tended to concur with Bringuier and others in their belief that Oswald was seeking to infiltrate their ranks and obtain information about their activities.

As noted, the committee believed the Clinton witnesses to be telling the truth as they knew it. It was, therefore, inclined to believe that Oswald was in Clinton, La., in late August–early September 1963, and that he was in the company of David Ferrie, if not Clay Shaw. The committee was puzzled by Oswald's apparent association with Ferrie, a person whose anti-Castro sentiments were so distant from those of Oswald, the Fair Play for Cuba Committee campaigner. But the relationship with Ferrie may have been significant for more than its anti-Castro aspect, in light of Ferrie's connection with G. Wray Gill and Carlos Marcello.

The committee also found that there was at least a possibility that Oswald and Guy Banister were acquainted. The following facts were considered:

The 544 Camp Street address stamped on Oswald's FPCC handouts was that of the building where Banister had his office;

Ross Banister told the committee that his brother had seen Oswald handing out FPCC literature during the summer of 1963;[263]and

Banister's secretary, Delphine Roberts, told the committee she saw Oswald in Banister's office on several occasions, the first being when he was interviewed for a job during the summer of 1963.[29][237]

The committee learned that Banister left extensive files when he died in 1964.[238] Later that year, they were purchased by the Louisiana State Police from Banister's widow.[239] According to Joseph Cambre of the State

---

[29]The committee did not credit the Roberts' testimony standing alone. It came late in the investigation and without corroboration or independent substantiation, and much of Roberts' other testimony lacked credibility.

police, Oswald's name was not the subject of any file, but it was included in a file for the Fair Play for Cuba Committee.[240] Cambre said the FPCC file contained newspaper clippings and a transcript of a radio program on which Oswald had appeared.[241] The committee was not able to review Banister's files, since they had been destroyed pursuant to an order of the superintendent of Louisiana State Police that all files not part of the public record or pertinent to ongoing criminal investigations be burned.[242]

Additional evidence that Oswald may have been associated or acquainted with Ferrie and Banister was provided by the testimony of Adrian Alba, proprietor of the Crescent City Garage which was next door to the Reily Coffee Co. where Oswald had worked for a couple of months in 1963. (The garage and the coffee company were both located less than a block from 544 Camp Street.) Although Alba's testimony on some points was questionable, he undoubtedly did know Oswald who frequently visited his garage, and the committee found no reason to question his statement that he had often seen Oswald in Mancuso's Restaurant on the first floor of 544 Camp.[243] Ferrie and Banister also were frequent customers at Mancuso's.[244]

(6) *Summary of the evidence.*—In sum, the committee did not believe that an anti-Castro organization was involved in a conspiracy to assassinate President Kennedy. Even though the committee's investigation did reveal that in 1964 the FBI failed to pursue intelligence reports of possible anti-Castro involvement as vigorously as it might have, the committee found it significant that it discovered no information in U.S. intelligence agency files that would implicate anti-Castroites. Contact between the intelligence community and the anti-Castro movement was close, so it is logical to suppose that some trace of group involvement would have been detected had it existed.

The committee also thought it significant that it received no information from the Cuban Government that would implicate anti-Castroites. The Cubans had dependable information sources in the exile communities in Miami, New Orleans, Dallas and other U.S. cities, so there is high probability that Cuban intelligence would have been aware of any group involvement by the exiles. Following the assassination, the Cuban Government would have had the highest incentive to report participation by anti-Castroites, had it existed to its knowledge, since it would have dispelled suspicions of pro-Castro Cuban involvement. The committee was impressed with the cooperation it received from the Cuban Government, and while it acknowledged this cooperation might not have been forthcoming in 1964, it concluded that, had such information existed in 1978, it would have been supplied by Cuban officials.

On the other hand, the committee noted that it was unable to preclude from its investigation the possibility that individuals with anti-Castro leanings might have been involved in the assassination. The committee candidly acknowledged, for example, that it could not explain Oswald's associations—nor at this late date fully determine their extent—with anti-Castro Cubans. The committee remained convinced that since Oswald consistently demonstrated a left-wing Marxist ideology, he would not have supported the anti-Castro movement. At the same time, the committee noted that Oswald's possible association with Ferrie might be distinguishable, since it could not be simply termed an anti-Castro association. Ferrie and Oswald may have had a personal friendship unrelated to Cuban activities. Ferrie was not Cuban, and though he actively supported the anti-Castro cause, he had other interests. For one, he was employed by Carlos Marcello as an investigator.[245] (It has been alleged that Ferrie operated a service station in 1964, the franchise for which was reportedly paid by Marcello.) [246] The committee concluded, therefore, that Oswald's most significant apparent anti-Castro association, that with David Ferrie, might in fact not have been related to the Cuban issue.

In the end, the committee concluded that the evidence was sufficient to support the conclusion that anti-Castro Cuban groups, as groups, were not involved in the assassination, but it could not preclude the possibility that individual members may have been involved.

4. THE COMMITTEE BELIEVES, ON THE BASIS OF THE EVIDENCE AVAILABLE TO IT, THAT THE NATIONAL SYNDICATE OF ORGANIZED CRIME, AS A GROUP, WAS NOT INVOLVED IN THE ASSASSINATION OF PRESIDENT KENNEDY, BUT THAT THE AVAILABLE EVIDENCE DOES NOT PRECLUDE THE POSSIBILITY THAT INDIVIDUAL MEMBERS MAY HAVE BEEN INVOLVED

Lee Harvey Oswald was fatally shot by Jack Ruby at 11:21 a.m. on Sunday, November 24, 1963, less than 48 hours after President Kennedy was assassinated. While many Americans were prepared to believe that Oswald had acted alone in shooting the President, they found their credulity strained when they were asked to accept a conclusion that Ruby, too, had not acted as part of a plot. As the Warren Commission observed,

> * * * almost immediately speculation arose that Ruby had acted on behalf of members of a conspiracy who had planned the killing of President Kennedy and wanted to silence Oswald.[1].

The implications of the murder of Oswald are crucial to an understanding of the assassination of itself. Several of the logical possibilities should be explicit:

> Oswald was a member of a conspiracy, and he was killed by Ruby, also a conspirator, so that he would not reveal the plot.

> Oswald was a member of a conspiracy, yet Ruby acted alone, as he explained, for personal reasons.

> Oswald was not a member of a conspiracy as far as Ruby knew, but his murder was an act planned by Ruby and others to take justice into their own hands.

> Both Oswald and Ruby acted alone or with the assistance of only one or two confederates, but there was no wider conspiracy, one that extended beyond the immediate participants.

If it is determined that Ruby acted alone, it does not necessarily follow that there was no conspiracy to murder the President. But if Ruby was part of a sophisticated plot to murder Oswald, there would be troublesome implications with respect to the assassination of the President. While it is possible to develop an acceptable rationale of why a group might want to kill the President's accused assassin, even though its members were not in fact involved in the assassination, it is difficult to make the explanation sound convincing. There is a possibility, for example, that a Dallas citizen or groups of citizens planned the murder of Oswald by Ruby to revenge the murders of President Kennedy or Patrolman J. D. Tippit, or both. Nevertheless, the brief period of time between the two murders, during which the vengeful plotters would have had to formulate and execute Oswald's murder, would seem to indicate the improbability of such an explanation. A pre-existing group might have taken action within 48 hours, but it is doubtful that a group could have planned and then carried out Oswald's murder in such a short period of time.

(a) The Warren Commission investigation

The Warren Commission looked at Ruby's conduct and associations from November 21 through November 24 to determine if they reflected a conspiratorial relationship with Oswald.[2] It found no "* * * grounds for believing that Ruby's killing of Oswald was part of a conspiracy."[3] It accepted as true his explanation that his conduct reflected "genuine shock and grief" and strong affection for President Kennedy and his family.[4] As for numerous phone contacts Ruby had with underworld figures in the weeks preceding the assassination, the Commission believed his explanation that they had to do with his troubles with the American Guild of Variety Artists, rather than reflecting any sinister associations that might have been related to the President's assassination.[5]

The Commission also found no evidence that Ruby and Oswald had ever been acquainted, although the Commission acknowledged that they both lived in the Oak Cliff section of Dallas, had post office boxes at the terminal annex, and had possible but tenuous third party links. These included Oswald's landlady, Earlene Roberts, whose sister, Bertha Cheek, had visited Ruby at his nightclub on November 18,[6] and a fellow boarder at Oswald's roominghouse, John Carter, who was friendly with a close friend and employee of Ruby, Wanda Killam.[7]

The Commission also looked to Ruby's ties to other individuals or groups that might have obviated the need for direct contact with Oswald near the time of the assassination. Ruby was found not to be linked to pro- or anti-Castro Cuban groups;[8] he was also found not to be linked to "illegal activities with members of the organized underworld."[9] The Commission noted that Ruby "disclaimed that he was associated with organized criminal activities," and it did not find reason to disbelieve him. [10] The evidence "fell short" of demonstrating that Ruby "was significantly affiliated with organized crime."[11] He was, at worst, "familiar, if not friendly" with some criminal elements, but he was not a participant in "organized criminal activity."[12] Consequently, the Commission concluded that "the evidence does not establish a significant

179

link between Ruby and organized crime."[13] And in its central conclusion about Jack Ruby, the Commission stated that its investigation had "yielded no evidence that Ruby conspired with anyone in planning or executing the killing of Lee Harvey Oswald."[14] For the Warren Commission, therefore, Ruby's killing of Oswald had no implications for Oswald's killing of the President.

(b) The committee investigation

Like the Warren Commission, the committee was deeply troubled by the circumstances surrounding the murder of the President's accused assassin. It, too, focused its attention on Jack Ruby, his family and his associates. Its investigation, however, was not limited to Ruby, Oswald and their immediate world. The committee's attention was also directed to organized crime and those major figures in it who might have been involved in a conspiracy to kill the President because of the Kennedy administration's unprecedented crackdown on them and their illicit activities.

(1) *Ruby and organized crime*.—The committee, as did the Warren Commission, recognized that a primary reason to suspect organized crime of possible involvement in the assassination was Ruby's killing of Oswald. For this reason, the committee undertook an extensive investigation of Ruby and his relatives, friends and associates to determine if there was evidence that Ruby was involved in crime, organized or otherwise, such as gambling and vice, and if such involvement might have been related to the murder of Oswald.

The evidence available to the committee indicated that Ruby was not a "member" of organized crime in Dallas or elsewhere, although it showed that he had a significant number of associations and direct and indirect contacts with underworld figures, a number of whom were connected to the most powerful La Cosa Nostra leaders. Additionally, Ruby had numerous associations with the Dallas criminal element.

The committee examined the circumstances of a well-known episode in organized crime history in which representatives of the Chicago Mafia attempted in, 1947, a move into Dallas, facilitated by the bribery of members of the Dallas sheriff's office.[15] The Kefauver committee of the

U.S. Senate, during its extensive probe of organized crime in the early 1950's, termed this attempt by the Chicago syndicate to buy protection from the Dallas authorities an extraordinary event, one of the more brazen efforts made during that postwar period of criminal expansion.

In the years since the assassination, there had been allegations that Ruby was involved in organized crime's 1947 attempt to move into Dallas, perhaps as a frontman for the Chicago racketeers.[16] During discussions of the bribe offer, Dallas Sheriff Steve Guthrie secretly taped conversations in which the Chicago mob representative outlined plans for its Dallas operation.[17] They spoke of establishing a nightclub as a front for illegal gambling. It happens that Ruby moved from Chicago to Dallas in 1947 and began operating a number of night-clubs.[18] While the FBI and the Warren Commission were aware in 1964 of the alleged links between Ruby and those involved in the bribery attempt, a thorough investigation of the charges was not undertaken.[19]

The committee frankly realized that because this incident occurred 32 years in the past, it would be difficult, if not impossible, to answer all the allegations fully and finally. Nevertheless, the committee was able to develop substantial evidence from tape recordings made by the sheriff's office, detailed law enforcement documents and the testimony of knowledgeable witnesses.

As a result, the committee concluded that while Ruby and members of his family were acquainted with individuals who were involved in the incident, including Chicago gangsters who had moved to Dallas, and while Ruby may have wished to participate, there was no solid evidence that he was, in fact, part of the Chicago group. [20] There was also no evidence available that Ruby was to have been involved in the proposed gambling operation had the bribery attempt been successful, or that Ruby came to Dallas for that purpose.[21]

The committee found it reasonable to assume that had Ruby been involved in any significant way, he would probably have been referred to either the tape recordings or the documentation relating to the incident, but a review of that available evidence failed to disclose any reference to Ruby.[22] The committee, however, was not able to interview former Sheriff Guthrie, the subject of the bribery attempt and the one witness who maintained to the FBI in 1963–64 that Ruby was significantly involved in the Chicago syndicate plan.[1][23]

The committee also examined allegations that, even before the 1947 move to Dallas, Ruby had been personally acquainted with two professional killers for the organized crime syndicate in Chicago, David Yaras and Lenny Patrick.[25] The committee established that Ruby, Yaras and Patrick were in fact acquainted during Ruby's years in Chicago, particularly in the 1930's and 1940's.[26] Both Yaras and Patrick admitted, when questioned by the FBI in 1964, that they did know Ruby, but both said that they had not had any contact with him for 10 to 15 years.[27] Yaras and Patrick further maintained they had never been particularly close to Ruby, had never visited him in Dallas and had no knowledge of Ruby being connected to organized crime. [28] Indeed, the Warren Commission used Patrick's statement as a footnote citation in its report to support its conclusion that Ruby did not have significant syndicate associations.[29]

On the other hand, the committee established that Yaras and Patrick were, in fact, notorious gunmen, having been identified by law enforcement authorities as executioners for the Chicago mob[30] and closely associated with Sam Giancana, the organized crime leader in Chicago who was murdered in 1975. Yaras and Patrick are believed to have been responsible for numerous syndicate executions, including the murder of James Ragan, a gambling wire service owner.[31] The evidence implicating Yaras and Patrick in syndicate activities is unusually reliable.[32] Yaras, for example, was overheard in a 1962 electronic surveillance discussing various underworld murder contracts he had carried out and one he had only recently been assigned. While the committee found no evidence that Ruby was associated with Yaras or Patrick during the 1950's or 1960's,[33] it concluded that Ruby had probably talked by telephone to Patrick during the summer of 1963.[34]

---

[1]With reference to Guthrie's claim that Ruby's name had been mentioned frequently in the discussions with Chicago underworld representatives, the committee's review of the tape recordings failed to disclose such references. Portions of the tapes were unintelligible and two entire recordings were discovered by investigators in 1964 to be missing, so the evidence was not conclusive.[24]

While Ruby apparently did not participate in the organized crime move to Dallas in 1947, he did establish himself as a Dallas nightclub operator around that time. His first club was the Silver Spur, which featured country and western entertainment. Then he operated the Sovereign, a private club that failed and was converted into the Carousel Club, a burlesque house with striptease acts. Ruby, an extroverted individual, acquired numerous friends and contacts in and around Dallas, some of whom had syndicate ties.

Included among Ruby's closest friends was Lewis McWillie. McWillie moved from Dallas to Cuba in 1958 and worked in gambling casinos in Havana until 1960.[35] In 1978, McWillie was employed in Las Vegas, and law enforcement files indicate he had business and personal ties to major organized crime figures, including Meyer Lansky and Santos Trafficante.[36]

Ruby traveled to Cuba on at least one occasion to visit McWillie.[37] McWillie testified to the committee that Ruby visited him only once in Cuba, and that it was a social visit.[38] The Warren Commission concluded this was the only trip Ruby took to Cuba,[39] despite documentation in the Commission's own files indicating Ruby made a second trip.[40]

Both Ruby and McWillie claimed that Ruby's visit to Cuba was at McWillie's invitation and lasted about a week in the late summer or early fall of 1959.[41] The committee, however, obtained tourist cards from the Cuban Government that show Ruby entered Cuba on August 8, 1959, left on September 11, reentered on September 12 and left again on September 13, 1959.[42] These documents supplement records the committee obtained from the Immigration and Naturalization Service (INS) indicating that Ruby left Cuba on September 11, 1959, traveling to Miami, returned to Cuba on September 12, and traveled on to New Orleans on September 13, 1959.[43] The Cuban Government could not state with certainty that the commercial airline flights indicated by the INS records were the only ones Ruby took during the period.[44]

Other records obtained by the committee indicate that Ruby was in Dallas at times during the August 8 to September 11, 1959, period.[45] He apparently visited his safe deposit box on August 21, met with FBI Agent

Charles W. Flynn on August 31,[2] and returned to the safe deposit box on September 4.[47] Consequently, if the tourist card documentation, INS, FBI and bank records are all correct, Ruby had to have made at least three trips to Cuba. While the records appeared to be accurate, they were incomplete. The committee was unable to determine, for example, whether on the third trip, if it occurred, Ruby traveled by commercial airline or some other means. Consequently, the committee could not rule out the possibility that Ruby made more trips during this period or at other times.

Based on the usual nature of the 1-day trip to Miami from Havana on September 11–12 and the possibility of at least one additional trip to Cuba, the committee concluded that vacationing was probably not the purpose for traveling to Havana, despite Ruby's insistence to the Warren Commission that his one trip to Cuba in 1959 was a social visit.[48] The committee reached the judgment that Ruby most likely was serving as a courier for gambling interests when he traveled to Miami from Havana for 1 day, then returned to Cuba for a day, before flying to New Orleans.[49] This judgment is supported by the following:

    McWillie had made previous trips to Miami on behalf of the owners of the Tropicana, the casino for which he worked, to deposit funds;[50]

    McWillie placed a call to Meyer Panitz, a gambling associate in Miami, to inform him that Ruby was coming from Cuba, resulting in two meetings between Panitz and Ruby;[51]

    There was a continuing need for Havana casino operators to send their assets out of Cuba to protect them from seizure by the Castro government;[52]

    The 1-day trip from Havana to Miami was not explained by Ruby, and his testimony to the Warren Commission about his travels to Cuba was contradictory.[53]

The committee also deemed it likely that Ruby at least met various organized crime figures in Cuba, pos-

---

[2]In March 1959, Ruby told the FBI he wished to assist the Bureau by supplying on a confidential basis criminal information that had come to his attention. Between April and October 1959, Ruby met with Agent Flynn eight times and gave him a small bit of information about thefts and related offenses. On November 6, 1959, Flynn wrote that Ruby's information had not been particularly helpful, that further attempts to develop Ruby as a PCI (potential criminal informant) would be fruitless and that the file on Ruby should be closed. [46]

sibly including some who been detained by the Cuban government.[54] In fact, Ruby told the Warren Commission that he was later visited in Dallas by McWillie and a Havana casino owner and that they had discussed the gambling business in Cuba.[3][55]

As noted by the Warren Commission, an exporter named Robert McKeown alleged that Ruby offered in 1959 to purchase a letter of introduction to Fidel Castro in hopes of securing the release of three individuals being held in a Cuban prison.[57] McKeown also claimed Ruby contacted him about a sale of jeeps to Cuba.[4][58] If McKeown's allegations were accurate, they would support a judgment that Ruby's travels to Cuba were not merely for a vacation. (The committee was unable to confirm or refute McKeown's allegations. In his appearance before the committee in executive session, however, McKeown's story did not seem to be credible, based on the committee's assessment of his demeanor.)[61]

It has been charged that Ruby met with Santos Trafficante in Cuba sometime in 1959.[62] Trafficante, regarded as one of the nation's most powerful organized crime figures, was to become a key participant in Castro assassination attempts by the Mafia and the CIA from 1960 to 1963.[63] The committee developed circumstantial evidence that makes a meeting between Ruby and Trafficante a distinct possibility,[64] but the evidence was not sufficent to form a final conclusion as to whether or not such a meeting took place.

While allegations of a Ruby link to Trafficante had previously been raised, mainly due to McWillie's alleged close connections to the Mafia leader, it was not until recent years that they received serious attention. Trafficante had long been recognized by law enforcement officials as a leading member of the La Cosa Nostra, but he did not become the object of significant public attention in connection with the assassination of the President until his participation in the assassination plots against Castro was disclosed in 1975.

---

[3]Earlier, though both he and McWillie denied it, Ruby apparently sent a coded message to McWillie in Havana, containing various sets of numerals, a communication Ruby transmitted to McWillie via McWillie's girlfriend. [56]

[4]Ruby denied this to the Warren Commission, stating he did not have sufficient contacts to obtain jeeps at the time.[59] The Warren Commission noted that Ruby "made preliminary inquiries, as a middleman" in regard to the possible sale of jeeps to Cuba, but stated that he "was merely pursuing a moneymaking opportunity."[60]

In 1976, in response to a freedom of information suit, the CIA declassified a State Department cablegram received from London on November 28, 1963. It read:

On 26 November 1963, a British journalist named John Wilson, and also known as Wilson-Hudson, gave information to the American Embassy in London which indicated that an "American gangster-type named Ruby" visited Cuba around 1959. Wilson himself was working in Cuba at that time and was jailed by Castro before he was deported.

In prison in Cuba, Wilson says he met an American gangster-gambler named Santos who could not return to the U.S.A. * * * Instead he preferred to live in relative luxury in a Cuban prison. While Santos was in prison, Wilson says, Santos was visited frequently by an American gangster type named Ruby.[65]

Several days after the CIA had received the information, the Agency noted that there were reports that Wilson-Hudson was a "psychopath" and unreliable. The Agency did not conduct an investigation of the information, and the Warren Commission was apparently not informed of the cablegram. The former staff counsel who directed the Commission's somewhat limited investigation of organized crime told the committee that since the Commission was never told of the CIA's use of the Mafia to try to assassinate Castro from 1960 to 1963, he was not familiar with the name Santos Trafficante in 1964.[66]

The committee was unable to locate John Wilson-Hudson. (According to reports, he had died.) Nor was the committee able to obtain independent confirmation of the Wilson-Hudson allegation. The committee was able, however, to develop corroborative information to the effect that Wilson-Hudson was incarcerated at the same detention camp in Cuba as Trafficante.[67]

On June 6, 1959, Trafficante and others who controlled extensive gambling interests in Cuba were detained as part of a Castro government policy that would subsequently lead to the confiscation of all underworld holdings in Cuba.[68] They were held in Trescornia, a minimum security detention camp.[69] According to documentation supplied by the Cuban Government, Trafficante was released from Trescornia on August 18, 1959.[70] Tourist card documentation, also obtained by the committee, as well as various Warren Commission documents, indicate Ruby's first trip to Cuba began on August 8, 1959.[71] Thus, Ruby was in Cuba during part of the final days of Trafficate's detention at Trescornia.[72]

McWillie testified before the committee that he had visited another detainee at Trescornia during that period, and he recalled possibly seeing Trafficante there. McWillie claimed, however, he did not say more than "hello" to him.[73] McWillie further testified it was during that period that Ruby visited him in Havana for about a week, and that Ruby tagged along with him during much of his stay.[74] McWillie told the committee that Ruby could have gone with him to visit Trescornia, although he doubted that Ruby did so.[75] McWillie testified that he could not clearly recall much about Ruby's visit.[76]

Jose Verdacia Verdacia, a witness made available for a committee interview by the Cuban Government, was the warden at Trescornia in August 1959.[77] Verdacia told the committee that he could not recall the name John Wilson-Hudson, but he could remember a British journalist who had worked in Argentina, as had Wilson-Hudson, who was detained at Trescornia.[78]

In his own public testimony before the committee, Trafficante testified that he did not remember Ruby ever having visited him at Trescornia. Trafficante stated,

There was no reason for this man to visit me. I have never seen this man before. I have never been to Dallas, I never had no contact with him. I don't see why he was going to come and visit me.[79]

Trafficante did, however, testify that he could recall an individual fitting British journalist John Wilson-Hudson's description, and he stated that the man was among those who were held in his section at Trescornia.[80]

The importance of a Ruby-Trafficante meeting in Trescornia should not be overemphasized. The most it would show would be a meeting, at that a brief one. No one has suggested that President Kennedy's assassination was planned at Trescornia in 1959. At the same time, a meeting or an association, even minor, between Ruby and Trafficante would not have been necessary for Ruby to have been used by Trafficante to murder Oswald.[81] Indeed, it is likely that such a direct contact would have been avoided by Trafficante if there had been a plan to execute either the President or the President's assassin, but, since no such plot could have been under consideration in 1959, there would not have been a particular necessity for Trafficante to avoid contact with Ruby in Cuba.

The committee investigated other aspects of Ruby's activities that might have shown an association with organized crime figures. An extensive computer analysis of his telephone toll records for the month prior to the President's assassination revealed that he either placed calls to or received calls from a number of individuals who may be fairly characterized as having been affiliated, directly or indirectly, with organized crime.[82] These included Irwin Weiner, a Chicago bondsman well-known as a frontman for organized crime and the Teamsters Union;[83] Robert "Barney" Baker, a lieutenant of James R. Hoffa and associate of several convicted organized crime executioners; [84] Nofio J. Pecora, a lieutenant of Carlos Marcello, the Mafia boss in Louisiana;[85] Harold Tannenbaum, a New Orleans French Quarter nightclub manager who lived in a trailer park owned by Pecora;[86] McWillie, the Havana gambler;[87] and Murray "Dusty" Miller, a Teamster deputy of Hoffa and associate of various underworld figures. [88] Additionally, the committee concluded that Ruby was also probably in telephonic contact with Mafia executioner Lenny Patrick sometime during the summer of 1963.[89] Although no such call was indicated in the available Ruby telephone records, Ruby's sister, Eva Grant, told the Warren Commission that Ruby had spoken more than once of having contacted Patrick by telephone during that period.[90]

The committee found that the evidence surrounding the calls was generally consistent—at least as to the times of their occurrence—with the explanation that they were for the purpose of seeking assistance in a labor dispute.[91] Ruby, as the operator of two nightclubs, the Carousel and the Vegas, had to deal with the American Guild of Variety Artists (AGVA), an entertainers union.[92]. Ruby did in fact have a history of labor problems involving his striptease performers, and there was an ongoing dispute in the early 1960's regarding amateur performers in Dallas area nightclubs.[93] Testimony to the committee supported

188

the conclusion that Ruby's phone calls were, by and large, related to his labor troubles.[94] In light of the identity of some of the individuals, however, the possibility of other matters being discussed could not be dismissed.[95]

In particular, the committee was not satisfied with the explanations of three individuals closely associated with organized crime who received telephone calls from Ruby in October or November 1963.[96]

Weiner, the Chicago bondsman, refused to discuss his call from Ruby on October 26, 1963, with the FBI in 1964, [97] and he told a reporter in 1978 that the call had nothing to do with labor problems.[98] In his executive session testimony before the committee, however, Weiner stated that he had lied to the reporter, and he claimed that he and Ruby had, in fact, discussed a labor dispute.[99] The committee was not satisfied with Weiner's explanation of his relationship with Ruby. Weiner suggested Ruby was seeking a bond necessary to obtain an injunction in his labor troubles, yet the committee could find no other creditable indication that Ruby contemplated seeking court relief, nor any other explanation for his having to go to Chicago for such a bond.[100]

Barney Baker told the FBI in 1964 that he had received only one telephone call from Ruby (on Nov. 7, 1963) during which he had curtly dismissed Ruby's plea for assistance in a nightclub labor dispute.[101] The committee established, however, that Baker received a second lengthy call from Ruby on November 8.[102] The committee found it hard to believe that Baker, who denied the conversation ever took place, could have forgotten it. [103]

The committee was also dissatisfied with the explanation of a call Ruby made on October 30, 1963, to the New Orleans trailer park office of Nofio J. Pecora, the long-time Marcello lieutenant.[104] Pecora told the committee that only he would have answered his phone and that he never spoke with Ruby or took a message from him.[105] The committee considered the possibility that the call was actually for Harold Tannenbaum, a mutual friend of Ruby and Pecora who lived in the trailer park, although Pecora denied he would have relayed such a message.[106]

Additionally, the committee found it difficult to dismiss certain Ruby associations with the explanation that they were solely related to his labor problems. For example, James Henry Dolan, a Dallas AGVA representative, was reportedly an acquaintance of both Carlos Marcello and Santos Trafficante.[107] While Dolan worked with Ruby on labor matters, they were also allegedly associated in other dealings, including a strong-arm attempt to appropriate the proceeds of a one-night performance of a stage review at the Adolphus Hotel in Dallas called "Bottoms Up." [108] The FBI, moreover, has identified Dolan as an associate of Nofio Pecora.[109] The committee noted further that reported links between AGVA and organized crime figures have been the subject of Federal and State investigations that have been underway for years.[5] [110] The committee's difficulties in separating Ruby's AGVA contacts from his organized crime connections was, in large degree, based on the dual roles that many of his associates played.[6]

In assessing the significance of these Ruby contacts, the committee noted, first of all, that they should have been more thoroughly explored in 1964 when memories were clearer and related records (including, but not limited to additional telephone toll records) were available. Further, while there may be persuasive arguments against the likelihood that the attack on Oswald would have been planned in advance on the telephone with an individual like Ruby, the pattern of contacts did show that individuals who had the motive to kill the President also had knowledge of a man who could be used to get access to Oswald in the custody of the Dallas police. In Ruby, they also had knowledge of a man who had exhibited a violent nature and who was in serious financial trouble. The calls, in short, established knowledge and possible availability, if not actual planning.

(2) *Ruby and the Dallas Police Department.*—The committee also investigated the relationship between Ruby and the Dallas Police Department to determine whether members of the department might have helped Ruby get access to Oswald for the purpose of shooting him.[111] Ruby had a friendly and somewhat unusual relationship with the Dallas Police Department, both collectively and with individual officers, but the committee found little evidence of any significant influence by Ruby within the force

---

[5]According to FBI records, AGVA has been used frequently by members of organized crime as a front for criminal activities.

[6]Although it was dissatisfied with the explanations it received for these calls, the committee also noted that the individuals called may have been reluctant to admit that Ruby was seeking their assistance in an illegal effort to settle his labor problems.

that permitted him to engage in illicit activities.[112] Nevertheless, Ruby's close relationship with one or more members of the police force may have been a factor in his entry to the police basement on November 24, 1963.[113]

Both the Warren Commission and a Dallas Police Department investigative unit concluded that Ruby entered the police basement on November 24, 1963, between 11:17 a.m., when he apparently sent a telegram, and 11:21, when he shot Oswald, via the building's Main Street ramp as a police vehicle was exiting, thereby fortuitously creating a momentary distraction.[114] The committee, however, found that Ruby probably did not come down the ramp,[115] and that his most likely route was an alleyway located next to the Dallas Municipal Building and a stairway leading to the basement garage of police headquarters. [116]

The conclusion reached by the Warren Commission that Ruby entered the police basement via the ramp was refuted by the eyewitness testimony of every witness in the relevant area, only Ruby himself excepted.[117] It was also difficult for the committee to reconcile the ramp route with the 55-second interval (derived from viewings of the video tapes of the Oswald murder) from the moment the police vehicle started up the ramp and the moment Ruby shot Oswald.[118] Ruby would have had to come down the ramp after the vehicle went up, leaving him less than 55 seconds to get down the ramp and kill Oswald. Even though the Warren Commission and the Dallas police investigative unit were aware of substantial testimony contradicting the ramp theory,[119] they arrived at their respective conlusions by relying heavily on Ruby's own assertions and what they perceived to be the absence of a plausible alternative route.[120]

The committee's conclusion that Ruby entered from the alley was supported by the fact that it was much less conspicuous than the alternatives,[121] by the lack of security in the garage area and along the entire route,[122] and by the testimony concerning the security of the doors along the alley and stairway route.[123] This route would also have accommodated the 4-minute interval from Ruby's departure from a Western Union office near police headquarters at 11:17 a.m. to the moment of the shooting at 11:21.[124]

Based on a review of the evidence, albeit circumstantial, the committee believed that Ruby's shooting of Oswald was not a spontaneous act, in that it involved at least some premeditation.[125] Similarly, the committee believed that it was less likely that Ruby entered the police basement without assistance, even though the assistance may have been provided with no knowledge of Ruby's intentions. The assistance may have been in the form of information about plans for Oswald's transfer or aid in entering the building or both.[7][126]

The committee found several circumstances significant in its evaluation of Ruby's conduct. It considered in particular the selectively recalled and self-serving statements in Ruby's narration of the events of the entire November 22–24 weekend in arriving at its conclusions. [127] It also considered certain conditions and events. The committee was troubled by the apparently unlocked doors along the stairway route and the removal of security guards from the area of the garage nearest the stairway shortly before the shooting;[128] by a Saturday night telephone call from Ruby to his closest friend, Ralph Paul, in which Paul responded to something Ruby said by asking him if he was crazy;[129] and by the actions and statements of several Dallas police officers, particularly those present when Ruby was initially interrogated about the shooting of Oswald.[130]

There is also evidence that the Dallas Police Department withheld relevant information from the Warren Commission concerning Ruby's entry to the scene of the Oswald transfer.[131] For example, the fact that a polygraph test had been given to Sergeant Patrick Dean in 1964 was never revealed to the Commission, even though Dean was responsible for basement security and was the first person to whom Ruby explained how he had entered the basement.[132] Dean indicated to the committee that he had "failed" the test, but the committee was unable to locate a copy of the actual questions, responses and results.[133]

(3) *Other evidence relating to Ruby.*—The committee noted that other Ruby activities and movements during the period immediately following the assassination—on November 22 and 23—raised disturbing questions. For example, Ruby's first encounter with Oswald occurred over 36 hours before he shot him. Ruby was standing within a

---

[7]While the Warren Commission did not make reference to it in its report, Ruby refused in his first interviews with the FBI, Secret Service and the Dallas police to indicate how he entered the basement or whether anyone had assisted him. In later interviews, Ruby stated he had walked down the ramp.

few feet of Oswald as he was being moved from one part of police headquarters to another just before midnight on November 22.[134] Ruby testified that he had no trouble entering the building, and the committee found no evidence contradicting his story. The committee was disturbed, however, by Ruby's easy access to headquarters and by his inconsistent accounts of his carrying a pistol. In an FBI interview on December 2, 1963, he said he had the pistol during the encounter with Oswald late in the evening of November 22. But when questioned about it by the Warren Commission, Ruby replied, "I will be honest with you. I lied about it. It isn't so, I didn't have a gun."[135] Finally, the committee was troubled by reported sightings of Ruby on Saturday, November 23, at Dallas police headquarters and at the county jail at a time when Oswald's transfer to the county facility had originally been scheduled. These sightings, along with the one on Friday night, could indicate that Ruby was pursuing Oswald's movements throughout the weekend.

The committee also questioned Ruby's self-professed motive for killing Oswald, his story to the Warren Comission and other authorities that he did it out of sorrow over the assassination and sympathy for the President's widow and children. Ruby consistently claimed there had been no other motive and that no one had influenced his act. [136] A handwritten note by Ruby, disclosed in 1967, however, exposed Ruby's explanation for the Oswald slaying as a fabricated legal ploy.[137] Addressed to his attorney. Joseph Tonahill, it told of advice Ruby had received from his first lawyer, Tom Howard, in 1963: "Joe, you should know this. Tom Howard told me to say that I shot Oswald so that Caroline and Mrs. Kennedy wouldn't have to come to Dallas to testify. OK?" [137]

The committee examined a report that Ruby was at Parkland Hospital shortly after the fatally wounded President had been brought there on November 22, 1963. Seth Kantor, a newsman then employed by Scripps-Howard who had known Ruby, later testified to the Warren Commission that he had run into him at Parkland and spoken with him briefly shortly before the President's death was announced.[139] While the Warren Commission concluded that Kantor was mistaken,[140] the committee determined he probably was not. The committee was impressed by the opinion of Burt W. Griffin, the Warren Commission counsel who directed the Ruby investigation and wrote the Ruby section of the Warren report. Griffith told the committee he had come to believe, in light of evidence subsequently brought out, that the Commission's conclusion about Kantor's testimony was wrong.[141]

Subsequent to Ruby's apprehension, he was given a polygraph examination by the FBI in which he denied that he had been involved with any other person in killing Oswald, or had been involved in any way in the assassination of President Kennedy.[142] The Warren Commission stated it did not rely on this examination in drawing conclusions, although it did publish a transcript of the examination.[143] The FBI in 1964 also expressed dissatisfaction with the test,[144] based on the circumstances surrounding its administration. A panel of polygraph experts reviewed the examination for the committee and concluded that it was not validly conducted or interpreted. [145] Because there were numerous procedural errors made during the test, the committee's panel was unable to interpret the examination.[146]

Finally, the committee analyzed the finances of Ruby and of his family to determine if there was any evidence of financial profit from his killing of the accused assassin. [147] It was an analysis the Warren Commission could not perform so soon after the assassination.[148] Some financial records, including tax returns, could not be legally obtained by the committee without great difficulty, and others no longer existed.[149] Nevertheless, on the basis of the information that it did obtain, the committee uncovered no evidence that Ruby or members of his family profited from the killing of Oswald.[150] Particular allegations concerning the increased business and personal incomes of Ruby's brother Earl were investigated, but the committee found no link between Earl Ruby's finances and the Oswald slaying.[151] Earl Ruby did say he had been approached by the Chicago bondsman and associate of organized crime figures, Irwin Weiner, who made a business proposition to him in 1978, the day before Earl Ruby was to testify before the committee.[152] Earl Ruby said he declined the offer,[153] while Weiner denied to the committee he ever made it.[154] The committee was not able to resolve the difference between the two witnesses.

(4) *Involvement of organized crime.*—In contrast to the Warren Commission, the committee's investigation of the possible involvement of organized crime in the assassination was not limited to an examination of Jack Ruby.

194

The committee also directed its attention to organized crime itself.

Organized crime is a term of many meanings. It can be used to refer to the crimes committed by organized criminal groups—gambling, narcotics, loan-sharking, theft and fencing, and the like.[155] It can also be used to refer to the criminal groups that commit those crimes.[156] Here, a distinction may be drawn between an organized crime enterprise that engages in providing illicit goods and services and an organized crime syndicate that regulates relations between individual enterprises—allocating territory, settling personal disputes, establishing gambling payoffs, etc.[157] Syndicates, too, are of different types. They may be metropolitan, regional, national or international in scope; they may be limited to one field of endeavor—for example, narcotics—or they may cover a broad range of illicit activities.[158]

Often, but not always, the term organized crime refers to a particular organized crime syndicate, variously known as the Mafia or La Cosa Nostra,[159] and it is in this sense that the committee has used the phrase. This organized crime syndicate was the principal target of the committee investigation.[160]

The committee found that by 1964 the fundamental structure and operations of organized crime in America had changed little since the early 1950's, when, after conducting what was then the most extensive investigation of organized crime in history, the Kefauver committee concluded:

1. There is a nationwide crime syndicate known as the Mafia, whose tentacles are found in many large cities. It has international ramifications which appear most clearly in connection with the narcotics traffic.

2. Its leaders are usually found in control of the most lucrative rackets in their cities.

3. There are indications of a centralized direction and control of these rackets, but leadership appears to be in a group rather than in a single individual.

4. The Mafia is the cement that helps to bind the * * * syndicate of New York and the * * * syndicate of Chicago as well as smaller criminal gangs and individual criminals through the country.

5. The domination of the Mafia is based fundamentally on "muscle" and "murder." The Mafia is a se-

cret conspiracy against law and order, which will ruthlessly eliminate anyone who stands in the way of its success in any criminal enterprise in which it is interested. It will destroy anyone who betrays its secrets. It will use any means available—political influence, bribery, intimidation, et cetera, to defeat any attempt on the part of law enforcement to touch its top figures * * *.[161)

The committee reviewed the evolution of the national crime syndicate in the years after the Kefauver committee and found continuing vitality, even more sophisticated techniques, and an increased concern for the awareness by law enforcement authorities of the danger it posed to the Nation.[162] In 1967, after having conducted a lengthy examination of organized crime in the United States, the President's Crime Commission offered another description of the power and influence of the American underworld in the 1960's:

Organized crime is a society that seeks to operate outside the control of the American people and their governments. It involves thousands of criminals, working within structures as complex as those of any large corporation, subject to laws more rigidly enforced than those of legitimate governments. Its actions are not impulsive but rather the result of intricate conspiracies, carried on over many years and aimed at gaining control over whole fields of activity in order to amass huge profits.[163]

An analysis by the committee revealed that the Kennedy administration brought about the strongest effort against organized crime that had ever been coordinated by the Federal Government.[164] John and Robert Kennedy brought to their respective positions as President and Attorney General an unprecedented familiarity with the threat of organized crime—and a commitment to prosecute its leaders—based on their service as member and chief counsel respectively of the McClellan Committee during its extensive investigation of labor racketeering in the late 1950's.[165] A review of the electronic surveillance conducted by the FBI from 1961 to 1964 demonstrated that members of La Cosa Nostra, as well as other organized crime figures, were quite cognizant of the stepped-up effort against them, and they placed responsibility for it directly upon President Kennedy and Attorney General Kennedy.[166]

During this period, the FBI had comprehensive electronic coverage of the major underworld figures, particularly those who comprised the commission.[8][167] The committee had access to and analyzed the product of this electronic coverage; it reviewed literally thousands of pages of electronic surveillance logs that revealed the innermost workings of organized crime in the United States.[168] The committee saw in stark terms a record of murder, violence, bribery, corruption, and an untold variety of other crimes.[169] Uniquely among congressional committees, and in contrast to the Warren Commission, the committee became familiar with the nature and scope of organized crime in the years before and after the Kennedy assassination, using as its evidence the words of the participants themselves.

An analysis of the work of the Justice Department before and after the tenure of Robert Kennedy as Attorney General also led to the conclusion that organized crime directly benefited substantially from the changes in Government policy that occurred after the assassination. [170] That organized crime had the motive, opportunity and means to kill the President cannot be questioned.[171] Whether it did so is another matter.

In its investigation of the decisionmaking process and dynamics of organized crime murders and intrasyndicate assassinations during the early 1960's, the committee noted the extraordinary web of insulation, secrecy, and complex machinations that frequently surrounded organized crime leaders who ordered such acts.[172] In testimony before the Senate on September 25, 1963, 2 months before his brother's assassination, Attorney General Kennedy spoke of the Government's continuing difficulty in solving murders carried out by organized crime elements, particularly those ordered by members of the La Cosa Nostra commission. Attorney General Kennedy testified that:

> * * * because the members of the Commission, the top members, or even their chief lieutenants, have insulated themselves from the crime itself, if they want to have somebody knocked knocked off, for instance,

---

[8]The ruling council of 9 to 12 Mafia leaders who collectively rule the national crime syndicate.

the top man will speak to somebody who will speak to somebody else who will speak to somebody else and order it. The man who actually does the gun work, who might get paid $250, or $500, depending on how important it is, perhaps nothing at all, he does not know who ordered it. To trace that back is virtually impossible.[173]

The committee studied the Kennedy assassination in terms of the traditional forms of violence used by organized crime and the historic pattern of underworld slayings. While the murder of the President's accused assassin did in fact fit the traditional pattern—a shadowy man with demonstrable organized crime connections shoots down a crucial witness—the method of the President's assassination did not resemble the standard syndicate killing.[174] A person like Oswald—young, active in controversial political causes, apparently not subject to the internal discipline of a criminal organization—would appear to be the least likely candidate for the role of Mafia hit man, especially in such an important murder. Gunmen used in organized crime killings have traditionally been selected with utmost deliberation and care, the most important considerations being loyalty and a willingness to remain silent if apprehended. These are qualities best guaranteed by past participation in criminal activities.[175]

There are, however, other factors to be weighed in evaluating the method of possible operation in the assassination of President Kennedy. While the involvement of a gunman like Oswald does not readily suggest organized crime involvement, any underworld attempt to assassinate the President would in all likelihood have dictated the use of some kind of cover, a shielding or disguise.[176] The committee made the reasonable assumption that an assassination of a President by organized crime could not be allowed to appear to be what it was.

Traditional organized crime murders are generally committed through the use of killers who make no effort to hide the fact that organized crime was responsible for such murders or "hits."[177] While syndicate-authorized hits are usually executed in such a way that identification of the killers is not at all likely, the slayings are nonetheless committed in what is commonly referred to as the "gangland style."[178] Indeed, an intrinsic characteristic of the typical mob execution is that it serves as a self-apparent message, with the authorities and the public readily perceiving the nature of the crime as well as the general identity of the group or gang that carried it out.[179]

The execution of a political leader—most particularly a President—would hardly be a typical mob execution and might well necessitate a different method of operation. The overriding consideration in such an extraordinary crime would be the avoidance of any appearance of organized crime complicity[180]

In its investigation the committee noted three cases, for the purposes of illustration, in which the methodology employed by syndicate figures was designed to insulate and disguise the involvement of organized crime.[181] These did not fit the typical pattern of mob killings, as the assassination of a President would not.[182] While the atypical cases did not involve political leaders, two of the three were attacks on figures in the public eye.[183]

In the first case, the acid blinding of investigative reporter Victor Riesel in April 1956, organized crime figures in New York used a complex series of go-betweens to hire a petty thief and burglar to commit the act.[184] Thus, the assailant did not know who had actually authorized the crime for which he had been recruited.[185] The use of such an individual was regarded as unprecedented, as he had not been associated with the syndicate, was a known drug user, and outwardly appeared to be unreliable.[186] Weeks later, Riesel's assailant was slain by individuals who had recurited him in the plot.[187]

The second case, the fatal shooting of a well-known businessman, Sol Landie, in Kansas City, Mo., on November 22, 1970, involved the recruitment, through several intermediaries, of four young Black men by members of the local La Cosa Nostra family. [188] Landie had served as a witness in a Federal investigation of gambling activities directed by Kansas City organized crime leader Nicholas Civella. The men recruited for the murder did not know who had ultimately ordered the killing, were not part of the Kansas City syndicate, and had received instructions through intermediaries to make it appear that robbery was the motive for the murder. [189] All of the assailants and two of the intermediaries were ultimately convicted.

The third case, the shooting of New York underworld leader Joseph Columbo before a crowd of 65,000 people in June 1971, was carried out by a young Black man with a petty criminal record, a nondescript loner who appeared to be alien to the organized crime group that had recruited him through various go-betweens. [190] The gunman was shot to death immediately after the shooting of Columbo, a murder still designated as unsolved. [191] (Seriously wounded by a shot to the head, Columbo lingered for years in a semiconscious state before he died in 1978.)

The committee found that these three cases, each of which is an exception to the general rule of organized crime executions, had identifiable similarities. [192] Each case was solved, in that the identity of the perpetrator of the immediate act became known. [193] In two of the cases, the assailant was himself murdered soon after the crime. [194] In each case, the person who wanted the crime accomplished recruited the person or persons who made the attack through more than one intermediary. [195] In each case, the person suspected of inspiring the violence was a member of, or connected to, La Cosa Nostra. [196] In each case, the person or persons hired were not professional killers, and they were not part of organized criminal groups. [197] In each case, the persons recruited to carry out the acts could be characterized as dupes or tools who were being used in a conspiracy they were not fully aware of. [198] In each case, the intent was to insulate the organized crime connection, with a particular requirement for disguising the true identity of the conspirators, and to place the blame on generally nondescript individuals. [199] These exceptions to the general rule of organized crime violence made it impossible for the committee to preclude, on the basis of an analysis of the method of the assassination, that President Kennedy was killed by elements of organized crime.[200]

In its investigation into the possibility that organized crime elements were involved in the President's murder, the committee examined various internal and external factors that bear on whether organized crime leaders would have considered, planned and executed an assassination conspiracy. [201] The committee examined the decisionmaking process that would have been involved in such a conspiracy, and two primary propositions emerged. [202] The first related to whether the national crime syndicate would have authorized and formulated a conspiracy with the formal consent of the commission, the ruling council of Mafia leaders. [203] The second related to whether an individual organized crime leader, or possibly a small combination of leaders, might have conspired to assassinate the President through unilateral action, that is, without the involvement of the leadership of the national syndicate.[204]

The most significant evidence that organized crime as an institution or group was not involved in the assassination of President Kennedy was contained in the electronic surveillance of syndicate leaders conducted by the FBI in the early 1960's.[205] As the President's Crime Commission noted in 1967, and as this committee found through its review of the FBI surveillance, there was a distinct hierarchy and structure to organized crime.[206] Decisions of national importance were generally made by the national commission, or at least they depended on the approval of the commission members.[207] In 1963, the following syndicate leaders served as members of the commission: Vito Genovese, Joseph Bonanno, Carlo Gambino, and Thomas Lucchese of New York City; Stefano Magaddino of Buffalo; Sam Giancana of Chicago; Joseph Zerilli of Detroit; Angelo Bruno of Philadelphia and Raymond Patriarca of Providence. [208] The committee's review of the surveillance transcripts and logs, detailing the private conversations of the commission members and their associates, revealed that there were extensive and heated discussions about the serious difficulties the Kennedy administration's crackdown on organized crime was causing.[209]

The bitterness and anger with which organized crime leaders viewed the Kennedy administration are readily apparent in the electronic surveillance transcripts, with such remarks being repeatedly made by commission members Genovese, Giancana, Bruno, Zerilli, Patriarca and Magaddino.[210] In one such conversation in May 1962, a New York Mafia member noted the intense Federal pressure upon the mob, and remarked, "Bob Kennedy won't stop today until he puts us all in jail all over the country. Until the commission meets and puts its foot down, things will be at a standstill."[211] Into 1963, the pressure was continuing to mount, as evidenced by a conversation in which commission member Magaddino bitterly cursed Attorney General Kennedy and commented on the Justice Department's increasing knowledge of the crime syndicate's inner workings, stating, "They know

201

everything under the sun. They know who's back of it—they know there is a commission. We got to watch right now—and stay as quiet as possible."[212]

While the committee's examination of the electronic surveillance program revealed no shortage of such conversations during that period, the committee found no evidence in the conversations of the formulation of any specific plan to assassinate the President.[213] Nevertheless, that organized crime figures did discuss possible violent courses of action against either the President or his brother, Attorney General Robert F. Kennedy—as well as the possible repercussions of such action—can be starkly seen in the transcripts.[214]

One such discussion bears quoting at length. It is a conversation between commission member Angelo Bruno of Philadelphia and an associate, Willie Weisburg, on February 8, 1962.[215] In the discussion, in response to Weisburg's heated suggestion that Attorney General Kennedy should be murdered, Bruno cautioned that Kennedy might be followed by an even worse Attorney General:

WEISBURG. See what Kennedy done. With Kennedy, a guy should take a knife, like all them other guys, and stab and kill the [obsenity], where he is now. Somebody should kill the [obscenity], I mean it. This is true. Honest to God. It's about time to go. But I tell you something. I hope I get a week's notice, I'll kill. Right in the [obscenity] in the White House. Somebody's got to get rid of this [obscenity].

BRUNO. Look, Willie, do you see there was a king, do you understand. And he found out that everybody was saying that he was a bad king. This is an old Italian story. So, he figured. Let me go talk to the old woman. She knows everything. So he went to the old wise woman. So he says to her: "I came here because I want your opinion." He says: "Do you think I'm a bad king?" She says: "No, I think you are a good king." He says: "Well how come everybody says I'm a bad king?" She says: "Because they are stupid. They don't know." He says: "Well how come, why do you say I'm a good king?" "Well," she said, "I knew your great grandfather. He was a bad king. I knew your grandfather. He was worse. I knew your father. He was worse than them. You, you are worse than them, but your son, if you die,

202

your son is going to be worse than you. So its better to be with you." [All laugh.] So Brownell—former Attorney General—was bad. He was no [obscenity] good. He was this and that.

WEISBURG. Do you know what this man is going to do? He ain't going to leave nobody alone.

BRUNO. I know he ain't. But you see, everybody in there was bad. The other guy was good because the other guy was worse. Do you understand? Brownell came. He was no good. He was worse than the guy before.

WEISBURG. Not like this one.

BRUNO. Not like this one. This one is worse. Right? If something happens to this guy * * * [laughs].[216]

While Angelo Bruno had hoped to wait out his troubles, believing that things might get better for him as time went by, such was not to be the case during the Kennedy administration. The electronic surveillance transcripts disclose that by mid-1963, Bruno was privately making plans to shut down his syndicate operations and leave America, an unprecedented response by a commission member to Federal law enforcement pressure.[217]

Another member of the mob commission, Stefano Magaddino, voiced similar anger toward the President during that same period.[218] In October 1963, in response to a Mafia family member's remark that President Kennedy "should drop dead," Magaddino exploded, "They should kill the whole family, the mother and father too. When he talks he talks like a mad dog, he says, my brother the Attorney General."[219]

The committee concluded that had the national crime syndicate, as a group, been involved in a conspiracy to kill the President, some trace of the plot would have been picked up by the FBI surveillance of the commission. [220] Consequently, finding no evidence in the electronic surveillance transcripts of a specific intention or actual plan by commission members to have the President assassinated, the committee believed it was unlikely that it existed. The electronic surveillance transcripts included extensive conversations during secret meetings of various syndicate leaders, set forth many of their most closely guarded thoughts and actions, and detailed their involvement in a variety of other criminal acts, including murder.[221] Given the far-reaching possible consequences of an assassination plot by the commission, the committee found that such a conspiracy would have been the subject of serious discussion by members of the commission, and that no matter how guarded such discussions might have been, some trace of them would have emerged from the surveillance coverage.[222] It was possible to conclude, therefore, that it is unlikely that the national crime syndicate as a group, acting under the leadership of the commission, participated in the assassination of President Kennedy.[223]

While there was an absence of evidence in the electronic surveillance materials of commission participation in the President's murder, there was no shortage of evidence of the elation and relief of various commission members over his death.[224] The surveillance transcripts contain numerous crude and obscene comments by organized crime leaders, their lieutenants, associates and families regarding the assassination of President Kennedy. [225] The transcripts also reveal an awareness by some mob leaders that the authorities might be watching their reactions.[226] On November 25, 1963, in response to a lieutenant's remark that Oswald "was an anarchist * * * a Marxist Communist," Gianaca exclaimed, "He was a marksman who knew how to shoot."[227] On November 29, 1963, Magaddino cautioned his associates not to joke openly about the President's murder, stating, "You can be sure that the police spies will be watching carefully to see what we think and say about this."[228] Several weeks later, during a discussion between Bruno and his lieutenants, one participant remarked of the late President, "It is too bad his brother Bobby was not in that car too."[229]

While the committee found it unlikely that the national crime syndicate was involved in the assassination, it recognized the possibility that a particular organized crime leader or a small combination of leaders, acting unilaterally, might have formulated an assassination conspiracy without the consent of the commission.[230]

In its investigation of the national crime syndicate, the committee noted factors that could have led an organized crime leader who was considering an assassination to withhold it from the national commission.[231] The committee's analysis of the national commission disclosed that it was splintered by dissension and enmity in 1963.

Rivalry between two blocks of syndicate families had resulted in a partial paralysis of the commission's functions. [232]

One significant reason for the disarray was, of course, the pressure being exerted by Federal law enforcement agencies. [233] In the fall of 1963, Attorney General Kennedy noted,

* * * in the past 2 years, at least three carefully planned commission meetings had to be called off because the leaders learned that we had uncovered their well-concealed plans and meeting places.

The Government's effort got an unprecedented boost from the willingness of Joseph Valachi, a member of the "family" of commission member Vito Genovese of New York, to testify about the internal structure and activities of the crime syndicate, a development described by Attorney General Kennedy as "the greatest intelligence breakthrough" in the history of the Federal program against organized crime.[234] While it was not until August 1963 that Valachi's identity as a Federal witness became public, the surveillance transcripts disclose that syndicate leaders were aware as early as the spring of 1963 that Valachi was cooperating with the Justice Department. [235] The transcripts disclose that the discovery that Valachi had become a Federal informant aroused widespread suspicion and fear over the possibility of other leaks and informants within the upper echelons of the syndicate.[236] The televised Senate testimony by Valachi led to considerable doubt by syndicate leaders in other parts of the country as to the security of commission proceedings, with Genovese rapidly losing influence as a result of Valachi's actions.[237]

The greatest source of internal disruption within the commission related to the discovery in early 1963 of a secret plan by commission member Joseph Bonanno to assassinate fellow members Carlo Gambino and Thomas Lucchese.[238] Bonanno's assassination plan, aimed at an eventual takeover of the commission leadership, was discovered after one of the gunmen Bonanno had enlisted, Joseph Columbo, informed on him to the commission. [239] The Bonanno conspiracy, an unheard-of violation of commission rules, led to a long series of acrimonious deliberations that lasted until early 1964.[240] Bonanno refused to submit to the judgment of the commission, and his colleagues were sharply divided over how to deal with his betrayal, Gambino recommending that Bonanno be handled with caution, and Giancana urging that he be murdered.[241]

The committee concluded, based on the state of disruption within the commission and the questions that had arisen as to the sanctity of commission proceedings, that an individual organized crime leader who was planning an assassination conspiracy against President Kennedy might well have avoided making the plan known to the commission or seeking approval for it from commission members.[242] Such a course of unilateral action seemed to the committee to have been particularly possible in the case of powerful organized crime leaders who were well established, with firm control over their jurisdictions.[243]

The committee noted a significant precedent for such a unilateral course of action. In 1957, Vito Genovese engineered the assassination of Albert Anastasia, then perhaps the most feared Mafia boss in the country.[244] Six months earlier, Genovese's men had shot and wounded Frank Costello, who once was regarded as the single most influential organized crime leader.[245] Both the Anastasia assassination and the Costello assault were carried out without the knowledge or consent of the national commission.[246] Genovese did, however, obtain approval for the crimes after the fact.[247] It was an extraordinary sequence of events that Attorney General Kennedy noted in September 1963, when he stated that Genovese "* * * wanted Commission approval for these acts—which he has received." The Genovese plot against Anastasia and Costello and the ex post facto commission approval were integral events in the rise to dominance of organized crime figures for the years that followed. It directly led to the assemblage of national syndicate leaders at the Apalachin conference 3 weeks after the Anatasia murder, and to the rise of Carlo Gambino to a position of preeminence in La Costa Nostra.[248]

(5) *Analysis of the 1963–64 investigation.*—In its investigation, the committee learned that fears of the possibility that organized crime was behind the assassination were more common among Government officials at the time than has been generally recognized. Both Attorney General Kennedy and President Johnson privately voiced suspicion about underworld complicity.[249] The Attor-

ney General requested that any relevant information be forwarded directly to him, and there was expectation at the time that the recently created Warren Commission would actively investigate the possibility of underworld involvement.[250]

The committee found, however, that the Warren Commission conducted only a limited pursuit of the possibility of organized crime complicity.[251] As has been noted, moreover, the Warren Commission's interest in organized crime was directed exclusively at Jack Ruby, and it did not involve any investigation of the national crime syndicate in general, or individual leaders in particular.[252] This was confirmed to the committee by J. Lee Rankin, the Commission's general counsel, and by Burt W. Griffin, the staff counsel who conducted the Ruby investigation. [253] Griffin testified before the committee that "* * * the possibility that someone associated with the underworld would have wanted to assassinate the President * * * [was] not seriously explored" by the Warren Commission.[254]

The committee similarly learned from testimony and documentation that the FBI's investigation of the President's assassination was also severely limited in the area of possible organized crime involvement. While the committee found that the Bureau was uniquely equipped, with the Special Investigative Division having been formed 2 years earlier specifically to investigate organized crime, the specialists and agents of that Division did not play a significant role in the assassination investigation.[255] Former Assistant FBI Director Courtney Evans, who headed the Special Investigative Division, told the committee that the officials who directed the investigation never consulted him or asked for any participation by his Division. [256] Evans recalled, "I know they sure didn't come to me. We had no part in that that I can recall."[257] Al Staffeld, a former FBI official who supervised the day-to-day operations of the Special Investigative Division, told the committee that if the FBI's organized crime specialists had been asked to participate, "We would have gone at it in every damn way possible."[258]

Ironically, the Bureau's own electronic surveillance transcripts revealed to the committee a conversation between Sam Giancana and a lieutenant, Charles English, regarding the FBI's role in investigating President Kennedy's assassination.[259] In the December 3, 1963 conversation, English told Giancana: "I will tell you something, in another 2 months from now, the FBI will be like it was 5 years ago. They won't be around no more. They say the FBI will get it (the investigation of the President's assassination). They're gonna start running down Fair Play for Cuba, Fair Play for Matsu. They call that more detrimental to the country than us guys."[260]

The committee found that the quality and scope of the investigation into the possibility of an organized crime conspiracy in the President's assassination by the Warren Commission and the FBI was not sufficient to uncover one had it existed. The committee also found that it was possible, based on an analysis of motive, means and opportunity, that an individual organized crime leader, or a small combination of leaders, might have participated in a conspiracy to assassinate President Kennedy. The committee's extensive investigation led it to conclude that the most likely family bosses of organized crime to have participated in such a unilateral assassination plan were Carlos Marcello and Santos Trafficante.[261] While other family bosses on the commission were subjected to considerable coverage in the electronic surveillance program, such coverage was never applied to Marcello and almost never to Trafficante.[262]

(6) *Carlos Marcello.*—The committee found that Marcello had the motive, means and opportunity to have President John F. Kennedy assassinated,[263] though it was unable to establish direct evidence of Marcello's complicity.

In its investigation of Marcello, the committee identified the presence of one critical evidentiary element that was lacking with the other organized crime figures examined by the committee: credible associations relating both Lee Harvey Oswald and Jack Ruby to figures having a relationship, albeit tenuous, with Marcello's crime family or organization.[264] At the same time, the committee explicitly cautioned: association is the first step in conspiracy; it is not identical to it, and while associations may legitimately give rise to suspicions, a careful distinction must always be drawn between suspicions suspected and facts found.

As the long-time La Cosa Nastra leader in an area that is based in New Orleans but extends throughout Louisiana and Texas, Marcello was one of the prime targets of Justice Department efforts during the Kennedy administration.[265] He had, in fact, been temporarily removed from the country for a time in 1961 through deportation proceedings personally expedited by Attorney General Kennedy.[266] In his appearance before the committee in executive session, Marcello exhibited an intense dislike for Robert Kennedy because of these actions, claiming that he had been illegally "kidnaped" by Government agents during the deportation.[267]

While the Warren Commission devoted extensive attention to Oswald's background and activities, the committee uncovered significant details of his exposure to and contacts with figures associated with the underworld of New Orleans that apparently had escaped the Commission. [268] One such relationship actually extended into Oswald's own family through his uncle, Charles "Dutz" Murret, a minor underworld gambling figure.[269] The committee discovered that Murret, who served as a surrogate father of sorts throughout much of Oswald's life in New Orleans, was in the 1940's and 1950's and possibly until his death in 1964 an associate of significant organized crime figures affiliated with the Marcello organization.[270]

The committee established that Oswald was familiar with his uncle's underworld activities and had discussed them with his wife, Marina, in 1963.[271] Additionally, the committee found that Oswald's mother, Marguerite Oswald, was acquainted with several men associated with lieutenants in the Marcello organization. One such acquaintance, who was also an associate of Dutz Murret, reportedly served as a personal aide or driver to Marcello at one time.[272] In another instance, the committee found that an individual connected to Dutz Murret, the person who arranged bail for Oswald following his arrest in August 1963 for a street disturbance, was an associate of two of Marcello's syndicate deputies. (One of the two, Nofio Pecora, as noted, also received a telephone call from Ruby on October 30, 1963, according to the committee's computer analysis of Ruby's phone records.) [273]

During the course of its investigation, the committee developed several areas of credible evidence and testimony indicating a possible association in New Orleans and elsewhere between Lee Harvey Oswald and David W. Ferrie, a private investigator and even, perhaps, a pilot for Marcello before and during 1963.[274] From the evidence available to the committee, the nature of the Oswald-Ferrie association remained largely a mystery. The committee established that Oswald and Ferrie apparently first came into contact with each other during Oswald's participation as a teenager in a Civil Air Patrol unit for which Ferrie served as an instructor, although Ferrie, when he was interviewed by the FBI after his detainment as a suspect in the assassination,[275] denied any past association with Oswald.

In interviews following the assassination, Ferrie stated that he may have spoken in an offhand manner of the desirability of having President Kennedy shot, but he denied wanting such a deed actually to be done.[276] Ferrie also admitted his association with Marcello and stated that he had been in personal contact with the syndicate leader in the fall of 1963. He noted that on the morning of the day of the President's death he was present with Marcello at a courthouse in New Orleans.[277] In his executive session testimony before the committee, Marcello acknowledged that Ferrie did work for his lawyer, G. Wray Gill, on his case, but Marcello denied that Ferrie worked for him or that their relationship was close.[278] Ferrie died in 1967 of a ruptured blood vessel at the base of the brain, shortly after he was named in the assassination investigation of New Orleans District Attorney Jim Garrison.

The committee also confirmed that the address, 544 Camp Street, that Oswald had printed on some Fair Play for Cuba Committee handouts in New Orleans, was the address of a small office building where Ferrie was working on at least a part-time basis in 1963.[279] The Warren Commission stated in its report that despite the Commission's probe into why Oswald used this return address on his literature, "investigation has indicated that neither the Fair Play for Cuba Committee nor Lee Oswald ever maintained an office at that address."[280]

The committee also established associations between Jack Ruby and several individuals affiliated with the underworld activities of Carlos Marcello.[281] Ruby was a personal acquaintance of Joseph Civello, the Marcello associate who allegedly headed organized crime activities in Dallas; he also knew other individuals who have been linked with organized crime, including a New Orleans nightclub figure, Harold Tannenbaum, with whom Ruby

210

was considering going into partnership in the fall of 1963.[282][9]

The committee examined a widely circulated published account that Marcello made some kind of threat on the life of President Kennedy in September 1962 at a meeting at his Churchill Farms estate outside New Orleans.[284] It was alleged that Marcello shouted an old Sicilian threat, "Livarsi na petra di la scarpa!" "Take the stone out of my shoe!" against the Kennedy brothers, stating that the President was going to be assassinated. He spoke of using a "nut" to carry out the murder.[285]

The committee established the origin of the story and identified the informant who claimed to have been present at the meeting during which Marcello made the threat. [286] The committee also learned that even though the FBI was aware of the informant's allegations over a year and half before they were published in 1969, and possessed additional information indicating that the informant may in fact have met with Marcello in the fall of 1962, a substantive investigation of the information was never conducted.[287] Director Hoover and other senior FBI officials were aware that FBI agents were initiating action to "discredit" the informant, without having conducted a significant investigation of his allegations.[288] Further, the committee discovered that the originating office relied on derogatory information from a prominent underworld figure in the ongoing effort to discredit the informant.[289] An internal memorandum to Hoover noted that another FBI source was taking action to discredit the informant, "in order that the Carlos Marcello incident would be deleted from the book" that first recounted the information.[290]

The committee determined that the informant who gave the account of the Marcello threat was in fact associated with various underworld figures, including at least one person well-acquainted with the Marcello organization. [291] The committee noted, however, that as a consequence of his underworld involvement, the informant had

[9]Law enforcement files have long contained information suggesting that Joseph Campisi, a restaurant owner in Dallas, occupied a position in organized crime. The committee's investigation did not confirm or refute the allegation, but it did establish that Ruby visited Campisi's restaurant on the evening of November 21 and that Ruby was visited in jail after the shooting of Oswald by Campisi and his wife. Further, Campisi acknowledged a longstanding business and personal relationship with Marcello. [283]

a questionable reputation for honesty and may not be a credible source of information.[292]

The committee noted further that it is unlikely that an organized crime leader personally involved in an assassination plot would discuss it with anyone other than his closest lieutenants, although he might be willing to discuss it more freely prior to a serious decision to undertake such an act. In his executive session appearance before the committee, Marcello categorically denied any involvement in organized crime or the assassination of President Kennedy. Marcello also denied ever making any kind of threat against the President's life.[293]

As noted, Marcello was never the subject of electronic surveillance coverage by the FBI. The committee found that the Bureau did make two attempts to effect such surveillance during the early 1960's, but both attempts were unsuccessful.[294] Marcello's sophisticated security system and close-knit organizational structure may have been a factor in preventing such surveillance.[10] A former FBI official knowledgeable about the surveillance program told the committee, "That was our biggest gap * * *. With Marcello, you've got the one big exception in our work back then. There was just no way of penetrating that area. He was too smart."[296]

Any evaluation of Marcello's possible role in the assassination must take into consideration his unique stature within La Cosa Nostra. The FBI determined in the 1960's that because of Marcello's position as head of the New Orleans Mafia family (the oldest in the United States, having first entered the country in the 1880's), the Louisiana organized crime leader had been endowed with special powers and privileges not accorded to any other La Cosa Nostra members.[297] As the leader of "the first family" of the Mafia in America, according to FBI information, Marcello has been the recipient of the extraordinary privilege of conducting syndicate operations without having to seek the approval of the national commission.[298]

Finally, a caveat, Marcello's uniquely successful career in organized crime has been based to a large extent on a policy of prudence; he is not reckless. As with the case of

---

[10]In addition Marcello was considered by his FBI case agent to be a legitimate businessman, which may account for the fact that the case agent was less than enthusiastic about pressing an investigation of the Louisiana Mafia leader. [295]

the Soviet and Cuban Governments, a risk analysis indicated that he would be unlikely to undertake so dangerous a course of action as a Presidential assassination. Considering that record of prudence, and in the absence of direct evidence of involvement, it may be said that it is unlikely that Marcello was in fact involved in the assassination of the President. On the basis of the evidence available to it, and in the context of its duty to be cautious in its evaluation of the evidence, there is no other conclusion that the committee could reach. On the other hand, the evidence that he had the motive and the evidence of links through associates to both Oswald and Ruby, coupled with the failure of the 1963–64 investigation to explore adequately possible conspiratorial activity in the assassination, precluded a judgment by the committee that Marcello and his associates were not involved.

(7) *Santos Trafficante.*—The committee also concentrated its attention on Santos Trafficante, the La Cosa Nostra leader in Florida. The committee found that Trafficante, like Marcello, had the motive, means, and opportunity to assassinate President Kennedy.[299]

Trafficante was a key subject of the Justice Department crackdown on organized crime during the Kennedy administration, with his name being added to a list of the top 10 syndicate leaders targeted for investigation.[300] Ironically, Attorney General Kennedy's strong interest in having Trafficante prosecuted occurred during the same period in which CIA officials, unbeknown to the Attorney General, were using Trafficante's services in assassination plots against the Cuban chief of state, Fidel Castro.[301]

The committee found that Santos Trafficante's stature in the national syndicate of organized crime, notably the violent narcotics trade, and his role as the mob's chief liaison to criminal figures within the Cuban exile community, provided him with the capability of formulating an assassination conspiracy against President Kennedy. Trafficante had recruited Cuban nationals to help plan and execute the CIA's assignment to assassinate Castro. (The CIA gave the assignment to former FBI Agent Robert Maheu, who passed the contract along to Mafia figures Sam Giancana and John Roselli. They, in turn, enlisted Trafficante to have the intended assassination carried out.)[302]

In his testimony before the committee, Trafficante admitted participating in the unsuccessful CIA conspiracy

213

to assassinate Castro, an admission indicating his willingness to participate in political murder.[303] Trafficante testified that he worked with the CIA out of a patriotic feeling for his country, an explanation the committee did not accept, at least not as his sole motivation.[304]

As noted, the committee established a possible connection between Trafficante and Jack Ruby in Cuba in 1959. [305] It determined there had been a close friendship between Ruby and Lewis McWillie, who, as a Havana gambler, worked in an area subject to the control of the Trafficante Mafia family.[306] Further, it assembled documentary evidence that Ruby made at least two, if not three or more, trips to Havana in 1959 when McWillie was involved in underworld gambling operations there. [307] Ruby may in fact have been serving as a courier for underworld gambling interests in Havana, probably for the purpose of transporting funds to a bank in Miami.[308]

The committee also found that Ruby had been connected with other Trafficante associates—R. D. Matthews, Jack Todd, and James Dolan—all of Dallas.[309]

Finally, the committee developed corroborating evidence that Ruby may have met with Trafficante at Trescornia prison in Cuba during one of his visits to Havana in 1959, as the CIA had learned but had discounted in 1964.[310] While the committee was not able to determine the purpose of the meeting, there was considerable evidence that it did take place.[311]

During the course of its investigation of Santos Trafficante, the committee examined an allegation that Trafficante had told a prominent Cuban exile, José Aleman, that President Kennedy was going to be assassinated.[312] According to Aleman, Trafficante made the statement in a private conversation with him that took place sometime in September 1962.[313] In an account of the alleged conversation published by the Washington Post in 1976, Aleman was quoted as stating that Trafficante had told him that President Kennedy was "going to be hit."[314] Aleman further stated, however, that it was his impression that Trafficante was not the specific individual who was allegedly planning the murder.[315] Aleman was quoted as having noted that Trafficante had spoken of Teamsters Union President James Hoffa during the same conversation, indicating that the President would "get what is coming to him" as a result of his administration's intense efforts to prosecute Hoffa.[316]

During an interview with the committee in March 1977, Aleman provided further details of his alleged discussion with Trafficante in September 1962.[317] Aleman stated that during the course of the discussion, Trafficante had made clear to him that he was not guessing that the President was going to be killed. Rather he did in fact know that such a crime was being planned.[318] In his committee interview, Aleman further stated that Trafficante had given him the distinct impression that Hoffa was to be principally involved in planning the Presidential murder.[319]

In September 1978, prior to his appreance before the committee in public session. Aleman reaffirmed his earlier account of the alleged September 1962 meeting with Trafficante. Nevertheless, shortly before his appearance in public session, Aleman informed the committee staff that he feared for his physical safety and was afraid of possible reprisal from Trafficante or his organization. In this testimony, Aleman changed his professed understanding of Trafficant's comments. Aleman repeated under oath that Trafficante had said Kennedy was "going to be hit," but he then stated it was his impression that Trafficante may have only meant the President was going to be hit by "a lot of Republican votes" in the 1964 election, not that he was going to be assassinated.[320]

Appearing before the committee in public session on September 28, 1978, Trafficante categorically denied ever having discussed any plan to assassinate President Kennedy.[321] Trafficante denied any foreknowledge of or participation in the President's murder. [322] While stating that he did in fact know Aleman and that he had met with him on more than one occasion in 1962, Trafficante denied Aleman's account of their alleged conversation about President Kennedy, and he denied ever having made a threatening remark against the President.[323]

The committee found it difficult to understand how Aleman could have misunderstood Trafficante during such a conversation, or why he would have fabricated such an account. Aleman appeared to be a reputable person, who did not seek to publicize his allegations, and he was well aware of the potential danger of making such allegations against a leader of La Costa Nostra. The committee noted, however, that Aleman's prior allegations and testimony before the committee had made him understandably fearful for his life.

The committee also did not fully understand why Aleman waited so many years before publicly disclosing the alleged incident. While he stated in 1976 that he had reported Trafficante's alleged remarks about the President to FBI agents in 1962 and 1963, the committee's review of Bureau reports on his contacts with FBI agents did not reveal a record of any such disclosure or comments at the time.[324] Additionally, the FBI agent who served as Aleman's contact during that period denied ever being told such information by Aleman.

Further, the committee found it difficult to comprehend why Trafficante, if he was planning or had personal knowledge of an assassination plot, would have revealed or hinted at such a sensitive matter to Aleman. It is possible that Trafficante may have been expressing a personal opinion, "The President ought to be hit," but it is unlikely in the context of their relationship that Trafficante would have revealed to Aleman the existence of a current plot to kill the President. As previously noted with respect to Carlos Marcello, to have attained his stature as the recognized organized crime leader of Florida for a number of years, Trafficante necessarily had to operate in a chacteristically calculating and discreet manner. The relationship between Trafficante and Aleman, a business acquaintance, does not seem to have been close enough for Trafficante to have mentioned or alluded to such a murder plot. The committee thus doubted that Trafficante would have inadvertently mentioned such a plot. In sum, the committee believed there were substantial factors that called into question the validity of Aleman's account.

Nonetheless, as the electronic surveillance transcripts of Angelo Bruno, Stefano Magaddino and other top organized crime leaders make clear, there were in fact various underworld conversations in which the desirability of having the President assassinated was discussed.[325] There were private conversations in which assassination was mentioned, although not in a context that indicated such a crime had been specifically planned.[326] With this in mind, and in the absence of additional evidence with which to evaluate the Aleman account of Trafficante's alleged 1962 remarks, the committee concluded that the conversation, if it did occur as Aleman testified, probably occurred in such a circumscribed context.

As noted earlier, the committee's examination of the FBI's electronic surveillance program of the early 1960's disclosed that Santos Trafficante was the subject of minimal, in fact almost nonexistent, surveillance coverage. [327] During one conversation in 1963, overheard in a Miami restaurant, Trafficante had bitterly attacked the Kennedy administration's efforts against organized crime, making obscene comments about "Kennedy's right-hand man" who had recently coordinated various raids on Trafficante gambling establishments.[328] In the conversation, Trafficante stated that he was under immense pressure from Federal investigators, commenting, "I know when I'm beat, you understand?"[329] Nevertheless, it was not possible to draw conclusions about Trafficante's actions based on the electronic surveillance program since the coverage was so limited. Finally, as with Marcello, the committee noted that Trafficante's cautious character is inconsistent with his taking the risk of being involved in an assassination plot against the President. The committee found, in the context of its duty to be cautious in its evaluation of the evidence, that it is unlikely that Trafficante plotted to kill the President, although it could not rule out the possibility of such participation on the basis of available evidence.

(8) *James R. Hoffa.*—During the course of its investigation, the committee also examined a number of areas of information and allegations pertaining to James R. Hoffa and his Teamsters Union and underworld associates. The long and close relationship between Hoffa and powerful leaders of organized crime, his intense dislike of John and Robert Kennedy dating back to their role in the McClellan Senate investigation, together with his other criminal activities, led the committee to conclude that the former Teamsters Union president had the motive, means and opportunity for planning an assassination attempt upon the life of President John F. Kennedy.

The committee found that Hoffa and at least one of his Teamster lieutenants, Edward Partin, apparently did, in fact, discuss the planning of an assassination conspiracy against President Kennedy's brother, Attorney General Robert F. Kennedy, in July or August of 1962.[330] Hoffa's discussion about such an assassination plan first

217

became known to the Federal Government in September 1962, when Partin informed authorities that he had recently participated in such a discussion with the Teamsters president.[331]

In October 1962, acting under the orders of Attorney General Kennedy, FBI Director Hoover authorized a detailed polygraph examination of Partin.[332] In the examination, the Bureau concluded that Partin had been truthful in recounting Hoffa's discussion of a proposed assassination plan.[333] Subsequently, the Justice Department developed further evidence supporting Partin's disclosures, indicating that Hoffa had spoken about the possibility of assassinating the President's brother on more than one occasion.[334]

In an interview with the committee, Partin reaffirmed the account of Hoffa's discussion of a possible assassination plan, and he stated that Hoffa had believed that having the Attorney General murdered would be the most effective way of ending the Federal Government's intense investigation of the Teamsters and organized crime.[335] Partin further told the committee that he suspected that Hoffa may have approached him about the assassination proposal because Hoffa believed him to be close to various figures in Carlos Marcello's syndicate organization.[336] Partin, a Baton Rouge Teamsters official with a criminal record, was then a leading Teamsters Union official in Louisiana. Partin was also a key Federal witness against Hoffa in the 1964 trial that led to Hoffa's eventual imprisonment.[337]

While the committee did not uncover evidence that the proposed Hoffa assassination plan ever went beyond its discussion, the committee noted the similarities between the plan discussed by Hoffa in 1962 and the actual events of November 22, 1963. While the committee was aware of the apparent absence of any finalized method or plan during the course of Hoffa's discussion about assassinating Attorney General Kennedy, he did discuss the possible use of a lone gunman equipped with a rifle with a telescopic sight,[338] the advisability of having the assassination committed somewhere in the South,[339] as well as the potential desirability of having Robert Kennedy shot while riding in a convertible.[340] While the similarities are present, the committee also noted that they were not so unusual as to point ineluctably in a particular direction.

President Kennedy himself, in fact, noted that he was vulnerable to rifle fire before his Dallas trip. Nevertheless, references to Hoffa's discussion about having Kennedy assassinated while riding in a convertible were contained in several Justice Department memoranda received by the Attorney General and FBI Director Hoover in the fall of 1962.[341] Edward Partin told the committee that Hoffa believed that by having Kennedy shot as he rode in a convertible, the origin of the fatal shot or shots would be obscured.[342] The context of Hoffa's discussion with Partin about an assassination conspiracy further seemed to have been predicated upon the recruitment of an assassin without any identifiable connection to the Teamsters organization or Hoffa himself.[343] Hoffa also spoke of the alternative possibility of having the Attorney General assassinated through the use of some type of plastic explosives.[344]

The committee established that President Kennedy himself was notified of Hoffa's secret assassination discussion shortly after the Government learned of it. The personal journal of the late President's friend, Benjamin C. Bradlee, executive editor of the Washington Post, reflects that the President informed him in February 1963 of Hoffa's discussion about killing his brother.[345] Bradlee noted that President Kennedy mentioned that Hoffa had spoken of the desirability of having a silenced weapon used in such a plan. Bradlee noted that while he found such a Hoffa discussion hard to believe, "the President was obviously serious" about it.[346]

Partly as a result of their knowledge of Hoffa's discussion of assassination with Partin in 1962, various aides of the late President Kennedy voiced private suspicions about the possibility of Hoffa complicity in the President's assassination.[347] The committee learned that Attorney General Robert F. Kennedy and White House Chief of Staff Kenneth O'Donnell contacted several associates in the days immediately following the Dallas murder to discuss the possibility of Teamsters Union or organized crime involvement.[348]

As noted in the account of Ruby's telephone records, the committee confirmed the existence of several contacts between Ruby and associates of Hoffa during the period of October and November 1963,[349] including one Hoffa aide whom Rogert Kennedy had once described as

219

one of Hoffa's most violent lieutenants.[350] Those associates, Barney Baker, Irwin Weiner and Dusty Miller, stated that Ruby had been in touch with them for the sole purpose of seeking assistance in a night-club labor dispute.[351]

The committee learned that Attorney General Kennedy and his aides arranged for the appointment of Charles Shaffer, a Justice Department attorney, to the Warren Commission staff in order that the possibility of Teamster involvement be watched. Shaffer confirmed to the committee that looking into Hoffa was one purpose of his appointment.[352]

Yet, partly as a result of the Commission's highly circumscribed approach to investigating possible underworld involvement, as well as limited staff resources, certain areas of possible information relating to Hoffa—such as the Ruby telephone calls—were not the subject of in-depth investigation.[353] Nevertheless, in a lengthy Commission memorandum prepared for the CIA in February 1964, the Teamsters Union had been listed first on a list of potential groups to be investigated in probing "ties between Ruby and others who might have been interested in the assassination of President Kennedy."[354]

During the course of its investigation, the committee noted the existence of other past relationships between Ruby and associates of Hoffa, apart from those disclosed by a review of the Ruby phone records. Two such figures were Paul Dorfman, the Chicago underworld figure who was instrumental in Hoffa's rise to power in the labor movement, and David Yaras, the reputed organized crime executioner whose relationship to Ruby dated back to their early days in Chicago.[355]

The committee also confirmed that another Teamsters official, Frank Chavez, had spoken to Hoffa about murdering Robert Kennedy in early 1967, shortly before Hoffa went to Federal prison.[356] During that incident, Hoffa reportedly sharply rebuked his aide, telling him that such a course of action was dangerous and should not be considered.[357]

In an interview with a newsman several weeks before his disappearance and presumed murder, Hoffa denied any involvement in the assassination of President Kennedy, and he disclaimed knowing anything about Jack Ruby or his motivations in the murder of Oswald. Hoffa also denied that he had ever discussed a plan to assassinate Robert Kennedy.[358]

As in the cases of Marcello and Trafficante, the committee stressed that it uncovered no direct evidence that Hoffa was involved in a plot on the President's life, much less the one that resulted in his death in Dallas in November 1963. In addition, and as opposed to the cases of Marcello and Trafficante, Hoffa was not a major leader of organized crime. Thus, his ability to guarantee that his associates would be killed if they turned Government informant may have been somewhat less assured. Indeed, much of the evidence tending to incriminate Hoffa was supplied by Edward Grady Partin, a Federal Government informant who was with Hoffa when the Teamster president was on trial in October 1962 in Tennessee for violating the Taft-Hartley Act.[11]

It may be strongly doubted, therefore, that Hoffa would have risked anything so dangerous as a plot against the President at a time that he knew he was under active investigation by the Department of Justice.[12]

Finally, a note on Hoffa's character. He was a man of strong emotions who hated the President and his brother, the Attorney General. He did not regret the President's death, and he said so publicly. Nevertheless, Hoffa was not a confirmed murderer, as were various organized crime leaders whose involvement the committee considered, and he cannot be placed in that category with them, even though he had extensive associations with them. Hoffa's associations with such organized crime leaders grew out of the nature of his union and the industry whose workers it represented. Organized crime and the violence of the labor movement were facts of life for Hoffa; they were part of the milieu in which he grew up and worked. But when he encountered the only specific plot against a Kennedy that came to the attention of the committee (the suggestion from Frank Chavez), he rejected it.

The committee concluded, therefore, that the balance of the evidence argued that it was improbable that Hoffa had anything to do with the death of the President.

[11]Hoffa was in fact facing charges of trying to bribe the jury in his 1962 trial in Tennessee on November 22, 1963. The case was scheduled to go to trial in January 1964. Hoffa was ultimately convicted and sentenced to a prison term. Partin was the Government's chief witness against him.

[12]The committee found no evidence to indicate that Hoffa was under electronic surveillance.

(c) Summary and analysis of the evidence

The committee also believed it appropriate to reflect on the general question of the possible complicity of organized crime members, such as Trafficante or Marcello, in the Kennedy assassination, and to try to put the evidence it had obtained in proper perspective.

The significance of the organized crime associations developed by the committee's investigation speaks for itself, but there are limitations that must be noted. That President Kennedy's assassin and the man who, in turn, murdered him can be tied to individuals connected to organized crime is important for one reason: for organized crime to have been involved in the assassination, it must have had access to Oswald or Ruby or both.

The evidence that has been presented by the committee demonstrates that Oswald did, in fact, have organized crime associations. Who he was and where he lived could have come to the attention of those in organized crime who had the motive and means to kill the President. Similarly, there is abundant evidence that Ruby was knowledgeable about and known to organized crime elements. Nevertheless the committee felt compelled to stress that knowledge or availability through association falls considerably short of the sort of evidence that would be necessary to establish criminal responsibility for a conspiracy in the assassination. It is also considerably short of what a responsible congressional committee ought to have before it points a finger in a legislative context.

It must also be asked if it is likely that Oswald was, in fact, used by an individual such as Marcello or Trafficante in an organized crime plot. Here, Oswald's character comes into play. As the committee noted, it is not likely that Oswald was a hired killer; it is likely that his principal motivation in the assassination was political. Further, his politics have been shown to have been generally left-wing, as demonstrated by such aspects of his life as his avowed support of Fidel Castro. Yet the organized crime figures who had the motive and means to murder the President must be generally characterized as right-wing and anti-Castro. Knitting these two contradictory strands together posed a difficult problem. Either the assassination of President Kennedy was essentially an apolitical act undertaken by Oswald with full or partial knowledge of who he was

222

working for—which would be hard to believe—or Oswald's organized crime contacts deceived him about their true identity and motivation, or else organized crime was not involved.

From an organized crime member's standpoint, the use of an assassin with political leanings inconsistent with his own would have enhanced his insulation from identification with the crime. Nevertheless, it would have made the conspiracy a more difficult undertaking, which raises questions about the likelihood that such a conspiracy occurred. The more complicated a plot becomes, the less likely it will work. Those who rationally set out to kill a king, it may be argued, first design a plot that will work. The Oswald plot did in fact work, at least for 15 years, but one must ask whether it would have looked workable 15 years ago. Oswald was an unstable individual. Shortly before the assassination, for example, he delivered a possibly threatening note to the Dallas FBI office. With his background, he would have been an immediate suspect an assassination in Dallas, and those in contact with him would have known that. Conspirators could not have been assured that Oswald or his companion would be killed in Dealey Plaza; they could not be sure that they could silence them. The plot, because of Oswald's involvement, would hardly have seemed to be a low risk undertaking.

The committee weighed other factors in its assessment of Oswald, his act and possible co-conspirators. It must be acknowleged that he did, in the end, exhibit a high degree of brutal proficiency in firing the shot that ended the President's life, and that, as an ex-marine, that profiency may have been expected. In the final analysis, it must be admitted that he accomplished what he set out to do.

Further, while Oswald exhibited a leftist political stance for a number of years, his activities and associations were by no means exclusively left-wing. His close friendship with George de Mohrenschildt, an oilman in Dallas with right-wing connections, is a case in point. Additionally, questions have been raised about the specific nature of Oswald's pro-Castro activities. It has been established that on at least one occasion in 1963, he offered his services for clandestine paramilitary actions against the Castro regime, though, as has been suggested, he may have merely been posing as an anti-Castro activist. That the evidence points to the possibility that Oswald was also associated in 1963 with

David Ferrie, the Marcello operative who was openly and actively anti-Castro, is troubling, too. Finally, the only Cuba-related activities that have ever been established at 544 Camp Street, New Orleans, the address of an office building that Oswald stamped on some of his Fair Play for Cuba Committee handouts, were virulently anti-Castro in nature.

Thus, the committee was unable to resolve its doubts about Lee Harvey Oswald. While the search for additional information in order to reach an understanding of Oswald's actions has continued for 15 years, and while the committee developed significant new details about his possible organized crime associations, particularly in New Orleans, the President's assassin himself remains not fully understood. The committee developed new information about Oswald and Ruby, thus altering previous perceptions, but the assassin and the man who murdered him still appear against a backdrop of unexplained, or at least not fully explained, occurrences, associations and motivations.

The scientific evidence available to the committee indicated that it is probable that more than one person was involved in the President's murder. That fact compels acceptance. And it demands a re-examination of all that was thought to be true in the past. Further, the committee's investigation of Oswald and Ruby showed a variety of relationships that may have matured into an assassination conspiracy. Neither Oswald nor Ruby turned out to be "loners," as they had been painted in the 1964 investigation. Nevertheless, the committee frankly acknowledged that it was unable firmly to identify the other gunman or the nature and extent of the conspiracy.

5. THE SECRET SERVICE, FEDERAL BUREAU OF INVESTIGATION, AND CENTRAL INTELLIGENCE AGENCY WERE NOT INVOLVED IN THE ASSASSINATION OF PRESIDENT KENNEDY

As the symbolic leader of the Nation, the President means many things to many people. His loss is keenly felt; it is a traumatic event. The President is also more than the symbolic leader of the Nation; in fact, he holds both political and military power, and his death is an occasion for its transfer. It was, therefore, understandable that in foreign and domestic speculation at the time of President Kennedy's assassination, there was a suggestion of complicity by agencies of the U.S. Government. This was one of the principal reasons for the Warren Commission's creation.

With the publication of the Commission's report, the question was quieted, if not completely stilled. Nevertheless, critics continued to imply hat the Secret Service, the FBI or the CIA had somehow been involved in the tragedy in Dallas, and the Warren Commission itself came to be viewed by some as part of a Government effort to conceal the truth. With the revelation of the illegal domestic programs of the FBI and the foreign assassination plots of the CIA by the Senate Select Committee to Study Governmental Operations with Respect to Intelligence Activities in 1976, speculation was rekindled that Government itself may have been involved in the President's death.

The committee carefully considered various charges of Government complicity and coverup. A major portion of its resources were devoted to examining a variety of allegations directed at the Secret Service, the FBI, and the CIA as well as the Warren Commission. As the investigation proceeded, the committee carefully sought evidence that Government agents had foreknowledge of an assassination, took advantage of it after the event, or afterwards covered up information relevant to ascertaining the truth. The committee made a conscientious effort, for example, to determine if the autopsy materials were authentic. Had they been tampered with, it would have raised the most serious of questions. The committee also carefully assessed the performance of the Secret Service in the planning and execution of the Dallas trip for signs that it may have actively sought to bring about the President's death. In addition, the committee carefully examined the relationship, if any, that Lee Harvey Oswald might have had with various governmental agencies, particularly the FBI and CIA. Over the years, there has been speculation that Oswald might have been an FBI informant or an agent of the CIA. However Oswald is seen—patsy or perpetrator —his relatonship to the agencies of the Government was crucial to assessing the question of Government complicity. If he had had a relationship with one or more of the agencies, serious issues would be raised. If he had not, the question would be less pressing.

(a) The Secret Service

The committee's investigation of alleged Secret Serivce complicity in the assassination was primarily, although not exclusively, concerned with two questions. One, did the Secret Service facilitate the shooting by arranging a motorcade route that went through the heart of downtown Dallas and past the Texas School Book Depository? Two, did any Secret Service personnel engage in conduct at the site of the assassination that might indicate complicity in the assassination? The committee's investigation involved extensive file reviews, interviews, depositions, and hearings. Former White House personnel, Secret Service agents, Dallas Police Department officers, Texas public officials and private citizens who had witnessed the assassination were interviewed or questioned. In addition, relevant files and documents of former White House staff, the Secret Service, and the Dallas Police Department pertaining to the planning of the motorcade route were reviewed. These included the Secret Service's contingency plans for the Dallas trip that set forth scheduling, security factors and related considerations for the motorcade route.

(1) *Connally testimony.*—Governor John B. Connally testified at a public hearing that he first heard of the possibility of a Presidential trip to Texas during his gubernatorial campaign in the spring of 1962, when Vice President Johnson told him the President wanted to make a fundraising visit to the State.[1] Connally said he discussed the trip with the President himself in El Paso, Tex., in June 1963, and in October he went to the White House to help formulate plans.[2] According to former White House aides, President Kennedy expressed a desire to make use of a motorcade during the trip,[3] since he had found it a useful political instrument during his campaign for the Presidency. Further, the Dallas luncheon engagement under discussion involved only a limited speaking appearance, and Kennedy believed a motorcade would broaden his public exposure.[4]

The decision to use a motorcade was opposed initially by Governor Connally, who testified that he thought it would fatigue the President. [5] Frank Erwin, executive secretary of the Texas Democratic Committee, also opposed the motorcade, but for a different reason. He testified that because of Adlai Stevenson's ugly confronta-

226

tion with rightwing extremists only weeks earlier, he was concerned about the possibility of a similar embarrassing and potentially difficult situation.[6] These objections, however, were overruled by the White House.[7]

(2) *Choice of the motorcade route.*—Once the motorcade decision was made, the choice of a route was dependent more upon the selection of a site for the President's luncheon speech than upon security considerations. The White House staff at first favored the Dallas Women's Building near the Dallas County Fairgrounds because its capacity was greater than that of the alternative site, the Trade Mart, a commercial center with more limited facilities.[8] The White House staff felt that the Women's Building would have permitted more of the President's supporters to attend.

According to Jerry Bruno, a White House advance man, the route to the Women's Building would have led the motorcade to proceed along Main Street eastward to the Fairgrounds, which lay to the southeast of the business district. Access to Main Street on the west side of Dealey Plaza would have been by a cloverleaf from the expressway. Using this route, the motorcade would have proceeded at a relatively high speed (40 to 50 mph) into Dealey Plaza and it would maintain this speed until it reached the intersection of Main and Houston Streets where crowds would have gathered.[9] Had it taken this route, the motorcade would not have passed directly in front of the Texas School Book Depository at the slow (approximately 11 mph) speed that it did enroute to the Trade Mart.

In his testimony, Forrest Sorrels, the special agent-in-charge of the Dallas Secret Service office in 1963, indicated that the Secret Service also preferred the Women's Building as the luncheon site because, as a single story structure, it would have been easier to secure than the Trade Mart.[10] For political reasons, however, Governor Connally insisted on the Trade Mart,[1][11] and the White House acquiesced to his wishes so it could avoid a dispute with the Governor, whose assistance was needed to assure the political success of the trip.[12]

Accordingly, a motorcade to the Trade Mart was

---

[1]Connally in effect indicated he would not support the fundraising visit if the Trade Mart was not the luncheon site.

planned and since the purpose of the motorcade was to permit the President to greet well-wishers in downtown Dallas, the route that was chosen was west along Main, right on Houston, then left on Elm Street, proceeding past the book depository, and through Dealey Plaza. Main Street, according to Governor Connally, had been the usual route for ceremonial occasions,[13] such as a procession in 1936—although in the opposite direction—in honor of President Roosevelt, the last President to have traveled through Dallas in a motorcade.

While the Secret Service was consulted regarding alternative luncheon sites, its role in the ultimate decision-making process was secondary to that of Governor Connally and the White House staff.[14] Similarly, once the actual motorcade route had been set, also without significant Secret Service input, it was the White House staff, not the Secret Service, who made the decision to publish the route in Dallas newspapers. Presidential aides wanted to assure maximum public exposure for President Kennedy.[15]

The committee found no evidence, therefore, suggesting that the selection of a motorcade route involved Secret Service complicity in a plot to assassinate the President.[2] [18]

(3) *Allegation a Secret Service agent was on the grassy knoll.*—After the assassination, several witnesses stated they had seen or encountered Secret Service agents behind the stockade fence situated on the grassy knoll area and in the Texas School Book Depository.[19] Other witnesses reported Secret Service agents leaving the motorcade and running to various locations in Dealey Plaza. [20] Warren Commission critics have alleged that these Secret Service agents either participated in the assassination itself or were involved in a coverup of the evidence. [21]

None of the witnesses interviewed by the committee was able to provide further corroborating information concerning their original statements. The majority, however,

---

[2] The decision not to use a bubble top on the President's limousine was made by White House staff aides just minutes before the motorcade got underway. The Secret Service was not involved in the decision. [16] The bubble top, in any event, was not a bulletproof barrier designed to protect the limousine occupants. It served merely to shield them from inclement weather. [17]

indicated that they were mistaken in their original interpretation of events.[22] Committee interviews or depositions with 11 of the 16 agents[3] who were on duty with the motorcade and with their supervisors produced evidence that only one agent had left the motorcade at any time prior to the arrival at Parkland Hospital. This agent, Thomas "Lem" Johns, had been riding in Vice President Johnson's followup car. In an attempt to reach Johnson's limousine, he had left the car at the sound of shots and was momentarily on his own in Dealey Plaza, though he was picked up almost immediately and taken to Parkland Hospital.[23] In every instance, therefore, the committee was able to establish the movement and the activities of Secret Service agents. Except for Dallas Agent-in-Charge Sorrels, who helped police search the Texas School Book Depository, no agent was in the vicinity of the stockade fence or inside the book depository on the day of the assassination. [24]

Significantly, most of the witnesses who made identifications of Secret Service personnel stated that they had surmised that any plain-clothed individual in the company of uniformed police officers must have been a Secret Service agent.[25] Because the Dallas Police Department had numerous plainclothes detectives on duty in the Dealey Plaza area.[26] the committee considered it possible that they were mistaken for Secret Service agents.

One witness who did not base his Secret Service agent identification merely upon observing a plainclothesman in the presence of uniformed police officers was Dallas police officer Joseph M. Smith. Smith, who had been riding as a motorcycle escort in the motorcade, ran up the grassy knoll immediately after the shooting occurred. He testified to the Warren Commission that at that time he encountered a man who stated that he was a Secret Service agent and offered supporting credentials. Smith indicated that he did not examine these credentials closely, and he then proceeded to search the area unsuccessfully for suspicious individuals.[27]

The committee made an effort to identify the person who talked to Patrolman Smith. FBI Special Agent James P. Hosty stated that Frank Ellsworth, then an agent for

---

[3]One of the agents not interviewed had died. Affidavits were obtained from the remaining four.

the Alcohol, Tobacco and Firearms Bureau of the Treasury Department, had indicated that he had been in the grassy knoll area and for some reason had identified himself to someone as a Secret Service agent.[28] The committee deposed Ellsworth, who denied Hosty's allegation. [29]

The committee did obtain evidence that military intelligence personnel may have identified themselves as Secret Service agents or that they might have been misidentified as such. Robert E. Jones, a retired Army lieutenant colonel who in 1963 was commanding officer of the military intelligence region that encompassed Texas, told the committee that from 8 to 12 military intelligence personnel in plain-clothes were assigned to Dallas to provide supplemental security for the President's visit. He indicated that these agents had identification credentials and, if questioned, would most likely have stated that they were on detail to the Secret Service.[30]

The committee sought to identify these agents so that they could be questioned. The Department of Defense, however, reported that a search of its files showed "no records * * * indicating any Department of Defense Protective Services in Dallas."[31] The committee was unable to resolve the contradiction.

(4) *Conclusion.*—Based on its entire investigation, the committee found no evidence of Secret Service complicity in the assassination.

(b) The Federal Bureau of Investigation

In the weeks that followed the assassination, it was alleged in several newspaper articles that Lee Harvey Oswald had been an FBI informant. Consequently, the Warren Commission expended considerable effort addressing the question. Testimony was taken form FBI Director J. Edgar Hoover, Assistant to the Director Alan H. Belmont, and FBI Special Agents John W. Fain, John L. Quigley and James P. Hosty, Jr.[1] "All declared, in substance, that Oswald was not an informant or agent of the FBI, and that he did not act in any other capacity for the FBI, and that no attempt was made to recruit him in any capacity." In addition, "Director Hoover and each Bureau agent, who according to the FBI would have been responsible for or aware of any attempt to recruit Oswald * * * provided the Commission with sworn affidavits to this effect."[1] This testimony was corroborated by the Warren Commission's independent review of FBI files.[3]

Nevertheless, the allegation that Oswald was associated in some capacity with the FBI persisted.[4] There are three main reasons for this that may be traced to actions by the Bureau.

First, Oswald's address book contained the name, address, telephone number and automobile license plate number of Special Agent James P. Hosty. That entry has been a source of controversy, especially since this information was not contained in an FBI report to the Warren Commission in December 1963, one that purportedly contained the contents of the address book.

Second, based on FBI contacts with Oswald in Fort Worth in 1962 and New Orleans and Dallas in 1963, rum that he was an informant for the Bureau continued to circulate.

Third, shortly after the assassination, Dallas FBI agent Hosty destroyed a note that had been delivered to his office allegedly by Oswald shortly before the Assassination. When that conduct was finally made public in 1975 it aroused great suspicions, especially since it had not been previously revealed, even to the Warren Commission. [5]

The committee attempted to investigate each of the alleged links between Oswald and the FBI. It conducted extensive file reviews, interviews, depositions, and hearings. Testimony was taken from present and former FBI officials and employees as well as from private citizens claiming to have relevant information. On occasion, formal explanations were sought directly from the FBI. Even though the testimony of two special agents of the FBI appeared to be seriously lacking credibility on two of the major issues (the destruction of the Oswald note and the omission of Hosty's name from a report purporting to contain a list of the entries in Oswald's notebook), the results of the committee's investigation were consistent with the con-

---

[1] Nine of the 10 affidavits executed by FBI agents denying that Oswald had been an informant were revised before the FBI submitted them to the Warren Commission. It had been alleged that these affidavits may have been materially altered. The committee found that none of the affidavits had been materially altered before delivery to the Warren Commision. The essential difference between the preliminary drafts and the final affidavits was that the drafts were witnessed by fellow FBI agents, whereas the final affidavits were witnessed by notaries public. In a few instances, minor changes of words or phrases were made, although none affected substance. [2]

clusions reached by the Warren Commission. The committee found no credible evidence that Oswald was an FBI informant.

(1) *Early rumors that Oswald was an informant.*—Shortly after the assassination of President Kennedy, rumors that Oswald had been an FBI informant began to circulate. This allegation was discussed in articles by Joseph C. Goulden, Alonzo Hudkins, and Harold Feldman, among others.[6] The committee's review of these articles indicated that they set forth the rumors and speculation concerning the informant issue, but they offered no direct evidence supporting the allegation. Moreover, Hudkins admitted to the committee that his involvement with the issue began when he and another newsman discussed by telephone a mythical FBI payroll number for Oswald in order to test their suspicion that they were under FBI surveillance. Hudkins told the committee that he was subsequently contacted by the FBI and asked what he knew about Oswald's alleged informant status, and that shortly afterward a newspaper article appeared in which the FBI denied any relationship with Oswald.[7] Neither Hudkins nor Goulden was able to give the committee any additional information that would substantiate the informant allegation.[8] The committee was unable to locate Feldman.

(2) *The Hosty entry in Oswald's address book.*—After the assassination, Dallas police found Oswald's address book among his possessions and turned it over to the FBI in Dallas. It contained FBI Special Agent Hosty's name, address, telephone number and car license plate number. [9] Dallas FBI agent recorded some of the entries in the address book and, on December 23, 1963, sent a report to the Warren Commission. This report, however, did not include the Hosty entry.[2][10]

The committee's review of the December 23 report established the likelihood that page 25 of that document, the page that logically would have contained the Hosty entry had it been properly included,[3] had been retyped. The page was numbered in the upper left-hand corner, whereas all other pages of the report—save page 1, the retyping

[2]On January 25, 1964, the FBI independently questioned the Dallas office concerning the omission and later sent to the Warren Commission a report, dated February 11, 1964, that did include the Hosty entry. In addition, in a letter dated January 27, 1964, the FBI informed the Commission of the inclusion of the Hosty data in Oswald's address book.
[3]This determination was based on a comparison of the other entries from Oswald's address book that did appear on page 25.

232

of which had been clearly recorded—were numbered at the bottom center. In addition, the horizontal margins of page 25 were unusually wide.

The former special agent who had coordinated the FBI's Dallas investigation and had submitted the December 23, 1963, report, testified in a committee executive session that he had ordered the contents of Oswald's notebook transcribed for the purpose of indicating any investigative leads.[11] The agent acknowledged that page 25 of the report would have contained the Hosty entry had it been included, and that both the numbering of that page and its unusually wide horizontal margins indicated it had been retyped.[12] Nevertheless, he stated that the page had not been retyped to mislead anyone, and indicated that the only reason the Hosty entry had been omitted from his report was because the original office memorandum setting out investigative leads generated from Oswald's address book had failed to include it. [13]

A second special agent, the one who had prepared the original office memorandum that was incorporated into the December 23, 1963, report, testified that the Hosty entry had not been included because it was not considered to be of significance as an investigative lead.[14] This agent contended it had already been known that Hosty had called at the home of Ruth and Michael Paine looking for Oswald prior to the assassination, so the entry of his name and related data in Oswald's book would not have been of potential evidentiary value.[15]

The committee did not accept the explanation that the Hosty entry was omitted from the report because it was not of lead significance, since the FBI's December 23, 1963, report included other entries from Oswald's address book that clearly had no lead significance at the time. For example, by December 23, it was generally known that the Oswalds had been living at the Paine home, yet the Ruth Paine address book entry was included in the report.[16] Similarly, a Robert W. Oswald entry that referred to Oswald's brother would not have been significant as a lead at that time.[17] Numerous other examples could be given.[18] Moreover, the agent who prepared the memorandum failed to include in it several entries that he acknowledged could not automatically be dismissed as lacking in lead significance (e.g., numbers and letters of the alphabet whose meaning was not then known).[19]

Finally, in the December 23 report that was given to the Warren Commission, the FBI did not indicate that the report of the address book's contents had been limited to those items of lead significance.[4][20]

When the committee apprised the FBI of the testimony of the two agents (first, the agent who coordinated the investigation; second, the one who prepared the memorandum that was incorporated in the December 23, report), the Bureau initiated its own inquiry. It produced an FBI airtel (an interoffice telegram) dated December 11, 1963, that seemed to verify that the second agent's original instructions were to set out investigative leads, rather than to transcribe the complete contents of the address book.[21] The FBI investigation also led to the discovery of a "tickler" copy of the December 23 report that did contain the Hosty entry on page 25[5][22] The two agents were then reinterviewed by FBI investigators.

Based on his review and analysis of FBI documents, the second agent substantially revised the testimony he had given the committee. He told the Bureau investigators that since his assignment was to review the information contained in Oswald's address book and to set out appropriate leads where necessary, he initially reproduced by dictation those entries in the address book that he thought might require investigative action. He recalled that he was vitally concerned with accuracy; consequently, he initially included the Hosty entry. Nevertheless, he explained that when he later had time to determine what investigative work remained to be done with regard to the address book, he decided that it was not necessary to include the Hosty data in his second dictation of an investigative "lead sheet."[23]

A December 8, 1977, report of the FBI interview with the second agent records his recollection in further detail:

> He specifically recalls that by the time of the second dictation, he had had the opportunity to check on the Hosty entry to the extent that he was aware of

---

[4]The agent who prepared the memorandum testified he did not know it would be incorporated in other reports and sent to the Warren Commission. The agent who coordinated the investigation was the one who actually prepared the report for transmission to the Warren Commission.

[5]The term "tickler" refers to a copy of a report that is placed in a file for the purpose of reminding the file keeper of further action that must be taken with respect to the subject of the report.

Hosty's visits to the Paine residence and that the address book entry reflected the Dallas FBI Field Office telephone number and the license number of the Government vehicle assigned to Hosty.

Upon learning these facts, he was convinced that the Hosty entry was not required in a "lead sheet" since it did not require further investigative attention. In addition, he was unofficially aware, through office conversations, that Hosty was being criticized not only in the media, but also by the FBI hierarchy, for his conduct of the Oswald case. Since he realized that a "lead sheet" would receive wide dissemination in the Dallas Field Office, he was doubly convinced that the Hosty data should not be included in the "lead sheet" —Hosty's connection to the Oswald case was officially known and had been explained in previous reports, and, furthermore, he did not wish to cause Hosty any unnecessary unpleasantness or exposure. At that time he never considered that Hosty might have been a target of Lee Harvey Oswald, and, further, any contention that Hosty was involved in an assassination conspiracy would have been so preposterous that he would not even have thought of it. He, therefore, did not dictate the Hosty data and thereby excluded it from the product of his second dictation which was, in effect, an office memorandum to be used only as a "lead worksheet." He also never considered that the "Lead sheet" might have been converted to a report insert and disseminated outside the FBI. Had he known it would be, he would have considered that the memorandum or "lead sheet" should have reflected all the entries in the address book, to include Hosty's name, since to do otherwise would not have been an accurate reporting of the entire contents of the address book.

He could not recall specifically what may have occasioned the redoing of page 25 after the second dictation, but it is possible that it became necessary because either he or someone else noticed that the "Ministry of Finances of the U.S.S.R." information should have been attributed to the same page in the address book as was the "Katya Ford" and "Delean Ford" information. This error was made by him during his first dictation and may have persisted through

235

the second dictation, thereby necessitating an additional change which caused page 25, to be numbered as it appears in the December 23, 1963, report.

[The second agent] concluded by stating that his recall of these events was triggered only by a review and discussion of all the pertinent documents retrieved. Until viewing the tickler version of the address book contents which reproduced the entries more identically than the "lead sheet" version with its editorializations, he had no specific recall with regard to his first dictation.[24]

When the first agent was reinterviewed by the FBI, he was unable to explain the origin of the headquarters tickler copy. In addition, after reviewing the December 11, 1963, FBI headquarters airtel to the Dallas office, he indicated that, contrary to his earlier recollection, he never instructed the second agent to transcribe the address book. That order had apparently been issued by another special agent.[25]

Bureau interviews with the former special-agent-in-charge of the Dallas office in 1963 and six other special agents who were involved in the assassination investigation generated no additional information concerning how the tickler copy of the December 23, 1963, report on the contents of the address book came to reside in FBI headquarters. Nor did they shed new light on the circumstances surrounding the omission of the Hosty entry from the copy of the report that was sent to the Warren Commission. Laboratory tests for fingerprints were inconclusive.[26] They did not indicate who had worked on the tickler copy of the December 23 report. Laboratory tests did determine, however, that the typewriter used to prepare page 25 of the December 23 report had also been used to prepare all but 10 pages of the report.

The committee also sought testimony from Special Agent Hosty concerning the circumstances by which his name was entered in Oswald's notebook and why this particular entry might have been omitted from the December 23, 1963, report. Hosty stated that he had been assigned to internal security cases on both Lee Harvey Oswald and his wife Marina.[27] He recalled that he spoke briefly to Marina Oswald twice during the first week of November 1963 and that he had had no other contacts with her.[28]

On this first occasion, he had given Ruth Paine, with whom Marina Oswald was residing, his name and telephone number and had told her to call him if she had any information on Oswald to give him.[29] It was Hosty's belief that Ruth Paine probably gave this information to Oswald. Hosty added that Oswald could have obtained the address of the Dallas FBI office from the front page of any Dallas telephone book.[30] Hosty believed that during his second visit to the residence, while he was talking to Ruth Paine, Marina Oswald went outside and copied his license plate number.[31] He suggested that Oswald may have wanted this data so he could write his self-serving letter of protest to the Soviet Embassy in Washington.[32] In addition, he stated that it is possible that Oswald wanted this information so that he could complain to the FBI in Dallas.[33] Hosty indicated that he could think of no good reason for withholding the references to him in Oswald's address book from the report on the address book that was sent to the Warren Commission, as this information was already well-known at the Dallas Police Department.[34] The committee also learned that Hosty dictated two memoranda in December 1963 that included the fact that his name and address were in Oswald's address book. In addition, FBI headquarters was aware of the Hosty entry in the address book; it had been made public by the media, and the FBI had advised the Warren Commission of it on January 27, 1964.

Based on all this evidence, the committee concluded that there was no plan by the FBI to withhold the Hosty entry in Oswald's address book for sinister reasons. This conclusion was based on several factors, the most important of which was the discovery of the tickler copy of the December 23, 1963 report.[6]

The committee considered the fact, on the other hand, that information about the entry was withheld. One explanation might be that it was unintentional, although the evidence was also consistent with an explanation that one or more Dallas FBI agents sought to protect Hosty from personal embarrassment by trying—ineffectually, as it turned out—to exclude his name from the reporting. The

---

[6]The leadership of the FBI as of 1978, was deserving of credit, in the committee's estimate, for its efforts to find the truth about the Hosty entry in Oswald's address book. The committee doubted that the tickler copy of the December 23 memorandum would have been found if FBI officials had not been interested in resolving the issue.

committee, though it deemed the incident regrettable, found it to be trivial in the context of the entire investigation.

(3) *FBI contacts with Oswald (Fort Worth, 1962)*.— Oswald was interviewed twice by FBI agents in Fort Worth in 1962 shortly after his return from the Soviet Union.[35] Special Agent Fain, who had been assigned the Oswald internal security case in Fort Worth, and Special Agent Burnett Tom Carter conducted the initial Oswald interview at the Fort Worth FBI office on June 26, 1962. In his report of this interview, Fain described Oswald as cold, arrogant and uncooperative. He also reported that when asked if he would be willing to submit to a polygraph examination, Oswald refused without giving a reason.[36]

On August 16, 1962, Fain and Special Agent Arnold J. Brown reinterviewed Oswald, this time in Fain's automobile near Oswald's Fort Worth residence.[37] The fact that the interview was conducted in Fain's car has been cited as an indication that Oswald was being developed as an informant.

Fain, Carter, and Brown submitted affidavits to the Warren Commission asserting Oswald was not an informant. [38] All three were interviewed by the committee, and they affirmed their previous positions.

Fain told the committee that in the first encounter, Oswald displayed a bad attitude and gave incomplete answers [39] while Carter remembered Oswald as arrogant, uncooperative, and evasive.[40] Fain said the second contact was necessitated by Oswald's bad attitude and incomplete answers in the first interview. In the second interview, Fain explained, Oswald invited him and Brown into his home, but decided to conduct the interview in his car so not to upset or frighten Oswald's wife.[41] Brown told the committee that his memory was hazy, but he did recall that he and Fain met Oswald as he was returning from work and that they interviewed him in or near Fain's car, possibly for the sake of convenience.[42]

The committee found the statements of these three FBI agents credible. They had legitimate reasons for contacting Oswald because his background suggested he might be a threat to the internal security of the United States. They corroborated each other's accounts of the two interviews of Oswald, and their statements were entirely consistent with reports written shortly after these interviews occurred. Given Oswald's documented unwillingness to co-operate, there was little reason to believe that he would have been considered by these agents for use as an informant.

(4) *FBI contacts with Oswald* (*New Orleans, 1963*).—The committee interviewed the special agent in charge of the FBI office in New Orleans in 1963 and three special agents who handled the Oswald case in that city, and it found their statements that Oswald had not been an FBI informant to be credible.

Harry Maynor, the special agent in charge of the New Orleans FBI office in 1963, explained that if Oswald had been an FBI informant in New Orleans, he would have known about it because of his supervisory position; if Oswald had been paid for any information, he would have approved the payments. Maynor noted that he had submitted an affidavit to the Warren Commission in which he had stated that no effort was made to develop Oswald as an informant.[43]

. Similarly, former Special Agent Milton Kaack, who had been assigned the FBI security investigation of Oswald, told the committee that Oswald had never been an FBI informant. Kaack explained that if Oswald had been an FBI informant, he would have known about it by virtue of having been assigned the internal security case on him.[7] [44]

The statements of Maynor, Kaack, and two other former FBI employees were considered in the context of allegations made by three witnesses, William S. Walter, Orest Pena, and Adrian Alba.

On August 9, 1963, Oswald was arrested in New Orleans for disturbing the peace after he had gotten into a fight with anti-Castro Cubans while distributing Fair Play for Cuba Committee leaflets. FBI Special Agent John L. Quigley interviewed Oswald the following day in a New Orleans jail.[45] Quigley's willingness to meet with Oswald in jail has been cited as evidence that Oswald was an FBI informant. Moreover, in connection with this incident, William S. Walter, who was an FBI security clerk in New Orleans in 1963, told the committee that he had been on duty on the day this interview occurred. In response to

---

[7] The committee asked Kaack why he had not submitted an affidavit to this effect to the Warren Commission. In response, Kaack indicated that this had not been done because no one had requested it.

Quigley's request for a file check on Oswald, he had determined that the New Orleans FBI office maintained both a security file and an informant file on Oswald.[46]

In a committee interview, Quigley, who had submitted an affidavit to the Warren Commission asserting that Oswald had not been an FBI informant,[47] reaffirmed his position. He explained that he interviewed Oswald at Oswald's request, and that he then checked the file indices at the New Orleans office and found that Oswald was the subject of a security investigation assigned to Special Agent Kaack. He advised that the indices check provided no indication that Oswald had ever been an FBI informant. He added that if Oswald had been an informant, he would have known about it by virtue of this indices search.[48]

The committee could find no independent basis for verifying Walter's testimony about an Oswald informant file, but another allegation made by him, unrelated to the informant issue, led the committee to reject his testimony in its entirety. In a committee deposition, Walter stated that on November 17, 1963, while he was on night duty as an FBI security clerk, he received a teletype from FBI headquarters warning of a possible assassination attempt against President Kennedy during the forthcoming trip to Dallas on November 22 or 23, 1963.[49] Walter recalled that the teletype was addressed to all special agents in charge of FBI field offices and that it instructed them to contact criminal, racial and hate group informants in order to determine whether there was any basis for the threat.[50] Walter contended that this teletype was removed from the New Orleans FBI office files soon after the Kennedy assassination.[51]

Walter admitted that he did not publicly allege the existence of this teletype until 1968.[52] At that time, the FBI instituted an investigation that failed to find any corroboration for Walter's story. According to the Bureau, no record of a teletype or any other kind of communication reporting that there would be an attempt to assassinate President Kennedy in Texas could be found. Over 50 FBI employees of the New Orleans FBI office were interviewed by the Bureau, and none of them stated that they had any knowledge of any such teletype.[53] In 1975, the Bureau reinvestigated the teletype allegation after Walter claimed he had retained a replica of the teletype and that it had been sent to all FBI field offices. The FBI examined the text of the alleged replica and determined that it varied in format and wording from the standard. The Bureau also reported that searches at each of its 59 field offices yielded no evidence indicating the existence of such a teletype.[54]

Walter advised the committee that he did not know of anyone who could definitely substantiate his teletype allegation, although he suggested that his former wife, Sharon Covert, who also had worked for the FBI in New Orleans, might be able to do so.[55] Sharon Covert, however, advised the committee that she could not support any of Walter's allegations against the FBI and that Walter had never mentioned his allegations to her during their marriage.[56]

New Orleans Special Agent in Charge Maynor also denied that he had been contacted by Walter in regard to an assassination threat.[57]

More fundamentally, however, the committee was led to distrust Walter's account of the assassination teletype because of his claim that it had been addressed to the special agents in charge of every FBI field office. The committee found it difficult to believe that such a message could have been sent without someone 15 years later—a special agent in charge or an employee who might have seen the teletype—coming forward in support of Walter's claim. The committee declined to believe that that many employees of the FBI would have remained silent for such a long time. Instead, the committee was led to question Walter's credibility. The committee concluded that Walter's allegations were unfounded.

Orest Pena, a bar owner in New Orleans, testified that during the early 1960's he was an FBI informant who reported to Special Agent Warren D. deBrueys.[58] He told the committee that on several occasions he saw Oswald in the company of deBrueys and other Government agents in a restaurant and that he believed Oswald and deBrueys knew each other very well.[8] Finally, Pena alleged that Special Agent deBrueys was "transferred" to Dallas at the same time Oswald was "transferred" there. He added that he was "very, very, very sure" that deBrueys

---

[8] In this regard, William Walter testified that after the assassination of President Kennedy he found a single file pertaining to Oswald in SAC Harry G. Maynor's locked file cabinet. Walter stated that he did not recall the title of the file, and acknowledged that it may not have been an informant file, but he remembered that the name of FBI Special Agent Warren D. deBrueys appeared on the file jacket. As noted, the committee did not find Walter to be a credible witness.

went to Dallas before the assassination of President Kennedy.[59]

Pena maintained that a few days before he went to testify before the Warren Commission, deBrueys threatened him physically and warned him not to make any accusations against him. Pena also stated that Warren Commission staff counsel Wesley J. Liebeler did not cooperate with him and did not let him talk freely, so he decided to "keep [his] mouth shut."[60]

In testimony before the committee, deBrueys denied that Oswald was his informant, that he had ever met Oswald, or that he had ever knowingly talked to him by telephone. [61] He acknowledged that he did use Pena informally as an occasional source of information because of his position as a bar owner in New Orleans, but he declined to characterize Pena as an informant because of the absence of any systematic reporting relationship.[62] He also denied having threatened Pena prior to Pena's Warren Commission testimony.[63] Finally, deBrueys testified that he was transferred to Dallas in 1963, but that this was the result of a temporary assignment to assist in the assassination investigation.[64] The transfer did not coincide with Oswald's move from New Orleans to the Dallas area.[9]

FBI files served to corroborate relevant aspects of deBrueys' testimony. DeBrueys' personal file indicates that the only time he was transferred to Dallas was to work on the assassination investigation, and that he was in Dallas from November 23, 1963, until January 24, 1964. In addition, there is no Bureau record of Pena ever having served as an informant. This, too, supported deBrueys' testimony that Pena was never used on any systematic basis as a source of information.

Pena, moreover, was unable to explain adequately why he waited until 1975 to make this allegation, and he declined to testify specifically that Oswald was, in fact, an FBI informant. Pena's responses to committee questions

---

[9]The committee also asked deBrueys why he did not submit an affidavit to the Warren Commission on the informant issue. In response, deBrueys testified that he was surprised not to have been called upon to submit an affidavit to the Warren Commission. He believed that he had signed an affidavit on the informant issue at Bureau headquarters within the past few years, but no longer recalled the specifics of this action. The Bureau informed the committee that, pursuant to regulations, deBrueys had submitted to the U.S. Attorney General a written synopsis of his testimony before the Senate Select Committee on Intelligence. In this synopsis, deBrueys stated that he had denied under oath that Oswald was his informant or that he had ever knowingly spoken to Oswald.

on the informant issue and others were frequently evasive.[65] The committee found, therefore, that he was not a credible witness.

Adrian Alba testified before the committee that he was an employee and part owner of the Crescent City Garage in New Orleans and that in the summer of 1963 he had become acquainted with Oswald, who worked next door at the Reily Coffee Co.[66] He related that one day an FBI agent entered his garage and requested to use one of the Secret Service cars garaged there. The FBI agent showed his credentials, and Alba allowed him to take a Secret Service car, a dark green Studebaker. Later that day or the next day, Alba observed the FBI agent in the car handing a white envelope to Oswald in front of the Reily Coffee Co. There was no exchange of words. Oswald, in a bent position, turned away from the car window and held the envelope close to his chest as he walked toward the Reily Coffee Co. Alba believed that he observed a similar transaction a day or so later as he was returning from lunch, but on this occasion he was farther away and failed to see what was handed to Oswald. Alba did not recall when the Secret Service car was returned or by whom. He never questioned Oswald about these incidents.[67]

Alba did not relate his account of the transactions between Oswald and the FBI agent when he testified before the Warren Commission.[68] He told the committee in 1978 that he first remembered these incidents in 1970, when his memory was triggered by a television commercial showing a merchant running to and from a taxi to assist a customer.[69]

The committee examined Alba's records for possible corroboration. These records indicated that in 1963 several Secret Service agents had signed out two Studebakers, a Ford and a Chevrolet at various times, but the records did not indicate that any FBI agents had signed out any of these cars.[70]

The committee regarded Alba's testimony, at least on this point, to be of doubtful reliability and outweighed by the evidence provided by the former FBI personnel stationed in New Orleans.

(5) *FBI contacts with Oswald (Dallas, 1963).*—According to a 1964 FBI memorandum, an FBI agent, later identified as Will Hayden Griffin of the Dallas field office, allegedly stated in 1964 that Oswald was definitely an

243

FBI informant and that FBI files in Washington would prove that fact.[71] Griffin, however, advised the committe that he had never made such an allegation. Moreover, in 1964, he had executed an affidavit specifically denying this allegation.[72] Griffin's position is consistent with that of other Dallas FBI personnel.

J. Gordon Shanklin, who was special-agent-in-charge of the Dallas FBI office in 1936, submitted an affidavit to the Warren Commission in which he denied that Oswald was an FBI informant.[73] In a committee interview, he again stated that Oswald was never an informant for the FBI in Dallas, and he added he had not even heard of Oswald prior to President Kennedy's assassination.[74]

Special Agent James P. Hosty, Jr., testified that Oswald had not been an FBI informant.[75] Hosty had submitted an affidavit to this effect to the Warren Commission.[10] Hosty told the committee that he had never interviewed Oswald before the assassination of President Kennedy. From his testimony, it appeared that his only contacts with Oswald had been indirect, in the form of two occasions that he had conversed with Marina Oswald and Ruth Paine. He added that Oswald was neither an informant for Special Agent Fain in Fort Worth nor an informant for any FBI agent in New Orleans. Had Oswald been an informant in either case, Hosty insisted he would have known about it by virtue of having been assigned the internal security case on Oswald in Dallas.[76]

Hosty also addressed the purported Griffith allegation. He testified to the committee that Griffin knew that Jack Ruby had been a potential criminal informant for the FBI in Dallas. He suggested that someone could have heard Griffith talking about Ruby's contacts with the FBI and might then have repeated the story with the mistaken assertion that Griffin was talking about Oswald.[77]

In support of Hosty's explanation, Shanklin stated to the committee that the Dallas office did send the potential criminal informant file on Ruby to FBI headquarters in Washington after the Kennedy assassination. He added that he did not know whether this file was sent to the Warren

---

[10]In addition to Hosty and Shanklin, several other FBI agents in Dallas executed affidavits for the Warren Commission denying that Oswald was an informant: Assistant Special-Agent-in-Charge Kyle G. Clark, former Special-Agent-in-Charge Curtis O. Lynum, and Special Agent Kenneth C. Howe.

Commission.[11][78] Griffin told the committee in a second interview that soon after the Kennedy assassination he learned that the FBI in Dallas had approached Ruby in order to obtain information from him. He advised that, although his recollection was unclear, he might have seen an FBI informant file on Ruby and then may have talked to persons outside the Bureau about the FBI's contacts with Ruby.[79]

(6) *The destruction of Oswald's note.*—Approximately 2 or 3 weeks before the assassination of President Kennedy, Oswald allegedly delivered a note addressed to Hosty at the FBI office in Dallas.[80] The varying accounts of the note's contents suggest that it was threatening or complaining in tone, ordering Hosty to stop bothering Oswald's wife.[81] Several hours after Oswald was murdered by Jack Ruby, Hosty, according to his own admission, destroyed the note after having been instructed to do so by J. Gordon Shanklin, the special-agent-in-charge of the Dallas FBI office.[82] Shanklin denied that he knew anything about the note until a reporter asked him about it in 1975.[83] Between 1963 and 1975, the existence of the note and its destruction were kept secret by the Dallas FBI Office.

In his committee testimony. Hosty stated that the note, according to his memory, did not contain Oswald's name and that he first determined that the note might have been from Oswald on the day of the assassination of President Kennedy. Hosty explained that soon after Oswald's arrest, he was instructed to sit in on the interrogation of Oswald at the Dallas Police Department, and that when he identified himself to Oswald, Oswald became upset and stated that Hosty had been bothering his wife, Marina. Hosty suggested that Special-Agent-in-Charge Shanklin, who was told by another FBI agent about Oswald's reaction to Hosty, probably made the same connection between Oswald and the anonymous note. Hosty advised that he was surprised that Shanklin wanted him to destroy the note because the note's contents were not particularly significant.[84]

Hosty recalled that the note was complaining in tone, but that it contained no threats and did not suggest that

---

[11]The committee found no evidence that this file was ever sent to the Warren Commission, although details of the association were furnished to the Commission by letter.

Oswald was prone to violence. Hosty stated that he destroyed the note because Shanklin, his superior, ordered him to do so. When asked what motivation Oswald might have had for writing this note, Hosty suggested that Oswald might have wanted to prevent Hosty from contacting his wife because he was afraid that she would tell Hosty about Oswald's trip to Mexico in the fall of 1963 and of his attempt to shoot Gen. Edwin Walker in the spring of 1963.[85]

The committee regarded the incident of the note as a serious impeachment of Shanklin's and Hosty's credibility. It noted, however, that the note, if it contained threats in response to FBI contacts with Oswald's wife, would have been evidence tending to negate an informant relationship. The committee noted further the speculative nature of its findings about the note incident. Because the note had been destroyed, it was not possible to establish with confidence what its contents were.

(7) *Conclusion.*—In summary, although there have been many allegations of an Oswald-FBI informant relationship, there was no credible evidence that Oswald was ever an informant for the Bureau. Absent a relationship between Oswald and the FBI, grounds for suspicions of FBI complicity in the assassination become remote.

(c) The Central Intelligence Agency[1]

In 1964, the CIA advised the Warren Commission that the Agency had never had a relationship of any kind with Lee Harvey Oswald. Testifying before the Commission, CIA Director John A. McCone indicated that:

Oswald was not an agent, employee, or informant of the Central Intelligence Agency. The Agency never contacted him, interviewed him, talked with him, or solicited any reports or information from him, or communicated with him directly or in any other manner * * * Oswald was never associated or connected directly or indirectly in any way whatsoever with the Agency.[1]

McCone's testimony was corroborated by Deputy Director Richard M. Helms.[2] The record reflects that once

---

[1] For a brief history of the CIA and description of its organizational structure, see Section I D 4 infra.

these assurances had been received, no further efforts were made by the Warren Commission to pursue the matter.

Recognizing the special difficulty in investigating a clandestine agency, the committee sought to resolve the issue of Oswald's alleged association with the CIA by conducting an inquiry that went beyond taking statements from two of the Agency's most senior officials. The more analytical approach used by the committee consisted of a series of steps:

> First, an effort was made to identify circumstances in Oswald's life or in the way his case was handled by the CIA that possibly suggested an intelligence association.

> Then, the committee undertook an intensive review of the pertinent files, including the CIA's 144-volume Oswald file and hundreds of others from the CIA, FBI, Department of State, Department of Defense and other agencies.

> Based on these file reviews, a series of interviews, depositions and executive session hearings was conducted with both Agency and non-Agency witnesses. The contacts with present and former CIA personnel covered a broad range of individuals, including staff and division chiefs, clandestine case officers, area desk officers, research analysts, secretaries and clerical assistants. In total, more than 125 persons, including at least 50 present and former CIA employees, were questioned.[2]

The results of this investigation confirmed the Warren Commission testimony of McCone and Helms. There was no indication in Oswald's CIA file that he had ever had contact with the Agency. Finally, taken in their entirety, the items of circumstantial evidence that the committee had selected for investigation as possibly indicative of an intelligence association did not support the allegation that Oswald had an intelligence agency relationship.

This finding, however, must be placed in context, for the institutional characteristics—in terms of the Agency's strict compartmentalization and the complexity of its

---

[2]The committee also attempted to identify CIA employees who may have had the motive, means and opportunity to assassinate President Kennedy. In this regard, no useful information was generated from selected file reviews. An effort was also made to locate a man identified as Maurice Bishop who was said to have been a CIA officer who had been seen in the company of Lee Harvey Oswald. The effort to find "Bishop" was likewise unsuccessful.

enorous filing system—that are designed to prevent penetration by foreign powers have the simultaneous effect of making congressional inquiry difficult. For example, CIA personnel testified to the committee that a reivew of Agency files would not always indicate whether an individual was affiliated with the Agency in any capacity. [3] Nor was there always an independent means of verifying that all materials requested from the Agency had, in fact, been provided. Accordingly, any finding that is essentially negative in nature—such as that Lee Harvey Oswald was neither associated with the CIA in any way, nor ever in contact with that institution—should explicitly acknowledge the possibility of oversight.

To the extent possible, however, the committee's investigation was designed to overcome the Agency's security-oriented institutional obstacles that potentially impede effective scrutiny of the CIA. The vast majority of CIA files made available to the committee were reviewed in undeleted form.[4] These files were evaluated both for their substantive content and for any potential procedural irregularities suggestive of possible editing or tampering. After review, the files were used as the basis for examination and cross-examination of present and former Agency employees. Each of the present and former Agency employees contacted by the committee was released from his secrecy oath by the CIA insofar as questions relevant to the committee's legislative mandate were concerned. Because of the number of Agency personnel who were interrogated,[5] it is highly probable that any significant inconsistencies between the files and witnesses' responses would have been discovered by the committee.

During the course of its investigation, the committee was given access by the CIA to information based on sensitive sources and methods that are protected by law from unauthorized disclosure. The committee noted that in some circumstances disclosure of such information in detail would necessarily reveal the sensitive sources and methods by which it was acquired. With respect to each item of such information, the committee carefully weighed the possible advancement of public understanding that might accrue from disclosure of the details of the information against the possible harm that might be done to the national interests and the dangers that might result to individuals. To the extent required by the balancing process, sections of this report were written in a somewhat conclusionary manner in order to continue the protection of such classified information.

(1) *CIA personnel in the Soviet Russia Division.*[3]—Since Oswald spent time in the Soviet Union, a subject of special attention by the committee was the Russia-related activities of the CIA. In addition to obtaining testimony from former Directors McCone and Helms, the committee interviewed the chiefs of the Soviet Russia Division from 1959 to 1963. In each case, the committee received a categorical denial of any association of the CIA with Oswald. [6]

To investigate this matter further, the committee interviewed the persons who had been chiefs or deputy chiefs during 1959–62 of the three units within the Soviet Russia Division that were responsible respectively for clandestine activities, research in support of clandestine activities, and the American visitors program.[4] The heads of the clandestine activity section stated that during this period the CIA had few operatives in the Soviet Union and that Oswald was not one of them. Moreover, they stated that because of what they perceived to be his obvious instability, Oswald would never have met the Agency's standards for use in the field.[5][7] The heads of the Soviet Russia Division's section that sought the cooperation of visitors to the Soviet Union informed the committee that they met with each person involved in their program and that Oswald was not one of them.[8] These officials also devised the committee that "clean-cut" collegiate types tended to be used in this program, and that Oswald did not meet this criterion.[9] Finally, the officers in charge of the Soviet Russia Division's research section in support of clandestine activities indicated that, had Oswald been contacted by the Agency, their section would probably have been informed, but that this, in fact, never occurred.[10]

---

[3]Classified analyses of these issues, written in undeleted form, are in the committee's files.

[4]The visitors program sought the cooperation, for limited purposes, of carefully selected persons traveling in the Soviet Union. For this unit, only the years 1959–61 were covered. Nevertheless, since every American traveler who was involved in this program was contacted before visiting the Soviet Union, the relevant year for Lee Harvey Oswald was 1959, the year he departed from the United States.

[5]One officer acknowledged the remote possibility that an individual could have been run by someone as part of a "vest pocket" (private or personal) operation without other Agency officials knowing about it. But even this possibilityy, as it applies to Oswald, was negated by the statement of the deputy chief of the Soviet Russia clandestine activities section. He commented that in 1963 he was involved in a review of every clandestine operation ever run in the Soviet Union, and Oswald was not involved in any of these cases.

(2) *CIA personnel abroad.*—Turning to particular allegations, the committee investigated the statement of former CIA employee James Wilcott, who testified in executive session that shortly after the assassination of President Kennedy he was advised by fellow employees at a CIA post abroad that Oswald was a CIA agent who had received financial disbursements under an assigned cryptonym.[6] [11] Wilcott explained that he had been employed by the CIA as a finance officer from 1957 until his resignation in 1966. In this capacity, he served as a fiscal account assistant on the support staff at a post abroad from June 1960 to June 1964. In addition to his regular responsibilities, he had performed security duty on his off-hours in order to supplement his income. This put him in contact with other employees of the post who would come by the office and engage in informal conversations. On the day after President Kennedy's assassination, Wilcott claimed he was informed by a CIA case officer that Oswald was an agent.[12] He further testified that he was told that Oswald had been assigned a cryptonym and that Wilcott himself had unknowingly disbursed payments for Oswald's project.[13] Although Wilcott was unable to identify the specific case officer who had initially informed him of Oswald's agency relationship, he named several employees of the post abroad with whom he believed he had subsequently discussed the allegations.[14]

Wilcott advised the committee that after learning of the alleged Oswald connection to the CIA, he never rechecked official Agency disbursement records for evidence of the Oswald project. He explained that this was because at that time he viewed the information as mere shop talk and gave it little credence.[15] Neither did he report the allegations to any formal investigative bodies, as he considered the information hearsay.[16] Wilcott was unable to recall the agency cryptonym for the particular project in which Oswald had been involved,[17] nor was he familiar with the substance of that project. In this regard, however, because project funds were disbursed on a code basis, as a

---

[6]A cryptonym is a code designation for an agency project, program or activity or an organization, agency or individual (for whom a legal signature is not required) having a sensitive operational relationship with the agency. Cryptonyms are used in communications only to the extent necessary to protect sensitive information from disclosure to unauthorized persons. They are used (1) when disclosure of the true identity of persons, organizations or activities would be detrimental to the interest of the U.S. Government or to the persons, organizations or activities concerned; or (2) to prevent disclosure of a sensitive operational relationship with the agency.

disbursement officer he would not have been apprised of the substantive aspects of projects.

In an attempt to investigate Wilcott's allegations, the committee interviewed several present and former CIA employees selected on the basis of the position each had held during the years 1954–64. Among the persons interviewed were individuals whose responsibilities covered a broad spectrum of areas in the post abroad, including the chief and deputy chief of station, as well as officers in finance, registry, the Soviet Branch and counterintelligence.

None of these individuals interviewed had ever seen any documents or heard any information indicating that Oswald was an agent.[18] This allegation was not known by any of them until it was published by critics of the Warren Commission in the late 1960's.[19] Some of the individuals, including a chief of counterintelligence in the Soviet Branch, expressed the belief that it was possible that Oswald had been recruited by the Soviet KGB during his military tour of duty overseas, as the CIA had identified a KGB program aimed at recruiting U.S. military personnel during the period Oswald was stationed there.[20] An intelligence analyst whom Wilcott had specifically named as having been involved in a conversation about the Oswald allegation told the committee that he was not in the post abroad at the time of the assassination.[21] A review of this individual's office or personnel file confirmed that, in fact, he had been transferred from the post abroad to the United States in 1962.[22]

The chief of the post abroad from 1961 to 1964 stated that had Oswald been used by the Agency he certainly would have learned about it.[23] Similarly, almost all those persons interviewed who worked in the Soviet Branch of that station indicated they would have known if Oswald had, in fact, been recruited by the CIA when he was overseas.[24] These persons expressed the opinion that, had Oswald been recruited without their knowledge, it would have been a rare exception contrary to the working policy and guidelines of the post abroad.[52]

Based on all the evidence, the committee concluded that Wilcott's allegation was not worthy of belief.

(3) *Oswald's CIA file.*—The CIA has long acknowledged that prior to the President's assassination, it had a personality file on Oswald, that is, a file that contained data about Oswald as an individual. This file, which in Agency terminology is referred to as a 201 file, was opened

on December 9, 1960.[26] The Agency explained that 201 files are opened when a person is considered to be of potential intelligence or counterintelligence significance.[27] The opening of such a file is designed to serve the purpose of placing certain CIA information pertaining to that individual in one centralized records system. The 201 file is maintained in a folder belonging to the Directorate for Operations, the Agency component responsible for clandestine activities.[28]

The existence of a 201 file does not necessarily connote any actual relationship or contact with the CIA. For example, the Oswald file was opened, according to the Agency, because as an American defector, he was considered to be of continuing intelligence interest.[29] Oswald's file contained no indication that he had ever had a relationship with the CIA. Nevertheless, because the committee was aware of one instance (in an unrelated case) where an Agency officer had apparently contemplated the use of faked files with forged documents,[30] special attention was given to procedural questions that were occasioned by this file review.

(4) *Why the delay in opening Oswald's 201 file?*—A confidential State Department telegram dated October 31, 1959, sent from Moscow to Washington and forwarded to the CIA, reported that Oswald, a recently discharged Marine, had appeared at the U.S. Embassy in Moscow to renounce his American citizenship and "has offered Soviets any information he has acquired as [an] enlisted radar operator."[31] At least three other communications of a confidential nature that gave more detail on the Oswald case were sent to the CIA in about the same time period.[32] Agency officials questioned by the committee testified that the substance of the October 31, 1959, cable was sufficiently important to warrant the opening of a 201 file.[33] Oswald's file was not, however, opened until December 9, 1960.[34]

The committee requested that the CIA indicate where documents pertaining to Oswald had been disseminated internally and stored prior to the opening of his 201 file. The agency advised the committee that because document dissemination records of relatively low national security significance are retained for only a 5-year period, they were no longer in existence for the years 1959–63.[35][8]

---

[8]None of these documents were classified higher than confidential.

Consequently, the Agency was unable to explain either when these documents had been received or by which component.

An Agency memorandum, dated September 18, 1975, indicates that Oswald's file was opened on December 9, 1960, in response to the receipt of five documents: two from the FBI, two from the State Department and one from the Navy.[36] This explanation, however, is inconsistent with the presence in Oswald's file of four State Department documents dated in 1959 and a fifth dated May 25, 1960. It is, of course, possible that the September 18, 1975, memorandum is referring to State Department documents that were received by the Directorate for Plans[9] in October and November of 1960 and that the earlier State Department communications had been received by the CIA's Office of Security but not the Directorate for Plans. In the absence of dissemination records, however, the issue could not be resolved.

The September 18, 1975, memorandum also states that Oswald's file was opened on December 9, 1960, as a result of his "'defection' to the U.S.S.R. on October 31, 1959 and renewed interest in Oswald brought about by his queries concerning possible reentry into the United States." [37] There is no indication, however, that Oswald expressed to any U.S. Government official an intention to return to the United States until mid-February 1961.[38] Finally, reference to the original form that was used to start a file on Oswald did not resolve this issue because the appropriate space that would normally indicate the "source document" that initiated the action referred to an Agency component rather than to a dated document.[10] [39]

The committee was able to determine the basis for opening Oswald's file on December 9, 1960, by interviewing and then deposing the Agency employee who was directly responsible for initiating the opening action. This individual explained that the CIA had received a request from the State Department for information concerning American defectors. After compiling the requested information, she responded to the inquiry and then opened a 201 file on each defector involved.[40]

---

[9]The Directorate for Plans was the predecessor of the Directorate of Operations.
[10]The Agency indicated that it is customary to refer to a component when the opening action is taken on that component's authority.

This statement was corroborated by review of a State Department letter which indicated that such a request, in fact, had been made of the CIA on October 22, 1960. Attached to the State Department letter was a list of known defectors; Oswald's name was on that list. The CIA responded to this request on November 21, 1960, by providing the requested information and adding two names to the State Department's original list.[41]

Significantly, the committee reviewed the files of 11 individuals on the original State Department list and determined that files were opened in December 1960 for each of the five (including Oswald) who did not have 201 files prior to receipt of the State Department inquiry. In each case, the slot for "source document" referred to an Agency component rather than to a dated document.[42]

Even so, this analysis only explained why a file on Oswald was finally opened; it did not explain the seemingly delay in the opening of the file. To determine whether such a delayed opening was unusual, the committee reviewed the files of 13 of the 14 persons on the CIA's November 21, 1960, response to the State Department and of 16 other defectors (from an original list of 380) who were American-born, had defected during the years 1958–63, and who had returned to the United States during that same time period. Of 29 individuals whose files were reviewed, 8 had been the subject of 201 files prior to the time of their defection. In only 4 of the remaining 21 cases were 201 files opened at the time of defection. The files on the 17 other defectors were opened from 4 months to several years after the defection.[43] At the very least, the committee's review indicated that during 1958–63, the opening of a file years after a defection was not uncommon. In many cases, the opening was triggered by some event, independent of the defection, that had drawn attention to the individual involved.

(5) *Why was he carried as Lee Henry Oswald in his 201 file?*—Oswald's 201 file was opened under the name Lee Henry Oswald.[44] No Agency witness was able to explain why. All agency personnel, however, including the person who initiated the file opening, testified that this must have been occasioned innocently by bureaucratic error.[45] Moreover, the committee received substantial testimony to the effect that this error would not have prevented the misnamed file from being retrieved from the

254

CIA's filing system during a routine name trace done under the name Lee Harvey Oswald.[46]

(6) *The meaning of "AG" under "Other Identification" in Oswald's 201 file.* The form used to initiate the opening of a 201 file for Lee Harvey Oswald contains the designation AG in a box marked "Other Identification." Because this term was considered to be of potential significance in resolving the issue of Oswald's alleged Agency relationship, the CIA was asked to explain its meaning.

The Agency's response indicated that "AG" is the OI ("Other Identification") code meaning "actual or potential defectors to the East or the Sino/Soviet block including Cuba," and that anyone so described could have the OI code "AG." This code was reportedly added to Oswald's opening form because of the comment on the form that he had defected to the Soviet Union in 1959.[47]

An Agency official, who was a Directorate of Operations records expert and for many years one who had been involved in the CIA's investigation of the Kennedy assassination, gave the committee a somewhat different explanation of the circumstances surrounding the term "AG" and its placement on Oswald's opening form. This individual testified that "AG" was an example of a code used to aid in preparing computer listings of occupational groupings or intelligence affiliations. He explained that these codes always used two letters and that, in this case, the first letter "A" must have represented communism, while the second letter would represent some category within the Communist structure.[48]

His recollection was that at the time of the assassination, the "AG" code was not yet in existence because there were no provisions then in effect within the Agency for indexing American defectors. He recalled that it was only during the life of the Warren Commission that the CIA realized that its records system lacked provisions for indexing an individual such as Oswald. Consequently, the CIA revised its records manual to permit the indexing of American defectors and established a code for its computer system to be used for that category. Although this witness did not know when the notation "AG" was added to Oswald's opening sheet, he presumed that it must have been following the addition of the American defector code, thus placing the time somewhere in the middle of the Warren Commission's investigation. He explained that it was

255

difficult to determine when any of the notations on the opening sheet had been made, since it was standard procedure to update the forms whenever necessary so that they were as reflective as possible of the available information.[11][49]

Finally, this witness testified that the regulations regarding the use of this occupation and intelligence code specifically prohibited indicating that a particular person was either an employee of the Agency or someone who was used by the Agency. This prohibition was designed to prevent anyone from being able to produce any kind of categorical listing of CIA employees, contacts or connections.[50]

(7) *Why was Oswald's 201 file restricted?*—the form used to initiate the opening of Oswald's 201 file contains a notation indicating that the file was to be "restricted."[51] This indication was considered potentially significant because of the CIA's practice of restricting access to agents' files to persons on a "need-to-know" basis. Further investigation revealed, however, that restricting access to a file was not necessarily indicative of any relationship with the CIA.

The individual who actually placed the restriction on Oswald's file testified that this was done simply to allow her to remain aware of any developments that might have occurred with regard to the file.[52] The restriction achieved this purpose because any person seeking access to the file would first have to notify the restricting officer, at which time the officer would be apprised of any developments.

This testimony was confirmed by a CIA records expert who further testified that had the file been permanently charged to a particular desk or case officer, as well as restricted, the possibility of a relationship with the CIA would have been greater.[53] There is no indication on Oswald's form that it had been placed on permanent charge.

Finally, the committee reviewed the files of four other defectors that had been opened at the same time and by the same person as Oswald's, and determined that each of the files had been similarly restricted. Each of these

---

[11]The CIA, after considering this witness' recollection of the origin of the AG code, adhered to its original position regarding this issue.

other individuals was on the lists of defectors that had been exchanged by the CIA and State Department. None of the files pertaining to these other defectors had any evidence suggestive of a possible intelligence agency association.

(8) *Were 37 documents missing from Oswald's 201 file?*—in the course of reviewing Oswald's 201 file, the committee discovered an unsigned memorandum to the Chief of Counterintelligence, Research and Analysis, dated February 20, 1964, which stated that 37 documents were missing from Oswald's 201 file.[54] According to the memorandum, this statement was based on a comparison of a machine listing of documents officially recorded as being in the 201 file and those documents actually physically available in the file.[55] While the memorandum mentioned that such a machine listing was attached, no such attachment was found in the 201 file at the time of the committee's review. The memorandum itself bears the classification "Secret Eyes Only" and was one of the documents that had been fully withheld from release under the Freedom of Information Act.[56]

In response to a committee inquiry, the CIA advised that, because Oswald's file had been so active during the course of the Warren Commission investigation, up-to-date machine listings were produced periodically. On this basis, the Agency stated that

* * * it must be assumed that whoever was responsible for maintaining the Oswald file brought this file up-to-date by locating the 37 documents and placing them in the file.[57]

Because this response was incomplete, the author of the memorandum was deposed. He testified that once a document had been registered into a 201 file by the Agency's computer system, physical placement of the document in the file was not always necessary.[58] On this basis, he explained, the items listed in the memorandum were not missing but rather had either been routinely placed in a separate file because of their sensitivity or were being held by other individuals who needed them for analytical purposes.[59] He further stated that in the course of his custodianship of Oswald's file, he had requested perhaps as many as 100 computer listings on the

257

contents of the Oswald file. While there had been many instances in which one or more documents had been charged out to someone, he stated that he had never discovered that any documents were actually missing.[60] According to his testimony, the 37 documents were, in fact, available, but they were not located in the file at the time.[61] The committee regarded this to be a plausible explanation.

(9) *Did the CIA maintain a duel filing system on Oswald?*—The committee was aware of the possibility that a dual filing system (one innocuous file and one that contained operational detail of a relationship with the CIA) could have been used to disguise a possible relationship between Oswald and the Agency. This awareness became a concern with the discovery that at least two Agency officers had contemplated the use of faked files and forged documents to protect the ZR Rifle project from disclosure.[12][62] The implications of this discovery in terms of the possibility that the Oswald file might also have been faked were disturbing to the committee.

In the Oswald case, two items were scrutinized because they were potentially indicative of a dual filing system. The first was a photograph of Oswald that had been taken in Minsk in 1961; the second was a copy of a letter that had been written to Oswald by his mother during his stay in the Soviet Union. At the time of President Kennedy's assassination, both of these items were in the CIA's possession, but neither was in Oswald's 201 file.

The photograph of Oswald taken in Minsk shows him posing with several other people. According to the CIA, the picture was found after the assassination as a result of a search of the Agency's graphics files for materials potentially relevant to Oswald's stay in the Soviet Union. [64] The Agency advised that this photograph, as well as several others not related to Oswald, were routinely obtained in 1962 from some tourists by the CIA's Domestic Contacts Division, an Agency component that regularly sought information on a nonclandestine basis from Americans traveling aboard in Communist countries.[65]

---

[12]ZR Rifle was an executive action (assassination of foreign leader) program unrelated to the Oswald case. Former CIA Director Helms testified that the assassination aspect of ZR Rifle was never implemented and, in fact, was discontinued as soon as it was brought to his attention. [63]

Committee interviews with the tourists in question confirmed that the photograph, along with 159 other photographic slides, had routinely been made available to the Domestic Contacts Division. Neither tourist had heard of Oswald prior to the assassination or knew which photographs had been of interest to the Agency.[66]

CIA records indicate that only 5 of the 160 slides initially made available were retained.[67] Committee interviews with the two CIA employees who had handled the slides for the Domestic Contacts Division established that Oswald had not been identified at the time that these photographic materials were made available.[68] One of these employees stated that the Oswald picture had been retained because it depicted a Soviet Intourist guide; the other employee indicated that the picture had been kept because it showed a crane in the background.[69] Of these two employees, the one who worked at CIA headquarters (and therefore was in a position to know) indicated that the photograph of Oswald had not been discovered until a post-assassination search of the Minsk graphics file for materials pertaining to Oswald.[70]

Accordingly, this photograph was not evidence that the CIA maintained a dual filing system with respect to Oswald. The picture apparently was kept in a separate file until 1964, when Oswald was actually identified to be one of its subjects.

The committee's investigation of a copy of a letter to Oswald from his mother that was in the Agency's possession similarly did not show any evidence of a dual filing system. This letter, dated July 6, 1961, and sent by Marguerite Oswald, was intercepted as a result of a CIA program [71] known as HT-Lingual,[13] the purpose of which was to obtain intelligence and counterintelligence information from letters sent between the United States and Russia. Typically, intercepted letters and envelopes would be photographed and then returned to the mails. [72]

In response to a committee inquiry, the CIA explained that because of HT-Lingual's extreme sensitivity, all materials generated as a result of mail intercepts were stored in a separate project file that was maintained by

---

[13]The HT-Lingual program was no longer in effect in 1978. Prior to that time, it had been found to be illegal.

the counterintelligence staff.[73] Consequently, such items were not placed in 201 files. This explanation was confirmed by the testimony of a senior officer from the counterintelligence staff who had jurisdiction over the HT-Lingual project files.[14][74]

(10) *Did Oswald ever participate in a CIA counterintelligence project?*—The committee's review of HT-Lingual files pertaining to the Oswald case[15] resulted in the discovery of reproductions of four index cards, two with reference to Lee Harvey Oswald and two to Marina Oswald, which were dated after the assassination of President Kennedy. The pages containing the reproductions of these cards were stamped "Secret Eyes Only." [75]

The first card regarding Lee Harvey Oswald, dated November 9, 1959, states that Oswald is a recent defector to the U.S.S.R. and a former marine. It also bears the notation "CI/Project/RE" and some handwritten notations.[76] The second card on Oswald places him in Minsk. It contains background information on him and states that he "reportedly expresses a desire for return to the United States under certain conditions." This card is dated August 7, 1961, and also bears the notation "Watch List."[77] These cards, particularly the reference to "CI/Project/RE," raised the question of whether Oswald was, in fact, involved in some sort of counterintelligence project for the CIA.

The committee questioned former employees of the CIA who may have had some knowledge pertaining to the HT-Lingual project in general and these cards in particular. Some of these employees recognized the cards as relating to the HT-Lingual project, but were unable to identify the meaning of the notation, "CI/Project/RE."[78]

One employee, however, testified that the "CI Project" was "simply a name of convenience that was used to de-

---

[14]Since Oswald was known to have sent or received more than 50 communications during his stay in the Soviet Union, the committee also questioned why the Agency ostensibly had just one letter in its possession directly related to Oswald. In essence, the Agency's response suggested that HT-Lingual only operated 4 days a week, and, even then, proceeded on a sampling basis.

[15]Although the Agency had only one Oswald letter in its possession, the HT-Lingual files were combed after the assassination for additional materials potentially related to him. Approximately 30 pieces of correspondence that were considered potentially related to the investigation of Oswald's case (even though not necessarily directly related to Oswald) were discovered. None of these was ultimately judged by the CIA to be of any significance. These materials, however, were stored in a separate Oswald HT-Lingual file.

scribe the HT-Lingual project"; [79] another testified that "CI Project" was the name of the component that ran the HT-Lingual project. This person also explained that "RE" represented the initials of a person who had been a translator of foreign language documents and that the initials had probably been placed there so that someone could come back to the translator if a question arose concerning one of the documents.[80] Another employee indicted that the "Watch List" notation on the second card referred to persons who had been identified as being of particular interest with respect to the mail intercept program.[81]

The committee requested the CIA to provide an explanation for the terms "CI/Project/RE" and "Watch List" and for the handwritten notations appearing on the index cards. In addition, the committee requested a description of criteria used in compiling a "Watch List."

With respect to the meaning of the notation "CI/Project/RE," the CIA explained that there existed an office within the counterintelligence staff that was known as "CI/Project," a cover title that had been used to hide the true nature of the office's functions. In fact, this office was responsible for the exploitation of the material produced by the HT-Lingual project. The Agency further explained that "RE" represented the initials of a former employee.[82]

In responding to a request for the criteria used in compiling a "Watch List," the CIA referred to a section of the "Report to the President by the Commission on CIA Activities Within the United States," which states:

> Individuals or organizations of particular intelligence interest (one should also add counterintelligence interest) were specified in watch lists provided to the mail project by the counterintelligence staff, by other CIA components, and by the FBI. The total number of names on the Watch List varied, from time to time, but on the average, the list included approximately 300 names, including about 100 furnished by the FBI. The Watch List included the names of foreigners and of U.S. citizens.[83]

Thus, the full meaning of the notation is that on November 9, 1959, an employee whose initials were RE placed Oswald's name on the "Watch List" for the HT-Lingual project for the reason stated on the card—that Oswald was a recent defector to the U.S.S.R. and a former Marine.[84]

The response went on to state that the handwritten number, No. 7–305, which also appears on the first card, is a reference to the communication from the CI staff to the Office of Security expressing the CI staff's interest in seeing any mail to or from Oswald in the Soviet Union. Finally, the other handwritten notation, "N/R–RI, 20 Nov. 59" signifies that a name trace run through the central records register indicates that there was no record for Lee Oswald as of that date.[16][85]

The agency's explanation of the meaning of the second card was that on August 7, 1961, the CIA staff officer who opened the Oswald 201 file requested that Oswald's name be placed on the "Watch List" because of Oswald's expressed desire to return to the United States, as stated on the card. The handwritten notation indicates, in this instance, that Oswald's name was deleted from the "Watch List" on May 28, 1962.[86]

With reference to the two cards on Marina Oswald, the Agency stated that her name was first placed on the "Watch List" on November 26, 1963, because she was the wife of Lee Harvey Oswald. The second card served the purpose of adding the name Marina Oswald Porter to the "Watch List" on June 29, 1965, after she had remarried. Both names were deleted from the list as of May 26, 1972.[87]

Thus the statements of former CIA employees were corroborated by the Agency's response regarding the explanation of the index cards in the CIA's HT-Lingual files pertaining to Oswald. The explanations attested that the references on the cards were not demonstrative of an Agency relationship with Oswald, but instead were examples of notations routinely used in connection with the HT-Lingual project.

(11) *Did the CIA ever debrief Oswald?*—The CIA has denied ever having had any contact with Oswald,[88] and its records are consistent with this position. Because the

---

[16]This, of course, is contrary to the Agency's record that indicates the receipt of a telegram concerning Oswald on Oct. 31, 1959, and of two telegrams from the Navy concerning him on No. 3 and 4, 1959.

Agency has a Domestic Contacts Division that routinely attempts to solicit information on a nonclandestine basis from Americans traveling abroad,[89] the absence of any record indicating that Oswald, a returning defector who had worked in a Minsk radio factory, had been debriefed has been considered by Warren Commission critics to be either inherently unbelievable (that is, the record was destroyed) or indicative that Oswald had been contacted through other than routine Domestic Contact Division channels.[90]

After reviewing the Agency's records pertaining to this issue, the committee interviewed the former chief of an Agency component responsible for research related to clandestine operations within the Soviet Union. He had written a November 25, 1963, memorandum indicating that, upon Oswald's return from the Soviet Union, he had considered "the laying of interviews [on him] through the [Domestic Contacts Division] or other suitable channels."[17][91] The officer indicated that Oswald was considered suspect because the Soviets appeared to have been very solicitous of him. For this reason, a nonclandestine contact, either by the Domestic Contacts Division or other "suitable channels" such as the FBI or the Immigration and Naturalization Service, was considered.[92] The officer stated, however, that to his knowledge no contact with Oswald was ever made. Moreover, if a debriefing had occurred, the officer stated that he would have been informed. Finally, he said that Oswald was considered a potential lead, but only of marginal importance, and therefore the absence of a debriefing was not at all unusual. [93]

The committee interviewed five other Agency employees who were in a position to have discussed Oswald in 1962 with the author of this memorandum, including the person who replaced the author of the memorandum as chief of the research section. None of them could recall such a discussion.[94] Interviews with personnel from the Soviet Russia Division's clandestine operations section, the visitors program and the clandestine activity research sec-

---

[17]The November 25, 1963 memorandum indicates that the possibility of an Oswald contact was discussed during the summer of 1960, but the author indicated that the conversation actually took place during the summer of 1962, shortly before his transfer to a new assignment. During the summer of 1960, the author was not on active assignment.

tion failed to result in any evidence suggesting that Oswald had been contacted at any time by the CIA.[96]

The author of the November 25, 1963, memorandum also informed the committee that the CIA maintained a large volume of information on the Minsk radio factory in which Oswald had worked. This information was stored in the Office of Research and Reports.[96]

Another former CIA employee, one who had worked in the Soviet branch of the Foreign Documents Division of the Directorate of Intelligence in 1962, advised the committee that he specifically recalled collecting intelligence regarding the Minsk radio plant. In fact, this individual claimed that during the summer of 1962, he reviewed a contact report from representatives of a CIA field office who had interviewed a former marine who had worked at the Minsk radio plant following his defection to the U.S.S.R. This defector, whom the employee believed may have been Oswald, had been living with his family in Minsk.[97]

The employee advised the committee that the contact report had been filed in a volume on the Minsk radio plant that should be retrievable from the Industrial Registry Branch, then a component of the Office of Central Reference. Accordingly, the committee requested that the CIA provide both the contact report and the volume of materials concerning the Minsk radio plant. A review by the committee of the documents in the volumes on the Minsk radio plant, however, failed to locate any such contact report.[98]

Since the Minsk radio plant seemed to be a logical subject of CIA concern, the committee theorized that questions about it would have been included in the debriefing of defectors. The committee therefore asked the Agency for a statement regarding its procedures for debriefing defectors. In response, the CIA stated that between 1958 and 1963 it had no procedure for systematically debriefing overseas travelers, including returning defectors. Instead, the Agency relied upon the FBI both to make such contacts and report any significant results. [99]

Two investigate this question further, the committee reviewed the files of 22 other defectors to the Soviet Union (from an original list of 380) who were born in America and appeared to have returned to the United

States between 1958 and 1963.[18] Of these 22 individuals, only 4 were interviewed at any time by the CIA. These four instances tended to involve particular intelligence or counterintelligence needs, but this was not always the case.[100]

Based on this file review, it appeared to the committee that, in fact, the CIA did not contact returning defectors in 1962 as a matter of standard operating procedure. For this reason, the absence of any Agency contact with Oswald on his return from the Soviet Union could not be considered unusual, particularly since the FBI did fulfill its jurisdictional obligation to conduct defector interviews. [101]

(12) *The Justice Department's failure to prosecute Oswald.*—When Oswald appeared at the U.S. Embassy on October 31, 1959, to renounce his American citizenship, he allegedly threatened to give the Soviets information he had acquired as a Marine Corps radar operator. [102] The committee sought to determine why the Justice Department did not prosecute Oswald on his return to the United States for his offer to divulge this kind of information.

A review of Oswald's correspondence with the American Embassy in Moscow indicates that on February 13, 1961, the embassy received a letter in which Oswald expressed a "desire to return to the United States if * * * some agreement [could be reached] concerning the dropping of any legal proceedings against [him]." [103] On February 28, 1961, the embassy sought guidance from the State Department concerning Oswald's potential liability to criminal prosecution.[104] The State Department, however, responded on April 13, 1961, that it was

not in a position to advise Mr. Oswald whether upon his desired return to the United States he may be amenable to prosecution for any possible offenses committed in violation of the laws of the United States * * *.[105]

In May 1961, Oswald wrote the embassy demanding a "full guarantee" against the possibility of prosecution.[106]

---

[18]An effort was also made to review only the files of those who had defected between 1958 and 1963. Not all of the 22 defectors, however, met this criterion.

He visited with Embassy Consul Richard Snyder on July 16, 1961, and denied that he had ever given any information to the Soviets.[107] Snyder advised Oswald on an informal basis that, while no assurances could be given, the embassy did not perceive any basis for prosecuting him.[108]

There is no record that the State Department ever gave Oswald any assurances that he would not be prosecuted. Upon his return to the United States, Oswald was interviewed twice by the FBI. On each occasion, he denied ever having given information to the Soviet Union. [109]

In response to a committee request, the Department of Justice indicated that prosecution of Oswald was never considered because his file contained no evidence that he had ever revealed or offered to reveal national defense information to the Soviet Union.[110] In a subsequent response, the Department acknowledged the existence of some evidence that Oswald had offered information to the Soviet Union, but stated that there were, nevertheless, serious obstacles to a possible prosecution:

It [the Department file] does contain a copy of an FBI memorandum, dated July 3, 1961, which is recorded as having been received in the Justice Department's Internal Security Division on December 10, 1963, which states that the files of the Office of Naval Intelligence contained a copy of a Department of State telegram, dated October 31, 1959, at Moscow. The telegram, which is summarized in the FBI report, quoted Oswald as having offered the Soviets any information he had acquired as a radar operator. The FBI report did not indicate that the information to which Oswald had access as a radar operator was classified.

Oswald returned to the United States on June 13, 1962. He was interviewed by the FBI on June 26, 1962, at Fort Worth, Tex., at which time he denied furnishing any information to the Soviets concerning his Marine Corps experiences. He stated that he never gave the Soviets any information which would be used to the detriment of the United States.

In sum, therefore, the only "evidence" that Oswald ever offered to furnish information to the Soviets is his own reported statement to an official at the U.S. Embassy in Moscow. That statement, of course, was contradicted by his denial to the FBI, upon his return to the United States, that he had ever made such an offer.

In the prosecution of a criminal case, the Government cannot establish a prima facie case solely on a defendant's unsupported confession. The Government must introduce substantial independent evidence which would tend to establish the trustworthiness of the defendant's statement. See, *Opper* v. *United States* U.S. 84 (1954).

Accordingly, in the absence of any information that Oswald had offered to reveal classified information to the Soviets, and lacking corroboration of his statement that he had proferred information of any kind to the Russians, we did not consider his prosecution for violation of the espionage statutes, 18 U.S.C. 793, 794.[111]

Based upon this analysis, the committee could find no evidence that Oswald received favorable treatment from either the State Department or the Justice Department regarding the possibility of criminal prosecution.

(13) *Oswald's trip to Russia via Helsinki and his ability to obtain a visa in 2 days.*—Oswald's trip from London to Helsinki has been a point of controversy. His passport indicates he arrived in Finland on October 10, 1959. The Torni Hotel in Helsinki, however, had him registered as a guest on that date, although the only direct flight from London to Helsinki landed at 11:33 p.m., that day. According to a memorandum signed in 1964 by Richard Helms, "[i]f Oswald had taken this flight, he could not normally have cleared customs and landing formalities and reached the Torni Hotel downtown by 2400 (midnight) on the same day."[112] Further questions concerning this segment of Oswald's trip have been raised because he had been able to obtain a Soviet entry visa within only 2 days of having applied for it on October 12, 1959.[113][19]

The committee was unable to determine the circumstances surrounding Oswald's trip from London to Helsinki. Louis Hopkins, the travel agent who arranged Oswald's

---

[19]Since Oswald arrived in Helsinki on October 10, 1959, which was a Saturday, it is assumed that his first opportunity to apply for a visa would have been on Monday, October 12.

initial transportation from the United States, stated that he did not know Oswald's ultimate destination at the time that Oswald booked his passage on the freighter *Marion Lykes*.[114] Consequently, Hopkins had nothing to do with the London-to-Helsinki leg of Oswald's trip. In fact, Hopkins stated that had he known Oswald's final destination, he would have suggested sailing on another ship that would have docked at a port more convenient to Russia.[115] Hopkins indicated that Oswald did not appear to be particularly well-informed about travel to Europe. The travel agent did not know whether Oswald had been referred to him by anyone.[116]

A request for any CIA and Department of Defense files on Louis Hopkins resulted in a negative response. The committee was unable to obtain any additional sources of information regarding Oswald's London-to-Helsinki trip.

The relative ease with which Oswald obtained his Soviet Union entry visa was more readily amenable to investigation. This issue is one that also had been of concern to the Warren Commission.[117] In a letter to the CIA dated May 25, 1964, J. Lee Rankin inquired about the apparent speed with which Oswald's Soviet visa had been issued. Rankin noted that he had recently spoken with Abraham Chayes, legal adviser to the State Department, who maintained that at the time Oswald received his visa to enter Russia from the Soviet Embassy in Helsinki, normally at least 1 week would elapse between the time of a tourist's application and the issuance of a visa. Rankin contended that if Chayes' assessment was accurate, then Oswald's ability to obtain his tourist visa in 2 days might have been significant.[118]

The CIA responded to Rankin's request for information on July 31, 1964. Helms wrote to Rankin that the Soviet Consulate in Helsinki was able to issue a transit visa (valid for 24 hours) to U.S. businessmen within 5 minutes but if a longer stay were intended, at least 1 week was needed to process a visa application and arrange lodging through Soviet Intourist.[119] A second communication from Helms to Rankin, dated September 14, 1964, added that during the 1964 tourist season, Soviet consulates in at least some Western European cities issued Soviet tourist visas in from 5 to 7 days.[120]

In effort to resolve this issue, the committee reviewd classified information pertaining to Gregory Golub, who was the Soviet Consul in Helsinki when Oswald was issued his tourist visa. This review revealed that, in addition to his consular activities, Golub was suspected of having been an officer of the Soviet KGB. Two American Embassy dispatches concerning Golub were of particular significance with regard to the time necessary for issurance of visas to Americans for travel into the Soviet Union. The first dispatch recorded that Golub disclosed during a luncheon conversation that:

Moscow had given him the authority to give Americans visas without prior approval from Moscow. He [Golub] stated that this would make his job much easier, and as long as he was convinced the American was "all right" he could give him a visa in a matter of minutes * * *.[121]

The second dispatch, dated October 9, 1959, 1 day prior to Oswald's arrival in Helsinki, illustrated that Golub did have the authority to issue visas without delay. The dispatch discussed a telephone contact between Golub and his consular counterpart at the American Embassy in Helsinki:

* * * Since that evening [September 4, 1959] Golub has only phoned [the U.S. consul] once and this was on a business matter. Two Americans were in the Soviet Consulate at the time and were applying for Soviet visas thru Golub. They had previously been in the American consulate inquiring about the possibility of obtaining a Soviet visa in 1 or 2 days. [The U.S. Consul advised them to go directly to Golub and make their request, which they did. Golub phoned [the U.S. Consul] to state that he would give them their visas as soon as they made advance Intourist reservations. When they did this, Golub immediately gave them their visas * * *.[20] [122]

Thus, based upon these two factors, (1) Golub's authority to issue visas to Americans without prior approval from Moscow, and (2) a demonstration of this authority, as reported in an embassy dispatch approximately 1 month

[20]Evidently Oswald had made arrangements with Intourist. On his arrival at the Moscow railroad station on October 16, he was met by an Intourist representative and taken to the Hotel Berlin where he registered as a student. [123]

269

prior to Oswald's appearance at the Soviet Embassy, the committee found that the available evidence tends to support the conclusion that the issuance of Oswald's tourist visa within 2 days after his appearance at the Soviet Consulate was not indicative of an American intelligence agency connection.[21]

(14) *Oswald's contact with Americans in the Soviet Union.*—Priscilla Johnson McMillan, author of "Marina and Lee," became a subject of the committee's inquiry because she was one of two American correspondents who had obtained an interview with Oswald during his stay in Moscow in 1959. The committee sought to investigate an allegation that her interview with Oswald may have been arranged by the CIA.[124]

John McVickar, a consul at the American Embassy, testified that he had discussed Oswald's case with McMillan, and that he thought "* * * she might help us in communicating with him and help him in dealing with what appeared to be a very strong personal problem if she were able to talk with him."[125] McVickar stated, however, that he had never worked in any capacity for the CIA, nor did he believe that McMillan had any such affiliation.[126] McVickar's State Department and CIA files were consistent with his testimony that he had never been associated with the CIA.

McMillan gave the following testimony about the events surrounding her interview with Oswald. In November 1959, she had returned from a visit to the United States where she covered the Camp David summit meeting between President Eisenhower and Premier Khrushchev. On November 16, 1959, she went to the American Embassy to pick up her mail for the first time since her return to the Soviet Union. The mail pickup facility was in a foyer near the consular office. Consular Officer John A. McVickar came out of this office and welcomed McMillan back to the Soviet Union. They exchanged a few words, and, as she was leaving, McVickar commented that at her hotel was an American who was trying to defect to the Soviet Union. McVickar stated that the American would not speak to "any of us," but he might speak to McMillan because she was a woman. She recalled that as she was leaving, Mc-

---

[21]If anything, Oswald's ability to receive a Soviet entry visa so quickly was more indicative of a Soviet interest in him.

Vickar told her to remember that she was an American.
[127]

McMillan proceeded to her hotel, found out the American's room number, knocked on his door and asked him for an interview. The American, Lee Harvey Oswald, did not ask her into the room, but he did agree to talk to her in her room later that night.[128] No American Government official arranged the actual interview. McMillan met with Oswald just once. She believed that McVickar called her on November 17, the day after the interview, and asked her to supper. That evening they discussed the interview. McVickar indicated a general concern about Oswald and believed that the attitude of another American consular official might have pushed Oswald further in the direction of defection. McVickar indicated a personal feeling that it would be a sad thing for Oswald to defect in view of his age, but he did not indicate that this was the U.S. Government's position.[129]

McMillan also testified that she had never worked for the CIA, nor had she been connected with any other Federal Government agency at the time of her interview with Oswald.[130] According to an affidavit that McMillan filed with the committee, her only employment with the Federal Government was as a 30-day temporary translator.[131]

Finally, McMillan testified that because of her background in Russian studies, she applied for a position with the CIA in 1952 as an intelligence analyst. The application, however, was withdrawn.[132] She acknowledged having been debriefed by an Agency employee in 1962 after returning from her third trip to the Soviet Union, but explained that this contact was in some way related to the confiscation of her notes by Soviet officials.[133][22]

The committee's review of CIA files pertaining to Ms. McMillan corroborated her testimony. There was no in-

---

[22]In her affidavit McMillan discussed the circumstances surrounding this encounter in some detail: "In November 1962, I had a conversation with a man who identified himself as a CIA employee * * * I agreed to see him in part because the confiscation of my papers and notes had utterly altered my situation—I now had no hope of returning to the U.S.S.R. and was free for the first time to write what I knew. I was preparing a series of articles for The Reporter which would contain the same information about which [the CIA employee] had expressed a desire to talk to me. Finally, during the latter part of my 1962 trip to the U.S.S.R., I had been under heavy surveillance and the KGB knew what Soviet citizens I had seen. Many of those I had talked to for the Reporter articles were Russian 'liberals' (anti-Stalin and pro-Khrushchev). What reprisals might befall those whom I had interviewed I did not know, but since my notes

dication in these files suggesting that she had ever worked for the CIA. In fact, the Agency did not even debrief her after her first two trips to the Soviet Union. An interview with the former Agency official who had been deputy chief and then chief of the visitors program during the years 1958 to 1961 similarly indicated that McMillan had not been used by the CIA in the program.[134]

There was information in McMillan's file indicating that on occasion during the years 1962–65 she had provided cultural and literary information to the CIA. None of this information was, however, suggestive in any way of a clandestine relationship. Accordingly, there was no evidence that McMillan ever worked for the CIA or received the Agency's assistance in obtaining an interview with Oswald.[23]

Richard E. Snyder was the consular official in the U.S. Embassy in Moscow who handled the Oswald case. It was Snyder with whom Oswald had met in 1959 when he sought to renounce his American citizenship.[135] Two years later, when Oswald initiated his inquiries about returning to the United States, Snyder again became involved in the case.[136] Warren Commission critics have alleged that Snyder was associated in some way with the CIA during his service in the Moscow Embassy.[137]

In his committee deposition, Richard Snyder acknowledged that for an 11-month period during 1949–50 he worked for the CIA while he was on the waiting list for a foreign service appointment with the State Department. [138] Snyder testified, however, that since resigning from the CIA in March 1950, he had had no contact with the CIA other than a letter written in 1970 or 1971 inquiring about employment on a contractual basis.[139][24]

The committee reviewed Snyder's files at the State Department, Defense Department and the CIA. Both the State Department and Defense Department files are consistent with his testimony. Snyder's CIA file revealed that,

were now part of the KGB files, I felt that it might help them if the CIA knew that which the KGB already knew. My meeting with—the CIA employee—which occurred at the Brattle Inn, Cambridge, was a reversal of my usual effort to avoid contact with the CIA, and the subject matter was confined to my impressions of the Soviet literary and cultural climate."

[23]Nor was there any basis, based on McMillan's testimony, CIA files or evidence provided by McMillan's publisher, Harper and Row, to support the allegation that the CIA financed or was otherwise involved in publishing "Marina and Lee."

[24]Snyder also denied contact with any other intelligence service while active as a foreign service officer.

at one time prior to 1974, it had been red flagged and maintained on a segregated basis. The file contained a routing indicator that stated that the file had been red flagged because of a "DCI [Director of Central Intelligence] statement and a matter of cover" concerning Snyder.[140]

In response to a committee inquiry, the CIA indicated that the DCI statement presumably refers to comments which former Director Richard Helms had made in 1964 concerning the Oswald case, when Helms was Deputy Director for Plans.[25] The CIA also stated that Snyder's file had been flagged at the request of DDO/CI (Directorate of Operations/Central Intelligence) to insure that all inquiries concerning Snyder would be referred to that office. The Agency was unable to explain the reference to "cover," because, according to its records, Snyder had never been assigned any cover while employed. Further, the Agency stated that "[t]here is no record in Snyder's official personnel file that he ever worked, directly or indirectly, in any capacity for the CIA after his resignation on 26 September 1950."[142]

The committee did not regard this explanation as satisfactory, especially since Snyder's 201 file indicated that for approximately 1 year during 1956–57 he had been used by an Agency case officer as a spotter at a university campus because of his access to others who might be going to the Soviet Union, nor was the Agency able to explain specifically why someone considered it necessary to red flag the Snyder file.

The remainder of the Snyder file, however, is consistent with his testimony before the committee concerning the absence of Agency contacts. In addition, the CIA personnel officer who handled Snyder's case in 1950 confirmed that Snyder had, in fact, terminated his employment with the CIA at that time. Moreover, he added that Snyder had gone to the State Department as a bona fide employee without any CIA ties.[143] This position was confirmed by a former State Department official who was familiar with State Department procedures regarding CIA employees. In addition, this individual stated that at no time from 1959 to 1963 did the CIA use the State De-

---

[25]Responding to a newspaper allegation that Oswald had met with CIA representatives in Moscow, Richard Helms wrote a memorandum to the Warren Commission on March 18, 1964, in which he stated the "desire to state for the record that the allegation carried in this press report is utterly unfounded as far as the CIA is concerned." [141]

partment's overseas consular positions as cover for CIA intelligence officers.[144]

The CIA's failure to explain adequately the red-flagging of Snyder's file was extremely troubling to the committee. Even so, based on Snyder's sworn testimony, the review of his file and the statements of his former personnel officer, a finding that he was in contact with Oswald on behalf of the CIA was not warranted.

Dr. Alexis H. Davison was the U.S. Embassy physician in Moscow from May 1961 to May 1963. In May 1963, the Soviet Union declared him persona non grata in connection with his alleged involvement in the Penkovsky case.[145] After the assassination of President Kennedy, it was discovered that the name of Dr. Davison's mother, Mrs. Hal Davison, and her Atlanta address were in Oswald's address book under the heading "Mother of U.S. Embassy Doctor."[146] In addition, it was determined that the flight that Oswald, his wife and child took from New York to Dallas on June 14, 1962, had stopped in Atlanta.[147] For this reason, it has been alleged that Dr. Davison was Oswald's intelligence contact inMoscow.[148]

In a committee interview, Dr. Davison stated that he had been a physician in the U.S. Air Force and was stationed in Moscow as the US. Embassy physician from May 1961 to May 1963. In this capacity, it was his duty to perform physical examinations on all Soviet immigrants in the United States. He recalled that most of these immigrants were elderly, but he remembers two young women, one who was a mathematics teacher from the south of Russia and one who was married to an American. The individual who was married to the American was frightened by the prospect of going to the United States. She stated that she was going to Texas with her husband. Davison told her that if she and her husband traveled through Atlanta on their way to Texas, his mother, a native-born Russian, would be happy to see her. He gave his mother's name and address in Atlanta to the woman's husband, who was "scruffy looking." This was not an unusual thing to do, since his family had always been very hospitable to Russians who visited Atlanta. In retrospect, he assumed that he gave his mother's name and address to either Lee or Marina Oswald, but he was uncertain about this.[149]

After the assassination of President Kennedy, Davison was interviewed first by a Secret Service agent and later by an FBI agent in connection with the entry of his mother's name and address in Oswald's address book. The FBI agent also interviewed Davison's mother, Natalia Alekseevna Davison. Davison indicated that the Secret Service and the FBI were the only Government agencies to interview him about his contact with the Oswalds.[150]

Davison stated that in connection with his assignment as U.S. Embassy physician in Moscow, he had received some superficial intelligence training. This training mainly involved lectures on Soviet life and instructions on remembering and reporting Soviet names and military activities. [151]

Davison admitted his involvement in the Penkovsky spy case. During his tour of duty in Moscow, Davison was asked by an Embassy employee, whose name he no longer remembered, to observe a certain lamppost on his daily route between his apartment and the Embassy and to be alert for a signal by telephone. Davison agreed. According to his instructions, if he ever saw a black chalk mark on the lamppost, or if he ever received a telephone call in which the caller blew into the receiver three times, he was to notify a person whose name he also no longer remembered. He was told nothing else about the operation. Davison performed his role for approximately 1 year. On just one occasion, toward the end of his stay in the Soviet Union, he observed the mark on the lamppost and his wife received the telephone signal. As instructed, he reported these happenings. Shortly thereafter, the Soviets reported that they had broken the Penkovsky spying operation. The Soviets declared Davison persona non grata just after he left Moscow, his tour of duty having ended. He did not recall any intelligence debriefings on the Penkovsky case. [152]

Davison denied under oath participating in any other intelligence work during his tour in Moscow.[153] The deputy chief of the CIA's Soviet Russia clandestine activities section from 1960 to 1962 confirmed Davison's position, characterizing his involvement in the Penkovsky case as a "one shot" deal.[154] In addition, a review of Davison's CIA and Department of Defense files showed them to be consistent with his committee testimony.

Accordingly, there was insufficient evidence for concluding that Dr. Davison was an intelligence contact for Oswald in Moscow.

(15) *Alleged intelligence contacts after Oswald returned*

from Russia.—George de Mohrenschildt was an enigmatic man—a geologist-businessman who befriended Oswald in Texas in 1962,[155] thus causing considerable speculation based on the contrasting backgrounds of the two men. De Mohrenschildt, who committed suicide in 1977, was sophisticated and well educated, a man who moved easily among wealthy Texas oilmen and a circle of white Russians in Dallas, many of whom were avowed conservatives. Oswald, because of his background and his Marxist ideological positions, was shunned by most of the people de Mohrenschildt counted among his friends.

In his Warren Commission testimony, de Mohrenschildt stated that he believed he had discussed Oswald with J. Walton Moore, whom he described as "a Government man —either FBI or Central Intelligence."[156] He said that Moore was known as the head of the FBI in Dallas, and that Moore had interviewed him in 1957 when he returned from a trip to Yugoslavia. [157] De Mohrenschildt indicated that he had asked Moore and Fort Worth attorney Max Clark about Oswald, to reassure himself that it was "safe" for the de Mohrenschildts to assist him and was told by one of these persons, "the guy seems to be OK." [158] This admitted association with J. Walton Moore employee of the CIA, gave rise to the question of whether de Mohrenschildt had contacted Oswald on behalf of the CIA.[159]

In 1963, J. Walton Moore was employed by the CIA in Dallas in the Domestic Contacts Division.[160] According to Moore's CIA personnel file, he had been assigned to the division in 1948. During the period April 1, 1963, to March 31, 1964, he was an overt CIA employee assigned to contact persons traveling abroad for the purpose of eliciting information they might obtain. He was not part of a covert or clandestine operation.

In an Agency memorandum dated April 13, 1977, contained in de Mohrenschildt's CIA file, Moore set forth facts to counter a claim that had been recently made by a Dallas television station that Oswald had been employed by the CIA and that Moore had known him. In that memorandum, Moore was quoted as saying that, according to his records, the last time he had talked with de Mohrenschildt was in the fall of 1961. Moore said that he had no recollection of any conversation with de Mohrenschildt concerning Oswald. The memorandum also said that Moore recalled only two occasions when he had met de Mohrenschildt—first, in the spring of 1958, to discuss a mutual interest in China; and then in the fall of 1961, when de Mohrenschildt and his wife showed films of their Latin American walking trip.[161]

Other documents in de Mohrenschildt's CIA file, however, indicated more contact with Moore than was stated in the 1977 memorandum. In a memorandum dated May 1, 1964, submitted to the Acting Chief of the Domestic Contacts Division of the CIA, Moore stated that he had known de Mohrenschildt and his wife since 1957, at which time Moore obtained biographical data on de Mohrenschildt following his trip to Yugoslavia for the International Cooperation Administration. Moore also wrote in that 1964 memorandum that he had seen de Mohrenschildt several times in 1958 and 1959. De Mohrenschildt's CIA file contained several reports submitted by de Mohrenschildt to the CIA on topics concerning Yugoslavia.[162]

De Mohrenschildt testified before the Warren Commission that he had never been in any respect an intelligence agent.[163] Further, the committee's interview with Moore and its review of the CIA's Moore and de Mohrenschildt files showed no evidence that de Mohrenschildt had ever been an American intelligence agent. (In this regard, the committee noted that during 1959–63, upon returning from trips abroad, as many as 25,000 Americans annually provided information to the CIA's Domestic Contacts Division on a nonclandestine basis.[164] Such acts of cooperation should not be confused with an actual Agency relationship.)[26]

Prior to visiting Mexico in September 1963, Oswald applied in New Orleans for a Mexican tourist card. The tourist card immediately preceding his in numerical sequence was issued on September 17, 1963,[167] to William G. Gaudet, a newspaper editor. Two days later, Gaudet departed on a 3- or 4-week trip to Mexico and other Latin American countries.[168] This happened to coincide with Oswald's visit to Mexico City between September 27, 1963, and October 3, 1963.[169] After the assassination, Gaudet advised the FBI during an interview

---

[26]De Mohrenschildt's file also contains a reference to an occasion when he may have been involved in arranging a meeting between a Haitian bank officer and a CIA or Department of Defense official.[165] The Department of Defense official, when interviewed by the committee, stated that the meeting was arranged by Department of Defense officials and that de Mohrenschildt's presence (in the company of his wife) was unanticipated. [166] The committee did not regard this incident as evidence of a CIA relationship.

that he had once been employed by the CIA.[170] Speculation about Gaudet's possible relationship with Oswald arose when it was discovered that the Warren Commission Report contained a list, provided by the Mexican Government, purporting to include all individuals who had been issued Mexican tourist cards at the same time as Oswald, a list that omitted Gaudet's name.[171]

In a committee deposition, Gaudet testified that his contact with the CIA was primarily as a source of information (obtained during his trips abroad). In addition, he explained that he occasionally performed errands for the Agency.[172] Gaudet stated that his last contact with the CIA was in 1969, although the relationship had never been formally terminated.[173]

The committee reviewed Gaudet's CIA file but found neither any record reflecting a contact between him and the Agency after 1961, nor any indication that he had "performed errands" for the CIA. A memorandum, dated January 23, 1976, also indicated the absence of any further contact after this time:

> The Domestic Collections Division (DCD) has an inactive file on William George Gaudet, former editor and publisher of the Latin American Report. The file shows that Gaudet was a source of the New Orleans DCD (Domestic Contacts Division) Resident Office from 1948 to 1955 during which period he provided foreign intelligence information on Latin American political and economic conditions resulting from his extensive travel in South and Central America in pursuit of journalistic interests. The file further indicates that Gaudet was a casual contact of the New Orleans Office between 1955 and 1961 when, at variout times, he furnished fragmentary intelligence.[174]

Gaudet said he could not recall whether his trip to Mexico and other Latin American countries in 1963 involved any intelligence-related activity.[175) He was able to testify, however, that during that trip he did not encounter Oswald, whom he had previously observed on occasion at the New Orleans Trade Mart.[176][27] Gaudet

---

[27]Gaudet testified that he had never met Oswald, although he had known of him prior to the assassination because Oswald had distributed literature near his office. Gaudet also stated that on one occasion he observed Oswald speaking to Guy Banister on a street corner.

stated that he was unaware at the time his Mexican tourist card was issued that it immediately preceded Oswald's, and he could not recall having seen Oswald on that day. [177] Finally, Gaudet said he did not have any information concerning the omission of his name from the list published in the Warren Commission Report.[178]

Based upon this evidence, the committee did not find a basis for concluding that Gaudet had contacted Oswald on behalf of the CIA. Although there was a conflict between Gaudet's testimony and his CIA file concerning the duration of his Agency contacts as well as the performance of errands, there was no indication from his file or testimony that Gaudet's cooperation involved clandestine activity. Again, it should be stressed that the Domestic Contacts Division, which was the Agency component that was in touch with Gaudet, was not involved in clandestine operations.

(16) *Alleged intelligence implications of Oswald's military service.*—The committee reviewed Oswald's military records because of allegations that he had received intelligence training and had participated in intelligence operations during his term of Marine service.[179] Particular attention was given to the charges that Oswald's early discharge from the corps was designed to serve as a cover for an intelligence assignment and that his records reflected neither his true security clearance nor a substantial period of service in Taiwan. These allegations were considered relevant to the question of whether Oswald had been performing intelligence assignments for military intelligence, as well as to the issue of Oswald's possible association with the CIA.

Oswald's Marine Corps records bear no indication that he ever received any intelligence training or performed any intelligence assignments during his term of service. As a Marine serving in Atsugi, Japan, Oswald had a security clearance of confidential, but never received a higher classification.[180] In his Warren Commission testimony, John E. Donovan, the officer who had been in charge of Oswald's crew at the El Toro Marine base in California, stated that all personnel working in the radar center were required to have a minimum security clearance of secret. [181] Thus, the allegation has been made that the security clearance of confidential in Oswald's records is inaccurate. The committee, however, reviewed files belonging to four enlisted men who had worked with Oswald either in Japan or California and found that each of them had a security clearance of confidential.[182][28]

It has been stated that Oswald claimed to have served in Taiwan.[183] The committee's review of his military records, including unit diaries that were not previously studied by the Warren Commission, indicated, however, that he had not spent substantial time, if any, in Taiwan. These records show that, except for a 3½ month period of service in the Philippines, Oswald served in Japan from September 12, 1957, until November 2, 1958.[184] Although Department of Defense records do indicate that MAG (Marine Air Group) 11, Oswald's unit, was deployed to Taiwan on September 16, 1958, and remained in that area until April 1959, an examination of the MAG 11 unit diaries indicated that Oswald was assigned at that time to a rear echelon unit.[185] The term rear echelon does not, on its face, preclude service with the main unit in Taiwan, but the Department of Defense has specifically stated that "Oswald did not sail from Yokosuka, Japan on September 16, 1958. He remained aboard NAS Atsugi as part of the MAG–11 rear echelon."[29][186]

Oswald's records also reflect that on October 6, 1958, he was transferred within MAG 11 to a Headquarters and Maintenance Squadron subunit in Atsugi, Japan.[187] He reportedly spent the next week in the Atsugi Station Hospital.[188] On November 2, 1958, Oswald left Japan for duty in the United States.[189]

Accordingly, based upon a direct examination of Oswald's unit diaries, as well as his own military records, it does not appear that he had spent any time in Taiwan. This finding is contrary to that of the Warren Commission that Oswald arrived with his unit in Taiwan on September 30, 1958, and remained there somewhat less than a week,[190] but the Commission's analysis apparently was made without access to the unit diaries of MAG11.[30]

Moreover, even if Oswald, in fact, did make the trip

---

[28]John E. Donovan, Oswald's commanding officer, did have a security clearance of secret.

[29]This is contrary to statements attributed to Lieutenant Charles R. Rhodes by Edward J. Epstein in his book, "The Secret World of Lee Harvey Oswald." Rhodes maintains, according to Epstein, that Oswald did make the trip with the main unit but was sent back to Japan on October 6, 1958.

[30]Similarly, a message sent on November 4, 1959, from the Chief of Naval Operations concerning Oswald, which states that he had "served with Marine Air Control Squadrons in Japan and Taiwan," [191] may have been issued without checking unit diaries which indicated that Oswald had not been so deployed.

with his unit to Taiwan, it is clear that any such service there was not for a substantial time. The unit arrived at Atsugi on September 30, 1958, and by November 2, 1958, Oswald had left from Japan to complete his tour of duty in the United States.[192]

Finally, with one exception, the circumstances surrounding Oswald's rapid discharge from the military do not appear to have been unusual. Oswald was obligated to serve on active duty until December 7, 1959, but on August 17 he applied for a hardship discharge to support his mother. About 2 weeks later the application was approved.[193][31]

It appeared that Oswald's hardship discharge application was processed so expeditiously because it was accompanied by all of the necessary documentation. In response to a committee inquiry, the Department of Defense stated that ". . . to a large extent, the time involved in processing hardship discharge applications depended on how well the individual member had prepared the documentation needed for consideration of his or her case."[195] A review of Oswald's case indicates that his initial hardship discharge application was accompanied by all of the requisite documentation. Oswald had met the preliminary requirements of having made a voluntary contribution to the hardship dependent (his mother) and of applying for a dependent's quarters allotment[32] to alleviate the hardship.[196] Even though all of the supporting affidavits for the quarters allotment had not been submitted at the time that the hardship discharge application was filed, the endorsements on the application indicated that the reviewing officers were aware that both the requisite voluntary contribution and the application for a quarters allotment had been made.[197] Moreover, that application was accompanied by two letters and two affidavits attesting to Marguerite Oswald's inability to support herself.[198]

Documents provided to the committee by the American Red Cross indicate that Oswald had sought its assistance and therefore was probably well advised on the requisite documentation to support his claim.[199] Indeed, Red

---

[31] By September 4, 1959, Oswald had been informed that he would be discharged on September 11, 1959. [194] This explains why he was able to tell passport officials on that day that he expected to depart the United States for Europe on September 21, 1959.
[32] A dependent's quarters allotment is one that is jointly paid to the dependent by the serviceman and the service.

Cross officials interviewed Marguerite Oswald and concluded that she "could not be considered employable from an emotional standpoint."[200] The Fort Worth Red Cross office indicated a quarters allotment was necessary for Marguerite Oswald, rather than a hardship discharge for Lee, and assisted her in the preparation of the necessary application documents.[201] Nevertheless, Oswald informed the Red Cross office in El Toro, Calif., where he was then stationed, that he desired to apply for a hardship discharge.[202]

The unusual aspect of Oswald's discharge application was that, technically, his requisite application for a quarters allowance for his mother should have been disallowed because Marguerite's dependency affidavit stated that Oswald had not contributed any money to her during the preceding year.[203] Even so, the first officer to review Oswald's application noted in his endorsement, dated August 19, 1959, that "[a] genuine hardship exists in this case, and in my opinion approval of the 'Q' [quarters] allotment will not sufficiently alleviate this situation." [204] This quotation suggests the possibility that applications for quarters allotments and hardship discharges are considered independently of one another. In addition, six other officers endorsed Oswald's application.[205] The committee was able to contact three of the seven endorsing officers (one had died); two had no memory of the event,[206] and one could not recall any details.[207] The committee considered their absence of memory to be indicative of the Oswald case having been handled in a routine manner.

Based on this evidence, the committee was not able to discern any unusual discrepancies or features in Oswald's military record.

(17) *Oswald's military intelligence file.*—On November 22, 1963, soon after the assassination, Lieutenant Colonel Robert E. Jones, operations officer of the U.S. Army's 112th Military Intelligence Group (MIG). Fort Sam Houston, San Antonio, Tex., contacted the FBI offices in San Antonio and Dallas and gave those offices detailed information concerning Oswald and A. J. Hidell, Oswald's alleged alias.[208] This information suggested the existence of a military intelligence file on Oswald and raised the possibility that he had intelligence associations of some kind.[209]

The committee's investigation revealed that military intelligence officials had opened a file on Oswald because he was perceived as a possible counterintelligence threat. Robert E. Jones testified before the committee that in June 1963 he had been serving as operations officer of the 112th Military Intelligence Group at Fort Sam Houston, Tex.[33] Under the group's control were seven regions encompassing five States: Texas, Louisiana, Arkansas, New Mexico and Oklahoma. Jones was directly responsible for counterintelligence operations, background investigations, domestic intelligence and any special operations in this five-State area.[210] He believed that Oswald first came to his attention in mid-1963 through information provided to the 112th MIG by the New Orleans Police Department to the effect that Oswald had been arrested there in connection with Fair Play for Cuba Committee activities. [211] As a result of this information, the 112th Military Intelligence Group took an interest in Oswald as a possible counterintelligence threat.[212] It collected information from local agencies and the military central records facility, and opened a file under the names Lee Harvey Oswald and A. J. Hidell.[213] Placed in this file were documents and newspaper articles on such topics as Oswald's defection to the Soviet Union, his travels there, his marriage to a Russian national, his return to the United States, and his pro-Cuba activities in New Orleans.[214]

Jones related that on November 22, 1963, while in his quarters at Fort Sam Houston, he heard about the assassination of President Kennedy.[215] Returning immediately to his office, he contacted MIG personnel in Dallas and instructed them to intensify their liaisons with Federal, State and local agencies and to report back any information obtained. Early that afternoon, he received a telephone call from Dallas advising that an A. J. Hidell had been arrested or had come to the attention of law enforcement authorities. Jones checked the MIG indexes, which indicated that there was a file on Lee Harvey Oswald, also known by the name A. J. Hidell.[216] Pulling the file, he telephoned the local FBI office in San Antonio to notify the FBI that he had some information.[217] He soon was in telephone contact with the Dallas FBI office, to which he summarized the documents in the file. He believed that one person with whom he spoke was FBI

---

[33]Questions had been raised about the contents of some FBI communications on November 22, 1963, that reflected information allegedly provided by military intelligence. In his testimony, Jones clarified several points and corrected several errors in these communications.

Special-Agent-in-Charge J. Gordon Shanklin. He may have talked with the Dallas FBI office more than one time that day.[218]

Jones testified that his last activity with regard to the Kennedy assassination was to write an "after action" report that summarized the actions he had taken, the people he had notified and the times of notification.[219] In addition, Jones believed that this "after action" report included information obtained from reports filed by the 8 to 12 military intelligence agents who performed liaison functions with the Secret Service in Dallas on the day of the assassination.[220] This "after action" report was then maintained in the Oswald file.[221] Jones did not contact, nor was he contacted by, any other law enforcement or intelligence agencies concerning information that he could provide on Oswald.[222] To Jones' knowledge, neither the FBI nor any law enforcement agency ever requested a copy of the military intelligence file on Oswald. [223] To his surprise, neither the FBI, Secret Service, CIA nor Warren Commission ever interviewed him.[224] No one ever directed him to withhold any information; on the other hand, he never came forward and offered anyone further information relevant to the assassination investigation because he "felt that the information that [he] had provided was sufficient and . . . a matter of record. . . ."[226]

The committee found Jones' testimony to be credible. His statements concerning the contents of the Oswald file were consistent with FBI communications that were generated as a result of the information that he initially provided. Access to Oswald's military intelligence file, which the Department of Defense never gave to the Warren Commission, was not possible because the Department of Defense had destroyed the file as part of a general program aimed at eliminating all of its files pertaining to nonmilitary personnel. In response to a committee inquiry, the Department of Defense gave the following explanation for the file's destruction:

1. Dossier AB 652876 Oswald, Lee Harvey, was identified for deletion from IRR (Intelligence Records and Reports) holdings on Julian date 73060 (1 March 1973) as stamped on the microfilmed dossier cover. It is not possible to determine the actual date when

physical destruction was accomplished, but is credibly surmised that the destruction was accomplished within a period not greater than 60 days following the identification for deletion. Evidence such as the type of deletion record available, the individual clerk involved in the identification, and the projects in progress at the time of deletion, all indicate the dossier deletion resulted from the implementation of a Department of the Army, Adjutant General letter dated 1 June 1971, subject: Acquisition of Information Concerning Persons and Organizations not Affiliated with the Department of Defense (DOD) (Incl 1). Basically, the letter called for the elimination of files on non-DOD affiliated persons and organizations.

2. It is not possible to determine who accomplished the actual physical destruction of the dossier. The individual identifying the dossier for deletion can be determined from the clerk number appearing on the available deletion record. The number indicates that Lyndall E. Harp was the identifying clerk. Harp was an employee of the IRR from 1969 until late 1973, at which time she transferred to the Defense Investigative Service, Fort Holabird, Md., where she is still a civil service employee. The individual ordering the destruction or deletion cannot be determined. However, available evidence indicates that the dossier was identified for deletion under a set of criteria applied by IRR clerks to all files. The basis for these criteria were [sic] established in the 1 June 1971 letter. There is no indication that the dossier was specifically identified for review or deletion. All evidence shows that the file was reviewed as part of a generally applied program to eliminate any dossier concerning persons not affiliated with DOD.

3. The exact material contained in the dossier cannot be determined at this time. However, discussions with all available persons who recall seeing the dossier reveal that it most probably included: newspaper clippings relating to pro-Cuban activities of Oswald, several Federal Bureau of Investigation reports, and possibly some Army counterintelligence reports. None of the persons indicated that they remember any significant information in the dossier. It should be noted here that the Army was not asked to investigate the

assassination. Consequently, any Army-derived information was turned over to the appropriate civil authority.

4. At the time of the destruction of the Oswald dossier, IRR was operating under the records disposal authority, contained in the DOD memorandum to Secretaries of the Military Departments, OASD(A), 9 February 1972, subject: Records Disposal Authority (Incl 2). The memorandum forwards National Archivist disposal criteria which is similar in nature to the requirements outlined in the 1 June 1971 instructions. It was not until 1975 that the Archivist changed the criteria to ensure non-destruction of investigative records that may be of historical value.[226]

Upon receipt of this information, the committee orally requested the destruction order relating to the file on Oswald. In a letter dated September 13, 1978, the General Counsel of the Department of the Army replied that no such order existed:

Army regulations do not require any type of specific order before intelligence files can be destroyed, and none was prepared in connection with the destruction of the Oswald file. As a rule, investigative information on persons not directly affiliated with the Defense Department can be retained in Army files only for short periods of time and in carefully regulated circumstances. The Oswald file was destroyed routinely in accordance with normal files management procedures, as are thousands of intelligence files annually.[227]

The committee found this "routine" destruction of the Oswald file extremely troublesome, especially when viewed in light of the Department of Defense's failure to make this file available to the Warren Commission. Despite the credibility of Jones' testimony, without access to this file, the question of Oswald's possible affiliation with military intelligence could not be fully resolved.

(18) *The Oswald photograph in Office of Naval Intelligence files.*—The Office of Naval Intelligence's (ONI) Oswald file contained a photograph of Oswald, taken at the approximate time of his Marine Corps induction. It was contained in an envelope that had on it the language

"REC'D 14 November 1963" and "CIA 77978."[228] These markings raised the possibility that Oswald had been in some way associated with the CIA.

In response to a committee inquiry, the Department of Defense stated that the photograph had been obtained by ONI as a result of an October 4, 1963 CIA request for two copies of the most recent photographs of Oswald so that an attempt could be made to verify his reported presence in Mexico City. The requested copies, however, were not made available to the CIA until after the President's assassination.[34] Because of the absence of documentation, no explanation could be given for how or when the Office of Naval Intelligence received this particular photograph of Oswald.[229]

The committee's review of CIA cable traffic confirmed that cable No. 77978, dated October 24, 1963, was in fact a request for two copies of the Department of the Navy's most recent photograph of Lee Henry [sic] Oswald. Moreover, review of other cable traffic corroborated the Agency's desire to determine whether Lee Harvey Oswald had, in fact, been in Mexico City.[230]

The committee concluded, therefore, that the ONI photograph of Oswald bearing a reference to the CIA, was not evidence that Oswald was a CIA agent. Again, however, the destruction of the military file on Oswald prevented the committee from resolving the question of Oswald's possible affiliation with military intelligence.

(19) *Oswald in Mexico City.*—The committee also considered whether Oswald's activities in Mexico City in the fall of 1963 were indicative of a relationship between him and the CIA. This aspect of the committee's investigation involved a complete review both of alleged Oswald associates and of various CIA operations outside of the United States.[231]

The committee found no evidence of any relationship between Oswald and the CIA. Moreover, the Agency's investigative efforts prior to the assassination regarding Oswald's presence in Mexico City served to confirm the absence of any relationship with him. Specifically, when apprised of his possible presence in Mexico City, the Agency both initiated internal inquiries concerning his background and, once informed of his Soviet experience,

---

[34]As noted, the military file on Oswald, presumably including the ONI photograph, was destroyed by the Department of Defense.

notified other potentially interested Federal agencies of his possible contact with the Soviet Embassy in Mexico City.[232]

Conclusion

Based on the committee's entire investigation, it concluded that the Secret Service, FBI, and CIA were not involved in the assassination. The committee concluded that it is probable that the President was assassinated as a result of a conspiracy. Nothing in the committee's investigation pointed to official involvement in that conspiracy. While the committee frankly acknowledged that its investigation was not able to identify the members of the conspiracy besides Oswald, or the extent of the conspiracy, the committee believed that it did not include the Secret Service, Federal Bureau of Investigation, or Central Intelligence Agency.

D. Agencies and Departments of the U.S. Government Performed With Varying Degrees of Competency in the Fulfillment of Their Duties; President John F. Kennedy Did Not Receive Adequate Protection; a Thorough and Reliable Investigation into the Responsibility of Lee Harvey Oswald for the Assassination Was Conducted; the Investigation into the Possibility of Conspiracy in the Assassination Was Inadequate; the Conclusions of the Investigations Were Arrived at in Good Faith, but Presented in a Fashion That Was Too Definitive

1. THE SECRET SERVICE WAS DEFICIENT IN THE PERFORMANCE OF ITS DUTIES

The assassination of President Kennedy was the first and only such crime since the Secret Service was assigned responsibility for full-time protection of the President in 1901, as a result of the assassination of William McKinley.[1] When originally formed in 1865, the Secret Service had not been given responsibility for Presidential protection, even though that was the year Lincoln was murdered.[2] Its primary purpose was to deal with counterfeiting, which had become a national outrage in the period before 1862 when a standardized national currency was adopted.[3] By the end of the 1860's, the new agency had all but eliminated the problem.[4]

For the balance of the 19th century, the Secret Service engaged in various criminal detection activities. It investigated the Ku Klux Klan in the 1870's,[5] Spanish espionage in the 1890's,[6] organized crime in New York City in the 1880's and 1890's,[7] and syndicated gambling in Louisiana at the turn of the century.[8]

Even with the assignment of Presidential protection as its primary purpose, the Secret Service was not always given the necessary annual appropriations to carry out the task.[9] It was not until 1908 that the agency's mission was better defined[10] and, at that, for an ironic reason.

When the Secret Service exposed the participation in land fraud schemes by Members of Congress from several Western States, legislation was passed restricting the operations of the Agency and creating a new Federal law enforcement body that ultimately would become the Federal Bureau of Investigation.[11] Indeed, the original FBI men were eight agents transferred from the Secret Service.[12]

The law left the Secret Service with two concerns: Treasury matters, or counterfeiting, and protection of the President.[13] On occasion, however, it was given special assignments. During World War I, the Agency was concerned with German saboteurs,[14] and in 1921 it investigated the roles of Secretary of the Interior Albert B Fall and Atty. Gen. Harry M. Daugherty in the Teapot Dome Scandal.[15] From about 1930 on, however, the Secret Service was an anticounterfeiting agency with the additional assignment of protecting the President. In its protective role, on only two occasions before November 22, 1963, was it tested by an actual assault on a President. In February 1932, the car in which President Roosevelt was riding was fired on in Miami, killing the mayor of Chicago, Anton Cermak.[16] In November 1950, members of the Puerto Rican Nationalist Party tried to force their way into Blair House, the temporary home of President Truman.[17]

(a) *The Secret Service possessed information that was not properly analyzed, investigated, or used by the Secret Service in connection with the President's trip to Dallas; in addition, Secret Service agents in the motorcade were inadequately prepared to protect the President from a sniper.*

President Kennedy posed a problem for the Secret Service from the start. As a policymaker, he was liberal and innovative, startlingly so in comparison with the cautious approach of President Eisenhower.[18] His personal style was known to cause agents assigned to him deep concern. He traveled more frequently than any of his predecessors, and he relished contact with crowds of well-wishers. He scoffed at many of the measures designed to protect him and treated the danger of assault philosophically.[19] If someone wanted to kill him, he reasoned, it would be very difficult to prevent.[20] Commenting on the relationship between the President and the Secret Service, Presidential Assistant Kenneth O'Donnell told Gerald Behn, Special Agent-in-Charge of the White House Detail, "Politics and protection don't mix."[21]

The core of the Presidential security arm of the Secret Service is the White House Detail, which in 1963 was composed of 36 special agents.[22] In addition, there were six special agent-drivers, eight special agents assigned to the Kennedy family and five special officers detailed to the Kennedy home in Hyannisport, Mass. On the trip to Texas, there were 28 special agents in the Presidential entourage.[23]

In all, out of 552 employees in November 1963, there were 70 special agents and 8 clerks—or 14 percent of the total Secret Service work force—assigned to protect the President and Vice President directly or to the Protective Research Section, a preventive intelligence division charged with gathering and evaluating threat information and seeing that it is usefully disseminated.[24] In addition, there were 30 employees in the office of the Chief of the Secret Service, plus 313 agents and 131 clerks in 66 field offices, all of whom were on call to assist in Presidential protection.[25]

The time when the most manpower was needed in 1963 (as it was in 1978) was when the President traveled and was exposed to crowds of people in open spaces. On such occasions, the Secret Service called on municipal, county, and State law enforcement agencies for personnel who assisted in the preparation of large-scale protective plans. [26]

(1) *The committee approach.*—From the beginning of its investigation of the Secret Service, the committee realized the great importance of the Protective Research Section, renamed the Office of Protective Research in October 1965. This office is the memory of the Secret Service and is responsible for analyzing threat data.[27] By reviewing PRS files and interviewing its personnel, the committee sought to clarify just how much the Secret Service knew about the nature and degree of the dangers the President faced in the fall of 1963 and to learn what protective tactics had been devised in response to them.

The committee took care to distinguish between major and minor threats to the President in order that it could concentrate on the followup action to the significant ones. A threat was considered major if: (a) it was verbal or communicated by a threatening act, or (b) it created a danger great enough to require either an in-depth and intense investigation by the Secret Service or other law inforcement agency, or a cancellation or alteration of the President's planned trip itinerary.

The committee examined all threat profile investigations from March to December 1963 and incorporated into its analysis information on some major threat activities dating back to March 1961.[28]

The committee also considered the following questions in its investigation of Secret Service threat activity files, questions raised by the Kennedy assassination itself:

Were there indications of a conspiracy behind threats to harm persons under Secret Service protection?

Was there information developed in investigations of earlier threats that might have been useful in the investigation of the assassination?

Was the pertinent information in Secret Service files made available to the Warren Commission?

The committee began its investigation of Secret Service performance by reviewing the Warren Commission's findgings on it. Although the Commission had considered both the question of intelligence-gathering and threat identification and the question of physical protection, it had relied primarily on a study conducted by the Secret Service in response to the President's assassination and to limited questioning of Secret Service personnel in depositions and hearings. The Commission's findings, in turn, stressed inadequate liaison between the Secret Service and other Government agencies in intelligence-gathering;[29] the need for broader criteria and automatic data processing in the assimilation of intelligence data by the Protective Research Section;[30] and the need for closer working arrangements between the PRS and the advance survey teams that handled preparations for Presidential trips.[31]

With respect to physical protection of the President, the Commission found that some aspects could have been improved, citing specifically the need for closer coordination and clearer definition of responsibilities among Secret Service headquarters, advance and protective detail agents, and local police authorities;[32] the failure to arrange for prior inspection of buildings along the motorcade route;

[33] and a lack of discipline and bad judgment by some members of the Secret Service protective detail in Dallas, who were drinking on the night before the assassination. [34]

In its investigation, the committee relied heavily on Protective Research Section files. In addition, it took extensive testimony under oath from agents and officials who occupied pertinent positions in the Secret Service in 1963.

The committee's investigation confirmed that the Warren Commission's suggestions for improved Secret Service performance were well founded. The committee also noted that there were additional issues not addressed by the Warren Commission. One important one not analyzed by the Commission was whether the information that the Secret Service did possess prior to November 22, 1963, was properly analyzed and acted upon. The committee found that the Secret Service did in fact possess information that was not properly analyzed and disseminated within the Secret Service. Consequently, it was not put to use with respect either to a protective investigation or to physical protection of President Kennedy in advance of the trip to Dallas.

The Warren Commission had found that the Secret Service should have taken a broader view of information that was considered a threat to the President.[35] The committee also took a closer took at Secret Service files to see if they contained what could have been recognized as significant threats that were simply overlooked in connection with the Dallas trip.

The committee discovered that the 1963 Protective Research Section files had since been summarized and computerized,[36] and the original files then destroyed. The committee thus reviewed the computerized summaries of PRS case files for the period March to December 1963. [37] The summaries indicated that during this period, the PRS received information on over 400 possible threats to the President, approximately 20 percent of which could have been attributed to political motivation. The committee then reviewed the trip files for 1963 to determine which threats the Secret Service had recognized as significant.[38] Although there are other concepts of significance, the committee decided to limit its review to those that actually caused cancellation of a trip, an alteration of the President's planned itinerary, or an intensive preliminary investigative effort by the Secret Service. By limiting the definition in this way, the committee believed it could reach a clear determination of the manner in which the Secret Service responded to significant threats.

The Secret Service "trip files" actually consisted of two basic documents—a preliminary survey report, reflecting the basic plans for a trip, and a final survey report, prepared after a trip had been completed, and incorporating any changes that had been made in the original plan.[39] These files were intended by the Secret Service to reflect princepal problems encountered on each trip. A comparison of the preliminary and final reports should have revealed not only alterations of the President's itinerary, but the reasons for such changes. Because the final survey reports did not always reveal the specific nature of threats, [40] other files on investigations conducted prior to the President's trips in 1963 were also reviewed, and interviews with agents who worked on each trip were conducted.

(2) *Significant threats in 1963*.—The committee's review determined there were three significant threats to the President in the March to December 1963 period: first, a postcard warned that he would be assassinated while riding in a motorcade—this resulted in additional protection being provided when the President went to Chicago in March;[41] second, a threat in connection with a November 2 trip to Chicago that was canceled;[42] third, a threat in connection with a trip to Miami on November 18,[43][1] resulting in an extensive preliminary investigation. The nature of the threats on November 2 and November 18 revealed these had been the reason for the Secret Service to have investigated individuals identified with them in terms of future danger to the President.[45]

The committee was unable to determine specifically why the President's trip to Chicago, scheduled for November 2, was canceled. The possibilities range from the condition of his health[46] to concern for the situation in South Vietnam following the assassination of President Diem[47] to the threat received on October 30.[48] On that date, the Secret Service learned that an individual

---

[1] A Miami journalist later reported that a decision was made to transport President Kennedy from Miami International Airport to a Miami Beach hotel by helicopter to avoid exposing him to assassins by having him ride in a motorcade. The committee could find no documentation for this report. [44]

named Thomas Arthur Vallee, a Chicago resident who was outspokenly opposed to President Kennedy's foreign policy, was in possession of several weapons.[49] Further, Vallee's landlady reported that he had requested time off from his job on November 2.[50] Vallee was subsequently interviewed, surveilled and eventually arrested by the Chicago police, who found an M–1 rifle, a handgun and 3,000 rounds of ammunition in his automobile.[51] Vallee was released from custody on the evening of November 2.[52]

The committee found that the Secret Service learned more about Vallee prior to the President's trip to Dallas on November 22: he was a Marine Corps veteran with a history of mental illness while on active duty;[53] he was a member of the John Birch Society[54] and an extremist in his criticism of the Kennedy administration;[55] and he claimed to be an expert marksman.[56] Further, he remained a threat after November 2, because he had been released from jail.[57]

The committee also learned that the information the Secret Service obtained on Vallee was not forwarded to the agents responsible for the President's trip to Texas on November 21–22, although it was transmitted to the Protective Research Section upon receipt on October 30.[58] The potential significance of Vallee as a threat was illustrated by the Secret Service's reports, which included a notation on November 27, 1963 of the similarity between his background and that of Lee Harvey Oswald,[59] and a record of extensive, continued investigation of Vallee's activities until 1968.[60]

In addition, the committee obtained the testimony of a former Secret Service agent, Abraham Bolden, who had been assigned to the Chicago office in 1963. He alleged that shortly before November 2, the FBI sent a teletype message to the Chicago Secret Service office stating that an attempt to assassinate the President would be made on November 2 by a four-man team using high-powered rifles, and that at least one member of the team had a Spanish-sounding name.[61] Bolden claimed that while he did not personally participate in surveillance of the subjects, he learned about a surveillance of the four by monitoring Secret Service radio channels in his automobile and by observing one of the subjects being detained in his Chicago office.[62]

According to Bolden's account, the Secret Service succeeded in locating and surveillance of two of the threat subjects who,[63] when they discovered they were being
watched, were arrested and detained on the evening of
November 1 in the Chicago Secret Service office.[64]

The committee was unable to document the existence
of the alleged assassination team. Specifically, no agent
who had been assigned to Chicago confirmed any aspect of
Bolden's version.[65] One agent did state there had been
a threat in Chicago during that period, but he was unable
to recall details.[66] Bolden did not link Vallee to the
supposed four-man assassination team, although he claimed
to remember Vallee's name in connection with a 1963 Chicago case.[67] He did not recognize Vallee's photograph
when shown it by the committee.[68]

The questionable authenticity of the Bolden account
notwithstanding, the committee believed the Secret Service
failed to make appropriate use of the information supplied it by the Chicago threat in early November 1963.

Similarly, the Secret Service failed to follow up fully on
a threat in Miami, also in November 1963. On November
9, 1963, an informant for the Miami police, William
Somersett, had secretly recorded a conversation with a
rightwing extremist named Joseph A. Milteer, who suggested there was a plot in existence to assassinate the
President with a high-powered rifle from a tall building.
[69] Miami Police intelligence officers met with Secret
Service agents on November 12 and provided a transcript
of the Somersett recording.[70] It read in part:

> SOMERSETT. I think Kennedy is coming here No-
> vember 18 to make some kind of speech. I don't
> know what it is, but I imagine it will be on TV.
> MILTEER. You can bet your bottom dollar he is
> going to have a lot to say about the Cubans; there
> are so many of them here.
> SOMERSETT. Well, he'll have a thousand body-
> guards, don't worry about that.
> MILTEER. The more bodyguards he has, the easier
> it is to get him.
> SOMERSETT. What?
> MILTEER. The more bodyguards he has, the easier
> it is to get him.

SOMERSETT. Well, how in the hell do you figure would be the best way to get him?

MILTEER. From an office building with a high-powered rifle.

* * * * * * *

SOMERSETT. They are really going to try to kill him?

MILTEER. Oh, yeah; it is in the working.

* * * * * * *

SOMERSETT. * * * Hitting this Kennedy is going to be a hard proposition. I believe you may have figured out a way to get him, the office building and all that. I don't know how them Secret Service agents cover all them office buildings everywhere he is going. Do you know whether they do that or not?

MILTEER. Well, if they have any suspicion, they do that, of course. But without suspicion, chances are that they wouldn't.

During the meeting at which the Miami Police Department provided this transcript to the Secret Service, it also advised the Secret Service that Milteer had been involved with persons who professed a dislike for President Kennedy and were suspected of having committed violent acts, including the bombing of a Birmingham, Ala., church in which four young girls had been killed. They also reported that Milteer was connected with several radical rightwing organizations and traveled extensively throughout the United States in support of their views.[71]

Although it would have been possible to read Milteer's threats as hollow speculation, the Secret Service did not dismiss them lightly. The case agent in the Miami office forwarded a report and a recording of the Somersett-Milteer conversation to the Protective Research Section. [72] Robert I. Bouck, special agent in charge of PRS, then requested that the Miami office make discreet inquiries about Milteer.[73]

On November 18, 1963, Special Agent Robert Jamison of the Miami Secret Service office, in an interview with Somersett, had him place a telephone call to Milteer at his home in Valdosta, Ga., to verify he was in that city. [74] In addition, Jamison learned that Somersett did not know the identity of any violence-prone associates of Milteer in the Miami area.[75] The November 26 Miami field office report indicated that the information gathered "was furnished the agents making the advance arrangements before the visit of the President * * *."[76] PRS then closed the case, and copies of its report were sent to the Chief of Secret Service and to field officers in Atlanta, Philadelphia, Indianapolis, Nashville, Washington, and Miami.[77]

The Milteer threat was ignored by Secret Service personnel in planning the trip to Dallas. PRS Special Agent-in-Charge Bouck, who was notified on November 8 that the President would visit Miami on November 18, told the committee that relevant PRS information would have been supplied to the agents conducting advance preparations for the scheduled trip to Miami,[78] but no effort was made to relay it to Special Agent Winston G. Lawson, who was responsible for preparations for the trip to Dallas,[2] or to Forrest Sorrels, special agent-incharge of the Dallas office. Nor were Sorrels or any Secret Service agent responsible for intelligence with respect to the Dallas trip informed of the Milteer threat before November 22, 1963. [80]

Following the assassination, Somersett again met with Milteer. Milteer commented that things had gone as he had predicted. Somersett asked if Milteer actually had known in advance of the assassination or had just been guessing. Milteer asserted that he had been certain beforehand about the inevitability of the assassination.[81]

Bouck and Inspector Thomas Kelley, who was assigned to represent the Secret Service in the investigation of the Kennedy assassination, testified to the committee that threat information was transmitted from one region of the country to another if there was specific evidence it was relevant to the receiving region.[82] The fact was, however, that two threats to assassinate President Kennedy with high-powered rifles, both of which occurred in early November 1963, were not relayed to the Dallas region.

(3) *Inspection of the motorcade route.*—During the Secret Service check of the Dallas motorcade route, Special Agent-in-Charge Sorrels commented that if someone wanted to assassinate the President, it could be done with

---

[2]Lawson, on November 8, visited the PRS office in Washington to check geographical indexes. They revealed no listing of any individual or group that posed a potential danger to the President in the territory of the Secret Service regional office that included Dallas and Fort Worth. [79]

a rifle from a high building.[83] President Kennedy himself had remarked he could be shot from a high building and little could be done to stop it.[84] But such comments were just speculation. Unless the Secret Service had a specific reason to suspect the occupants or activities in a certain building, it would not inspect it.[85] The committee found that at the time of the Dallas trip, there was not sufficient concern about the possibility of an attack from a high building to cause the agents responsible for trip planning to develop security precautions to minimize the risk.

The Warren Commission commented that a building survey conducted under a "level of risk" criterion might well have included the Texas School Book Depository.[86] Although the agent in the lead vehicle had some responsibility to scan the route for danger,[87] this would have been woefully inadequate to protect against a concealed sniper. Television films taken in Dallas on November 22, 1963 show foot patrolmen facing the motorcade but not the crowd or the buildings.[88] The police captain in charge of security on the route was not instructed to have his men watch the buildings, although they were ordered to watch the crowds.[89] The committee found that if the threats that the PRS was aware of had been communicated to agents responsible for the Dallas trip, additional precautions might have been taken.[3]

(4) *Performance at the time of the assassination.*—The committee concluded that Secret Service agents in the motorcade were inadequately prepared for an attack by a concealed sniper. Using films and photographs taken of the motorcade at the time of the firing of the shots and immediately thereafter, the committee studied the reactions of Secret Service agents.[96] In addition, the com-

---

[3]The committee's investigation of the Vallee and Milteer threats dealt primarily with the Secret Service response to them. It also, however, investigated any actual connection they might have had with the assassination. In the Vallee case, the committee contacted relatives and his union [90] and visited his most recent known address [91] but was unable to develop additional information. Although Milteer as well as Somersett had since died, the committee did obtain the names and addresses of rightwing associates of Milteer. It found no connection to Oswald or Ruby or their associates. [92] The committee also investigated information that Milteer had called a friend from Dallas on the morning of November 22, 1963, [93] as well as an allegation that Milteer appeared in a photograph of the Presidential motorcade in Dallas. [94] The committee's investigation—which included an analysis of the photograph in question by forensic anthropologists—could find no evidence that Milteer was in Dallas on the day of the assassination. [95] In its investigation, therefore, the committee was unable to find a connection between the threat in Chicago or the threat in Miami with the assassination in Dallas.

mittee questioned agents who had been in the motorcade with respect to their preparedness to react to gunfire.

The Committee found that, consistent with the protective procedures and instructions they had been given,[97] the Secret Service agents performed professionally and reacted quickly to the danger. But the committee also found that a greater degree of awareness of the possibility of sniper fire could have decreased reaction time on the part of the agents and increased the degree of protection afforded the President.[4]

No actions were taken by the agent in the right front seat of the Presidential limousine to cover the President with his body, although it would have been consistent with Secret Service procedure for him to have done so.[99] The primary function of the agent was to remain at all times in close proximity to the President in the event of such emergencies.[100] The committee found that the instructions to the driver of the limousine were inadequate to maximize his recognition of, and response to, such emergencies.[101] He should have been given the responsibility to react instantaneously on his own initiative and to take evasive action. Instead, his instructions were to act only at the judgment of the agent in the right passenger seat, who had general supervisory responsibilities. [102]

The committee found from its acoustical analysis that approximately 8.3 seconds elapsed from the first shot to the fatal head shot.[103] Under the circumstances, each second was crucial, and the delay in taking evasive action while awaiting instructions should have been avoided. Had the agents assigned to the motorcade been alert to the possibility of sniper fire, they possibly could have convinced the President to allow them to maintain protective positions on the rear bumper of the Presidential limousine, and both shielded the President and reacted more quickly to cover him when the attack began. The committee recognized, however, that President Kennedy consistently rejected the Secret Service's suggestions that he permit agents to ride on the rear bumper of the Presidential limousine or permit motorcycles to ride parallel to the limousine and in close proximity to it.[104]

---

[4] The committee, of course, noted that if sniper fire had been expected, the motorcade should have been canceled. The committee learned that instruction received by Secret Service agents in 1978 in responding to a variety of emergency threats and attacks was far more intensive than it was in 1963. [98]

Although the conduct of the agents was without firm direction and evidenced a lack of preparedness,[105] the committee found that many of the agents reacted in a positive, protective manner. Agent Clint Hill, assigned to protect the First Lady, reacted almost instanteneously.[106] Agent Thomas "Lem" Johns left Vice President Johnson's follow-up car in an effort to reach the Vice President's limousine, but he was left behind momentarily in Dealey Plaza as the procession sped away to Parkland Hospital.[107] Photographic analysis revealed that other agents were beginning to react approximately 1.6 seconds after the first shot.[108]

In reviewing the reactions of the agents, the committee also reexamined the allegation that several had been out drinking the evening before and the morning of the assassination.[109] Four of the nine agents alleged to have been involved were assigned to the motorcade and had key responsibilities as members of the President's follow-up car.[110] The supervisor of the agents involved advised that each agent reported for duty on time, with full possession of his mental and physical capabilities and was entirely ready to perform his assigned duties.[111] Inspector Thomas Kelley, who was in charge of an evaluation of Secret Service performance in the assassination, testified before the committee that an investigation of the drinking incident led to a conclusion that no agent violated any Secret Service rule.[112]

In an effort to reach its own conclusion about the drinking incident, the committee reviewed film coverage of the agents' movements at the time of the shooting. The committee found nothing in the reactions of the agents that would contradict the testimony of the Secret Service officials.[113]

(b) *The responsibility of the Secret Service to investigate the assassination was terminated when the Federal Bureau of Investigation assumed primary investigative responsibility.*

The committee found that the investigation by the Secret Service after the assassination was terminated prematurely when President Johnson ordered that the FBI assume primary investigative responsibility.[114] Although the initial investigative efforts of the Secret Service lacked coordination, individual field offices with information that might have been related to the assassination had started their own investigations and pursued them aggressively.

How the Secret Service responded after the assassination is illustrated by the investigation conducted by the Chicago Secret Service office. After the assassination, the acting special agent-in-charge of the Chicago field office wrote an urgent report indicating he had received reliable information about "a group in the Chicago area who (sic) may have a connection with the JFK assassination."[115] This report was based on information received after the assassination from a reliable informant who reported a conversation he had had on November 21, 1963.[116] The informant, Thomas Mosley, reported that for some time he had been involved in negotiating the sale of illegal arms with a Cuban exile, an outspoken critic of President Kennedy named Homer S. Echevarria.[117] On November 21, Echevarria had said his group now had "plenty of money" and that they were prepared to proceed with the purchases "as soon as we [or they] take care of Kennedy."[118]

After receiving the initial report, the Secret Service surveilled subsequent meetings between Mosley and Echevarria,[119] received reports from Mosley about the conversations,120] and discussed the progress of the investigation with the local FBI office.[121] By December 3, 1963, a fuller picture of Echevarria was obtained[122] and reported to the Protective Research Section.[123] By that date, it appeared that Echevarria was a member of the 30th of November (Cuban exile) Movement,[124] that an associate of his who had also spoken directly with Mosley about the arms sales was Juan Francisco, Blanco-Fernandez, military director for the Cuban Student Revolutionary Directorate (DRE),$125]⁵ and that the arms purchases were being financed through Paulino Sierra Martinez, a Cuban exile who had become a Chicago lawyer.[126] Mosley inferred from his conversation with Echevarria and Blanco that Sierra's financial backers consisted in part of "hoodlum elements" who were "not restricted to Chicago." [127]

The committee's investigation provided substantial corroboration for the Secret Service's concern about the Mosley allegations. The committee found that the 30th of November Movement was receiving financial backing through the Junta del Gobierno de Cuba en el Exilio

---

⁵As previously noted, the FBI had learned that the Miami-based DRE had a representative in New Orleans, Carlos Bringuier, who had contact with Oswald in the summer of 1963 (see section I C 3 on anti-Castro Cuban exiles).

(JGCE), a Chicago-based organization led by Sierra. JGCE was essentially a coalition of predominantly right-wing anti-Castro groups.[128] It had been formed in April 1963 and abolished abruptly in January 1964.[129] During its short life, JGCE apparently acquired enormous financial backing, secured at least in part from organized gambling interests in Las Vegas and Cleveland.[130] JGCE actively used its funds to purchase large quantities of weapons and to support its member groups in conducting military raids on Cuba.[131] The affiliates of JGCE, in addition to the 30th of November Movement, included Alpha 66, led by Antonio Veciana Blanch,[6] and the MIRR, whose leader was the militant anti-Castro terrorist, Orlando Bosch Avila.[132]

The Secret Service recognized the need to investigate the alleged plots by Cuban exile groups more fully, especially that of Echevarria's 30th of November group. [133] But when the progress of the investigation was discussed with the FBI, the FBI responded that the 30th of November group was not likely to have been involved in any illegal acts.[134][7] The Secret Service initially was reluctant to accept this representation in light of the evidence it had developed that indicated the group was in fact involved in illegal activities,[137] and therefore began preparations to place an undercover agent in Echevarria's groups to investigate his activities more closely.[138] On November 29, 1963, however, President Johnson created the Warren Commission and gave the FBI primary investigative responsibility.[139] Although the Secret Service understood the President's order to mean primary, not exclusive, investigative responsibility,[140] the FBI, according to testimony of former Secret Service Chief James J. Rowley and Inspector Thomas J. Kelley, soon made it clear that it did not consider the Secret Service to be an equal collaborator in the post-assassination investigation. Rowley testified that "in the ultimate," there was "no particular jurisdiction" on the part of the Secret Service to cooperate in the post-assassination investigation.[141] Inspector Kelley testified that an order

---

[6]See section I C 3 on anti-Castro Cuban exiles.
[7]As discussed in the section on the FBI investigation, the Bureau's Nationalities Intelligence Section, the most knowledgeable about anti-Castro Cuban exile activities, did not actively participate in the investigation, nor did the Bureau ever fully investigate the question of Cuban involvement. [135] After the Secret Service provided the results of its Echevarria investigation to the FBI, the FBI conducted only a limited investigation and closed the case on him. [136]

came down not only to the Secret Service but to the Dallas Police Department that the FBI would take "full responsibility,"[142] not joint responsibility, for the post-assassination investigation of conspiracies.

In summary, the committee concluded that the Secret Service did in fact possess information that was not properly analyzed and put to use with respect to a protective investigation in advance of President Kennedy's trip to Dallas. Further, it was the committee's opinion that Secret Service agents in the Presidential motorcade in Dallas were not adequately prepared for an attack by a concealed sniper. Finally, the committee found that the investigation by the Secret Service of a possible assassination conspiracy was terminated prematurely when President Johnson ordered that the FBI assume primary investigative responsibility.

2. THE DEPARTMENT OF JUSTICE FAILED TO EXERCISE INITIATIVE IN SUPERVISING AND DIRECTING THE INVESTIGATION BY THE FEDERAL BUREAU OF INVESTIGATION OF THE ASSASSINATION

The position of Attorney General was created by law in 1789, but not until after the Civil War did the role of the chief legal officer of the U.S. Government acquire its modern institutional forms. Since the post was (and is) appointive, the Department of Justice was established in 1870 to insure continuity from one administration to another. Over time, the Department increasingly took the lead in major Federal prosecutions and other Federal legal matters.

In the aftermath of the assassination of President Kennedy, the Justice Department participated in various discussions with White House and FBI officials, and it had a major part in the formation of the Warren Commission. The committee found, however, that the Department largely abdicated what should have been important responsibilities in the continuing investigation.

The committee determined, for example, that during the critical early days before there was a Warren Commission, officials at Justice did not exercise any significant role in shaping, monitoring or evaluating the FBI's investigation, desipte the Bureau's organizational status as an agency within the Department.[1] Similarly, the committee discovered little indication that Justice Department officials moved to mount a sophisticated criminal investigation, including its conspiracy implications, an investigation that could have relied on the enormous resources of the Department—its specialized investigative sections and attorneys, as well as the powers and capabilities of a Federal grand jury and the granting of immunity.[2] There was, the committee concluded, ample reason for the Department to have become so involved, since various officials contacted by the committee agreed that Federal jurisdiction existed, in spite of some confusion over each of the applicable statutes.

In examining the performance of the Department of Justice in the Kennedy assassination, the committee took into account the importance of the understandable personal situation of Attorney General Robert F. Kennedy during the period following his brother's death. The committee found that the Attorney General's deep-felt grief in fact significantly affected the Government's handling of the investigation, and that this effect was magnified by the inability of Attorney General Kennedy's deputies to take a strong position with FBI Director J. Edgar Hoover on the course of the investigation.

The committee did note that officials at Justice, notably Deputy Attorney General Nicholas deB. Katzenbach, were instrumental in creating the Warren Commission, in effect transferring the focus of the investigation from the FBI to a panel of distinguished Americans. Nevertheless, as before, the Department exercised little authority in the investigation that followed the formation of the Commission.[3]

In testimony at a public hearing of the committee, Katzenbach said he believed it would have been distasteful and of questionable propriety for Robert Kennedy to have presided over the investigation of his brother's death.[4] He insisted there had been a need for a special investigative body that could make use of the resources of a number of Federal agencies.[5] The committee agreed with Katzenbach's general points.

The committee observed, nevertheless, that it was regrettable that the Department of Justice was taken out of the investigation, for whatever reason. It was unfortunate that it played so small a role in insuring the most thorough investigation of President Kennedy's assassination. The promise of what the Department might have realized in fact was great, particularly in the use of such evidence-gathering tools such as a grand jury and grants of immunity.

3. THE FEDERAL BUREAU OF INVESTIGATION PERFORMED WITH VARYING DEGREES OF COMPETENCY IN THE FULFILLMENT OF ITS DUTIES

(a) *The Federal Bureau of Investigation adequately investigated Lee Harvey Oswald prior to the assassination and properly evaluated the evidence it possessed to assess his potential to endanger the public safety in a national emergency*

(b) *The Federal Bureau of Investigation conducted a thorough and professional investigation into the responsibility of Lee Harvey Oswald for the assassination*

(c) *The Federal Bureau of Investigation failed to investigate adequately the possibility of a conspiracy to assassinate the President*

(d) *The Federal Bureau of Investigation was deficient in its sharing of information with other agencies and departments*

(1) *History of the FBI.*—Until after the turn of the century Federal agencies and departments were responsible for their own investigations. The Department of Justice was primarily a prosecutorial body, although it had been given statutory authority to perform investigations in 1891. In 1907, Atty. Gen. Charles J. Bonaparte proposed an investigative force in the Justice Department and went ahead with it despite objections in Congress. His successor, George Wickersham, named the force the Bureau of Investigation.[1]

By the end of World War I, the Bureau was firmly established as the main investigative arm of the Federal Government, its size increasing fivefold from 1916 to 1920. The two major influences on this growth were: (1) the war itself, which confronted the Bureau with the task of enforcing President Wilson's alien enemy proclamations and with the problems of draft evasion and enemy espionage; and (2) the passage of the Mann Act, which gave the Federal Government jurisdiction over certain interstate criminal activities. Both made increased personnel and budgetary demands on the Bureau.[2]

After the war—in the period 1919 to 1924—two successive Attorneys General abused the power of the Bureau of Investigation. A. Mitchell Palmer, in his campaign against Bolshevist radicals, acted with questionable legality. After the bombing of his home in June 1919, Palmer created a General Intelligence Division within the Bureau to deal with radicalism. He named a young Justice Department attorney, J. Edgar Hoover, to head the Division. It used covert as well as overt means to gather information on suspected radicals.[3]

In 1920, Attorney General Palmer also directed the wholesale deportation of members of the American Communist Party and the Communist Labor Party. This led to the controversial "Palmer raids," which diminished the standing of American Communists and came to symbolize the misuse of police power for a political purpose.

Then came the Harding administration, under which Harry Daugherty, the President's campaign manager, was named Attorney General. He in turn appointed his friend, William S. Burns, of the Burns Detective Agency, to run the Bureau. Burns was antiradical and antilabor as well, and he continued the questionable tactics of wiretapping and surreptitious entry in investigative work. Although the primary target continued to be Communists, the Bureau dealt a heavy blow to the Ku Klux Klan.[4]

Harlan Fiske Stone, a New York attorney and civil libertarian, was appointed Attorney General by Calvin Coolidge in 1924. Stone was a reformer, and he named Hoover Director of the Bureau of Investigation, with a mandate to clean it up. Hoover created a structure and a set of policies that were to endure for the nearly 50 years of his tenure. He also established the independence of the Bureau within the Department of Justice.[1]

The Bureau stayed out of the limelight until the 1930's, when the emergence of a resourceful criminal underworld, feeding on the public response to Prohibition, became a national menace. The Bureau was recognized as the single law enforcement agency in the country that could cope with crime of such a national scope.

In 1933, public outrage over the kidnapping of Charles Lindbergh's infant son led to enactment of the so-called "Lindbergh Law." It added kidnapping to the list of interstate crimes that came under the jurisdiction of the Bureau.

Then, in 1934, there was a major expansion of Federal criminal laws when Congress passed a package of nine new statutes. They dealt with such crimes as killing or assaulting a Federal law enforcement officer, fleeing across a State line to avoid apprehension or prosecution, extortion

---

[1]Hoover accepted the directorship with the assurance from Stone that he would have a free hand in running it and that it would be completely divorced from politics.

involving interstate commerce.[5] That same year, Bureau agents were granted authority to go beyond general investigative powers and to serve warrants and subpoenas, to make seizures and arrests and to carry arms. They were soon to be tagged "G-men" by the underworld.

The Bureau was renamed in 1935, becoming the Federal Bureau of Investigation, and by the end of the decade it was able to point to an array of accomplishments, for example:

A Division of Identification with central fingerprint records;

An FBI laboratory with up-to-date scientific law enforcement techniques; and

A National Police Academy for training State and local law enforcement officers.[6]

The Bureau had no internal security or counterintelligence functions until they were established, beginning in 1936, by a series of Presidential orders coupled with a secret oral agreement between Hoover and President Roosevelt. The FBI was authorized to store intelligence information collected by other Federal agencies.

In 1939, a written directive was issued providing that the FBI take charge of investigative work relating to "espionage, sabotage, and violation of neutrality regulations." Subversive activities were not specifically mentioned until 1950, in an Executive order by President Truman.[7]

The FBI's primary responsibility during World War II was enforcement of laws dealing with espionage, sabotage, and conscription. It also handled the apprehension of enemy aliens. (Hoover was one of the few Government officials who opposed the relocation of Japanese citizens as a violation of their civil rights.)[8]

The FBI also conducted foreign intelligence in South America, attempting to gather information on activities detrimental to U.S. interests. FBI involvement in foreign intelligence was ordered terminated after World War II when the Central Intelligence Agency was formed.

After World War II, the fear of communism was such that internal security activities against it were acceptable to most Americans. The FBI's actions were based on statutes that covered membership in the Communist Party, including the Smith Act, the Internal Security Act of 1950, and the Communist Control Act of 1954.[9]

J. Edgar Hoover himself defined as disloyal any acts

that could pose a threat to the Government, and even after the anti-Communist fervor of the McCarthy era had subsided, the internal security operations of the FBI continued at a high pace. By 1960, Hoover had developed a force of agents who employed sophisticated investigative techniques and enjoyed unusual independence. Hoover himself had become a formidable figure who deftly handled Presidents, Attorneys General, and Members of Congress. He was looked upon as an extraordinary crime fighter, and FBI appropriations passed without serious opposition after pro forma hearings.

(2) *The FBI investigation*—From the beginning of its examination of the performance of the FBI in the Kennedy investigation, the committee was impressed with the extraordinary work that was done in certain aspects of the case. The thoroughness and efficiency of the collection and processing of such a mass of evidence, for example, could hardly be overstated. What can be said in criticism of the Bureau must be placed in the context of the superior performance of the vast majority of the agents who worked long hours on the investigation. Nevertheless, the committee did find some deficiencies and shortcomings in the FBI investigation.

The FBI was the only Federal agency to conduct a full field investigation in the period immediately after the assassination, the period in which the evidentiary components at the crime scene for solving a homicide are assembled in the great majority of cases. Thereafter, the FBI continued to assume an overwhelming share of the burden of the investigation. Since the Warren Commission did not have its own investigative staff, the Bureau was responsible for the investigative raw product including the evidence upon which the Commission's deliberations about a possible domestic conspiracy were to be based.[10]

The committee concluded from its lengthy study of the roles of the FBI, Secret Service, CIA and other Federal agencies that assisted the Warren Commission that the final determinations of who was responsible for President Kennedy's murder and whether there had been a conspiracy were based largely on the work of the FBI.[11] With an acute awareness of the significance of its finding, the committee concluded that the FBI's investigation of whether there had been a conspiracy in President Kennedy's assassination was seriously flawed. The conspiracy aspects of the investigation were characterized by a limited approach and an inadequate application and use of available resources.[12]

The committee concluded that the FBI's investigation into a conspiracy was deficient in the areas that the committee decided were most worthy of suspicion organized crime, pro- and anti-Castro Cubans, and the possible associations of individuals from these areas with Lee Harvey Oswald and Jack Ruby. In those areas in particular, the committee found that the FBI's investigation was in all likelihood insufficient to have uncovered a conspiracy.

Given the FBI's justifiable reputation as one of the most professional and respected criminal investigative agencies in the world, its effort in the Kennedy assassination was expected to be of the highest degree of thoroughness and integrity. Indeed, it was an effort of unparalleled magnitude in keeping with the gravity of the crime, resulting in the assignment of more Bureau resources than for any criminal case in its history.[13] In terms of hours worked, interviews conducted and tests performed, the FBI's response was, in fact, unexcelled. It was so wide-ranging that it could not be easily summarized, as could the FBI's investigation of the assassination in 1968 of Dr. Martin Luther King, Jr. Over 80 Bureau personnel were sent to Dallas, over 25,000 interviews were conducted, and 2,300 reports, consisting of 25,400 pages were prepared.[14]

The FBI collected and examined the physical evidence with an impressive array of scientific equipment and personnel. By means of unusually rapid compilation of test results, laboratory and field personnel of the bureau were able to trace elements of the physical evidence to Oswald, and a series of sophisticated techniques led to early identification of Oswald's rifle as the murder weapon.[15] Then, using spectrographic, fingerprint, textile, and other analyses, the Bureau was able to assemble a substantial mass of evidence that led to the identification of Oswald as a possible gunman.[16] Based on the committee's independent evaluation of the FBI's test results, the committee found that the FBI's performance in the investigation was at its best in the area of scientific anlysis. Similarly, the FBI's ability to compile an abundance of disparate documentary evidence pertaining to Oswald's background and activities at the time of the assassination was highly commendable; it made full and efficient use of hundreds of FBI personnel.[17]

On the other hand, a qualitative assessment of aspects of the investigation raised some perplexing questions. From an appraisal of the structure of the operation, the committee detected weaknesses in both formulation and execution. The committee found evidence of organizational fragmentation,[18] an allocation of duties among various divisions of the Bureau that considerably, if unintentionally, compromised the quality of the effort to investigate the possiblity of a conspiracy[19]²

The assassination investigation was divided between two main divisions of the FBI, the General Investigative Division and the Domestic Intelligence Division. A primary responsibility of the General Investigative Division[21] was assembly of the basic facts of the assassination by means of testing and analysis of physical evidence.[22] Traditionally, the General Investigative Division handled FBI murder investigations, and it was the official in charge of the bank robbery desk in that Division who supervised the assassination investigation, since, according to the Bureau's manual of operations, jurisdiction for assaults on Federal officials was appropriately assigned to his desk.

The committee's conclusion that conspiracy was a blind spot in the FBI's investigation was reflected in the observation of the assistant FBI director in charge of the General Investigative Division, who said that while the Division was charged with investigating who specifically fired the shot or shots that killed President Kennedy, whether persons other than Oswald were involved was an "ancillary matter" that was not part of his division's responsibility.[23] He also characterized the investigation by saying, "* * * we were in the position of standing on the corner with our pocket open, waiting for someone to drop information into it, and we utilized what was fed to us, and disseminated it * * * to the Warren Commission."[24]

Within the General Investigative Division, the probe of Jack Ruby was delegated to the Civil Rights Division on the theory that Ruby violated Oswald's civil rights by killing him.[25] While the committee, in its investigation,

²The former assistant director, since deceased, who coordinated the FBI's conspiracy investigation himself characterized the effort in testimony before the Senate Select Committee to Study Governmental Operations with Respect to Intelligence Activities as rushed, chaotic, and shallow, despite the enormity of paperwork that was generated. [20]

found that Ruby's links to various organized crime figures were contained in reports received by the FBI in the weeks following his shooting of Oswald, the Bureau was seriously delinquent in investigating the Ruby-underworld connections.[26] The committee established that the Bureau's own organized crime and Mafia specialists were not consulted or asked to participate to any significant degree. [27] The assistant director who was in charge of the organized crime division, the Special Investigative Division, told the committee, "They sure didn't come to me * * * We had no part in that that I can recall."[28] The committee also determined that the Bureau's lack of interest in organized crime extended to its investigation of Oswald.

The Domestic Intelligence Division was responsible for the FBI's investigation of Oswald's activities, associations, and motivations, and it was assigned to consider all questions of a possible foreign conspiracy.[29] The assistant director who ran this phase of the investigation, however, had been one of several FBI officials and agents who were disciplined by Director Hoover following the assassination for what the Inspection Division determined to have been deficient performance in the investigation of Oswald prior to the assassination. The disciplinary action was kept a Bureau secret. Not even the Warren Commission was informed of it.

Within the Domestic Intelligence Division, the investigation of Oswald and a possible conspiracy was assigned to a team of agents from the Bureau's Soviet section because Oswald had been an avowed Marxist who had defected to the Soviet Union.[30]

While numerous specialists on Cuban affairs and exile activities were assigned to the Domestic Intelligence Division, the committee found that they were seldom consulted on the assassination or asked to participate in the investigation, despite the reported connections between both Oswald and Ruby and individuals active in Cuban revolutionary activities.[31] Supervisors of Cuba-related activities at the Bureau in the early 1960's told the committee they were unaware of any investigation of the Cuban issue with respect for the assassination. Similarly, the committee found that neither the Domestic Intelligence Division nor FBI headquarters authorized an intelligence investigation into possible foreign complicity in the assassination.[32]

While the FBI Domestic Intelligence Division had some

of the most sophisticated investigators and resources at its disposal, the committee concurred with the conclusion of the Senate select committee when it stated in 1976: "Rather than addressing its investigation to all significant circumstances, including all possibilities of conspiracy, the FBI investigation focused narrowly on Lee Harvey Oswald."[33]

The committee further concluded that the critical early period of the FBI's investigation was conducted in an atmosphere of considerable haste and pressure from Hoover to conclude the investigation in an unreasonably short period of time.[34] The committee also noted that Hoover's personal predisposition that Oswald had been a lone assassin affected the course of the investigation, adding to the momentum to conclude the investigation after limited consideration of possible conspiratorial areas. While Hoover continued to press conspiracy leads, his apparent attitude was reflected in a telephone conversation with President Johnson on November 24, 1963, just hours after Oswald had been shot of death by Ruby. Hoover said: "The thing I am most concerned about * * * is having something issued so we can convince the public that Oswald is the real assassin."[35] Two days later, on November 26, 1963, Hoover received a memorandum from an assistant director stating that, "* * * we must recognize that a matter of this magnitude cannot be fully investigated in a week's time."[36] In a notation on the memo, indicating his impatience, Hoover jotted: "Just how long do you estimate it will take. It seems to me we have the basic facts now."[37] Three days later, on November 29, in a memorandum regarding a conversation he had with President Johnson earlier that day, Hoover stated:

I advised the President that we hope to have the investigation wrapped up today, but probably won't have it before the first of the week, due to an additional lead being pursued in Mexico.[38]

The committee also concurred with other House and Senate committees that the FBI failed to cooperate fully with the Warren Commission. The committee found the Bureau's relationship with the Commission to have been distinctly adversarial and that there were limited areas in which the FBI did not provide complete information to the Commission and other areas in which the Bureau's information was misleading.[39] An entry from Oswald's notebook containing the name, address and phone number of an FBI agent in Dallas, for example, was initially withheld from the Warren Commission.[40] In addition, the same special agent in Dallas destroyed a note he had received, apparently from Oswald, within 2 weeks of the assassination.[41] The note, in which Oswald reportedly threatened the agent,[42] was flushed down a toilet several hours after Oswald was murdered by Ruby. The existence of the note was also withheld from the Warren Commission and did not come to light for over 12 years. [43]

Warren Commission General Counsel J. Lee Rankin addressed himself to instances of FBI misconduct in testimony before the committee:

> * * * it just raises doubt about the way our government has been conducted and the fact that it seems to be more important to people that they protect their particular agency or bureau than their own country. It does not prove that there was ever a conspiracy. By that I mean conspiracy to kill President Kennedy. But there may have been a conspiracy as far as the Commission was concerned, and what they were going to do to it, and it has worked. [44]

The committee also found that the FBI was deficient in failing to inform the Warren Commission that a number of Bureau officials had been disciplined by Hoover for deficiencies in the security investigation of Oswald prior to the assassination.[45] These same officials were subsequently assigned to the post-assassination investigation of Oswald and the possible conspiratorial involvement of others. Hoover had ordered an investigation shortly after the assassination to determine whether Bureau personnel had adequately probed Oswald's potential for subversive actions or violence and whether he should have been listed on the Bureau's security index.[46] The FBI Inspection Division concluded that there had been numerous deficiencies in the preassassination investigation and recommended various forms of disciplinary action or censure for five field agents, one field supervisor, three special agents-in-charge, four headquarters supervisors, two headquarters section chiefs, one inspector, and one assistant director.[47]

Subsequently, Hoover did in fact carry out most of the disciplinary actions recommended. A former assistant director stated that such action was taken in strict secrecy so that the Warren Commission would not become aware of the deficiencies. The committee found that Hoover's action in ordering the official disciplining[48] of some of these personnel went beyond what was justified, and that the Bureau's preassassination security investigation of Lee Harvey Oswald had been adequate.[3] Nevertheless, the circumstances of such disciplinary action should have been communicated to the Warren Commission, particularly since a number of the personnel disciplined participated in the assassination investigation.

The committee determined further that in several instances Hoover's pledge to the Warren Commission that the FBI would continue to investigate information it received in years to come on the President's murder was not kept. The committee found specific cases in which the Bureau did not follow up on such information provided to it.[49] Two examples relate to leads received from underworld sources.

In the first instance, the Bureau received information from Chief Justice Warren regarding organized crime figure John Roselli's claim of personal knowledge relating to Cuban or underworld complicity. The Bureau declined to investigate the information and did not take any action until President Johnson personally intervened.[50] In the second instance, the Bureau received information from a source in 1967 regarding a reported meeting at which New Orleans Mafia leader Carlos Marcello had allegedly made a threat against the life of President Kennedy.[51] Rather that investigating the information, Bureau personnel took repeated action to discredit the source.[52]

To summarize, the committee found that the Bureau performed with varying degrees of competency in the investigation of the President's death. Its investigation into

---

[3]The committee examined the basis for this disciplinary action and found the action to have been unwarranted. The actions of the agents involved were appropriate under the circumstances as they knew them. That Oswald turned out to be an assassin should not have been used to fault the agents, since they had no reason to suspect that would be the case when they were dealing with him. If the agents were to be faulted in Oswald's case, they would have to have been faulted in all similar cases, and the Bureau's conduct in security matters would have to have been radically altered.

the complicity of Lee Harvey Oswald prior to and after the assassination was thorough and professional. Nevertheless, it failed to conduct an adequate investigation into the possibility of a conspiracy in key areas, and it was deficient in its sharing of information with the Warren Commission.

4. THE CENTRAL INTELLIGENCE AGENCY WAS DEFICIENT IN ITS COLLECTION AND SHARING OF INFORMATION BOTH PRIOR TO AND SUBSEQUENT TO THE ASSASSINATION

Created by the National Security Act of 1947,[1] the CIA was, in fact, a postwar outgrowth of the Office of Strategic Services (OSS). The head of OSS, though never a CIA official, was William J. Donovan, who in World War II adopted the British approach of combining the intelligence activities of various agencies into one office.

Toward the end of World War II, President Roosevelt sought Donovan's advice on a permanent intelligence apparatus. Donovan's classified reply, leaked to the press 3 months later, described an "all-powerful intelligence service . . . [which] would supersede all existing Federal police and intelligence units."[2] The reaction among the heads of existing intelligence and investigative agencies was predictably negative. Few wanted to see the OSS become more powerful.

President Roosevelt's death turned out to be a serious blow to OSS—nearly crippling, for President Truman abolished the wartime agency without consulting Donovan or the Joint Chiefs of Staff. As a result, the United States was handicapped by a serious intelligence gap in immediate postwar international struggles.

(a) Establishment of the CIA

Unification of the Armed Forces was the main objective of the 1947 act. It also created the National Security Council, of which the CIA was to be the intelligence coordinating unit. Under the act, the CIA was charged with four responsibilities:

To advise the NSC on intelligence matters relating to national security;

To make recommendations on the coordination of intelligence activities;

To correlate, evaluate and disseminate intelligence; and

To engage in additional intelligence activities and national security functions at the direction of the NSC.

The Agency was given no law enforcement functions.

In its early years, the CIA was hampered by internal organizational difficulties and bad relationships with other agencies. The turnover of directors was rather rapid— Lt. Gen. Hoyt S. Vandenberg in 1946, Adm. Roscoe H. Hillenkoetter in 1947, Lt. Gen. Walter Bedell Smith in 1950, Allen W. Dulles in 1952.

Dulles, who had been a wartime master spy, had strong opinions as to the type of men who should be named to top posts in the Agency. At Senate Armed Services Committee hearings on the National Security Act, he testified that the CIA:

> * * * should be directed by a relatively small but elite corps of men with a passion for anonymity and a willingness to stick at that particular job. They must find their reward in the work itself, and in the service they render their Government, rather than in public acclaim.[3]

In addition, in its formative period the CIA was subjected to the harangues of Senator Joseph R. McCarthy, who demanded a purge of Agency personnel. The upshot was a severe tightening of employment standards, as well as a restriction within the Agency on the expression of political viewpoints.

Although the CIA is not required to make public its organizational structure, it is known to consist of five main entities—the Office of the Director and four Directorates. The Director and Deputy Director, only one of whom may be a military officer, are appointed by the President. The four Directorates are as follows:

The Directorate of Operations—the clandestine services unit, which is comprised of a number of geographical operating divisions supplemented by functional staffs.

The Directorate of Intelligence—its responsibility is to analyze and then synthesize raw intelligence information into finished intelligence products.

The Directorate of Science and Technology—it is responsible for basic research and development; it operates technical systems and analyzes highly technical information.

The Directorate of Administration—the Agency's housekeeping department.

At one time there were also a number of proprietary organizations, front groups and social or political institutions that were run by the CIA or on its behalf. The best known proprietaries were Radio Free Europe and Radio Liberty, both established in the early 1950's. Among the front organizations were airlines and holding companies to support clandestine operations. In early 1967, it was learned that the CIA had for years been subsidizing the country's largest student organization, the National Student Association. Eventually, it became known that the Agency had channeled money to a number of business, labor, religious, charitable, and educational organizations.

(b) Rockefeller Commission investigation of CIA activities

In 1974 and 1975, in response to charges that the CIA had engaged in large-scale spying on American citizens and had compiled dossiers on many citizens, a commission headed by Vice President Rockefeller investigated whether domestic CIA activities exceeded the Agency's statutory authority. Mail intercepts, infiltration of dissident groups, illegal wiretaps and break-ins were among the subjects of the investigation.

The Rockefeller Commission concluded that the "great majority of the CIA's domestic activities comply with its statutory authority * * * Nevertheless, over the 28 years of its history, the CIA has engaged in some activities that should be criticized and not permitted to happen again— both in light of the limits imposed on the Agency by law and as a matter of public policy."[4]

(c) The committee investigation

As the committee examined the Agency's role in the investigation of the death of the President, it focused its investigation in these areas:

The Agency's handling of the Oswald case prior to the assassination;

CIA support of the Warren Commission investigation; and Developments relevant to the Kennedy assassination after publication of the Warren report.

318

The committee's investigation proceeded on the basis of interviews, depositions and hearings. Evidence was received from present and former CIA officials and employees, as well as members and staff attorneys of the Warren Commission. The CIA personnel who testified or were interviewed were assured in writing by the Acting Director of Central Intelligence that their secrecy obligation to the CIA was not in effect with respect to questions relevant to the committee's inquiry.[5] To the extent possible, the committee pursued investigative leads by interviewing Cuban and Mexican citizens. Further, an extensive review of CIA and FBI files on Oswald's activities outside of the United States was undertaken. The CIA materials made available to the committee were examined in unabridged form.[6]

Much of the information obtained by the committee came from present and former officials and employees of the CIA and dealt with sensitive sources and methods of the Agency. Since these sources and methods are protected by law from unauthorized disclosure, this report of the CIA investigation was written with the intention of not disclosing them. Much of what is presented is, therefore, necessarily conclusionary, since detailed analysis would have required revealing sensitive and classified sources and methods.[1]

(1) *CIA preassassination performance—Oswald in Mexico City.*—An individual identified as Lee Harvey Oswald came to the attention of the CIA in the fall of 1963 when he made a trip to Mexico City. The committee examined the efforts of the CIA to determine the true identity of the individual, the nature of his visit to Mexico and with whom, if anyone, he might have associated while there.

CIA headquarters in Washington, D.C., was informed on October 9, 1963, that a person who identified himself as Oswald had contacted the Soviet Embassy in Mexico City on October 1, 1963. Headquarters was also advised that Oswald had spoken with an individual possibly identified as Soviety Consul Kostikov on September 28, 1963, and that a photograph, apparently of an American, had been obtained. This photograph, which was thought by some Agency personnel to be of Oswald, did not purport to be a positive identification of him. The subject of the photograph was described as approximately 35 years old, 6 feet

---

[1]Staff studies reflecting a comprehensive examination of the issues and containing pertinent information and analysis were classified and stored at the National Archives.

tall, with an athletic build, a balding top, and receding hairline.[7]

During October 1963,[2] CIA intelligence sources abroad determined that Oswald had visited the Soviet Embassy or the Cuban consulate in Mexico City at least 5 times for the purpose of obtaining an intransit visa to Russia via Cuba.[8] Once CIA headquarters determined that Oswald was a former defector to the Soviet Union, his activity in Mexico City was considered to be potentially significant by both headquarters personnel and CIA intelligence sources abroad.[9] Headquarters, however, was not informed about Oswald's visa request nor of his visits to the Cuban consulate. As a result, while other interested Federal agencies were apprised of Oswald's contact with the Soviet Embassy, they were not informed about his visa request or of his visit to the Cuban consulate.[10]

The committee considered the possibility that an imposter visited the Soviet Embassy or Cuban consulate during one or more of the contacts in which Oswald was identified by the CIA. This suspicion arose, at least in part, because the photograph obtained by the CIA in October 1963 was shown after the assassination by the FBI to Oswald's mother as possibly showing her son. (Mrs. Oswald maintained the person in the picture was her son's killer, Jack Ruby.) [11] In addition, the description, based on the photograph, that the CIA had received in its first report of Oswald's contact with the Soviet Embassy in Mexico City, in fact bore no resemblance to Oswald[12] The man in the photograph was clearly neither Oswald nor Ruby, and the CIA and FBI were unable (as was the committee) to establish the identity of the individual in the photograph. The overwhelming weight of the evidence indicated to the committee that the initial conclusion of Agency employees that the individual in the photograph was Oswald was the result of a careless mistake. It was not, the committee believed, because the individual was posing as Oswald. In fact, the committee established that the photograph was not even obtained at a time when Oswald was reported to have visited the Soviet Embassy in Mexico City.[13]

The question of an Oswald imposter was also raised in a FBI letterhead memorandum to the Secret Service dated

---

[2]The Agency maintained that prior to the assassination, its field sources had not actually linked Oswald to the person who visited the Cuban consulate in October 1963. Testimony obtained directly from these sources, however, established that this connection had in fact been made in early October 1963.

November 23, 1963. It was based in part upon information received by CIA headquarters on October 9, 1963, that on October 1, 1963, Oswald had contacted the Soviet Embassy in Mexico City:

The Central Intelligence Agency advised that on October 1, 1963, an extremely sensitive source had reported that an individual identified himself as Lee Oswald, who contacted the Soviet Embassy in Mexico City inquiring as to any messages. Special Agents of this Bureau, who have conversed with Oswald in Dallas, Tex., have observed photographs of the individual referred to above and have listened to a recording of his voice. These Special Agents are of the opinion that the above-referred-to individual was not Lee Harvey Oswald.[14]

In response to a committee inquiry, the FBI reported that no tape recording of Oswald's voice was in fact ever received. The Bureau esplained that its Dallas office only received the report of a conversation to which Oswald had been a party. This explanation was independently confirmed by the committee. A review of relevant FBI cable traffic established that at 7:23 p.m. (CST) on November 23, 1963, Dallas Special Agent-in-Charge Shanklin advised Director Hoover that only a report of this conversation was available, not an actual tape recording. On November 25, the Dallas office again apprised the Director that "[t]here appears to be some confusion in that no tapes were taken to Dallas * * * [O]nly typewritten [reports were] supplied * * *."[15]

Shanklin stated in a committee interview that no recording was ever received by FBI officials in Dallas.[16] Moreover, former FBI Special Agents James Hosty, John W. Fain, Burnett Tom Carter, and Arnold J. Brown, each of whom had conversed with Oswald at one time, informed the committee they had never listened to a recording of Oswald's voice.[3][17]

Finally, on the basis of an extensive file review and detailed testimony by present and former CIA officials and employees, the committee determined that CIA headquarters never received a recording of Oswald's voice.[18] The committee concluded, therefore, that the information in

---

[3]The committee did not contact the three other FBI special agents who had also conversed with Oswald at one time.

the November 23, 1963, letterhead memorandum was mistaken and did not provide a basis for concluding that there had been an Oswald imposter.

The committee did, however, obtain independent evidence that someone might have posed as Oswald in Mexico in late September and early October 1963. The former Cuban consul in Mexico City, Eusebio Azcue, testified that the man who applied for an in-transit visa to the Soviet Union was not the one who was identified as Lee Harvey Oswald, the assassin of President Kennedy on November 22, 1963. Azcue who maintained that he had dealt on three occasions in Mexico with someone who identified himself as Oswald, described the man he claimed was an imposter as a 30-year-old white male, about 5 feet 6 inches in height, with a long face and a straight and pointed nose. [19]

In addition, the committee interviewed Silvia Duran, a secretary in the Cuban consulate in 1963. Although she said that it was in fact Oswald who had visited the consulate on three occasions, she described him as 5 feet 6, 125 pounds, with sparse blond hair, features that did not match those of Lee Harvey Oswald.[20] The descriptions given by both Azcue and Duran do bear a resemblance—height aside—to an alleged Oswald associate referred to in an unconfirmed report provided by another witness, Elena Garro de Paz, former wife of the noted Mexican poet, Octavio Paz. Elena Garro described the associate, whom she claimed to have seen with Oswald at a party, as "very tall and slender [with] * * * long blond hair * * * a gaunt face [and] a rather long protruding chin."[4][21]

Two other points warranted further investigation of the imposter issue. The Oswald who contacted the Russian and Cuban diplomatic compounds reportedly spoke broken, hardly recognizable Russian, yet there is considerable evidence that Lee Harvey Oswald was relatively fluent in this language.[22] In addition, Silvia Duran told the committee that Oswald was not at the Cuban consulate on September 28, 1963, a day the consulate was closed to the public.[23] The committee obtained reliable evidence of a sensitive nature from another source, however, that a person who identified himself as Oswald met with Duran at the consulate that day.[24]

The imposter issue could, of course, have been easily re-

---

[4]Elena Garro's allegation is discussed in more detail in section I C 2, supra.

solved had photographs of the person or persons in question been taken at the entrance to the Cuban consulate and Soviet Embassy. The Cuban Government maintained to the committee that the Cuban consulate was under photographic surveillance. In fact, the Cuban Government provided the committee with photographs of the alleged surveillance camera location.[25] The committee had other reports that the CIA had obtained a picture of Oswald that was taken during at least one of his visits to the Soviet Embassy and Cuban consulates.[26] The CIA, however, denied that such a photograph had been obtained, and no such pictures of Oswald were discovered by the committee during its review of the Agency's files.[27]

Despite the unanswered questions, the weight of the evidence supported the conclusion that Oswald was the individual who visited the Soviet Embassy and Cuban consulate. Silvia Duran, who dealt with Oswald at three different times, told the committee she was certain that the individual who applied for an in-transit visa to Russian via Cuba was Oswald.[28] She specifically identified the individual in the photograph on Oswald's visa application form as the Lee Harvey Oswald who had visited the Cuban consulate.[29] Moreover, Duran stated that Oswald's visa application was signed in her presence.[30]

Duran's statements were corroborated by Alfredo Mirabal who succeeded Azcue as Cuban consul in Mexico City in 1963. Mirabal testified that on two occasions, from a distance of 4 meters, he had observed Oswald at the Cuban consulate and that this was the same person who was later photographed being shot by Jack Ruby.[31] Further, the committee was given access by the Cuban Government to Oswald's original visa application, a carbon copy of which had been supplied to the Warren Commission. Testimony before the committee established that each of these forms had been signed separately.[32] The application papers were photographed, and the signature on them was then studied by the committee's panel of handwriting experts. The panel's analysis indicated that the signature on both forms was that of Lee Harvey Oswald.[5][33] Finally, reliable evidence of a sensitive nature provided to the committee by the CIA tended to indicate that the person who

---

[5]Cuban Consul Azcue indicated to the committee that consulate practice in 1963 prohibited applications from being removed from the consulate premises to be filled out elsewhere. Silvia Duran stated, however, that applications could be filled out elsewhere.

contacted the Soviet Embassy was the same Lee Harvey Oswald who had visited the Cuban consulate.[34]

It can be said that the fact that the Agency's field sources noted Oswald's movements outside the United States was an indication of effective intelligence work. Nevertheless, the CIA's handling of the Oswald case prior to the assassination was deficient because CIA headquarters was not apprised of all information that its field sources had gathered with respect to Oswald, and headquarters, in turn, was thereby prevented from relaying a more complete résumé of Oswald's actions in Mexico City to the FBI, which was charged with responsibility for the Oswald security case.

The committee was unable to determine whether the CIA did in fact come into possession of a photograph of Oswald taken during his visits to the Soviet Embassy and Cuban consulate in Mexico City, or whether Oswald had any associates in Mexico City. Nevertheless, other information provided by the CIA, as well as evidence obtained from Cuban and Mexican sources, enabled the committee to conclude that the individual who represented himself as Lee Harvey Oswald at the Cuban consulate in Mexico was not an imposter.

(2) *The CIA and the Warren Commission*—The CIA took the position that it was not to conduct a police-type investigation of the assassination of President Kennedy. According to the testimony of former Director Richard M. Helms, its role was to provide support for the Warren Commission's effort by responding to specific inquiries. [35] Nevertheless, because the CIA was the Commission's primary source of information beyond U.S. territorial limits with respect to the question of foreign complicity in the assassination, the committee sought to evaluate both the quality of the CIA's handling of the foreign conspiracy question and the Agency's working relationship with the Commission.[6]

The Senate Select Committee to Study Governmental Operations with Respect to Intelligence Activities also studied the performance of the intelligence agencies in conducting their investigation of the assassination and their relationship with the Warren Commission. The Senate committee's report emphasized the Agency's failure to pur-

---

[6]Results of the committee's investigation of how effectively the CIA pursued the question of foreign complicity can be found in sections II C 1 and 2.

sue certain leads to a possible Cuban Conspiracy or Apprise the Warren Commission of CIA assassination plots against Fidel Castro.[36] In response, the CIA prepared a Task Force Report (1977 TFR) on the accuracy of the Senate committee's analysis. In its investigation, the committee reviewed the 1977 TFR[7] and used it as a starting point in assessing the timeliness and effectiveness of the CIA's responses to the Warren Commission's periodic requests for information.[37]

The CIA investigation of the Kennedy assassination was focused at the outset on Oswald's trip to Mexico. It was managed at Washington headquarters by the desk officer responsible for intelligence activity related to Mexico. Immediately following the assassination, the desk officer was instructed by Richard Helms, then Deputy Director for Plans, to coordinate efforts to compile and evaluate incoming information pertaining to the assassination. The desk officer was assigned this responsibility due to his past experience conducting internal CIA security investigations and because Oswald had visited Mexico 2 months prior to the assassination.[38] The cable traffic this officer coordinated was voluminous.

By late December 1963, it had become apparent that the CIA's interest in information related to the assassination had extended beyond Oswald's trip to Mexico. It encompassed Oswald's defection to the Soviet Union as well as the possible involvement of foreign powers in an assassination conspiracy. Consequently, responsibility for coordinating CIA investigative efforts was shifted to the counterintelligence staff, which had worldwide resources and expertise in investigating sabotage, guerrilla activities and counterespionage.[39]

The second phase of the Agency information collection effort, designed principally to respond to the work of the Warren Commission, was coordinated by Raymond Rocca, Chief of Research and Analysis (CI/R & A) for the counterintelligence staff. CI/R & A was the counterintelligence staff component particularly concerned with research and analysis related to counterintelligence and the formulation of policy based on the analysis. Rocca was the CIA's working-level contact point with the Warren Commission; consequently he was in a position to reivew most CIA information pertaining to the assassination, which com-

---

[7]For the committee's analysis of the significance of information that the CIA failed to provide the Warren Commission, see section I C 2.

prised a heavy volume of incoming cable traffic.[40] Due to compartmentalization, however, Rocca did not have access to all materials potentially relevant to the Warren Commission investigation. For example, Rocca had no knowledge of efforts by the CIA to assassinate Fidel Castro in the early 1960's.[41]

An examination of the functioning of the Warren Commission indicated to the committee that its staff assumed the CIA would expeditiously provide it with all relevant information rather than merely furnish data in response to specific requests.[42] An analysis by the committee showed that the Warren Commission's view was not shared by certain high-ranking officials of the Agency, including Deputy Director Helms. In fact, the CIA did not always respond to the Commission's broad request for all relevant material. In testimony to the committee, Helms said the CIA's general position was that it should forward information to the Commission only in response to specific requests.[43] Helms indicated that he did not inform the Warren Commission of the anti-Castro plots because he was never "asked to testify before the Warren Commission about * * * [CIA] operations."[44] This attitude caused, in the view of the Senate committee, an interpretation of the Warren Commission investigation that was too narrow in scope.[45][8]

The CIA also failed to provide the Warren Commission with all information in its possession pertaining to Luisa Calderon, a Cuban consulate employee in Mexico City suspected of having ties to the Cuban intelligence service. Calderon, who was alleged in 1964 by a Cuban defector to have been in contact with an American who might have been Oswald during the period of time of Oswald's visit to Mexico City, engaged in a conversation approximately 5 hours after the assassination in which she indicated pos-

---

[8]The committee agreed that this was an unacceptable explanation for the CIA's failure to inform the Warren Commission of the anti-Castro plots. It was apparent that the Commission was unable to make a specific request for information about the plots since it was unaware of their existence. In this regard, the observations of the Senate committee are worth quoting:

"Why senior officials of the FBI and the CIA permitted the investigation to go forward, in light of these deficiencies, and why they permitted the Warren Commission to reach its conclusion without all relevant information is still unclear. Certainly, concern with public reputation, problems of coordination between agencies, possible bureaucratic failure and embarrassment, and the extreme compartmentalization of knowledge of sensitive operations may have contributed to these shortcomings. But the possibility exists that senior officials in both agencies made conscious decisions not to disclose potentially important information." [46]

sible foreknowledge of the assassination.[9] The Warren Commission, however, was not apprised by the CIA of this conversation. (The CIA was unable to explain the omission, but the committee uncovered no evidence to suggest that it was due to anything but careless oversight.) [47]

With the exception of that which was obtained from sensitive sources and methods, CIA information, in general, was accurately and expeditiously provided to the Warren Commission. In cases of sensitive sources and methods, rather than provide the Commission with raw data that would have meant revealing the sources and methods, the substance of the information was submitted in accurate summary form.[48]

As a case in point, the committee determined that within two days of the President's assassination, CIA headquarters received detailed reports of Oswald's contacts with the Soviet Embassy and Cuban consulate in Mexico City in late September and early October 1963.[49] Accurate summaries of this material were given to the Warren Commission on January 31, 1964, but direct access to the original material (which would have revealed sources and methods that were sensitive) was not provided until April 1964, when Warren Commission investigators traveling abroad met with a CIA representative who provided it to them. [50] One Warren Commission staff member who reviewed the original material wrote an April 22, 1964, memorandum, which indicated the impact of this material:

> [The CIA representative's] narrative plus the material we were shown disclosed immediately how incorrect our previous information had been on Oswald's contacts with the Soviet and Cuban Embassies [in Mexico City]. Apparently, the distortions and omissions to which our information had been subjected had entered some place in Washington, because the CIA information that we were shown by [the CIA representative] was unambiguous on almost all

---

[9]The substance of that conversation is covered in section I C 2 on a possible Cuban conspiracy. The CIA maintained that the original Agency report summarizing this conversation was inaccurately translated and that, when accurately translated, it was apparent that there was no basis for sending the original conversation to the Warren Commission. The committee, however, considered the CIA's revised translation of the report and did not regard it as definitive. Moreover, even if the Agency's revised translation were accepted, the substance of the report remained essentially unchanged. Accordingly, using either translation as the basis for analysis, the Warren Commission should have been apprised of this conversation.

the crucial points. We had previously planned to show the [CIA representative] [Commission Assistant Counsel W. David] Slawson's reconstruction of Oswald's probable activities at the Embassies to get [his] opinion, but once we saw how badly distorted our information was we realized that this would be useless. Therefore, instead, we decided to take as close notes as possible from the original source materials at some later time during our visit.[51]

The committee did note that these distortions may have merely been the product of the staff member's inaccurate analysis of the available material, since the record reflected that he had reviewed a CIA memorandum dated January 31, 1964, that accurately summarized these records.[52] Nevertheless, as a result of his direct review of the original source materials, he was able to clarify considerably his analysis of Oswald's activities in Mexico City.

Another instance in which the CIA's concern for protecting its sensitive sources and methods resulted in delayed access by the Warren Commission had to do with a photograph that was referred to when CIA headquarters was informed on October 9, 1963, that Oswald had contacted the Soviet Embassy in Mexico City. The photograph was described as apparently depicting an American initially believed by some CIA personnel to be Oswald.[53] It was also the photograph that was apparently shown to Marguerite Oswald after the assassination.[54]

The circumstances of the photograph's origin as well as the fact that the individual in the photograph bore no resemblance to Oswald were known to the CIA shortly after the assassination.[55] Nevertheless, the Warren Commission was not told those details by the CIA until late March 1964.[56][10] The Commission had requested an explanation of the photograph on February 12, 1964, having inadvertently learned of its existence from the testimony of Marguerite Oswald.[60]

---

[10]One CIA officer indicated that since the photograph was not of Oswald, there was no need to inform the Warren Commission about it, thereby jeopardizing a sensitive CIA source and method.[57] Further, CIA documents show that even when the Commission sought an explanation of the photograph, the Agency's concern for the protection of its sources and methods inhibited immediate compliance with the request. [58] The committee believed, nonetheless, that as the photograph was referred to in the first report that CIA headquarters received on Oswald's contact wtih the Soviet Embassy,[59] it was directly relevant to the Warren Commission investigation and should have been made available promptly.

The committee did not conclude that the CIA's handling of information derived from sensitive methods and sources, in fact, substantially impeded the progress of the Warren Commission, but it did find that the Agency's policy with respect to this information was inconsistent with the spirit of Executive Order 11130 that "[a]ll executive departments and agencies are directed to furnish the Commission with such facilities, services and cooperation as it may request from time to time."

(3) *Post-Warren report CIA investigation.*—The committee found that the CIA, as had the FBI, showed little or no inclination to develop information with respect to the President's assassination once the Warren Commission had issued its report. Three cases in point that emerged in the aftermath of the investigation and seemed relevant enough to warrant more careful consideration than they received have been described previously in this report.

In the case of Yuri Nosenko, the Soviet defector who claimed that, as an officer of the KGB, he handled the Oswald file,[11] the CIA failed to capitalize on a potential source of critical evidence. By employing inexperienced interrogators who lacked interest in or knowledge of Oswald or the assassination, and by subjecting Nosenko to hostile interrogation, the CIA lost an opportunity to elicit information that might have shed light on Oswald, his wife Marina, and a possible KGB connection to them. In the cases of two Mexican citizens who claimed to have had contacts with Oswald in Mexico City in the fall of 1963, Elena Garro de Paz and Oscar Contreras,[12] the CIA took only perfunctory action, consequently failing to gain insight into actions by Oswald that might have had a bearing on the assassination.

5. THE WARREN COMMISSION PERFORMED WITH VARYING DEGREES OF COMPETENCY IN THE FULFILLMENT OF ITS DUTIES

(*a*) *The Warren Commission conducted a thorough and professional investigation into the responsibility of Lee Harvey Oswald for the assassination*

(*b*) *The Warren Commission failed to investigate adequately the possibility of a conspiracy to assassinate the President. This deficiency was attributable in part to the failure of the Commission to receive all the*

---

[11]See section I C 1.
[12]See section I C 2.

  relevant information that was in the possession of
  other agencies and departments of the Government
(c) *The Warren Commission arrived at its conclusions,*
  based on the evidence available to it, in good faith
(d) *The Warren Commission presented the conclusions in*
  its report in a fashion that was too definitive

  President John F. Kennedy was the fourth American
President to be assassinated, but his death was the first
that led to the formation of a special commission for the
purpose of making a full investigation. In earlier assassinations, the investigations had been left to existing judicial
bodies:
    In the case of Abraham Lincoln in 1865, a mili-
  tary commission determined that John Wilkes Booth
  was part of a conspiracy, and the Office of the Judge
  Advocate General of the U.S. Army saw to the prosecution of six defendants, four of whom were hanged.
    The assassins of James A Garfield in 1881 and
  William McKinley in 1901 were promptly tried in
  courts of law and executed.
  In the aftermath of the Kennedy assassination, it was
decided by President Lyndon B. Johnson and his advisers
that a panel of distinguished citizens should be given the
responsibility for finding the full facts of the case and reporting them, along with appropriate recommendations,
to the American people.
  The Commission was authorized by Executive Order
11130 to set its own procedures and to employ whatever
assistance it deemed necessary from Federal agencies, all of
which were ordered to cooperate to the maximum with
the Commission, which had, under an act of Congress,
subpoena power and the authority to grant immunity to
witnesses who claimed their privilege against self-incrimination under the fifth amendment.[1]
  Chief Justice Earl Warren was selected by President
Johnson to head the Commission. Two senior Members of
the Senate, Richard B. Russell, Democrat of Georgia,
and John Sherman Cooper, Republican of Kentucky, were
chosen to serve on the Commission, as were two from the
House of Representatives, Hale Boggs, Democrat of Louisiana, and Gerald Ford, Republican of Michigan. Two
attorneys who had long been active in Government service,
Allen W. Dulles, former Director of the CIA, and John

J. McCloy, former president of the World Bank, were also named.[2] J. Lee Rankin, former Solicitor General of the United States, was sworn in as General Counsel on December 16, 1963, and 14 attorneys were appointed within a few weeks to serve as assistant counsel.[3]

The Commission did not employ its own investigative staff. Instead, it relied on agencies in place—the FBI and Secret Service for domestic aspects, the CIA for activities involving foreign countries.

In September 1964, following a 9-month effort, the Warren Commission published a report that not only included its conclusions and recommendations, but also a detailed analysis of the case. The Commission had seen its task to be:

* * * to uncover all the facts concerning the assassination of President Kennedy and to determine if it was in any way directed or encouraged by unknown persons at home or abroad.

While the committee concluded that the Warren Commission failed in significant areas to investigate "all the facts and circumstances" surrounding the tragic events in Dallas, the committee also found that assigning the responsibility for that failure needed to be approached with utmost caution and care. In large measure, the Warren Commission's inadequacies in investigating important aspects of the President's assassination were the result of failures by the CIA and the FBI to provide it with all relevent evidence and information.[4]

It has been the contention of the CIA and FBI that they gave full and complete responses to all specific requests of the Warren Commission, placing responsibility with the Commission for assuming it would receive the relevant materials automatically.[5] This apparent misunderstanding, in the view of the committee, compromised the effectiveness of the process by which the Warren Commission arrived at its conclusions.

The committee observed that during the course of its hearings, numerous former Warren Commission members and staff attorneys testified that the general atmosphere of Government had changed during the years since President Kennedy's death. They repeatedly noted that they had been significantly more disposed toward trusting the CIA and FBI in 1963 and 1964 than they would have been in 1978.[6]

As it began to prepare its report on the performance of the Warren Commission, the committee took note of the high level of professionalism, dedication, and integrity it found to have characterized the members and staff of the Commission. The committee noted that criticisms leveled at the Commission had often been biased, unfair, and inaccurate. Indeed, the committee believed that the prevailing opinion of the Commission's performance was undeserved. The competence of the Commission was all the more impressive, in the opinion of the committee, in view of the substantial pressure to elicit findings of the committee, in view of the substantial pressure to elicit findings in only 9 months.[7] It was evident to the committee that the Commission could have productively used several more months for its investigation, although the committee recognized that this was a judgment based on the benefit of years of hindsight.

Nevertheless, the committee made the judgment that the time pressures under which the Warren Commission investigation was conducted served to compromise the work product and the conclusions of the Commission.[8] Early in the life of the Commission, it was working under internal deadlines of March or April 1964 for completion of the investigation, June 1 for a draft report and June 30 for a final report to the American public. Although these deadlines were finally abandoned, the committee found that the Commission staff was in fact under heavy pressure to meet them. President Johnson, among others in his administration, was anxious to have the investigation completed in advance of the 1964 Presidential conventions, out of concern that the assassination could become a political issue.[9]

The committee also found that most of the attorneys recruited for the Commission staff were promised their work would require no more than 3 or 4 months. Additionally, a number of lawyers were hired on a part-time basis.[10] Eventually, the realities of the task began to be apparent.

It was not until March that staff attorneys did any real field work in Dallas and elsewhere, and it was the middle of March before an investigation of Jack Ruby could get underway, since he was on trial for murder in Dallas. Nevertheless, a number of senior staff counsel, those who directed important areas of the case, left their jobs with the

Commission by early summer 1964, over 4 months before the investigation officially ended.[11]

The committee found that the Commission demonstrated a high degree of competency and good judgment in its central determination that Lee Harvey Oswald was the assassin of President Kennedy. [12] Contrary to the allegations of some critics, the Commission was not part of a sinister Government coverup of the truth. The committee found that the Commission acted in good faith, and the mistakes it made were those of men doing their best under difficult circumstances. That being said, on the subject that should have received the Commission's most probing analysis—whether Oswald acted in concert with or on behalf of unidentified co-conspirators the Commission's performance, in the view of the committee, was in fact flawed.[13] In its effort to fix responsibility for this failure, the committee, as noted, found one of the primary causes was the absence of the full and proper cooperation of the FBI and the CIA, along with the time pressures and the desire of national leaders to allay public fears of a conspiracy.[14]

Virtually all former Warren Commission members and staff contacted by the committee said they regarded the CIA-Mafia plots against Fidel Castro to be the most important information withheld from the Commission.[15] They all agreed that an awareness of the plots would have led to significant new areas of investigation and would have altered the general approach of the investigation. [16] J. Lee Rankin, who was the Commission's General Counsel, said he was outraged on learning in 1975 of the CIA's use of underworld figures for Castro assassination plots. Rankin stated to the committee:

Certainly * * * it would have bulked larger, the conspiracy area * * * we would have run out all the various leads and * * * it is very possible that we could have come down with a good many signs of a lead down here to the underworld.[17]

Burt W. Griffin, a Commission assistant counsel who directed much of the investigation of the possible involvement of organized crime and Cuban exiles, told the committee:

There was no showing that Oswald had any connection with organized crime. Therefore, there was no

333

reason to think that simply because Ruby was involved in organized crime, that this would have been linked to the assassination of the President.

We needed to fill that in, in some way, but that is why the Cuban link is so important. If we had known that the CIA wanted to assassinate Castro, then all of the Cuban motivations that we were exploring about this made much, much more sense. If we had further known that the CIA was involved with organized criminal figures in an assassination attempt in the Caribbean, then we would have had a completely different perspective on this thing.

But because we did not have those links at this point, there was nothing to tie the underworld in with Cuba and thus nothing to tie them in with Oswald, nothing to tie them in with the assassination of the President.[18]

Apart from the inability of the Commission to obtain all of the information it needed from the CIA and FBI, the committee found inherent inadequacies in its investigation of an assassination conspiracy.[19] It was, for example, limited in approach and resources.[20] In the crucial areas of organized crime, Cuban exiles and other militant groups, and foreign complicity, the attorneys assigned were lacking in experience and knowledge. Moreover, the committee found little to indicate that outside experts in these areas were ever consulted by the Commission.

The committee also discovered certain basic deficiencies in the capacity of the Commission to investigate effectively the murder of a President. In the words of a Commission assistant counsel: "The style of the Commission's own staff * * * was not one of criminal investigators."[21] The committee found, further, that the Commission consciously decided not to form its own staff of professional investigators, choosing instead to rely on an analysis by its lawyers of the investigative reports of Federal agencies, principally the FBI and CIA.[22] And even though its staff was composed primarily of lawyers, the Commission did not take advantage of all the legal tools available to it. An assistant counsel told the committee: "The Commission itself failed to utilize the instruments of immunity from prosecution and prosecution for perjury with respect to witnesses whose veracity it doubted."[23] While the Commission did go beyond the expected role of traditional factfinding panels serving a President, its inability to break out of the mold of such blue-ribbon bodies severely restricted its effectiveness in investigating the assassination of the President and the murders of Dallas police officer J. D. Tippit and Lee Harvey Oswald.

The committee also found fault with the manner in which the conclusions of the Warren Commission were stated, although the committee recognized how time and resource limitations might have come into play. There were instances, the committee found, in which the conclusions did not appropriately reflect the efforts undertaken by the Commission and the evidence before it.[24] In the Warren report, the Commission overstated the thoroughness of its investigation and the weight of its evidence in a number of areas, in particular that of the conspiracy investigation.[25] The Commission did not candidly enumerate its limitations due to time pressures, inadequate resources or insufficient information. Instead the language employed in the report left the impression that issues had been dealt with more thoroughly than they actually had. This was due in part, according to attorneys who worked for the Commission, to pressure from Commission members to couch the report in the strongest language possible. As an example, the Commission declared in the beginning paragraph of its conclusions section,

No limitations have been placed on the Commission's inquiry; it has concluded its own investigation, and all Government agencies have fully discharged their responsibility to cooperate with the Commission in its investigation.[26]

This, in the opinion of the committee, was an inaccurate portrayal of the investigation.

On conspiracy, the Commission stated, "* * * if there is any * * * evidence [of it], it has been beyond the reach of all the investigative agencies and resources of the United States and has not come to the attention of this Commission."[27] Instead of such definitive language, the Commission should have candidly acknowledged the limitations of its investigation and denoted areas where there were shortcomings.

As the committee's investigation demonstrated, substantive new information has been developed in many areas since the Warren Commission completed its work. Particu-

335

lar areas where the committee determined the performance of the Commission was less than complete include the following:

Oswald's activities and associations during the periods he lived in New Orleans;

The circumstances surrounding the 2½ years Oswald spent in the Soviet Union;

The background, activities, and associations of Jack Ruby, particularly with regard to organized crime;

The conspiratorial and potentially violent climate created by the Cuban issue in the early 1960's, in particular the possible consequences of the CIA-Mafia assassination plots against Castro and their concealment from officials of the Kennedy administration;

The potential significance of specific threats identified by the Secret Service during 1963, and their possible relationship to the ultimate assassination of the President;

The possible effect upon the FBI's investigation from Director Hoover's disciplining agents for their conduct of the Oswald security case;

The full nature and extent of Oswald's visit to Mexico City 2 months prior to the assassination, including not only his contact with the Soviet and Cuban diplomatic offices there, and the CIA's monitoring of his activities there, but also his possible associations and activities outside of those offices;

The violent attitude of powerful organized crime figures toward the President and Attorney General Robert Kennedy, their capacity to commit murder, including assassination, and their possible access to Oswald through his associates or relatives; and

Analysis of all available scientific evidence to determine the number of shots fired at the President.

In conclusion, the committee found that the Warren Commission's investigation was conducted in good faith, competently, and with high integrity, but that the Warren Report was not, in some respects, an accurate presentation of all the evidence available to the Commission or a true reflection of the scope of the Commission's work, particularly on the issue of possible conspiracy in the assassination. It is a reality to be regretted that the Commission failed to live up to its promise.

II

FINDINGS OF THE SELECT COMMITTEE ON ASSASSINATIONS IN THE ASSASSINATION OF DR. MARTIN LUTHER KING, JR., IN MEMPHIS, TENN., APRIL 4, 1968

INTRODUCTION: THE CIVIL RIGHTS MOVEMENT AND DR. KING

Dr. Martin Luther King, Jr., an eloquent Baptist minister from Atlanta, Ga., was one of the most prominent figures in the civil rights movement in America during its period of most visible achievement, 1955 to 1968. A disciple of nonviolence and love, Dr. King became the victim of savage violence, killed by a sniper's bullet as he stood on the balcony of a Memphis, Tenn., motel on April 4, 1968. His death signaled the seeming end of a period of civil rights progress that he had led and for which his life had become a symbol. Dr. King's legacy is one of profound change in the social fabric, not only for Black Americans, but for all citizens. But for some, after his death, as a Washington Post writer observed, "* * * his army of conscience disbanded, the banners fell, the movement unraveled * * *."

HISTORY OF CIVIL RIGHTS VIOLENCE[1]

Dr. King's tragic death in Memphis in 1968 was not, unfortunately, a historical aberration. The first Blacks arrived in colonial America at Jamestown, Va., in 1619 as slaves from Africa. As they were dispersed among Southern plantations, they were deprived of their traditions and separated from the rest of the population by custom and law. Their fate was determined by the white majority.

Civil rights violence dates back at least to the mid-18th

century, with the slave revolts of that period and their brutal suppression by whites. Roaming bands of runaway slaves in the South attacked plantations, and, in 1775, fears of a general slave uprising led to the annihilation of at least one group of Blacks by white soldiers in Georgia.

After the American Revolution, with the invention of the cotton gin, slavery in the South intensified. Black Americans provided most of the labor to support the economy of that region. Laws restricting Black mobility and educational opportunity were adopted by Southern legislatures, while the rights of slaveholders were jealously protected. Involuntary servitude was, however, outlawed in the North, and leaders of the new Nation such as Benjamin Franklin, John Jay, and John Woolman called for an end to slavery.

During the 1830's, sentiment for emancipation of slaves solidified. The movement for the abolition of slavery, led by "radicals," sparked violence throughout the United States. In 1835, a proslavery band seized abolitionist William Lloyd Garrison and dragged him through the streets of Boston. Two years later, the presses of the radical Alton, Ill., Observer were destroyed, and its editor, Elijah P. Lovejoy, was shot to death by white vandals.

In the 1850's, violence presaged the struggle that was to tear the Union asunder. The pillaging and burning of Lawrence, Kans., by a proslavery mob on May 21, 1856, led abolitionist John Brown to launch a bloody retaliatory raid on Potawatamie, Kans., 3 days later. The massacre touched off a guerrilla war that lasted until Kansas was granted statehood in 1861. In 1859, Brown seized the Federal arsenal at Harpers Ferry, W. Va., in the hope of arming a Black force that would free slaves in the South. The arsenal was recaptured 2 days after Brown's raid, and Brown was hanged following his trial and conviction of treason, conspiracy, and murder.

Sectional differences led to the Civil War that fractured the Union in 1861; it lasted 4 years and became one of the bloodiest military conflicts in U.S. history. Blacks served a limited role in the Union Army; over 200,000 of them were inducted. Their presence in battle infuriated Confederate military leaders, some of whom approved a no-prisoner policy for Blacks. Combat reports indicate that Black prisoners were murdered by Southern troops following, for example, the 1864 Battles of Fort Pillow,

Tenn., Poison Spring, Ark., and the Crater at Petersburg, Va.

In the decade following the Northern victory in 1865 and the freeing of slaves from bondage, a spate of laws, engineered to guarantee the rights of newly emancipated Blacks, were adopted. They included the 13th, 14th, and 15th amendments and 7 civil rights acts. The promise of equality during postwar Reconstruction, the period of reestablishment of the seceded States into the Union, however, was not realized. Reforms were ultimately defeated by Southern white intransigence and violence. With emancipation, a wave of murders swept the South, and Reconstruction became the bloodiest period of civil rights violence in U.S. history, as the caste system of segregation was violently institutionalized. Militant groups such as the White Leagues and the Ku Klux Klan organized to oppose the new challenge to white supremacy.

Outbursts of violence were commonplace throughout the South during this period:

According to General Philip Sheridan, commander of troops in Louisiana and Texas during Reconstruction, 3,500 civil rights advocates were slain in Louisiana alone in the decade following the Civil War, 1,884 of them in 1868 alone.

When Blacks in Memphis, Tenn. appealed for their civil rights in 1866, rampaging white terrorists burned homes and churches in the Black section of that city and massacred 47 Blacks.

The killing of 27 delegates by a white mob at the Louisiana State Convention in New Orleans in 1866 was described by one observer as a "systematic massacre of Negroes by whites."

Of 16 Blacks elected as delegates to the Mississippi Constitutional Convention in 1868, two were assassinated by whites.

In the Alabama election campaign of 1870, four Black civil rights leaders were murdered when they attended a Republican rally.

White terrorists took control of Meridian, Miss., in 1871 after they killed a Republican judge and lynched an interracial group of civil rights leaders.

In the Mississippi election campaign of 1874, several Black leaders in Vicksburg were attacked and murdered by members of the Ku Klux Klan.

339

During the Louisiana election campaign of 1878, Klan gunmen fired on Blacks in Caddo Parish, killing 40 by one account, as many as 75 by another.

Systematic violence, designed to terrify Blacks asserting their right to vote, led Attorney General Alfonso Taft to declare in 1876, "It is the fixed purpose of the Democratic Party in the South that the Negro shall not vote and murder is a common means of intimidation to prevent them."

Radical Reconstruction in the South was defeated by 1877, and the last of the Black militias in the South were dissolved. Southern legislatures adopted laws to deprive Blacks of all opportunity for political or civil participation and to segregate all facilities for education, travel, and public accommodation. Despite the waning of Reconstruction, mob violence and lynching occurred almost unchecked in the South until World War I. Blacks were removed from public affairs by intimidation.

In the 1890's, the legislatures of all Southern States disenfranchised Black citizens. With its 1903 ruling in *Giles* v. *Harris,* the U.S. Supreme Court sanctioned this practice. A few years earlier, in 1896, the Court had also approved racial segregation, finding in *Plessy* v. *Ferguson* that "separate but equal" facilities were acceptable under the Constitution. As the Black vote disappeared in the South, the murder of civil rights leaders decreased dramatically, only to be replaced by other forms of white terrorism: riots and lynching. The National Association for teh Advancement of Colored People (NAACP) was founded in 1909 to deal with this intimidation at the expense of further assertion of Black political authority.

EQUALITY IN EDUCATION—THE 20TH CENTURY OBJECTIVE[2]

The civil rights movement that became a major social and political force in the 1950's, and matured in the 1960's, grew out of the efforts of organizations founded during the first half of the 20th century. One prominent organization of this period, the NAACP, was responsible for the gradual emergence of the Black protest movement. It sought an end to racial segregation primarily through the court system by providing counsel to Blacks whose rights had been denied. It also pushed for reform in the Congress and in State legislatures and initiated programs to educate the public about existing racial injustice. The National Urban League worked on behalf of middle-class Blacks. The Congress of Racial Equality (CORE), a pacifist organization founded

340

in 1942, attacked discrimination in places of public accommodation in Northern and Border States. CORE took the lead in nonviolent direct action, organizing, for example sit-ins in Chicago on 1943, bus rides and stand-ins at Chicago's Palisades Pool in 1947–48, and in 1947, the Journey Reconciliation, a harbinger of later freedom rides. These activities of CORE, in fact, presaged the work of Dr. Martin Luther King's Southern Christian Leadership Conference in the late 1950's and 1960's.

With the signs of civil rights progress in the 1940's, particularly judicial responses to the NAACP, a mass movement began to develop. The U.S. Supreme Court prohibited all-white primary elections and delcared unconstitutional racially restrictive real estate covenants. In 1941, President Franklin D. Roosevelt issued an Executive order urging fair employment practices in response to the threats of mass demonstrations from A. Philip Randolph, president of the Brotherhood of Sleeping Car Porters. The President's Committee on Civil Rights recommended the enactment of fair employment legislation in 1947, and in 1948, President Harry S. Truman barred segregation in the Armed Forces and Government agencies. The Congress, however, did not act on civil rights issues until 1957.

The modern civil rights movement set its roots in the field of education. The NAACP had initiated litigation in the 1930's to end segregation in education. At the beginning of 1954, 17 States and the District of Columbia required segregation in public schools, while three other States permitted localities to adopt the practice. Then, on May 17, 1954, the U.S. Supreme Court announced its unanimous decision in *Brown* v. *Board of Education* that segregation in public schools was unconstitutional. In delivering the opinion of the Court, Chief Justice Earl Warren said that "separate education facilities are inherently unequal." A year later, the Court followed with a ruling that the process of public school desegregation must proceed with "all deliberate speed," thus choosing a policy of gradualism rather than requiring desegregation by a fixed date as urged by the *Brown* plaintiffs through their NAACP attorneys.

The *Brown* decision signaled the beginning of a long struggle, for it was not readily accepted in the South. Segregationist and States rights groups emerged to oppose the goal of integration, and militant organizations such as the White Citizens Councils and the Ku Klux Klans attracted a new following. Violence was resumed. On August 28,

1955, for example, a white mob in Mississippi kidnapped and lynched Emmett Till, a 14-year-old boy from Chicago who had been visiting his relatives.

A NEW LEADER EMERGES

Many historians believe the beginning of the modern Black revolt against inequality was marked in Montgomery, Ala., on December 1, 1955. Four Black passengers were asked by the driver of a downtown bus to give up their seats. Rosa Parks, a 42-year-old Black seamstress, refused and was arrested under a local segregation ordinance. In protest, Black leaders organized a boycott of the Montgomery bus system that lasted 382 days, ending only when the U.S. Supreme Court ordered the buses integrated.

The bus boycott was guided by the words of a 27-year-old Baptist minister who emerged as a fresh and dynamic force among Blacks. Preaching the "Christian doctrine of love operating through the Gandhian method of nonviolence," Dr. Martin Luther King, Jr., represented a new leadership. In Montgomery, he demonstrated that nonviolent direct action could be used effectively to achieve social justice. From that time until his death in 1968, Dr. King's life was inextricably interwoven with the events of the civil rights movement.

Dr. King was born in Atlanta, Ga., on January 15, 1929, the son of a Baptist minister, Martin Luther King, Sr., and the maternal grandson of another Baptist minister. He enrolled at Atlanta's all-Black Morehouse College at age 15 and, in his junior year, decided to enter the clergy. In 1947, he was ordained a minister at his father's Ebenezer Baptist Church in Atlanta. The following year, he continued his studies at the Crozer Theological Seminary in Chester, Pa. He was elected president of his class in his senior year and was named outstanding student when he graduated first in his class. At Crozer, he became acquainted with the work of Christian social theologians, as well as Mohandas K. Gandhi's doctrine of nonviolent direct action, Satyagraha (Sanskrit for truth-force), and Henry David Thoreau's essay, "On the Duty of Civil Disobedience."

With a fellowship he received to pursue his doctorate, King entered graduate school at Boston University in 1951. His doctoral thesis compared the conceptions of god in the thinking of Paul Tillich and Harry Helson Weiman. He received his doctorate in the spring of 1955.

In Boston, he met Coretta Scott, a graduate of Antioch College who was attending the New England Conservatory of Music. They were married in June 1953, and in the ensuing years had four children: Yolanda, Martin Luther III, Dexter Scott, and Bernice.

At the beginning of 1954, as he continued work toward his doctorate, Martin Luther King was hired as pastor of the Dexter Avenue Baptist Church in Montgomery, Ala., the city where he was to begin his civil rights career.

As president of the Montgomery Improvement Association (MIA), Dr. King led the bus boycott with the assistance of Montgomery Black leaders E. D. Nixon, a civil rights activist who had worked with A. Philip Randolph's Brotherhood of Sleeping Car Porters, Reverend Ralph David Abernathy, and Reverend E. N. French. At the first meeting of the MIA on December 5, 1955, Dr. King enunciated the principle from which he would never waver: "We will not resort to violence. We will not degrade ourselves with hatred. Love will be returned for hate." In the tradition of Gandhi, leader of the struggle for Indian independence and an advocate of passive resistance, Dr. King urged his followers to forswear violence and to work for ultimate reconciliation with their opponents by returning good for evil.

After mass arrests, threats and physical attacks, including the dynamiting of Dr. King's home, the Montgomery bus boycott ended successfully in December 1956. That month the Southern Regional Council announced that 25 other Southern cities had desegregated their buses either voluntarily or as the result of boycotts.

Despite the successful Montgomery bus boycott, 1956 was also marked by disappointments to the rising hopes of Black Americans. The admission of Autherine Lucy to the University of Alabama in February was met by white mob violence. To avert further disturbances, she was expelled by university officials. That decision was upheld by a Federal district court and the University of Alabama remained segregated until 1963. Also in 1956, 101 members of Congress from the 11 States that had comprised the Confederacy signed the Southern Manifesto, which declared that the school desegregation decisions of the Supreme Court were a "clear abuse of judicial power." Noting that neither the Constitution nor the 14th amendment mentioned education and that the *Brown* decision had abruptly reversed precedents established in *Pless* v. *Ferguson* and subsequent cases, the manifesto signers vowed "to use all lawful means to bring about a reversal of this decision which is contrary to the Constitution and to prevent the use of force in its implementation."

A PHILOSOPHY OF NONVIOLENCE

White resistance notwithstanding, the civil rights movement continued its growth in 1957. Recognizing the need for a mass movement to capitalize on the Montgomery bus boycott, Black leaders formed the Southern Christian Leadership Conference (SCLC) early in the year, and the boycott leader, Dr. Martin Luther King, Jr., was elected its first president. Adopting a nonviolent approach and focusing on the South, the SCLC was dedicated to the integration of Blacks in all aspects of American life.

In May 1957, to commemorate the third anniversary of the Supreme Court's *Brown* ruling on school desegregation, Dr. King led a prayer pilgrimage in Washington, D.C., the first large-scale Black demonstration in the capital since World War II. In his first national address, Dr. King returned to a theme that had lain dormant for 80 years, the right to vote. "Give us the ballot," he pleaded, "and we will no longer have to worry the Federal Government about our basic rights * * * we will quietly and nonviolently, without rancor or bitterness, implement the Supreme Court's decision." Dr. King was on his way to becoming one of the most influential Black leaders of his time, a symbol of the hopes for equality for all Americans.

It was a time of fast-moving events, actions and counteractions, in a continuing conflict. On September, 9, 1957, President Dwight D. Eisenhower signed the first Civil Rights Act since 1875. The law markedly enlarged the Federal role in race relations. It established a Civil Rights Commission and a Civil Rights Division in the Department of Justice. Most important, it gave the Attorney General authority to seek injunctions against obstruction of voting rights.

That same month, in Little Rock, Ark., violent rioting erupted over the integration of Central High School. Nine Black students were successfully enrolled, but not before 1,000 paratroopers and 10,000 National Guardsmen were sent into the beleaguered city. The appearance of Federal troops in Little Rock brought back unpleasant memories of Reconstruction, and the price of progress was a polarization of southern attitudes. Meanwhile, as Dr. King continued to carry the civil rights banner, he became the victim of a near fatal assault on September 20, 1957. As he was autographing copies of his first book, "Stride Toward Freedom," in a Harlem department store, a deranged Black woman, Izola Curry, stabbed him with an 8-inch letter opener. Though the weapon penetrated near his heart, Dr. King recovered after 2 weeks of hospitalization.

1960: THE YEAR OF THE SIT-INS

Civil rights activism intensified in 1960, the year of the sit-ins. On February 1, 1960, four Black students dedicated to nonviolent direct action sat at the lunch counter of a Greensboro, N.C. Woolworth's store. Though they were refused service, the students sat at the counter until the store closed, and each succeeding day they returned with more students. The sit-in movement spread to cities in Virginia, Maryland, South Carolina, Tennessee, Alabama, Kentucky, and Florida. Recognizing the need for organization of this new movement, the SCLC provided the impetus for the Student Nonviolent Coordinating Committee (SNCC) in April 1960.

The sit-ins that continued throughout the year became a successful means to protest. By the end of 1960, Blacks were being served at lunch counters in hundreds of southern stores.

Inevitably, there was white resistance. As the sit-ins set the pace of a campaign to open up public facilities of all sorts, there were thousands of arrests and occasional outbreaks of violence. Dr. King was arrested with other demonstrators at an Atlanta, Ga., department store sit-in in October 1960. Trespass charges were dropped against him at his trial, but he was sentenced to 4 months hard labor at the Reidsville State Prison Farm on the pretext that he had violated probation for an earlier minor traffic offense. National concern for Dr. King's safety prompted the intercession of Democratic Presidential candidate John F. Kennedy, which led to the civil rights leader's release. Some observers believed this action contributed to Kennedy's narrow election victory over Vice President Richard M. Nixon a week later by attracting Black support.

Violence increased with attempts to integrate the interstate transportation system in 1961, the year of the freedom rides. They began in May when members of CORE boarded two buses in Washington, D.C., and set out for

New Orleans, determined to test southern segregation laws on buses as well as in terminals en route. Trouble broke out when the buses reached Alabama. One bus was burned and stoned by whites in Anniston, and, in Birmingham, protestors on the second bus were brutally beaten by a mob awaiting their arrival. Another group of students left Atlanta, Ga., for Montgomery, Ala., the following week. Attorney General Robert F. Kennedy sent 500 Federal marshals to protect them, but the students arrived before the marshals and were savagely beaten. The next evening an angry throng of whites surrounded a church where Dr. King was scheduled to speak. The marshals and federalized National Guard troops had to rescue the congregation and Dr. King from the mob. Although the freedom riders met with little violence in Mississippi, they did have to reckon with an unsympathetic legal system. Over 300 demonstrators were arrested for breach of the peace and for disobeying police orders to disperse in segregated Mississippi terminals.

In response to the attacks on freedom riders, Attorney General Kennedy petitioned the Interstate Commerce Commission (ICC) to adopt stricter regulations against segregation. On September 22, 1961, the ICC announced new rules prohibiting segregation on interstate buses and in terminals.

Across-the-board desegregation of all public facilities in Albany, Ga., was the focus of a campaign led by Dr. King from late 1961 through the summer of 1962. The city reacted by arresting over 1,100 demonstrators during the campaign, including Dr. King and his colleague, Reverend Abernathy. City officials stubbornly refused to confer with Black leaders and steadfastly rejected proposals for desegregation. By September 1962, public parks, pools, and libraries had been closed or sold to white business groups. The Albany campaign received national attention, but it failed to crack the southern resistance symbolized by the city. From the Albany defeat Dr. King learned that the scattergun approach of simultaneously attacking all aspects of segregation was ineffective.

On the other hand, the admission of the first Black student to the all-white University of Mississippi in the fall of 1962 marked a significant integrationist victory. James Meredith, an Air Force veteran, had been enrolled at Jackson State College when he decided to transfer to "Ole Miss." With the assistance of the NAACP, he filed suit when he was rejected. After 16 months of litigation, the Fifth Circuit Court of Appeals, ruled that he had been turned down solely because of his race and ordered that he be accepted. Outright obstruction by State officials led the court to order that Mississippi's Gov. Ross Barnett and Lt. Gov. Paul Johnson pay fines unless they stop interfering with its ruling. On October 1, 1962, 320 Federal marshals arrived at Oxford to escort Meredith to his dormitory. This action set off a riot that left 2 persons killed and 375 injured before it was quelled by Federal troops. When the tear gas cleared, Meredith was the first Black student to enter "Ole Miss." Despite Governor Barnett's vow to continue to fight his enrollment, Meredith graduated in August 1963.

1963: A YEAR OF TRIUMPH AND DESPAIR

Dr. King led an all-out attack in the spring of 1963 on racial discrimination in Birmingham, Ala., which he described as "the most segregated city in the United States." Civil rights activists sought removal of racial restrictions in downtown snack bars, restrooms and stores, as well as nondiscriminatory hiring practices and the formation of a biracial committee to negotiate integration. Sit-ins, picket lines and parades were met by the police forces of Eugene "Bull" Connor, commissioner of public safety, with hundreds of arrests on charges of demonstrating without a permit, loitering and trespassing.

On Good Friday, April 12, 1963, Dr. King, Reverend Abernathy and Rev. Fred Shuttlesworth were arrested for leading a demonstration in defiance of an injunction obtained by Bull Connor. Dr. King was placed in solitary confinement and refused access to counsel. During his incarceration, he penned his "Letter from the Birmingham Jail," a response to a statement by eight leading local white clergymen—Protestant, Catholic, and Jewish—who had denounced him as an outside agitator and urged Blacks to withdraw their support for his crusade. In this eloquent statement, Dr. King set forth his philosophy of nonviolence and enumerated the steps that preceded the Gandhian civil disobedience in Birmingham. Specifically citing southern segregation laws, he wrote that any law that degraded people was unjust and must be resisted. Nonviolent direct action, Dr. King explained, sought to foster tension and dramatize an issue "so it can no longer be ignored."

Dr. King was released from jail on April 20, 1963. The

Birmingham demonstrations continued. On May 2, 500 Blacks, most of them high school students, were arrested and jailed. The next day, a group of demonstrators was bombarded with brickbats and bottles by onlookers, while another cluster of 2,500 protestors was met by the forces of Police Commissioner Connor, with his snarling dogs and high-pressure firehoses.

Worldwide attention was being focused on the plight of Blacks whose reasonable demands were being met by the unbridled brutality of the Birmingham police. Senator Wayne Morse of Oregon said Birmingham "would disgrace a Union of South Africa or a Portuguese Angola." The outcry led to negotiations with the city, and Dr. King suspended his campaign on May 8. Two days later, an agreement was reached to desegregate lunch counters, restrooms, fitting rooms, and drinking fountains in department stores and to promote Blacks over a 60-day period. The following day, however, the bombings of a desegregated hotel and the home of Dr. King's brother, Rev. A. D. King, led to a disturbance by hundreds of Blacks that lasted until State troopers arrived to assist local police. Calm was restored. Dr. King was considered victorious because of the attention he had attracted to racial injustice. One by one public facilities in Birmingham were opened to Blacks.

Birmingham became a rallying cry for civil rights activists in hundreds of cities in the summer of 1963. Marches were held in Selma, Ala., Albany, Ga., Cambridge, Md., Raleigh and Greensboro, N.C., Nashville and Clinton, Tenn., Shreveport, La., Jackson and Philadelphia, Miss., as well as in New York and Chicago.

This period was also one of tragedy. On June 12, 1963, the day after President Kennedy's dramatic call for comprehensive civil rights legislation, Medgar Evers, NAACP field secretary for Mississippi, was shot to death in front of his Jackson home. Evers had been instrumental in James Meredith's efforts to enter the University of Mississippi, and a month before his death had launched an antisegregation drive in Jackson. Byron de la Beckwith, a fertilizer salesman, was charged with the murder and tried twice; both trials ending in hung juries. In September 1963, attention reverted to Birmingham, Ala., when the 16th Street Baptist Church was bombed, killing four Black girls, aged 11 to 14, in their Sunday school class. The tragedy was compounded by the deaths of two Black youths, killed later that day in an outburst of violence that followed the bombing.

The climactic point of the campaign for Black equality came on August 28, 1963, when Dr. King led 250,000 followers in the march on Washington, a nonviolent demonstration of solidarity engineered by A. Philip Randolph and Bayard Rustin to dramatize Black discontent and demand an open, desegregated society with equal justice for all citizens regardless of race. A goal of the march was passage of a comprehensive civil rights bill to insure integrated education, equal assess to public accommodations, protection of voting rights and nondiscriminatory employment practices. In his address, acclaimed as the most memorable moment of the day, Dr. King recounted his dream for an integrated society:

I have a dream that one day this Nation will rise up, live out the true meaning of its creed: "We hold these truths to be self-evident that all men are created equal." I have a dream that one day on the red hills of Georgia sons of former slaves and the sons of former slaveowners will be able to sit down together at the table of brotherhood. I have a dream that on day even the State of Mississippi, a State sweltering with the heat of injustice * * * will be transformed into an oasis of freedom and justice. I have a dream that my four little children will one day live in a nation where they will not be judged by the color of their skin but by the content of their character.

Dr. King pledged to continue to fight for freedom and concluded:

When we allow freedom to ring * * * from every town and every hamlet, from every State and every city, we will be able to speed up that day when all of God's children, Black men and white men, Jews and Gentiles, Protestants and Catholics will be able to join hands and sing in the words of the old Negro spiritual, "Free at last! Free at last! Great God A'Mighty, we are free at last!"

The march provided new impetus to the civil rights movement and helped solidify the recognition of Dr. King as one of the most important spokesmen for the Black cause.

Within weeks of President Kennedy's assassination on November 22, 1963, his successor, President Lyndon B. Johnson, asked the Congress to end its deadlock and submit strong civil rights legislation for his approval. Congress responded by passing the Civil Rights Act of 1964, which contained provisions that: Guaranteed Blacks the right to vote; guaranteed access to public accommodations, such as restaurants, hotels, and amusement areas; authorized the Federal Government to sue to desegregate public facilities, including schools; mandated nondiscrimination in Federal programs; and required equal employment opportunity. In addition, on February 5, 1964, poll taxes, a device that had been used to prevent Blacks from voting, were barred with the adoption of the 24th amendment.

CORE and SNCC recruited 1,100 northern college students in a drive to register on the voting rolls as many of Mississippi's 900,000 Blacks as possible in the freedom summer voter registration campaign of 1964. The campaign came to the forefront of public attention on August 4 when the bodies of three civil rights workers—James E. Chaney, Andrew Goodman, and Michael Schwerner—were found buried in a dam near Philadelphia, Miss. The three men, missing since June 21, had been shot to death. Eighteen whites, including several police officers, were arrested and charged with conspiracy to deprive the victims of their civil rights. Dismissed by Federal District Court Judge W. Harold Cox, the charges were reinstated in 1968 after the U.S. Supreme Court decided that the Federal Government could prosecute State officials, as well as private persons who conspire with them, who deprive persons of their constitutional rights.

The year 1964 also marked an important personal achievement for Dr. King. On December 10, he was awarded the Nobel Peace Prive in Oslo, Norway. At age 35, he was the youngest recipient of the award in history and the second Black American after Dr. Ralph J. Bunche, the 1950 award winner. Not only was the award a recognition of Dr. King's role in the nonviolent struggle for civil rights in the United States, but to many it signified official international recognition of the Black protest movement.

In 1965, civil rights advocates, led by Dr. King, focused their attention on Black voting rights. At least two-thirds of Alabama's eligible Black voters were not registered at the beginning of the year. In Selma, Ala., on January 2, 1965, Dr. King announced a voter registration drive centering on that city, an attempt to dramatize the need for a Federal voting rights law. The violence directed against demonstrators in Selma, along with harassment by State and local authorities, aroused sentiment for such legislation. In February, Jimmy Lee Jackson, a civil rights worker from Perry County, Ala., became the first martyr of the campaign, when he was killed by gunfire in a clash between demonstrators and State troopers. Dr. King organized but did not lead an initial march from Selma to the State capital, Montgomery, on March 7. The demonstrators were turned back just outside Selma by State troopers with nightsticks, tear gas, and bull whips. On March 9, 1,500 Black and white marchers, this time led by Dr. King, made a second attempt to reach Montgomery, despite a Federal court injunction. They were again met by a phalanx of State troopers just outside Selma. Rather than force a confrontation, Dr. King asked his followers to kneel in prayer and then instructed them to return to Selma. His caution cost him the support of many young militants who already mocked him with the title, "De Lawd." That evening in Selma, three white ministers were attacked and brutally beaten by white thugs. Rev. James Reeb, a Unitarian pastor from Boston, died 2 days later as a result of his injuries.

On March 13, President Johnson addressed a joint session of Congress to propose enactment of a strong voting rights bill. In one of the most memorable speeches of his Presidency, Johnson said:

At times history and fate meet at a single time in a single place to shape a turning point in man's unending search for freedom. So it was at Lexington and Concord. So it was last week in Selma, Ala.

In Alabama, the twice-aborted march from Selma to Montgomery began for a third time on March 21, led by two Black Nobel Peace Prize winners, Dr. King and Dr. Bunche. On March 25, when the civil rights marchers reached Montgomery, their ranks had swelled to 50,000. In an impassioned address on the statehouse grounds, Dr.

King noted that the Black protest movement was recognizing gains and no amount of white terrorism would stop it. He said:

* * * I know some of you are asking today, "How long will it take?" I come to say to you this afternoon, however difficult the moment, however frustrating the hour, it will not be long, because truth pressed to earth will rise again.

How long? Not long, because no lie can live forever.

How long? Not long, because you will reap what you sow.

How long? Not long, because the arm of the moral universe is long but it bends toward justice.

While the march was considered a success, the tragedy that had plagued it from the outset continued. A civil rights transportation volunteer, Viola Liuzzo of Detroit, was shot to death as she drove a marcher home to Selma. Four Ku Klux Klan members were arrested for her murder, three of whom were eventually convicted of violating Mrs. Luizzo's civil rights sentenced to 10 years in prison.

The Selma campaign led to the passage of the Voting Rights Act, signed into law by President Johnson on August 6, 1965. The act provided for direct action through use of Federal examiners to register voters turned away by local officials. The Department of Justice moved swiftly to suspend voter qualification devices such as literacy tests in several Southern States, and within 3 weeks of the law's enactment, Johnson announced that over 27,000 Blacks had been registered by Federal examiners in three Southern States.

Divisions in the ranks of Black Americans became painfully apparent in 1965. Militants labeled Dr. King's nonviolence a tool of the white power structure. The February 21 assassination of Malcolm X, a former leader of the Black Muslims who had called for Black separation, underscored growing problems among Blacks. Three Black men were arrested for the Harlem shooting of Malcom X.

In early 1965, Dr. King suggested that the SCLC wage a campaign in northern cities for better housing for Blacks and nondiscriminatory employment practices. He spoke several times in the North. That summer he attacked patterns of de facto segregation in Chicago, and led a number of marches in predominantly Black neighborhoods of that city. It was also in 1965 that he first indicated a nexus between Federal Government spending for the Vietnam war and cuts in Federal assistance to the poor.

The euphoria over the August 6, 1965, signing of the Voting Rights Act subsided a week later when the Watts section of Los Angeles exploded in the Nation's worst race riot since 1943. It lasted 6 days and left 35 dead, 900 injured, over 3,500 arrested and $46 million of property damage. Dr. King received a mixed welcome in Watts, as he preached nonviolence in the wake of the tragic disturbance. He urged massive Federal assistance for the northern urban poor who suffered from economic discrimination and de facto segregation, the underlying causes of the Los Angeles violence.

The Watts riot demonstrated the depth of the urban race problems in the North. At the beginning of 1966, Dr. King launched a campaign against discrimination in Chicago, focusing his attack on substandard and segregated housing. He moved to a Chicago slum tenement in January and promised to organize tenants and lead a rent strike if landlords did not improve living conditions in the ghetto. Mayor Richard Daley met with Black leaders several times, but he took no concrete action to promote better housing or to implement nondiscriminatory employment practices. Violence against demonstrators plagued rallies and marches led by Dr. King in the spring and summer of 1966. At the end of July, he pressed his drive for better housing into Chicago's all-white neighborhoods. Demonstrators were jeered and attacked during these marches, and Dr. King himself was stoned in a parade through the Gage Park section on August 5. Although he was stunned by the vehement reaction of northern whites to civil rights activities, Dr. King planned a march through the all-white suburb of Cicero because demands for better housing were not acknowledged by the city. He canceled the Cicero protest, however, when the city administration and Chicago business leaders agreed to meet with civil rights leaders. The city officials and Black leaders signed a summit agreement that manifested a commitment to open housing. Though Dr. King considered the agreement a victory and moderate Black leaders saw it as setting a new precedent by forcing the mayor to the conference table, restive Black militants criticized it as a middle class sellout. The agreement ultimately had little effect on the plight of Chicago Blacks, and Dr. King's campaign was defeated by the combination of Mayor Richard Daley's intransigence and the complexities of northern racism. A positive byproduct of the effort was the SCLC's Operation Bread Basket that attacked economic ills and attempted to create new jobs for Blacks.

During 1966, the Black protest movement crumbled into several factions. SNCC, led by Stokely Carmichael, and CORE, under Floyd McKissick, adopted the slogan "Black Power," symbolizing radicalization of the movement. The term dramatically came to the attention of the public during the Meredith march in June. On June 6, 1966, James Meredith had been shot and wounded shortly after he began a 220-mile "March Against Fear" from Memphis, Tenn., to Jackson, Miss. He had hoped to embolden Blacks to register and vote, as well as to demonstrate the right of Blacks to move freely in the South. On the day after the assassination attempt, the leaders of five major civil rights organizations, Dr. King of the SCLC; Roy Wilkins, NAACP; Whitney Young, Jr., National Urban League; Floyd McKissick, CORE; and Stokely Carmichael, SNCC, converged in Memphis to pick up Meredith's march. Dr. King attempted to walk the line between the militancy of SNCC and CORE and the moderate tactics of the NAACP and the Urban League. During the 3-week Meredith march, however, the differing views of King and Carmichael became increasingly apparent. The SCLC president continued to advocate nonviolence, cooperation with whites and racial integration, while Carmichael urged Blacks to resist their white "oppressors" and "seize power."

The marches reached their destination, Jackson, on June 26. While Meredith and King addressed the marchers, it was Carmichael's plea for Blacks to build a power structure "so strong that we will bring them whites to their knees every time they mess with us" that attracted the most attention. In July 1966, CORE adopted "Black Power" rather than integration as its goal. The NAACP disassociated itself from the "Black Power" doctrine.

Urban riots in 1966 by angry and frustrated Blacks did not compare to the magnitude of the Watts riot a year earlier, but violence spread to more cities, 43 for the year, including Washington, D.C., Baltimore, Dayton, St. Louis, Brooklyn, Cleveland, Milwaukee, and Atlanta. By the end of the summer, 7 persons were dead, over 400 injured, 3,000 arrested; property damage was estimated at over $5 million.

1967 was a year of widespread urban violence, sanctioned by some Black militant leaders while abhorred by moderates who saw the uprising as ultimately counterproductive to Black interests. It appeared to some that the phase of the Black protest movement characterized by nonviolent demonstrations led by Dr. King was coming to an end. Many civil rights leaders thought violent upheaval inevitable. In an April 16, 1967, news conference, Dr. King warned that at least 10 cities "could explode in racial violence this summer."

Urban racial violence did plague over 100 cities in 1967. During the spring, minor disturbances had occurred in Omaha, Louisville, Cleveland, Chicago, San Francisco, Wichita, Nashville, and Houston. Then in June, Boston and Tampa experienced serious disorders. The most devastating riot since Watts in 1965 occurred, however, in Newark. from June 12 to 17, 1967, an outburst that resulted in 25 deaths, 1,200 persons injured, and over 1,300 arrested. The following month Detroit was the site of the worst urban race riot of the decade, one that left 43 dead, over 2,000 injured and more than 3,800 arrested. Rioting continued around the country, with outbreaks in Phoenix, Washington, D.C., and New Haven, among other cities. According to a report of the Senate Permanent Committee on Investigations released in November 1967, 75 major riots occurred in that year, compared with 21 in 1966; 83 were killed in 1967, compared with 11 in 1966 and 36 in 1965.

On July 27, 1967, President Johnson established the National Advisory Commission on Civil Disorders, chaired by Illinois Gov. Otto Kerner, to investigate the origins of the disturbances and to make recommendations to prevent or contain such outbursts. On July 26, Dr. King, with Roy Wilkins, Whitney Young, and A. Philip Randolph. issued a statement from NAACP headquarters calling on Blacks to refrain from rioting and urging them to work toward improving their situation through peaceful means.

Violence flared early in 1968 as students at South Carolina State College, on February 5, organized a protest against segregation at a local bowling alley. Following the arrests of several demonstrators on trespassing charges, a clash between students and police left eight injured. On February 8, renewed conflicts on the campus led to the shooting deaths of three Black students. The bowling alley was ultimately integrated, but only after the National Guard was called in. Still, sporadic disruptions continued.

On Feburary 29, a jolting summary of the final report of the National Advisory Commission on Civil Disorders was made public. The Commission found that the urban riots of 1967 were not the result of any organized conspiracy, as fearful whites had charged. Rather, it concluded that the United States was "moving toward two separate societies, one Black, one white—separate and unequal." The report warned that frustration and resentment resulting from brutalizing inequality and white racism were fostering violence by Blacks. The Commission suggested that the Nation attack the root of the problems that led to violence through a massive financial commitment to programs designed to improve housing, education, and employment opportunities. This advice was significant because it came not from militants, but from moderates such as Illinois Governor and Commission Chairman Kerner, New York City Mayor and Commission Vice Chairman John V. Lindsay, NAACP executive board chairman Roy Wilkins and Senator Edward W. Brooke of Massachusetts. In the conclusion of its report, the Commission quoted the testimony of social psychologist Dr. Kenneth B. Clark, who referred to the reports of earlier violence commissions:

I read that report * * * of the 1919 riot in Chicago, and it is as if I were reading the report of the investigating committee on the Harlem riot of 1935, the report of the investigating committee of the Harlem riot of 1943, the report of the McCone Commission on the Watts riot.

I must in candor say to you members of this Commission: it is a kind of Alice in Wonderland, with the same moving picture reshown over and over again, the same recommendations, and the same inaction.

Black leaders generally felt vindicated by the report. On March 4, 1968, Dr. King described it as "a physician's

356

warning of approaching death of American society] with a prescription to life. The duty of every American is to administer the remedy without regard for the cost and without delay."

In December 1967, Dr. King had announced plans for a massive campaign of civil disobedience in Washington to pressure the Federal Government to provide jobs and income for all Americans. In mid-March, he turned his attention from this Poor People's Campaign to a strike of sanitation workers in Memphis, Tenn., and thus began his last peaceful crusade.

THE ROAD TO MEMPHIS [3]

A quest for world peace and an end to economic deprivation for all American citizens, regardless of race, were uppermost in Dr. King's mind during the last year of his life, as manifested by his staunch opposition to the Vietnam war and his Poor People's Campaign, an effort designed to dramatize the scourge of poverty in the United States. In March 1968, he interrupted his planning of the Poor People's March on Washington to travel to Memphis, Tenn., where he hoped to organize a nonviolent campaign to assist the poorly paid, mostly Black sanitation workers who were on strike for better pay, better working conditions, and recognition of their union.

By 1967, American forces in Vietnam had grown to over 500,000, and more than 6,000 Americans had died in the escalating Southeast Asian conflict.[4] Opposition to U.S. involvement in Vietnam had begun to intensify. Dr. King was among those who called for disengagement and peaceful settlement.

The press pointed to Dr. King's address at New York City's Riverside Church on April 4, 1967, as the time when the SCLC president publicly disclosed his opposition to the Vietnam war, even though he had made similar statements and had been urging a negotiated settlement since early 1965.[5] He attacked the foreign policy of the Johnson administration, emphasizing the connection between wasteful military sending and its harmful effect on the poor, as social programs were dropped in favor of Vietnam-related expenditures. He warned that this pattern was an indication of the "approaching spiritual death" of the Nation. Dr. King described the United States as the "greatest purveyor of violence in the world today," and said that the high proportion of fatalities among Black soldiers in Vietnam demonstrated "cruel manipulation of the poor" who bore the burden of the struggle. On April 15, 1967, at a rally at the United Nations, he called for a halt to U.S. bombing.

Dr. King was stunned by the vehement reaction to his call for peace, especially from his colleagues in the civil rights movement. For example, Urban League president Whitney Young and NAACP executive director Roy Wilkins strongly condemned Kings' pacifism.[6] Moderate Black leaders feared that the generally sympathetic Johnson administration would be antagonized by the SCLC president's ministrations, while Dr. King argued that war priorities diverted valuable resources that could be used to improve the condition of America's Blacks. At the same time, his indefatigable belief in nonviolence was increasingly challenged by younger, more militant Blacks who did not renounce the use of violence to achieve their goals. A King biographer, David L. Lewis, wrote that by early 1967, "the verdict was that Martin was finished."[7]

In late 1967, in keeping with his belief that the problem of domestic poverty was exacerbated by use of Government funds to finance the war in Vietnam, Dr. King turned his attention to the plight of the poor in America. At an SCLC meeting in Atlanta in December 1967, he presented a plan for a nonviolent demonstraton by a racially integrated coalition of the poor, to take place in Washington, D.C., in April 1968. Using creative nonviolence, these ignored Americans would demand an economic bill of rights with the objectives of a guaranteed annual income, employment for the able-bodied, decent housing, and quality education. Dr. King planned that the poor would demonstrate, beginning on April 20, until the Government responded to their demands. He wrote:

We will place the problems of the poor at the seat of the Government of the wealthiest Nation in the history of mankind. If that power refuses to acknowledge its debt to the poor, it will have failed to live up to its promise to insure life, liberty, and the pursuit of happiness to its citizens.

In the face of criticism of his antiwar views by moderate Blacks and rejection of his tireless devotion to nonviolence by militants. Dr. King also hoped to use the Poor People's Campaign to broaden his base of support and buoy the SCLC. In the opinion of Dr. King's closest associate, Reverend Abernathy, SCLC vice-president-at-large in 1968, and Dr. King's successor as president of the organization, SCLC influence had declined since the Selma, Ala., voter registration campaign in 1965. Stymied in its efforts to deal with the urban racism of the North, the SCLC had seen a decline in financial contributions after the 1966 Chicago drive for better housing and nondiscriminatory employment practices. Abernathy described the SCLC's failure to implement new policies in Chicago as "the SCLC's Waterloo."

Public sentiment for a negotiated settlement in Vietnam intensified in early 1968, following the bloody Tet offensive during which the National Front attacked almost every American base in Vietnam and destroyed the U.S. Embassy in Saigon. Dr. King continued his criticism of the Johnson administration's escalation of U.S. involvement in Southeast Asia. In a March 16, 1968, address to delegates at the California Democratic Council's statewide convention in Anaheim, he urged that Johnson's nomination be blocked by the Democratic Party that year, charging that the President's obsession with the war in Vietnam was undercutting the civil rights movement.[8] According to one writer, this was Dr. King's first public call for President Johnson's defeat.[9] Although he did not endorse either of the Democratic peace candidates, Senator Eugene B. McCarthy or Senator Robert F. Kennedy, he did praise the civil rights record of each aspirant.

During the weekend of March 16 to 17, 1968, Dr. King told Rev. James Lawson of Memphis, Tenn., that he would be willing to make an exploratory trip to Memphis to speak on behalf of striking sanitation workers. He was expected to appear there on Monday night, March 18, 1968. Reverend Lawson had first contacted Dr. King in late February 1968 in the hope that the SCLC president could assist the garbage workers in pressing their demands, as well as avert further violence between the strikers and the police.

At the heart of the Memphis strike was the issue of racial discrimination.[10] As the result of heavy rains in Memphis on January 31, 1968, Black crews of sanitation workers had been sent home without pay, while white city employees had been allowed to work and received a full day's wage. On the following day, two Black sanitation workers took shelter from the rain in the back of a compressor garbage truck. The truck malfunctioned, and the two were crushed to death. These events were the catalyst for a strike of Memphis sanitation workers, 90 percent of whom were Black; they were protesting the problems faced by the workers: low wages, unsafe working conditions, lack of benefits such as medical protection and racial discrimination on the job. On February 12, 1968, all but 200 of the 1,300 Memphis workers walked off their jobs. The American Federation of State, County and Municipal Employees (AFSCME) supported the strike and demanded a pay raise, recognition of AFSCME as sole bargaining agent, seniority rights, health and hospital insurance, safety controls, a meaningful grievance and other benefits.

Newly elected Memphis Mayor Henry Loeb III rejected the demands, labeling the strike illegal and refusing to negotiate until the workers returned to their jobs. Using the slogan "I am a man," Blacks believed that union representation was tantamount to their recognition as human beings. The racial issue became a central theme and the NAACP intervened in the strike.

When the Memphis City Council refused to hear their demands for union recognition on February 23, 1968, the striking workers had responded with their first march. They were ruthlessly dispersed by police indiscriminately using mace and nightsticks. Several marchers were injured. On the following day, the city obtained an injunction against further marches.

Deeply affected by the violence, Black ministers in Memphis, including Lawson, Rev. Samuel B. Kyles, and Rev. H. Ralph Jackson, formed a strike support organization, Community on the Move for Equality (COME) and called for a boycott of downtown stores. Beginning on February 26, COME organized a large number of Black Memphians to support the daily marches that continued for the duration of the strike, and COME leader Lawson invited Dr. Martin Luther King, Jr., to Memphis.

In the midst of organizing his Poor People's Campaign, Dr. King was reluctant to travel to Memphis when first approached by Lawson in late February. Rev. Andrew Young, in 1968 the executive vice-president of SCLC, told the committee that the SCLC staff initially opposed a King trip to Memphis. Dr. King eventually agreed, however, to make an initial trip in an attempt to discourage further violence, rearranging his schedule and flying to Memphis on March 18, 1968. He saw the poorly paid, badly organized, mostly Black garbage workers as epitomizing the problems of the poor in the United States.

On the evening of March 18, Dr. King gave a well-received address to a throng of 17,000 strikers and their supporters. Encouraged by his reception, he announced he would head a citywide demonstration and sympathy strike of other workers on Friday, March 22. As the result of a recordbreaking snowstorm, the march was rescheduled for Thursday, March 28. In the meantime, efforts to settle the strike failed as Mayor Loeb tenaciously continued to reject union demands.

At about 11 a.m. on March 28, 2 hours after the march had originally been scheduled to begin, Dr. King arrived at the Clayborn Temple in Memphis to lead the demonstrators. By this time, the impatient and tense crowd of about 6,000 persons had heard rumors that police had used clubs and mace to prevent a group of high school students from joining the demonstration.

The march, led by Dr. King and Reverend Abernathy, began shortly after 11. As it proceeded along Beale Street toward Main, several Black youths broke store windows with signpost clubs. Police, clad in gas masks and riot gear, blocked Main Street. Abernathy and Dr. King were somewhere in the middle of the procession, not at its head, when they heard the shattering of glass. Some teenagers at the rear of the march began breaking windows and looting stores. When violence appeared imminent, Dr. King asked Reverend Lawson to cancel the march. SCLC aides commandeered a private automobile, and Dr. King was hustled away to safety at the Holiday Inn-Rivermont Hotel.

As Lawson pleaded with the marchers to return to Clayborn Temple, police moved toward Main and Beale where youths met them with picket signs and rocks. Tear gas was fired into the mob of young Blacks and stragglers who were unable to make their way back to the starting point. Police dispersed the crowd with nightsticks, mace and finally guns. In the ensuing melee, 60 persons were injured, and Larry Payne, a 16-year-old Black youth, was killed by police gunfire. Much of the violence was attributed to the Invaders, a group of young Black militants. A curfew was ordered following the riot, and Tennessee Gov. Buford Ellington called out 3,500 National Guard troops.

Dr. King was upset and deeply depressed by the bloody march. Never before had demonstrators led by Dr. King perpetrated violence, according to Abernathy. The press excoriated Dr. King for inciting the tragic confrontation, even though he was quick to state that his staff had not planned the march and it had been poorly monitored. The Memphis debacle was labeled a failure of nonviolence direct action.

Three members of the militant Invaders visited Dr. King on the morning following the violence, Friday, March 29. They acknowledged their role in inciting the disturbance but explained that they merely wanted a meaningful role in the strike. Dr. King said he would do what he could, but stated emphatically that he could not support a group that condoned violence. At a press conference later that morning, he announced that he would return to Memphis the following week to demonstrate that he could lead a peaceful march.[11] He and Abernathy then left Memphis for Atlanta at 3 p.m. Both Jesse Jackson and Andrew Young, members of the SCLC executive board in 1968, told the committee that they believed Dr. King would not have returned to Memphis if the March 28 demonstration had been nonviolent. Following the Memphis incident, critics, including civil rights leaders such as Roy Wilkins of the NAACP, were doubtful that Dr. King could control a demonstraton and asked that he cancel the Poor People's Campaign to avoid another bloody eruption.

On Sunday, March 30, 1968, in Atlanta, Dr. King along with the SCLC executive staff, including Abernathy, Young, Jackson, James Bevel, Walter Fauntroy, and Hosea Williams decided it was crucial to resolve the Memphis dispute before marching on to Washington with the Poor People's Campaign. Abernathy said Dr. King, was "very delighted" by this plan, which would allow him to prove the efficacy of nonviolence. The next day, Dr. King preached at Washington's National Cathedral, urging human rights in the United States and withdrawal from Vietnam. He mentioned the Poor People's march and promised an orderly, nonviolent demonstration. That evening, President Johnson announced his decision not to seek reelection in 1968.

On Monday, April 1, an entourage of SCLC executive staff members arrived in Memphis to lay the groundwork for a peaceful demonstration in support of the striking garbage workers, preparation that regrettably had been ignored before the last march. Memphis was the focus of national attention the next day as hundreds of Blacks attended the funeral of riot victim Larry Payne.

Dr. King, with Abernathy and administrative assistant Bernard Scott Lee, arrived in Memphis on Wednesday, April 3. That morning their flight had been delayed in Atlanta for more than an hour by an extensive search for a bomb following a threat against Dr. King. Solomon Jones, a local mortuary employee who served as Dr. King's chauffeur during his Memphis visits, took Dr. King and Abernathy from the airport to the Lorraine Motel. Dr. King's April 3 return visit to Memphis had received heavy publicity. It was common knowledge that he would be staying at the Lorraine, and at least one radio station announced that he was booked in room number 306, according to Kyles.

On the morning of April 3, U.S. District Court Judge Bailey Brown issued a temporary restraining order against the SCLC-sponsored demonstration that was originally scheduled to occur on Friday, April 5. Dr. King was determined to lead the march despite the injunction, and the planned protest became a major attraction for Blacks and union leaders.

Tornado warnings were broadcast in Memphis during the afternoon of April 3, and heavy rain fell on the city that night. Despite the inclement weather, 2,000 persons gathered that evening at the Mason Temple Church and awaited Dr. King, who was scheduled to speak there. King had asked Reverend Abernathy to talk in his place, but then Abernathy saw the enthusiastic crowd waiting to hear the SCLC president, he telephoned Dr. King and urged him to give the address. King agreed to go to Mason Temple, where he gave one of the most stirring speeches of his career, the last public address of his life.

After alluding to the bomb scare that morning and other threats against him, Dr. King explained his return visit to Memphis despite such intimidation. Ambassador Young later remarked to the committee that the address was "almost morbid," and Abernathy noted that his friend appeared particularly nervous and anxious.

Dr. King concluded the speech with a reference to his own death:

* * * Well, I don't know what will happen now. We've got some difficult days ahead. But it really doesn't matter to me now, because I've been to the mountaintop. I won't mind.

Like anybody, I'd like to live a long life. Longevity has its place but I'm not concerned about that now. I just want to do God's will and He's allowed me to go up to the mountain. And I've looked over. And I've seen the Promised Land.

So I'm happy tonight. I'm not worried about anything. I'm not fearing any man. "Mine eyes have seen the glory of the coming of the Lord."

After the talk, Dr. King and Young had dinner at the home of Judge Ben Hooks, a Memphis Black leader. Later that evening, Dr. King's brother, Rev. A. D. King, arrived in Memphis from his home in Louisiville, Ky. He registered at the Lorraine Motel at 1 a.m. on April 4. Dr. King, who had not expected his brother in Memphis, visited with him until almost 4 a.m.

THE LAST MOMENTS: MEMPHIS, TENN., APRIL 4, 1968

Dr. King spent the last day of his life, Thursday, April 4, 1968, at the Lorraine Motel. Walter Lane Bailey, owner of the Lorraine, later recalled that the usually business-like SCLC president was particularly jovial that day, "teasing and cutting up."

At an SCLC staff meeting that morning, the march, planned for the next day, was postponed until the following Monday, April 8. In addition, that morning, SCLC general counsel Chauncey Eskridge appeared before Judge Bailey Brown in Federal court and argued that the city's injunction against the proposed demonstration should be lifted. In the meantime, four members of the Invaders presented a series of demands to Dr. King, including one for several thousand dollars. He refused to entertain their demands. After the men left, he told a group of executive board members that he would not tolerate advocates of violence on his staff and was angry that two Invaders had been assigned to work with the SCLC.

At about 1 p.m., Dr. King and Reverend Abernathy had a lunch of fried catfish at the motel, then Abernathy went to his room to take a nap, while Dr. King visited his brother in his room.

At about 4 p.m. on the afternoon of April 4, Abernathy was awakened from his nap by the telephone in his motel room. He answered, and Dr. King asked him to come to his brother's room, No. 201, so they could talk.

When Abernathy reached A. D.'s room, Dr. King told him that he and A.D. had called Atlanta and had spoken with their mother, who was pleased that her sons could get together in Memphis. He also said that they were all invited to the Kyles home for dinner. At King's direction, Abernathy called Mrs. Kyles to find out what she would be serving, and she said she would have a good dinner of prime rib roast and soul food such as chitterlings, greens, pig's feet and blackeyed peas.

At about 5 p.m., according to Abernathy, he and Dr. King returned to room 306 to shave and dress for dinner. He recalled Dr. King's use of an acrid, sulfurous depilatory to remove his heavy beard, part of his daily shaving ritual. As they were preparing to leave, Abernathy mentioned that he would not be able to attend the poor people's march in Washington in April because he had planned a revival at his West Hunter Street Baptist Church in Atlana for that same day. Dr. King told Abernathy he would not consider going to Washington without him and attempted to make arrangements for someone else to handle the Atlanta revival. He called Rev. Nutrell Long in New Orleans but was unable to reach him.

Dr. King then told Abernathy to go to the West Hunter Street Church and tell his congregation that,

* * * you have a greater revival, you have a revival where you are going to revive the soul of this Nation; where you are going to cause America to feed the hungry, to have concern for those who are downtrodden, and disinherited; you have a revival where you are going to cause America to stop denying necessities to the masses * * *.

Abernathy agreed to go to Washington with Dr. King.

At about 5:30 p.m., Kyles went to room 306 and urged Dr. King and Abernathy to hurry so they would get to dinner on time. "OK, Doc, it's time to go," he urged.

365

Kyles had arrived at the Lorraine at about 4 p.m. and had run into the Bread Basket Band, an SCLC singing group. He had been singing some hymns and movement anthems with them until shortly after 5 p.m. Dr. King assured Kyles that he had telephoned the preacher's home and that Mrs. Kyles had said dinner was not until 6. "We are not going to mess up her program," Dr. King insisted.

When he finished dressing, Dr. King asked Kyles if his tie matched his suit. He was in a good mood, according to Kyles, who told the committee that Dr. King teased him about dinner, saying he once had been to a preacher's house for ham and Kool-Aid, and the ham was cold. "I don't want to go to your house for cold food."

As Dr. King adjusted his tie. he and Kyles walked onto the balcony outside room 306. The room overlooked a courtyard parking lot and swimming pool. The two men faced west, toward the backs of several rundown buildings on Mulberry Street. Dr. King greeted some of the people in the courtyard below, and Kyles said hello to SCLC attorney Eskridge who had been in Federal court most of the day. Eskridge was challenging the injunction against the SCLC's proposed Monday march, and the court had decided to permit a demonstration, though it restricted the number of marchers and the route. After court had adjourned at 3 p.m., Eskridge went with Young to the Lorraine where they saw Dr. King in A. D.'s room and informed him of the ruling. At that time, Dr. King invited Eskridge to join him for dinner at the home of Reverend Kyles. Thus, Eskridge was standing in the Lorraine's courtyard parking lot shortly before 6 p.m., awaiting Dr. King's departure for dinner. Dr. King, leaning against the iron railing of the balcony, called to Eskridge and asked that he tell Jesse Jackson, a member of the SCLC's Chicago chapter, to come to dinner with him. Eskridge found Jackson, who was also in the courtyard, and invited him to dinner, suggesting that he change into something other than the turtleneck he was wearing.

Rev. James Orange of the SCLC advance team and James Bevel were also in the courtyard. Both had been assigned by the SCLC staff to work in Memphis with the Invaders in an effort to get the young militants to cool down. Orange had just arrived at the Lorraine with Marrell McCullough, a Memphis Police Department undercover officer. Orange and Bevel wrestled playfully in the courtyard. Dr. King spotted them and shouted to Bevel: "Don't let him hurt you."

Dr. King's chauffeur, Solomon Jones, was standing next to the funeral home limousine, which he had parked in front of room 207, below room 306. Jones had been parked in front of the Lorraine since 8:30 a.m. that morning, and he later recalled that this was the first time Dr. King had stepped out that day. Dr. King told Jones to get the car ready for their trip to Kyles' home, and Jones urged him to bring a top coat because it was chilly that evening. "Solomon, you really know how to take good care of me," Dr. King responded.

Dr. King's administrative assistant, Bernard Lee, along with Andrew Young and Hosea Williams, were also talking in the Lorraine parking lot, waiting for Dr. King to leave for dinner. Young recalled that Jones said, "I think you need a coat" to Dr. King. Ben Branch, leader of the Bread Basket Band, was also there, with Jesse Jackson. Dr. King called down to Branch, "Ben, make sure you play 'Precious Lord, Take My Hand' at the meeting tonight. Sing it real pretty."

"OK, Doc, I will," Branch promised.

Meanwhile, in room 306, Abernathy recalled that at some point shortly before 6 p.m., he and Dr. King put on their coats and were about to leave the motel. Abernathy hesitated and said, "Wait just a moment. Let me put on some aftershave lotion."

According to Abernathy, Dr. King replied, "OK, I'll just stand right here on the balcony."

Kyles recalled that Dr. King asked Abernathy to get his topcoat and then called to Jackson, "Jesse, I want you to go to dinner with us this evening," but urged him not to bring the entire Bread Basket Band. Kyles chided Dr. King, "Doc, Jesse had arranged that even before you had." Kyles then stood on the balcony with Dr. King for a moment, finally saying, "Come on. It's time to go." Kyles turned and walked away to go down to his car. After a few steps, Kyles called to lawyer Eskridge in the courtyard below. "Chauncey, are you going with me? I'm going to get the car."

At 6:01 p.m., as Dr. King stood behind the iron balcony railing in front of room 306, the report of a high-powered rifle cracked the air. A slug tore into the right side of his face, violently throwing him backward.

367

At the mirror in room 306, Abernathy poured some cologne into his hands. As he lifted the lotion to his face, he heard what sounded like a "firecracker." He jumped, looked out the door to the balcony and saw that Dr. King had fallen backward. Only his feet were visible, one foot protruding through the ironwork of the balcony railing. According to Abernathy, the bullet was so powerful it twisted Dr. King's body so that he fell diagonally backward. As Abernathy rushed out to aid his dying friend, he heard the cries and groans of people in the courtyard below.

Just below the balcony, Jones recalled that Young and Bevel shoved him to the ground just after the firecracker sound. He looked up and saw Abernathy come out of the room and then realized that the prone Dr. King had been shot. Lee, who had been talking with Young and Bevel, took cover behind a car and then noticed Dr. King's feet protruding through the balcony railing.

Memphis undercover policeman McCullough recalled that immediately before he heard the shot, he saw Dr. King alone on the balcony outside room 306, facing a row of dilapidated buildings on Mulberry Street. As he turned away from Dr. King and began to walk toward his car, McCullough, an Army veteran, heard an explosive sound, which he assumed was a gunshot. He looked back and saw Dr. King grasp his throat and fall backward. According to McCullough's account, he bolted up the balcony steps as others in the courtyard hit the ground. When he got to Dr. King's prone figure, the massive face wound was bleeding profusely and a sulfurous odor like gunpowder, perhaps Dr. King's depilatory, permeated the air. McCullough took a towel from a housekeeping tray and tried to stem the flow of blood.

Eskridge had heard a "zing" and looked up toward the balcony. He saw that Dr. King was down, and as Abernathy walked out onto the balcony, Eskridge heard him cry out "Oh my God, Martin's been shot." A woman screamed.

Abernathy recalled that when he walked out on the balcony, he had to step over his mortally wounded friend.

* * * the bullet had entered his right cheek and I patted his left cheek, consoled him, and got his attention by saying, "This is Ralph, this is Ralph, don't be afraid."

Kyles, who had started to walk toward his car, ran back to room 306. Young leaped up the stairs from the courtyard to Dr. King, whom he found lying face up, rapidly losing blood from the wound. Young checked Dr. King's pulse and, as Abernathy recalled, said, "Ralph, it's all over."

"Don't say that, don't say that," Abernathy responded.

Kyles ran into room 306. Abernathy urged him to call an ambulance. Kyles tried to make the call, but was unable to get through to the motel switchboard.

Lee, Jackson, and Williams had followed Young up the steps from the courtyard to room 306. Dr. King's still head lay in a pool of blood. Abernathy, kneeling over his friend, tried desperately to save Dr. King's life. Several of the men on that balcony pointed in the direction of the shot. Frozen in a picture taken by photographer James Louw, they were aiming their index fingers across Mulberry Street and northwest of room 306.

An ambulance arrived at the Lorraine about 5 minutes after Dr. King had been shot, accoding to Abernathy. By this time, police officers "cluttered the courtyard." Abernathy accompanied the unconscious Dr. King to the emergency room of St. Joseph Hospital. The 39-year old civil rights leaders, described by Abernathy as "the most peaceful warrior of the 20th Century," was pronounced dead at 7:05 p.m., April 4, 1968.

A. JAMES EARLE RAY FIRED ONE SHOT AT DR. MARTIN LUTHER KING, JR., THE SHOT KILLED DR. KING

Shortly after 6 p.m. on April 4, 1968, Dr. Martin Luther King Jr., was shot and mortally wounded as he stood on the second-floor balcony outside his room at the Lorraine Motel in Memphis, Tenn. He was pronounced dead at 7:05 p.m. at St. Joseph Hospital.

James Earl Ray, a 40-year-old convicted armed robber who had escaped from the Missouri State Penitentiary in Jefferson City, Mo., on April 23, 1967, pleaded guilty on March 10, 1969, in Shelby County (Tenn.) Criminal Court to the first degree murder of Dr. King. He was sentenced to 99 years at the State penitentiary.

(a) Biography of James Earl Ray

James Earl Ray was born on March 10, 1928, in Alton, Ill. The Ray family moved a few miles from Alton to Bowling Green, Mo., in 1930, and 5 years later they moved to near Ewing, Mo., where Ray received his elementary school education.

At age 16, Ray moved back to Alton, where he lived with his grandmother. He worked in the dye room of the International Shoe Tannery in nearby East Hartford, Ill. he was laid off in December 1945 and, 6 weeks later, enlisted in the Army. He was stationed in West Germany where he was charged with drunkenness and breaking arrest. Ray was discharged for ineptness and lack of adaptability for service in December 1948.

After his discharge, Ray returned to stay with his grandmother in Alton, Ill., and embarked on a life of odd jobs and jail sentences. He worked for the Dryden Rubber Co. in Chicago until he was laid off in September 1949, and then left for Los Angeles, Calif. On October 11, he was arrested for robbing a cafe and was sentenced to 90 days' imprisonment.

Upon his release from jail in Los Angeles in the spring of 1950, he traveled back to Illinois, where he worked until May 1952. During this time he attempted to earn his high school diploma at night. He robbed a cab driver of $11.90 on May 6, 1952. He was found guilty of robbery and incarcerated at the State penitentiary at Joliet and later at the State prison farm in Pontiac until his release on March 12, 1954.

Ray then moved to Quincy, Ill. On March 7, 1955, Ray and an accomplice, Walter Rife, broke into the Kellersville, Ill., post office and stole 66 postal money orders as well as a validating stamp. The two men fled to Miami, Fla., but were arrested in Missouri on their return. Ray pleaded guilty to the robbery and, on July 1, 1955, was sentenced to 45 months at the Federal penitentiary in Leavenworth, Kans.

Ray was paroled from Leavenworth in early 1959. He robbed two grocery stores in St. Louis, Mo., and one in Alton during the summer and fall of 1959. He was eventually captured and tried for the St. Louis robbery in December 1959. On March 17, 1960, he began serving a 20-year sentence at the Missouri State Penitentiary. Ray tried to escape in November 1961 and again in March 1966. Following the second attempt, he was examined at the State hospital in Fulton, Mo., and determined capable of standing trial for escape.

On April 23, 1967, Ray did escape from the Missouri State Penitentiary. Over the following 11½-month period, he traveled extensively in North America, residing in such cities as Chicago, Montreal, Birmingham, Los Angeles, and Atlanta. On the afternoon of April 4, 1968, posing as John Willard, Ray rented a room at a Memphis roominghouse near the Lorraine Motel. That day, Dr. Martin Luther King, Jr., was assassinated as he stood on the second floor balcony of the Lorraine Motel.

On May 7, 1968, the Shelby County Criminal Court named James Earl Ray in an indictment for the first-degree murder of Dr. King. An international manhunt culminated with Ray's capture at Heathrow Airport in London, England, on June 8, 1968. Following extradition proceedings in England, Ray was returned to the United States on July 19, 1968. Ray pleaded guilty to the murder of Dr. King on March 10, 1969. Judge W. Preston Battle sentenced him to 99 years in the penitentiary.

(b) The Committee's investigation

With Ray's background and the record of his arrest, trial, conviction, and sentence as background, the committee undertook an exhaustive investigation of all available evidence bearing on Ray's involvement in the assassination of Dr. King. It conducted eight extensive interviews with Ray at Brushy Mountain State Penitentiary in Petros, Tenn., where he is serving the 99-year sentence for the murder of Dr. King.[1] The committee also listened to 3 days of testimony by Ray in public session on August 16, 17, and 18, 1978, and it closely examined all known writings, tape recordings, transcripts and interviews made by or about Ray since his April 23, 1967, escape from the Missouri State Penitentiary. Further, the committee interviewed dozens of associates of Ray and hundreds of other witnesses, many of whom testified under oath in executive session or during 20 days of public hearings. Thousands of Government documents were scrutinized, particularly files of the Memphis Police Department and the FBI.[2] Records from other agencies, such as the Department of State and the Central Intelligence Agency, were also reviewed. Scientific evidence was thoroughly analyzed by experts in such areas as firearms, forensic pathology and engineering.

Based on its investigation, the committee determined that James Earl Ray fired the shot that killed Dr. Martin Luther King, Jr.

1. DR. KING WAS KILLED BY ONE SHOT FIRED FROM IN FRONT OF HIM

In March 1968, Dr. Martin Luther King, Jr., traveled to Memphis, Tenn., to lead a march in suppport of striking sanitation workers. The march was disrupted by violence and ended in a riot. Dr. King returned to Memphis

---

[1] Ray's interviews with the committee were published as appendices to the committee hearings. See Appendix to the Hearings before the Select Committee on Assassinations, U.S. House of Representatives, 95th Congress, 2d Session (Washington, D.C.: U.S. Government Printing Office, 1979), vol. IX-XI (hereinafter—Appendix to the HSCA-MLK Hearings,—).

[2] Because of widespread public allegations of FBI complicity in the assassination, the committee recognized that FBI files were potentially tainted. Ultimately, however, the committee's investigation uncovered no evidence to support the allegations (see section II D). The committee did note major deficiencies in the scope and method of the FBI's postassassination investigation (see section II E). Nevertheless, the committee was satisfied that it could consult FBI files as one of a number of sources of infirmation in the case.

on April 3, 1968, in an attempt to demonstrate that a peaceful march could succeed in achieving desired social and economic goals.[1]

Dr. King and his party were staying at the Lorraine Motel, a Black owned establishment near the waterfront area of Memphis. Dr. King was sharing room 306 with his associate, Dr. Ralph Abernathy, and it was on a balcony in front of that room, at 6:01 p.m. on April 4, 1968, that Dr. King was struck by a bullet and mortally wounded.[2]

Shortly after Dr. King was pronounced dead, his body was taken from St. Joseph Hospital to John Gaston Hospital, where an autopsy was performed by Dr. Jerry T. Francisco, the Shelby County medical examiner. He concluded that Dr. King's death was the result of a single "gunshot wound to the chin and neck with a total transection of the lower cervical and upper thoracic spinal cord and other structures of the neck."[3]

Following the submission of Dr. Francisco's report, questions were raised by critics of the investigation about the thoroughness of the report and the procedures that were followed. These included questions about whether Dr. Francisco properly traced the path of the bullet through Dr. King's body and performed all the normal procedures of a complete autopsy.

To resolve issues raised by the autopsy, the committee retained a panel of three noted forensic pathologists to review the medical evidence pertaining to the assassination. The panel examined all available relevant evidence, including clothing worn by Dr. King at the time of his death, bullet fragments recovered from his body, photographs, and slides taken during the course of the autopsy and microscopic slides and tissue blocks from the autopsy and neuropathology study. The panel also reviewed the report of the committee's firearms panel, as well as X-rays, medical reports, notes, and documents submitted by physicians who treated Dr. King.[3] The forensic pathology panel traveled to Memphis to view the crime scene and meet with Dr. Francisco and the physicians who treated Dr. King at St. Joseph Hospital.[4]

The panel determined that Dr. Francisco had not dissected the path of the bullet during the autopsy. Dr.

---

[3]A detailed discussion of Dr. Francisco's findings and the separate conclusions of the committee's forensic pathology panel are contained in XIII appendix to the HSCA–MLK hearings.

Michael Baden, chief medical examiner for New York City and spokesman for [5] the autopsy panel, testified that this decision resulted entirely from Dr. Francisco's "concerns about not causing any unnecessary deformity to the body" and "his sensitivity to the treatment of the dead." Dr. Baden also noted, however, that "tracing the bullet track proper at the time of the autopsy would have given additional information for questions that might arise later."[6]

The panel concluded, nevertheless, that the autopsy findings were generally accurate. Dr. Baden testified that Dr. King died as a result of a single gunshot wound caused by a bullet that entered the right side of the face approximately an inch to the right and a half inch below the mouth.[7] The bullet fratcured Dr. King's jaw exited the lower part of the face and reentered the body in the neck area.[8] It then severed numerous vital arteries and fractured the spine in several places, causing severe damage to the spinal column and coming to rest on the left side of the back. The bullet traveled in a downward, and rearward from a medial direction.[9]

The panel found that the wounds to Dr. King were caused by the bullet recovered from his body—Remington-Peters, a soft-point, metal-jacketed bullet fired from a distance by a high-velocity rifle.[10] Based on the examination of the evidence by the forensic pathology panel, the committee concluded that Dr. King died as a result of one shot fired from in front of him.

2. THE SHOT THAT KILLED DR. KING WAS FIRED FROM THE BATHROOM WINDOW AT THE REAR OF A ROOMINGHOUSE AT 422½ SOUTH MAIN STREET, MEMPHIS, TENN.

An important issue has always been the location of the assassin at the time the shot was fired. Unfortunately, precise directional and trajectory data could not be obtained in this investigation through forensic pathology for two reasons. One, a dissection of the bullet's path was not performed during the autopsy and could not be done at the time of the committee investigation. Two, it was not possible to determine Dr. King's exact position at the time of the shooting.[11]

From extrinsic evidence, the autopsy panel accepted that at the moment the bullet entered his body, Dr. King was at the balcony railing talking to someone on the pavement one story below.[12] Accordingly, the panel found that the bullet pathway was consistent with the shot coming from his right and above.[13] The autopsy panel concluded that the single bullet that struck Dr. King must have come from across Mulberry Street,[4] because Dr. King's body was facing in that direction and because a bullet coming from that direction would have traveled on a downward slope. The panel concluded, further, that the bullet was probably fired from the area of the rooming-house at 422½ South Main Street, but the panel could not determine, from the medical evidence alone, whether the shot was fired from the bathroom window on the second floor or from the shrubbery below the window.[14][5]

Because of the importance of determining as accurately as possible the location of the assassin, the committee retained Koogle and Pouls Engineering, Inc. of Albuquerque, N. Mex., to conduct engineering surveys at the scene of the assassination. The engineering consultant met the committee and committee medical panel members in Memphis in June 1978, and the firm proceeded to conduct an engineering survey, using sophisticated scientific equipment.[15]

Eyewitness testimony indicated that at the moment of the bullet's impact, Dr. King was standing on the motel balcony in front of room 306, conversing with associates in the courtyard below.[16] The engineering survey was based on scientific measurements of the rear of the rooming-house from that position and of the probable posture of Dr. King's body at the instant of impact—that is, with his head forward, looking down into the parking area and with a slight forward bend at the waist[17] While the consultant was unable to state with certainty, the vertical angle of the trajectory,[18] the geometric data was consistent with both the bathroom window at the rear of the rooming-house[19] and shrubbery within the garden area at the rear of 418–422½ South Main Street[20] as possible locations for the assassin.

Because the medical and engineering evidence was not conclusive as to the precise origin of the shot,[21] the committee used the testimony of witnesses at the scene to determine the most likely origin. Charles Quitman Ste-

[4]See MLK Exhibit F–19 (crime scene diagram), Hearings before the Select Committee on Assassinations, U.S. House of Representatives, 95th Congress, 2d Session (Washington, D.C.: U.S. Government Printing Office, 1979), vol. I, p. 77 (hereinafter HSCA–MLK Hearings).
[5]The panel was asked to concentrate on these two specific areas because the committee received eyewitness testimony supporting each as the firing location of the assassin.

phens, a roominghouse tenant who occupied room 6-B, maintained in a sworn affidavit given on June 13, 1968, that on two or three occasions during the afternoon of April 4, 1968, he "heard footsteps leaving room 5-B and going past [his] room and into the common bathroom at the end of the hall."[6] A second tenant, William Charles Anschutz, told FBI interviewers that during the afternoon of April 4, 1968, he made two attempts to use the bathroom and found it occupied on each occasion. He recalled that Stephens told him, through the door of room 6-B, that the bathroom was being used by the new tenant in 5-B.[22] This information became significant in light of the uncontroverted evidence that Ray did, in fact, rent room 5-B on the afternoon of April 4.

Neither Anschutz nor Stephens could recall for the committee details of these bathrooms visits by the occupant of room 5-B, but Stephens noted in a sworn statement that at the time of the assassination, he was seated at the kitchen table in room 6-B, when he heard a loud explosion that he recognized as a shot. After looking out the window toward the Lorraine Motel, he heard footsteps running in the hallway. He went to the door, opened it, looked out and observed a man with something under his arm turning the corner at the end of the hallway. Stephens was sure the individual had come from the bathroom adjoining his apartment because of the loudness of the shot. [23]

Stephens' sobriety on the afternoon of April 4 was called into question by the number of sources, and the committee did not rely on his testimony for an eyewitness identification of the assassin. It believed that he was sober enough, however, to determine that a loud explosion had occurred nearby and that he saw a man fleeing down the hallway.[24] Similarly, Anshutz heard a shot, opened his door and saw a man fleeing down the hallway from the direction of the bathroom.[25]

Witnesses in the vicinity of the Lorraine, including several officials of the Southern Christian Leadership Conference (SCLC) who were awaiting Dr. King for dinner, pointed in the direction of the rear of the roominghouse

---

[6]Grace Walden, who occupied room 6-B as Stephens' common-law wife, gave a variety of conflicting statements with respect to her observations immediately after the assassination. Since Ms. Walden's testimony became the subject of dispute and caused controversy, it is discussed in a separate section of this report. See section II A b infra.

THE ASSASSINATION OF PRESIDENT JOHN F. KENNEDY

UPI

One of the last photos
of John F. Kennedy alive.

THE ASSASSIN

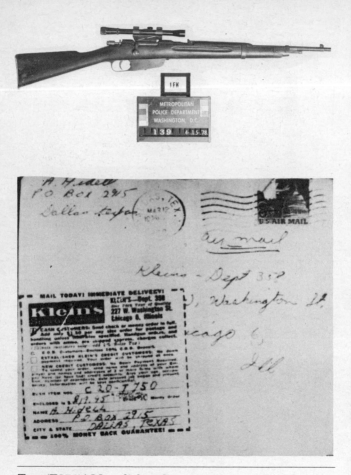

Top: (F276)* Mannlicher-Carcano 6.5-mm rifle ordered by Lee Harvey Oswald from Klein's, Chicago, Ill., and used to assassinate the president.

Bottom: (F504) Oswald's order for rifle, using alias.

*Committee exhibit number

(F382, F383) Front and back of signed photo
Oswald gave George De Mohrenschildt, dating it
"5/IV/63." Russian words reading "Killer of
Fascists—Ha-Ha-Ha" are in unknown hand.

THE PRESIDENT'S WOUNDS

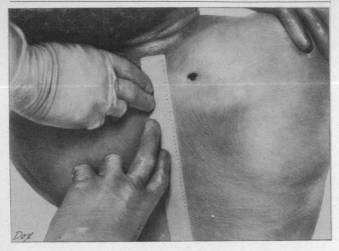

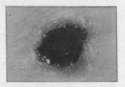

(F20) Committee's special drawing of
Kennedy's back entrance wound, made from
original autopsy photograph.

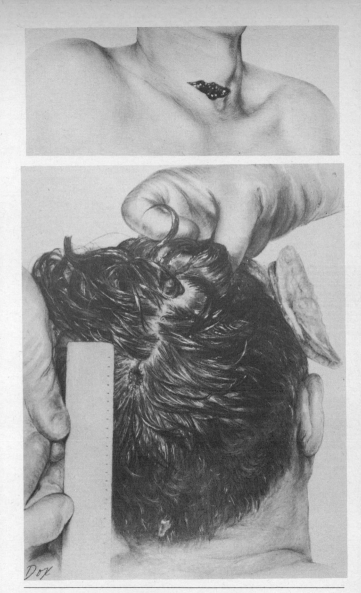

Top: (F36) Exit wound and tracheotomy.

Bottom: (F48) Entrance wound at back of head.

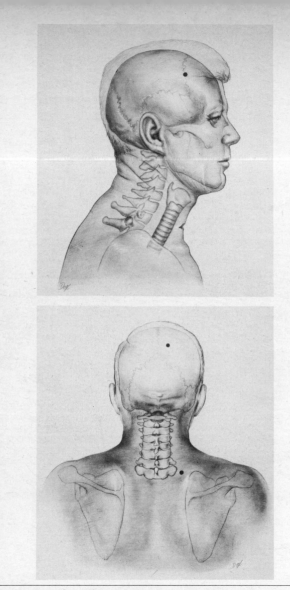

Top: (F58) Cutaway showing 2 exit wounds.

Bottom: (F307) The rear view showing 2 entry wounds.

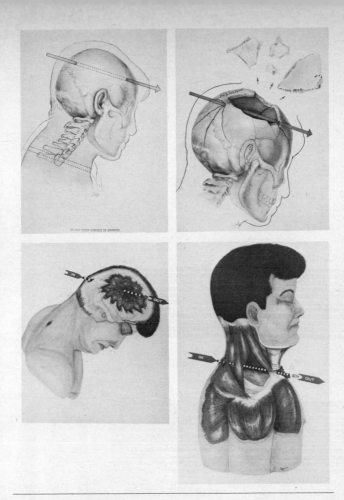

Top, left: (F65) Path of bullets
through head and neck.

Top, right: (F66) Path of bullet
through head (exploding view).

Bottom, left: (F68) Warren Commission drawing
showing path of bullet through head.

Bottom, right: (F47) Warren Commission drawing
of entry and exit neck wounds.

Diagrams of Bullet Wounds

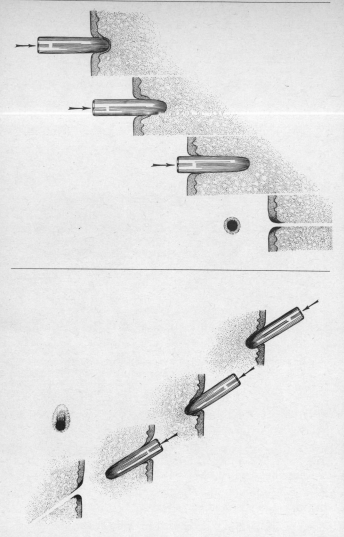

Top: (F23) Right-angle-entry abrasion collar.
Bottom: (F24) Acute-angle-entry abrasion collar.

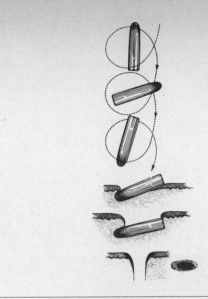

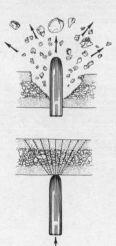

Top: (F72) Entry wound abrasion collar
formed by tumbling bullet.

Bottom: (F61) Entry showing beveling.

BULLET TRAJECTORIES
The Single Bullet

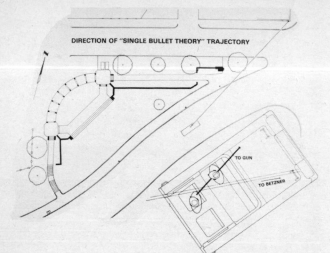

DIRECTION OF "SINGLE BULLET THEORY" TRAJECTORY

TO GUN

TO BETZNER

SLOPE OF "SINGLE BULLET THEORY" TRAJECTORY

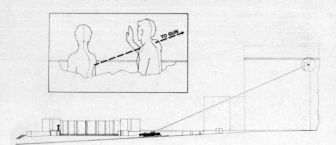

TO GUN

Top: (F144) Diagram at right shows
juxtaposition of Kennedy and Connally.

Bottom: (F145)

The President's Head Wound

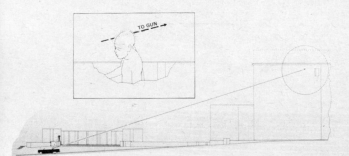

LINE OF SIGHT FROM ZAPRUDER CAMERA TO JFK/SLOPE
OF BULLET CAUSING HEAD WOUND

TO GUN →

Where the Shots Came from

(F122) School Book Depository with 3 ovals drawn around 6th-floor window. Size of oval reflects margin of error in calculations. Smallest shows point of origin if a straight line were drawn from Connally's back to Kennedy's neck exit

wound to Kennedy's back entry wound to oval. Second oval traces bullet from Kennedy's neck to his back to point of origin. Largest is from exit wound in Kennedy's head to entry wound in his head to point of origin.

THE ACOUSTICAL REPORT

Third Shot from Grassy Knoll

Acoustics expert Mark Weiss
pointing to general area of grassy knoll,
where 3rd shot originated.

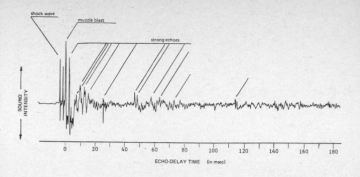

WAVEFORMS OF THE SOUNDS OF A GUNSHOT

(Weiss Fig. 1)

IMPULSES ON THE DPD RECORDING ASSOCIATED WITH ECHOES

(Weiss Fig. 7)

TABLE 1. LIST OF STRUCTURES IN DEALEY PLAZA THAT WOULD HAVE PRODUCED
ECHOES OF SUFFICIENT STRENGTH TO HAVE BEEN RECORDED ON THE
DPD TAPE

OBJECT NO.	IDENTIFICATION
1	South Shelter : south door, east post
2	South Shelter : east door, south post
3	South Shelter : east door, north post
4	North Shelter : south door, west post
5	North Shelter : south door, east post
6	North Shelter : east door, south post
7	North Shelter : east door, north post
8	Wall "A"[1]
9	Wall "A" : corner 1
10	Wall "A" : corner 2
11	Column "A"[2] : southwest corner
12	Wall "B"[3] : corner 1
13	Wall "B" : corner 2
14	Column "B"[4] : west corner
15	Wall at the north end of the reflecting pool
16	DAL-TEX Building : southwest corner
17	DCRB : northwest corner
18	DCRB : west wall (front of building)
19	DCRB : roof edge on west wall
20	DCRB : southwest corner
21	New DCCCB : northwest corner
22	DCRB - New DCCCB : alley wall between buildings

Notes:
1. Wall "A" is a concrete wall on the north side of Elm Street that runs
in an east-west direction. Corners 1 and 2 are at the east end
of the wall. The direction of the wall changes from east to northeast
at corner 1, and from northeast to north at corner 2.
2. Column "A" is a concrete column on the north side of Elm St. near the
intersection with Houston St.
3. Wall "B" is a concrete wall on the south side of Elm St. near the reflecting pool. It runs in a generally north-south direction. Corners
1 and 2 are at the northern end of the wall. The direction of the wall
changes from north to northeast at corner 1 and from northeast to east
at corner 2.
4. Column "B" is a concrete column on the south side of Elm St., at the
northern end of Wall "B".

(Weiss Table 1)

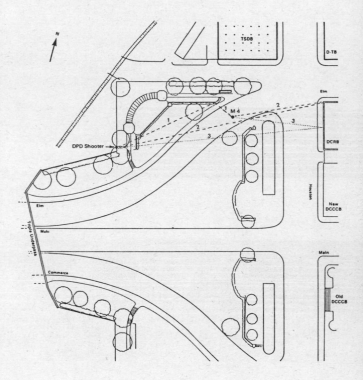

PATHS OF THREE MUZZLE BLAST ECHOES

(Weiss Fig. 5)

The Microphone

Top: (F668) Police Officer H. B. McLain on Main St.,
120 feet behind and to the left of president's limousine.

Bottom: (F671) McLain turning from Main onto Houston.

Top: Enlargement of movie film shows
McLain turning from Houston onto Elm,
just where acoustics expert located him
at about the time of the first shot.

Bottom: McLain testifying before the Committee.

SOME CONSPIRACY THEORIES

The "Umbrella Man"

(F130) Zapruder film showed
raised umbrella, lower left.

Top: (F130) "Umbrella Man" in
Dealey Plaza after assassination.

Bottom: (F130) Enlarged and computer-
enhanced photo of "Umbrella Man."

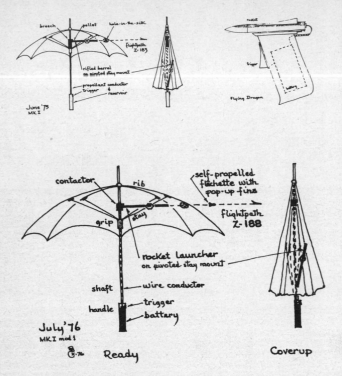

June '75
MK I

breech   pellet   hole-in-the-silk

flightpath
Z-183

rifled barrel
on pivoted stay mount

propellant conductor
trigger & reservoir

rocket

trigger

battery

Flying Dragon

contactor   rib

self-propelled
fléchette with
pop-up fins

flightpath
Z-188

grip   stay

rocket launcher
on pivoted stay mount

shaft   wire conductor

handle   trigger
battery

July '76
MK I mod 1

8
15-76

Ready   Coverup

Figure
63

THE PIECE

Above: (F406) Robert B. Cutler drawing
showing umbrella as rocket launcher.

Opposite: Louie Steven Witt, the "Umbrella
Man." The actual umbrella he used to heckle
Kennedy on 11/22/63 is open. Washington Post

The Mysterious Deaths

Top: (F541) 1967 London *Sunday Times* article.

Bottom: (F544)

TIMES NEWSPAPERS LIMITED

Registered office: P.O. Box no. 7, New Printing House Square,
Gray's Inn Road, London WC1X 8EZ
Telephone 01-837 1234 Telex 264971 Registered no. 894646 England

098644

Mr. G. Robert Blakey,
Chief Counsel and Director,
Select Committee on Assassinations,
U.S. House of Representatives,
3331 House Office Building, Annex 2,
Washington, D.C.20515,
U.S.A.   19th May, 1978

Dear Mr. Blakey,

   Kennedy deaths statistics - The Sunday Times 26 February 1967

     The Editor has passed me your letter of 25th April.

     Our piece about the odds against the deaths of the
Kennedy witnesses was, I regret to say, based on a careless
journalistic mistake and should not have been published. This
was realized by The Sunday Times' editorial staff after the
first edition - the one which goes to the United States and
which I believe you have - had gone out, and later editions
were amended.

     There was no question of our actuary having got his
answer wrong: it was simply that we asked him the wrong
question. He was asked what were the odds against fifteen
named people out of the population of the United States dying
within a short period of time, to which he replied - correctly -
that they were very high. However, if one asks what are the
odds against fifteen of those included in the Warren Commission
Index dying within a given period, the answer is, of course,
that they are much lower. Our mistake was to treat the reply
to the former question as if it dealt with the latter - hence
the fundamental error in our first edition report, for which
we apologize.

     None of the editorial staff involved in this story can
remember the name of the actuary we consulted, but in view of
what happened you will, I imagine, agree that his identity is
hardly material.

                         Yours sincerely,

                         Antony Whitaker,
                         Legal Manager.

(F543) *Sunday Times* letter to Committee
disavowing 1967 statistics.

The Two Oswalds

(F556) Six among the many photo
comparisons of Oswald made by Committee.

(F399) Selected comparisons of Oswald's
signatures at different times of his life.

THE CUBAN CONNECTION

(F429A) The Committee interview with Fidel
Castro in Cuba. At left, Richardson Preyer,
chairman of Kennedy subcommittee, and Louis
Stokes, chairman of the full committee.

Top: (Warren Comm. Pizzo Ex. 453A) Oswald
and unidentified companion distributing pro-Castro
literature in New Orleans, Aug. 1963. Committee
recommends further investigation of this man.

Bottom: (F408) Copy of Oswald's visa application
obtained by the Committee from Cuban government.

Top: (F437) Eusebio Azque, Cuban consul with whom Oswald spoke in Mexico City.

Bottom: (F433) Silvia Duran Tirado, Azque's secretary, who helped Oswald fill out visa application.

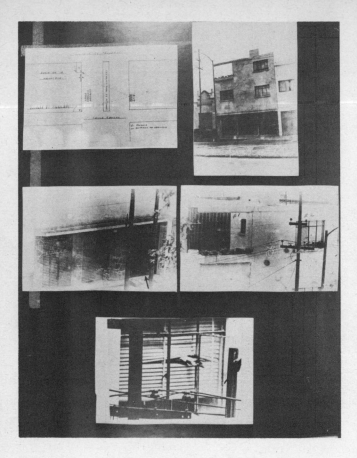

(F438) Composite provided by Cuban government shows alleged CIA surveillance post opposite Cuban embassy in Mexico City. Note camera poking through blinds at bottom.

Comm. Exh. 237

(Warren Comm. CE237)
The "Mystery Man" erroneously identified
in 1964 as Oswald at Russian embassy in Mexico
City. Photo supposedly taken in Sept. 1963.

ORGANIZED CRIME

Jack Ruby as he kills Lee Harvey Oswald. Wide World

(F583, F584) Obtained from Cuban government, front and back of Ruby's tourist cards show him entering and leaving Cuba twice in 1959.

JACK RUBY - TOLL CALLS - 1963

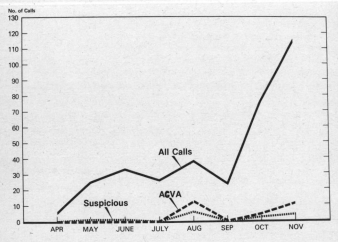

Organized Crime Program

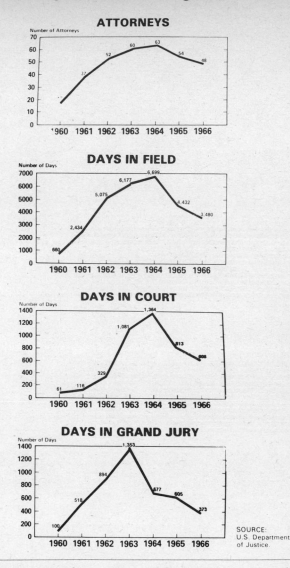

ATTORNEYS

Number of Attorneys

70, 60, 50, 40, 30, 20, 10, 0

'960 1961 1962 1963 1964 1965 1966

37, 52, 60, 63, 54, 48

DAYS IN FIELD

Number of Days

7000, 6000, 5000, 4000, 3000, 2000, 1000, 0

1960 1961 1962 1963 1964 1965 1966

660, 2,434, 5,075, 6,177, 6,699, 4,432, 3,480

DAYS IN COURT

Number of Days

1400, 1200, 1000, 800, 600, 400, 200, 0

1960 1961 1962 1963 1964 1965 1966

61, 116, 329, 1,081, 1,364, 813, 606

DAYS IN GRAND JURY

Number of Days

1400, 1200, 1000, 800, 600, 400, 200, 0

1960 1961 1962 1963 1964 1965 1966

100, 518, 894, 1,353, 677, 605, 373

SOURCE:
U.S. Department
of Justice.

(F552) Statistics showing rise and decline of
Justice Dept.'s efforts against organized crime.

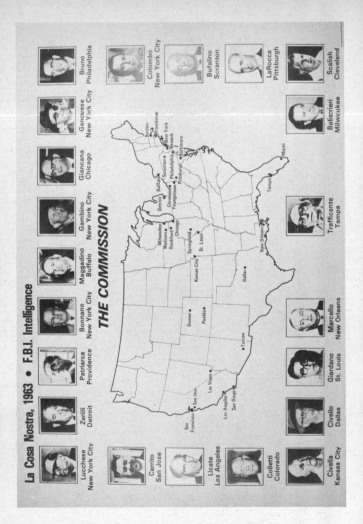

(F547B) Map of the U.S. showing
major organized crime families.

THE ASSASSINATION OF DR. MARTIN LUTHER KING, JR.

Dr. King pointing to
bullet hole made in
assassination attempt
in St. Augustine, 1964.
Wide World

Dr. King and colleagues on balcony where he was shot, the day before his assassination. Wide World

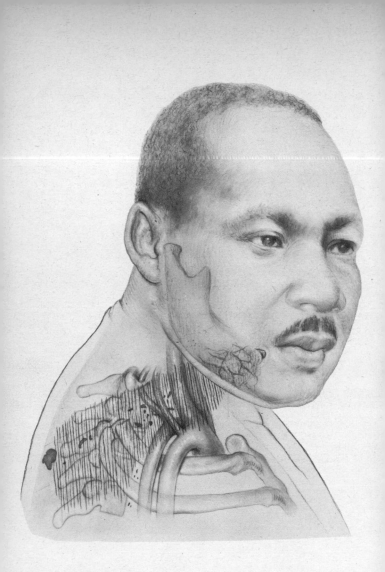

(F10) Drawing of Dr. King's head and
shoulders showing path of bullet.

THE SETTING

Top: (F16) Aerial view of crime scene, Memphis.

Bottom: (F19)

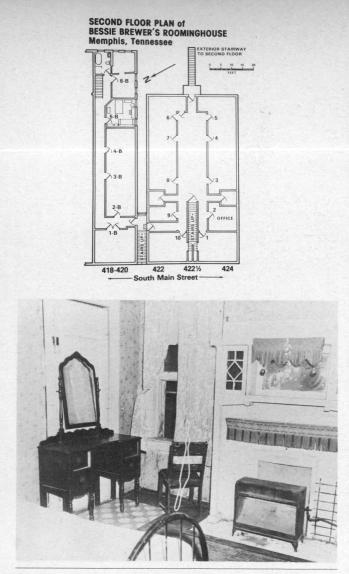

SECOND FLOOR PLAN of
BESSIE BREWER'S ROOMINGHOUSE
Memphis, Tennessee

EXTERIOR STAIRWAY
TO SECOND FLOOR

0 5 10 15 20
FEET

6-B

5-B

4-B

3-B

2-B

1-B

6

7

8

9

5

4

3

2 OFFICE

10

1

STAIRS UP

STAIRS UP

418-420   422   422½   424

← South Main Street →

Top: (F20) Ray's room was 5B; shot was
fired from bathroom at end of hall.

Bottom: (F15B) Ray's room.

Top: (F15C) View from rooming-house bathroom to King's balcony.

Bottom: (F15D) View from King's balcony to Ray's rooming house. Bathroom window from which Ray shot is outlined.

THE EVIDENCE

(F15F) Bundle Ray dropped in front of Canipe's
Amusement Co. contained newspaper and rifle.

FINAL **THE COMMERCIAL APPEAL** FINAL

MEMPHIS, TENN., THURSDAY MORNING, APRIL 4, 1968

128th YEAR—No. 95 ***** 96 PAGES PRICE 10 CENTS

TORNADO ALLEY — High winds and tornadoes swept several hill-South green last night, with widespread damage near Paragould, between Monticello and Star City, and north of Crawfordsville near the Tipton community in Arkansas. Another hit north of Memphis near Millington. Arrow near Burlington also says SW.

Tornado Strikes Near Millington; At Least 30 Hurt

An estimated 30 to 40 persons were injured when a tornado slammed through the Shady Lawn Trailer Court at 3300 Raleigh-Millington Road, near the climax of a night in which violent weather left persons dead in Arkansas and Tennessee.

Two persons were reported dead at Aloha, Tenn., 20 miles northwest of Memphis. Into last night and seven were known dead after an earlier tornado which ripped from the Star City, Ark. area before disappearing around Paglois.

King Challenges Court Restraint, Vows To March

But US Attorney Says Ban To Be Enforced, Even If Troops Needed

LBJ Going To Hawaii Today To Consult On Peace Moves, Set Stage For Red Meeting

US Wary Of Bid To Talk Of Peace On Enemy Terms

NEWS ANALYSIS

By JAMES RESTON

HANOI OFFER OF TALKS ACCEPTED BY JOHNSON

By MERRIMAN SMITH

PUSHING WEST —

Bridwell Urges Park Route OK

Says Council Should Decide; Sees No Easy Alternative

By LARRY SCRIBGIO

Top: Rifle used to kill King was found
in Ray's bundle.

Bottom: (F35) Purchase order for
rifle with Ray's signature, using alias.
Ray acknowledges signature as his.

RAY'S TRAVELS

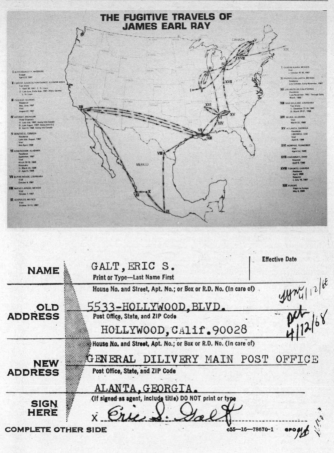

THE FUGITIVE TRAVELS OF
JAMES EARL RAY

NAME	GALT, ERIC S.		Effective Date
	Print or Type—Last Name First		
	House No. and Street, Apt. No.; or Box or R.D. No. (In care of)		JUN 4 1/12/68
OLD ADDRESS	5533-HOLLYWOOD, BLVD.		
	Post Office, State, and ZIP Code		oct 4/12/68
	HOLLYWOOD, Calif. 90028		
	House No. and Street, Apt. No.; or Box or R.D. No. (In care of)		
NEW ADDRESS	GENERAL DILIVERY MAIN POST OFFICE		
	Post Office, State, and ZIP Code		
	ALANTA, GEORGIA.		
SIGN HERE	(If signed as agent, include title) DO NOT print or type		
	x Eric S. Galt		

COMPLETE OTHER SIDE   c55—16—78670-1   gpo

Top: (F360) Map shows Ray's route from time
of his escape on 4/23/67 from Missouri State
Prison until his flight from U.S. on 5/6/68.
Ray was captured in London on 6/8/68.

Bottom: (F52) Postal change of address card
shows Ray, using alias, had begun stalking King
and knew in advance where he was going. Ray
acknowledges Galt signature as his.

PIEDMONT LAUNDRY 68
JAckson 5-8393
Atlanta, Georgia · Date April 1 19 68
Name Eric Galt
Address
Source   Mark   No 31

	DESCRIPTION	PRICE
	3-PC. SUIT	
	2-PC. SUIT	
1	COATS Beige ck.	45
1	TROUSERS Grey	45
	OVERCOATS	
	SHIRTS	
1	TIES Belt w/ laun 4/3 00 St	25
	JACKETS	
	DRESSES	1 15
	BELTS	
	SKIRTS	
	BLOUSES	
	SUITS	
	COATS	
	SWEATERS	
	BLANKETS	
		1 55

RETURN T

755

PIEDMONT LAUNDRY 68
JAckson 5-8393   Atlanta, Ga. April 1 68
Name Eric Galt

SOURCE	MARK	MARKER	LOT	PIN NO.
C 83	EG53	a	10	

½ HR.   REG   M T W T F S
NO STARCH   19-30
LT. STARCH ☐   ON HANGERS ☐
HVY. STARCH ☐ FLUFF DRY ☐ folded

Shirts (2-5)		Dresses		
Drawers				
Undershirts		Slips		
Pajamas				
Union Suits		Gowns		
Sox Pr.		Slacks		
Handkerchiefs		House Coats		
Polo Shirts		Uniforms		11
Shorts		Belts		1
Pants				
Coat				
Jackets				no Starch
Overall Comb.				folded
Bath Robes				
Bath Towels				
Wash		Serv. Chg.		.02
Laundry Bag		Tch. Curl		
Hand Fin.		Tch. Color		
Sheets				
Pillow Cases		TOTAL		

STARCH

ALTON BANK ROBBERY AND RAY FAMILY RESIDENCES

Bank of Alton

Residence of
William Maher
1945 to 1967

Residence of
James Earl Ray
Mid 1940's

Residence of
Lucille Maher Ray

Evidence
Abandoned

ALTON, ILLINOIS

Top: (F59) Ray's laundry receipts,
using Galt alias, show he returned to
Atlanta on 4/1/68 while stalking King.

Bottom: (F546) Alton bank robbery
on 7/13/67 probably financed Ray's
fugitive travels.

JAMES EARL RAY'S FINANCIAL LEDGER
4-23-67 TO 6-8-68

KNOWN EXPENSES

Lodging	$1,783.75
Food and drink	939.00
Gasoline	408.68
Miscellaneous	5,756.83

UNKNOWN EXPENSES

Miscellaneous (10% of known miscellaneous)	575.68
CASH ON HAND AT TIME OF ARREST	144.00
Total	$9,607.94

KNOWN INCOME

On hand at time of escape from prison (approximate)	$300.00
Net salary from Indian Trails Restaurant	664.34
Sale of 1959 Chrysler	45.00
London bank robbery	229.20
Total	$1,238.54

KNOWN EXPENSES LESS KNOWN INCOME ___ $8,369.40

INCOME ALLEGED TO HAVE BEEN RECEIVED FROM "RAOUL"

At U.S.-Canadian border -- 8-21-67	$1,500.00
In Birmingham -- 8-30-67	2,000.00
In Birmingham -- 8-30-67	1,000.00
In Nuevo Laredo, Texas -- 10-7-67	2,000.00
In New Orleans -- 12-17-67	500.00
In Birmingham -- 3-29-68	750.00
Total	$7,750.00

(F361) Ray claimed "Raoul" had financed his travels.

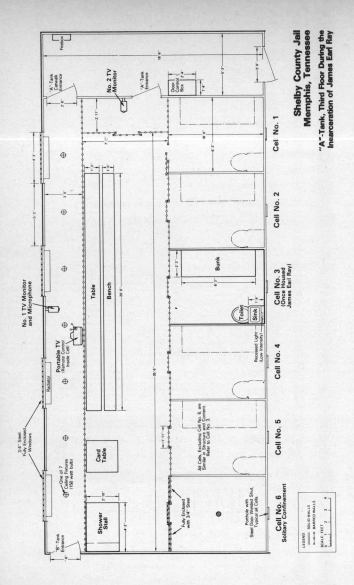

Shelby County Jail
Memphis, Tennessee

"A"-Tank, Third Floor During the
Incarceration of James Earl Ray

THE CONSPIRACY

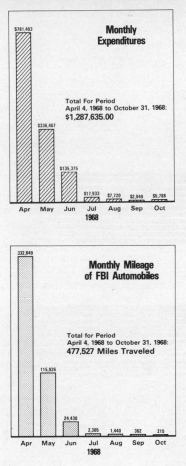

FBI INVESTIGATION OF KING ASSASSINATION:

Monthly Expenditures

$781,403

$336,467

$135,375

Total For Period
April 4, 1968 to October 31, 1968:
$1,287,635.00

$17,933 $7,720 $2,949 $5,788

Apr   May   Jun   Jul   Aug   Sep   Oct
1968

Monthly Mileage of FBI Automobiles

332,849

115,926

Total for Period
April 4, 1968 to October 31, 1968:
477,527 Miles Traveled

24,430

2,305   1,440   362   215

Apr   May   Jun   Jul   Aug   Sep   Oct
1968

(F500) Chart shows FBI conducted a "fugitive"
investigation and made little effort to
pursue Ray's connections after his capture.

ST. LOUIS CONSPIRACY (1)

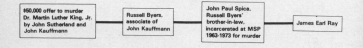

| $50,000 offer to murder Dr. Martin Luther King, Jr. by John Sutherland and John Kauffmann | Russell Byers, associate of John Kauffmann | John Paul Spica, Russell Byers' brother-in-law, incarcerated at MSP 1963-1973 for murder | James Earl Ray |

ST. LOUIS CONSPIRACY (2)

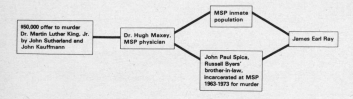

(F579A, F579B, F579C, F579E) Charts show possible connections between St. Louis conspiracy and Ray. Committee considers number 4 the most likely.

ST. LOUIS CONSPIRACY (3)

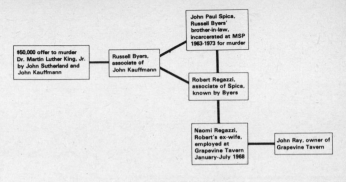

ST. LOUIS CONSPIRACY (4)

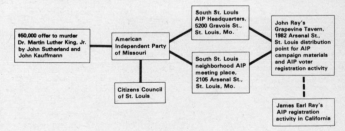

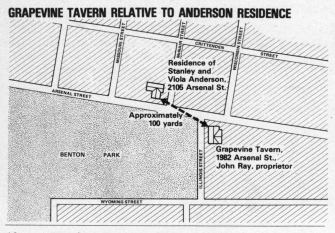

GRAPEVINE TAVERN RELATIVE TO ANDERSON RESIDENCE

MISSOURI STREET

McNAIR STREET

CRITTENDEN STREET

WISCONSIN STREET

STREET

ARSENAL STREET

Residence of
Stanley and
Viola Anderson,
2105 Arsenal St.

Approximately
100 yards

BENTON PARK

ILLINOIS STREET

Grapevine Tavern,
1982 Arsenal St.,
John Ray, proprietor

WYOMING STREET

Above: (F580) Anderson residence was the
South St. Louis headquarters for American
Independent Party campaign materials.

Opposite: (F580A) View from Anderson
residence to tavern owned by Ray's brother.

119 Ex –
Forman Dept
4-3-74

LAW OFFICES OF

PERCY FOREMAN
804 SOUTH COAST BUILDING
HOUSTON, TEXAS 77002

MAIN AT RUSK

CA 4-9321

Memphis
Thursday
Feb. 13,
1969

Mr. James Earl Ray,   260031
Shelby County Jail,
Memphis, Tennessee.

Dear James:

    I write this letter to put of record my analy-
sis of your case, my judgment concerning the probable outcome and my recommendantion as to the course of action we
should explore in your behalf. I also write it for my own
protection. Because I anticipate the coming of a time when
it will be needed for reference.

    I have spent several weeks reviewing the nature
of the case the State of Tennessee has against you. I have
surveyed jury sentiment in this county and jury verdicts in
other recent cases. And I have come to this conclusion:

    In my opinion, there is a little more than a 99%
chance of your receiving a death penalty verdict if your
case goes to trial. Furthermore, there is a 100% chance of
a guilty verdict. Neither I nor any other lawyer can change
the overwhelming evidence that has been assembled against
you. The above analysis of your chances would still obtain
even without the LOOK articles.

    As my client, you are entitled to my judgment. It
is based on my experience as attorney in more than 1,000
murder cases. If I am able to sqve your life by negotiation wi
with the Attorney General and the Court, I will consider it
one of the great accomplishments of my career in the court
room. I do not know whether I can get an agreement to waive
the death penalty or not. But if I can, it will have to be
NOW. I know that it can not be done after March 3, 1969.

    Please sign both pages of two copies of this let-
ter as evidence I have advised you to permit me to try to negotiate the waiver of the death penalty in consideration of
our entering a guilty plea for you.

James Earl Ray
James Earl Ray.

LAW OFFICES OF
PERCY FOREMAN
804 SOUTH COAST BUILDING
HOUSTON, TEXAS 77002

MAIN AT RUSK

CA 4-9321

Page 2 - JAMES EARL RAY - 2-13-69.

Sincerely yours,

Percy Foreman

PF-4

Memphis, Shelby Co., Jail,
Tennessee.
2 - 13 - 69.

I acknowledge receipt of the above letter and the advice and
recommendation contained therein. I have signed the first
page at the bottom, and I sign this one in acknowledgment
that I understand the analysis and recommendation thoroughly.

James Earl Ray
James Earl Ray.

Opposite and above: (F262) Letter to Ray
from his lawyer, Percy Foreman.

Above: Aerial view of
Tennessee State Prison,
where Ray is now.

Right: James Earl Ray
returned to prison after
his escape on 6/10/77.
Wide World

when asked by a Memphis police officer about the direction of the shot.[7]

Marrell McCullough, an undercover Memphis police officer, was one of the first people to reach Dr. King's body. He testified in a committee public hearing that, based on his police training and experience, he determined from the position of the fallen body that the shot had come from the area of the roominghouse.[26] Others in the courtyard, including Ben Branch and Jesse Jackson, also believed that the shot had come from the direction of the roominghouse.[27]

Solomon Jones, who was serving as Dr. King's driver and who was in the courtyard of the Lorraine at the time of the shot, told the committee in a sworn statement that he saw a movement of something white and "as tall as a human being" in the brush beneath the roominghouse after Dr. King was shot.[28] There had been speculation that Jones observed, in fact, the hasty retreat of an assassin. Jones told the committee, however, that he saw the object for only a brief time. He did not see a head or arms; he could not tell whether the object was Black or white, male or female; and he assumed the object was a human being simply because he could think of no other explanation.[29]

In addition, Jones stated that at the moment of the assassination, both Bernard Lee and Andrew Young "reached and got me on each shoulder and pulled me to the ground." He stated further that by the time he got up off the ground, policemen had "almost" arrived at the Lorraine Motel from a nearby firehouse.[30]

The committee believed that the movement Jones perceived actually occurred several moments after the shot. If it was, in fact, a person, it may have been a law enforcement officer responding to the shot.

Other evidence, while not weighted heavily, was nonetheless consistent with the bathroom of the roominghouse as the likely firing location of the assassin. A slight indentation in a windowsill in the bathroom was originally thought by Memphis police to have been caused by a rifle barrel. FBI analysis could not confirm that the murder weapon was the cause of the indentation, nor could the committee. The committee's firearms panel conducted a microscopic review and chemical analysis of the windowsill, but it too

---

[7]See MLK Exhibit F–454. VI HSCA–MLK Hearings, 420 (a photograph of several SCLC members pointing toward the roominghouse from the balcony of the Lorraine immediately following Dr. King's assassination).

could not confirm or eliminate the murder weapon or, in fact, any rifle or other object as the cause of the indentation.[31]

Similarly, scuff marks found in the bathrub could indicate that the assassin stood in the tub while taking aim through the bathroom window. The committee determined, in fact, that a clear shot at room 306 of the Lorraine could only have beem made from the bathroom if the assassin was standing in the bathtub. The committee, however, was unable to eliminate the alternative possibility that these marks, apparently made by someone wearing shoes, were left by police officers attempting to check possible shooting angles immediately after the assassination.

Although the scientific evidence did not independently establish the location of the assassin, when it was combined with witness testimony, it pointed strongly to the rear of the roominghouse. In light of the mutually corroborative testimony of Stephens and Anschutz, and the absence of significant evidence of an alternative firing location, the committee found that the shot that killed Dr. King was fired from the bathroom window at the rear of the roominghouse at 422–South Main Street.

3. JAMES EARL RAY PURCHASED THE RIFLE THAT WAS USED TO SHOOT DR. KING AND TRANSPORTED IT FROM BIRMINGHAM, ALA. TO MEMPHIS, TENN., WHERE HE RENTED A ROOM AT 422½ SOUTH MAIN STREET, AND MOMENTS AFTER THE ASSASSINATION, HE DROPPED IT NEAR 424 SOUTH MAIN STREET

Dr. King was killed by a Remington-Peters, soft-point, metal-jacket bullet fired from a high velocity .30–06 rifle. The committee determined that a rifle purchased by James Earl Ray on March 30, 1968, in Birmingham, Ala., and which was found in front of Canipe's Amusement Co., 424 South Main Street, moments after the assassination, was the type of rifle that could have fired the bullet that killed Dr. King.

From a combination of field investigation, scientific data, and admissions by Ray, the committee was convinced that Ray purchased the rifle, transported it to the scene of the crime and abandoned it near the scene immediately after the shooting. First, the evidence is conclusive that Ray purchased a .30–06 caliber Remington Gamemaster slide action rifle, serial No. 461476, model 760, with a Redfield variable telescopic sight, serial No. A 17350, and Weaver sight mount. This rifle, sight, and mount were recovered by police officers immediately after the assassination and were later designated exhibit "Q2" by the FBI. Ray repeatedly admitted, as he did under oath at a committee public hearing, that on March 29, 1968, he purchased a .243 caliber rifle and a telescopic sight at the Aeromarine Supply Co. in Birmingham. Further, Ray admitted that the next day he exchanged the .243 caliber rifle for a more powerful .30–06 Remington Gamemaster.[32] That rifle was identified as the rifle found in front of Canipe's Amusement Co. on April 4, 1968.

Ray's admission about the purchase and exchange was corroborated by the statements of U. L. Baker and Donald Wood, the Aeromarine employees who dealt with Ray on March 29 and 30. Wood, in fact, identified Ray as the man known to him as Harvey Lowmeyer who, on March 30, received the .30–06 rifle in exchange for the original .243 purchase.[33] In addition, the Aeromarine sales receipt reflects the initial purchase and subsequent exchange by Lowmeyer, the alias Ray admitted using at the time of the rifle purchase.[34]

The committee found significant Ray's use of an alias other than Eric S. Galt during a transaction that could be directly tied to the assassination. Ray had established identification as Eric S. Galt and used that name almost exclusively for 9 months preceding the assassination. When he rented an apartment or a room, bought a car, secured a driver's license, took dance lessons, rented a safe deposit box, visited a doctor, attended bartending school, and subscribed to a locksmith course, all everyday activities, he did so as Eric Starvo Galt.[35] On the other hand, in transactions directly linked to the assassination, and there the most incriminating, Ray deviated from his established identity. He used the name Harvey Lowmeyer only for the purchase of the rifle; [36] similarly, he used the name John Willard only to rent the room at Bessie Brewer's roominghouse at 422–South Main Street, Memphis.[8]

Although Ray claimed to have taken a slow drive through

---

[8]Ray testified that he made these name changes because he*knew his involvement in gunrunning with a person he knew only as Raoul was illegal. (A complete analysis of Ray's Raoul story appears at Section II A 6 infra.) This explanation is undermined, however, by Ray's use of the Galt alias at the New Rebel Motel in Memphis on April 3, 1968, where he planned to meet Raoul and exchange the rifle, as well as by his admitted involvement in past criminal endeavors, such as smuggling at the Canadian border, without similarly elaborate precautionary measures. The committee believed Ray reverted to the Galt alias at the New Rebel because his stay there was not powerfully incriminating and to disassociate himself further from the activities he had engaged in as Lowmeyer and Willard in preparation for the assassination.

Alabama and Mississippi from March 31 to April 4, authenticated documents and sworn testimony convinced the committee that Ray, in fact, returned to Atlanta and left there for Memphis no earlier than April 1 and possibly as late as April 3. Regardless, Ray admitted transporting the rifle from Birmingham to Memphis,[37] claiming that he gave it to Raoul at the New Rebel Motel on the evening of April 3, never to see it again.

Thus the committee established that Ray bought a .30–06 Remington Gamemaster in Birmingham and took it to Memphis. This same rifle—with Ray's fingerprints on it—was found on the sidewalk in front of 424 South Main Street moments after the assassination.

Ray also admitted renting room 5–B at Bessie Brewer's roominghouse, using the name John Willard.[38] In interviews with the committee, as well as in the original investigation, Mrs. Brewer recalled renting room 5–B to John Willard. She also noted that the tenant rejected the first room shown to him, one equipped with light house-keeping facilities, saying he only wanted a sleeping room. Willard then accepted 5–B, Mrs. Brewer recalled, which was in the rear of the building near the bathroom and which offered a vew of the front of the Lorraine Motel. [39][9] A man matching the general description of Ray was also seen at the time he rented the room by Charles Stephens and by Bertie Reeves, another resident of the roominghouse.[40]

As noted previously, both Stephens and Anschutz saw a man carrying a bundle that could have contained a rifle, fleeing down the hallway shortly after the shooting. Bernell Finley, who was shopping in Canipe's Amusement Co. at the time of the assassination, recalled hearing a sound like the backfiring of an automibile. A shortime later he saw a man walking by the front of the store, heard a noise and saw a bundle in the entranceway of the store. He then caught a glimpse of the profile of a man walking away in haste. [41] During his FBI interview, Finley described the man as a white male of average build wearing a dark suit. Shortly after he saw the man, Finley heard the screech of tires and saw a white Mustang pull away from the curb.[42]

---

[9]While room 5–B offered a view of the Lorraine Motel, it did not provide a steady, comfortable firing position, since a shooter would have to lean out the window to aim at the motel. The window of the bathroom at the end of the hall, fronting on the rear of the Lorraine, did not present this problem. See MLK exhibits F–19 (crime scene), I HSCA–MLK hearings, 77; F–20 (Bessie Brewer's roominghouse; second floor), I HSCA–MLK hearings, 79.

Guy Canipe, owner of the amusement company, told the committee he had no recollection of hearing the shot. He did remember hearing a thud at the front door and catching a glimpse of a dark-skinned white man passing the store.[43] In an earlier FBI interview, Canipe described the man as white, between 5 feet 10 inches and 6 feet tall, with a chunky build, wearing a dark suit and generally clean and neat in appearance. He also told the FBI that within moments of hearing the bundle drop, he saw a small white car pull away from the curb on Main Street.[44] Canipe did not recall this car [45] when he was interviewed by the committee. Julius Graham, another customer in Canipe's store, could not provide the committee with a description of the individual who dropped the bundle, but he did recall that a white Mustang passed the store heading north shortly after the bundle was dropped.[46]

The bundle dropped in front of Canipe's was recovered immediately afterward by Memphis police officers. It contained among other items two cans of Schlitz beer, the April 18 edition of the Memphis Commercial Appeal, a plastic bottle of aftershave lotion, a .30–06 rifle with a serial number matching that of the rifle purchased by Ray in Birmingham, ammunition, and a pair of binoculars.[47] The bundle also contained a portable radio with an identification number scratched off it. When the FBI was able to decipher the number, it was revealed to be Ray's Missouri State Penitentiary inmate number.[48]

The committee, in an effort to evaluate the available fingerprint evidence in the case, retained a fingerprint expert, Vincent Scalice of Forensic Control Systems. Scalice examined latent fingerprints lifted from the rifle, the binoculars, a Schlitz beer can and the front page of the Memphis Commercial Appeal. All were found to be the prints of James Earl Ray. Because of other commitments, Scalice could not complete the fingerprint identification, so the committee retained Darrell D. Linville and Ray Holbrook, fingerprint specialists for the Washington, D.C. Metropolitan Police Department. They subsequently identified Ray's prints on the telescopic sight on the rifle and on the bottle of aftershave lotion. No prints, either identifiable or unidentifiable, other than those identified as Ray's, were found on the rifle.[49]

Having determined that Ray purchased the rifle, that his prints were on the rifle, that no other prints were on the rifle, and that a man matching Ray's description dropped the rifle shortly after the shot, the committee turned to the firearms evidence in an effort to establish, if possible, that the Q2 rifle was the murder weapon.

The committee retained a panel of five of the foremost firearms examiners in the United States to review the ballistics evidence.[10] A total of 257 man-hours wese consumed the firearms examination, which consisted of 81 comparisons of Q64, the bullet taken from Dr. King's body, with test-fired bullets, a well as exhaustive microscopic, visual, and chemical analyses. Despite this effort, the panel was forced to conclude that "the bullet, exhibited Q64, cannot be identified or eliminated as having been fired from the rifle, Q2."[11][50]

The panel, however, did make the following positive determinations:

1. The Q64 bullet was a .30–06 caliber bullet of Remington-Peters manufacture.

2. The bullet was imprinted with six lands and six grooves and a right twist by the rifle from which it had been fired.

3. The Q2 rifle had general class characteristics of six lands and six grooves with a right twist.

4. The cartridge case (Q3) found in the Q2 rifle had been fired in the Q2 rifle.

5. The damage of Dr. King's clothing, when tested microscopically and chemically, revealed the presence of lead from a disintegrating bullet and also revealed the absence of nitrites (the presence of nitrites would have identicated a close-range discharge).

6.[The damage of the clothing was consistent with the caliber and condition of the Q64 bullet.[51]

While the firearms panel could not say conclusively that the rifle found in front of Canipe's, one with Ray's fingerprints on the stock and scope, fired the fatal shot, it did conclude that it was possible for the shot to have been

---

[10]Aside from the obvious importance of an accurate analysis of the firearms evidence, the committee noted that the firearms examination in the original FBI investigation was inconclusive. The FBI found it was "* * * not impossible to determine whether or not Q64 [the bullet removed from Dr. King's body] was actually fired from the Q2 rifle."

[11]It is a common misunderstanding that bullets can always be matched to guns. In fact, it is not always possible to match bullets to guns, and no significance should be attached to the failure. Indeed, the panel determined that the individual bullets that it fired from the Q2 rifle could not always be matched scientifically with the weapon, since the rifle apparently engraves inconsistent characteristics on successive rounds. See MLK firearms panel report. XIII HSCA–MLK hearings.

fired from that rifle. When the panel's conclusions were combined with Ray's admissions, fingerprint evidence, and the testimony of other witnesses, there was ample evidence for the committee to conclude that Ray had purchased the .30–06 rifle, transported it to Memphis, shot Dr. King and dropped the murder weapon in front of Canipe's Amusement Co. while fleeing from the scene of the crime.

4. IT IS HIGHLY PROBABLE THAT JAMES EARL RAY STALKED DR. KING FOR A PERIOD IMMEDIATELY PRECEDING THE ASSASSINATION

The committee considered allegations that Ray stalked Dr. King for a period of time preceding the assassination, and it developed evidence indicating a high probability that Ray did, in fact, pursue Dr. King from Los Angeles to Atlanta and ultimately to the Lorraine Motel in Memphis.

In all likelihood, the stalking began about March 17, 1968, the day that Ray left Los Angeles and drove eastward. Ray's decision to leave California was not impulsive. In discussions with his acquaintances from a bartending school earlier in March 1968, he had mentioned his plans to travel east on two separate occasions.[52] Moreover, Ray submitted a postal change of address card[12] with a forwarding address of Atlanta, Ga., Dr. King's home city, before leaving Los Angeles.

Ray, however, never conceded his intent to travel to Atlanta from Los Angeles. In an interview with Dan Rather of CBS in 1977, Ray flatly stated that he never knew he was going to Atlanta until he arrived in Birmingham, "* * * and there was no forwarding address [when I left Los Angeles] and, of course, that would be very damaging against me." [53] Similarly, in his public hearing testimony, Ray emphatically denied filing a change of address in Los Angeles, although he did acknowledge the possibility that he mentioned Atlanta during a telephone conversation with an associate of Raoul.[54] When the committee confronted Ray with the change of address card that he had filed in Los Angeles on March 17, indicating a temporary change of address to General Delivery, Atlanta, until April 25, Ray admitted the card was his and that he must have filed it before his departure from Los Angeles.[55] Ray could not explain his statement to Rather that an intent to

[12]See MLK exhibit F–52 (postal change of address card), II HSCA–MLK hearings, 50–51.

go to Atlanta was damaging.[56] Since Atlanta was the national headquarters of the SCLC, as well as Dr. King's home, the committee found Ray's anticipated travel to that city as the first significant indication of his interest in tracking the activities of Dr. King.

Ray's probable stalking of Dr. King continued with his trip to Selma, Ala., following his departure from Los Angeles. Dr. King was in the Selma area on March 21. Ray admitted being in Selma on March 22 (a motel registration card for his Galt alias confirms his stay there),[13] but his explanation for being there was not convincing. He claimed that while driving from New Orleans to Birmingham, allegedly to meet Raoul, he got lost and had to spend the night in Selma.[57] The committee noted, however, that in 1968 there were two direct routes from New Orleans to Birmingham, and that Selma was on neither of them. It was situated in between the two routes, about 45 miles out of the way. The committee further determined that it would have been difficult for Ray to have become lost between New Orleans and Birmingham.

The committee found Ray's activities following the purchase of the rifle relevant to the stalking theory. On March 28, the day after violence cut short a Memphis march led by Dr. King, Ray purchased a .243 caliber rifle in Birmingham.[58] On March 30, he exchanged it for a .30–06 Remington,[59] the rifle the committee concluded he used to assassinate Dr. King.

Ray testified that between March 30, and April 3, he took a slow drive through Alabama and Mississippi, stopping at different motels each night, on his way to meet Raoul in Memphis.[60] The committee could find no evidence, witness corroboration or documentation, to support this account.[14] On the other hand, there was substantial evidence indicating that Ray returned to Atlanta following the rifle purchase. Thus, Ray's movements roughly paralleled those of Dr. King, who returned to Atlanta from Memphis on March 30. Except for a trip to Washington, D.C., on

[13]See MLK exhibit F–53 (Flamingo Motel registration card), II HSCA-MLK hearings, 55.

[14]During his public hearing testimony, James Earl Ray's brother, Jerry, asserted that records that would have shown James' stay at the Southern Motel in Mississippi on April 1, 1968, had been destroyed by the FBI. The committee explored Jerry Ray's allegation—it took testimony from the manager of the motel, and it reviewed registration cards from the motel for the appropriate period. The committee determined that Jerry Ray's allegation was without merit.

March 31, Dr. King remained in Atlanta until April 3, 1968, when he returned to Memphis.[61]

Ray adamantly denied that he returned to Atlanta before proceeding to Memphis. At a public hearing of the comimittee, he testified, "I know I didn't return to Atlanta. If I did, I will just take the responsibility for the King case here on TV."[62]

The committee reviewed two incidents, however, that compellingly show that Ray did, in fact, return to Atlanta after purchasing the murder weapon in Birmingham. First, the committee established that, on March 31, Ray paid his Atlanta landlord, Jimmy Garner, for a second week's rent; he wrote his name on an envelope and gave it to Garner. [63] This payment was one of the 56 stipulations of material fact that Ray agreed to in his guilty plea.[64] In addition, a committee interview with Garner confirmed the date of the payment.[65] When Ray was confronted with Garner's statement, he claimed Garner was in error. He suggested that the issue of his presence in Atlanta could be cleared up by checking with the Piedmont Cleaners where he left his laundry on March 25, 26 or 27 and picked it up on April 5, 1968.[66]

While Ray was correct about the date he retrieved the clothing, both the laundry receipts[67] and the Piedmont Cleaners ledger, as well as the public testimony of a retired Piedmont employee, Annie Estelle Peters, proved that Ray left his laundry at Piedmont on April 1, 1968. [68] Ray's charge that the incriminating documents were somehow falsified was refuted by both the sworn public testimony of Mrs. Peters and the Piedmont ledger book.

The committee observed that while Ray was in Atlanta on April 1, both the Atlanta Constitution and the Atlanta Journal published stories about the volatile situation in Memphis and Dr. King's intention to return to the troubled city.[69] The committee believed that after learning from news accounts of Dr. King's intention to return to Memphis, Ray left Atlanta and headed for Memphis himself. After arriving in Memphis on April 3, Ray checked into the New Rebel Motel, on the outskirts of the city.[70] The next day he moved to a roominghouse adjacent to the Lorraine Motel.[71]

Rev. Samuel B. Kyles of Memphis, an associate of Dr. King, recalled that on April 3 he heard a radio broadcast reporting that Dr. King was staying at 306 of the

Lorraine.[72] Among Ray's possessions left in front of Canipe's, authorities recovered a copy of the Memphis Commercial Appel with a front page story about Dr. King, one that placed him at the Lorraine Motel for lunch on April 3. [73] Ray's fingerprint was found on the front page of the newspaper.[74]

With information that Dr. King was staying at the Lorraine available to Ray, the transfer from the New Rebel Motel to Bessie Brewer's roominghouse takes on special significance. The rear of the roominghouse faces the Lorraine, offering an ideal vantage point for one who was stalking Dr. King and waiting for an opportunity to assassinate him.[75]

Ray testified that he might have purchased the newspaper, but that he did not read it on April 4 and that he was not aware Dr. King was in Memphis. "I really wasn't aware that he was existing,"[76] he stated. In light of the high visibility of the sanitation worker's strike, Ray's natural sensitivity to the increased police activity because of his fugitive status, the radio and newspaper coverage of Dr. King's activities, and Ray's fingerprint on the April 4 edition of the Memphis Commercial Appeal, the committee concluded that Ray's denial was not worthy of belief.

The manner in which Ray selected his room at Bessie Brewer's roominghouse provided additional evidence of his intent to monitor Dr. King's movements. Room 8, the first room Ray was shown, was located toward the front (South Main Street) side of the building. It was across the hall from the office where Ray had approached Mrs. Brewer. It offered neither privacy nor the possibility of a view of the Lorraine Motel located to the rear of the building.[15] Ray rejected the room, telling Mrs. Brewer he wanted only a sleeping room and not an apartment.[77]

The second room, 5–B, was located in another wing of the building, away from the office and toward the rear of the building. Further, its window offered the possibility of a direct view of the Lorraine. The committee found no evidence that Ray entered the room and examined the view from the window before accepting it. Nevertheless, the privacy and its location at the rear of the building apparently made the room more acceptable to Ray.

Ray's monitoring of Dr. King was also indicated by his purchase of a pair of binoculars after renting the room.

---

[15]See MLK Exhibit F–20 (diagram, second floor, Bessie Brewer's roominghouse), I HSCA–MLK hearings, 79.

Ray admitted purchasing binoculars on the afternoon of April 4, 1968.[78] This admission was corroborated by a sales receipt from the York Arms Co., 162 South Main Street, Memphis, dated April 4, 1968; the statement of Ralph Carpenter, the sales clerk who sold the binoculars to Ray;[79] and Ray's fingerprint on the binoculars. The binoculars with the receipt were found in the bundle of evidence outside Canipe's. Although inexpensive, they would have enabled Ray to keep a close watch on movement at the Lorraine Motel from the rear of the roominghouse. Ray could have observed the Lorraine either from room 5–B, by leaning slightly out of the window, or from the bathroom at the end of the hall. Examination of room 5–B immediately after the assassination revealed that a dresser had been pushed from in front of the window and that a chair had been moved up to the window,[80] indicating that Ray had, in fact, used the window for surveillance of the Lorraine.

Thus, there is compelling circumstantial evidence that from March 17, 1968, Ray tracked Dr. King's movements from Los Angeles eastward, and then followed him to Selma, Ala., Atlanta, Ga., and ultimately Memphis, Tenn., where he rented a room from which he could observe Dr. King and purchased a pair of binoculars to assist him in his observations. The committee concluded that these were activities performed by Ray in preparation for assassinating Dr. King.

5. JAMES EARL RAY FLED THE SCENE OF THE CRIME IMMEDIATELY AFTER THE ASSASSINATION

The committee concluded that James Earl Ray shot Dr. King from the bathroom window on the second floor of the north wing of Bessie Brewer's roominghouse, fled from the building carrying a bundle containing the weapon and other items, and dropped the bundle in the entranceway of Canipe's Amusement Co. The evidence further indicated that Ray then drove from the area in a small white car, heading north. Police radio broadcasts shortly after the assassination identified a white Mustang with a single white occupant as the car and suspect seen fleeing the scene.[16]

After his flight from the immediate scene, the evidence established, moreover, that he drove for 11 hours to Atlanta, Ga., where he abandoned his automobile, picked up

[16]Ray acknowledged in public hearings that he purchased a 1966 white Mustang in Birmingham in August 1967 and that he drove the Mustang to the vicinity of the Brewer roominghouse in Memphis on the day of the assassination. See I HSCA–MLK hearings, 101.)

laundry, hastily packed some belongings at Garner's rooming-house, and then fled north to Canada.[81][17] Ray's flight alone provided substantial corroboration for Ray's involvement in the assassination. Thus, the committee questioned him about it at length in interviews and during his appearance at a committee public hearing.

Although Ray denied in his public testimony that he was at the roominghouse at the time the shot was fired, he admitted leaving Memphis in the Mustang shortly after 6 p.m. on April 4, 1968. He claimed that while returning from a service station shortly after 6 p.m., he saw a police roadblock near the roominghouse.[82] He gave as a reason for leaving Memphis his instinctive fear of police and his concern that something had gone wrong with Raoul's gunrunning scheme.[83]

By his own account, Ray proceeded to drive south toward New Orleans, planning to telephone Raoul's associates in that city to see whether they could explain what had happened at the roominghouse. Ray asserted that, up to this time, he was unaware of Dr. King's assassination in Memphis.[84]

During his second interview with the committee, Ray explained that somewhere south of Memphis he had turned on his car radio and heard, for the first time, of the attempt on the life of the civil rights leader. Ray claimed that at this time he saw no connection between the police activity around the roominghouse, Raoul and the reported assassination attempt:

STAFF COUNSEL. * * * [W]hen you first heard the bulletin that Dr. King had been shot did you in your mind then realize that this had nothing to do with you or Raoul?

RAY. I didn't even pay too much attention to that. There was another bulletin, and I listened to it, and I think music was on before it, and—

STAFF COUNSEL. But his question is that, when you heard that, did you at least then assume that that must have been what the police car was blocking the——

---

[17]Ray testified that he reached Toronto on April 6, 1968, after traveling by bus and train from Atlanta. In fact, his Toronto landlady Mrs. Feliksa Szpakowska, told authorities in 1968 that he had registered on April 8, 1968. While a stopover at some city between Atlanta and Toronto therefore seemed likely, the committee found no evidence to show there had been one.

RAY. No, no there was no connection there whatsoever.—[85]

Approximately 15 minutes later, while still driving toward
New Orleans and seeking a telephone to contact Raoul's
associates. Ray stated that he heard a second report that
announced that the police were seeking a person in a white
Mustang in connection with the assassination. At this time,
Ray decided that he was somehow involved in the assassination and that the police were looking for his white Mustang.[86] The realization caused Ray to change his plans immediately and head east for Atlanta. He was by then
convinced that Raoul was involved in the assassination,
and he feared that he had become the object of a nationwide manhunt. Ray was so certain of this involvement
that he said he threw out everything he had in the car, including some expensive photographic equipment, apparently thinking that these items might link him to the
assassination. [87] By his own account, he continued non-
stop for Atlanta.

Ray was asked to explain the thought process by which
he had concluded, based on the information available to
him, that Raoul was involved in the assassination. Ray
specified a general apprehension about the "guns," that is, the
gunrunning operation, and the involvement of a Mustang:

STAFF COUNSEL. Well, that's what I'm trying to pinpoint when you started to think Raoul may be involved in the shooting of Dr. King, what was it you
were thinking of? It can't be the broadcast about the
car, it's got to be some other things, and what were
they?

RAY. Well, of course, the guns was always a consideration. I thought that when I, I first pulled out of
the area in the car, but I hate to keep getting back to
this same thing, but the Mustang was what really
concerned me.

STAFF COUNSEL. That's why you wanted to get out
of there, but I'm trying to find out what is it that made
you decide or think Raoul may be involved in the
shooting of King?

RAY. Well, I think it was his association with the
Mustang, he was in the general area, and, of course,
the guns.* * *[88]

At another time, Ray described his thought process as follows:

> RAY. * * * The assumptions were step by step. The first assumption I made was when they started looking for the Mustang, was that they were looking probably for me. If they were looking for me, then the next assumption was that they might have been looking for this Raoul, and there may have been some offense committeed in this area.[89]

Ray's explanation for his flight from Memphis to Atlanta was crucial to his claim of innocence in light of the highly suspicious character of his conduct during the hours following the assassination. Consequently, the committee examined his account in great detail and found it unpersuasive.

First, there was no mention of the suspect's description, or of any of Ray's aliases—John Willard, for example—during the broadcasts that Ray heard. He, therefore, had little reason to suppose the authorities were looking for him.

Second, Ray testified in public hearings that he was unaware of Dr. King's presence at the Lorraine Motel.[90] Further, the radio broadcasts apparently made no mention of the Lorraine, Bessie Brewer's roominghouse or the addresses of either. There was no reason, therefore, to associate the police activity to the roominghouse with the reports of an assassination attempt on Dr.King.

Third, Raoul had never exhibited overt racial animosity or mentioned the possibility of shooting Dr. King during their extended period of criminal association.[91] There was no reason, therefore, to associate Raoul with the reported attempt on Dr. King's life.

Fourth, Ray claimed that he was in his own Mustang—away from the roominghouse—at the time of the assassination. In addition, he stated that by the time he returned to the vicinity of the roominghouse, police roadblocks had already been erected, a clear indication that the Mustang reported to have been seen leaving the crime scene had departed some time before. Thus, it is difficult to understand why Ray would have believed that the police were not looking for his Mustang.

Fifth, Ray's story of his flight assumes, as a necessary ingredient, Raoul's presence in the Memphis roominghouse. The committee, however, found no evidence to support the existence of Raoul on April 4, 1968, or any other time.

Finally, as an "innocent dupe," Ray's immediate danger stemmed from the possibility of an erroneous stop of his white Mustang and the subsequent discovery of his status as an escapee from Missouri State Penitentiary. Nevertheless, he accepted this risk and remained in the car for 11 hours during the drive from Memphis to Atlanta. This behavior was illogical, and it suggested that Ray believed the benefit to be gained in placing distance between himself and the area of the assassination outweighed the substantial risk of an arrest on an all points bulletin for the white, Mustang. The committee found Ray's decision to accept this risk comprehensible only if he knew of the bundle drop—and the substantial evidence he had left behind tying him directly to the assassination.

Ray's decision to flee south to Atlanta, rather than directly north to Canada, was also significant, since it too created an increased risk of arrest. The committee considered two explanations. First, Ray returned to Atlanta to receive money for the assassination. Second, there was highly incriminating evidence in Atlanta that Ray needed to eliminate before leaving the country.

The committee found no evidence to support the first explanation. Some evidence indicated that Ray had photographed Dr. King while in Atlanta,[18] raising the possibility that he had left photographs in the city. This possibility was perhaps corroborated by Ray's admission that he threw out his camera equipment during the drive from Memphis. Ultimately, however, the committee was unable to develop concrete evidence supporting this explanation for Ray's return to Atlanta. Nevertheless, the committee found Ray's conduct following the assassination, and his inadequate explanation for that conduct, to be significant additional evidence of his involvement in the assassination.

6. JAMES EARL RAY'S ALIBI FOR THE TIME OF THE ASSASSINATION HIS STORY OF "RAOUL," AND OTHERS ALLEGEDLY EXCULPATORY EVIDENCE ARE NOT WORTHY OF BELIEF

(a) Ray's alibi

One of the best defenses available to a criminal defendant is an alibi—"the plea of having been at the time of the commission of a [criminal] act elsewhere than at the place of its commission." If the defense can be established, the prosecution's case inevitably fails.

---

[18]This evidence was received in the form of a sworn deposition from a witness who requested anonymity.

The committee received substantial evidence that James Earl Ray was at Bessie Brewer's roominghouse during the hours immediately preceding the assassination; that he fired the murder weapon; that he fled the roominghouse; that he dropped a bundle in the doorway of Canipe's Amusement Co.; and that he fled from Memphis to Atlanta in his white Mustang immediately after the assassination.

Ray, however, asserted an alibi defense. He told the committee that he was not at the roominghouse at the moment Dr. King was murdered, but was, in fact, blocks away at a service station, attempting to get a flat tire fixed. It was upon his return from the service station to the roominghouse that he ran into the police roadblock that precipitated his flight from Memphis.[92]

Ray's story to the committee was not his first alibi for the assassination. He had told his attorney, Arthur Hanes, Sr., that at approximately 6 p.m. on April 4, 1968, he was sitting in his parked Mustang in front of 422½ South Main Street when Raoul came running out of the roominghouse, jumped in the back of the car, threw a white sheet over himself and told Ray to drive away. Ray told Hanes that he followed the instructions. After they had driven a few blocks, Raoul jumped out of the car, never to be seen again.[93] This story was also given to author William Bradford Huie, who was working with Hanes. Huie quoted it in his book about the King assassination, "He Slew the Dreamer."[94]

Ray changed his alibi to the gas station story after replacing Hanes with Percy Foreman as his defense counsel. [95] He relied on it to prove his innocence in his 1978 public testimony. When questioned as to why he switched alibis, Ray said the "white sheet" story was intended as a joke at the expense of Huie who had an interest in the Ku Klux Klan.[96] Ray claimed that he did not tell Hanes or Huie the true story because he was afraid they would give the information to the FBI whose agents would then be able to undermine it. Ray said he had planned to give the gas station account at his trial, when he took the witness stand in his own defense.

Chairman STOKES. All I want to know is why you didn't tell this man [Hanes] who is representing you in a Capital case the truth.

RAY. It wasn't I wasn't telling you the truth; I just

didn't tell him that. It was my intention to tell the jury that.

Chairman STOKES. You were going to spring this on your attorney at the trial?

RAY. Yes; that's correct.[97]

The committee was unable to understand why Ray, who planned to go to trial and take the stand, would have decided to withhold a valid alibi from his own attorney, especially since Ray faced the possibility of capital punishment. If the gas station story were true and Hanes had been told of it, he could have found witnesses to corroborate it and support Ray's testimony. By withholding his story, Ray guaranteed that his testimony, which was subject to impeachment because of his prior criminal record, would stand alone without independent corroboration.

The committee found it impossible to believe that Ray would have engaged in such risky trial tactics had the gas station story been anything more than an unsupportable fabrication.

Mark Lane, Ray's attorney at the time of the committee's public hearings, circulated Ray's gas station alibi and identified witnesses who allegedly saw Ray at a Texaco service station at the corner of Linden Avenue and Second Street in Memphis at the time of the assassination.[19] When the committee investigated Lane's account, however, it found no factual support for it. Coy Dean Cowden, one of the men who, according to Lane, saw Ray at the station, testified in public session that he was 400 miles away, in Port Naches, Tex., at the time of the assassination and therefore could have seen no one at a Memphis service station on the evening of April 4, 1968.[98] Cowden explained that he fabricated the story to assist a friend, Renfro Hays, who had been an investigator for Arthur Hanes, Sr.

Congressman EDGAR. Can you tell the committee why you told this false story with such serious implications to the National Enquirer and also to Mark Lane?

Mr. COWDEN. Yes. Renfro Hays was a fellow that

---

[19]Lane's account of Ray's gas station alibi appears in a paperback edition of "Code Name 'Zorro.'" See MLK Exhibit F–117, III HSCA–MLK Hearings, 518.

supported me for a period of about 4 months, completely, while I was unemployed. He befriended me in that he gave me food and lodging and he had the great ability to, you know, let you know, make you feel like that you really owed him something, you know, and really what he was trying to do was sell the movie rights, a book, I believe. There were several things that he mentioned from time to time that he was trying to market, and he would call on me, especially with Mark Lane and some other people that came by to talk to me from time to time, with basically this same story. This—story—I don't rember how many of us, not only Mark Lane and the National Enquirer, but this was to five or six different people. I do not know who they represented, what publication.[99]

The committee also investigated the whereabouts at the time of the assassination of Thomas I. Wilson, because he also could, according to Lane, substantiate Ray's alibi. Wilson had died by the time of the committee's investigation, but a friend of his, Harvey Locke, told committee investigators that he and Wilson were at a store blocks away from the Texaco station at the time of the assassination.[100]

Finally, Larce and Phillip McFall, coowners of the Texaco station in question, testified in public session that no white Mustang entered their station during the late afternoon of April 4, 1968.[101]

The committee, therefore, found that there was no evidentiary support for Ray's alibi.

(b) Ray's "Raoul" story

A character named Raoul had been the cornerstone of Ray's defense. It was Raoul who, according to Ray, directed him at every incriminating stage prior to the murder of Dr. King, from the purchase of the murder weapon in Birmingham, Ala. (ostensibly a sample to show prospective buyers in a gun-running scheme) to the rental of a room in Bessie Brewer's roominghouse (where the gun-running deal was to be negotiated). At Raoul's direction, Ray traveled to Memphis and purchased binoculars shortly before the assassination. Without Raoul, therefore, Ray would be left with no explanation for his highly incriminatory behavior.

The committee determined that much of Ray's Raoul story was flawed. Ray was unable to produce witnesses who saw him and Raoul together at anytime in their 9 months of association, and he had no explanation for the absence of Raoul's fingerprints on the murder weapon. Moreover, while Ray told the story of Raoul countless times over the years to lawyers, journalists, and congressional investigators, he was inconsistent on details as important as Raoul's physical description. Even in Ray's sworn testimony before the committee, his answers to questions about Raoul were vague, incongruous, and evasive. Ultimately, the committee gave no credence to Ray's story of Raoul. Ray's resulting inability to explain his inculpatory behavior must stand as one of the strongest indications of his involvement in the assassination of Dr. King.

(1) *Conflicting descriptions of Raoul.*—Ray's inability to give a complete and consistent description of Raoul was a strong indication of the invalidity of the story. Ray had ample opportunity to observe Raoul. Although he denied in sworn testimony before the committee spending a great deal of time with him, Ray did claim to have met with him from 12 to 15 times and to have engaged in 6 or 7 hours of conversation.[102]

The first publicized description of Raoul appeared in an article by William Bradford Huie in the November 12, 1968, edition of Look magazine. In this article, Ray was quoted as describing Raoul as a "blond Latin."[103] Huie subsequently published a book, "He Slew the Dreamer" that drew heavily on correspondence from Ray. In the book, Raoul was described as a "red-haired French Canadian."[104] During his testimony, Ray explained this inconsistency by stating that he had never mentioned blond hair to Huie and that the second description was correct.[105]

In subsequent interviews, however, Ray gave descriptions of Raoul that differed from the first two. In March 1977, Ray told CBS reporter Dan Rather that Raoul was an auburn-haired "Latin Spanish." [106] By September 1977, in Ray's interview with Playboy magazine, Raoul had become a "sandy-haired Latin." [107] Ray asserted that Playboy erroneously printed the description just as he alleged Huie had done 10 years before.[108]

(2) *Absence of witnesses to corroborate Raoul's existence.*—Significantly, Ray could not produce one witness to establish Raoul's existence, although his meetings with him were more than occasional, as this account shows:

Ray stated that he first met Raoul in July 1967 at the Neptune Bar in Montreal,[109] and he continued to meet with him there "several more times."[110] On August 21, 1967, they smuggled contraband across the United States-Canadian border at Detroit.[111] On August 28, 29 and 30, 1967, they met at the Starlite Cafe in Birmingham, Ala., and later on August 30, they went to Ray's residence at Peter Cherpes' roominghouse.[112] On October 7, 1967, they met at a motel in Nuevo Laredo, Mexico, crossed the border into Texas, and then drove back into Mexico with some unidentified contraband.[113] Ray recalled spending that night at the motel where he had originally met Raoul. Ray claimed, however, that he did not know where Raoul stayed.[114] The next morning they continued further into Mexico, past an interior customs point, and then parted company.[115] In mid-December, Ray met with Raoul in the LeBunny Lounge in New Orleans,[116] and on March 23, 1968, they met again in the Starlite Cafe in Birmingham.[117] That same day they traveled to Atlanta where Ray rented a room at Jimmy Garner's roominghouse.[118] They ate dinner together at a Peachtree Street diner and on the next day Raoul visited Ray in his room at Garner's roominghouse.[119] On March 29, after an absence from Atlanta, Raoul returned to Ray's room, and the two left together for Birmingham to purchase the rifle that was used in the assassination. Ray checked into the Travelodge Motel in Birmingham.[120] He could not remember whether Raoul accompanied him to Aeromarine Supply Co. or simply waited for him at the Travelodge. [121] In any event, they met at the Travelodge following the purchase of the rifle that was exchanged the next day. [122] On April 3, Ray met Raoul at the New Rebel Motel in Memphis and on April 4 at Jim's Grill.[123] Together they went to the room Ray had rented in Bessie Brewer's roominghouse,[124] the last place Ray ever saw Raoul.

The committee located and interviewed witnesses from the three roominghouses, Charpes', Garner's and Brewer's, where Ray maintained he had met Raoul. While these witnesses remembered seeing Ray, they did not recall seeing Ray with Raoul or with any other individual.

Other witnesses who allegedly could corroborate Raoul's existence—for example, Raoul's telephone contact in New Orleans [125] or his smuggling companion in Nuevo Laredo—were impossible to locate because of the inadequacy of Ray's descriptions. He could provide no names or addresses, and the smuggling accomplice was described only as Mexican with Indian-like features.[126]

The committee conducted an extensive investigation of Ray's activities during the preassassination period and yet uncovered no witnesses who would corroborate the existence of Raoul. Ray, who could only gain by such a discovery, provided no identifying characteristics, names or addresses that might have assisted the committee. The absence of corroborating witnesses was a strong indication that Ray fabricated the "Raoul" story.

(c) Preassassination transactions

The committee also found problems in Ray's account of crucial moments in his preassassination relationship with his alleged companion. For example, there was overwhelming evidence to substantiate Ray's purchase of the murder weapon and the binoculars that were found in the bundle in front of Canipe's Amusement Co. and his rental of room 5–B at Bessie Brewer's Memphis roominghouse. Ray did not deny these crucial preassassination transactions, but he contended that he engaged in them at the direction of Raoul as part of a gunrunning scheme.[127]

Each of these transactions was examined in minute detail, and no support was found for Ray's claims.

(1) *The rifle purchase.*—In his correspondence with Huie, Ray wrote that while in Atlanta, Raoul gave him a two-part role in the gunrunning operation. First, he was to buy a large bore deer rifle fitted with a scope; second, he was to inquire about the price of some "cheap" foreign rifles.[128] According to this version, Raoul told Ray about the plan at Garner's roominghouse on the day after their arrival in Atlanta.[129] In a later interview with the committee, however, Ray stated that Raoul did not outline the gunrunning scheme until the morning they left Atlanta for Birmingham, 6 days after his arrival in the city.[130] During his testimony before the committee, Ray reverted to the account he had given Huie in 1968.[131]

Whenever the plan was proposed, Ray said Raoul initially instructed him to make the weapon purchase in Atlanta. [132] Ray suggested that since he had an Alabama driver's license in the name of Eric S. Galt as identification, it would be easier to buy the rifle in Birmingham. Raoul agreed.[133] Ray's subsequent conduct, however, was inconsistent with this aspect of the Raoul story, for when he bought the rifle and ammunition in Birmingham, he did not use his established identity, Eric S. Galt, but rather a new alias, Harvey Lowmeyer, for which he had no documentation. When asked why he used the Lowmeyer name, Ray replied that he thought it would be safer to buy the guns under a different name.[134] This explanation contradicted his stated reason for traveling to Birmingham, since he could have purchased the rifle in Atlanta under the Lowmeyer alias, thus avoiding a 250-mile drive.

Once in Birmingham, Raoul and Ray decided to purchase the rifle at Aeromarine Supply Co.[135] Ray claimed that Raoul also instructed him to look into military surplus rifles for possible sale in their gunrunning operation. Ray told the committee that he inquired about the surplus rifles at Aeromarine.[136] The committee's investigation, however, failed to corroborate this aspect of Ray's story. In a sworn affidavit, U. L. Baker, the clerk who sold the first rifle to Ray, told the committee that Ray asked only general questions about deer hunting rifles and said nothing about foreign or military surplus rifles.[137]

Ray testified before the committee that in furtherance of the gunrunning scheme and on Raoul's instructions, he also purchased some military ammunition at Aeromarine. [138] Although ammunition with machinegun link marks was found in the bundle of Ray's belongings, he apparently did not purchase it at Aeromarine. Both Baker and Donald Wood, the store owner who sold the second rifle, said they did not sell military ammunition to Ray.[139] Further, the sales receipt for the exchange of the rifle and the purchase of commercial ammunition did not reflect the purchase of military ammunition.[140 Confronted with this evidence at a hearing, Ray said it had not changed his story, though he offered no explanation for the contradictory evidence, other than to suggest there must have been a second receipt.[141

(2) *Fingerprints on the rifle.*—The most significant problem with Ray's story of the rifle purchase was his inability to explain the absence of Raoul's fingerprints on the rifle. In both the fifth[142] and sixth[143] interviews with the committee, Ray stated that he brought the second rifle back to the Travelodge Motel, where Raoul examined it and approved the purchase. In the sixth interview, moreover, Ray conceded that Raoul handled the rifle. Ray's responses illustrate the vague and evasive manner in which he spoke of Raoul throughout his interviews with the committee.

STAFF COUNSEL. What did he do? How did he decide that it was OK? What did he do with the rifle?

RAY. I really couldn't say, he just looked at it and that was it.

STAFF COUNSEL. When you say he looked at it, Just like you check a rifle over I guess, you——

STAFF COUNSEL. Well, I wasn't there, how did he check it over?

RAY. Well he checked the mechanism and every—I don't remember all the details, maybe he checked the Mechanisms I think and just give it cursory glance and that would be it.

STAFF COUNSEL. Did he check, pick it up and check the weight to see if it, how heavy the rifle was?

RAY. I think he just said this was, this will do or something of that order.

STAFF COUNSEL. When you say he checked the mechanism, how did he check the mechanism?

RAY. I don't recall, see I don't I don't have the least idea of what the mechanism was all about.

STAFF COUNSEL. Well he took it out, did he take it out of the box?

RAY. Ah, yes I think it was in the box, yes.

STAFF COUNSEL. And he took it out of the box?

RAY. Yes, it was taken, it was taken out of the box and looked at yes.

STAFF COUNSEL. Now he did that, Raoul?

RAY. Yes.

STAFF COUNSEL. Did you lift it and check the weight and check the sight and look through the magnifying mechanism?

RAY. No, I, no the only time I looked at it, and I looked at it quite a bit when I first purchased it. I wanted to try to give the guy the impression that I knew what I was doing. But after that I never did touch it. There was never any touching of the sights or checking the mechanism or anything like that.

STAFF COUNSEL: From the time you purchased that rifle in Aeromarine, that was the last time that you touched the rifle?

RAY. Ah, yes, I would say so.

STAFF COUNSEL. And then after that Raoul picked up the rifle and checked it out, at the motel in Birmingham, is that right?

RAY. Yes.

STAFF COUNSEL. And then how did it get back into the package?

RAY. Well he must of put it there.

STAFF COUNSEL. And then he left the package with you?

RAY. Yes.[44]

Ray stated, during this exchange, that he never handled the rifle after Raoul examined it. (He had transported it to Memphis in a box, given it to Raoul at the New Rebel Motel, and never seen it again.) Yet when the rifle was examined after the assassination, two latent fingerprints of value were lifted from it, both belonging to Ray.[145] Ray was confronted, therefore, with the need to explain how Raoul, after handling the rifle, managed to remove all of his prints while leaving two of Ray's.

Ray addressed this problem in his public hearing testimony by asserting that his previous statements during committee interviews had been erroneous and that, when he took the second rifle back to the motel, no one was there.[146] Raoul had left town and did not see the second rifle until Ray gave it to him in Memphis.[147]

(3) *Rental of room 5–B at Bessie Brewer's rooming-house.*—Ray's sworn testimony concerning the April 4, 1968, rental of room 5–B at Bessie Brewer's Memphis roominghouse raised further doubts about his Raoul story. Ray told the committee that at the New Rebel Motel in Memphis the previous night, April 3, he and Raoul agreed to rent the room under the new alias John Willard.[148] Ray wrote that name on a slip of paper for Raoul so that he could rent the room if he arrived at the roominghouse first.

He mentioned that if he were not in a room at the South Main Street address when I arrived he would be in a bar and grill located on the ground floor of the building * * * .[149]

Sometime between 3 and 4 p.m. the next day, according to Ray's account, he drove to downtown Memphis where he parked his car in a commercial lot some distance from Bessie Brewer's roominghouse. Ray had to make at least three inquiries before he could locate the roominghouse. [150] When he arrived, he testified that he stopped briefly in the tavern downstairs, and then went into the rooming-house and registered as John Willard:

> Chairman STOKES. Well, when you got there, you didn't know whether he had taken a room in the name of John Willard or not then, did you?
> Mr. RAY. No, I didn't know whether he had or not.
> Chairman STOKES. And you didn't inquire, did you?
> Mr. RAY. No, I didn't make any inquiries.
> Chariman STOKES. So you just went right in, furnished your name as John Willard and got a room, even though he might have still been there already ahead of you and gotten the room?
> Mr. RAY. He very well could have, yes.[151]

There seemed to be only one explanation for Ray's willingness to stick to this story. He realized that if he said he had asked the landlady if John Willard had already arrived, she could deny any recollection of this inquiry, further undermining his Raoul story. He chose, therefore, cling to an illogical version of the events.

(4) *The binocular purchase.*—Ray testified that after the room was rented, Raoul told him to buy "a pair of binoculars with infrared attachments saying that the 'people' also wanted to examine some glasses."[152] Thus, the binocular purchase became another step in the gunrunning scheme. Ray testified further that after some initial difficulty locating the store, he entered the York Arms Co. on South Main Street and asked the clerk for infrared attachments for binoculars. The clerk replied that the store did not carry such equipment. He suggested, however, that Ray could purchase the attachments at an Army surplus store. Ray bought ordinary binoculars from the clerk and took them back to Raoul.[153]

As with the rifle purchase at Aeromarine, this aspect of the gunrunning scheme could not be corroborated. In 1968, Ralph Carpenter, the clerk at York Arms, identified James Earl Ray from several photographs he was shown by the FBI.[154] Carpenter stated that Ray asked to see a pair of binoculars that was in the window display. After learning the price, he bought a less expensive pair. It was established in a later committee interview with Carpenter that Ray said nothing about infrared attachments.[155]

In conclusion, Ray's story of Raoul was deficient on a

number of points. First, Ray's descriptions of Raoul's physical appearance and nationality changed significantly over the years. Second, the committee was unable to find—and Ray was unable to produce—one witness who could attest to Raoul's existence. Third, witnesses at Aeromarine Supply Co. in Birmingham, and York Arms Co. in Memphis, as well as documentary evidence from Aeromarine, failed to corroborate details of the gunrunning scheme. Finally, Ray's statements about Raoul over the years, and even during the committee's investigation, were inconsistent and contradictory.

The committee concluded that "Raoul," as described by Ray, did not exist.[20]

(d) Grace Walden Stephens

Aside from Ray's own account of his actions on April 4, 1968, the committee investigated other evidence that had been offered as exculpatory, including the testimony of Grace Walden Stephens.

A tenant of Bessie Brewer's roominghouse at 422½ South Main Street, Memphis, Charles Stephens, said he saw a man who fit the general description of James Earl Ray running down a hallway from the vicinity of the second-floor bathroom immediately after the shooting. [156] William Anschutz, another tenant, said he also saw the man, although he was unable to give a good description of him.[157]

It had been alleged that a third roominghouse tenant, Grace Walden who in 1968 was the common-law wife of Charles Stephens, saw a man who did not fit Ray's description fleeing down the hallway after the shooting.

Further, it had been alleged that because Walden would not agree to sign an affidavit identifying Ray as the assassin, even though she was offered a $100,000 reward to do so, was threatened by an FBI agent and a few days later arrested by Memphis police and taken to the mental ward of John Gaston Hospital. Three weeks later, the allegation continues, she was taken by armed guards to Western State Mental Hospital in Bolivar, Tenn., and committed.

Thus, there had been claims that a witness who could identify Dr. King's assassin as someone other than Ray was

---

[20]See section II B of the report for a discussion of the possibility that Ray's story of Raoul was created to conceal contact with one or both of his brothers.

silenced in an effort by the Government to convict Ray and conceal the identity of the true assassin.

Walden's alleged importance as an eyewitness prompted the committee to conduct a thorough investigation of her background, her story and the circumstances of her commitment to a mental institution. The committee learned that at the time of the assassination, Walden was living with Stephens in room 6–B of Bessie Brewer's roominghouse. Their room was adjacent to 5–B, the one Ray admitted renting under the alias of John Willard. The committee also learned that Walden had a history of arrests and convictions, going back to 1942, for a variety of offenses, including public drunkenness and driving while intoxicated.

At a public hearing on Walden's account and her reliability as a witness, the committee was told that Wayne Chastain, a Memphis newspaper reporter, was the first person to interview her after the assassination, that is, even before the police arrived on the scene. At that time, Walden described the man she had seen fleeing from the bathroom as short and wiry, with salt and pepper hair, wearing a colored plaid shirt and army jacket.[158] During a committee interview, Chastain asserted that he had interviewed Grace Walden on the night of April 4 and that she had told him she had seen a man come out of the bathroom with "a military jacket with a box."[159]

The committee's investigation revealed that Chastain's story is improbable, if not an outright fabrication. First, the committee determined that Memphis police were at the roominghouse within moments of the shooting[160] and were therefore most likely the first to take statements from any residents of the roominghouse, including Walden. Second, the committee found it to be highly improbable that Chastain even spoke to Walden that first evening, as the police had sealed off her portion of the roominghouse. Third, there is some question about whether Walden, admittedly bedridden that day, was able to see the bathroom door from her bed.[161] Finally, no mention of Chastain's interview appeared in any Memphis paper immediately after the assassination.

The committee's investigation did determine that Grace Walden had been interviewed numerous times, beginning immediately after the assassination, and had given several conflicitng stories.

Shortly after the shooting, Walden was interviewed in her room by Lt. Glynn King and Capt. R. L. Williams of the Memphis police. She told them that she and her husband had spent most of the day in their room. The tenant of room 5–B had been running back and forth between 5–B and the bathroom, and, about 2 minutes before the shot was fired, he had returned to the bathroom. After the shot, the person in the bathroom ran down the hall toward the front of the building. She said she was sick, did not get out of bed that day and did not see the man.[162]

She was interviewed again later that evening at Memphis police headquarters by a police lieutenant and an FBI agent and again on April 5 and April 24 by FBI agents. The committee's investigation revealed that at none of those interviews did Walden claim to have seen anyone fleeing from the bathroom or running down the hall.[163]

Robert Jensen, special agent in charge of the Memphis FBI field office in 1968, supervised the FBI's local investigation of the assassination. He told the committee that Walden's statement to Memphis agents was to the effect that she saw nothing following the shot that killed Dr. King because she was in bed all day. He also stated that she "* * * was never requested by the FBI or by anyone to sign an affidavit identifying James Earl Ray as a man she observed exiting the bathroom following the shot." In addition, Jensen explained that she was never offered a reward of $100,000 or any amount to sign such an affidavit, and she was never threatened for failing to sign such an affidavit.[164]

Thus, by April 25, 1968, Walden had said on numerous occasions that she did not see the man who exited the bathroom following the shot that killed Dr. King. In addition, a careful review by the committee of journalistic coverage of the assassination revealed numerous references to statements by Stephens and Anschutz, while there was no mention of any account by Walden.

In November 1968, however, Walden allegedly gave a statement to Renfro Hays,[21] an investigator for Ray's original attorney, Arthur Hanes, Sr., that she had seen a man fleeing from the bathroom who fit the description attributed to her by Chastain. The substance of that statement appeared in the October 1969 and April 1977 issues of Saga magazine.

Walden's statement to the committee on July 26, 1977,

---

[21]The committee noted that Renfro Hays subsequently persuaded Coy Dean Cowden to provide false corroboration for James Earl Ray's gas station alibi.

noted that she did recall seeing a man leave the bathroom, and though she could not describe him because he was moving rapidly, she was certain he was white.[165]

Walden's most recent public statement concerning the events surrounding the assassination occurred on the August 15, 1978, edition of NBC television's "Today" show. She said, "Charlie picked James Earl Ray out. I don't think the man looked anything like him. In the first place I think he was a nigger."[166]

Because of the differences in Walden's statements about whether she saw anyone at all and, if so, whether the man she saw was white or Black, the committee found that her testimony was virtually useless.

In view of allegations that Walden was committed to mental institutions beginning on July 8, 1968, because of her failure to agree that Ray was the assassin, the committee investigated the circumstances of her hospitalization. The investigation included: a careful review of pertinent medical and other records; interviews with individuals knowledgeable about Walden's commitment, treatment and release; and sworn public testimony from six persons who knew about the situation.

The investigation revealed that a few weeks after the assassination, Charles Stephens was taken into protective custody as a material witness and was accompanied everywhere by two police officers. On July 8, Stephens took Walden, who was complaining of a leg or ankle injury, to the hospital; they were accompanied by two plainclothes Memphis policemen. The trip was unrelated to the King assassination case, and no request was made that Walden be examined by a psychiatrist. [167]

After admission to the emergency room at John Gaston Hospital, Walden was examined by Dr. Mary Slechta, a staff psychiatrist, who concluded that she was suffering from psychotic depression and was dangerous to herself. [168] Since she was diagnosed as exhibiting "suicidal tendncies" and presenting a danger to herself, a record of arrest, called for by Memphis police procedures in all similar cases, was filed for Walden at the hospital.[169] The officers signing the arrest record stated "unequivocally" to the committee that no instructions were given by the Memphis Police Department, Shelby County Attorney General's office, the FBI or anyone else to have Walden committed to the John Gaston Hospital phychiatric ward. Both officers indicated.

* * * it was a matter of standard operating procedure for a record of arrest to be filed with respect to
each person who was diagnosed by a staff physician
to be dangerous to himself or others and to be in need
of admission for psychiatric treatment.

Other testimony corroborated the officers' statement.
[170]
During her stay at John Gaston, Walden complained that
she continued to hear voices, and on July 29, she attempted to hang herself with strips of bedding.[171]
An allegation that Walden was given "mind crippling
drugs" after her admission to the John Gaston psychiatric
ward and that this treatment led to a deterioration of her
condition and her commitment to Western State Mental
Hospital in Bolivar, Tenn., was found to be unsubstantiated. All treatment, including drug therapy, was found to
be within the range of generally accepted medical practice at that time.[172]
After Walden's suicide attempt on July 29, doctors at
John Gaston Hospital decided that due to her continued
depression and suicidal tendencies, she should be transferred to Western State Mental Hospital for further treatment.[173] A petition for commitment was filed with the
Shelby County Probate Court on July 29, 1968, by John
A. Henderson, administrator of John Gaston Hospital. Dr.
David Moore, supervising psychiatrist at John Gaston,
and Dr. Sidney Vick[174] certified that Walden's psychological condition indicated that she was a proper subject for
treatment and care in a psychiatric hospital.
Dr. Vick normally handled an average of 15 such commitments in a month, and he stated to the committee that,

* * * the judicial commitment of Grace E. Walden
was handled no differently than hundreds of other
judicial commitments handled by me over my 13-
year tenure.[175]

While testimony at the committee's public hearing and
official court record showed that Tennessee commitment
procedures in 1968 might not stand constitutional scrutiny
in 1978, they were applied equally to all in 1968, including to Grace Walden. The evidence showed that there
was no difference between the proceedings in the Walden

case and any of the several hundred other commitment proceedings held each year.[176] While there were references in Walden's medical records that noted she was "a witness in the King case," the committee determined that the question of her possible status as a witness had no bearing on her commitment.

Dr. James H. Druff, Dr. Jack C. Neale and Dr. Morris Cohen, who served successively as superintendent of Western State during Walden's commitment, testified before the committee that once committed, Walden received the appropriate treatment for somebody suffering from her condition—chronic organic brain syndrome, secondary to alcoholism. The symptomology of that disease includes impairment of memory, orientation, and judgment, a shallowness of affect and an impairment of all intellectual functions. The doctors agreed that her drug therapy, occupational therapy, and other treatment were well within the acceptable practice of medical and psychiatric standards then prevailing. In fact, her drug dose levels were on the moderate to low side. None of the drugs that she received were mind-crippling or dangerous to her case.[177]

They also agreed that she was incapable of caring for herself and should not have been released or discharged from the institution until appropriate outside support facilities were available. In 1978, when such facilities were available, Walden was released.[178]

The testimony revealed that all judgments about Walden's treatment and suitability for discharge were made on purely medical bases, and none of the superintendents was subjected to any pressure from any Federal, State, county, or municipal authorities concerning the commitment, treatment, or retention of Grace Walden.[179]

On the recommendation of the National Institute on Mental Health, the committee retained a psychiatric expert, Dr. Roger Peele, to review and evaluate the records from John Gaston Hospital and Western State Mental Hospital to determine whether Walden's hospitalization, insofar as it was reflected in the records, met acceptable professional standards of reasonable care and treatment.

Dr. Peele reported:

The treatment and medication afforded Walden were, in general, consistent with her diagnosis and fell well within the acceptable standard of psychiatric care. In addition, according to an examination of her records, Walden's medical history was consistent with her subsequent diagnosis.[180]

Concerning her transfer from John Gaston Hospital to Western State Hospital, Dr. Peele stated; "The 23-day length of hospitalization and the transfer to a State hospital were not inconsistent with the psychiatric practice in American psychiatry in 1968."

Taking into consideration these factors concerning Grace Walden:

> The numerous conflicting descriptions of what she saw or did not see on April 4, 1968;
>
> The evidence indicating there was nothing sinister in her commitment to John Gaston or Western State hospitals; and
>
> That her commitment was in no way related to her role as a possible witness in the King assassination investigation;

The committee concluded that Grace Walden's testimony would be of little or no value, and her statements to the effect that James Earl Ray was not the assassin of Dr. King were unworthy of belief.

In summary, after reviewing the evidence, the committee concluded that Grace Walden's alleged observation of someone other than Ray leaving the roominghouse bathroom was not worthy of belief. The committee further concluded that her commitment to John Gaston Hospital and Western State Mental Hospital was based on medical considerations and was not related to her role as a possible witness in the assassination investigation.

7. JAMES EARL RAY KNOWINGLY, INTELLIGENTLY, AND VOLUNTARILY PLEADED GUILTY TO THE FIRST DEGREE MURDER OF DR. MARTIN LUTHER KING, JR.

On March 10, 1969, James Earl Ray appeared before Judge W. Preston Battle of the Criminal Court of Shelby County, Tenn., and pleaded guilty to the first degree murder of Dr. Martin Luther King, Jr.[181][22] This plea re-resulted from negotiations between Ray's principal attorney

---

[22]A more detailed analysis of the guilty plea appears as part of an appendix to the public hearings. See staff report, "An Analysis of the Guilty Plea Entered by James Earl Ray: Criminal Court of Shelby County, Tenn., Mar. 10, 1969," XIII appendix to the HSCA–MLK hearings.

Percy Foreman, and Shelby County Attorney general Phil N. Canale. [182] Foreman was assisted in his representation of Ray by Hugh Stanton, Sr. and Hugh Stanton, Jr., [183] both of the Shelby County Public Defender's Office. The maximum penalty under Tennessee law in 1969 for first degree murder was death. [184] Nevertheless, under the terms of the prosecution's recommendation to the court, Ray was spared the death penalty and was sentenced to 99 years confinement in the State penitentiary. [185]

During the hearing before Judge Battle, the court questioned Ray extensively in an effort to determine the voluntariness of the plea and to insure that he knew the plea would result in the waiver of valuable rights. [186] In addition, as a condition of the plea, Ray agreed to a proposed stipulation of the material facts that set forth all the details of his whereabouts, and actions that the State advanced to support its case against him. [187] Ray ultimately agreed to the stipulations sought by the prosecution except one concerning his alleged political activities. A portion of the exchange between Ray and Judge Battle on March 10, 1969, indicated that Ray admitted his role in the assassination of Dr. King and voluntarily and understandingly entered his guilty plea:

The COURT. You are entering a plea of guilty to murder in the first degree as charged in the indictment as a compromise and settling your case on an agreed punishment of 99 years in the State penitentiary. Is that what you want to do?

ANSWER. Yes, I do.

The COURT. Is this what you want to do?

ANSWER. Yes, sir.

The COURT. Do you understand that you are waiving which means you are giving up a formal trial by your plea of guilty although the laws of this State require the prosecution to present certain evidence to a jury in all cases on pleas of guilty to murder in the first degree by your plea of guilty you are also waiving [the court explains Ray's rights in great detail] * * * Has anything besides this sentence of 99 years in the penitentiary been promised to you to plead guilty? Has anything else been promised to you by anyone?

ANSWER. No, it has not.

The COURT. Has any pressure of any kind of anyone in any way been used on you to get you to plead guilty?

ANSWER. No, no one in any way.

The COURT. Are you pleading guilty to murder in the first degree in this case because you killed Dr. Martin Luther King under circumstances that would make you legally guilty of murder in the first degree under the law as explained to your by your lawyer?

ANSWER. Yes, legally, yes.

The COURT. Is this plea of guilty to murder in the first degree with an agreed punishment of 99 years in the State penitentiary free, voluntarily and understandingly made and entered by you?

ANSWER. Yes, sir.

The COURT. Is this plea of guilty on your part the free act of your free will made with your full knowledge and understanding of its meaning and consequences?

ANSWER. Yes, sir.[188][23]

Within 3 days of the guilty plea, Ray recanted his admission and requested a new trial in a letter to Judge Battle dated March 13, 1969. [189] Ray followed this letter with another dated March 26, 1969, that echoed the first, also directed to Judge Battle. [190] Judge Battle died on March 31, 1969. He had not taken any action on Ray's request for a new trial. [191]

Following Judge Battle's death, on April 7, 1969, Ray filed a formal petition for a new trial. The court denied the motion at the conclusion of its hearing on Ray's petition on May 26, 1969.[192]

After exhausting his right of appeal under Tennessee law, Ray sought relief in the Federal courts by filing a petition for a writ of habeas corpus. On March 30, 1973, a Federal district court denied Ray's request for relief, ruling that Ray's constitutional rights had not been denied.[193] Ray subsequently appealed to the U.S. Court of Appeals for the Sixth Circuit. That panel reversed the district court on January 29, 1974, finding that the lower court improperly denied Ray an evidentiary hearing before it ruled on his motion.[194] The State of Tennessee appealed this decision to the U.S. Supreme Court, which refused to hear the

[23]A complete transcript of the guilty plea proceedings appears as MLK Exhibit F–80, III HSCA–MLK hearings, 52.

case on June 3, 1974.[195] The matter was returned to the district court, where an evidentiary hearing was held. On February 27, 1975, the district court ruled that Ray's constitutional rights had not been violated and denied his petition for a writ of habeas corpus.[196] Ray also appealed this decision, and on May 10, 1976, the Sixth Circuit Court of Appeals affirmed the lower court's decision, ruling that the evidence sustained a finding that Ray had voluntarily and knowingly pleaded guilty in State court to murder:

Considering "all of the relevant circumstances" surrounding Ray's plea * * * we agree with the district court that the plea was entered voluntarily and knowingly. As stated, Judge Battle very carefully questioned Ray as to the voluntariness of his plea before it was accepted on March 10, 1969. Ray specifically denied at that time that anyone had pressured him to plead guilty * * *.[197]

The court also noted that a February 18, 1969 letter, signed by Ray, authorizing Foreman to negotiate a guilty plea, supported the finding that the plea was voluntary; that he had not been prejudiced by his contracts with writer William Bradford Huie; that he had not shown inadequate investigation by his counsel; that he had failed to establish that Foreman gave him incompetent advice in urging him to plead guilty; and that he had not reasonably believed that he had no alternative to a guilty plea. The court also rejected Ray's contention that he had been denied effective assistance of counsel by police surveillance, interception of mail and delivery of attorney-client communications to the prosecution, since he had been unable to demonstrate that these activities affected the preparation of his defense.[24] The court concluded that Foreman's representation of Ray was "within the range of competence demanded of attorneys in criminal cases." [198]

Ray sought review of this decision in the U.S. Supreme Court. On December 13, 1976, the Supreme Court denied Ray's request for a writ of certiorari.[199]

Ray's immediate repudiation of his guilty plea started speculation that it had been part of an elaborate plot to

---

[24]The committee did review FBI files that clearly established that interception of Ray's mail had occurred. A detailed discussion of this matter is contained in the committee's evaluation of the performance of the FBI in the assassination investigation. See, infra, at sec. II E 2.

silence Ray and protect conspirators in the assassination. Consequently, the committee conducted a full factual and legal investigation of the plea to determine whether it was voluntarily entered and legally sufficient, applying appropriate legal standards in its assessment. Ray had maintained that a number of conditions rendered his guilty plea defective or involuntary,[200] including:

Irreconcilable conflicts of interest involving his attorneys, Percy Foreman and Arthur Hanes, Sr.;

Inadequate investigation by Foreman, Ray's chief defense counsel at the time of the guilty plea;

Mental coercion exerted by Foreman and the Federal Government to force Ray to plead guilty; and

Ray's belief that his guilty plea would not preclude his ability to secure a subsequent trial.

The committee reviewed each of the claims made by Ray.

(a) Irreconcilable conflicts of interest of Foreman and Hanes

Initially in conjunction with Arthur Hanes, Sr., Ray's first attorney, and then with Percy Foreman, Hanes' successor, Ray entered into contracts with William Bradford Huie for the literary rights to Ray's version of the assassination of Dr. King. Ray subsequently maintained that he signed these contracts only at the insistence of his attorneys.[201] The committee interviewed all parties to the contracts and reviewed information from the papers filed in Federal court in *Ray* v. *Foreman*[24] and *Ray* v. *Rose*.[25]

The investigation revealed that Ray, Hanes, and Huie entered into the first three-party contract on July 8, 1968, just under a month after Ray's arrest in London and 2 weeks before he was returned to the United States.[202] The contract gave Huie literary rights to Ray's story and provided for a three-way split of the proceeds. In September 1968, Ray and Hanes amended the initial contract's provision for Hanes' fee, limiting the total amount he could realize to $20,000 plus expenses.[203] After Foreman replaced Hanes, he assumed contractual rights similar to those of Hanes but without the $20,000 limit on his fee.[204] Ray maintained that these agreements put

---

[24]*Ray* v. *Foreman* was a civil action filed by Ray following his guilty plea. Named defendants included Foreman, Hanes, and Huie. Ray charged them with violation of his constitutional rights and sought to enjoin Huie's book, "He Slew the Dreamer."

[25]*Ray* v. *Rose* was Ray's habeas corpus action.

Hanes and Foreman in conflict with his best interests as their client.

A review by the committee of the sworn testimony given in *Ray* v. *Foreman* and *Ray* v. *Rose* indicated that Ray was an intelligent party to the literary contracts. In an interview with the committee, Hanes said the original and primary reason for entering into the contracts was to assure enough money to finance Ray's defense.[205] Ray maintained that Foreman was initially critical of the Hanes contract, and he then broke his word to him by entering into a similar literary contract with Huie. [206] Foreman, on the other hand, contended that he entered into the contract with Huie at Ray's request to secure funds to finance the defense.[207] When questioned about the arguably unconscionable nature of his fee arrangement with Ray, Foreman said that he took an assignment of all Ray's interest in the literary contract, at Ray's behest, and held it in trust to protect Ray from attachment, should Dr. King's widow successfully mount a civil suit against him for the wrongful death of her husband.[208] After examining Foreman's contracts with Ray, the committee rejected Foreman's contention that he intended simply to hold Ray's proceeds in trust. The contracts indicated an unconditional transfer of Ray's interest in the literary proceeds to the trust. Nevertheless, Foreman testified that he saw nothing wrong with the contract or with his fee of $165,000 plus expenses.[209]

A further review of pertinent court documents indicated that the financial interest of Huie and Foreman in the literary contract was not enhanced by Ray's guilty plea. In *Ray* v. *Rose*, all of the contractual obligations were subjected to judicial scrutiny. An examination of the contracts between Huie and the publishing houses that paid him to collect information and write about Ray showed that the value of Ray's story depreciated markedly once the guilty plea was entered, for it reduced public interest in the case.[210] This finding supported Foreman's claim that his only concern in urging Ray's guilty plea was saving his life and that the money he stood to gain from the literary contracts did not color his professional judgment.

The committee's conclusions concerning the Hanes-Huie-Ray and Foreman-Huie-Ray literary agreements were consistent with the findings in *Ray* v. *Rose*. In that case, the court found there was no evidence whatsoever to support Ray's allegation that the conflicts of interest with his attorneys caused him to plead guilty involuntarily.[211] The court reached this conclusion despite its finding that the fee arrangement originally negotiated by Hanes was in apparent violation of the American Bar Association's code of professional responsibility and its finding that Foreman's fee, had it been collectable, was unreasonable. [212]

The committee found no evidence from its interviews, reviews of documents and other investigative methods to support Ray's claim that the contractual agreements resulted in prejudice to his defense. While a conflict of interest did exist between Ray and his attorneys, it did not materially affect the quality of the representation Ray received. In addition, Hanes had disclosed the conflict to Ray, and Foreman warned Ray about such arrangements at the time he was hired. Thus, Ray was both a voluntary and intelligent party to the contracts.

(b) Foreman's failure to investigate the case

The committee reviewed, with the aid of the Congressional Research Service, Library of Congress, the judicial interpretations of the phrase "effective assistance of counsel," and applied these standards to the factual situation giving rise to Ray's claim that the assistance of counsel in the King case was ineffective.

Ray became dissatisfied with the representation of his first attorney, Arthur Hanes, Sr., primarily as a result of the relationship Hanes had established with author William Bradford Huie.[213] This dissatisfaction prompted Ray, through the efforts of his brothers, Jerry and John Ray, to contact Texas trial attorney Percy Foreman. On November 10, 1968, 2 days before Ray's scheduled trial, Foreman replaced Hanes.[214] Foreman succeeded in postoning the trial until March 3, 1969, to prepare a defense for Ray.[215]

Ray alleged that Foreman's investigation was deficient and that he was consequently deprived of the effective assistance of counsel.[216]

The committee examined the merits of this allegation. As with the conflict of interest issue, the committee referred to the court documents filed in Ray v. Rose and Ray v. Foreman. In addition, the committee interviewed Ray's defense attorneys, including Foreman, and investigators who were in their employ. Foreman's investigation was examined in light of the legal standard required of counsel in a criminal case to determine if he was prepared to take the Ray case to trial.

Foreman maintained that from the time he entered the case until the March 10, 1969, guilty plea, he devoted 80 to 90 percent of his time to Ray's defense.[217] He estimated that he spent between 30 and 75 hours in interviews with Ray.[218] He also said that he used eight senior law students from Memphis State University as investigators.[219] Foreman, however, was vague about the duties of these students,[220] as well as other aspects of his investigation. He apparently did speak to Huie, Attorney Arthur Hanes, Sr., Hanes' investigator Renfro Hayes, and some potential witnesses.[221] After a full review, however, the committee concluded that Foreman did not conduct a thorough and independent investigation into the death of Dr. Martin Luther King, Jr., on behalf of Ray. Foreman was unable to provide a list of witnesses he interviewed,[222] but the committee was able to conclude that many potential witnesses were never interviewed by Forman or his associates. Stanton did not complete a canvass of witnesses by the time of the guilty plea,[223] and Foreman's student investigators apparently never conducted a single interview.[224] In fact, one of the student investigators interviewed by the committee indicated that the students never did any investigating for Foreman. [225]

The committee's review of Shelby County jail logs contradicted Foreman's claim of 30 to 75 hours of consultations with Ray.[226] These hourly activity logs kept by Ray's jailers indicated that Foreman visited with Ray approximately 20 hours from the time he entered the case in November 1968 until the March 10, 1969, guilty plea. [227] According to the logs, Foreman spent an inordinately small amount of time with his client for a case of such magnitude.

Foreman differed with the findings of the committee review, and the committee found a possible explanation for the discrepancy: Security slackened as time progressed, and less accurate records may have been kept on Ray after initial interest in his case diminished.[228] Ray's recollection of the time Foreman spent with him, however, was consistent with the hours shown in the jail logs.[229]

Additionally, Arthur Hanes, Sr. told the committee

that he attempted to make his files on Ray's case available to Foreman, but Foreman only used a few of them. Hanes also noted that Foreman never fully questioned him about his personal knowledge of the case, even though Hanes had offered to help.[230]

Although Foreman may be faulted for not conducting a more thorough independent inquiry before he advised Ray to plead guilty, he did have at his disposal the results of investigations by William Bradford Huie, Arthur Hanes, Sr. and Renfro Hayes, as well as those of an investigation conducted by the Shelby County Public Defender's Office. The scope of the combined defense investigations was substantial,[231] the public defender's probably being the most comprehensive. Three investigators were assigned to the case and worked closely with Foreman. They interviewed numerous witnesses and followed up investigative leads,[232] and they retraced the investigation done for Arthur Hanes, Sr. by Renfro Hayes. (Much of that work was later found to be unreliable.) [233] The product of the public defender's work in Ray's defense filled between 10 and 12 files.[234]

The defense team uncovered and considered weaknesses in the State's case.[235] but when Foreman and co-counsels Hugh Stanton, Sr. and Hugh Stanton, Jr. discussed the evidence against Ray, they decided, even with the weaknesses, that the Government's case could not be beaten.[236] Despite Ray's protestations, the committee concluded that his decision to plead guilty was based primarily upon Foreman's recitation of the State's case against him.[237]

Ray was unable to demonstrate any actual prejudice to his case, and the committee believed that the level of representation Ray received from his attorneys, including Foreman, satisfied the standard established to measure effective assistance of counsel in the sixth circuit in 1968.

(c) *Coercion by Foreman and the Federal Government*

In his effort to repudiate his guilty plea, Ray maintained he had entered it against his will, under pressure from Foreman who misrepresented the facts to him and gave him bad advice.[238] While only Ray and Foreman were present at conversations out of which the plea arose, rendering much of what Ray alleged unverifiable, the committee was able to establish certain facts from the

416

record. On February 13, 1969, Foreman told Ray in a letter that if the case went to trial, there was a 100 percent chance he would be found guilty and a 99 percent chance he would get the death penalty. Foreman commented that it would be "one of the great accomplishments" of his career if he could save Ray's life with a negotiated plea. [239] Then, in a letter prepared by Foreman for Ray's signature and dated February 18, 1969, Ray authorized Foreman to negotiate a guilty plea for a term of years. It was stated in this letter that Foreman and Ray agreed it would be impossible to dispute certain incriminating evidence and that they believed a trial ending in a guilty verdict would result in a 99-year sentence or the electric chair.[240]

In its review of the district court's evidentiary hearing on Ray's petition for habeas corpus relief, the Sixth Circuit Court of Appeals summarized the lower court's reasons for its finding that Foreman had not induced the guilty plea.[241]

> The court found that most of Ray's allegations regarding Foreman's inducement of the guilty plea were not supported by the proof. Specifically, the court found that Foreman did not advise Ray, even if innocent, to plead guilty; that Foreman suggested to Ray that he would be better off financially with a guilty plea, but that this statement did not influence Ray in his decision; that Foreman did not advise Ray to plead guilty because he would be pardoned by John J. Hooker, Jr., who would be the next Governor of Tennessee; and that Foreman did not attempt to persuade Ray to plead guilty by telling him either that the prosecution was prepared to bribe a key witness against Ray, or that Foreman would exercise less than his best efforts if Ray insisted on a trial, or that Judge Battle would not allow him to change attorneys and that Foreman would not withdraw.

The committee found no evidence that would warrant a different judgment.

At his March 10, 1969, hearing, Ray answered questions put to him by Judge Battle, not as an intimidated man, but as a defendant convinced that he could not withstand the State's case against him. Ray indicated at the hearing that "no one in any way" pressured him to plead guilty.[242] As for his quick repudiation of that plea, the committee found this to be consistent with Ray's pattern of behavior. It noted that in 1959, shortly after he was arrested for robbing a supermarket, Ray made a statement to police admitting the crime. At the trial, however, Ray reversed his position, charging that his confession had been coerced by police brutality.[243]

Ray also claimed that part of the coercion to gain his guilty plea was the "brutal" conditions in the Shelby County jail during his pretrial incarceration, which had an ill effect on his physical condition.[244]

In its investigation of conditions at the jail, the committee determined that extraordinary measures were taken to safeguard Ray, as a result of the notoriety of the case. The precautions included: An entire cellblock to house Ray alone; steel doors on the entrances to the cellblock; steel plate covers on all the windows in the cellblock; two guards to watch Ray on each of three daily shifts; two closed-circuit television cameras to monitor the cellblock; constant illumination of the cellblock; special food selection; microphone surveillance within the cellblock.[245]

The committee determined that Dr. McCarthy DeMere was the person best qualified to comment on Ray's physical condition during his incarceration at the Shelby County jail and the possible effect of the special precautions. DeMere served as Ray's physician from the time of his return to Memphis from England on July 19, 1968, until he was taken to the Tennessee State Penitentiary following his guilty plea. DeMere testified on Ray's health and condition of confinement at a 1974 evidentiary hearing on Ray's petition for habeas corpus relief,[246] in an interview with the committee [247] and in a committee public hearing. [248] DeMere said Ray was in good health when he arrived and that it remained excellent during his stay at the jail. In fact, De Mere told the committee, Ray gained weight while he was in the jail. Although Ray complained at first to DeMere about the lights in his cell, he never complained of losing sleep. The only medical complaints he made during his stay in the Shelby County jail concerned occasional headaches and nosebleeds.

The facilities that Ray occupied were comparable to a good motel suite and compared favorably to a first-grade suite in an ordinary hospital, according to DeMere. Additionally, DeMere told the committee he never saw Ray depressed and that he never exhibited any nervous tension. DeMere concluded that Ray was in better health when he left the Shelby County jail than when he entered it.

Ray argued that another aspect of the coercion was harassment of his family by the Federal Government and Forman to get him to plead guilty. He charged specifically:

That the FBI threatened to have his father arrested and returned to a prison he had escaped from 40 years earlier;[249]

That the FBI burglarized the home of his sister, Carol Pepper;[250]

That his brother, John Ray, had been sentenced to 18 years for bank robbery, an excessive sentence compared to those of his codefendants;[251]

That Foreman told him that his brother, Jerry Ray, would be arrested and charged with conspiracy in the assassination if Ray did not plead guilty;[252] and

That Foreman tried to induce members of Ray's family to convince him he should plead guilty.[253]

The committee explored Ray's allegation concerning the FBI and Foreman. This task was complicated because Ray's word and that of members of his family provided the only support for his allegations. Given their probable bias, the committee was reluctant to accept such evidence without corroboration.

The committee found no independent evidence to support Ray's contention that the FBI burglarized his sister's house. The committee also determined that John Ray had been incarcerated on the bank charge almost 1½ years after James entered his guilty plea.[254] Ray's brother, Jerry, was the original source of the story that the FBI threatened to rejail their father, and the committee was unable to substantiate this story.

Ray's allegations concerning Foreman were equally difficult to confirm. During an interview with the committee at the Brushy Mountain State Penitentiary Petros, Tenn., Ray admitted that Foreman at no time said that the FBI had informed him of Jerry's imminent arrest, but Foreman had alluded to the possibility that he might be picked up. [255] No independent evidence was found to support the family's claim that Foreman tried to force them to induce Ray's plea.

The committee could not find substantiation for any of Ray's charges that his guilty plea was coerced—specifically, that his plea was induced by Foreman, that he was subjected to brutal conditions at the Shelby County jail, that his physical condition was permitted to deteriorate or that members of his family were pressured and harassed.

419

(d) Ray's belief a guilty plea would not preclude a new trial

Statements made by Ray both before and after his guilty plea raised questions about his understanding of the plea's finality. In an interview with the committee, Ray said his main purpose in entering the guilty plea was to get rid of Foreman.[256] He looked upon the plea as a technicality, a way out of jail in Memphis.[257] According to Ray, the guilty plea served as a convenient, harmless alternative to going to trial with Foreman, whom he no longer trusted; [258] going to trial with the public defender, whom he felt had neither the skill nor the resources to handle this major case; [259] and going to trial unrepresented. [260] Ray's background strongly indicated that he knew the guilty plea would effectively extinguish all of his legal remedies. First, he had previous experience with the appellate court system, as a result of his unsuccessful appeal of a [1959 robbery conviction.[261] In addition, he was fully apprised of the consequences of his guilty plea during the March 10, 1969, proceedings.

The committee believed, therefore, that Ray's plea was knowing, intelligent and voluntary and that constitutional requirements were satisfied. The committee further concluded that the plea was a significant indication of Ray's guilt in the assassination of Dr. King.

B. THE COMMITTEE BELIEVES, ON THE BASIS OF THE CIRCUMSTANTIAL EVIDENCE AVAILABLE TO IT, THAT THERE IS A LIKELIHOOD THAT JAMES EARL RAY ASSASSINATED DR. MARTIN LUTHER KING, JR., AS A RESULT OF A CONSPIRACY

As noted, the committee concluded that James Earl Ray was the assassin of Dr. King. Other aspects of the assassination remained to be examined. What was Ray's motive? Was he assisted in any way? Was there a conspiracy involved in Dr. King's death?

Several facts conditioned the thinking of law enforcement officials and the American public since the day of the assassination: Dr. King was an important leader of the civil rights movement; he was shot down in a southern city by a single shot from a high-powered rifle in the midst of a series of turbulent civil rights demonstrations; only one assailant was seen fleeing the scene. To most, there would seem to be reason to believe, therefore, that a lone assassin, acting out of racial animosity, committed the assassination.

1. THE FBI INVESTIGATION

Indeed, as the FBI's investigation in 1968 progressed after that tragic day in April, the theory that Ray was a lone, racially motivated assassin gained plausibility. With the identification of Ray as the probable assassin, an extensive background investigation began. Missouri State Penitentiary inmates provided evidence indicating his distaste for association with Black inmates. Further evidence of racial incidents was developed in California and Mexico that reflected both a volatile temper and a deep-seated racial prejudice. Finally, in early interviews with the FBI, members of Ray's family—and particularly his brothers—exhibited strong strains of racism. Although he held open the possibility of conspiracy, FBI Director J. Edgar Hoover's views had become clear by June 20, when he wrote a memorandum summarizing a discussion with Attorney General Ramsey Clark:

I said I think Ray is a racist and detested Negroes and Martin Luther King and there is indication that prior to the Memphis situation, he had information about King speaking in other towns and then picked out Memphis.(1)

This view of the assassination is reflected in the work of some prominent authors who have written on the subject. (2) In addition, committee interviews with FBI and Justice Department officials involved in the original investigation indicate a general consensus that Ray was a loner who was motivated in the assassination primarily by racial hatred. Finally, while a 1977 Justice Department Task Force proposed varying interpretations of Ray's ultimate motivation; (3)[1] it, too, agreed that he acted alone in the assassination.

The committee recognized that despite the results of earlier investigations, a respectable body of public opinion supported the theory that the King assassination was the product of a conspiracy. In addition, the committee was faced with a variety of well-publicized conspiracy allegations, most based on speculation and not founded on fact, and many of them inconsistent with one another.

2. THE COMMITTEE INVESTIGATION

The committee approached the issue of conspiracy with a range of investigative techniques. Where applicable, the committee relied on the skills of scientific experts, (4) retaining panels in the fields of forensic pathology, firearms, fingerprint analysis, handwriting analysis and polygraphy; it also contracted with an engineering firm for a survey of the assassination scene. Finally, the committee undertook an extensive program of file reviews, field interviews, depositions and hearings. Where necessary, immunity grants were employed to compel the testimony of witnesses who claimed their privilege against self-incrimination.

(a) Transactional analysis

A major undertaking in the field investigation was an examination of Ray's known transactions during the 14

---

[1]The task force report, while noting in Ray "a strong racist attitude toward Blacks." concluded that his motive was a combination of "apparent hatred for the civil rights movement; his possible yearning for recognition, and a desire for a potential quick profit."

months from his escape from the Missouri State Penitentiary in April 1967 to his arrest in London in June 1968. The committee closely examined each transaction for any indication that might lead to a finding of conspiracy on April 4, 1968. The committee traced every step of Ray's travels after his escape—to suburban Chicago, where he worked as a dishwasher; to the area of St. Louis, Mo., home of his brother, John Larry Ray; to Montreal and to a resort in the Laurentian Mountains, where he vacationed; to Birmingham, Ala., where he purchased an automobile; to Mexico and to Los Angeles, where he lived for 4 months until March 1968, except for a brief trip to New Orleans in December; and finally on his circuitous trip eastward, in mid-March 1968, a trip that ended with the assassination in Memphis and Ray's flight to Europe via Canada.

(b) Ray's associates examined

The committee conducted a similar examination of Ray's known or alleged associates, concentrating on those with whom he was actually or reportedly in contact during the 14-month period. They included members of his family, especially his two brothers, John and Jerry; the mysterious Raoul, Ray's alleged criminal associate; Charles and Rita Stein and Marie Martin, Ray's acquaintances in California; and several individuals alleged to have been associated with Ray.

In addition to closely examining Ray and his associates in an effort to find indications of conspiracy, the committee considered a variety of conspiracy leads to see if any could be independently established as valid or connected to Ray. The committee also investigated a variety of extremist organizations, including the Ku Klux Klan and the Minutemen, to determine if they were involved in the assassination or linked to Ray. Finally, the committee examined more than 20 specific conspiracy theories or allegations. Some were significant and received close attention; the committee looked at others, however, that could be, and were discredited by a routine check of facts.

By and large, the committee's investigation of suspect organizations and its exhaustive check of the specific theories and miscellaneous allegations produced negative results. In many cases these results were, in light of the mutually exclusive character of the allegations, predictable. The committee was satisfied, however, that its effort was not wasted, for it provided a sound evidentiary basis for settling a variety of long-lingering questions and eliminating deep concerns.[2]

3. INVESTIGATION OF RAY'S MOTIVE

Motive is, of course, an integral element of any murder. Its significance is readily apparent in an examination of criminal trials, where the absence of convincing evidence of motive will often lead to an acquittal. Such evidence is not, at least legally, a necessary element of the prosecutor's proof. Nevertheless, many juries are simply unwilling to convict a defendant for such a crime without first receiving a satisfactory explanation to the question, "Why?".

In addition, the question of motive is intertwined in the issue of conspiracy. Several different, yet complimentary, motives, if established, could be consistent with a single assassin theory. If, for example, Ray were found to possess a strain of virulent racism, a lone assassin theory would be viable. Similarly, if it was established that Ray were driven by a psychological need for recognition in the criminal community, his involvement in a notorious crime such as the assassination, without the help or urging of others, would likewise be understandable. Nevertheless, to the extent that a theory tied to Ray's racism or some other motive did not provide a satisfactory rationale, other explanations had to be sought. And with each additional explanation, its consistency with a lone assassin theory had to be tested anew.

In its examination of the question of motive, the committee was aware that its ability ultimately to resolve this issue was necessarily limited. Ray consistently denied his involvement in Dr. King's murder. The committee, therefore, did not have access to the most probative evidence—Ray's own explanation for his conduct. In the absence of a confession, the committee was forced to rely on the testimony of others and on an analysis of Ray's conduct. This evidence was valuable, but it was unsatisfactory for the purpose of understanding the complexities of Ray's psyche, which might lead to firm conclusions on the issue of motive.

---

[2] A discussion of the committee's investigation of private organizations and of miscellaneous conspiracy allegations appears in section II C of this report. The committee's discussion of possible official complicity appears in section II D of this report.

(a) Ray's racial attitudes examined

The committee's investigation of Ray's racial attitudes was extensive, in keeping with the significance of the issue. Ray, several family members, and a large number of Ray's associates were questioned on the subject. An effort was also made to explore the significance of certain alleged incidents in his past that have been identified as showing strong racial animosity.

It had been reported, for example, that while at Missouri State Penitentiary, Ray exhibited extreme hatred for Black prisoners and for Martin Luther King as well. (5) To verify this allegation, the committee reviewed some 70 FBI inmate interviews, compiling a smaller list of inmates who had worked with Ray, celled near or with him, or who professed knowledge of his personal life and habits. The committee then interviewed approximately 30 prison associates of Ray.[6] While some recalled that Ray had demonstrated anti-Black feelings, the majority said he was not a racist. On balance, therefore, the committee viewed the inmate testimony as essentially inconclusive. It could not be relied on as proof that Ray harbored the kind of deep-seated, racial animosity that might, on its own, trigger the assassination of Dr. King.

The committee also closely examined the facts surrounding two incidents with alleged racial overtones that occurred within a year before the assassination. They occurred in Canada and Mexico. William Bradford Huie, author of "He Slew the Dreamer," had written that a female companion of Ray in Canada in the summer of 1967 told him that Ray spoke disparagingly of Blacks during a dinner conversation. According to Huie, she said:

> I can't remember how the subject came up. But he said something like, "You got to live near niggers to know 'em." He meant that he had no patience with the racial views of people like me who don't "know niggers" and that all people who "know niggers" hate them.[7]

Despite the assistance of the Canadian authorities, the woman, a Canadian citizen living in Canada in 1978, declined to be interviewed, so the committee was able only to review the files of the Royal Canadian Mounted Police

(RCMP), which were attained by committee subpoena from local authorities. During the RCMP interview, the woman said Ray never indicated any hatred of Blacks and never mentioned Dr. King in her presence. Once more, therefore, the committee's evidence tended to pull in opposite directions.

The second incident that had been cited to show Ray's racism occurred when he was in Puerto Vallarta, Mexico, in October 1967. Manuela Aguirre Madrano who, using the professional name of Irma Morales, worked at a brothel named the Casa Susana, allegedly told in 1968 of an incident involving Ray, or "Galt," as he was calling himself at the time. Galt reportedly arrived at the Casa Susana about 9 p.m. on a Sunday. He and Morales drank together. At a nearby table, there was a group that included four Blacks, sailors who worked on a private yacht. Morales said Galt became angered at the Blacks, one or more of whom were laughing noisily. He told Morales he hated Blacks, and he went over to their table and insulted one of them. Then, he went to his car, returned and stopped to berate the Blacks again. When he got back to his own table, he asked Morales to feel his pocket. She noted he was carrying a pistol. Galt said he intended to kill the Blacks When one of them came over to Galt's table to try to make peace, Galt muttered another insult. When the Blacks left, Galt appeared to want to go after them, but Morales told him it was about time for the police to pay a 10 p.m. visit. Galt said he wanted nothing to do with the police. [8] This incident had since been reported in the writings of popular authors[9] and was often cited as support for the proposition that Ray harbored racial hatred toward Blacks.

When investigated by the committee, the evidence was contradictory With the assistance of the Mexican authorities, the committee reinterviewed Morales in Puerto Vallarta.[10] Her recollection of her association with Ray and of her period of employment at the Casa Susana seemed clear and exact; further, her memory on many subjects was corroborated by other evidence and testimony taken by the committee. Yet her description of the alleged incident varied significantly from the published reports.

Morales explained that she and "Galt" had been seated in the club when a Black sailor from a nearby table of both Black and white sailors touched her as he was attempting to maneuver past them. She recalled thinking that the sailor was drunk, causing him to stumble as he passed her. He reached out and touched her, she explained, in an effort to break his fall. Morales added that the sailor was escorted out by another sailor and that Galt did become angry. Nevertheless, it was her opinion that Galt's anger was prompted by the sailor touching her, and not because of his race. She said further that Ray never mentioned his feelings about Blacks to her. Indeed, she said that conversation had been quite limited because of the language barrier.

The committee found that Morales was a reliable witness on this point, who was certain of her recollections of the Casa Susana incident. It would appear, therefore, that the racial overtones of this incident were seriously distorted, both in the original reports and in subsequent popularized versions of the event.[11]

While two of the most widely circulated stories of Ray's racism did not withstand careful scrutiny, the committee noted that a number of Ray's reported actions or statements did tend to manifest racist attitudes. In sworn testimony before the committee, Alexander Anthony Eist, a former member of Scotland Yard who had extensive contact with Ray during the first hours of his confinement in London, as well as during trips between prison and the extradition hearings, recalled specific examples of anti-Black sentiments expressed by Ray.[12][3] In addition, Ray's interest in emigration to the white supremist nations of Rhodesia and South Africa, while probably just an effort to reach a country where English was spoken and where there might be sympathy for the assassination, could also be evidence of Ray's support of the general notion of white supremacy.[13]

The committee saw a need to scrutinize closely the evidence bearing on Ray's racial attitudes. In light of the

---

[3]The committee conducted an investigation of Eist's background in an attempt to establish his reliability as a witness. It learned that in 1976, Eist had been charged with conspiracy to commit corruption and conspiracy to prevent the course of justice. In 1978, however, Eist was found not guilty on all counts in a directed verdict. (See MLK Exhibit F–136, certificate of acquittal, IV HSCA–MLK Hearings, 28.) The committee further learned that Eist had given his account of conversations with Ray to three other persons previously, a London newspaper reporter in 1968 (see MLK Exhibit F–131. Owen Summers' statement, Nov. 2, 1978, IV HSCA–MLK Hearings, 46) and an American serviceman and his wife in 1977. (See MLK Exhibits F–132, 133, statements of David and Connie Meurinas, Nov. 2, 1978, IV HSCA–MLK Hearings, 49, 52.) The committee also noted that Eist was honorably retired with full pension from Scotland Yard. (See MLK Exhibit F–137, certificate of retirement, IV HSCA–MLK Hearings, 12.) The committee determined that Eist had testified in good faith and to the best of his recollection.

contradictory evidence, the committee was unwilling to conclude that deepseated hatred of Blacks was the sole or even the primary motivating factor in Ray's decision to murder Dr. King. While the committee was satisfied that Ray's lack of sympathy toward Blacks and the civil rights movement permitted him to undertake the assassination, it was equally convinced that the murder did not stem from racism alone.

(b) Ego gratification as a motive

The committee also examined the possibility that Ray assassinated Dr. King in an effort to gain recognition and gratification of his ego.[4] This psychological motive had chiefly been promoted by Huie in his book, "He Slew the Dreamer."[15] Huie supported this theory, in part, through an examination of Ray's activities in California in early 1968, prior to the assassination. He noted Ray's inability to secure legimate employment; Ray's dancing lessons, indicative of a "fantasy" of "doing the rhumba in some South American country from which he could never be extradited;"[16] and his consultation of "no fewer than eight different psychiatrists, hypnotists, the scientologists, trying to find relief from his depressions and feelings of inadequacy."[17] Huie concluded:

> Ray didn't want to remain a nobody among prisoners all his life. Ray wanted to make the "Top Ten" * * * Ray wanted to see his own face in full color on his favorite TV show. Ray thought that attention and recognition would relieve his feelings of inadequacy and make him feel like somebody.[18]

That the psychological motive could not be summarily dismissed was also evidenced by the testimony of Eist. Eist told the committee that during discussions with Ray pending his extradition, he had been able to establish a rapport with Ray and that Ray had expressed a feeling of pride for

---

[4]The committee carefully considered assembling a panel of psychiatrists to explore why Ray murdered Dr. King, and in particular the theory that he did so out of a need for ego gratification. A list of prominent candidates was compiled, and interviews were conducted with the doctors.[14] A clear majority raised objections to the proposed project; the main objection was the probability that Ray would refuse to cooperate. They also noted the current controversy over the validity of psychiatric examinations that are not based on extensive analysis of the subject himself. Based on this advice, as well as other considerations, the committee decided to forego the idea of a psychiatric panel.

his act. In particular, Eist recalled Ray's interest in the publicity he would receive in the news media:

> * * * He was continually asking me how could he hit the headlines in the newspapers, and he kept wanting news of publicity.
>
> *   *   *   *   *   *   *
>
> * * * In fact, he said to me, when I told him it hadn't really made too much of an impact in the British press, that is, as far as he was concerned, he was telling me, you haven't seen anything yet. I will be in the headlines one of these days. He was quite proud of the fact that he was going to make the headlines. [19]

The committee also interviewed a former inmate associate of Ray, George Ben Edmondson, who characterized Ray as a man in need of substantial egotistical fulfillment and who recalled speculation among Missouri State Penitentiary inmates that Ray killed Dr. King to gain a measure of self-importance.[20]

Taken as a whole, however, the evidence that Ray was motivated in the assassination by a pressing need for recognition was not substantial. Many of Ray's activities in Los Angeles, including his purchase of dance lessons, his enrollment in bartending school, and his employment of a professional psychiatrist and a hypnotist, may have merely manifested an effort to attain self-confidence. Similarly, the committee noted that there was an ego-satisfying dimension to Ray's purchase of a late-model sports car and his reported practice of regularly paying for drinks in a Los Angeles nightspot with $20 bills. To argue that Ray killed Dr. King to become somebody, however, necessarily must assume that Ray expected to be identified. The credible evidence did not support that possibility. While it has been argued that Ray dropped the bundle of evidence outside Canipe's Amusement Co. to insure his identification as the assassin, the committee rejected this theory. Investigation at the crime scene revealed that at the time of the assassination, at least 13 members of the Memphis Police Department were at a fire station south of Bessie Brewer's roominghouse on South Main Street.[22] Further, an official police car parked in the fire station parking lot protruded onto the sidewalk on the east side of South Main Street and would have been clearly visible to Ray as he fled south from the roominghouse. The committee believed that Ray threw the bundle of evidence down in a moment of panic, probably triggered by his seeing police activity or the police vehicle.[5]

In addition, Ray used two new aliases during the period immediately preceding the assassination and went to a Los Angeles plastic surgeon. Both acts reflect a concerted effort to avoid identification as the assassin. The committee was, therefore, unwilling to conclude that Ray's participation in the assassination resulted solely from a need for recognition and ego-fulfillment.

(c) The prospect of financial reward

Having found in neither race nor psychology adequate motivation for the assassination the committee considered a third possibility: financial reward. The committee found substantial evidence that Ray might have been lured by the prospect of money.

Once more, however, the evidence was not uncontroverted. First, while Ray had a background of financially motivated crime, none of it involved physical violence.[23] From his military discharge in 1948 to the King assassination 20 years later, Ray had spent 14 years in prison. In 1949, he had been convicted of burglary in California and sentenced to 8 months. Returning to the Midwest after serving that term, he was arrested for robbery in 1952 and served 2 years. Shortly after his release, he was, in 1955, convicted for forging an endorsement on a money order and sentenced to 3 years at Leavenworth Federal Penitentiary. In 1959, he was arrested in the armed robbery of a St. Louis grocery store and was sentenced to 20 years at the Missouri State Penitentiary under the State's habitual offender law. He was serving this term when he escaped from MSP, just short of a year before the assassination.

Apart from Ray's criminal record, there was the question of Ray's general character. Here the committee found significant the opinions of Ray's brothers, John and Jerry, both given at the time Ray was named in the King assassination and in hearings before the committee.

In an interview with the St. Louis Post-Dispatch[24] the

---

[5]During a taped interview with the committee, Eist recalled Ray admitting that he threw the gun away after seeing police activity. (III, MLK-HSCA hearings, 274.)

day following his brother's 1968 arrest, John Ray speculated on the possible motive:

> If my brother did kill King he did it for a lot of money—he never did anything if it wasn't for money —and those who paid him wouldn't want him sitting in a courtroom telling everything he knows.

In the committee's public hearings in November 1978, John Ray was asked if his statement was accurately recorded. He responded, "I expect so."[25]

Similar indications of Ray's willingness to commit crimes, and possibly the assassination, for money were voiced by Ray's second brother, Jerry Ray, around the time of the assassination. In a conversation with an acquaintance, Jerry's general response to a question concerning his brother's involvement in the assassination was:

> This is his business. I didn't ask him. If I was in his position and had 18 years to serve and someone offered me a lot of money to kill someone I didn't like anyhow and get me out of the country, I'd do it.[26]

In other conversations with the same individual,[27] Jerry stated that his brother had been paid a substantial sum for the assassination.[6]

Jerry Ray was questioned during public hearings concerning these statements. While denying his brother's knowing involvement in a conspiracy, his comments were illuminating to the search for Ray's motive:

> It might have been true. I can't remember exactly what I said, but I have told other people. I said if he done it there had to be a lot of money involved because he wouldn't do it for hatred or just because he didn't like somebody, because that is not his line of work.[28]

In a subsequent portion of his testimony, Jerry Ray described his initial feelings concerning the assassination:

---

[6]In committee testimony, Jerry Ray denied knowledge of a payoff in the assassination. Moreover, it is unclear whether his statements to the female acquaintance reflected his perception of the truth, speculation, or outright fabrication. The committee believed, however, that the statements were made as reported.

* * * before I knew anything about the murder, you know, before it happened, my kind of opinion was that he was involved some way; I didn't know if he was unknowingly involved or knowingly involved, but I knew there had to be a lot of money involved in it before he would get involved in anything like that. [29]

As in the earlier mentioned possibilities concerning motive, the evidence before the committee was not without contradictions. Ray's participation in a London bank robbery shortly before his arrest [30] and his impecunious condition at the time of his arrest were strong indications that if the assassination were financially motivated, he did not receive a payoff. Further, despite a major effort by the committee, no evidence of a payoff was uncovered. The committee noted, however, that contrary to popular impression, contract killings are not generally paid for in advance. Ray's failure to receive payment may have resulted from his panicky, unplanned flight abroad following the assassination. It is also possible that his coconspirators welshed on their payment to him.

Even though it could find no evidence of a payoff, the committee was convinced by Ray's lifetime pattern of crime for profit and by testimony about his general character that one explanation for the assassination probably lay in Ray's expectation of financial reward.[7]

(d) Conclusion on motive

In conclusion, the committee's investigation of Ray's motive revealed that while Ray's general lack of sympathy for Blacks or the civil rights movement would have allowed him to commit the assassination without qualms, his act did not stem from racism alone. The committee was convinced that while Ray's decision to assassinate Dr. King may have reflected a desire to participate in an important crime, his predominant motive lay in an expectation of monetary gain. This conclusion necessarily raised the possibility of conspiracy.[8]

---

[7] The committee considered and rejected the possibility that Ray's expectations of financial gain lay with the possibility of royalties, film rights and other forms of payment for his story. This theory would necessarily assume a plan to be identified after the crime, a theory that the committee had previously rejected.

[8] A detailed examination of several additional incidents examined by the committee during its motive investigation is included in a staff report

In its investigation of Ray's transactions and associates over the 14 months subsequent to his escape from Missouri State Penitentiary, the committee looked for associates during this period who had not previously been connected to Ray; activities or transactions with these associates of a criminal nature or that might indicate complicity in the assassination itself; and activities and transactions with known associates that had not been previously known or fully understood and that might have led to the assassination.

As a fugitive, Ray was on the move in 1967–68; he lived in second-rate motels and cheap roominghouses During much of the period, he was observed to be a man alone, a man without friends or lasting associates. In Mexico, his companions were prostitutes and bartenders.[31] In California, he was a regular visitor at the Sultan Room of the St. Francis Hotel, but he was normally alone unless conversing with employees of the bar.[32] While some of Ray's activities, such as his enrollment in dancing and bartending school in Los Angeles, brought him into regular contact with others, a close investigation of these activities revealed that significant friendships or associations never developed.[33] A large portion of the committee's evidence, therefore, provided no signs of association or of criminal involvement with individuals beyond the innocent relationships identified in previous investigation of the assassination.

(a) Transactions as evidence of associations

Despite this general picture of a lonely, uninvolved individual, the committee's investigation of three separate transactions provided definite evidence of association—in some instances criminal—with other individuals. They were Ray's activities in California on behalf of the American Independent Party; his brief, but possibly sinister, trip to New Orleans in December 1967; and his purchase of the murder weapon in Birmingham, Ala., at the end of March 1968. Much of the evidence of these transactions did not suggest a direct link to the assassination. It did convince

entitled Dr. Martin Luther King, Jr. Supplemental Studies Pertaining to the Motive of James Earl Ray. XIII Appendix to the IISCA–MLK Hearings, p. 241.

the committee, however, that the generally accepted image of Ray wandering aimlessly around the country until he reached a lonely decision to assassinate Dr. King was not a complete picture.

Ray's rather abrupt involvement with recruiting activity on behalf of the American Independent Party in California, while not criminal in nature, strongly suggested association with others.[9] Ray's life to this point had been, from all known indicators, apolitical. He was not a "joiner" or a "grassroots" volunteer. In addition, as a convicted felon and escaped convict, he could not expect to vote or to achieve a paid position in the California AIP. His recruitment of three individuals[34] to register in support of Governor Wallace of Alabama and the AIP, therefore, stood in stark contrast to a prior life of political inactivity. Further, Charles Stein, one of the three individuals recruited by Ray, recalled that Ray appeared familiar with the AIP headquarters, as well as with the registering procedures,[35] thus suggesting additional campaign activity not disclosed during the investigation. Standing alone, Ray's AIP activity raised the definite possibility of association with individuals unidentified during earlier investigations.

Of similar interest was the evidence on Ray's abrupt trip to New Orleans in December 1967. Ray's partner on the trip was California resident Charles Stein.[10] Stein was going to New Orleans to pick up his sister's children. The purpose of Ray's trip could not be determined, although the committee found it likely that Ray met secretly with another associate in New Orleans. The secretive nature of that meeting was significant, if not sinister. Stein was certain when he testified before the committee in executive session[37] that Ray had his own reason for the cross-country drive. He recalled that Ray told him about a place where he was to meet an associate or associates, and he

---

[9]In identifying the association of James Earl Ray with the American Independent Party and the Presidential campaign of George Wallace, the committee did not mean to imply that either the party or Wallace had any relation to the events in Memphis. As in all large movements or any nationwide campaign, not everyone in the movement or the campaign can be held responsible for the acts of all those in some way associated with it.

[10]The committee devoted a significant portion of its investigative resources to Stein. It was ultimately satisfied that his association with Ray was unrelated to the assassination, for four reasons: (1) pronounced personality differences between Ray and Stein; (2) evidence that they met only a day before the New Orleans trip; (3) Stein's emphatic and sworn denials of criminal involvement with Ray; and (4) extensive questioning of friends and relatives of Stein in New Orleans and Los Angles.[36]

434

said that once or twice en route to New Orleans, Ray stopped to make a telephone call. Stein speculated that in one of the calls, Ray informed an associate of his arrival time. Further, Stein recounted how Ray told him, after they had been in New Orleans for part of a day, that he had seen Stein walking in the French Quarter with his son. Ray explained he had been drinking in a Canal Street bar at the time, and Stein figured Ray had been with someone or else he would have called to him.

Stein also testified that Ray was ready to return to California the day after they arirved in New Orleans. His testimony and the willingness of Ray, an escaped prisoner, to drive several thousand miles, risking a random vehicle check, were additional reliable indications that Ray's purpose in going to New Orleans was to attend one brief but important meeting.[38][11]

The committee discovered sound indications that Ray was not alone, or at least not without someone to concult, when he purchased the murder weapon in Brimingham on March 29–30, 1968. First, the fact that he bought one rifle on the 29th, then exchanged it for another—the murder weapon—on the 30th, indicated the possibility of advice from an associate. In addition, Donald Wood, Jr., the clerk at Aeromarine Supply Co. where the rifle purchase and exchange took place, told the committee that while Ray was unaccompanied in his visits to the store, Ray said he had been advised by someone that the first rifle, a .243 caliber Remington, was not the one he wanted. [41] In an FBI interview days after the assassination, Wood recalled that Ray said he had been talking to his brother.[42] Ray told the committee he got his advice on the rifle purchase from Raoul.[43] The committee's investigation, however, provided no concrete evidence of the existence of a Raoul.[12] The committee concluded that the circumstances surrounding the rifle pur-

---

[11]The committee also received the sworn testimony of a New Orleans friend of Stein's. Anthony Charles De Carveiho, who stated that he brought Ray to the Provincial Motel for a meeting with an unidentified individual on the day of Ray's arrival in New Orleans. [39] Despite the committee's general feeling that De Carvelho was an honest and sincere witness, there were serious problems with his testimony. First, on several points his account was inconsistent with Stein's. Second, De Carvelho's statements concerning a Provincial Motel meeting in New Orleans did not appear in the reports of his FBI interviews conducted immediately following the assassination. [40] In the absence of independent corroboration of a Provincial Motel meeting, the committee decided to discount De Carvelho's testimony.

[12]See section II A of this report for discussion of Ray's "Raoul" story.

chase consistuted significant signs of unwitting aid, if not knowing complicity, in the assassination itself.[13]

A final indication of criminal association between Ray and others in the period before and after the assassination arose from an analysis of Ray's spending patterns. [44] The committee estimated that Ray spent approximately $9,000 during his 14 months of freedom. That figure included $1,800 for lodging, $900 for food and drink, $400 for gasoline and $5,700 for miscellaneous purchases—his cars, dance lessons, airline tickets, camera equipment, clothing, the rifle and so on. Except for 6 weeks as a dishwasher in a restaurant outside Chicago, for which he earned $664.34, Ray was unemployed over the 14 months. The committee concluded that the most likely source of his funding was criminal activity. In light of Ray's record of criminal ventures in combination with others, the committee felt that this criminal activity provided an additional indication of possible involvement with others.

Ray's explanation, which the committee rejected, was that he received a total of $7,750 from Raoul for two smuggling ventures at the Canadian and Mexican borders and for being available for future crimes, including the gunrunning operation which, Ray claimed, was the reason he went to Memphis.

Thus, the committee's analysis of Ray's AIP recruiting in California, his abrupt trip to New Orleans in December 1967, the Birmingham rifle purchase shortly before the assassination, and his spending habits provided ample evidence, not only of associates, but of criminal associations during the 14-month fugitive period. What had to be determined, therefore, was whether these associations could be linked to the assassination of Dr. King.

5. THE BROTHERS, JOHN AND JERRY RAY

The committee viewed the likelihood of a financial motive in the assassination as one general indication of conspiracy. The finding, however, brought the committee no closer to identifying Ray's accomplice(s). Similarly, while several of Ray's activities suggested his preassassination involvement with others, there was no immediate evidence of their identity. The committee's investigation, therefore, necessarily focused on the assassin's known associates, in-

---

[13]The committee's investigation of the rifle purchase is more thoroughly detailed in sec. II A 3.

cluding his brothers, Gerald William Ray and John Larry Ray.

The committee's decision to direct its attention to the brothers reflected a variety of considerations. Both had criminal backgrounds that included financially motivated crime.[45] In addition, the committee was struck by the substantial evidence turned up in the original investigation of Ray's contacts with one or another of the brothers throughout the preassassination period. In fact, the 1977 Justice Task Force criticized the FBI's original investigation for failing to investigate adequately the brothers' possible involvement with Ray both before and after the assassination.[46] Finally, on the assumption that there was a conspiracy, Ray's persistent refusals to identify his coconspirators in the years following the assassination would be most easily understood if his evidence implicated family members.[14]

Jerry Ray was born July 16, 1935, in Bowling Green, Mo., the fourth of nine Ray children and the third son. His criminal record shows convictions for grand larceny in 1954 and armed robbery in 1956, for which he served prison terms. His parole on the robbery conviction was to become final in August 1958, but he held up a gas station before it did, and he was returned to Menard State Penitentiary in Chester, Ill., where he served an additional 2 years.[48] Following his release from Menard in 1960, he worked at odd jobs in St. Louis and Chicago. In September 1964, he was hired as a night maintenance man at the Sportsman Country Club in Northbrook, Ill., a job he held until the summer of 1968.[49]

John Ray was born February 14, 1933, in Alton, Ill. His criminal record shows a conviction in 1953 for motor vehicle theft, for which he was sentenced to 5 to 10 years at Menard.[50] During the years following his release from the penitentiary in February 1960, he worked as a bartender, as an employee of the Greyhound bus depot in Chicago, and as a greenskeeper at the White Pine Golf Course near Chicago.[51] In 1964 and 1965, he worked for brief periods in Florida and in the Catskill Mountains

---

[14]In 1970, Ray refused to provide information to a Federal grand jury on the subject of conspiracy. While the terms of the proposed agreement with the Justice Department were unclear, Ray's attorney understood that this assistance might be rewarded by release from imprisonment and a new identity, Ray's stated reasons for not cooperating, according to his attorney, were that he felt he did not have enough information to satisfy the Justice Department; he only had enough to get himself killed. [47]

of New York. He then traveled to New York City, where he collected unemployment, and to the Chicago area, where he worked at various country clubs before his return to St. Louis in October 1966.[52] John had no formal employment in 1967, although he testified that he "believes" he was a painter then.[53] In January of 1968, he and sister, Carol Pepper, opened and operated the Grapevine Tavern at 1982 Arsenal Street in St. Louis.[54]

(a) Evidence of Ray's contact with his brothers, 1967–68

Since their first FBI interviews shortly after the assassination, Jerry and John Ray attempted to minimize the extent of their contact with their brother during the 14-month period from his prison escape to his arrest in London. On April 19, 1968,[55] Jerry told the FBI he had last seen James in 1964, but over the years he conceded this statement was false. Both Jerry[56] and James[57] told the committee of at least three meetings following James' escape from Missouri State Penitentiary. Two occurred while James was working at the Indian Trails Restaurant in Winnetka, Ill., from May 3 to June 24, 1967; the third came in August 1967 when James passed through Chicago on his way from Montreal to Birmingham and gave Jerry his 1962 Plymouth.

Jerry Ray's testimony before the committee reflected at least "two or three" telephone conversations, the last coming during James' December trip to New Orleans:

The last time I talked to him was about four months, approximately four months before King got killed, and I thought he was calling from Texas; but later he told me it was New Mexico.* * * [T]he call was under 3 minutes and just a friendly talk, you know, asking how my old man was and asking about Carol and John and everybody because I was the only contact he had with the whole family.[58]

When he was interviewed by the FBI in April 1968, John Ray said he had last seen James "2 to 4 years ago" during a visit to Missouri State Penitentiary and that prior to that, he had not seen his brother for some fifteen years.[59] Unlike Jerry, John persistently adhered to his original claim. In fact, in testimony before the committee, he insisted, as he had before, that he had been totally

438

unaware of his brother's escape from Missouri State Penitentiary until James was named on April 19, 1968, as the suspected assassin of Dr. King.[60] James also denied to the committee that he was in contact with John following his prison escape.[61]

Despite the testimony of the Ray brothers, the committee was convinced that there was substantially more contact among them than they were willing to concede. First, the evidence indicated that the Ray brothers were close. Several Missouri State Penitentiary inmates interviewed by the committee, when asked about James' closest associates, could only recall that he often mentioned a brother. Some of them remembered that he referred to his brother as a resident of St. Louis.[62] The committee also interviewed inmate associates of Jerry and John. One who had known them both, Harvey Lohmeyer, confirmed that the Ray family was close.[63][15]

The best evidence of the close relationship between the Ray brothers came from John Ray himself, who was quoted in a June 9, 1968, article in the St. Louis Post-Dispatch:[64]

John Ray said that he and another brother, Jerry, 32, Chicago, were the closest to James Ray * * * in the family. "James would do anything for us, and we for him. But he wasn't particularly sociable with strangers," said Ray.

In his appearance before the committee, John Ray was asked about the quote in the Post-Dispatch article:

Congressman FITHIAN. Then could you share the truth with the committee as to whether or not that does reflect your feeling toward your brother in June of 1968?

RAY. I already answered yes to that.[65]

The committee took note of other factors that suggested the likelihood of contacts between Ray and his two brothers. For example, Ray acknowledged he had been in the St. Louis area, where John lived, twice soon after his prison escape. The first visit occurred right after

---

[15] Although James Earl Ray did not know Lohmeyer, he used his name (spelling it Lowmeyer) when he purchased the murder weapon in Birmingham.

he broke out of prison in late April or early May 1967; [66] the second was on a return trip after he quit his job in Winnetka, Ill. Ray, in fact, told the committee the purpose for the second visit was "to see some of my relatives down there," although he added, "I never did see them."[67] Further, throughout his fugitive period—in locations as varied as Montreal, Los Angeles and Birmingham—Ray talked of recent or intended contact with a brother. Finally, the committee found significance in the fact that James and John—both largely apolitical from all accounts and, as conviced felons, unable to vote—began to campaign actively on behalf of the American Independent Party's "Wallace for President" campaign at almost exactly the same time. James, as noted, worked for the AIP in California, and John was active in St. Louis, Mo., where his Grapevine Tavern served as a distribution point for campaign literature.

The committee recognized that at the time of their initial interviews with authorities, John and Jerry Ray could well have chosen to conceal contact with their brother, even if innocent, in an attempt to protect him and avoid scrutiny during the assassination investigation. Another explanation, however, one that the committee deemed more credible, was that they were concerned with potential criminal liability stemming from contact with their brother.

The committee found that the evidence established that John Ray had foreknowledge of his brother's escape from Missouri State Penitentiary. It was equally apparent that Ray was assisted by both Jerry and John following his escape, making them potentially responsible as accessories after the fact to both James' escape and his interstate flight. Finally, the committee received substantial evidence indicating that James and John were involved in the Alton bank robbery in East Alton, Ill., on July 13, 1967. It was also shown that Jerry Ray was aware of their participation in this robbery and helped to distribute the proceeds of the crime to James during his fugitive period.[16] The evidence of Jerry Ray's actual involvement in that robbery was, on balance, insubstantial.

---

[16]Both John and Jerry Ray denied any involvement with James in criminal activity, most notably his escape from prison and the bank robbery in Alton, Ill. In light of the assassination in Memphis on April 4, 1968, these denials might well have represented an effort to avoid admitting an association that eventually matured into murder.

(b) Missouri State Penitentiary escape[17]

James Earl Ray escaped from Missouri State Pententiary on April 23, 1967, concealed in a box of bread in the back of a delivery truck. An investigation in 1967 concluded that Ray had escaped in a bread box, probably aided by at least one fellow inmate who placed bread on top of him.[68] Nevertheless, Ray asserted for years that he had escaped without assistance by scaling a prison wall.[69] Finally, in an interview with this committee, in December 1977, Ray confirmed the accuracy of the official version. He admitted he left the prison in a delivery truck bound for a nearby prison farm and jumped out of the truck as it slowed for an intersection. Ray stated further that, while he planned the escape alone, he was assisted in executing the plan by two inmates. He refused to identify them.[70]

Jerry Ray has, over the years, admitted meeting with James on at least three occasions during the weeks immediately following his escape from Missouri State Penitentiary.[71] On the last occasion, moreover, Jerry shared a room with James for one night in Chicago before putting his brother on a bus to Birmingham.[72] His involvement in facilitating James' interstate flight, therefore, seemed clear. John Ray, on the other hand, consistently maintained that he did not even know of the escape until after the King assassination. The committee's investigation, however, produced substantial evidence to contradict John's assertion.

Certainly the strongest single piece of evidence before the committee indicating John Ray's foreknowledge of his brother's escape plans was found in the Missouri State Penitentiary visitor records.[73] These records indicated nine visits by John during James' incarceration. The last four occurred during the year prior to the escape—on July 10, 1966, November 13, 1966, December 20, 1966, and April 22, 1967. The final visit was of particular interest to the committee since it was made on the day before the escape. Given the relative sophistication of James' escape plans and the need for inside assistance from fellow inmates to cover him with bread and to load the

---

[17]The committee also investigated the Missouri State Penitentiary escape for evidence of official complicity in the assassination. (See Section II D, infra.)

box on the truck, the committee believed that the escape had been planned by the time of John Ray's visit. It seemed reasonable, therefore, to assume that a discussion of the break occurred during their meeting. This assumption was supported, the committee found, by Ray's admitted trip to St. Louis, John's home city, within a week of his escape.[74]

During his testimony before the committee, John Ray was asked about the visits reflected in the prison records. His responses were inherently incredible, excellent examples of the obstructionist posture John Ray assumed throughout the committee's investigation:

STAFF COUNSEL. I have at this time introduced into the record MLK exhibit F–634, and I ask you whether this record accurately reflects the dates that you visited your brother, James Earl Ray, while he was incarcerated at the Missouri State Prison.

RAY. I could not remember any dates.

Chairman STOKES. Is the answer of the witness the fact that he does not recall those visits?

RAY. No; I do not recall them.

Chairman STOKES. Proceed * * *.

STAFF COUNSEL Mr. Ray, I am particularly concerned with the last visit that is reflected on that record. That is the visit on April 22, 1967. That was the day prior to the escape of your brother from Missouri State Prison.

I ask you at this time, do you have any recollection of visiting your brother James the day preceding his escape from the State prison.

RAY. I do not have no recollection of that.

STAFF COUNSEL. Do you have any reason to offer this committee at this time as to why this record before you would not be accurate?

RAY. I did not say it wasn't accurate. I just said I don't recall visiting that certain day.[75]

John Ray subsequently offered one explanation for the April 22, 1967, entry on the records:

* * * Jerry, my visiting pass, Jerry used it sometimes. I used it sometimes, and a guy named John Gawron, I believe, used it sometimes.[76]

442

After investigation, the committee rejected this explanation. The committee questioned both James and Jerry Ray about the possibility that someone posing as John visited the prison on April 22, 1967. James indicated in an interview that one of his brothers, and probably John, was the visitor:

John or Jerry, I'm not too positive now which one it was.
It was, I believe it was John. I'm not certain.[77][18]

Jerry Ray, when questioned on the same matter, did not recall using another's pass, and he denied emphatically visiting James the day prior to his escape:

RAY: I positively didn't visit him. That is a positive.
STAFF COUNSEL. Do you know if your brother John visited him on that day?
RAY. I don't know if John did. I know definitely I didn't.[79]

The committee found other evidence of John Ray's knowledge of, and participation in, Ray's escape and subsequent flight. In a letter to author George McMillan on March 5, 1973, John referred to the account of James' escape by Gerold Frank, the author of "An American Death.":

He [Frank] stated that Jimmy walked for days to get to St. Louis from Jefferson City when he escaped, when actually he had a car, and I.D. waiting for him in Jefferson City * * * He also made a phone car [sic] to a certain party in St. Louis to come down, and fix his car. The person who went and help him, also is doing time now in a Federal prison for a charge that I expect is a frameup.[80]

---

[18]During the same interview, Ray insisted that he did not tell the brother who visited him of his planned escape, since "that would have been illegal." He continued:

"I can't remember all what I told him, but I mean they all knew, both Jerry and John knew, that I was thinking about escaping. So, it wouldn't of been no revelation if I would of mentioned something about escaping. But there was no pre-arranged deal where he would be outside waiting in front of the prison, and I'd jump out and jump in the car." [78]

443

At the time he wrote the letter, John was serving time for a bank robbery conviction that he claimed was an FBI frameup.[19]

John allegedly made a similar admission to a longtime criminal associate of the Ray brothers, Walter Rife, who was incarcerated with him in Leavenworth during the early 1970's. In an unsworn interview with the committee, Rife stated that John told him that he had picked James up on a highway near Jefferson City following the escape. [82] The committee, however, found Rife's credibility on other matters highly suspect, and it gave little weight to this evidence.[20]

Further evidence of John's willing assistance to James' flight was found in the fact that James left the Missouri State Penitentiary with a social security number in the name of John L. Rayns, a number and alias previously used by John Ray.[83] During a committee interview, James described the number as:

> * * * one of my brother's old social security numbers, John L. Rayns, I believe it was. I don't recall the social security number. I didn't have the card. I got the number off him. We interchanged these numbers all the time. He used them. I used them. So I used that social security number.[84]

John Ray was questioned on James' possession of his social security number:

> Congressman FITHIAN. Now my question is, did you, prior to James Earl Ray's escape from Missouri State Penitentiary, furnish James either with your social security card or your social security number?
>
> RAY. Well, it is possible. Sometime I might have gave him a number. But it is also possible he might have had the number because he remembered probably that number. I did not give him no social security card. I did not have one.[85]

The evidence before the committee indicated John Ray had foreknowledge of his brother's prison escape. The

---

[19] John Ray told the committee in executive session that he fabricated this admission to McMillan, although he did acknowledge he was referring to himself when he wrote of a "certain party" who had been imprisoned in a "fameup." [81]

[20] See textual footnote, Section II–B 5(e).

evidence included: the Missouri State Penitentiary visitor records; the testimony of James that a brother, he believed John, was his visitor; John's letter to author George McMillan; John's alleged admission to Walter Rife; James' admitted possession of John's old social security number at the time of his escape; and James' trip to the St. Louis area shortly after the escape.

John's own denials—in particular, his claim that he first learned of the escape only when James had been named in the assassination—served to add to the force of the evidence.[21] The committee found, therefore, that John Ray was involved with his brother James in the escape from Missouri State Penitentiary.

(c) The Alton bank robbery

The committee devoted considerable effort to an investigation of Ray's finances following his escape from Missouri State Penitentiary on the theory that Ray's method of financing himself bore on the assassination. Indeed, the committee considered, but ultimately rejected, the theory that his escape and travels were part of a single scheme that culminated in the assassination. The committee also considered a variety of alternative sources of finances: payments from time to time from Raoul, as Ray claimed; from narcotic trafficking at Missouri State Penitentiary and during his flight; and from the robbery of the Bank of Alton, Alton, Ill., on July 13, 1967.[22]

As has been noted, the committee, after due deliberation, rejected Ray's Raoul story. Further, the committee found it highly unlikely that Ray left Missouri State Penitentiary with a substantial amount of money. Inmates interviewed by the committee characterized him as a "second-rate hustler" who engaged in bookmaking, narcotics and the smuggling of contraband, but who operated on a relatively small scale.[86] The committee also found it improbable that Ray would have engaged in the menial labor, of dishwashing, had he possessed a significant sum of money at the time of his escape.

---

[21]John Ray's testimony on the prison escape was given under a grant of immunity. Further, the statute of limitations had run out on any potential prosecutions stemming from his foreknowledge of and assistance in his brother's escape and flight. His false testimony in this area, therefore, did not stem from fear of subsequent prosecution.

[22]Prior to the committee's investigation, the Alton bank robbery had been investigated twice by the FBI—at the time of the crime and during the assassination investigation. The case remained officially unsolved.

The committee received evidence supporting the possibility that Ray trafficked in marihuana during his stays in Mexico and California.[23] In addition to an assertion in Huie's "He Slew the Dreamer" that Ray left Mexico with "his Mustang loaded with marihuana," [89] the committee identified witnesses in both Mexico and California who confirmed Ray's interest in, and occasional use of, marihuana.[90] One California witness, Ronald Dennino, provided sworn testimony indicating Ray's possession, on at least one occasion, of a kilo of marihuana.[91] Nevertheless, Dennino's evidence was hearsay, and when his alleged source of information, Marie Martin, was questioned —also under oath—she denied knowledge of Ray's trafficking in substantial amounts of marihuana.[92]

The committee was unable to locate evidence, beyond Dennino's testimony, indicating that Ray received substantial income from dealings in marihuana Thus, while the committee did not foreclose the possibility that Ray supplemented his income through small-scale marihuana traffiicking, there was no evidence that it constituted a primary source of income during his fugitive period.

On the other hand, the committee did obtain and analyze a substantial amount of evidence establishing the likelihood that James and John Ray robbed the Alton bank and that Jerry Ray, while probably not a participant in the robbery, was aware of his brothers' involvement and helped distribute funds from the robbery to James. The committee, therefore, concluded that the Alton bank robbery was the most likely explanation for Ray's financial independence during his fugitive period.

The Alton bank was help up by two masked gunmen at approximately 1:30 p.m. on July 13, 1967. One was described as a middle-aged white male, 5 feet 10 inches tall, 150 to 160 pounds; the other, a middle-aged white male, 5 feet 8 inches, 170 to 180 pounds. One was armed with a handgun, the other with a shotgun; both wore stocking masks and hats. Once inside the bank, the one with the shotgun stood guard, while the other collected $27,230 from behind the teller's counter. The two

---

[23]Ray acknowledged discussing marihuana with some "hippies" and a bartender in Puerto Vallarta, Mexico. [87] Nevertheless, he has denied, in a characteristically vague manner, any smuggling activity between Mexico and California:

"STAFF COUNSEL. Were you smuggling anything in particular? Were you smuggling anything from Mexico into, into California?

"RAY. Uh, no, no, not particularly. I was thinking about it one time." [88]

men then left the bank and walked westward to a near-by church parking lot. No further direct evidence was developed in the FBI's investigation of the robbery or in this committee's reexamination of the crime bearing on the manner, or the direction, of the robbers' flight from the immediate vicinity of the bank. At the time of the committee's investigation, none of the stolen money had been recovered.[93]

The committee first examined eyewitness and physical evidence bearing on the robbery. Because the bank robbers wore stocking masks, eyewitness descriptions were imprecise. Nevertheless, none of those that were given would eliminate the Ray brothers as suspects.[24] Moreover, the facts developed in the FBI's investigation—in particular, the apparent route of flight taken after the crime and the location of discarded evidence—provided some evidence of the involvement of James Earl Ray.

Ray had been born in Alton on March 10, 1928. After spending his early childhood elsewhere, he returned to Alton at the age of 16, joined a grandmother who ran a local roominghouse, and spent considerable time with his uncle, William Mayer, still a resident of the city in 1978.[94] While much of his subsequent life was spent either in the military or in jail, Ray had returned to Alton for periods in 1948 and again in 1954. On August 21, 1959, he and an accomplice robbed an Alton supermarket of about $2,000.[25] Against this background, Ray's familiarity with the city of Alton was self-evident, the committee determined.

In the FBI's investigation of the Alton bank robbery, it was established that the shotgun and partially burned clothes used during the robbery were discarded in a wooded area near the National Cemetery in Alton. This, area—a 3-minute car ride from the bank—is situated at the end of a dead end street, indicating that the suspects were familiar with the area around the cemetery and that the evidence drop was planned.[95] Further, the

[24]At the time of the original FBI interviews in April 1968, John Ray was described as 5 feet 10 inches to 5 feet 11 inches tall, 160 pounds, medium build; and Jerry Ray as 5 feet 9 inches tall, 178 pounds, medium-stocky build. James Earl Ray was described as 5 feet 10 inches tall, 165–174 pounds, medium build, on the wanted posted issued following his Missouri State Penitentiary escape in April 1967.

[25]Ray's accomplice was arrested, while Ray got away. He was subsequently identified, however, and on October 27, 1959 was indicted for this offense. By that time, however, he had been arrested for a super-market holdup in St. Louis (for which he was later sentenced to 20 years at Missouri State Penitentiary). He was, therefore, never brought to trial for the Alton supermarket robbery.

abandoned evidence was not found along the most direct route from the bank out of Alton, suggesting the robbers were confident they could elude capture without heading directly out of town. These considerations, standing alone, suggested a familiarity with the Alton area such as that possessed by James Earl Ray. In addition, the drop site for the incriminating evidence was near the home in 1967 of Ray's uncle, William Mayer, and in the general vicinity of former residences of Ray's mother and of Ray himself.[26][96]

The committee next investigated the whereabouts of the Ray brothers on the day of the robbery. James had quit his job at the Indian Trails Restaurant in Winnetka, Ill., on June 24, 1967, approximately three weeks prior to the bank robbery.[97] Before that time, while still in prison, he had decided to move to Canada,[98] as he later indicated in interviews with the committee. But instead of heading straight for Canada, Ray made two trips in the opposite direction. He first went to Quincy, Ill., where he stayed for approximately 12 days[99] before returning to Chicago for 4 to 5 days. In Chicago, he picked up his last weekly paycheck from the Indian Trails.[100] Then, on July 10 or 11[27] he drove to the St. Louis area, ostensibly to visit "family members."[101] Ray, however, told the committee he did not see any relatives, particularly not his brother John. In fact, Ray testified, he did not even know John's address, although, as noted, his brother was close enough to him to have visited him regularly in prison. [102]

The committee found Ray's trip to the St. Louis area 3 days before the bank robbery especially interesting, not only because it strongly suggested a meeting with John, but also because Alton, Ill., is only 20 miles north of St. Louis. When Ray appeared before the committee in a public hearing, the committee pressed to learn why he had not visited his St. Louis relatives on his earlier trip to Quincy, which is far closer to St. Louis than Chicago. In addition, the committee sought a logical explanation as to why, once he did return to St. Louis to see relatives, he did not see them. Ray's testimony on these points was

---

[26]The committee recognized that this analysis, in and of itself, could be applied to any number of Alton residents. It was given significance, nevertheless, as one of several components of the circumstantial evidence bearing on the robbery.

[27]This date was determined by using Ray's estimates of a 12-day stay in Quincy and a 4-to 5-day stay in Chicago.

crucial and, at the same time, characteristic of the evasive and illogical nature of much of his testimony before the committee. His responses are, therefore, quoted at length:

Congressman FITHIAN. *** if I remember my Illinois map, Quincy is a lot closer to the East St. Louis area than Chicago, and you have 12 days where you were in Quincy. *** Just for my own satisfaction, could you share with the committee why you didn't drop on over to East St. Louis and try to see your relatives in that 12-day period?

RAY. I have no particular reason. I always did like Quincy, Ill. I have lived there quite a bit, and I did intend to see my aunt, but I didn't. Many people I know had since died, since I have been in prison. I think the only person I really knew, and I think probably saw me, and I talked to him several times, was a bar owner named Ted Crowley.[28] Other than that I can't think of anyone that knew me. I know I inquired about several people and they had died.

Congressman FITHIAN. Here is my problem just in terms of logic. You were in the Chicago area and you decided to quit your job and you have already decided much earlier you are going to Canada, according to what you just told me, and then you quit your job and you go down 280 miles southwest to Quincy and spend 12 days there?

RAY. Yes, sir.

Congressman FITHIAN. You go back to the Chicago area. Then on the very eve of your departure for Montreal, you make a trip all the way down to the St. Louis area. I am having a little trouble with that just as a normal flow of movement. Could you help me out on that?

RAY. No. That may have been a little illogical. I don't know. Of course I had been in jail 6 years. Sometimes you do things that are not exactly logical. [104]

*   *   *   *   *   *   *

Congressman FITHIAN. Did you then see your relatives in the East St. Louis area?

RAY. No, I didn't.[105]

---

[28]In a sworn deposition, Ted Crowley stated that he knew James Earl Ray as a customer of his establishment—the Gem Tavern—in Quincy. He emphatically denied seeing Ray after his April 1967 escape from Missouri State Penitentiary. [103]

* * * * * * *

Congressman FITHIAN. So anyway your testimony to the committee is after you decided to go to Canada, you traveled the opposite direction to St. Louis, East St. Louis, for about 300 miles, in order to visit relatives, but you didn't visit your relatives? Is that your testimony?

RAY. Well, I visited a close friend down there named Jack Gawron.[29] Knew him on the street. He knew all my relatives and I sent a message via him. I don't know if he delivered it or not.[106]

The committee found Ray's explanation for his trip to St. Louis in July 1967 inadequate. His presence in the vicinity of Alton at the time of the bank robbery was highly incriminating, albeit circumstantially, of his participation in the robbery.

John Ray, of course, acknowledged that he was a St. Louis resident in July 1967;[107] Jerry was employed at the Sportsman's Club outside Chicago. The Alton bank robbery occurred on a Thursday, which, according to Jerry, was his day off.[108] Assuming Jery's recollection in testimony to the committee was correct, his presence in Alton could not be discounted.[30]

More important than familiarity with Alton and physical whereabouts, however, was the evidence bearing on the financial condition of James and John Ray during the period of the Alton bank robbery. At the time of his prison escape, Ray, according to his testimony, had about $250. [110] He got a job at the Indian Trails Restaurant in Winnetka, Ill., earning about $85 a week, so by the time he quit—on June 24, 1967[111]—he had netted $664.34, giving him a total cash accumulation of about $915.

During the same period, however, Ray purchased a 1959 Chrysler for $200.[112] Although he apparently lived fru-

---

[29]Gawron, now deceased, was interviewed by the FBI during the Bureau's investigation of the Alton bank robbery. He stated that James Earl Ray was involved in the crime. Subsequent investigation by the FBI, however, undermined Gawron's credibility. The committee, therefore, did not rely on Gawron's statements to the FBI in reaching its conclusions on the Alton bank robbery.

[30]In testimony before the committee, Jerry Ray was certain that his day off fell on Thursday. His recollection, however, was contradicted by his own 1968 interview with the FBI, as well as the 1968 statements of two officials of the Sportsman's Club—all of whom designated Tuesday, not Thursday, as his day off. [109] The committee found the 1968 statements more reliable. Due to the destruction of his employment records, however, the issue could not be firmly resolved.

gally, his living expenses placed a constant drain on his limited financial resources. During the first week of July, in fact, Ray drove approximately 300 miles from Quincy, Ill., to Chicago[113] to pick up his last paycheck of $77.53. His conduct was not that of a man of substantial means.

In late July, Ray's pattern of frugality abruptly changed significantly. On July 14, the day after the Alton bank robbery, he bought a 1962 Plymouth for $210 at a dealership in East St. Louis, Ill.,[114] having sold his Chrysler for $45. He then drove to Montreal, where he placed a $150 deposit on an apartment on July 18 and bought $250 worth of clothes on July 19.[115] On July 30, he began a 1-week vacation at Gray Rocks, a resort north of Montreal; his bill came to $200.[31][116]

Ray clearly had come into a substantial amount of money by mid-July, and it was evident that he received this income sometime after the first week in July, when he drove 300 miles from Quincy to Chicago to get a $77.53 paycheck.

The Alton bank robbery, coming the day before his extensive spending began, could have explained his new-found wealth. Ray, however, gave the committee a different story. He said he departed for Canada with $260 or $270,[117] and after 2 days in Montreal, he had almost exhausted his cash reserve—for food and lodging on the road, for the deposit on his apartment and for two visits to a $25 prostitute.[118] Ray's solution was to rob a Montreal brothel:

> That evening I returned to the aforementioned nightclub and, meeting the same girl, again accompanied her via taxi to her apartment. Inside her apartment I gave her another $25, but this time showed her the pistol Mr. Gawron had purchased for me, and told her I would go with her to wherever she was taking the money. When she aroused the manager into opening the office I put the pistol on him. We moved back into the office wherein I asked him for the money. Taking out his wallet, he offered me the small amount in it, approximately $5 to $10. When I told him I wanted the rest of the money he spoke

[31]See MLK exhibit F-362 (diagram of Ray's financial transactions during his fugitive period) V, HSCA–MLK hearings, 664.

about a cabinet nearby, and motioned to a container. Before leaving the office I had the manager lie on a bed and the girl remove her stockings and tie his hands and legs. I then had her get under the bed before departing. Later I found I had taken approximately $1,700 in mixed currency from the manager's office.[119]

The committee's investigation of the story, tracing it back to its origin, revealed several problems. First, Huie had written in "He Slew the Dreamer" that Ray had told him initially of an $800 whorehouse robbery, then changed it to a $1700 holdup of a Montreal food store.[120][32] In addition, Jerry Ray was reported to have told McMillan, the author, that James had fabricated the brothel robbery story.[121] Ray's story, moreover, was one that could not be easily confirmed or denied, since the manager of a brothel was not the type to report a robbery to police or cooperate with a congressional committee.[33] Ray agreed on this point during his public testimony:

> Congressman FITHIAN. Mr. Ray, from your experience would you expect the owner of an illegal house of prostitution to report a robbery like this to the police?
>
> RAY. No * * * I would think usually prostitution and gambling houses take care of their own legal problems.[122]

James Earl Ray was an experienced criminal, with an ability, evidenced by his April 1967 escape from Missouri State Penitentiary, to plan and execute criminal operations with some degree of sophistication. Moreover, his decision to travel to Canada was not precipitous. It was a course of action he had apparently settled on while still in prison. The committee found it difficult to believe, therefore, that Ray lingered in the United States for 2½ months, traveled to a strange city in Canada in a destitute condition, and then committed an armed robbery of a brothel manager.

---

[32]Ray's explanation to the committee was that he fed Huie and his first attorney, Arthur Hanes, Sr., a phony story as a test, fearing they were leaking information he gave them to the authorities (Ray testimony, I, HSCA–MLK hearings, 163).

[33]In fact, the committee was unable to locate the manager of the brothel.

452

A more sensible course of action would have been for him to escape from prison, make contact with John in St. Louis, and take employment at some distant point while a suitable crime could be planned. After the crime, he would flee to Canada, where he could live undetected and supported by the proceeds of the crime. The committee found that Ray's financial transactions in July 1967 strongly pointed to his receipt of unexplained income—probably from crime—and that the Alton bank robbery was the most likely source.

An examination of John Ray's travels and financial condition in 1967 was similarly revealing. His employment history in the 1960's was sporadic. He held a variety of jobs and spent at least one period on collecting unemployment insurance. In 1967, while living in St. Louis, he was not a salaried employee, although in interviews with the FBI and the committee, he said he had worked as a painter. Nonetheless, John went to San Francisco in July 1967 with $3,000 in cash,[123] his stated purpose being to purchase a tavern in California or in Reno, Nev.[124] Mrs. Charles F. Terry, manager of an apartment on Sutter Street in San Francisco, told FBI agents that he had resided in her building between July 23, 1967 (10 days after the Alton bank robbery) to August 15, 1967.[125]

In testimony before the committee, John Ray conceded he made the trip to California with approximately $3,000 in his possession and that he intended to purchase a tavern. John claimed, however, that the money constituted "savings" and not proceeds from the Alton bank robbery.[126]

In light of John Ray's work history, the committee was highly skeptical of his claim to have set aside $3,000 in "savings." His possession of this sizable sum, together with his decision to leave the St. Louis area almost simultaneously with James' trip north to Canada, provided additional circumstantial evidence of his participation in the Alton bank robbery and of a common plan by both Ray brothers to leave the St. Louis area immediately following the robbery.

(1) *Bank robbery modus operandi analysis.*—The committee also examined the conduct of the Ray brothers subsequent to the Alton bank robbery. It found strong evidence indicating John Ray's involvement in five bank robberies in 1969 and 1970 for which the modus op-

erandi[127] was substantially similar to that of the Alton bank robbery.[34] The evidence surrounding these robberies demonstrated several points. It undermines John's credibility, since he denied participation in each of them; it shows his character as a bank robber; and it demonstrates subsequent criminal activity by John that is similar to and consistent with his involvement in the Alton robbery.

The committee obtained the following information on the bank robberies from FBI files and through its own investigation:

At 10:45 a.m. on October 17, 1969, the Farmers Bank of Liberty, Ill., was robbed of $10,995 by two men wearing stocking masks and hats, one carrying a shotgun, the other a revolver. The one with the shotgun stood guard, while his accomplice collected the money from behind the counter. The stocking masks and an automobile were abandoned near the crime scene after an attempt to burn them.[128] John Ray's involvement in the robbery of the Bank of Liberty, Ill., was established through the sworn testimony of his accomplice, James Rogers, before the committee.[129] When confronted with this evidence, John Ray denied involvement in the robbery.[35]

At 1:05 p.m. on January 28, 1970, the Farmers & Traders State Bank of Meredosia, Ill., was robbed of $5,038 by two men wearing stocking masks and hats, one carrying a sawed-off shotgun, the other a revolver. The one with the shotgun stood guard, while his accomplice collected the money from behind the counter. The stocking masks and clothing were left in a wooded area.[131] John Ray's involvement in this bank robbery was established through the sworn testimony of James Rogers, [132] an accomplice, and by the unsworn statement of Ronald Goldenstein, a second accomplice during an interview with committee investigators.[133] Nevertheless, John Ray denied involvement in the robbery.[134]

At 1 p.m. on June 11, 1970, the Laddonia State Bank of Laddonia, Mo., was robbed of $13,975 by two men wearing stocking masks and hats, one carrying a sawed-off shotgun, the other a revolver. The one with the shotgun stood guard, while his accomplice collected the money

---

[34]While James was in prison during the 1960–70 period and could not have participated in the five bank robberies, the committee did obtain proof that he committed a bank robbery in London shortly before his arrest on June 8, 1968.

[35]John Ray asserted that since James Rogers was on Federal parole at the time of his testimony before the committee, he probably would testify to anything. [130]

from behind the counter. The stocking masks and an automobile were abandoned near the crime scene, and an attempt was made to burn them.[135] John Ray's involvement in the robbery was established by the sworn testimony of two accomplices, James Rogers and Clarence Haynes.[136] Haynes was convicted of the robbery. John Ray, nevertheless, denied involvement in the robbery.[137]

At 2 p.m. on July 29, 1970, the Bank of Hawthorne, Fla., was robbed of $4,514 by two men wearing stocking masks and hats, each carrying a revolver. One of the men stood guard, while his accomplice collected the money from a vault. The stocking masks were discarded following the robbery.[138] John Ray's involvement in the crime was established by the sworn testimony of James Rogers, [139] who was convicted of the robbery. John Ray admitted being with Rogers and a second convicted participant, Carl Kent, deceased, around the time of the robbery,[140] but he denied actual involvement or any knowledge of the involvement of others.[141]

At 1:20 p.m. on October 26, 1970, the Bank of St. Peters, Mo., was robbed of $53,128 by three men wearing stocking masks and hats, all carrying revolvers. Two of the men stood guard, while their accomplice collected the money from behind the counter. The stocking masks and clothing were left in a wooded area.[142] John Ray was tried and convicted by a jury for his participation in this robbery. Before the committee, however, he denied his involvement and claimed he had been framed.[143]

In light of evidence from a variety of sources indicating John Ray's involvement in these five robberies, and considering his conviction for robbery of the Bank of St. Peters, Mo., the committee found his denials unworthy of belief. His participation in these robberies and the similarities they bore to the Alton bank robbery provided additional circumstantial evidence of his involvement in the Alton bank robbery.

The committee also examined evidence of a subsequent bank robbery by James Earl Ray. On June 4, 1968, the Trustee Savings Bank of Fulham in London, England, was robbed by a lone gunman; the amount taken was approximately 100 pounds, or about $240 in U.S. currency. Physical evidence from the crime scene included a paper bag bearing a printed note which read: "Place all 5–10 pound notes in this bag."[144] Fingerprint comparisons by both the FBI and a committee consultant of a latent print taken from the bag identified it as the right thumbprint of James Earl Ray.[145] When confronted by this evidence, Ray still denied responsibility for the robbery.[146] Ray's denial was, in light of this physical evidence, unworthy of belief.

The committee believed that the denials themselves (by James, with respect to the London bank robbery; by John, with respect to four robberies of which he was accused by his accomplices, as well as a fifth for which he was convicted) provided an additional reason to believe that James and John participated in the Alton bank robbery.

The committee noted that James' refusal to admit the London bank robbery could not have been based on a fear of implicating others, for he had acted alone. Nor was there reason to believe that he was reluctant to associate himself with criminal activity, since he willingly told the committee about his alleged robbery of a brothel in Montreal and about his smuggling and gunrunning activities with Raoul. Likewise, John could not have been impelled to deny the robberies for fear of implicating accomplices, since he was aware of their cooperation with the committee, or for fear of prosecution, since the statute of limitations had tolled in the unprosecuted cases.

The committee believed that these denials, in the face of substantial evidence to the contrary, reflected a concern by John and James that an admission of involvement in any bank robbery might implicate them in the Alton holdup. This would, in turn, undermine Ray's Raoul story, the keystone of this defense in the assassination. It would also indicate a pattern of joint criminal behavior by the brothers that would possibly raise a question about their collusion in the assassination of Dr. King.

(d) A brother was Raoul

In its investigation of the Alton bank robbery, the committee determined it was unlikely that Jerry Ray was a participant. He had a steady job in the Chicago area at the time, and he did not take an abrupt trip or show signs of sudden wealth right after the Alton robbery, as did James and John. Nevertheless, the committee received significant evidence, both circumstantial and direct, indicating that Jerry knew of the involvement of his two brothers and that he participated directly in the distribution of the robbery proceeds to James at various times during his fugitive period.

Jerry Ray met several times with John and James during the period of the Alton robbery. In fact, by his own admission, James traveled to Chicago,[148] where Jerry lived, only a week before the robbery occurred. Further, a committee witness, who requested anonymity but who gave a deposition under oath,[149] reported a conversation in which Jerry revealed that John and James participated in the bank robbery, adding certain details about their preparation for it. The committee found particular significance in this reported statement by Jerry to the witness in light of his close relationship with his two brothers, one that afforded ample opportunity for them to have discussed the crime.[36]

Jerry's probable involvement in the distribution of funds from the robbery was revealed through a close analysis of James' Raoul story.[37] Except for employment at the Indian Trails Restaurant and an alleged robbery of a brothel in Montreal, Ray's only acknowledged source of income during the 14-month fugitive period was the payments he claims to have received from Raoul. The committee's evidence indicated the strong likelihood that Ray shared in the proceeds of the Alton bank robbery. His Raoul story was viewed, therefore, as a cover, not just for the assassination, but also for the bank robbery. The committee did find that there was some basis in fact for the Raoul story, because Ray's spending pattern indicated that he received money from some source at about the times he specified in his Raoul story. Since Ray was traveling throughout the United States and two foreign countries, Canada and Mexico, it is not unreasonable to suppose that he was reluctant to carry the entire proceeds of the robbery with him. At the same time, he was not free, as a fugitive, to transfer his funds through the banking system.[38] The committee believed, therefore, that the money he received was, in fact, his share of the Alton bank robbry proceeds, secured and periodically distributed to him by a brother, probably Jerry.

---

[36] Jerry Ray, in testimony before the committee, denied the statement to the witness.

[37] A detailed analysis of Ray's Raoul story appears in section II A, supra.

[38] Ironically, there was evidence that Ray, a bank robber, stored portions of his funds in a bank safety box in Birmingham.

In all, Ray claimed he received $7,750 from Raoul, in six payments:

Aug. 21, 1967, at the United States-Canadian border[150]	$1,500
Aug. 30, 1967, in Birmingham, Ala.[151]	2,000
Aug. 30, 1967, in Birmingham, Ala.[152]	1,000
Oct. 7, 1967, in Nuevo Laredo, Mexico[153]	2,000
Dec. 17, 1967, in New Orleans, La.[154]	500
Mar. 29, 1968, in Birmingham, Ala.[155]	750
Total	7,750

When added to the $1,700 Ray said he got in the holdup of a brothel in Montreal, his total reported income for the period came to $9,450.[39] Moreover, all of the alleged meetings with Raoul in which money was passed, except for the one in Nuevo Laredo, Mexico, coincided with statements about a recent or imminent meeting with a brother.

According to Ray's account, he first met Raoul at a bar in Montreal soon after he arrived in that city on July 18 (5 days after the Alton bank robbery).[16] He had three or four meetings[17] with him before he went on vacation at the Gray Rocks resort in the Laurentian Mountains, where he struck up a brief friendship with a woman who worked for the Canadian Government. In an interview with the Royal Canadian Mounted Police after the assassination, she said Ray told her he had been at the resort for about a week and that "he would be leaving within the next few days for Montreal to meet his brother."[158] In fact, he left the next day and returned to Montreal where, according to his story, he had several more meetings with Raoul.[59]

The committee established that John Ray was in San Francisco between July 23, and August 15, 1967,[160] so he could not have been the brother referred to by James. Consequently, this was one of several instances in which Ray's Raoul story seemed framed to conceal contact with Jerry.

Approximately 2 weeks after his return from Gray Rocks, on August 18 or 19, Ray went to Ottawa to visit the Canadian Government worker. She later reported to the RCMP.

He [Ray] stayed in Ottawa for 2 days and I showed him around Ottawa. * * * I don't recall him saying

---

[39]While the committee was unable to identify a third participant in the Alton bank robbery, it was reasonable to assume one existed. With two men in the bank, a third would be necessary outside to insure a speedy getaway. A three-way split of the robbery proceeds would have given Ray $9,075.

where he was coming from, but I assumed it was Montreal. * * * He mentioned that he was working for his brother in real estate and that he did not do much but was paid well. He also said that he had no problems with money and could always get some. [161]

According to his own account, Ray left Ottawa and, on August 21, he engaged in smuggling a package of contraband across the U.S. border for which Raoul paid him $1,500.[162] Ray then went to Birmingham, Ala. A week later, Raoul also arrived in that city. Raoul funded the purchase of a $2,000 1966 Mustang and gave Ray $500 for "living expenses" and another $500 for camera equipment.[163] On August 30, Raoul departed, instructing Ray to "lay low" and promising to contact him later to discuss "the business at hand and the matter of travel documents."[164] Between August 21, 1967, and August 30, 1967, then, Ray claimed to have received $4,500 from Raoul.

Ray's purchase of a $2,000 car in Birmingham on August 30, 1967, was established independently; clearly he then had a substantial amount of money. His rental of a safe deposit box on August 28, 1967,[165] indicated, however, that he had that money before the alleged arrival of Raoul, since Ray, in public hearing testimony, said he did not meet Raoul until that evening at the Starlite Cafe.[166] The committee found it significant, therefore, that both James and Jerry Ray admitted meeting in Chicago between Ray's departure from Canada and his arrival in Brimingham several days later.[167] Ray's Raoul fabrication, by which he tried to explain his receipt of at least $4,500, embraced a known and uncontroverted meeting with Jerry Ray.

The committee believed, based on Ray's meeting with Jerry on August 22, 1967—followed by his rental of a safe deposit box on August 28, 1967, and his purchase of an expensive automobile on August 30, 1967—that Ray receive substantial amounts of money, not from Raoul, but from Jerry. Further, the committee believed the most likely source of this money was the Alton bank robbery.

Ray also claimed to have met with Raoul during his December 1967 visit to New Orleans.[40] According to Ray,

[40] A detailed examination of the New Orleans trip appears in a staff report entitled "An Analysis of James Earl Ray's Trip to New Orleans, December 15–December 21, 1967," XIII HSCA–MLK hearings 265.

an associate of Raoul told him by telephone in early December to travel from Los Angeles to New Orleans later in the month to meet with Raoul. Ray said he made the trip with Charles Stein, met Raoul at the Le Bunny Lounge, discussed a gunrunning scheme planned for early May, and received $500 because he was "low on funds." [168]

In addition to hearing Ray's account, the committee examined evidence supplied by Mark O. Freeman, a clinical psychologist in Los Angeles whom Ray consulted in November and December 1967. Dr. Freeman's records indicated that Ray's last appointment was at 10 a.m. on December 14, the day before he departed for New Orleans. In an FBI interview, Dr. Freeman told of a telephone call from Ray subsequent to that appointment. FBI report stated:

The doctor recalled that Ray had telephone [sic] him at the office, after making the appointment for December 18, and told him he would be uanble to come to the office for the appointment as he had received information from his brother, that the latter had "found a job for him in the Merchant Marine in New Orleans, La." The doctor is not sure of the date or time that Ray telephone [sic] to cancel his last appointment; but feels sure that it was sometime after their 10 a.m. appointment on December 14 * * *.[169]

Dr. Freeman's statement, together with his appointment records, provided clear evidence that Ray's trip to New Orleans was more impulsive than his Raoul story indicated and that Ray planned to meet a brother in New Orleans. This inference was strengthened by the statements of Sharon Rhodes, a Los Angeles dance school instructor, both in her initial FBI interview [170] and in a statement to the committee.[171] In the FBI interview, she recalled a discussion with Ray following his New Orleans trip:

She believes he was a southerner, and she recalled that possibly the first or second week during January 1968, he did not attend dancing instruction, and upon his return, stated that he had vsited a brother in the State of Louisiana.[172]

In addition to the separate witness statements indicating Ray met with a brother in New Orleans, the committee obtained convincing evidence that he, in fact, received money on the trip. On the day of his return to Los Angeles, December 21, Ray paid $365, the balance of what he owed on the 50-hour dance course. Under his original agreement with the studio, he was obligated to pay only $50 a week.[173]

James did not identify the brother in New Orleans during his conversations with the California witnesses. The committee found it likely that Ray at least met with Jerry in New Orleans. Jerry was still employed at the Sportsman's Club in Chicago at the time, but he admitted to the committee that he went to St. Louis for Christmas that year. [174] St. Louis and New Orleans are only 675 miles apart, so it was at least reasonably possible for Jerry and James to have met. Further, both James and Jerry Ray conceded to the committee that they talked by telephone during James' drive from Los Angeles to New Orleans. The committee was unable, however, to rule out the possibility that it was John Ray—then an unemployed painter living in St. Louis who traveled to New Orleans to meet James. The committee was also unable to determine fully the purpose of the New Orleans meeting. If, in fact, it was to receive only $500, that would not seem to justify the risks Ray took in driving several thousand miles on the open highway.[41] The committee noted that the assassination occurred 3½ months after the New Orleans trip. While the possibility of a connection between the trip and the murder of Dr. King existed, the committee uncovered no direct evidence to that effect.[42]

(e) The brothers and the rifle purchase

The final contact with a brother that James Earl Ray tried to conceal with his Raoul ruse was considered by the committee to have been by far the most significant. It oc-

---

[41]A random vehicle check might well have resulted in his identification as an escapee from the Missouri State Penitentiary.

[42]Two circumstances surrounding the New Orleans trip did provide support for a link between the New Orleans trip and the murder. First, in Ray's account, Raoul proposed the gunrunning scheme for the first time in New Orleans. It was gunrunning, according to Ray, that brought him and Raoul to Memphis on the day before Dr. King's assassination. Second, there was Ray's abrupt activity on behalf of the American Independent Party on the morning of his departure for New Orleans. The committee developed evidence that individuals involved in the AIP movement in St. Louis engaged in a conspiracy that may well have been linked to the events in New Orleans and subsequently Memphis.

curred in Birminghm, Ala., on March 29 and 30, 1968, just days before the assassination of Dr. King, and its purpose, the committee concluded, was a transaction that suggested the likelihood that a brother was involved in a conspiracy in the assassination. The transaction was the purchase of the murder weapon.

Ray's testimony before the committee,[175] corroborated by a postal change of address that he mailed in Los Angeles,[176] established that he departed California for the Southeastern United States on March 17, 1968, approximately 2½ weeks prior to Dr. King's assassination.[43] On at least three occasions during the weeks immediately prior to his departure, Ray mentioned upcoming contact with a brother. On one of these occasions, moreover, he indicated a plan to meet that brother in Brimingham.

One of Ray's closest friends in Los Angeles was Marie Martin, a waitress at the Sultan Room in the St. Francis Hotel, who had a casual relationship with him over a period of several months. In an interview with the FBI on May 14, 1968, she reported that Ray, using the Galt alias, asked in late February if he could leave some barbells at her apartment.

Martin * * * told Galt to leave the weights outside of the door [to her apartment]. Galt called her later the same day on the phone and she asked him for some money for taking care of the weights. Galt claimed he was broke, but said he would leave her ten dollars * * * Galt claimed he was waiting for some money from his brother.[177]

In testimony to the committee, Martin repeated her recollection that Galt received money by mail from a brother:

I took it for granted it was on a regular basis because it seemed every now and then he was waiting for an envelope. He asked me, "When you pass the lobby, will you check my box?"[178]

---

[43] The committee received evidence that Ray went through St. Louis on his way east. The source of the evidence. Walter Rife, also said that Ray told him he "had a deal down there about some stuff to go into Cuba," conceivably a reference to the gunrunning operation. Ray never mentioned a trip to St. Louis. In addition, the committee found no evidence to corroborate the existence of a gunrunning operation. (See Section II A).

Martin's testimony provided the first indication of contact between Ray and a brother during a period proximate to the assassination.

On March 2, during graduation ceremonies at a bartending school Ray had attended in California, he was asked by the director of the school, Tomas Lau, what he planned to do. Ray's response was overheard by Richard Gonzalez, another student at the school, and reported to the FBI in an April 16 interview: "* * * Galt stated he was going to go to Birmingham, Ala., to visit his brother for about 2 weeks."[179] In a public hearing in August 1978, Ray told the committee that he met Raoul in Birmingham on March 23, exactly 3 weeks after he reportedly made the statement to Lau.[180] Six days thereafter, he and Raoul returned to Birmingham to purchase the rifle that was used to kill Dr. King.[181]

On March 9, Ray talked by telephone to Tomas Lau, who reported the conversation to the FBI following the assassination:

Lau recalls that approximately 1 week after Galt's graduation on March 2, 1968, Galt telephonically contacted him [Lau] at which time Lau advised him that he had a possible job opportunity for him as a bartender. Galt advised Lau that he was leaving town within 2 weeks for an undisclosed location to visit his brother and did not wish to take a job at this time. [182]

Precisely 2 weeks later, according to Ray's testimony to the committee, he met Raoul in Birmingham. The rifle purchase followed 6 days later.

More significant than the three allusions in California to a brother, however, was Ray's reference to a brother during the rifle purchase itself. On March 29, Ray went to the Aeromarine Supply Co. and bought a .243 caliber Winchester, using the name Harvey Lowmeyer.[44] He later decided to exchange the rifle for another, a transaction that was described by Donald Wood, a clerk at Aeromarine, in a signed FBI interview on April 5, 1968:

It was, as best I recall, either later that afternoon or early the following Saturday morning when this

---

[44] See MLK exhibit F-35 (Aeromarine receipt of rifle purchase), II, HSCA-MLK hearings, 89.

individual called on the telephone and stated that he had a conversation with his brother and decided that the gun he had purchased was not the gun he wanted and he requested whether he could exchange it for a Remington model 760, .30–06 caliber.[183]

Wood stated further that when Ray came to the store on Saturday, he told him that the Winchester was a big enough gun to bring down any deer in Alabama. "He stated in an offhand manner that he wanted the .30–06 caliber gun because he was going to use it to hunt in Wisconsin."[184]

Ray's version of the rifle purchase again seemed to be an effort to disguise contact with a brother through the character of Raoul. Ray stated that he and Raoul traveled to Birmingham from Atlanta and that Raoul gave him over $700 to purchase a "large deer bore rifle."[185] He bought the rifle and brought it back to the motel. Raoul disapproved of the choice and told Ray to exchange it for one chosen from a brochure.

Chairman STOKES. So, then, after you purchased the second rifle, at Raoul's direction, because he told you the first rifle was not adequate——

RAY. Yes, he pointed out in a brochure—I had a brochure with the second rifle.

Chairman STOKES. OK. He sent you back to get the second rifle and told you what kind to get, didn't he?

RAY. That is correct.

Chairman STOKES. And you did what he told you to do?

RAY. Yes, sir. * * * I made a phone call to Aeromarine Supply and I asked them about exchanging it and they said they could do it.[186]

Ray's use of the Harvey Lowmeyer alias also corroborated the possible involvement of a brother in the rifle purchase. Ray told the committee he got the name from a friend or criminal associate in Quincy, Ill.[187] Ray's last known visit to Quincy, however, had been in June and July of 1967, 9 months earlier. Further, the actual Harvey Lohmeyer[45] told the committee in an interview that while he knew John Ray and Jerry Ray from a period of

---

[45]The committee noted the slight spelling difference between Lowmeyer and Lohmeyer and decided it was due to an error made by Ray.

overlapping prison terms at Menard State Penitentiary in Chester, Ill., in the late 1950's, he did not know James Earl Ray.[188] The committee, therefore, believed it more likely that James got the idea for this alias from either John or Jerry Ray. In the absence of any evidence that James stockpiled aliases, Ray's use of "Harvey Lowmeyer" for the rifle purchase suggested contact with one or both brothers at that time.

Percy Foreman, Ray's attorney when Ray pled guilty to the assassination on March 10, 1969, testified in a committee hearing to admissions by Ray that his brother Jerry was with him at the time of the rifle purchse.[46] Foreman said:

> I cross-examined James Earl Ray for hours and the only name that he ever mentioned other than his own at any phase or time of his preparation for the killing * * * Dr. Martin Luther King * * * the only person's name that he ever mentioned to me was his brother, Jerry.
>
> Jerry was with him when he bought the rifle in Birmingham, the one he did not use because it was a low caliber. He took it back and traded it for a more powerful one that would be more likely to kill an individual. The smaller caliber was more suited for killing small animals. And Jerry was not with him, according to Ray's statement, when he bought the gun that killed Dr. Martin Luther King; but he was with him the day before at the same place where he bought another rifle for that purpose * * *.[189]

In his testimony before the committee, Jerry Ray repeatedly denied that he participated in the rifle purchase [190] or that he was the Raoul that James referred to. He also denied having transmitted any funds to James.[191] Finally, he suggested that James used the brother references as a means of disguising contact with Raoul:

> He would use the statement and he would go along—"My brother said this" and "My brother said that" or "He wanted the gun" or "I'm going to go visit him" or something. That was just a way of, you

<hr>

[46]The committee noted that certain statements by Foreman were at variance with other reliable evidence. (See discussion of guilty plea, at sec. II *supra*.) The committee therefore, discounted his testimony concerning Jerry Ray's involvement in the rifle purchase.

know, of saying he was going to meet somebody and instead of saying he was going to see Raoul, he wasn't going to tell everybody he was going to visit Raoul. [192]

The committee reviewed Jerry Ray's extensive testimony before the committee, as well as his prior statements to members of the press, FBI agents, authors and a number of private citizens, and it found his testimony self-serving and generally unworthy of belief. For example, the committee obtained evidence from several sources who requested confidentiality that Jerry Ray believed parts of the Raoul story were untrue, yet he continued to insist to the committee that such a character existed. Further, Jerry Ray admitted to the committee that he gave a false description of Raoul in a New York City radio interview in 1977;[193] that he falsely denied that James ever mentioned Dr. King in their conversations during prison visits over the 10 years following the assassination;[194] and that he falsely claimed his brother was not a beer drinker.[47][195] Jerry also admitted to the committee that he supplied McMillan, the author, with bank records he had falsified.[196]

Finally, during his testimony, Jerry told the committee that he had located the Mississippi motel where James had stayed during a drive from Birmingham to Memphis that James claimed he made after the rifle purchase. Jerry added that he had talked to individuals who indicated that the FBI had destroyed the motel records that reflected his stay. When the committee investigated his charge, however, it found the motel records still intact[48] and Jerry Ray's testimony an intentional distortion of the truth.[197]

The committee found Jerry Ray's public hearing testimony, including his denial of involvement in the Birmingham rifle purchase, unworthy of belief.[49]

The committee was at pains to make a careful assessment of the evidence bearing on the rifle purchase. No less

[47]The committee believed Jerry lied on this matter to support James' allegation that beer cans with Ray's fingerprints found in the bundle of evidence had been "planted" by authorities.
[48]The records did not, in fact, reflect Ray's stay at the motel.
[49]Authors Huie and McMillan had each alleged that Jerry Ray claimed to have received a telephone call from James the night before the assassination in which James predicted that the "big nigger has had it." A discussion of this evidence is contained in a staff report entilted "Supplemental Studies Pertaining to the Motive of James Earl Ray," XIII HSCA–MLK hearings, par. 64.

than four separate witnesses—Marie Martin, Richard Gonzalez, Tomas Lau, and Donald Wood—in separate interviews with authorities shortly after the assassination, provided evidence of Ray's receipt of money from, or contact with, a brother during the month preceding the rifle purchase. Wood's testimony tied that brother directly into the rifle purchase itself.

Both Jerry and James asserted that James' reference to a brother was meant to conceal his involvement with Raoul. [198] The committee's investigation produced no evidence to corroborate the existence of Raoul, so that proposed explanation was worthless. The committee believed that Ray's postassassination tale of Raoul was fabricated to conceal contacts with one or both brothers. The committee was, however, unable to establish the precise whereabouts of either John or Jerry for the period of the rifle purchase. John Ray stated in executive session that he was operating the Grapevine Tavern in St. Louis at the time, [199] and the committee while unwilling to credit John Ray's unsupported testimony, received no evidence that contradicted his assertion. Jerry Ray's working records were destroyed approximately 6 months before the committee contacted his employer, the Sportsman's Club near Chicago. Jerry's working hours at that time were 11 p.m. to 7 a.m.[200] If his recollection that Thursday was his day off was correct,[50] he could conceivably have gone to Birmingham, given advice on the initial rifle purchase on the afternoon of Friday, March 29, 1968, and returned in time to be on the job by 11 p.m. that night.

Finally, although James' presence at the Birmingham Travelodge was verified, the committee found no evidence of his brothers, or of any associates, at the motel with him.[201]

The committee also considered the possibility that James' contact with his brother was by telephone, rather than in person, but the relevant telephone records had been destroyed.

On balance, therefore, the committee believed the evidence convincing that James had some form of contact with a brother both before and during the rifle purchase. The committee had no direct evidence, which it was willing to credit, establishing the identity of the brother. Given

---

[50]The committee received significant evidence that Jerry Ray's day off was, in fact, Tuesday.

the limits on the evidence available to the committee, no more definitive statement could be made.

(f) Motive with respect to John and Jerry Ray

Since the evidence reflected a criminal association of Ray and his two brothers that was far more substantial than any of the three were willing to admit, and since that association appeared to extend to complicity in the assassination itself, it was appropriate to examine the question of motive with reference to John and Jerry.

The investigation of James Earl Ray's motive in the assassination revealed that while he was generally unsympathetic with the civil rights movement, he apparently did not harbor such an intense racial hatred that he would have acted in the assassination without other inducement. While Ray might have been attracted by the notoriety he would achieve for committing the crime, the committee found that his primary inducement was probably the expectation of financial gain.

The committee reviewed evidence bearing on the racial attitudes of John and Jerry Ray and found it clear and compelling. John Ray was found to be a man of pronounced racial bias. By his own admission, his place of business in 1968, the Grapevine Tavern in St. Louis, was a segregated establishment in a segregated neighborhood. [202] In addition, many of John Ray's remarks, both to the committee and at the time of the assassination, reflected strong opposition to the civil rights movement and to Dr. King himself. In his first interview with the FBI following the assassination—on April 22, 1968—he voiced approval of the murder of Dr. King. Quoting from the FBI report:

It is noted that Ray was initially uncooperative and said. "What's all the excitement about? He only killed a nigger. If he had killed a white man you wouldn't be here. King should have been killed 10 years ago."[51][203]

John Ray's testimony in public hearings, while modified

---

[51]When confronted with his statement, Ray stated, "I was probably drunk." [204] He added "* * * I ran a tavern in a racial neighhood. And everybody makes these statements, similar statements." [205]

in tone, provided additional evidence of his general racial attitudes:

> STAFF COUNSEL. Again, Mr. Ray my question was: What was your racial attitude toward Dr. King and the civil rights movement that he headed up in 1968?
>
> *   *   *   *   *   *   *   *
>
> RAY. I would guess you would say I was a mild segregationist, I guess.[206]

One of the strongest indications of John Ray's opposition to Dr. King, however, appears in a letter that he wrote from prison to George McMillan, the author, in June 1972.[207]

> *** the common man *** knows that King was not a saint as these try to picture him. There are millions of Rays in the United States with the same background and beliefs, who know that King not only was a rat but with his beaded eyes and pin ears looked like one.[52]

Over the years since Dr. King's assassination, Jerry Ray also overtly exhibited racist attitudes. He went to work in 1969 as a bodyguard for J. B. Stoner, leader of the National States Rights Party. The committee found it significant that he chose to work with the leader of an organizaion, which, shortly after Dr. King's death, had declared in The Thunderbolt, the party newspaper, that:

> The man who shot King was actually upholding the law of the land and enforcing the injunction of the U.S. District Court of Memphis which had forbidden King's marches. The white man who shot King *** should be given the Congressional Medal of Honor and a large annual pension for life, plus a Presidential pardon.[209]

Jerry Ray's support for the views expressed in The Thunderbolt was confirmed in a letter he later wrote on "J. B. Stoner for United States Senator" stationery:

---

[52]When questioned in executive session about this letter, John Ray stated, "I more or less might have said that to get McMillan's goat for not paying me the $700." [208]

I am sure when history is written my brother James Earl Ray, and the Hon. Gov. George Wallace will be heroes along side of J. B. Stoner.[210][53]

Finally, Jerry Ray's racism was confirmed by the testimony of Dr. Edward Fields, secretary of the National States Rights Party, who characterized Jerry as a "segregationist."[212]

Both Jerry and John Ray, therefore, manifested in their general attitudes pronounced racial bias, as well as willingness to commit crime for financial gain, attitudes that would be consistent with their participation in the assassination of Dr. King.

6. EVIDENCE OF A CONSPIRACY IN ST. LOUIS

An offer on Dr. King's life that existed in St. Louis in late 1966 or early 1967 was brought to the attention of the committee in March 1978 by the FBI.[213] A Bureau informant contact report dated March 19, 1974, had been discovered during a file review in an unrelated investigation.[214][54] It indicated that in the fall of 1973 an informant advised that Russell G. Byers of St. Louis had told him he had been offered $10,000 or $20,000 by a St. Louis lawyer, than deceased, to kill Dr. King.

The committee began its investigation of the lead by contacting Byers, who initially denied knowledge of the offer. After consulting with his attorney, however, Byers agreed to cooperate, but only in response to a subpoena and if he were granted immunity. A subpoena was issued, and when Byers appeared before an executive session of the committee on May 9, 1978, he was granted immunity under title II of the Organized Crime Control Act of 1970. Byers' testimony in committee public hearings was also given under an immunity grant.[215]

---

[53]When asked about this letter in public hearings, Jerry Ray conceded he was its author, but he insisted it was a joke. [211] While the letter may well have been an attempt at humor, the committee believed that its contents offered strong evidence of pronounced racism and anti-Semitism.

[54]The informant contact report had not been disseminated by the St. Louis FBI field office, so there had been no official investigation of the information it contained. The FBI conducted interviews in 1978 with the two former special agents, since retired, who had handled the informant. It was determined that the failure to follow up on the information resulted from inadvertence on the part of the agents who stated, in retrospect, that they should have acted on the lead. The current leadership of the Bureau is to be commended for creating a climate within the Bureau where an informant report of this character could be forwarded to a congressional committee rather than ignored or destroyed.

(a) The Byers allegation

Byers gave the following account to the committee: [216]

He was contacted in late 1966 or early 1967 by John Kauffmann, whom he had known since 1962 as a former stockbroker and operator of the Bluff Acres Motel and a drug manufacturing company, both located in Imperial, Mo. Kauffmann had, in return for payment, permitted Byers to store stolen merchandise, including stolen cars, at his motel. Kauffmann asked Byers if he would like to make $50,000, and Byers asked what he would have to do to earn it. Kauffmann told him to meet him at 6:30 that evening, which Byers did, and together they drove to the home in Imperial of John Sutherland, a St. Louis patent attorney. The three men met in a study that Byers described as decorated with Confederate flags and Civil War memorabilia. There was a rug replica of a Confederate flag as well, and Sutherland was wearing what appeared to Byers to be a Confederate colonel's hat.

After some social conversation, Byers asked Sutherland what he would have to do for the $50,000. Sutherland said he would have to kill, or arrange to have killed, Dr. Martin Luther King. Byers, who told the committee he did not know at the time who Dr. King was, asked where that amount of money would come from. Sutherland told him he belonged to a secret southern organization that had plenty of money. According to Byers, no names were mentioned. Byers said he neither accepted nor rejected the offer, indicating he would think it over. Outside the door of Sutherland's home, however, he told Kauffmann he was not interested.[55] He said he saw Sutherland only once again at a water company meeting and that he soon severed his ties with Kauffmann, having learned he was involved in an illegal drug operation. Byers indicated he feared he would end up murdered or in the penitentiary if he got involved in drugs.

To determine if Byers' story was credible, the committee initiated a full-scale investigation of Byers, Kauffmann, and Sutherland. Dozens of associates of each were inter-

---

[55]The committee subpoenaed Beulah Kauffmann, the widow of John Kauffmann, to appear in executive session. (In light of her conviction on drug charges in 1967, Mrs. Kauffmann's testimony was regarded with some skepticism by the committee.) She confirmed that her late husband and Sutherland had been business associates with Wallace supporters. She also recalled that Kauffmann had taken Byers to Sutherland's home on one occasion but that Sutherland was not home. [217]

viewed or deposed, and several were called to testify in executive session. In addition, files of local, State and Federal agencies were reviewed.

Although the investigation was hampered by the death of many of the principals, the committee uncovered enough evidence to be convinced that the Byers allegation was essentially truthful. There was in existence, in 1966 or 1967, a St. Louis conspiracy actively soliciting the assassination of Dr. King. The committee found that Byers was a logical target for solicitation in such a conspiracy even though he testified that he did not know why Kauffmann would have approached him.[218] The committee learned that Byers had a reputation, at the time of the offer, for associating with people known to have a propensity for violence. More specifically, his brother-in-law, John Paul Spica, had been convicted of the contract murder of a St. Louis businessman.[219] Kauffmann and Sutherland could well have been led to believe, the committee reasoned, that while Byers might not have been willing to undertake the murder himself, he could have established contact with people willing to accept the offer.

Nevertheless, the committee sought further corroboration for Byers' account, realizing that his criminal record raised substantial doubts concerning his credibility.[220] In addition, questions were raised by his failure to approach authorities with his information in 1968. Byers himself explained that he had not wanted to get involved in any way or attract attention to his criminal activities. [221] He did say however, that he told two St. Louis attorneys, Lawrence Weenick[56] and Murray Randall, about his meeting with Kauffmann and Sutherland. According to Byers, Weenick was told in 1974. Byers had two conversations with Randall, one in 1968 and the other in 1974.[222]

Byers waived his attorney-client privilege with Weenick and Randall, and they were interviewed by the committee.[223] Their accounts to staff counsel and committee investigators essentially supported the testimony Byers had given in executive session. The two attorneys were then subpoenaed to appear at a committee public hearing. Weenick testified that in 1974 or 1975, while he was representing Byers in several civil matters, Byers told him he had been offered $50,000 by Kauffmann and Sutherland to

---

[56]Weenick also represented Kauffmann in his 1967 drug case.

murder Dr. Martin Luther King and that Byers gave him the impression that, while the offer was seriously made, he (Byers) never took it seriously. Weenick was pressed by the committee on his assessment of Byers' credibility. He replied:

> * * * Byers had absolutely no reason to tell me this at the time he told it to me, or any other time. Whether he made it up or not, I don't know. There was—there seems to be no credible reason why he would have made it up and told it to me and to Mr. Randall, and evidently to this other person who was an FBI informant. * * *
> * * * I can't say for certain that he is not lying, but I certainly don't know what his motive would be for doing so.[224]

When Randall, who had since become a judge in the Court of Criminal Corrections in St. Louis, learned he might be subpoenaed to testify before the committee in public session, he attempted to avoid an appearance, arguing that his testimony would be of no value and expressing concern over the effect the publicity could have on his reelection to the bench. He complained to staff counsel, [225] committee investigators,[226] the chairman of the committee,[227] and another member of Congress. To support his position about the value of his testimony, he raised—for the first time with the committee —doubts he said he had about Byers' credibility. He offered the speculation that Byers might have concocted the story in 1973 and told it to a person he suspected of being an FBI informant to test his suspicion. According to Randall's theory, if the FBI subsequently contacted Byers about the King assassination, he would have his suspicions about the informant confirmed.[228]

Nevertheless, Randall was called to testify, as was Weenick, at a public hearing on November 29, 1978.[229] He said he first met Byers in 1967 when Byers pled guilty to a stolen car charge. He next saw him when he assisted him in incorporating a business in 1968. He then stated to the committee that he had run into Byers at the court-house in 1974, shortly before he left private practice to take the bench. Byers asked his advice on the procedures for claiming immunity in a grand jury investigation, saying he thought he might be questioned by Federal authorities about his knowledge of a plot to assassinate Dr. King. Byers then told Randall a story that reflected in essential details Byers' testimony before the committee and the story Byers told Weenick. During his committee testimony, Randall said he did not remember that Byers had told him of the King offer prior to the 1974 meeting.[230][57] In response to questioning, Randall also repeated his speculation about Byers and the informant, conceding it was only "speculation, * * * "my belief and opinion."[231]

The committee accepted the basic outlines of Judge Randall's testimony. Indeed, he added valuable detail to the story told by Byers. As such, his testimony contributed to the work of the committee. Nevertheless, the committee found that Judge Randall's memory that only one conversation took place was in error. The committee also rejected Randall's speculation about Byers' possible effort to unmask an FBI informant. It believed that the theory was offered to undermine the witness' own testimony in order to discourage the committee from compelling his public appearance.[58] In addition, the committee found Randall's speculation about Byers' story to be implausible. Byers was a relatively sophisticated and experienced criminal, and he would have known such a ploy would not work. It would only have served to expose him to an FBI investigation that he, with a long history of dealing in stolen property, would have wanted to avoid. The very significance of his information would have subjected him to increased scrutiny. The committee's chief investigator testified that, based on his experience, Byers' more likely course of action would have been to discontinue dealing with the suspected informant.[232] Moreover, it was considered highly unlikely that the FBI would have approached Byers in such a way, since this would have risked making Byers aware of the role of the informant.

The committee agreed with Weenick's testimony that Byers had no motive to lie about the offer. Unlike many sources of King death threats, who have fabricated in-

[57]During an earlier conversation with the committee, Randall recalled a 1968 meeting with Byers during which Byers told him that some prominent people were involved in Dr. King's murder. Byers also recalled a 1968 discussion with Randall about the offer for the assassination of Dr. King.

[58]Judge Randall's theory was undermined by the likelihood of a 1968 conversation about the offer as well as by the statement of a St. Louis police detective who told the committee that a St. Louis Post-Dispatch reporter had been looking into a rumor in 1971 or 1972 of Byers' involvement with a patent attorney in the King assassination. [233] The committee was unable to contact the reporter, who had died in 1974.

formation for publicity, Byers' conduct since 1967 has demonstrated a consistent unwillingness to get involved in the investigation of the King assassination. He did not volunteer his information to the committee; he refused to cooperate until he was subpoenaed and granted immunity.

The committee's conclusion that Byers' testimony of a serious conspiracy to kill Dr. King in the St. Louis area was essentially truthful was independently substantiated by the sworn testimony of an unpaid informant for the Jefferson County, Mo., sheriff's office in 1967 and 1968. This witness spent 3 years thereafter with a State police agency. He requested anonymity, since he was concerned that his failure to take more vigorous action in 1968 with the information might damage his reputation, destroy his marriage and injure his career in private industry.[59] The committee decided, based on these considerations and a judgment that the witness was candid and forthcoming, to grant his request for anonymity and refer to him in this report as witness A.[234]

As a sheriff's office informant, witness A spent much time at the Buff Acres, the motel operated by Kauffmann in Imperial, Mo. He had been asked to investigate numerous individuals who frequented the motel. He testified that Kauffmann was accepting stolen property in exchange for room rent, running a prostitution ring out of the motel and dealing in drugs. He then recounted conversation he had heard at the motel regarding a standing offer to murder Dr. King:

> * * * there was a frequent remark whenever any more than two of the members got together, if they were hard up for money, somebody would say, "Well, we can always make $20,000 or $30,000 for, killing Martin Luther King," or, on another occasion, and quite frequently, "We can always make $20,000 or $30,000 if we kill the big nigger for John."

Asked who John was, witness A replied, "John Kauffmann."[235]

The committee found certain elements of the Sutherland/Kauffmann conspiracy particularly interesting. First, it provided a source of funds that could explain the in-

---

[59]He stated that he gave the information to two officers he worked with but pursued it no further. When interviewed by the committee, Lt. Wally Ganzman said he could not recall the incident, but he did not deny that it occurred. The second officer had since died.

volvement of a financially motivated criminal such as Ray. The committee had noted that if in fact the Alton bank robbery involved three people—as circumstances seemed to indicate—James' expenditures in his fugitive period would have almost completely exhausted his share of $9,077 by the time of the assassination.[236] Even if a two-way split were assumed, his funds would have been substantially depleted. In either case, he would have been interested in a new source of income at about the time of the assassination.

Second, the Sutherland-Kauffmann conspiracy was located in the St. Louis area. The principals lived there, and the offers were made there—both Sutherland's offer to Byers and the standing offer at Kauffmann's motel. James Earl Ray visited St. Louis at least twice during his fugitive period, and his brother John was a permanent resident. Given the circulation of the offer among the area's criminal elements, at least at the Buff Acres Motel, it seemed entirely possible that word of the offer might reach the Ray family.

(b) The backgrounds of Kauffmann and Sutherland

John Kauffmann was born April 7, 1904, and died April 1, 1974.[237] He was a lifelong St. Louis resident, involved in a variety of business activities, including the manufacture of gliders and real estate development. From the early 1960's to his death, he owned and resided at the Bluff Acres Motel in Barnhardt, Mo. His widow, Beulah, still lived there in 1978.

Kauffmann's criminal record [238] disclosed that he was arrested and convicted for the manufacture and sale of amphetamines in 1967.[60] The committee reviewed the files of the Federal drug case that led to Kauffmann's arrest and conviction.[239] They revealed he had been operating a legitimate drug company that marketed a cough mixture called Fixaco. Through the company, he was ordering amphetamine sulfate powder in bulk and making amphetamine pills from the powder. Kauffmann sold an estimated 1 million pills illegally to undercover Federal agents in 1967.

Testimony given at Kauffmann's narcotics trial revealed a link between his illegal drug operation and the Missouri

---

[60] Kauffmann was free on an appeal bond at the time of Dr. King's assassination.

State Penitentiary where James Earl Ray was incarcerated until his escape in April of 1967.[240] A Federal informant indicated that some of the illegal contraband was delivered to the prison by one of Kauffmann's accomplices. During an interview with the committee, one of Kauffmann's codefendants disclosed that Kauffman had arranged for an additional delivery to the Missouri State Penitentiary on the day of his arrest.[241]

Kauffmann's criminal record did not reflect a conviction for any crimes of violence. Nevertheless, the committee learned that a Federal narcotics agent was ambushed and shot just after talking to an informant about Kauffmann. This incident occurred shortly after Kauffmann's arrest, but following disclosure that the victim was a Federal agent who had worked undercover on the Kauffmann case.[242] Kauffmann also once told an undercover agent he had threatened a person who owed him money in order to scare him.[243]

In addition, while the committee was unable to obtain information that would provide substantial details on Kauffmann's political attitudes, it did establish that he was associated with John Sutherland in efforts to establish an American Party chapter in the St. Louis area in 1967–68. The American Party supported the candidacy of Governor George Wallace of Alabama. Examination of numerous American Party petitions filed with the Missouri Secretary of State for the 1968 Presidential election showed Kauffmann's signature as either circulating officer or as notary public.[244]

John Sutherland, a descendant of early colonists, was born in Charlottesville, Va., October 19, 1905. He died in 1970.[245] He was a 1926 graduate of Virginia Military Institute, with a degree in electrical engineering; he received a bachelor of laws degree from City College of Law and Finance, St. Louis, 1931, and a master of laws degree from Benton College of Law. He held a commission in the U.S. Army Reserve from 1926 to 1936, though he apparently never served on active duty. He was married in 1930 to Anna Lee of Atlanta.[61][246]

Sutherland practiced patent law in St. Louis. He was a lifelong resident of the St. Louis area and had no criminal record.

[61]John Sutherland's widow, Anna Lee Sutherland, confirmed in a committee interview that her husband had been extremely outspoken in his racial views and strongly anti-Black. She also confirmed that her husband's den was decorated with Confederate paraphernalia, including

A number of associates of Sutherland were interviewed by the committee. One characterized him as a "die-hard southerner" who "never let the Civil War die."[247] Others described him as a "strong Wallace supporter," anti-Black, an "outspoken conservative," and opposed to civil rights, integration, and the Supreme Court.[248] There were several associates, however, who said that they could not conceive of Sutherland's involvement in an assassination plot.

Sutherland belonged to a number of social and professional organizations, and he was active politically throughout his adult life. A segregationist or anticivil rights strain was apparent in many of these organizations. For example, information obtained from FBI St. Louis field office files indicated that Sutherland was the founder and chairman of the steering committee of the first St. Louis Citizens' Council in 1964.[249] The local group had ties to a parent organization in the deep South with stated principles of "States rights" and "racial integrity."[250]

Available information indicated that Sutherland withdrew from an active leadership role in the citizens' council after the first year of its existence.[251] Gordon Baum, the field director of the St. Louis organization in 1978, stated during a committee interview that, to his knowledge, Sutherland had ceased formal ties with the citizens council prior to 1967.[252] Other members, however, indicated that Sutherland's name was well known in citizens council activities and that he had served as an adviser on the group's activities until his death in 1970.[253]

Sutherland was associated with a second organization of interest to the committee, the Southern States Industrial Council (SSIC), headquartered in Tennessee. The SSIC was an organization of businessmen and industrial leaders, and its policies as of 1967 reflected opposition to the civil rights movement and a suspicion of Communist infiltration of the "Negro movement."[254] Sutherland served as a regional director of the association and was an associate of its 1968 president, Theodore Sensing.[255] The committee's examination of the council developed evidence that some of its members were unsympathetic to Dr. King.

a Confederate flag. She volunteered that Sutherland had been an active member of the Southern States Industrial Council and at one time had inquired into possible membership in the National States Rights Party. Mrs. Sutherland said John Kauffmann had not been a close associate of her husband, and she disclaimed any knowledge of an offer to kill Dr. King or a discussion of such an offer.

Sensing, for example, addressed the Daughters of the American Revolution in Washington on April 15, 1968, less than 2 weeks after the King assassination. While Sensing called it a "senseless, tragic crime" and recommended that the killer ". . . be apprehended if possible, and brought to trial for his crime," he also used the occasion to criticize Dr. King and those associated with him. He stated at one point, "It is not too much to say, in fact, that Martin Luther King, Jr., brought this crime upon himself." Holding Dr. King to account for his attitude toward civil disobedience, Sensing speculated that the assassin, ". . . may well have said to himself, 'I think Martin Luther King should be killed. I realize there is a law against murder, but in this case, I think the law was unjust.' " [256] While this speech did not, of course, provide any evidence of complicity by members of SSIC in the assassination, it did give an indication of the political persuasion of Sutherland's associates.

The committee was unable to identify the secret southern organization to which Sutherland referred as the source of payment when he allegedly made the offer to Byers. It did, however, establish that he belonged to at least two organizations with extreme segregationist leanings,[62] and it developed evidence of pronounced racial bias in Sutherland himself.

A committee investigation of Sutherland's financial condition revealed that he left an estate valued at more than $300,000.[258]

Based on this background investigation, the committee concluded that the two principals, Sutherland and Kauffmann, met the criteria for being serious conspirators:

> They had the motive, i.e., Sutherland's avowed social and political attitudes, and Kauffmann's readiness to earn money legally or illegal;
>
> They had the monetary means, either from Sutherland's own funds or from associates; and
>
> They actively sought the opportunity to carry out a plot, as evidenced at least by their solicitation of Byers.

---

[62]Sutherland was also a member of the Order of the Veiled Phophet, a social organization with membership restricted to caucasians. It was the target of protest by St. Louis civil rights organizations for its restricted membership policies. [257]

(c) Connectives to James Earl Ray

The committee turned finally to an examination of the possibility that the Sutherland-Kauffmann offer might have reached James Earl Ray. Four possible connectives were explored.[63]

The first connective was John Paul Spica, brother-in-law of Russell Byers and a fellow inmate of Ray at Missouri State Penitentiary.

The committee determined that Spica was convicted and imprisoned in 1963 for the contract murder of a St. Louis businessman. Missouri State Penitentiary records showed that he was incarcerated from 1963 to 1973 and that for at least part of that time he occupied a cell in the same cell block and same tier of the prison as Ray.[259]

In executive session testimony before the committee, Spica acknowledged that he was acquainted with Ray, but he denied close contact with him.[260] Committee interviews with prison officials and other inmates, on the other hand, indicated a much closer friendship between Spica and Ray than Spica admitted.[261] Spica also testified that he knew nothing of the offer to Byers by Sutherland and Kauffmann.[262]

Byers testified during public hearings that he visited Spica regularly[64] until his conviction, in December 1967, on a Dyer Act charge (interstate transportation of stolen automobiles). Nevertheless, he stated emphatically that he did not discuss the Sutherland-Kauffmann offer with him.[263]

In light of Spica's incarceration at Missouri State Penitentiary until 1973, his only potential role in the assassination might have been as a conduit of information between Byers and Ray. The committee found no evidence to contradict the denials of both Spica and Byers that the Sutherland-Kauffmann offer was discussed prior to the assassination. Finally, the committee believed that active planning for the assassination of Dr. King did not begin until early March 1968, a period when Ray had discussions with California associates about his plans to travel

---

[63]Of the four connectives considered, the committee deemed the first three to be possible but less likely, while the fourth was regarded as possible and more likely. Consistent with its duty to be cautious in its evaluation of the evidence, the committee acknowledged that none of the four connectives could be firmly established.

[64]Byers alleged visits to Spica could not be substantiated by the committee's investigation. Prison authorities informed the committee that visiting records for the pertinent period were missing from Spica's file.

east. Thus, if Ray did receive word of the Kauffmann-Sutherland plot while still in Missouri State Penitentiary, it would have to be assumed that Ray stored it away for later consideration.

The second possible connective developed by the committee was Dr. Hugh Maxey, a medical officer at the Missouri State Penitentiary. Committee interviews with relatives and associates of John Kauffmann indicated that Kauffman and Maxey were associated for several years.[264] Mrs. Kauffman characterized it as a purely social relationship, one that lasted from the early 1960's until Kauffmann was sent to Federal prison for the sale of amphetamines.[265]

The committee looked into other reasons for an association between Maxey and Kauffman. It was learned, for example, that Maxey assisted Kauffmann in obtaining the services of parolees in work release programs.[266] In addition, the committee received allegations that Maxey was involved with Kauffmann in the distribution of amphetamines in the prison.[267] While the existence of an amphetamine problem at the prison was confirmed, the committee found no evidence to support the charge that Maxey was involved in illegal distribution.

An examination of prison records established that Maxey had contact with James Earl Ray at the prison and, further, that Ray pushed a food cart in the prison hospital on occasion.[268] Thus, an opportunity for significant contact between the two existed.

Maxey, who was over 80 and of failing health when he was interviewed by the committee, denied his own involvement in illegal drug distribution. He characterized his relationship with Kauffmann as social and declined to discuss the association further. Finally, Maxey stated that he had contact with James Earl Ray only as a patient. He denied any knowledge of an offer to kill Dr. King circulating at the prison during his employment there.[269]

The committee's investigation did not substantiate a Maxey connective. The committee was unable to establish firmly any criminal activities shared by Maxey and Kauffman; thus, the likelihood that the two would have discussed the Sutherland offer seemed slim. In addition, while the opportunity existed for extensive contact between Ray and Maxey, there was no evidence that any relationship developed beyond that of doctor and patient.

The third connective explored by the committee was

Naomi Regazzi, an employee of the Grapevine Tavern when it was operated by John Ray in 1968. Byers told the committee that he was acquainted with a St. Louis resident named Robert Regazzi and that Regazzi and Spica also knew each other. The significance of this was amplified by the fact that Naomi Regazzi, a former wife of Robert, was a bartender at the Grapevine Tavern in St. Louis from January to July 1968.

In an attempt to substantiate this connective, the committee heard testimony from a number of people. Byers stated that to the best of his recollection, he did not discuss the offer with Regazzi.[270] Spica, also questioned under oath, confirmed that he knew Regazzi, but asserted there was no friendship between them. Spica further stated that he had had no knowledge of an offer to kill Dr. King, [271] thus making it impossible for him to have passed the offer to Regazzi. Regazzi, in an interview with the committee, claimed that he had no knowledge of events leading to the King assassination. He said he had been separated from Naomi during the period of her employment at the Grapevine, so he could not have communicated an offer to her, had he known about it.[272]

Finally, the committee subpoenaed Naomi Regazzi to testify under oath in executive session. She confirmed her employment at the Grapevine between January 1, 1968, and July 1968. She recalled seeing her ex-husband during this period only when he wanted to see their son. She stated that he was never in the Grapevine itself.[273] Finally, she testified that she did not know Byers personally, and she could recall no discussion concerning an offer to kill Dr. King at the Grapevine. She added that she discussed Dr. King with John Ray only after the assassination, when he confirmed that the assassination suspect was his brother.[274]

While Naomi Regazzi, who had become Naomi Denny, could have brought information concerning the offer on Dr. King's life to John Ray's tavern, the committee found no evidence that she, in fact, did. Mrs. Denny was separated from Robert Regazzi as of 1965 or 1966, and her relationship with him afterwards was limited to his visits to see their son.[275] It would seem unlikely under these circumstances that they would have discussed an offer for the murder of Dr. King. In addition, Byers did not recall telling Regazzi of the offer, and both Regazzi and his former wife denied having heard of it. The committee noted that an examination of Mrs. Denny's testimony indicated that she was not always candid. The connective remained unsubstantiated.

The fourth and final connective between Kauffmann, Sutherland, and James Earl Ray was the American Party campaign of Alabama Governor George C. Wallace for the Presidency in the late months of 1967 and early months of 1968. Both Sutherland and Kauffman supported the party, also known as the American Independent Party. In fact, Floyd Kitchen, an organizer for the American Party in St. Louis in 1968 and Missouri State chairman of the American Independent Party, indicated to the committee in a sworn statement that his AIP salary of $600 a month was paid by Sutherland.[276] Additionally, committee interviews with persons who were officials of the American Party in 1968, revealed that Sutherland was active at both the local and national levels of the party and was a candidate for Presidential elector.[277]

Former associates of Sutherland reported that his strong support of the American Party was based in large degree on the party's conservative position on civil rights. The committee also learned that considerable support for the American Party campaign was drawn from the White Citizens Council in St. Louis, an organization dedicated to racial separation. As has been noted, Sutherland was a member of the council.

John Ray was apparently active in the 1968 American Party campaign. His support for Wallace was reflected in an article in the St. Louis Post-Dispatch:

John Ray said he last saw his brother at the prison. "He and I are both strong supporters of George C. Wallace * * * so maybe we talked about him a little."[278]

Jerry Ray's attitude toward Governor Wallace was characterized by Edward Fields, secretary of the National States Rights Party and editor of The Thunderbolt, who said that Jerry "is very strongly for George Wallace and always has been a strong Wallace supporter."[279]

John Ray's Grapevine Tavern was a distribution point for American Party campaign literature, as the committee's investigation developed from sources including his brother, Jerry.[280] Further, John helped transport prospective party registrants to the registration office.[281] During the same general period, evidence before the committee indicated, James Earl Ray was engaging in AIP campaign activities in California.[65] These activities by John and James Earl Ray were considered significant by the committee in that they indicated a common pursuit strongly suggesting a link between the brothers that neither was willing to admit. Further, James' persistent denials of his AIP activity, despite clear and convincing evidence to the contrary,[66] necessarily raised the additional question: What, beyond the activity itself, was he trying to conceal? Ray's concern about his AIP activities was best reflected in his curious sensitivity about one of the proposed "stipulations of fact" that he was asked to sign as part of the proceedings leading to his guilty plea in March 1969.[282] The stipulation involved an admission that he had taken three California residents to register for Wallace. Ray, through his attorney, Percy Foreman, deleted the reference to Wallace headquarters. No other stipulations in the 56-paragraph document were altered.[67]

John Ray's interest in AIP politics also seemed out of character, since he apparently had never evidenced it before 1967 or 1968 and since, as a convicted felon, he was not able to vote. For this reason, and because of demonstrated ties between both Sutherland and Kauffmann and the AIP, the committee's investigation was focused on this connection.

It was determined that a significant amount of AIP campaign activity occurred in the neighborhood of the Grapevine Tavern. For example, Viola Anderson, who lived only one block from the Grapevine Tavern,[283] was active in both the St. Louis Citizens Council and the American Party.[284] In fact, her residence was a neighborhood campaign headquarters in the south St. Louis area and a likely place for John Ray to have acquired his Wallace campaign paraphernalia.[68]

[65]James was also involved in transporting registrants to a local AIP headquarters.
[66]Three witnesses—Charles Stein, Rita Stein, and Marie Martin—gave sworn statements to the committee concerning Ray's AIP activities.
[67]Ray told the committee that he objected to other stipulations and that his attorney, Percy Foreman, refused to make the requested changes. (James Earl Ray testimony, Aug. 18, 1978, III, HSCA–MLK hearings. 19–20). In light of the fact that Ray's initials, as well as Foreman's, appear on each page of the draft stipulations, (MLK exhibit F–79, III, HSCA–MLK hearings, 46) the committee was unwilling to accept this explanation.
[68]Though Mrs. Anderson died in 1977, her widower, Stanley Anderson, confirmed her party activities. Anderson further acknowledged to committee investigators that his late wife had met Sutherland, but stated she was not close to him. Although Anderson said he could not remember

484

The committee also closely examined Glen Shrum, since deceased, a close friend of Viola Anderson and one who was instrumental in American Party organization in the Third Congressional District, the district in which John Ray's tavern was located. Shrum was described to the committee as an activist member of radical right-wing organizations, such as John Birch Society and the Minutemen. Further, he reportedly attended meetings of the National States Rights Party, and he may have been in contact with the Ku Klux Klan.[286] His friends also indicated to the committee that he held strong opinions on civil rights, leading him to be openly critical of Federal legislation and court actions dealing with equality for Blacks.[287]

The committee contacted several American Party and White Citizens' Council members, who said that several informal meetings were held in the neighborhood in which Ray's tavern was located during the 1968 campaign. Reportedly, Shrum attended many of them.[288] In addition, Shrum was apparently at least an occasional patron of the Grapevine Tavern, raising the realistic likelihood of a contact with John Ray.[289]

Ultimately, however, the committee's investigation of the St. Louis conspiracy proved frustrating. Only circumstantial evidence was developed. Direct evidence that would connect the conspiracy in St. Louis to assassination was not obtained. Several of the principals and possible suspects were, of course, no longer living, and others were clearly not inclined to be truthful with the committee, even when faced with the possibility of perjury or contempt prosecutions. Nevertheless, in light of the several alternate routes established by the evidence through which information of the offer could have reached James Earl Ray, the committee concluded it was likely that he was aware of the existence of the St. Louis conspiracy.[69]

---

ever meeting John Ray, he volunteered that he and his wife and another party worker visited the Grapevine on at least one occasion. Finally, Anderson denied ever hearing of an offer to assassinate Dr. King, but he indicated, after repeating questioning, that conversations critical of Dr. King's activities occurred frequently at meetings he and his wife attended prior to the assassination. [285] During his public appearance before the committee, John Ray denied knowing either Viola Anderson or her husband, and he stated that he attended no American Party meetings at their residence. (John Ray testimony, VIII HSCA—MLK hearings, 591–592).

[69]John Ray denied under oath knowing John Sutherland, John Kauffmann, or Russell Byers, and he stated that he never heard or participated in conversations at the Grapevine of an offer to fund the assassination of Dr. King. [290]

The committee concluded that there was a likelihood of conspiracy in the assassination of Dr. King. To summarize, several findings were central to the committee's conspiracy and conclusion. First, James Earl Ray was the assassin of Dr. King, and Raoul, as described by Ray, did not exist. In reaching these conclusions, the committee rejected the possibility that James Earl Ray was an unwitting "fall guy" manipulated by others. The committee found, rather, that Ray acted with full knowledge of what he was doing in the murder of Dr. King.

Second, an analysis of Ray's conduct before the assassination provided compelling indications of conspiracy. Ray was not, in fact, a man without significant associations. His financing, in all likelihood supplied by the Alton bank robbery in July 1967, was strong evidence of significant criminal associations with his brothers during the preassassination period. Further, his campaign activities in California, viewed against the background of his 1967–68 fugitive status, his apolitical nature and his consistent refusal to admit the activities, also strongly suggested involvement with others. Ray's trip to New Orleans, too, was significant. The abrupt nature of his departure from Los Angeles, the risks he took on the road, his receipt of money during the visit and the speedy termination of his mission all indicated Ray's involvement with others in an important meeting with a preplanned purpose.

Third, the analysis of Ray's motive was crucial to the conspiracy conclusion. After examining Ray's behavior, his character and his racial attitudes, the committee found it could not concur with any of the accepted explanations for Ray as a lone assassin. Historically, Ray was a financially motivated criminal. While unsympathetic to the civil rights movement, he did not manifest the type of virulent racism that might have motivated the assassination in the absence of other factors. While the committee recognized the presence of other possible motives—racism or psychological needs—it concluded that the expectation of financial gain was Ray's primary motivation. The committee's finding on motive, therefore, carried conspiratorial implications.

Just as significant in the committee's ultimate conclusions on conspiracy was the evidence bearing on the complicity of the brothers, John and Jerry Ray. Three factors, negative in character, raised the possibility of the involvement of one or both brothers.

First, despite an exhaustive and far-reaching field investigation, neither the committee nor previous investigators were able to identify significant associates of the assassin other than his brothers. The possibility of their involvement in the assassination was necessarily increased by the absence of alternatives.

Second, despite an offer of assistance from the Justice Department, Ray refused to provide credible evidence on the subject of conspiracy. His self-sacrificial posture was possibly explained as an effort to protect his brothers.

Third, the Ray brothers consistently attempted to conceal the true scope of their preassassination contact with each other. John and James denied any contact at all. This conduct could be explained by a sense of family loyalty. Nevertheless, it also raised the possibility that preassassination contact, if revealed, would lead to implication in a conspiracy.

Additional positive factors ultimately convinced the committee of the likelihood of the involvement of one or both brothers in the assassination. James was, of course, a fugitive from Missouri State Penitentiary. Automatically, this should have led him to limit the duration of meetings with his brothers. Nevertheless, substantial contact in a variety of forms apparently persisted throughout the preassassination period. Much of this contact, moreover, was criminal in nature. Both John and Jerry met with and assisted James during the months immediately following his escape from Missouri State Penitentiary. In addition, John clearly had foreknowledge of the escape plans and provided James with an alias and social security number for immediate use. More significantly, the committee found it highly likely that John and James robbed the Bank of Alton in Alton, Ill., on July 13, 1967. Jerry knew of the robbery and assisted in distributing the proceeds to James throughout his fugitive travels. There was evidence of the receipt of money by James from a brother as late as February 1968, only weeks before the assassination. Further, the committee concluded that James' trip to New Orleans in December 1967 could best be understood as a meeting with one or both of his brothers, with circumstantial evidence suggesting it was Jerry Ray. The purpose of that meeting, beyond the transfer of funds, could not be firmly established, but its sinister significance was clear. Finally, there was strong circumstantial evidence of the involvement of a brother in a consulting capacity during

487

Ray's purchase of the murder weapon itself, although the evidence was insufficient to determine the identity of the brother or the nature of the contact.

Nevertheless, the evidence with respect to Ray and his brothers contained one serious flaw: by itself, it provided no convincing explanation for their combination in a plot on Dr. King's life. The committee did receive strong evidence of pronounced racist attitudes in both John and Jerry. Yet, the committee believed it unlikely that James or his brothers would have killed Dr. King solely for racial reasons. The development of additional evidence on a credible St. Louis-based plot, therefore, became a crucial element in the committee's conspiracy analysis.

The committee found that there was substantial evidence to establish the existence of a St. Louis-based conspiracy to finance the assassination of Dr. King. A serious effort to solicit Russell Byers was made by John Sutherland and John Kauffmann in late 1966 or early 1967, apparently on behalf of a wider authority. In addition, knowledge of Kauffman's role in the effort to broker the assassination was circulated and frequently mentioned at his Bluff Acres Motel in 1967. According to witness A, it was perceived as a standing offer. The committee frankly acknowledged that it was unable to uncover a direct link between the principals of the St. Louis conspiracy and James Earl Ray or his brothers. There was no direct evidence that the Sutherland offer was accepted by Ray, or a representative, prior to the assassination. In addition, despite an intensive effort, no evidence was found of a payoff to Ray or a representative either before or after the assassination.

Despite this, the committee believed that there was a likelihood that word of the standing offer on Dr. King's life reached James Earl Ray prior to the assassination. This conclusion was based on several considerations. John was a permanent resident of St. Louis from October 1966 forward. Ray himself was in the St. Louis area on at least two occasions during his early fugitive period—once immediately after his escape, and again in July 1967 when he participated in the robbery of the Bank of Alton. It was possible that either John or James or both received word of the standing offer through criminal associates in the St. Louis area. It was more likely, however, that John Ray heard of the offer through AIP campaign activities in and around the Grapevine Tavern. George Wallace's Presidential bid stirred up intense support in the Grapevine's neighborhood—the south St. Louis area. Race relations and the civil rights movement became subjects of daily, and increasingly polarized, debate. At the same time, Dr. King's efforts in the civil rights movement were expanding to encompass opposition to the Vietnam war and support for the economically oppressed—to culminate in a Poor People's Campaign in Washington. The committee found it reasonable to believe that with an increase in the intensity of the St. Louis AIP campaign effort, and the heightened visibility of Dr. King, discussion of the Sutherland offer could well have come to James Earl Ray's attention. This possibility was only strengthened by Sutherland's heavy involvement in the AIP effort in St. Louis. Kauffmann also did significant work with Sutherland on behalf of the party. In addition, the committee found at least two individuals who knew Sutherland, were active in the AIP campaign, and who had been in the Grapevine Tavern. Finally, John Ray's tavern was used as a local distribution point for AIP campaign literature and paraphernalia. It was in these campaign activities that the committee found the most likely connective between James Earl Ray and the St. Louis conspiracy. In sum, the committee believed that the weight of the evidence bearing on James and his brothers, taken in combination with the evidence of the St. Louis-based conspiracy, established the likelihood of a conspiracy in the death of Dr. King.

Because of a failure of the evidence, the committee's ultimate conclusion must, however, be phrased in terms of alternatives. The committee believed that the St. Louis conspiracy provided an explanation for the involvement of Ray and one or both brothers in the assassination. The manner of their involvement could have taken one of two forms. James Earl Ray may simply have been aware of the offer and acted with a general expectation of payment after the assassination; or he may have acted, not only with an awareness of the offer, but also after reaching a specific agreement, either directly or through one or both brothers, with Kauffmann or Sutherland. The legal consequences of the alternative possibilities are, of course, different. Without a specific agreement with the Sutherland group, the conspiracy that eventuated in Dr. King's death would extend only to Ray and his brother(s); with a specific agreement, the conspiracy would also encompass Sutherland and his group. In the absence of additional evidence, the committee could not make a more definite statement. The committee believed, nevertheless, that the evidence provided the likely outlines of conspiracy in the assassination of Dr. King.

It is unfortunate that this information was not developed in 1968, when it could have been pursued by law enforcement agencies equipped with tools not available to the committee and at a time when the principals were still alive and witnesses' memories were more precise.[70] It is a matter on which reasonable people may legitimately differ, but the committee believed that the conspiracy that eventuated in Dr. King's death in 1968 could have been brought to justice in 1968.

---

[70]John Kauffmann was still alive in 1978 when the information of the St. Louis conspiracy first came to the attention of the FBI.

C. The Committee Believes, on the Basis of the Evidence Available to It, That No Private Organizations or Individuals, Other Than Those Discussed Under Section B, Were Involved in the Assassination of Dr. King

Since the assassination of Dr. Martin Luther King, Jr., numerous conspiracy allegations have been advanced by authors, independent investigators, attorneys for James Earl Ray and Ray himself. The committee examined these as well as others that were uncovered during a review of agency files or were otherwise brought to the committee's attention during the course of its investigation. Some of the leads merited exhaustive investigation. All were pursued until it was determined to the satisfaction of the committee that there was no link to the King assassination.

1. RIGHT WING, EXTREMIST ORGANIZATIONS

The committee investigated right wing, segregationist, extremist groups and individuals to find out if their outspoken opposition to Dr. King and their demonstrated propensity for violence might have resulted in their involvement in the assassination. FBI files on the Minutemen, Ku Klux Klan, and other extremist organizations were examined, and while the committee found no evidence that these organizations had anything to do with the assassination, the committee did discover conspiracy allegations that warranted additional field investigation beyond that performed in the original investigation.

(a) The Minutemen[1]

A review of FBI files on the Minutemen revealed a possible plot against Dr. King's life that had received some

---

[1] The Minutemen organization was fervently anti-Communist. In 1968, it believed that leftist infiltration of the Government had progressed to the extent that America could no longer be saved by the traditional political process. Members were trained in guerrilla warfare techniques. Dr. King was viewed by the Minutemen as a Communist and an enemy of the American people.

The committee found numerical estimates of Minutemen membership in 1968 to be unreliable.

attention by law enforcement officials shortly before Dr. King's death. On January 15, 1968, Vincent DePalma, a close associate of Robert B. DePugh, the founder of the Minutemen, told a Denver agent of the Bureau of Alcohol, Tobacco and Firearms (ATF) that he had defected from the Minutemen and wished to supply information.[1] DePalma revealed that there were 19 Minutemen strike teams across the United States assigned to assassinate several prominent persons, including Dr. King, in the event DePugh was ever imprisoned.[2] According to DePalma, the Minutemen also planned to incite race riots in the summer of 1968.[3]

After it received this information from the ATF, the FBI attempted unsuccessfully to locate DePalma, who had said he was moving to Oregon.[4] As for DePugh, he disappeared in February 1968 following his indictment by a Federal grand jury in Seattle, Wash., for conspiracy to commit bank robbery. The FBI made no further attempts to investigate the threat until shortly after Dr. King's assassination, when one of DePalma's Minutemen associates, Edward Baumgardner, told a reporter that the artist's drawing of the suspected assassin resembled DePalma.[5] Baumgardner was interviewed several times by the FBI. He said that he and DePalma were members of a Minutemen strike team that had been formed at a training camp in Colorado during the summer of 1967. Baumgardner repeated the information that DePalma had provided ATF and said DePalma had been assigned the code name Willard. (James Earl Ray used the alias John Willard when renting a room in a roominghouse in Memphis on April 4, 1968.)[6]

DePalma was located by the FBI several days after Dr. King was killed. He again detailed information on the Minutemen strike teams that had targeted Dr. King and on Minutemen plans to precipitate race riots in the summer of 1968 as a means of facilitating a takeover of the Government.

Work records showed that DePalma was in Newport, R.I., on April 4, 1968. Information he furnished during 3 days of interviews was verified by several FBI offices.[7] DePugh and his chief associate in the Minutemen, Walter Peyson, remained fugitives until their capture in July 1969. There was nothing in the FBI files to reflect they were ever interviewed regarding possible involvement of the Minutemen in the assassination of Dr. King.

The committee found that the DePalma lead had not been fully investigated by the FBI, so it examined it anew. It found that DePalma had been murdered in an unsolved gangland slaying in January 1978 in Los Angeles.[8] The committee did locate and interview four persons who had attended the Colorado training camp in the summer of 1967. Both Jerry Brooks,[9] an associate of DePugh's for at least 12 years, and Mary Tollerton,[10] DePugh's secretary until late 1967, denied knowing of any plot to kill Dr. King. Although Brooks told of other assassination plots by the Minutemen and of intelligence files on Dr. King and other "subversives," Tollerton claimed that these activities were not serious. Tollerton added that DePugh had trouble keeping the organization together in 1968 while avoiding capture, so he could not have been involved in Dr. King's assassination. Walter Peyson[11] and Robert DePugh,[12] brought to Washington under subpoena, testified under oath that they were not involved in any plot to kill Dr. King. They insisted that all discussions of assassination plots and strike teams were mere paper propaganda. [13] Both Peyson and DePugh also explained that because DePalma and Baumgardner were believed to be infiltrators, they were often fed false information.[14]

As a final investigative step, the committee compiled a list of all individuals associated with the Minutemen in the cities visited by James Earl Ray following his escape in April 1967 from Missouri State Penitentiary. This list was cross-checked against a list of known or possible Ray associates. The results were negative.

Based on the testimony it heard, interviews with the assistant U.S. attorney who prosecuted DePugh and Peyson in 1966 and ATF agents who had encountered DePugh, extensive file reviews, and the Ray associates name check, the committee concluded there was insufficient evidence to indicate that the Minutemen were involved in Dr. King's death.

(b) *Klan organizations*

A review of extensive FBI files on a number of Ku Klux Klan organizations revealed approximately 25 Klan-related leads to potential conspiracies in the assassination of Dr. King. Four of them warranted the attention of the committee.

1. Information from a Mobile, Ala., FBI report indi-

cated an informant had told the Bureau that Sidney Barnes[2] and several others had gone to Birmingham, Ala., in the fall of 1963 to kill Dr. King.[15] The FBI also learned that a secret meeting had been held in Birmingham before the September 15, 1963, bombing of a Birmingham church that left four young Black girls dead. Barnes, William Potter Gale, Noah Jefferson Carden and John C. Crommelin attended this meeting.[16]

The FBI had attempted to determine the whereabouts of the participants in the 1963 Birmingham meeting during the week following Dr. King's assassination.[17] The Bureau files reflected that the FBI ended its investigation of Barnes after it found no indication he was away from his home before or after the assassination.[18]

When the committee approached Barnes for an interview, he refused to cooperate.[19] The committee, however, extensively interviewed an individual who was deeply involved in racial violence in the South in the mid-1960's and who was willing to provide the committee with detailed information. This person, who was considered very reliable by the committee, said he had met Barnes in 1963. He characterized Barnes as an independent right winger who, despite deep-seated racial animosity, had never been involved in violence. This source also told the committee he had been in contact with Barnes and Noah Jefferson Carden during March and April 1968, and he recalled no indications of their participation in a conspiracy to kill Dr. King.[20]

Additional interviews[21] and file reviews by the committee failed to reveal evidence that would indicate Barnes was in any way involved in Dr. King's death.

2. In an interview with an agent of the Dallas FBI field office on April 22, 1968, Myrtis Ruth Hendricks, accompanied by Thomas McGee, maintained she had overheard discussions of a conspiracy to kill Dr. King.[22] Hendricks said that while working as a waitress at John's Restaurant in Laurel, Miss., on April 2, 1968, she heard the owner, Deavours Nix, say he "had gotten a call on King." Nix was then head of intelligence and the grand director of the Klan Bureau of Investigation for the White Knights of Ku Klux Klan of Mississippi (WKKKKOM), the most

---

[2] An extensive committee investigation resulted in no evidence of a direct link between Barnes and any specific Klan organizations. He did have close associates in Klan organizations, however, including the White Knights of the Ku Klux Klan in Mississippi.

violent Klan organization during 1967 and 1968. Hendricks said that on April 3, 1968, she saw in Nix's office a rifle with a telescopic sight in a case, which two men put in a long box in the back of a 1964 maroon Dodge. Hendricks alleged that on the following day, Nix received a phone call announcing Dr. King's death before the news was broadcast on the radio. Hendricks left Laurel shortly after Dr. King's death to join her boyfriend, Thomas McGee, in Texas.[3]

The Bureau had independently confirmed that John's Restaurant was a gathering place for known Klan members and that members had been there on April 3 and 4, 1968. Nevertheless, it found no corroboration of the Hendricks rifle story. The committee's review of FBI files concerning the White Knights' activities uncovered informant information similar to the Hendricks allegation. In addition, statements attributed to Samuel H. Bowers, the imperial wizard of the WKKKKOM, in John's Restaurant on April 5, 1968, raised the possibility of his involvement in the assassination.[23] As a result of this information and an indication that it was not developed further in the FBI investigation, the committee pursued the lead.

Myrtis Hendricks denied the substance of her allegation when contacted by the committee.[24] While admitting that she had worked for Nix, she said she was afraid of her former boyfriend, Thomas McGee, but refused to elaborate further. The committee's attempt to interview FBI informants who had furnished relevant information was unsuccessful.[25] The informants were either unavailable or uncooperative.[26] Although the committee initially issued subpoenas to Nix, Bowers and McGee, time and cost constraints prevented their appearance in executive session. [27]

The committee was, however, able to question at length a former member of the White Knights who had participated in racial violence in the 1960's. This witness, who was considered reliable and well-informed on the activities of the White Knights, could provide no information to indicate that Bowers or any other member of the White Knights was involved in Dr. King's death. Further, he re-

_____
[3]The committee noted that Laurel, Miss., the scene of these alleged activities, lies between New Orleans and Birmingham. James Earl Ray traveled between these two cities in March 1968.

marked that it would not have been characteristic for members of the White Knights to leave Mississippi and go to an unfamiliar locale to commit the assassination.

The committee concluded that in light of Hendricks' refusal to repeat her original allegation and the absence of evidence of a connection with James Earl Ray, the lead be discounted.

3. On June 15, 1968, 1 week after Ray's arrest, a long-distance telephone operator in Racine, Wis., contacted the FBI with information she believed pertinent to the King assassination. She said she had placed calls for an unknown male caller on June 11, 1968, to three numbers in North Carolina.[28] She added that in one call she overheard a man who identified himself as "Robert" ask for his money so he could leave the country immediately.[29] In a separate call, "Robert" referred to the Klan as the source of this money and said he feared that Ray would "spill his guts" when he got back in the country.[30]

The Bureau identified the subscribers to the three North Carolina telephone numbers as a used car dealer and his two brothers.[31] Local law enforcement officials told the Bureau that a third brother was involved with stolen cars and bad checks.[32] When interviewed by the Bureau, the two brothers had denied any knowledge of the telephone calls or their brother's activities.[33] The FBI found no connection between the subscribers to the numbers and any Klan organizations. No further attempts to pursue this lead were initiated by the Bureau.

The committee decided to examine this allegation further, despite the FBI's conclusions in 1968. An attempt to locate the source of the information through the Wisconsin Telephone Co. revealed that the supposed operator had never been employed by that company. Based on this information, the committee concluded that the lead was not based on credible evidence and not worthy of further investigation.

4. The most significant Klan-related lead involved informant information that implied a financial relationship between Arthur Hanes, Sr., James Earl Ray's attorney in 1968, and Robert Shelton, Imperial Wizard of the United Klans of America (UKA). This information indicated Shelton's Klan organization had contributed to Ray's defense through his attorney and, further, that Shelton had made arrangements with Hanes to review the jury list for Ray's trial in order to identify potentially sympathetic ju-

rors. While neither of these acts were illegal, cooperation between the leader of the UKA and Ray's attorney, if proven, would have raised the possibility of preassassination agreement between the UKA and Ray, especially in light of Ray's choice of Hanes as his attorney following his arrest.

In January 1978, George Wilson,[34] a former midwestern leader of the UKA, told the committee that the UKA had contributed $10,000 to Hanes when he was representing Ray, under the pretense of paying for Hanes' legal representation of a group of North Carolina Klansmen. [35] Wilson said this payment was mentioned in a speech allegedly made at a Klan meeting by Furman Dean Williams, Grand Dragon of the South Carolina UKA. The statement was made in the presence of other persons whom Wilson also named.

Two documents in the FBI file covering the murder of Dr. King indicated that two sources independently corroborated some of Wilson's information.

Source A alleged that Shelton advised that in August 1968 the defense was in need of money for Ray's defense. Shelton inquiry whether Klan members would be willing to donate money for Ray's defense. Shelton added that he intended to review the jury list in Ray's case when it was available.[36]

Source B learned that a UKA board meeting was held in 1969, and attended by Hanes and Melvin Sexton, the UKA secretary who handled Klan finances,[4] among others. The meeting was convened to discuss the Klan's national defense fund, a fund to assist members arrested while participating in Klan activities. Hanes' defense of klansmen in North Carolina for $12,500 was specifically mentioned. After Hanes left the meeting, Sexton allegedly commented on the King assassination and said he had a piece of paper for Hanes pertaining to the Ray case.[37]

The committee's file review also revealed documentation of a contact between Shelton and Hanes in June and August 1968 relating to legal assistance of Shelton by Hanes. The document did not, however, specifically refer to Hanes' representation of Ray.[38] The committee was unable to locate any FBI documents indicating that the

[4]The Imperial Board of the UKA consisted of the national officers of the Klan. Robert Shelton, who had begun serving a sentence for contempt of Congress in February 1969, was absent from the meeting. The contempt conviction resulted from Shelton's refusal to testify before the House Un-American Activities Committee.

Bureau attempted to interview Hanes, Shelton, Sexton or other principals concerning cooperation between the Klan and Hanes during Ray's trial.

The committee's initial interest in Ray's choice of Hanes as his first attorney following his June 1968 arrest, combined with the FBI informant material, led to an extensive investigation by the committee to ascertain the nature of the Hanes-Shelton relationship.[39] First, George Wilson was interviewed at length.[40] Then, sources A and B were contacted by the FBI and, after giving consent, were interviewed by the committee. The committee found no indication of a motive to lie on the part of Wilson or either of the informants. Further, no financial remuneration was offered in return for information, and there was no sign of a personal vendetta against Hanes, Shelton, or Sexton.

In addition, Shelton,[41] Sexton,[42] Hanes,[43] Williams,[44] and James Robertson Jones,[45] Grand Dragon for North Carolina in 1967 and 1968, testified before the committee in executive session. Williams and Jones stated under oath that they knew nothing of an understanding or agreement between Hanes and Shelton or Sexton for funding or any other assistance for Ray's defense.[46] Hanes, Shelton and Sexton vigorously denied ever considering such an arrangement.[47]

The committee also uncovered discrepancies between the testimony of Hanes and that of Shelton and Sexton. For example, Hanes and Sexton disagreed substantially regarding the duration of their friendship and whether Hanes helped establish the Klan's national defense fund.[48] Further, the Klansmen and Hanes attempted to minimize their association, specifically denying meetings between July 1968 and July 1969 that had been reported to the FBI. While these contacts were important in establishing the credibility of the witnesses, they did not bear specifically on Dr. King's assassination and, therefore, were not pursued further. The discrepancies between the testimony of Hanes and Sexton regarding the duration of their friendship and whether Hanes took part in establishing the national defense fund could have been explained by the lapse of time or by an attempt by Hanes to minimize his relationship with Sexton and the legal work he did for him.

While the committee was unable ultimately to resolve all conflicts in the evidence, it found no indications of an agreement between the UKA and James Earl Ray prior to

Dr. King's assassination. The committee concluded that there was no evidence that Ray and members of the United Klans of America entered into a conspiracy to assassinate Dr. King.

(c) *J. B. Stoner*

J. B. Stoner, a Georgia attorney and virulent segregationist, had represented numerous defendants in racially motivated crimes against Blacks.[49] A founder and leader of the frantically anti-Black and anti-Semitic National States Rights Party,[50] Stoner frequently excoriated Dr. Martin Luther King, Jr., and his campaign for racial integration in the South.[5] After Dr. King's assassination, the FBI investigated Stoner's activities on April 4, 1968. [52] Once the FBI established that Stoner had been speaking at an NSRP rally in Meridian, Miss., on that day, it eliminated him as a suspect in Dr. King's murder.[53]

Stoner became James Earl Ray's attorney in 1969,[54] and he represented John L. Ray[55] and Jerry W. Ray[56] in separate criminal matters in 1970. In addition, Jerry Ray was employed as a bodyguard for Stoner in 1969. Based on Stoner's blatant racism and his relationship with the three Ray brothers, the committee decided further to investigate his possible involvement in the assassination.

Th committee's review of FBI files on Stoner revealed that, in the late 1950's, Stoner was a suspect in a series of bombings directed against Black and Jewish targets throughout the South.[57] Although no charges and been brought at the time, Stoner was under indictment in 1978 for the 1958 bombing of a Birmingham church.[58] An undercover Birmingham police officer who took part in the bombing investigation said Stoner had a proven propensity for violence.[59] In testimony before the committee, Dr. Edward R. Fields, a close friend of Stoner and a leader of the NSRP, provided the committee with the names of other segregationists with violent backgrounds whom Stoner knew.[60] In addition, Stoner, Dr. Fields, and several codefendants were indicted in 1963 for obstruction of justice in connection with their efforts to thwart desegregation efforts in Birmingham, Ala.[61] The

[5]Stoner participated in a July 26, 1964, Klan rally at which Dr. King was burned in effigy.[51] He was also quoted in the NSRP newspaper, Thunderbolt, with the following reaction to Dr. King's death: "He has been a good nigger now since 6 or 7 o'clock." (MLK exhibit F–593. VII. HSCA–MLK Hearings, p. 331.)

case was dismissed in 1964 for deficiences in the wording of the complaint.[62]

Stoner has been extremely active politically. In 1964, he was a candidate for Vice President of the United States on the NSRP ticket.[63] He ran unsuccessful campaigns for Governor of Georgia in 1970,[64] for Senator from Georgia in 1972[65] and for Governor of Georgia in 1978.[66]

The first apparent contact between Stoner and members of the Ray family occurred following James Earl Ray's apprehension in London on June 8, 1968.[67] Although it has been suggested that Stoner and Ray or other members of the family had contact before the assassination, [68][6] the committee found no evidence of such an association.[70] Ray maintained that he first heard of Stoner when Stoner's Patriotic Legal Fund contacted him in London with an offer to finance his defense.[71] Ray refused the offer at the time.[72] Stoner apparently first met with Ray in late 1968 and discussed a civil suit against Time Inc. to stop pretrial publicity.[73] Stoner did not represent Ray, however, until after his March 10, 1969, guilty plea to the murder of Dr. King. Ray retained Stoner as cocounsel in the motion for a new trial.[74]

Stoner had indicated publicly that he had information about a conspiracy to assassinate Dr. King,[75] but when he testified before the committee, he denied any knowledge of an assassination plot.[76] Further, when asked specific questions relating to James Earl Ray and the assassination, Stoner declined to answer, as was his duty on the basis of the attorney-client privilege.[77] (At the time of Stoner's testimony, Ray had executed waivers of attorney-client privilege for all of his previous attorneys except Arthur Hanes, Jr., and Stoner.[78] Ray later executed a waiver for Hanes[79] but refused to waive his privilege for Stoner.)

For several reasons—his relationship with the three Ray brothers, his racist views, his demonstrated propensity for violence, as well as his recalcitrant behavior before the committee—led to a suspicion that Stoner might have had information about the assassination that he would not divulge. The committee found no evidence, however, that

---

[6]Harry Avery, commissioner of corrections for the State of Tennessee in March 1969, claimed that following Ray's guilty plea, Jerry Ray told him that Stoner had been an attorney for Jerry and James 2 years before the assassination. [70] The committee was unable to find evidence to support this allegation.

Stoner in fact participated in the plot to assassinate Dr. King.

(d) William Hugh Morris

J. B. Stoner told the committee in 1978 that William Hugh Morris offered him $25,000 in the late 1950's to locate a skilled marksman to assassinate Dr. King.[80] Stoner, who had contended repeatedly that the FBI was responsible for Dr. King's death, said he believed Morris was a Bureau informant.[81] Stoner said he told Morris that for $5,000 in advance, he would kill Dr. King with a bomb,[82] but Morris explained that the persons financing the assassination wanted it done with a rifle.[83] Stoner contended that he asked for the $5,000 up front to insure his receipt of the money beforehand, although he had no intention of carrying out the assassination.[84] Stoner believed the offer was part of an FBI plot to entrap him.[85]

Stoner testified before the committee that there were no witnesses to his discussion with Morris, but, he said, Morris had approached Asa Carter, a Stoner associate, with the same offer.[86]. Carter told the committee that he had been active in white supremacist groups in the 1950's and 1960's, but he denied that he had been offered a contract to kill Dr. King.[87] Carter added, however, that threats on Dr. King's life were commonplace in the 1960's.[88]

In an attempt to resolve the Stoner allegation, the committee reviewed FBI files concerning Morris and questioned him extensively in interviews and under oath. The committee learned that the elderly Morris had been actively involved in Klan organizations most of his adult life and, in 1978, was the Imperial Wizard and Emperor of the Federated Knights of Ku Klux Klan, an organization with over 1,000 members in at least 7 States.[89] Morris' only known criminal conviction had occurred in 1949 when he was charged with contempt of court for refusing to provide a Jefferson County, Ala., grand jury with a list of the Alabama members of the Federated Knights of Ku Klux Klan.

In executive session testimony before the committee, Morris vehemently denied ever engaging in a conversation about a bounty on Dr. King's life with Stoner, Carter, or anyone else.[90] Morris stressed that he was never involved in violence or advocated its use in effectuating the Klan's principles.[91] Nevertheless, in its review of the FBI files concerning Morris, the committee found several FBI intelligence reports, based on informant information, that indicated Morris, at an October 1961 Klan meeting, had said southern racial problems could be eliminated by the murder of Dr. King.[92] Morris then apparently boasted that he had a New Orleans underworld associate who would kill anyone for a price.[93] Under oath, Morris denied making these statements.[94]

For a brief period in the 1960's, while Morris was active in the Klan, he also served as an informant to Federal, State and local law enforcement officials.[95] Although Morris readily admitted this activity, he explained that he had never been paid and that he had never provided original information to any law enforcement agency. [96] Rather, Morris contended that he had been merely a conduit between agencies for information which the FBI, the Alabama attorney general and the Birmingham police obtained from their own independent sources.[97] He claimed his underlying objective in acting as an informant was to ascertain the identities of actual informers in the Klan organizations.[98]

Morris said he believed that Stoner had lodged the allegation to discredit him.[99] He explained that he and an undercover Birmingham police detective had been regarded by the Alabama attorney general's office as key witnesses against Stoner in the 1958 bombing of the Bethel Baptist Church in Birmingham.[100]

The committee uncovered no evidence to support Stoner's allegation against Morris and concluded that Morris was not involved in the assassination of Dr. King.

2. CONSPIRACY ALLEGATIONS: MEMPHIS

(a) Citizen's band radio broadcast

At approximately 6:36 p.m. on April 4, 1968, an unidentified citizen's band radio operator in Memphis was heard broadcasting over channel 17.[101] He stated he was pursuing a white Mustang driven by the killer of Dr. King. The CB operator, contrary to lawful radio procedure, never identified himself. He announced that he was chasing the white Mustang east on Summer Avenue from Parkway Street at a high rate of speed and requested a land line to communicate to the police department.[102] The broadcast was made about 33 minutes after the first announcement over police radio that Dr. King had been shot.

A Memphis CB operator, William Herbert Austein, among others, heard the original broadcast. As he was driving through the intersection of Jackson Avenue and Hollywood Street, Austein halted a Memphis police cruiser driven by Lt. Rufus Bradshaw [103] Austein relayed information received from the unknown CB operator to the police,[104] and for the remainder of the broadcast, Austein received transmissions over the CB unit in his automobile, and they were relayed by Bradshaw to Memphis police headquarters.[115]

Shortly after 6:36 p.m., in response to a request from Austein, the unidentified operator said that he was pursuing the Mustang east on Summer Avenue from Highland Street.[106] In subsequent transmissions, the operator told Austein he was accompanied by two white males in a blue Pontiac, and they were chasing the Mustang east on Summer Avenue from Waring. They then followed the Mustang north on Mendenhall Road from Summer Avenue. At approximately 6:41 p.m., the chase proceeded north on Jackson Avenue toward Raleigh, a suburb northeast of Memphis, according to the broadcast.[107] At approximately 6:44 p.m., the operator reported that he had just chased the white Mustang through a red light at the intersection of Jackson and Stage Roads at 95 miles per hour.[108]

At this point, Memphis police began to suspect that the broadcast was a hoax.[109] Two units of the Shelby County Sheriff's Department, stationed at an intersection at the very moment the Mustang and Pontiac were supposed to have passed through, informed the dispatcher they had seen no one.[110]

At approximately 6:45 p.m., the unidentified operator broadcast his position as going out Austin Peay Highway and said the occupant of the Mustang was shooting at him. [111] In the CB operator's final broadcast at approximately 6:48 p.m., he said he was approaching Millington Road heading to a naval base from Austin Peay Highway.[112]

In its subsequent investigation of this CB broadcast, the Memphis Police Department concluded it had been a hoax

503

and that the chase had never occurred.[113] The FBI, relying on the field investigation by the Memphis police, concurred.[114]

The committee also concluded that a chase as described in the mysterious postassassination CB broadcast never occurred and that the broadcast was in fact a hoax. The committee noted first that at approximately 6:44 p.m., the moment the chase was said to have sped through the intersection of Stage and Jackson Roads at 95 miles per hour, officers in two patrol cars from the Shelby County Sheriff's Department, stationed at the intersection, saw nothing unusual.[115]

Further, the committee's examination of a map of the route revealed that the chase covered about 10.5 miles from the first transmission at approximately 6:36 p.m. to the transmission at approximately 6:44 p.m. that described the blue Pontiac passing through the intersection of Jackson and Stage.[116] For the two automobiles to have covered such a distance in that time—10.5 miles in 8 minutes—they had to have averaged a speed of 78 miles per hour. A large segment of the alleged chase route was on a busy artery that was, at the time, crowded with rush-hour traffic. Under such conditions, a high speed chase such as that described in the broadcast would have attracted considerable attention, caused numerous traffic infractions and undoubtedly given rise to citizen complaints. The committee's examination of Memphis Police Department records revealed no supporting evidence of such a chase on April 4, 1968.

Investigative records of the Memphis police and the FBI indicated that an 18-year-old CB enthusiast, Edward L. Montedonico, Jr., was considered the most likely perpetrator of the hoax, although prosecution was not recommended.[117] Memphis police officers chiefly responsible for the investigation told the committee that Montedonico was considered the prime suspect.[118]

The committee's investigation into the identity of the broadcaster, although hampered by Montedonico's refusal to cooperate,[119] revealed that the evidence relied upon by the Memphis Police Department and the FBI in naming Montedonico as the suspect was apparently based on an erroneous interpretation of a key witness statement.[120] Additionally, an extensive background investigation of Montedonico failed to reveal incriminating evidence.[121] Indeed, the committee uncovered specific exculpatory evidence relating to Montedonico as the broadcaster,[122] and the committee's own consultants, Federal Communications Commission engineers, doubted that Montedonico was responsible for the hoax.[123]. Ultimately, Montedonico decided to cooperate with the committee, and he denied under oath that he made the broadcast.[124]

Additional possible suspects were identified and interviewed in the course of the committee's investigation of the CB broadcast.[125] The committee also made an effort to pinpoint the broadcast by identifying all operators who had overheard the broadcast and by obtaining technical data concerning their location, their equipment and the strength of the signal they had received.[126] The committee used FCC engineers in an attempt to identify the broadcaster.[127] As stated by the FCC in its report to the committee,[128] however, the interval of 10 years made virtually impossible a task that would have been difficult even in 1968. The committee, therefore, was unable to identify the broadcaster.

The committee considered indications that the broadcast was a conspiratorial act. For instance, the broadcaster asked for a land line relay to police headquarters, a request that shows he wanted the information to get to the police and suggests he had more than a hoax in mind. Further, the broadcaster attempted to lead police to the northern part of Memphis, while the most accessible route out of town from the vicinity of the Lorraine Motel was to the south, the direction the committee believed James Earl Ray did indeed follow.

Although its failure to identify the broadcaster prevented the committee from determining definitively whether the broadcast was in any way linked conspiratorially to the assassination of Dr. King, several factors indicated it probably was not a conspiratorial act. The broadcast came a full 35 minutes after the assassination, so it could not have assisted in the immediate flight of the assassin out of Memphis. A description of the suspected assassin's white Mustang had been broadcast over the police radio at 6:10, so a CB operator who had been monitoring police calls would have had the description of the automobile. Moreover, the broadcaster did not use the best means of penetrating the police network. He used channel 17, one of the lesser used CB frequencies. Consequently, while the identity of the CB operator remained undetermined, the committee found that the evidence was insufficient to conclude that the Memphis CB broadcast was linked to a conspiratorial plot to kill Dr. King.

(b) John McFerren

The committee's review of Memphis FBI files revealed that John McFerren approached agents on April 8, 1968, with information concerning the assassination.[129] McFerren said that on the afternoon of April 4, 1968, while he was shopping at the Liberto, Liberto, and Latch Produce Store in Memphis, he overheard a "heavy set white male," later identified as Frank Liberto,[7] the company's president, talking on the telephone.[130] McFerren asserted that Liberto indicated that his brother in New Orleans, La., was going to pay $5,000 to someone to kill a person on a balcony.[131] After hearing of Dr. King's death later that day and observing a sketch of the assassin in the newspaper the following day, he felt an individual that had been employed at Liberto, Liberto and Latch Produce during the last year might be the fugitive assassin. [132] Based on McFerren's story, a writer, William Sartor, hypothesized that organized crime was responsible for the King assassination. In his investigation, Sartor attempted to connect Frank Liberto with organized crime figures in Memphis and New Orleans.[133][8]

In its 1968 investigation of McFerren's allegation, the FBI and Memphis Police Department interviewed Liberto and members of his family in New Orleans, and James W. Latch, vice president of Liberto, Liberto, and Latch Produce. All those interviewed denied any involvement in, or knowledge of, Dr. King's assassination. Both Frank Liberto and his business partner, Latch, however, admitted making disparaging remarks about Dr. King in the presence of their customers.[134]

Because Liberto lived in the Memphis area and because of reports that he had displayed pronounced racial bias, the committee determined that McFerren's story warranted additional investigation. It conducted extensive interviews of Liberto.[135] members of his family,[136] neighbors[137] and business associates,[138] in addition to checking the backgrounds of Liberto and his brother through the FBI and municipal police departments. Liberto

[7] The committee received additional allegations with respect to Frank Liberto from Morris Davis (see sec. IIc(5) (a) infra).
[8] See text, infra, at subsection IIc(3) (a) for a discussion of Sartor's information.

and members of his family provided the committee essentially the same information they had given the FBI in 1968. Liberto stated under oath that, while on occasion he had made disparaging remarks concerning Dr. King, he did not recall making the April 4, 1968, statements attributed to him by McFerren.[139] Although an indirect link between Liberto's brother, Salvatore, and an associate of New Orleans organized crime figure Carlos Marcello was established.[140] no evidence was found to substantiate the claim that Frank Liberto or Carlos Marcello was involved in the assassination.

In its attempt to evaluate McFerren's credibility, the committee interviewed local police and FBI agents who had received information from him. McFerren had a reputation for furnishing the officials with information that could not be substantiated.[141] The committee noted, however, that this evaluation by law enforcement officers may have been tainted by McFerren's work as a Black civil rights activist who frequently lodged complaints of police brutality.

Extensive interviews of McFerren by the FBI in 1968 [142] and the committee [143] revealed inconsistencies in his basic allegation that could not be reconciled. For instance, McFerren had told the original investigators, as well as the committee, that James Earl Ray had worked at the Liberto produce company before the assassination, either in the fall or early winter of 1967.[144] McFerren also told members of the committee staff that at this time, Ray had "jungle rot" on his cheek and neck.[145] The committee, however, had no evidence of Ray's presence in Memphis during the period alleged by McFerren, and persons who had seen Ray during that period did not recall a similar skin disease.

McFerren also claimed he had positively identified James Earl Ray to the FBI as the individual who worked at the produce company before the assassination.[146] An FBI memorandum concerning this incident revealed that McFerren eliminated all photographs (including one of Ray) of Bureau suspects that he reviewed. McFerren only claimed that Ray closely resembled the person who worked at the market after a picture of Ray was pointed out to him.[147]

On the basis of witness denials, lack of corroborating evidence and McFerren's questionable credibility, the committee concluded that his allegation was without foundation and that there was no connection between his story and the assassination of Dr. King.

3. CONSPIRACY ALLEGATIONS: NEW ORLEANS[9]

(a) William Sartor

Writer William Sartor, in an unpublished manuscript, advanced the possibility, among other allegations, that organized crime participated in Dr. King's assassination. The committee focused its attention on Sartor's contention that, in New Orleans in December 1967, James Earl Ray met with Charles Stein and three persons who were connected with organized crime and white supremacist groups.[148] The meeting allegedly was held at either the Town & Country Motel, owned by New Orleans Mafia boss Carlos Marcello, or the Provincial Motel, where Ray stayed from December 17 to 19, 1967.[149]

Sartor, who died in 1971,[150] had provided no information about how he discovered that such a meeting occurred, and he wrote that he was not aware of the subject of the meeting.[151] In support of his speculation that this meeting was in some way linked to the assassination of Dr. King, however, Sartor pointed to the following considerations:

> The proximity in time between the meeting and the assassination;
>
> The occurrence of the meeting in a city Sartor described as a bastion of racist thinking;
>
> The location of the meeting at either one of two hotels that Sartor suggested were guest houses for an underworld clientele; and
>
> Ray's statement to author William Bradford Huie that he left New Orleans with $2,500 cash and the promise of $12,000 more for doing one last big job in 2 to 3 months.[152]

Sartor wrote that Sam DiPianzza, Sol La Charta and Lucas Dilles were also at the meeting. DiPianzza and La Charta were described by Sartor as involved in organized crime, as well as avid racists. Dilles, also a racist, was allegedly connected with the late Leander Perez, Louisiana political boss and virulent segregationist.[153]

---

[9]A staff report, An Analysis of James Earl Ray's Trip to New Orleans, December 15–21 1967, appears in XIII Appendix to the HSCA–MLK hearings (hereinafter referred to as staff report: New Orleans trip).

Further investigation by the committee revealed that the correct spelling for names of the persons alluded to by Sartor was Salvadore "Sam" DiPiazza, Dr. Lucas A. DiLeo, and Salvadore La Charda.

Sartor also speculated that Ray may have been told during this meeting that Carlos Marcello would protect him after the assassination because Sartor believed both DiPiazza and La Charda had direct ties to Marcello.[154]

The committee checked the backgrounds of the three persons named by Sartor. DiPiazza, a suburban New Orleans resident, was a gambler and bookmaker with reputed connections to Marcello and other underworld figures. Approximately 3 weeks before the alleged meeting, DiPiazza was sentenced to 10 years in prison on a gambling conviction. Although he was free on bond at the time of the alleged meeting, he denied in a committee interview ever meeting with Ray.[155] DiLeo, a practicing physician in a New Orleans suburb, had a record for such minor offenses as disturbing the peace, resisting arrest, and assault. When questioned by the committee, he maintained that he never had heard of the Provincial Motel but admitted he was familiar with the Town & Country Motel where he had stayed once 20 years earlier. He stated that he had never met or spoken with Ray or Marcello.[156] Salvadore La Charda, formerly Chief Juvenile Probation Officer in the St. Bernard Parish Sheriff's Office, committed suicide in June 1968. He had no criminal record.[157] DiLeo and DiPiazza were unable to account for their whereabouts on December 17 through 19, 1968.

A review of the Provincial Motel records indicated that the persons named by Sartor had not registered at the motel while Ray was there. Town & Country records were no longer available. Both Charles Stein[10][158] and Carlos Marcello[159] told the committee they knew of no such meeting with Ray or the others.

In his manuscript, Sartor named two sources of his information. Carlton Pecot, the first Black police officer in New Orleans and the director of a Federal education program aiding minority students in 1978, appeared to be the primary source of Sartor's New Orleans information. When questioned under oath by the committee with regard to

---

[10]A major field investigation of Charles Stein was performed by the committee in light of his association with Ray in California and on the New Orleans trip. The committee concluded that Stein was not involved in the assassination. (See staff report: New Orleans, XIIII, appendix to the HSCA–MLK hearings, par. 10.)

Sartor's reliability and the accuracy of his notes, Pecot claimed, however, that he was unfamiliar with most of the facts and statements in Sartor's manuscript.[160] Pecot did recall meeting with Sartor five to eight times to assist with his investigation of relevant leads in the King case. [161]

Robert Lyons, another purported Sartor source, told the FBI in 1968 that Sartor had attributed false information to him that in reality originated with Sartor.[162]

The committee found no support for Sartor's contention that Ray met with persons involved in organized crime in New Orleans before the assassination.

(b) Raul Esquivel

In 1969, Charles Stein gave Dave Larsen and Jerry Cohen, investigative reporters for the Los Angeles Times, a New Orleans telephone number that Stein said was Ray's contact number for his alleged criminal accomplice, Raoul. Larsen and Cohen discovered that the subscriber to the number was Troop B of the Louisiana State Police. Assigned to that suburban New Orleans barracks was trooper Raul Esquivel. The reporters theorized that Esquivel might be the Raoul to whom Ray had referred.

In an attempt to determine whether Stein actually received this number from Ray or merely represented it as Ray's contact number so he could sell it, the committee reviewed the entire FBI investigation of the information and the FBI interviews with Larsen, Cohen, and Stein. Larsen and Cohen were interviewed by the committee, and Stein testified in executive session.

The committee received several different accounts about how Stein originally obtained this number and the conversations that led Larsen and Cohen to believe that the number belonged to a Ray contact. There were allegations that the phone number was in Ray's handwriting;[163] that the phone number was in Stein's handwriting;[164] that Ray gave Stein the number and told Stein it was where he could be reached;[165] that Ray told Stein he could get a weather report at the number;[166] that Ray never gave Stein the number but Stein saw the telephone number on a paper in Ray's car and copied it,[167] that Stein never gave the reporters the number at all because they only offered him $15 or $20 for the note;[168] and, finally, that Stein obtained the number of a highway patrol office from a service station attendant to check road conditions.

Although the committee could not find satisfactory proof that this number actually came from Ray, it conducted a full investigation of Raul Esquivel's background and his whereabouts on the dates in 1967 and 1968 that Ray alleged he met with Raoul.[11] The committee found that Raul Esquivel was not the Raoul implicated in the assassination by Ray. Criminal indexes of Federal and local law enforcement agencies failed to reveal any intelligence data indicating that Esquivel had a criminal background. His record as a Louisiana State trooper was unblemished except for one complaint of use of excessive force, a charge later found by the office of the U.S. attorney to lack prosecutive merit.[169] Work records for 1967 and 1968 indicated that Esquivel could not have met Ray at the times and places Ray alleged he was with Raoul. Moreover, in a sworn statement to the committee, Esquivel denied ever having met with Ray, or with a person using any of Ray's known aliases, or with Charles Stein.[170] Finally, Esquivel did not fit any of the physical descriptions of Raoul provided by Ray.[171] The committee concluded that there was no evidence linking Esquivel with Ray or the assassination of Dr. King, and that the Larsen-Cohen theory was unsupported by fact.

(c) Reynard Rochon

According to author George McMillan's unpublished notes from interviews with Jerry Ray, James Earl Ray had a New Orleans drug contact named "Eddie."[172] McMillan made the notes while working on "The Making of an Assassin," a biography of James Earl Ray. While McMillan's notes were unclear, it appeared that Jerry Ray told McMillan that James made money on drugs he secured from "Eddie" and then delivered them to Los Angeles.[173] Jerry recalled that James asked him to contact this person in New Orleans and tell him that James had not disclosed their relationship to authorities, which Jerry claimed he did.[174]

In notes of a much later interview, McMillan noted that Jerry referred to "The Fence" in New Orleans and sug-

---

[11] A similar investigation had also been conducted by the FBI during the 1968 investigation.

gested to McMillan that James carried drugs for this person to Los Angeles.[175] Jerry seemed to indicate "The Fence" was Reynard J. Rochon and that he had twice met with Rochon.[176] Jerry claimed he received money each time he met Rochon and implied, according to McMillan's notes, that the money was paid to induce James not to expose his relationship with "The Fence."[177] Jerry told McMillan that "The Fence" knew James as Harvey Lowmeyer but was aware that James intended to kill King. [178]

It was unclear from McMillan's notes whether "Eddie," "The Fence" and Reynard J. Rochon were supposed to be the same person. As a result, the committee asked McMillan, but he could not recall with any certainty whether Jerry was using "Eddie" and "The Fence" as nicknames for Rochon.[179] McMillan said that after he learned from his own investigation that Reynard Rochon was a postal worker, he dropped the matter.[180]

The committee, although able to confirm Jerry's presence in New Orleans on the dates he purportedly met with this person,[181] uncovered no evidence that the meetings he described took place. A complete background check on Rochon was conducted through the Drug Enforcement Administration,[182] the FBI [183] and the New Orleans Police Department; no records were found indicating any criminal activities. Finally, the committee deposed Rochon, a successful Black accountant in New Orleans, concluding he had never met with James Earl Ray.[184] Rochon vigorously denied that he had been known by the nicknames "Eddie" or "The Fence" [185] or that he ever trafficked in narcotics.[186]

The committee was unable to ascertain why either James Earl Ray or his brother, Jerry Ray, might choose to implicate Rochon in Ray's 1967 and 1968 activities. The committee concluded that there was no connection between Rochon and either Ray brother and that the allegation was without foundation.

(d) Herman Thompson

James Earl Ray maintained that, following his October 6, 1967, departure from Birmingham, he drove through Baton Rouge, La., and called a telephone number he had been given by his mysterious coconspirator, Raoul. The subscriber to this number, according to Ray, was to give

512

him instructions about his next rendezvous with Raoul.
[187]

The committee hoped to identify and locate the subscriber to that Baton Rouge telephone number. Ray's conflicting accounts about this part of his journey, however, cast doubt on the Baton Rouge story.

In a March 3, 1977, interview with CBS reporter Dan Rather, Ray indicated that his destination was New Orleans when he left Birmingham, Ala., in October 1967. [188] Ray claimed he called the number Raoul had given him when he reached Baton Rouge and the party that answered told Ray his next meeting with Raoul had been changed to Nuevo Laredo, Mexico.[189]

During the committee's third interview with Ray 6 weeks after the Rather interview, he indicated, however, that he knew his destination was Nuevo Laredo when he left Birmingham.[190] Ray said he called a number given him by Raoul while driving through Baton Rouge, but he never spoke with the subscriber of the number because the line was busy when he made the call. Ray later received more detailed instructions concerning his next meeting with Raoul by calling a New Orleans number Raoul had given him.[191]

Ray told the committee that he had the name of the subscriber to the Baton Rouge number.[192] At the time he called the number, he said he was unaware of the subscriber's identity, but he later discovered the name by spending several hours skimming through a local telephone book in a Baton Rouge motel.[193] Once he found a number ending with the correct last two digits, he explained, he looked at the whole number until he found the one Raoul had given him.[194] Ray's efforts ultimately led him to the name Thompson.[195] Ray contended he had never spoken with Thompson and never mentioned Thompson's name to Raoul.[196]

The person Ray identified was Herman Thompson. Thompson had been an assistant chief criminal deputy of the East Baton Rouge Sheriff's Department for 26 years. In 1978, Thompson resided at the same address and had the same telephone number as in 1967.[197]

Thompson was a cooperative committee witness, who submitted to a deposition following an interview. He stated under oath that he never knew anyone named or nicknamed Raoul.[198] Although he had heard of James Earl Ray in connection with the King assassination, he denied ever meeting or speaking with Ray or anyone using Ray's known aliases.[199] The committee did attempt to determine whether Ray may have maliciously implicated Thompson as a means of settling a grudge or aiding a fellow inmate. Thompson could not recall ever arresting, incarcerating or transporting any person who had contact with either Leavenworth Federal Penitentiary or Missouri State Penitentiary where Ray had been an inmate.[200]

Thompson stated that he was never a member of any white extremist organization [201] and that he never had any usual complaints or disciplinary actions filed against him while he worked with the sheriff's department. [202] Thompson's former employer confirmed his statements to the committee.

The committee found no evidence to indicate that Herman Thompson was involved in the assassination or with an individual named Raoul. The committee concluded, further, that Ray's allegation was merely an attempt to gain credence for his Raoul story and to raise an implication of official complicity in the assassination.

(e) Jules Ricco Kimble

In June 1968, The Toronto Star named Jules Ricco Kimble as a possible criminal associate of James Earl Ray in 1967.[203] A reporter for the newspaper wrote that Kimble, a member of the right-wing Minutemen, had lived within a few blocks of Ray's 1967 Montreal residence and had met Ray in both Montreal and New Orleans.[204]

Upon receipt of this information following the assassination, the FBI reviewed its files on Kimble. They reflected that Kimble had an extensive criminal record and associations in 1967 with the Ku Klux Klan. [205] The files did not establish ties between Kimble and the Minutemen.[206]

In light of Kimble's criminal background and his possible presence in Montreal during the period Ray resided in the city, July and August 1967, the committee decided that the allegation warranted further investigation. The committee interviewed Toronto Star reporters André Salwyn [207] and Earl MacRae, [208] who had developed this lead, and reviewed an investigative report on the Kimble lead prepared by the RCMP. The reporters recalled the story in detail. Their recollections, however, as well as the version of the allegation that appeared in the RCMP report, [209] differed on several major points. For instance, Salwyn alleged that MacRae got the lead from author, William Bradford Huie, for whom he was doing research in 1968.[210] and MacRae said that Salwyn received the information from a police contact in Montreal. [211] RCMP files, however, indicated that a newspaper article regarding James Earl Ray's residence in Montreal aroused Salwyn's curiosity, and the reporter subsequently discovered Kimble had lived in the same area.[212] Salwyn wrote that a person whose name was actually Raoul drove a white Mustang with Louisiana plates, equipped with guns and a police radio. [213] RCMP files indicated that this person, named Kimble, made daily calls to New Orleans, listened to police broadcasts, carried guns and made racist comments.[214]

The committee performed a thorough background check of Kimble. Files from the offices of Jim Garrison, New Orleans district attorney in 1968, Joseph Oster, a former investigator for the Louisiana Labor-Management Commission of Inquiry, the FBI, and the CIA reflected that Kimble had an extensive criminal background, including active participation in the Ku Klux Klan in 1967.[215] There was no indication, however, that Kimble was involved in narcotics smuggling and gunrunning, the criminal activities that James Earl Ray attributed to his contact, Raoul.

Extensive interviews with Oster, who was familiar with Kimble's history,[216] and Kimble's former wife[217] indicated that Kimble was in New Orleans in December 1967 when Ray visited that city, although he apparently did not visit Montreal until after Ray had left that city in August 1967. Although generally uncooperative during his interview, Kimble confirmed that he did not go to Canada until September 1967.[218] Kimble also denied meeting Ray or a person using any of Ray's aliases.[219]

The committee found no evidence to support a Ray-Kimble connection or to indicate that Kimble was involved in any plot to kill Dr. King.

(f) Randy Rosenson

In a 1977 interview with the Canadian Broadcasting Co., James Earl Ray intimated that Randolph Erwin Rosenson might have information about Raoul, the mysterious figure who Ray maintained was responsible for the King assassination. Ray asserted that while cleaning his Mustang when he was in Mexico in November 1967, a few weeks after Raoul had been in the car, he found a business card with Rosenson's name on it.[220]

Although Ray apparently withheld this information for 10 years and was elusive about the nature of Rosenson's possible involvement, the committee conducted an exhaustive investigation of Rosenson's background, associates and movements in the 1960's. It uncovered evidence indicating that Rosenson and Ray had had several opportunities to meet prior to the assassination of Dr. King.

Evidence developed by the committee showed that Rosenson had traveled to Mexico in late 1965 and early 1966.[221] According to Ray, Raoul was dealing in unspecified contraband, perhaps narcotics or stolen cars, in Mexico in late 1967. In addition, Rosenson's operation of a traveling carnival business gave him mobility.[222] The committee surmised that he may have been in some of the same cities Ray visited after escaping from the Missouri State Penitentiary in 1967. For example, Rosenson often traveled to New Orleans to visit friends and relatives, although the committee found no evidence that he was in New Orleans in December 1967 when Ray drove there from Los Angeles and allegedly met Raoul.[223] The committee did establish, however, that Rosenson was in Los Angeles and Birmingham, Ala., at the same time as Ray in 1967.[224] Rosenson and Ray used the same Birmingham bank.[225] Rosenson was also in the Birmingham area in March 1968 when Ray was purchasing the murder weapon there.[226] Finally, Rosenson traveled in many of the same New Orleans circles as Ray's associate Charles Stein, a former New Orleans resident who lived in Los Angeles in 1967. Both Rosenson and Stein were known to the New Orleans Police Department for similar criminal conduct. [227] They also had mutual acquaintances, frequented the same bars, and had retained the same lawyer.[228]

Rosenson was interviewed by the committee on at least six occasions, and he appeared before the committee in executive session. He repeatedly denied knowing Ray, any Ray family members or any known Ray associates, including a Raoul, or Charles Stein. Further he emphatically denied any involvement in the King assassination and could provide no reason why Ray would implicate him. [229]

Despite the opportunities for Ray and Rosenson to have met, an extensive field investigation, including interviews of

Rosenson's relatives, friends, business associates, criminal contacts, and numerous law enforcement officials, failed to establish a definite link between Ray and Rosenson.[230] The committee concluded that Rosenson was not involved with Ray in a conspiracy to assassinate Dr. King.

4. CONSPIRACY ALLEGATIONS: ATLANTA

(a) Edna Mathews Lancaster

Edna Mathews Lancaster told the committee in late 1977 that she was associated with a group of people, including James Earl Ray, who met at a laundry where she worked in Mableton, Ga., to plot the assassination of Dr. King. [231] According to Mrs. Lancaster, this group, which she called "the secret American Revolutionary Army," not only planned but carried out the assassination.[232] She claimed she had met James Earl Ray in the early 1950's when he and her husband were stationed in the Army in California.[233]

The committee reviewed FBI files concerning this allegation in an attempt to check Lancaster's story. The files reflected that after providing a similar, although not identical story, Lancaster had named several persons who allegedly could verify certain aspects of her account.[234] When subsequently interviewed by the FBI, each person had denied any knowledge of the discussions, and most characterized Lancaster as an unbalanced person with an overactive imagination.[235] During interviews conducted by the committee, Lancaster's husband [236] and former employees [237] of the Mableton laundry reported that she had a severe drinking problem and was generally unstable. In addition, they denied any knowledge of an assassination plot.

The committee found that Edna Mathews Lancaster was not a credible person. Its investigation revealed substantial variations in her story over the years to accommodate new revelations about the CIA, FBI, and prominent figures associated with various assassinations and government scandals.[238] A further indication of Lancaster's lack of credibility was her son's statement to the committee that his mother had convinced him that James Earl Ray was his father.[239]

The committee concluded that Lancaster's story was not worthy of further investigation.

(b) Claude and Leon Powell

In January 1976, Leon Powell contacted the FBI about a possible conspiracy involving the King assassination. In February 1978, he testified before the committee concerning the details of the allegation.[240] According to Powell, he and his brother Claude Powell were in an Atlanta bar known as "Pete's," or "Pete Bailey's," in the fall of 1967 when Arnold Ray Godfrey, a mutual friend, told them he could put them in touch with a person who would pay a large sum of money to anyone willing to kill Dr. King. [241] Several days later, at the same bar, Claude and Leon were approached by a white male who introduced himself only as Ralph.[242] After indicating that he was the person to whom Godfrey had referred, Ralph displayed an open briefcase full of money.[243] Ralph said it contained $25,000 and promised that if they took the job, they would receive $25,000 more when it had been completed.[244] The Powells hesitated to accept the offer, and Ralph closed his briefcase and left the bar.[245] Leon said he never saw or heard from this person again.[246]

In its investigation of the assassination of Dr. King, the FBI interviewed Claude Powell, who essentially corroborated his brother's story. The FBI also conducted polygraph examinations of both brothers.[247] Leon's examination was inconclusive,[248] while responses by Claude to questions about the assassination plot indicated his responses were not deceptive.[249] After a full investigation of the Powell allegation, the FBI was unable to corroborate or discredit the story. The matter was turned over to the Department of Justice for possible submission to the Federal grand jury. No further action was taken by the Department.[250]

After reviewing FBI files concerning the Powell brothers, the committee conducted an extensive field investigation. It interviewed the FBI agent who first received this information[251] and also made an effort to locate "Ralph" through interviews of associates of Arnold Ray Godfrey and of customers of Pete's Bar.[252] In addition, a composite drawing of Ralph was released by the committee to national news organizations; it did not lead to his identification.[12] The committee investigated several possible

---

[12]The committee noted that the composite was released along with several unrelated photographs and another unrelated composite. Within

links between Ralph's offer to the Powells in Atlanta and John Sutherland's offer to Russell Byers in St. Louis, primarily because of their similarity and proximity in time.[13] Nevertheless, the committee found no evidence linking the two offers.

The committee was unable to locate any witnesses to the alleged Ralph offer other than the Powell brothers. Thus, their credibility became a crucial issue. Both brothers had a history of alcohol abuse and a reputation for violence.[253] Annie Lois Campos, Leon Powell's former wife, testified in executive session that Leon told her about the offer in 1973 or 1974 when he was under the influence of alcohol.[254] In executive session testimony before the committee, Arnold Ray Godfrey flatly denied ever discussing the assassination with the Powells.[225] Claude Powell resisted the committee's subpoena, indicating he feared for his life, and subsequently pleaded guilty to contempt of Congress for his refusal to testify.

As a result of Claude's refusal to cooperate and the absence of corroborating evidence to support the allegation, the committee was unable to investigate this allegation further. Although the committee concluded that the Powell brothers' story was credible, it was not able to uncover any evidence that would link it to the assassination of Dr. King.

(c) Robert Byron Watson

Robert Byron Watson maintained that on March 28, 1968, exactly 1 week before the assassination, he overheard a conversation concerning a plot to kill Dr. King in Memphis on April 4, 1968 in Magellan's Art Gallery in Atlanta, Ga. [257] Watson, then 14, worked at the gallery after school. [258] He identified those involved in the discussion as Harold Eugene Purcell and Jerry Adams, co-owners of the gallery, as well as their associates, Lawrence Meier and Bayne S. Culley. Several other persons were also present. [259] According to Watson, Jerry Adams emphasized that the date and time of the assassination attempt would be "exactly 1 week from then and about the

---

days, individuals in the photographs were identified. No identification of either composite was made.
[13]The Sutherland offer to Byers is discussed in sec. II B of this report.

same time of day." [260] Adams further said he had just learned King would be in Memphis. Purcell allegedly made reference to "framing a jailbird," as in the assassination of President John F. Kennedy. [261]

Watson said he told his mother that afternoon where and when King was to be murdered but withheld the details from authorities until after the assassination. [262] Lawrence Meier allegedly confronted Watson after James Earl Ray's arrest and threatened him with violence if he talked about what he had overheard. [263]

Watson outlined his allegation in numerous letters to the committee. In order to evaluate Watson's credibility, as well as his story, the committee reviewed all available documents on the allegation.

Watson's allegation had been covered extensively in the Atlanta newspapers and was investigated by the Atlanta Police Department, but the police found no evidence to substantiate it. [264]

In its review of Atlanta police files, the committee noted that in 1970, Bernard Fensterwald, an attorney for James Earl Ray during his habeas corpus action, looked into Watson's allegation. Fensterwald's investigator, Ken Smith, verified some aspects of the allegation but could not produce any reliable documentation to support key elements of the story. [265] Subsequently, Fensterwald commissioned Cleve Backster, an established polygrapher, to examine Watson about the allegation. The results indicated Watson was 90–95 percent truthful. [266]

The committee's review of the FBI's assassination investigation revealed that in April 1971, Watson admitted fabricating the Magellan Gallery story about to plot to kill Dr. King. [267] Watson made the story up because he believed someone at the Magellan Gallery had defrauded his mother of $50,000.[268]

Watson told various accounts of the plot to the committee and to other sources. [269] He vacillated significantly on the time of day of the meeting, and, in November 1977, Watson revealed for the first time that the conspirators mentioned Ray's name. [270]

Finally, the committee noted that Dr. King did not publicly announce his decision to return to Memphis until March 29, [271] the day after Watson allegedly overheard the conversation.

The committee concluded that Watson was an unreliable witness and that his story was false.

5. CONSPIRACY ALLEGATIONS: BIRMINGHAM

(a) Morris Davis

In early 1977, Morris Davis provided the committee with information that Frank Liberto, two members of the SCLC and others were involved in a conspiracy to kill Dr. King. [272] Davis claimed that in 1967 or 1968, he became acquainted with Dr. Gus J. Prosch, [273] a Birmingham, Ala., doctor who in 1970 was convicted for possession of a large cache of illegal weapons and for income tax evasion. [274] According to Davis, he often met Prosch in early 1968 at the Gulas Restaurant in Birmingham. During one of these meetings, Prosch allegedly introduced Davis to an associate, Frank Liberto. [275] Davis said he witnessed a meeting in Gulas' parking lot of Prosch and Liberto with Rev. Ralph D. Abernathy, a close friend of Dr. King, and Rev. Fred Shuttlesworth, also a friend of Dr. King. [276] A week later, Prosch and Liberto again met at the Gulas Restaurant, this time with a man introduced to Davis as Eric Galt. Davis also asserted that he saw a subsequent meeting of these persons at the restaurant on March 29, 1968.[277]

Davis maintained that on April 3, 1968, he met Prosch at the Gulas Restaurant and agreed to drive with him to the Aeromarine Supply Co. (Ray bought the weapon used to kill Dr. King at Aeromarine on March 30, 1968.) Prosch allegedly went in the store and returned 15 minutes later with a large wooden crate that he put in the trunk of the car.[278] They then drove back to the restaurant where, in the parking lot, Prosch opened the crate and showed Davis a rifle inside.[279] Davis claimed that Prosch told him that he and Liberto had accepted a contract from Abernathy and Shuttlesworth to kill Dr. King for $265,000 and that this weapon would be used in the killing.[280] Eric Galt, who had already purchased a similar rifle at Aeromarine, was to be the decoy.[281] Galt was to meet Liberto in Detroit after the assassination and collect $25,000 as payment for his participation in the murder.[282]

Davis told the committee that Prosch often used the name John Willard at the Gulas Restaurant to avoid being recognized as a doctor.[283] Davis also claimed that the Eric Galt he met was identical to photographs he had seen of James Earl Ray.[284]

Davis, who had a background of supplying reliable information to the Drug Enforcement Administration, told the committee he had approached the FBI several times with this information since 1970.[285][14]

A review of the FBI file concerning the murder of Dr. King revealed a December 1976 interview with Davis during which he supplied similar information. In light of Davis' background and the serious nature of the allegation, the committee conducted a thorough investigation of his story. Davis and those persons named in his allegation were extensively interviewed by the committee.

During executive session testimony, Dr. Ralph B. Abernathy denied any knowledge of such a plot.[286] Rev. Fred Shuttlesworth also said he knew of no such conspiracy to kill Dr. King.[287] Frank Liberto stated under oath that he had never been to Gulas Restaurant in Birmingham and never had met Prosch, Abernathy, or Shuttlesworth. [288]

The committee questioned Donald Wood of the Aeromarine Supply Co. about Gus Prosch.[289] Wood recalled that Prosch was a regular customer at Aeromarine from 1968 until 1970. When Prosch was arrested for possession of illegal weapons, Wood pulled all invoices and receipts pertaining to Prosch's purchases, made copies of them and set them aside.[290] A review of these receipts by the committee indicated the purchase of two pistols on March 25, 1968, and a purchase of a semiautomatic rifle on April 5, 1968. There is no record of Prosch buying any weapons on April 3, 1968.[291] Wood mentioned that a customer would use a large wooden crate only if buying more than one rifle. All single rifles were packed in cardboard boxes.

The committee then located and interviewed Prosch. [292] He denied involvement in any plot to kill Dr. King and denied knowing any of the persons connected with the allegation, including Davis.

As a result of its investigation, the committee called into question Morris Davis' credibility. Further interviews with Davis revealed basic inconsistencies in his story that could not be reconciled.[293] Davis additionally claimed that various Government agencies and prominent individuals associated with Government scandals were involved in the assassinations of President Kennedy and Dr. King.[294]

---

[14]Davis explained he had been arrested and imprisoned shortly after the assassination and not released until 1970.

Davis refused, however, to provide the committee with the source of this information.

After a thorough field investigation, the committee was unable to corroborate Davis' allegation and found that his allegation was false.

(b) Walter Maddox

Walter and Virginia Maddox owned and operated the South Birmingham Travelodge Motor Inn [295] when James Earl Ray registered there as Eric Starvo Galt on March 29, 1968. When questioned by the committee concerning Ray and his alleged companion Raoul, Walter Maddox recalled that at approximately that time there were three men living at the motel, one of whom was called Raoul by his companions.[296] Maddox added that one of the men was named Billy Fisher and that they resided there for almost a year and that they left without paying $1,500 room rent. [297][15]

The committee reviewed the financial records of the motel in the Travelodge executive offices and found that Billy E. Fisher had stayed at this motel between May 1965 and February 1966.[298] Fisher was subsequently questioned by the committee and admitted that he and two companions, Jack Cunningham of Biloxi, Miss., and Leroy Roell of Jackson, Miss., had spent considerable time at the Travelodge Motor Inn during this period.[299] Fisher said the three were attempting to obtain financial backing in Birmingham to purchase a motel in Huntsville, Ala. [300]

Leroy Roell, who in 1978 owned two Travelodge Inns in Jackson, Miss., was questioned by committee staff and confirmed Fisher's story.[301] Roell stated he had lost $30,000 in the venture and therefore had a vivid recollection of it.[302]

Although attempts to locate Jack Cunningham were unsuccessful, both Fisher and Roell stated they assumed the Raoul referred to by Walter Maddox was actually Leroy Roell.[303] Given this explanation and the 2- to 3-year difference between Roell's residence and Ray's stay at

---

[15]The committee noted that the person referred to as Raoul by Ray allegedly spent substantial time in Canada, Mexico, and New Orleans, while Ray never indicated he stayed in Birmingham for more than brief periods. The committee believed, nevertheless, that the lead warranted investigation.

the motel, as evidenced by motel records, the committee concluded there was no connection between the three men and James Earl Ray.

6. CONSPIRACY ALLEGATIONS: LOUISVILLE

(a) Clifton Baird

A former Louisville, Ky., police officer, Clifton Baird, raised the possibility of FBI complicity in Dr. King's assassination. He testified before the committee in 1977 that, on September 18, 1965, another Louisville police officer, Arlie Blair, offered him $500,000 to kill Dr. King.[304] Blair allegedly told Baird that an organization he belonged to was willing to pay someone to assassinate Dr. King. [305] Baird refused the offer.[306] The next day he overheard several Louisville police officers and FBI agents discussing the offer at Louisville police headquarters during afternoon rollcall.[307] In an effort to document this apparent conspiracy, Baird tape recorded a conversation on September 20, 1965, in which Blair again referred to the $500,000 bounty.[308] Baird turned this recording over to the committee.[16]

Blair testified under oath that he had no recollection of offering Baird any money to kill Dr. King and denied he had been a member of any organization seeking to assassinate Dr. King.[309] Blair did not deny, however, that his voice was on Baird's recording, and he explained his inability to recall the conversation was the result of a general physical and mental deterioration caused by alcoholism. [310]

Baird told the committee the names of five other police officers and three FBI agents he believed participated in the conversation he overheard on September 19, 1965. [311] Each police officer named was questioned either by deposition or in executive session. Each claimed to have no knowledge of any meeting or discussion concerning an offer to kill Dr. King.[312]

Special Agent William Duncan, FBI liaison with the Louisville Police Department in 1965, testified in executive session that he did remember the discussion of an offer to assassinate Dr. King.[313] According to Duncan, however, the discussion was part of a practical joke initiated by Sgt. William Baker of the Louisville police.[314] Duncan testi-

---

[16]The tape was transcribed by the committee. It contained references to a previous discussion about "knocking off" Dr. King.

fied that sometime in the mid-60's, he was at police headquarters when Sergeant Baker asked him to help "put some
boys on."[315] Duncan agreed. At Baker's direction, he
went to the rollcall area and confirmed a rumor that there
was a reward of $250,000 or $500,000 on the head of Dr.
King and that the Ku Klux Klan or the Communist Party
was the source of the offer.[316] Duncan testified that he
recalled adding that Special Agent Robert Peters and
Special Agent-in-Charge Bernard C. Brown would confirm
the offer.[317] Duncan testified that he made this statement
concerning verification solely to lend credence to the
story.[318] Duncan followed this description of the offer
by mentioning to the committee the poor relationship between FBI Director J. Edgar Hoover and Dr. King.[319]
Duncan recalled that he made his statement to a group of
three to six people, primarily uniformed officers, whose
identities he could not recall.[320] He did not remember any other remarks and said he left the room almost
immediately after he made the statement. [321] Although
he did not know to whom the joke was directed, Duncan
testified that he believed it was a gag and characterized
Baker as a practical joker.[322] He was certain that no
one connected with the FBI urged that he make this remark[323] and testified that no other FBI agent was present during his statement about Dr. King.[324]

The committee interviewed three other FBI agents from
the Louisville office, Special Agent Robert Peters, Special
Agent Warren L. Walsh (retired), and Special Agent-in-
Charge Bernard C. Brown. Each denied any knowledge of
an offer to kill Dr. King.[325] Peters, who testified in
executive session, stated that in his opinion Sergeant
Baker would not have concocted such a story even as a
joke.[326] Since Baker had since died, it was difficult for
the committee to determine his motive or whether he actually knew of an assassination conspiracy.

Retired Louisville police officer Vernon Austin, in a
designated counsel statement, maintained that he did not
know of such an offer but added that he believed Baker
was capable of fabricating this information.[327].

The committee conducted a thorough background investigation of Clifton Baird, including a review of medical
and criminal records.[328] It concluded that Baird was
highly credible. Results of a technical evaluation of Baird's
tape conducted by the FBI indicated that it was consistent
with those known to have been used in 1965.[329] The

committee reviewed the personal files and attendance records for all the officers allegedly involved. The documents indicated that all but two officers were on duty on September 19, 1965.[330] Both officers, however, testified that it was possible they came into the office on their designated day off.[331]

Duncan's testimony supported a finding that the 1965 conversation did take place. It may be that someone hearing such an offer, such as Baird did, would consider it serious. There was no evidence, however, to support a finding that an actual conspiracy existed or that the events in Louisville in September 1965 were in any way connected with the assassination in Memphis in April 1968. The committee concluded that both Duncan and Baker purposefully circulated a rumor of an offer to kill Dr. King. Their conduct reflected, in the committee's view, an absence of professionalism. The committee found no evidence contrary to Duncan's statement that he acted alone and not at the direction of any FBI official or agent.

(b) Charles Lee Bell

Charles Lee Bell claimed in an interview with the committee that Albert Ridley and Bishop Eubanks Tucker allegedly told him in 1967 and 1968 that Louisville, Ky., was an alternate site for the assassination of Dr. King, if the attempt in Memphis failed. Ridley was to funnel Cuban money from a man named Cordova, an underworld figure, to Louisville police and to an FBI agent assigned to Louisville to insure that protection was withdrawn from Dr. King when he came to Louisville.[333] Bell claimed that Bishop Tucker learned of the plot from Reverand A. D. King, Dr. King's brother, who in turn was told by a Black director of safety for the city of Louisville.[334]

Bell told the committee that a number of persons, including Huey Newton and Stokely Carmichael, knew of the conspiracy,[335] since Black militants were receiving aid from the Cubans and wanted Dr. King killed because of his commitment to nonviolence.[336] Bell added that he had worked as an FBI informant for years[337] and was certain the FBI did not kill Dr. King.[338] He also provided elaborate details of an alleged 1977 plot to kill Ambassador Andrew Young, again involving Ridley and Cordova.[339]

Bell came to the attention of the committee when his

attorney, James Skinney, notified the committee that Bell had information on the King assassination. Despite a long criminal history[340] that cast doubt on Bell's veracity, the committee staff questioned him twice while he was incarcerated in Georgia[341] and reviewed a 23-page account of the allegation that he provided.[342] Although Bell recounted contradictory details in several different versions of his story, the committee attempted to verify the information he provided.

The committee identified and interviewed the only Black Director of Safety in Louisville's history, A. Wilson Edwards.[343] Edwards, who knew both Bishop Tucker and Reverend A. D. King, denied knowning Bell and further stated that he did not live in Louisville from 1968 through 1970.[344]

The committee also interviewed Thomas Kitchen. According to Bell, Kitchen was an FBI agent assigned to Louisville and an alleged participant in the conspiracy. Kitchen told the committee he had not been assigned to Louisville until 1972, and he had served there as special agent-in-charge until 1975.[345] Kitchen denied knowing Bell, Ridley, or Cordova, but admitted they may have known him as the special agent-in-charge in Louisville. [346]

The committee attempted to locate other persons who Bell said could verify the conspiracy, but efforts to find them failed.[347] Both Reverend A. D. King and Bishop Eubanks Tucker had died before the committee's 1977 probe of the Bell contention. Given the lack of witness corroboration of this allegation, the death of two central figures and Bell's questionable background, the committee concluded his story was not credible and did not merit further investigation.

7. CONSPIRACY ALLEGATIONS: ST. LOUIS

(a) Delano Elmer Walker

Delano Elmer Walker told the committee that some time in 1965, he received a $500 down payment from three unidentified white men for his participation in a plot to assassinate Dr. King.[348] Walker alleged that the men approached him with this offer in St. Louis, Mo., while he was under the influence of alcohol.[349] Only after discussing the proposition with his wife, Ruth Ann, did Walker decide to report the plan to Sheriff Ken Buckley in

Farmington, Mo.[350] Walker asserted that his meeting with the sheriff and an FBI agent ended when they decided he was insane.[351] Soon afterward, according to Walker, he was committed to a mental health facility.[352] Walker was sentenced to 18 months in Missouri State Penitentiary in October 1967, following an assault conviction. [353]

In June 1968, Walker's physician, Dr. C. W. Chastain, contacted a San Francisco magazine and reported that the FBI had questioned him extensively in 1965 regarding Walker's allegation.[354] After learning of that contact, the committee located Dr. Chastain and verified this FBI questioning.[355] Dr. Chastain explained that, in 1977, Walker and his wife had described the King offer in detail. [356] Dr. Chastain mentioned that Sheriff Ken Buckley of Farmington, Mo., believed Walker's story.[357]

The committee interviewed both Delano[358] and Ruth Ann Walker[359] about the allegation and received substantially different accounts from each. While Walker said that he had offered to use his gun to murder Dr. King, [360] his wife explained that he did not purchase the weapon until 1970.[361] Mrs. Walker stated that Delano told her the assassination offer was initiated at their house in Elvins, Mo., not at a tavern in St. Louis.[362] She also said she did not see the down payment money that Delano supposedly showed her on the day of the agreement.[363] Walker could not locate the documents that he said would support his allegation, specifically a card noting the name of the tavern where the offer was made and his wife did not know of such a card.[364]

The inconsistencies in details of Walker's story, his inability to provide leads to the identities of those who made the offer, and his mental problems led to the committee's conclusion that this allegation was not worthy of further investigation.

8. CONSPIRACY ALLEGATIONS: MIAMI

(a) William Somersett

The committee explored a conspiracy allegation that originated with William Somersett, a long-time informant in Miami who died in 1970.[365] Somersett had worked with various law enforcement agencies, including the FBI and the Miami Police Department.[366] He achieved notoriety with his story that, just weeks before the 1963 assassination of President John F. Kennedy, he received information that the President would be killed by someone in an office building with a high-powered rifle.[17]

According to an article in Miami Magazine, Somersett attended a National Labor Relations Board meeting in Washington on April 1, 1968, at which he overheard a conversation among longshoremen and sanitation workers indicating that Dr. King, on his next visit to Memphis would be killed for meddling in the sanitation strike.[367] Somersett reportedly told a Miami police officer of the death threat on April 3, 1968, the day before the assassination.[368]

A review of FBI and Miami Police Department files on Somersett revealed a career of supplying law enforcement officials with valuable and reliable information since the 1950's.[369] In the early 1960's, however, the FBI discontinued Somersett as an informant because of his increasing unreliability.[370] The files showed Somersett had repeatedly supplied information about political assassinations.[371] In addition to the Kennedy and King death threats, he also reported to the FBI and the Secret Service alleged conspiracies to kill Presidents Johnson and Nixon. [372] These allegations had been investigated and found to be unsupported by independent evidence.

The committee sought to verify Somersett's story by interviewing the Miami police officer to whom he said he allegedly reported the King death threat. Detective Sgt. Charles Sapp was questioned under oath by the committee. He said he remembered receiving the information on April 3, the day before the assassination.[373] Further, on April 25, 1968, memorandum he wrote [374][18] (the earliest documentation the Miami Police Department could locate pertaining to the matter) was not the first document he had prepared concerning Somersett's information on the King assassination. He maintained that an earlier departmental memo would reflect his receipt of the information prior to the assassination.

Following Sapp's deposition, an earlier police memoran-

---

[17]Somersett did not pass this information to authorities until after the President's assassination.
[18]The April 25, 1968 memorandum reflected Sapp's receipt of information on the King assassination from Somersett, but the implication of the memorandum was that Somersett did not provide the information to Sapp until days after the assassination.

dum by Sapp, dated April 17, 1968, was discovered in the files of a former prosecutor in the State attorney's office. [376] The document indicated that on April 16, the State attorney's office asked Sapp to contact Somersett to determine if he had any information pertaining to the King murder.[377] The memo indicated further that Sapp contacted Somersett on April 17, 1968. Somersett told him that he had learned of a death threat against Dr. King "on the eve of his death."[378] When questioned about this document, Sapp insisted that there was still an earlier memorandum, dated April 14, 1968, that would reflect Somersett's transmittal of the information to him before the assassination. [379] No additional reports, however, were discovered by the committee. In addition, the clear implication of the April 17 memorandum was that Sapp contacted Somersett for the first time on that date. The committee concluded, therefore, that, despite Sapp's recollection, he did not receive the information from Somersett until a week after the assassination of Dr. King.

The committee also questioned several other police officers to whom Sapp said he relayed Somersett's information prior to April 4.[380] These individuals, however, did not recall receiving the account before the assassination.[381] The committee believed that these veteran police officers would have recalled receipt of the information before the assassination, had it in fact been received.

The committee also attempted to determine whether there was an NLRB meeting on April 1, 1968, in Washington. Several agencies and labor organizations, including the NLRB, were contacted. The committee discovered that available files did not reflect such a meeting.[382]

Further, the committee found a number of inconsistencies between the police reports and Sapp's recollection. Thus, the committee concluded that Sapp did not know of Somersett's story before Dr. King's death, but learned of it after the assassination, probably on April 17, 1968.

The committee was unable to uncover any evidence supporting the purported plot described by Somersett to Sapp. Indeed, the committee found it improbable that sanitation workers would plot to kill Dr. King, a supporter of their strike. In view of Somersett's background of informing law enforcement officials of unfounded assassination plots and the lack of evidence to corroborate his allegation, the committee found that Somersett's information was without substance.

(a) Otis Moore

Otis Humphrey Moore alleged that, while he was stationed at Ford Hood, Tex., in April 1965,[383] an unnamed white male offered him $50,000 to assassinate Dr. King. [384] The conversation took place in an unknown bar outside Temple, Tex.[385] Moore said when he returned to the bar shortly after Dr. King's murder in April 1968, a new building stood in its place.[386]

Also present at the bar during the 1965 conversation, according to Moore, was a man he described as a "million dollar" lawyer from Dallas.[387] Moore believed the prominent attorney's presence in the rundown bar indicated his involvement in serious plans to kill Dr. King, although the supposed lawyer did not participate in the conversation.[388] Moore, however, could give no leads to identify the man.[389]

The committee interviewed Moore after he wrote that he had "certain information that, I am sure, will give a clue to the people really involved in the conspiracy * * *." [390] Moore provided the committee with a detailed narrative and records of attempts he made to tell his story to, among others, the FBI,[391] the Senate Select Committee to Study Government Operations with Respect to Intelligence Activities,[392] Senator Edward M. Kennedy,[393] and the Board of Ebenezer Baptist Church, Atlanta, Ga., the church of Dr. King's father, Rev. Martin Luther King, Sr.[394]

In an attempt to evaluate Moore's credibility, the committee reviewed relevant FBI files on him and discovered that Moore's wife had said he was extremely drunk on the night he returned home with the assassination story.[395]

The vagueness of Moore's allegation and the interval since he allegedly came upon the offer made corroboration of this story virtually impossible. Further, the lack of geographical and time proximity to the assassination of Dr. King in Memphis in 1968 reduced the significance of Moore's allegations. No further action was taken on the lead.

10. CONSPIRACY ALLEGATIONS: NEW YORK

(a) Myron Billett

Myron Billett, a convicted felon, claimed that in the spring of 1968, during a meeting he attended of organized crime figures Sam Giancana and Carlos Gambino, as well as CIA and FBI agents, an offer was proposed for the assassination of Dr. King.[396] Billet said he drove Giancana to this meeting at the Skyview Motel near Binghamton, N.Y.[397] Martin Bishop and Lee Leland, allegedly of the CIA, offered Giancana and Gambino money to kill King.[398] Giancana and Gambino refused because, as Giancana supposedly commented, the CIA had messed up the assassination of President John F. Kennedy. [399] Billett also claimed he had been to a similar meeting attended by Giancana, Lee Harvey Oswald, Jack Ruby and others in 1963 in Dallas, Tex., where an offer to kill President Kennedy was made.[400]

Billett originally came to the committee's attention when a Washington, D.C. newspaper printed a story concerning his conspiracy allegation. At the time Billett was interviewed by the committee, he was in prison for armed robbery and manslaughter convictions. Although cooperative with the committee, Billett changed important details of his story several times.[401]

In its investigation of Billett's story, the committee tried to verify the names of the alleged CIA and FBI agents. None of the alleged agents existed.[402] Although Billett said he had a close relationship with several persons involved in organized crime, he could not supply details that would enable the committee to verify these associations.[403] Giancana and Gambino were dead in 1977 when this allegation was investigated.

The committee found that Billett's story about the meetings involving the assassinations of President Kennedy and Dr. Martin Luther King was not credible.[404]

D. No Federal, State or Local Government Agency Was Involved in the Assassination of Dr. King

Allegations of government complicity in the assassination of Dr. Martin Luther King have been made by attorneys for James Earl Ray, authors of books and articles, even prominent civil rights leaders, and they have aroused suspicion in the minds of political leaders as well as the general public. For the most part, the charges have been pointed at agencies assigned to investigate the assassination, specifically the FBI and the Memphis Police Department, or authorities at the Missouri State Penitentiary, from which Ray escaped a year before the assassination. The committee examined each of those agencies in light of the allegations.

1. THE FEDERAL BUREAU OF INVESTIGATION

Speculation that the FBI—or, more probably, members of that organization, including highly placed Bureau officials—might have had a role in the assassination originated in the early 1970's, when the public became aware of COINTELPRO, the Bureau's counterintelligence program that had Dr. King as one of its targets. When, in 1976, the report on the investigation of the Senate Select Committee to Study Governmental Operations with Respect to Intelligence Activities was published and the full scope of the attempt by the FBI to discredit Dr. King became recognized, suspicions were widely rekindled.†

In November 1975, as the Senate committee was completing its investigation, the Department of Justice formed a Task Force to examine the FBI's program of harassment directed at Dr. King, the Bureau's security investiga-

---

†The origin, scope, rationale, techniques and targets of the Bureau's COINTEL program are traced in Book III of the Final Report of the Senate Select Committee to Study Governmental Operations with Respect to Intelligence Activities, S. Rept. 94–755, 94th Cong., 2d sess. 1–77 (1976). The efforts of the Bureau against Dr. King, the security investigation as well as COINTELPRO, also appear as a case study. *Id.* at 81–183. For this reason, those programs will not be reviewed here except as necesary for background or as they focus on the question of responsibility in the assassination. See also *infra* sec. II D.

tion of him, his assassination and the criminal investigation that followed. One aspect of the Task Force study was to determine "whether any action taken in relation to Dr. King by the FBI before the assassination had, or might have had, an effect, direct or indirect, on that event."

In its report, the Task Force criticized the FBI not for the opening, but for the protracted continuation of, its security investigation of Dr. King:

> We think the security investigation which included both physical and technical surveillance, should have been terminated * * * in 1963. That it was intensified and augmented by a COINTELPRO type campaign against Dr. King was unwarranted; the COINTELPRO type campaign, moreover, was ultra vires and very probably * * * felonious. [1]

The Task Force concluded, however, that the evidence was overwhelming that Ray was a lone assassin, and it found no evidence of FBI involvement.

The question of FBI complicity lingered, nonetheless, and alleged deficiencies in the FBI assassination investigation raised the possibility of a coverup after the fact. Because of these persistent doubts and because the committee questioned both the method and the reasoning behind the Justice Department's report, a decision was made to reexamine the question of involvement by the FBI in the assassination.

Ultimately, the committee found no evidence that the FBI intentionally brought about the death of Dr. King. In reaching that conclusion, it sought answers to specific questions that bore on FBI complicity:

Did the counterintelligence program, initiated in August 1967 against the Southern Christian Leadership Conference and in March 1968 against Dr. King, result in Dr. King's staying at the Lorraine Motel in Memphis on April 4, 1968?

Did the Bureau pay members of the Invaders, an organization of young Black activists in Memphis, or act through its informants in the Invaders, to incite the violence on March 28 that led Dr. King to return to Memphis?

Did the Bureau have foreknowledge of the assassination through surveillance, informants or other means, on which it did not act?

Did the Bureau, through the use of an undercover agent or informant, act with James Earl Ray in the assassination of Dr. King?

The committee began its analysis with a review of the investigations by the Senate committee and the Justice Department. It then turned to the FBI files generated during both the agency's security investigation[1] and COINTEL-PRO[2] against Dr. King and the SCLC.

While the files reviewed by the committee contained substantial detail and were invaluable in providing an understanding of the nature and scope of the FBI's operations, certain decisions and actions were often ambiguous or unexplained. In addition, there were critical periods of time for which documentation was either scarce or nonexistent. For these reasons, the committee chose to supplement its file review with extensive interviews of FBI field agents and headquarters personnel. These interviews were initially unsworn, but because of the gravity of the issues and the serious implications of the FBI's campaign to undermine Dr. King's stature as a civil rights leader, extensive testimony was taken under oath in executive session and in public hearings. With the exception of J. Edgar Hoover, Director of the Federal Bureau of Investigation; Clyde Tolson, his Associate Director; and William C. Sullivan, Assistant Director of the Domestic

---

[1] In October 1962, the FBI opened its security investigation of the SCLC and its president, Dr. King. The investigation was authorized by the Attorney General. The initial purpose of the investigation was to examine what, if any, Communist influence existed in the SCLC. The committee concurred with the 1977 Justice Department study in its conclusion that no evidence existed that Dr. King was a Communist or ever was affiliated with the Communist Party; that the SCLC under Dr. King was ever anything other than an organization devoted to civil rights; that Dr. King's alleged Communist advisors never "sold" Dr. King any course of action that could be identified as Communist; and that the security investigation should have been terminated shortly after it commenced. Indeed, as the 1977 report noted, one adviser was not influential and the other disassociated himself from the party in 1963 "because it failed adequately to serve the civil rights movement."

[2] COINTEL-type atcivities against Dr. King and the SCLC are best dated from December 1963, although Dr. King was not formally targeted until March 1968. Their purpose was not only to gather information, but to use it to undermine Dr. King and his influence in the civil rights movement. Activities of this type with regard to Communist Party and white hate groups were known in a general way to various advisers to the President and congressional leaders, but their extension to the Socialist Workers Party, the Black Nationalists (that, according to the Bureau, included the SCLC and Dr. King) and the New Left was known only to the Bureau. The FBI's effort to discredit Dr. King and to undermine the SCLC touched every aspect of Dr. King's life, including his private life, which was subjected to extensive electronic surveillance. Religious leaders and institutions were contacted and leaks were made to the press. Members of Congress, White House officials, and other Washington leaders were contacted.

Intelligence Division, all of whom were deceased,[3] FBI officials and agents whose testimony was considered essential to a thorough examination of the issue of FBI complicity were interviewed.

(a) The Lorraine Motel issue

The committee investigated the possibility that the FBI's COINTELPRO effort influenced Dr. King's decision to be in Memphis on April 4, 1968, and, more specifically, to stay at the Lorraine Motel. The committee determined that Dr. King had been designated as a man to be discredited as early as December 1963.[2] On August 25, 1967, FBI headquarters directed 22 field offices, including Memphis, to commence COINTELPRO activities against "Black Nationalist—Hate Groups."[3] The purpose of the directive, as reflected in supporting documents, was to expose, disrupt, misdirect or otherwise neutralize the activities of specified organizations, including the Southern Christian Leadership Conference (SCLC). Instructions were issued "that no opportunities be overlooked for counterintelligence action."[4]

On March 4, 1968, a second memo was issued, expanding the COINTELPRO effort to include 44 field offices and for the first time specifically naming Dr. King.[5] Several goals of COINTELPRO were set out. One of them was to "[p]revent the rise of a 'messiah' who could unify and electrify the militant black nationalist movement." The memo continued,

> Malcolm X might have been such a "messiah"; Martin Luther King, Stokely Carmichael, and Elijah Muhammad all aspire to this position * * * King could be a very real contender for this position should he abandon his supposed obedience to white, liberal doctrines (nonviolence) and embrace Black Nationalism.[6]

For the first time, specific reporting requirements were established, with the first response due from all offices within 10 days. Imagination and initiative were stressed, although

---

[3]The committee frankly acknowledged that its investigation of the FBI was severely restricted by its inability to put questions on the Bureau's campaign to discredit Dr. King to these three top officials, since they had been primarily responsible for it.

specific operations were to be approved by headquarters to avoid embarrassment to the Bureau.[7]

The committee found no evidence of COINTELPRO initiatives against Dr. King or the SCLC from the Memphis field office in response to the March 4 memorandum. FBI files did reflect a March 14, 1968, response from the Memphis field office,[8] but it contained no reference to Dr. King or the SCLC.

From the testimony of FBI personnel as well is that of members of the SCLC and the Invaders, the committee found that Dr. King's decision to return to Memphis and stay at the Lorraine Motel was not influenced by COINTELPRO initiatives. While it was apparent that the FBI learned of Dr. King's decision to return to Memphis from an informant within SCLC, there was no evidence that the informant influenced the decision itself.[4]

The testimony of Ralph Abernathy, Dr. King's close associate and successor as the leader of SCLC, established that Dr. King's decision to return to Memphis after the March 28 violence was a personal choice, made after some debate with his SCLC colleagues. It stemmed from Dr. King's desire to erase the effects of the highly publicized violence on the success of the upcoming Poor People's Campaign.[10]

The committee explored the possibility that a March 29, 1968, FBI headquarters COINTELPRO initiative directed at Dr. King influenced his decision to stay at the Lorraine Motel when he returned to Memphis on April 3. [11] The headquarters memorandum from G. C. Moore, Chief of the Racial Intelligence Section, to William C. Sullivan, Assistant Director in charge of the Domestic Intelligence Division, recommended release of a news item, which read in part:

The fine Hotel Lorraine in Memphis is owned and patronized exclusively by Negroes but King didn't go there after his hasty exit [from] the demonstration

---

[4]The committee learned of the identity of the SCLC informant when he acknowledged his former status in a committee interview; he was also asked about the nature of his relationship with the Bureau; the instructions he received, particularly during March and April 1968; the type of information he sought; FBI counterintelligence activities against Dr. King and SCLC; and FBI activities in Memphis in April 1968. [9] The committee also reviewed his FBI informant file. Based on this independent investigation, the committee found that while the informant was in Memphis periodically during March and April 1968, there was no indication that he influenced events that took place there.

of March 28]. Instead, King decided the plush Holiday Inn Motel, white-owned, operated, and almost exclusively white patronized was the place to "cool it." There will be no boycott of white merchants for King, only for his followers.

The memo was initialed by Hoover, who indicated his approval, and by Sullivan and Moore. The notation, "handled 4/3/68," was written at the bottom. The committee was unable to determine the meaning of the notation.[5] The committee received testimony which it credited, from Dr. Abernathy that Dr. King's normal practice was to stay at the Lorraine Motel when he was in Memphis and that his choice of the Lorraine on April 3 reflected this past practice.[12] Given Dr. Abernathy's testimony, the committee was satisfied that the March 29 memorandum did not cause Dr. King to stay at the Lorraine.

The FBI's intent in drafting the memorandum, however, remained an open issue. If its purpose was to cause Dr. King to take a room at the Lorraine, its intent remained sinister, no matter what the reasons were for the choice of lodgings. On the other hand, if the purpose was to embarrass Dr. King, it was simply one of many COINTELPRO initiatives that had no connection with the assassination.

An examination of Ray's conduct in Memphis led the committee to conclude that the latter is the more credible alternative. Dr. King returned to Memphis and checked into the Lorraine on the morning of April 3, 1968. Ray arrived in Memphis on the evening of April 3. Yet Ray chose to stay at the New Rebel Motel and did not check into the roominghouse at 422½ South Main Street until the afternoon of April 4. To assume the FBI's purpose on March 29 was to set Dr. King up for assassination at the Lorraine is to assume that the Bureau had control over Ray's movements. Ray's presence at the New Rebel on April 3 was evidence that it did not have such control. The committee concluded, therefore, that the drafters of the March 29

<hr/>

[5]The committee interviewed Special Agent Harold Leinbaugh who wrote the "handled" notation on the memo. He stated that while he had no recollection of the COINTELPRO initiative, he could offer two possible interpretations of the notation. It could mean simply that the proposal had been received by the Mass Media Section where he worked at the time, or it might signify actual placement of the proposed editorials with a friendly news outlet. Leinbaugh added that if a proposal was not considered newsworthy, no effort was made to pass it to cooperative media outlets.

memorandum did not intend to set Dr. King up for assassination at the Lorraine.

(b) The inciting of violence by informants issue

The committee investigated the possibility that the violence that interrupted the sanitation workers march in Memphis on March 28, 1968, leading to Dr. King's return to the city, was provoked by FBI agents or FBI or law enforcement informants working within a militant organization known as the Invaders.

The Invaders came into being in late 1967 when a number of Black youths, politically conditioned by the Vietnam war, the civil rights movement and economic conditions in Memphis, created what they envisioned would be a coalition of groups to challenge the established leadership of Memphis. The coalition came to be known as the Black Organizing Project; its most widely known group was the Invaders.

The committee found evidence that some members of the Invaders, resorting to inflammatory rhetoric and acts of violence, encouraged the disturbances that marred the sanitation workers march. In its investigation of the Invaders, the committee took testimony from several former members (the organization had since been disbanded), some of whom had provided written releases authorizing the FBI to turn over their files, investigative or informant. In addition, the committee reviewed reports of Invader activities in the files of the FBI and the Memphis Police Department, and it took testimony from FBI agents who controlled informants in Memphis and monitored the activities of groups and individuals connected with the sanitation strike. Finally, the committee took testimony from Marrell McCullough, an undercover Memphis police officer who had infiltrated the Invaders in 1968.

The investigation established the existence of five FBI informants who provided intelligence on the racial situation to the Memphis field office; their reporting touched on Invader activities. [13] The committee then gained access to the headquarters and field office files the FBI maintained on them. In accordance with an understanding that had been worked out with the FBI, all information that might identify the informants was excised before the files were turned over to the committee. The committee specified the informant it considered most likely to have been influential in Invader activities, and the FBI was asked to approach him and determine if he would agree to be interviewed by the committee. An interview was arranged, and the informant was questioned about the nature of the information provided to the Bureau as well as the nature of the instructions given the informant by Bureau personnel.[14] The other four informants were not in a position to have influenced Invader activities. Nevertheless, reviews of their files were conducted. Nothing in the committee's investigation, file review or interview of the informant indicated that FBI informants were used as agent provcateurs during the March 28 violence.

Two serious discrepancies between the testimony of the informant, as opposed to the files and the word of the relevant FBI agents, however, did arise as a result of the committee's interview. The FBI informant denied having provided certain information that had been attributed to him and placed in his informant file. He also denied ever having received any instructions from the FBI as to the conduct of his informant activities. [15] The committee could only speculate about the significance of the discrepancies, and believed such speculation would have served no useful purpose. The committee was forced to conclude, however, that the discrepancy tarnished the evidence given by both the Bureau and the informant, and it left the committee with a measure of uncertainty about the scope of FBI involvement with the Invaders.

Marrell McCullough, the undercover Memphis police officer whose intelligence on the Invaders was transmitted regularly to the local FBI office, was in the parking lot of the Lorraine Motel at the time of the assassination and was among the first to reach the fallen Dr. King. Since there had been allegations that McCullough was a Federal agent, the committee was particularly interested in his testimony. He denied having had any connections with the FBI or any other Federal agency, and he specifically stated he had no part in provoking violence on March 28, 1968. [16] Members of the Invaders supported his testimony, and while the FBI and other intelligence agencies received his intelligence regularly from the Memphis Police Department, the committee could find no evidence that the Bureau or any other agency was aware of McCullough's role or his identity as an undercover police officer.[17]

The committee noted, further, that in an interview by the FBI shortly after the assassination, McCullough was treated no differently than other eyewitnesses, indicating the FBI was unaware of his official ties to the Memphis Police Department. [18] Thus, the committee found that McCullough was not employed by the FBI or any Federal agency. Nor did he have knowledge, as far as the committee could determine, that his information was being transmitted to the Bureau or the Federal Government.[19]

While the committee found no basis for a conclusion that the FBI, directly or through its informants, provoked the violence on March 28, FBI files and sworn testimony to the committee did indicate an awareness by members of the Memphis field office of the potential for disturbances. [20] The committee reviewed a memorandum indicating that the Bureau received information prior to the march that violence was likely to occur. [21] Agents of the field office at the time confirmed it. One or two hours before the march, an FBI informant reported that participants had purchased several hundred two-by-two sticks to which they had attached cardboard placards, and that there was a possibility they would be used in a violent manner.[22] This information was corroborated by Memphis police sources who provided an additional report that members of the Invaders were distributing the sticks to "impressionable youngers between the ages of 10 and 13."[23]

The Memphis office notified FBI headquarters and kept close contact with the Memphis police, but no steps were taken to relay the warning either to the strike leaders or to Dr. King and his associates. [24] The committee believed such preventive steps should have been taken, even though the FBI had no authority to provide protection to the strike participants. The committee stressed, however, that it found no evidence that the FBI's failure to warn the strike leaders or Dr. King and his party indicated a plan to disrupt the march.

(c) The FBI foreknowledge issue

While the committee believed the FBI was guilty of no more than unwarranted neglect in its failure to alert the organizers of the march of the threat of violence, it considered the issue of foreknowledge of the assassination to be potentially much more significant. The committee noted that the FBI—in particular, the Memphis field office—closely monitored developments in the sanitation strike. [25] Further, the committee found that Dr. King's Washington spring project, the upcoming march on Washington, was the subject of great concern at FBI headquarters. [26] Consequently, the committee found it curious that in its review of the King security file it found a scarcity of intelligence pertaining to Dr. King's activities between March 28 and April 4, 1968.

The committee was told by agents in the Memphis field office at the time that the absence of data on Dr. King for that period was indicative only of the fact that the main area of FBI coverage in Memphis was the sanitation strike.[27] Moreover, Memphis agents adamantly maintained in sworn testimony that no efforts were made to monitor Dr. King physically or electronically following his arrival in that city on April 3. [28] Finally, a thorough review of FBI files produced no evidence that documentation of a surveillance of Dr. King's activities in Memphis had been destroyed.[6]

The committee also reasoned that, as ironic as it may seem, the presence of the FBI COINTELPRO initiatives against Dr. King up to the day of his death could be used to show that FBI headquarters did not have foreknowledge of his assassination. It would hardly have been necessary to continue a nationwide program of harassment against a man soon to be killed. In a review of all COINTELPRO files on Dr. King, the committee found substantial evidence that the harassment program showed no signs of abatement as the fateful day approached. For example, the Mobile, Ala., FBI field office proposed using an unwitting minister, one influential in Selma, Ala., and somewhat hostile to Dr. King for personal reasons, to effect a COINTELPRO objective.[29] The minister was to be sent an anonymous letter stating that Dr. King was using Blacks for personal aggrandizement, that demonstrators would be stranded without food or shelter, and that there might be violence. A copy of the letter would be sent to the Selma Times Journal with a suggestion that the paper interview the minister. On April 2, headquarters authorized Mobile to issue the letter, suggesting that it be mailed from Baltimore to disguise the origin.[7][30] Con-

---

[6] A committee review of a separate FBI file on the Memphis sanitation workers strike did in fact show that Dr. King's participation in the March 28 demonstration and a press conference that followed had been covered. Thus, the absence of similar references to Dr. King's activities in the King security file became more understandable.

[7] Of similar import was an April 2, 1968, request from the FBI to the Justice Department for authorization to implement electronic surveillance on Dr. King's SCLC headquarters in Atlanta. (see e.g., testimony of Ramsey Clark, Nov. 28, 1978. VII HSCA–MLK Hearings, 140.)

sequently, the committee could find no indication in its interviews of agents or its file reviews that the FBI had foreknowledge of the assassination of Dr. King.

(d) The FBI assistance for Ray issue

The committee investigated the possibility that the FBI, either through an agent or informant, may have acted with James Earl Ray in the assassination of Dr. King.

The committee first sought to identify all persons who met with Ray during the period of his incarceration at Missouri State Penitentiary and from the time of his escape from MSP on April 23, 1967, to the day of the assassination, April 4, 1968. A list was compiled of 663 possible Ray associates, fellow inmates at MSP, criminal associates and other persons known to have had even fleeting contact with Ray. The list included individuals associated with establishments frequented by Ray, or registered at motels, hotels, and roominghouses where Ray stayed during his fugitive period.

The committee also identified the FBI agents in Jefferson City, Mo., where Missouri State Penitentiary is located and those assigned to the unlawful flight case following Ray's MSP escape.

From the list of known, probable, or possible Ray associates, the FBI was asked to indicate if any were informants, and the Bureau acknowledged in fact that three of them had at one time or another supplied information to the Bureau on a regular basis. Two of these informants were not active in 1967–68; one did have a confidential relationship with the Bureau in 1968.[32]

Independent of information supplied by the Bureau, the 1968 informant was interviewed by the committee.[33] He acknowledged his relationship with the Bureau and indicated that:

> His confidential relationship with the FBI dated back to the late 1950's;[34] and
>
> He had known Ray casually while the two men were serving terms together at Missouri State Penitentiary in the early 1960's.[35]

It was also learned that the informant left MSP nearly 3 years before the assassination and was returned there shortly after Ray's escape.[36] The committee checked the respective whereabouts of the two men during the period

543

in 1967 when they were both at liberty and could find no evidence that they had been in contact.

Seven key FBI agents were questioned with respect to a direct connection between Ray and the Bureau, one of whom was in that Jefferson City field office for the entire period of Ray's detention at MSP.[37] From these interviews, no direct contact between Ray and the FBI either at MSP or during the fugitive period could be established. The interviews also failed to indicate a contact between the Bureau and any individual who was also in contact with Ray from the time of his escape to the assassination.

Based on this investigation, the committee found no evidence that Ray had contact either at Missouri State Penitentiary or during the fugitive period with any FBI agent or active FBI informant. In the absence of known, contact between Ray and the FBI, either through an agent or an informant, the committee found no evidence that Ray acted with the FBI, either knowingly or unwittingly, in the assassination.[8]

(e) FBI surveillance files in the National Archives

From the beginning of the committee's investigation, James Earl Ray had suggested that his innocence or the FBI's role in the assassination of Dr. King might be revealed by an examination of FBI documents and tape recordings that are sealed and stored in the National Archives as a result of a court order in *Lee* v. *Kelly*.[9]
[38] In its effort to seek information from every possible source, the committee sought access to these materials. [39] Permission was obtained from the court for the committee to have access to the files deposited in the Archives. [40] The access sought and obtained was the minimum necessary to ascertain the relevancy of the material to the work of the committee. Every effort was made to minimize the invasion of the privacy associated with the review.

A review was conducted in the latter part of Decem-

---

[8]The committee frankly acknowledged that contact between Ray and the Bureau could have been made indirectly through several intermediaries. Nevertheless, since there was no reasonable way to investigate this theoretical possibility (absent a concrete lead), no investigation was undertaken to explore it.

[9]An action filed in 1977 by Bernard Lee, a former member of the executive board of SCLC, named as defendants Clarence Kelley, who had been Director of the FBI, and other former FBI officials. In the suit, Lee sought to recover damages for alleged violations by the FBI of his civil rights through the use of illegal electronic surveillance in the 1960's.

ber 1978 of an inventory of the materials, approximately 845 pages in length. Each entry in the inventory included the serial number of the document, the date it was written, the name of the individual who originated it, and the person to whom it was directed. In addition, a separate portion of the inventory catalogued the tapes that were produced during the various electronic surveillances that were conducted on Dr. King, written transcripts of some of those tapes, and handwritten logs and notes made by the agents who supervised the surveillance.

While the entire inventory was examined, the portion relating to the actual tapes and transcriptions of the tapes was of particular interest. The committee's review determined that the earliest item in this category in the inventory was dated February 18 through 20, 1964. The latest entry was dated May 16, 1966. This information was compared with an internal FBI memorandum dated April 18, 1968, from Charles D. Brennan to William C. Sullivan. [41] The purpose of the memorandum was to identify all of the microphone and wiretap installations that had been employed by the Bureau during the course of its security investigations of Dr. King and the SCLC. [42] While the memorandum indicated that the last electronic surveillance of Dr. King terminated on November 30, 1965, as opposed to the May 16, 1966, termination date[10] contained in the inventory, neither document indicated that electronic surveillance was directed at Dr. King after mid-1966. The committee's file review uncovered a memorandum, apparently issued for record purposes, from Atlanta Special Agent in Charge Joseph Ponder, dated June 23, 1966.[43] It recounted a June 21, 1966, order from headquarters to remove an existing technical surveillance on SCLC headquarters. This would indicate that the technical surveillance of King through the SCLC tap continued at least until June 21, 1966, in Atlanta. These dates are consistent with information given to the Senate Select Committee to Study Governmental Operations With Respect to Intelligence Activities by the Bureau on July 21, 1965, in response to a request concerning electronic surveillance of Dr. King from January 1, 1960, until April 5, 1968.[44]

The discrepancies existing between these various dates were not considered significant by the committee. Former

---

[10]The May 16, 1966, date was established when the committee discovered a reference to a surveillance log for that date. Surveillance logs are normally created to provide an index for an ongoing tap.

Attorney General Ramsey Clark testified that, during the tenure, authorizations for electronic surveillance by the Bureau were severely curtailed. [45] The committee's investigation revealed that during 1968 the Bureau tried unsuccessfully to have Clark authorize electronic surveillance of SCLC and Dr. King.[46] The committee's investigation uncovered no evidence that the Bureau ever disregarded the Attorney General's refusal to authorize the requested surveillance. Given their distance in time from the assassination, it is extremely improbable, moreover, that the actual tapes, transcripts, and other materials underlying these intercepts would have information pertaining to the assassination. Because of the invasion of privacy that a review of the raw materials would have entailed, the committee decided it was not necessary to undertake one. It would have been ironic indeed, if a committee, out of a concern for what happened to Dr. King, unnecessarily invaded his privacy.

2. MEMPHIS POLICE DEPARTMENT

In its investigation of possible official complicity in the assassination, the committee considered allegations suggesting that the Memphis Police Department facilitated Dr. King's murder.[11] For example, there had been wide dissemination of a theory that a Black detective was removed from his post at a fire station adjacent to the Lorraine Motel so that he would not interfere with the assassination.[47]

To resolve questions concerning the possible complicity of the MPD, the committee conducted extensive interviews with Memphis police officials, officials of the Southern Christian Leadership Conference and citizen witnesses; it also took sworn testimony in depositions and hearings. Further, the committee reviewed the pertinent files of the MPD, the FBI, and the Department of Justice.

With regard to possible MPD complicity in the assassination, four main issues were explored:

Why was an MPD security detail assigned to Dr. King withdrawn on April 3, 1968?

[11]As director of fire and safety in Memphis in 1968, Frank C. Holloman was responsible for the performance of the Memphis Police Department. Because of Holloman's extensive background with the FBI, the actions of the Memphis Police Department had been viewed by some as additional evidence of FBI complicity in the assassination.

546

Why was Detective Edward Redditt removed from his observation post at a fire station next to the Lorraine on April 4, 1968?

Why were two Black firemen transferred from the same fire station shortly before the assassination?

Were the alleged deficiencies in the postassassination conduct of the MPD intentionally designed to faciliate the escape of the assassin?

(a) Withdrawal of the security detail

On April 3, 1968, at approximately 10:30 a.m., Dr. King arrived at the airport in Memphis where he was met by a four-man security detail ordered by Chief of Detectives W. P. Huston and led by Inspector Don H. Smith (since retired). [48] The purpose of the detail was to provide physical protection for Dr. King, and it was apparently provided at the initiative of the Memphis Police Department because of the violence that had occurred during Dr. King's visit to Memphis the previous week. It did not appear to the committee that Dr. King or members of his party requested that the MPD provide security.[12][49]

At the airport, the security detail asked members of Dr. King's party what their schedule was to be during their stay in Memphis. Rev. James Lawson, a Memphis minister who had been instrumental in getting Dr. King to come to Memphias on March 28, responded that theyhadnotmade up their minds; Inspector Smith testified that he inferred from Lawson's response that security detail would not be welcome.[51] Mrs. Tarlese Matthews, a member of Dr. King's party, specifically told the police that a security detail had not been requested. Inspector Smith said he perceived that the detail was not welcome.[52] Detective Edward Redditt, who was at the airport, was also told that Dr. King's party did not want protection.

The security detail followed Dr. King from the airport to the Lorraine Motel, arriving at approximately 11:20 a.m. At the request of Inspector Smith, another security unit, composed of an inspector and two additional Memphis police officers, arrived at the Lorraine to assist.[53]

---

[12]The committee tried to determine if Dr. King was provided protection by the MPD on earlier trips to Memphis but it could not resolve the question. [50] the committee decided, however, that this did not fundamentally affect its assessment of the removal of the detail on Apr. 3, 1968.

Shortly after noon, the detail followed Dr. King to the Centenary Methodist Church, where it secured the front and rear entrances.[54] As they were returning to the Lorrain at approximately 2:15 p.m.,[55] Dr. King's party took side routes and avoided the main streets, giving Inspector Smith the impression, he testified, that Dr. King's party was trying to lose the detail.[56]

Inspector Smith further testified that his belief that Dr. King and his party did not want the detail was reinforced by their refusal to tell police officers where they were going or how long they were to remain at a given stop, and the security detail just had to "tag along." [57] At approximately 5 p.m., Smith telephoned Chief of Detectives Huston and requested permission to remove the detail due to this apparent lack of cooperation.[58] According to Smith, Huston had a quick conference with "someone" while Smith held the phone, and he then granted the request.[59]

According to Henry Lux, who subsequently became police chief and who had since retired, Houston's conference was with Police Chief James MacDonald, now also retired. Lux stated that Huston told MacDonald that Smith's request was based on the failure of the King party to cooperate with the security detail. [60] While Lux told the committee that Huston authorized Smith to secure the detail after receiving permission from MacDonald, [61] MacDonald stated he had no recollection of Huston's decision to remove the detail or of his requesting permission to do so. [62]

Having obtained permission from Huston, Smith testified, he withdrew the detail shortly after 5 p.m. No attempt was made to inform anyone in Dr. King's party that it was being pulled back.[63]

Regardless of the attitude of Dr. King and of members of his party toward the security detail, the committee believed that in light of Dr. King's prominence, the violence that attended the March 28 demonstration, the tension in Memphis and the numerous threats that had been made on Dr. King's life, it was highly improper for the security detail to have been withdrawn. The committee also believed it improper for members of Dr. King's party not to have been informed of the withdrawal of the detail. The committee noted that Frank Holloman, director of fire and safety in Memphis at the time, maintaining he had not been informed of these decisions,[13] concurred in 1978 that they were wrong. [64]

The security detail was removed over 24 hours prior to Dr. King's assassination. All the evidence the committee obtained indicated that the detail was removed because of an evident sense of exasperation at what was perceived to be an uncooperative attitude on behalf of Dr. King's party. Its removal was not, the committee found, a part of a conspiracy to strip Dr. King of his protection in order to facilitate the assassination.

(b) The removal of Detective Redditt

In conjunction with its assessment of the withdrawal of Inspector Smith's security detail, the committee investigated the allegation that Detective Edward Redditt, who had been assigned to a security detail near the Lorraine, was removed two hours prior to the assassination. The fact of Detective Redditt's April 4 removal from his post at the firehouse across from the Lorraine Motel was uncontested. The nature of the assignment that Redditt had on April 3 and 4, 1968—whether it was security or surveillance—was central to an assessment of the significance of his removal. Redditt and his partner, Patrolman W. B. Richmond, met Dr. King at the airport on April 3, 1968, [65] on orders from Inspector Graydon Tines, who was in charge of the Inspectional Bureau. [66] Redditt claimed that he was ordered to go to the airport and report to a detail headed by Inspector Smith that was to provide security for Dr. King.[67] At the airport, Redditt said, he was threatened by Mrs. Tarlese Matthews, a young Black woman who had met Dr. King's party.[68] He also testified that a member of Dr. King's party told him security was not wanted.[69]

Redditt said that he and Richmond followed Dr. King to the Lorraine. Upon arriving at the Lorraine, he saw Smith talk to members of Dr. King's party and then proceed to make a phone call. After the phone call, he said Smith moved the men back to the sidewalk away from the patio area.[70] Redditt testified Smith made another phone call and then ordered the security detail withdrawn. [71] Redditt testified that he spoke with Smith and then

---

[13]The committee noted that retired Chief of Police Henry Lux stated that Holloman was not consulted when the decision to withdraw the detail was transmitted by Huston to Smith.

decided by himself to "set up security" in the firehouse.
[72]

The committee observed that Redditt's claim to have
been assigned to security for Dr. King at the airport was
not supported by the facts. In fact, Redditt's role was that
of surveillance and not security. Inspector Tines, who ordered Redditt to the airport, was in charge of the Inspectional Bureau in 1968, of which the Intelligence Section
was part. He testified in executive session that he ordered
Redditt and Richmond to go to the airport for surveillance
purposes, "* * * just to find out who was coming in and
who all was around the airport." [73] The surveillance at
the airport, as well as for the remainder of Dr. King's
stay in Memphis, was ordered, "* * * not only because
Dr. King was a controversial public figure, but also because he had been meeting with local Black militants
while in Memphis on prior visits."[74]

Patrolman Richmond, Redditt's partner, stated he understood his assignment to be surveillance and that no one
ever told him they were part of a security detail.[75] Inspector Smith also testified that neither Redditt nor Richmond had been assigned to the security detail on April 3,
and he would have been aware of it if they had been.[76]
Redditt conceded that he did not even speak to Inspector
Smith at the airport or beforehand. [77]

Finally, Redditt's account of the events after he arrived at the Lorraine was clearly in error. Smith's security
detail was not, as Redditt claimed, removed right after
King arrived at the Lorraine. As previously described, Dr.
King's party arrived at the Lorraine at approximately
11:30 a.m. Smith's security detail stayed with the party
during its trip to Centenary Church, and it was not removed until approximately 5 p.m. Redditt apparently did
have Dr. King under surveillance during this period, and
his own report to Tines, dated April 4, 1968, was entitled
"Surveillance of MLK, Jr., and related activities."[78] It
appeared, in fact, that Redditt may have set up at the firehouse shortly after King arrived at the Lorraine. A
memorandum prepared for Assistant Chief W. E. Routt
by Tines noted that Redditt was on "surveillance" at the
firehouse while Smith's detail was on "security" for King
and that that was one reason Redditt's reports, while they
corroborated Smith's, contained more detail about who
came and went from the area.[79]

The committee noted that when questioned about why

he would be chosen to be on a security detail, Redditt first claimed he believed he was chosen because he had provided security for Dr. King in the past. [80] He later admitted he had never previously provided security for Dr. King.[81]

The committee did not believe Redditt's representation that on April 3, 1968, he was assigned to the airport as part of a security detail for Dr. King, headed by Inspector Smith, [82] and remained in that capacity until the withdrawal of Smith's security detail. The committee found that Redditt's sole function was to observe Dr. King from the moment of his arrival at the airport.

The nature of Redditt's activities while he was at the firehouse was then explored by the committee. This was considered more significant than his activities at the airport on April 3, since Redditt concededly would have been at the firehouse on April 4, 1968, at the time of the assassination, had he not been removed some 2 hours earlier. After Smith's security detail was withdrawn, Redditt first testified he set up a kind of "security surveillance" at the firehouse. He characterized it as "still giving security in some way, form, or fashion." [83]

During his testimony, the committee explored with Redditt his characterization of his job at the firehouse as "security." The committee noted that both Inspector Tines [84] and his partner, Richmond,[85] characterized Redditt's job at the firehouse as one of surveillance. Further, the committee observed, Reddit did not physically accompany Dr. King to and from the Clayborn Temple on the evening of April 3, after he set up his post at the firehouse, as he would have done had he been providing physical protection or security for Dr. King. [86] In addition, Redditt admitted to the committee that the firehouse was at least 180 feet away from Dr. King's room, and he was in no position to provide physical protection for Dr. King.[87] His actions at the firehouse, such as the covering of most of the windows with newspaper so that he could see out without being noticed from the street, [88] further demonstrated to the committee that he was surveilling, not providing security for Dr. King. Finally, the committee showed him his own statement given April 10, 1968, in which he stated his assignment on April 3 and 4, 1968, was "* * * to keep Dr. Martin Luther King under surveillance and observation while he was in the city." [89]

When confronted with the evidence that his job on the day of the assassination was to surveil Dr. King, and not to provide security, Redditt conceded that this was correct. Finally, Redditt admitted it would be "absolutely false" to characterize his function as one of security on the day of the assassination.[90]

The committee observed that Redditt previously had appeared on television with various authors,[91] granted interviews to the BBC, and actively participated in the public forum, knowingly allowing the nature of his job on the day of the assassination to be misrepresented and exploited by advocates of conspiracy theories. The committee believed that Redditt's participation in such activities was reprehensible. In a committee hearing, Redditt retraced statements made to the BBC and others that he had provided security for Dr. King on the day of the assassination.[92] Redditt also formally apologized to the committee if statements he had made might have caused people to misinterpret the nature of his assignment on the day of the assassination.[93]

Despite the clear evidence that Redditt's function was surveillance and not security, the committee explored the reason for Redditt's removal from the firehouse 2 hours prior to the assassination, since it had been alleged that Redditt had a plan that he had shared with Richmond in case of trouble on the scene[94] and that Redditt's removal faciliated the escape of the assassin.

Redditt first stated he had a contingency plan in case of trouble near the Lorraine. The plan was to have Richmond remain looking out the window, while he would go to Main Street.[95] Redditt stated he communicated this plan to Richmond and his superiors.[96] During the hearing, the committee informed Redditt that his partner, Richmond, had stated that Redditt never communicated a plan to him.[97] Similarly, Redditt was informed that Inspector Tines had testified he had no knowledge of a contingency plan formulated by Redditt. [98]

Redditt then equivocated and acnowledged that he was "almost sure" he had devised a plan because "you usually in your own mind think of ways to protect yourself."[99] He first stated that he perhaps only discussed it with Richmond, and not his superiors.[100] He then conceded that there was no defined plan he had communicated to anyone and that the formulation of any plan was only in his mind.[101] He eventually admitted that he did not have even a definitive plan in his own mind.[102]

The committee found that Redditt did not communicate a plan relating to what he would do in the event of trouble to anyone. Indeed, he did not have a concrete plan formulated in his own mind. Thus, his removal obviously could not have been an intentional attempt to facilitate the escape of the assassin. The committee believed, as Redditt ultimately testified, that allegations that he was removed to facilitate the assassination were without substance.[103]

The committee concluded that Redditt was removed from his surveillance post 2 hours prior to the assassination primarily because his superiors perceived a threat on his life. Their perception and evaluation of the threat was apparently reinforced by previous threats that had been made against Redditt.

On March 8, 1968, Redditt wrote a memorandum to Tines relating a threat made to him by people sympathetic to the sanitation strike. The memo noted that he was warned not to attend a meeting because people planned to harm him and strike sympathizers saw him as "the type of Negro that was not needed."[104] Other threats were made directly to Redditt on April 3 and 4,[105] although it was unclear if these were brought to the attention of Redditt's supervisors by the time they had ordered his removal.

There was conflicting evidence as to the specific source of the threat that prompted the meeting that resulted in Redditt's removal. Tines testified that on April 4, Lt. E. H. Arkin told him that Philip Manuel, an investigator for the Permanent Subcommittee on Investigations of the U.S. Senate, had received information that someone was en route to Memphis to kill a police lieutenant.[106] Arkin, however, believed he was called into the office by Tines and told of the threat.[107] Tines believed he then discussed this with Chief McDonald and Fire and Safety Director Holloman.[108] Holloman testified he could not remember who first told him of the threat on Redditt's life. [109] Arkin was sent to get Redditt and bring him back to headquarters.[110]

As to who was present in the meeting at headquarters when Redditt was brought back, the testimony was conflicting. McDonald only remembered Holloman, Redditt, and himself being there.[111] Tines recalled that Manuel and he were also present.[112] Holloman rememberd that an agent of the Secret Service was there,[113] and Redditt rcalled that Holloman introduced a person at the meeting as a representative of the Secret Service.[114]

Redditt was informed at the meeting that there was a contract on his life, that he was being relieved from duty at the firehouse[115] and that he and his family were to be placed under police protection.[116]

Holloman testified he believed the threat might have bccn passed to the Memphis police by the Secret Service, [117] A check by the committee with the Secret Service, however, revealed no contact with the Memphis Police Department that might have resulted in Redditt's being relieved of his post.[118] Holloman testified he was not informed of the substance of an internal MPD memorandum dated April 4, 1968, and titled "Information concerning assassination plot of possibly Det. Reddit."[119] The memorandum referred to Philip Manuel as transmitting information concerning a possible plot to kill a Negro lieutenant in Memphis. Holloman did not recall if he was aware of this threat when he made the decision to relieve Redditt, though he did not believe it was the basis for his decision.[120] Tines[121] and Arkin,[122] however, recalled that the threat relayed by Manuel was the basis for the decision to relieve Redditt.

When interviewed by the committee, Manuel stated he had no independent recollection of the Redditt affair, but he did remember receiving a call from his office in Washington informing him that a confidential source had stated a Black Tennessee policeman's life was in danger. He knew from reading files that Redditt's life had previously been threatened, and he therefore believed the threat was directed to Redditt. He so informed the Memphis Police Department. The committee deposed Manuel's confidential source who stated that he personally told Manuel over the phone of the threat, but he also informed him that the target was a police sergeant in Knoxville. The source further said he did not leave messages in Washington, that he telephoned information only to Manuel direct.[124]

The committee believed, on the basis of Manuel's testimony, as well as that of Arkin and Tines, that Manuel believed the threat to be directed at Redditt and that some officials of the MPD believed this also, as confirmed in the April 4, 1968, memorandum from Tines to McDonald. [125] The committee, therefore, concluded that this threat was the one that resulted in the meeting where the decision to transfer Redditt was made.

The committee questioned Tines and Holloman about an internal MPD memorandum [126] from Arkin to Tines that indicated Arkin had received information at 4:15 p.m. on April 4, 1968, that the threat Manuel had passed along was directed at a Black sergeant in Knoxville and not, as had first been reported, a Black lieutenant in Memphis. The memorandum stated the information had been incorrectly transmitted from Washington. Tines maintained, [127] as did Holloman, [128] that they did not receive this information prior to the decision to remove Redditt. It appeared that this information was being received by Arkin as Holloman was holding his meeting with Redditt.

Redditt himself, in a statement he gave on April 10, 1968, at police headquarters, stated Tines relieved him because of a threatening phone call Redditt received at the firehouse on the afternoon of April 4, 1968, another threat Redditt had received at the airport on Dr. King's arrival, and the report from the Justice Department indicating his life was in danger. [129] It seems likely that Redditt would have discussed the other threats on his life in the meeting with Holloman concerning Redditt's removal from duty because of a specific threat.[14]

The committee believed that Redditt was removed because his superior perceived real danger to his safety. In addition, Richmond was not removed; he remained at the firehouse surveillance post. The committee found that Redditt's removal was not part of any plot to facilitate the assassination of Dr. King.

(c) The transfer of two Black firemen

Two Black firemen, Floyd Newsum and Norvell E. Wallace, were transferred on April 3, 1968, from the firehouse where Redditt and Richmond were conducting a surveillance. It has been charged that their transfers were part of a conspiracy to facilitate the assassination and the assassin's escape. [130]

Newsum stated that in April 1968, he was working the B shift at fire station No. 2 of the Memphis Fire Depart-

---

[14]This likelihood was supported by Police Chief McDonald's memory that Redditt's transfer was the cumulative result of all the prior threats on his life.

ment and was assigned to a truck company that required a minimum of five men. B shift did not work the 24-hour period from 7 a.m., April 3, to 7 a.m., April 4, but it was scheduled to work the following 24-hour period. Consequently, Newsum would have been at the firehouse at the time of the assassination. [131]

According to Newsum, sometime on the night of April 3, while he was at the Mason Temple rally where Dr. King spoke, a message was left with his daughter for him to call the fire station. When he did at about 11:30 p.m., he was told to report the following morning to company 31 in Frazier (North Memphis), not to fire station No. 2.[15][132]

The transfer appeared to be uncalled for, since the company to which he was detailed already had the minimum number of men to operate, [133] while his regular company would be left one man short. Thus, Newsum's transfer meant that another man would have to be transferred to his former company. Newsum stated that he subsequently placed a telephone call to another member of his regular company and learned that such a transfer had in fact been made. [134] An examination of Memphis Fire Department records supported Newsum with respect to his characterization of personnel transfers and personnel levels of the companies involved. [135]

On April 3, 1968, Wallace was working the A shift at fire station No. 2, where he was assigned to a pumper company that required a minimum force of five.[136] A shift had begun work at 7 a.m., April 3, and was to be relieved at 7 a.m., April 4. At approximately 10 p.m. on April 3, Wallace recalled, he was detailed to pumper company 33 at the Memphis Airport, where he was an extra man.[137]

Evidence obtained by the committee demonstrated that the transfers of Newsum and Wallace were prompted by a request from Redditt. Tines testified that Redditt or Arkin informed him there was "a fireman or firemen" at the firehouse who Redditt believed would hinder the functioning of the surveillance post and that he was asked "if there was some way they could be moved."[138] Tines then called either Chief Hamilton or Williams of the fire department and requested they be transferred.[139]

Tines' testimony is corroborated by a memorandum he received from Redditt. Dated April 4, 1968, it referred

---

[15]See MLK exhibit F–19 (crime scene diagram), I HSCA–MLK hearings, 77.

to Newsum as being very sympathetic with the sanitation strike and possibly the cause of the threats he had received.[140] When confronted by the committee with the memorandum, Redditt acknowledged that his request could have been the reason the firemen were transferred. [141]

In an interview with the committee, Newsum acknowledged he had been very sympathetic with the strike, that his support for it was well known, and that he had in fact passed information to persons affiliated with the strike. [142] He conceded that his reporting of information may have had something to do with his transfer,[143] since such activity on his behalf would have jeopardized the surveillance post.

While Wallace did not have a history of specific activities that would account for his transfer, it appeared that his transfer was prompted by Redditt's request to Tines. Wallace's and Newsum's supervisor, James O. Barnett, recalled that the transfers were made because someone in the police department was uncomfortable with Black firemen sympathetic to the strike in the vicinity of the surveillance post.[144]

The committee found that the transfers of Newsum and Wallace were made at the request of the Memphis Police Department out of a concern for the security of the surveillance post. Redditt himself was the person who initiated the request. The committee found that the transfers in no way facilitated the assassination or the escape of the assassin. The firemen obviously had no protective or surveillance responsibilities. Allegations that the transfers were part of a conspiracy to assassinate Dr. King were determined to be groundless.[16]

---

[16]Many of the allegations of conspiracy the committee investigated were first raised by Mark Lane, the attorney, who represented James Earl Ray at the committee's public hearings. As has been noted, the facts were often at variance with Lane's assertions. For example, Coy Dean Cowden did not see James Earl Ray at a service station at the time of the assassination (section II A 6 a). Further, Grace Walden was not hospitalized to prevent her from testifying and presenting exculpatory information on behalf of Ray (section II A 6 c); and the FBI did not lure Dr. King to the Lorraine Motel for the purpose of setting him up for assassination (section II D 1). Finally, the committee found that Detective Edward Redditt was not relieved of his post to strip Dr. King of security, that Detective Edward Redditt was not relieved of his post to strip Dr. King of security, and Firemen Newsum and Wallace were not transferred to assure the escape of an assassin.

In many instances, the committee found that Lane was willing to advocate conspiracy theories publicly without having checked the factual basis for them. In other instances, Lane proclaimed conspiracy based on little more than inference and innuendo. Lane's conduct resulted in public misperception about the assassination of Dr. King and must be condemned.

(d) The postassassination performance of the Memphis police

The committee also investigated the possibility that the postassassination conduct of the Memphis Police Department was indicative of an official effort to facilitate the escape of the assassin. When Dr. King was shot at approximately 6 p.m. on April 4, 1968, there were from 53 to 66 law enforcement officers within a mile of the Lorraine Motel [145] Included in this force were six "tact" or tactical units, each consisting of three or four vehicles. The purpose of the tact units was to respond to any disorder or emergency.[17][146] One of the units (tact 10) was on a rest break at fire station 2 within 100 yards of the Lorraine Motel. [147]

Aside from the 12 officers in tact 10, there were two other officers in the immediate vicinity of the motel—Patrolman Richmond, in his observation post at fire station 2 and Marrell McCullough, an undercover officer who was in the Lorraine parking lot[148]

Despite the presence of so many law enforcement officers, James Earl Ray was able to assassinate Dr. King, gather his belongings and successfully flee the scene without being observed by a single policeman. Ray's ability to avoid detection has led to speculation that there may have been official complicity in the assassination by Memphis officials. This suspicion has even been voiced by members of the Memphis Police Department.[149]

Consequently, the committee closely scrutinized the actions of key law enforcement personnel following the shooting. The committee sought to determine: (1) what actually occurred following Dr. King's assassination; (2) whether this conduct constituted irregular or substandard performance on the part of the local law enforcement personnel; and (3) if this conduct indicated official complicity in the murder of Dr. King.

Ray was able to escape the scene without detection for two main reasons: All of the officers rushed toward the Lorraine immediately after the shot, leaving South Main

[17]The tact units had been patrolling the streets immediately surrounding the Lorraine until, in response to a request from someone in Dr. King's party, they were ordered to pull back so as not to be visible from the Lorraine. (See MLK exhibit F–193, affidavit of William O. Crumby, IV, MSCA–MLK hearings, 279.)

Street unsecured; and there was, in fact, no contingency plan for units in case of trouble near the Lorraine. Right after Dr. King was shot, McCullough, who was standing in the parking lot of the Loraine, ran to Dr. King's side in an effort to render aid.[150] Simultaneously, Richmond ran from his observation post to a telephone several feet away and placed a call to the intelligence section at police headquarters to inform them of the assassination.[151]

Eleven members of tact 10 had been on a rest break at the fire station for several minutes,[152] while one member had remained in the lead patrol vehicle to monitor the radio.[153] Upon realizing Dr. King was shot, the 11 men in the firehouse hurriedly exited the building and started to rush toward the Lorraine. Most dropped over a 10-foot retaining wall at the rear of the fire station in their rush toward the Lorraine.[154] Some of them then went to the balcony, while others continued north and then west back to South Main Street.[155] The commander of the unit remained at the edge of the retaining wall for a few moments, from which he saw most of the men running to the Lorraine. He then returned to South Main Street where he moved northward toward the roominghouse. [156] The other patrolman who had not gone over the wall also remained at its edge for a few moments. He then went to the lead patrol vehicle to radio news of the assassination.[157]

The lead patrol vehicle was parked adjacent to the firehouse. Upon realizing something had happened, the member of the unit who had stayed in the vehicle ran a short distance along the side of the firehouse. He then returned to the vehicle and radioed news of the shooting to the police dispatcher.[158] After he was joined by the member of the unit who had returned to the car, they pulled out and turned south on Main Street to get to the Lorraine.[159]

The focus of attention of all members of the Memphis Police Department was on the Lorraine. During this time, Ray apparently exited the roominghouse on South Main, moved southward, dropped his bundle into the inset doorway of Canipe's Amusement Co., entered his white Mustang parked just south of Canipe's and sped northward on South Main. It seemed likely that Ray dropped the bundle with its incriminating evidence because he either observed the members of tact 10 departing the firehouse to rush to the Lorraine, or else because he spotted the lead tact 10 vehicle parked on the north side of the firehouse and protruding on the sidewalk.

Ray's departure in the Mustang apparently preceded the arrival on South Main of two officers from tact 10 by only a matter of seconds. The two approached the roominghouse on South Main from opposite directions after having first concentrated their attention on the Lorraine.[160]

The failure of the units patrolling the general vicinity to have a contingency plan in case of trouble near the Lorraine also contributed to Ray's ability to escape. The assassination took place at approximately 6:01 p.m. Although members of the Memphis Police Department were aware of the event almost immediately, it was not until approximately 6:03 p.m., after receiving confirmation, that the dispatcher transmitted its occurrence over the air.[161] Immediately thereafter, patrol cars and units in the general vicinity began moving toward the immediate area of the Lorraine. This activity, however, duplicated the individual actions of both the undercover policeman and the members of tact 10. Further, it was not until 6:06 p.m., almost 5 minutes after the assassination, that the dispatcher ordered the two-block area around the Lorraine and the roominghouse sealed off. [162] By this time, Ray had almost certainly left the vicinity of the Lorraine and was headed out of Memphis.

Other questions about the performance of the Memphis Police Department have been raised. They pertained to the extent of the MPD fugitive search, the failure of the MPD to issue an all points bulletin for the white Mustang, and its failure to establish roadblocks on the major arteries leading out of Memphis.

At 6:07 p.m., the dispatcher was advised by a member of tact 10 that the murder weapon had been recovered in front of 424 South Main Street and that the suspect had run south on South Main.[163] At 6:08 p.m., the description of the suspect was broadcast as a young, well-dressed white male, and at 6:10 p.m., the description of the suspected getaway car as a late model white Mustang was broadcast.[164]

Memphis Police Department records reflecting the actions of the general ward cars and tact units with respect to the extent of the fugitive search conducted immediately following the assassination do not exist. The committee, however, was able to reconstruct a board outline of these actions through an examination of the April 4, 1968, MPD radiotapes and a series of interviews with individuals involved.

The transcript of the April 4, 1968, Memphis Police Department radio transmissions immediately following the assassination reflected that the general ward cars halted at least three white Mustangs.[165] though it was impossible for the committee to ascertain the actual number of such vehicles halted.[166] Nevertheless, field interviews conducted by the committee revealed that none of the city's tact units engaged in a fugitive search following the assassination.[167] This meant that an approximate total of from 48 to 110 patrol vehicles and from 186 to 440 Memphis law enforcement officers never responded to the 6:10 p.m. broadcast of the white Mustang. According to Memphis Police Department officials, the reason for the failure of the tact units to engage in the search was that their primary concern was with the rioting firebombing and looting that occurred throughout the city following news of the assassination.[168] This was corroborated in interviews with various members of miscellaneous tact units.[169]

The committee's investigation further revealed that, contrary to established Memphis Police Department procedures, roadblocks were not established on major arteries leaving Memphis, and an all points bulletin (APB) for a white Mustang was never broadcast to the surrounding jurisdictions, including Arkansas, Mississippi, and Alabama. [170] The committee's investigation revealed that, in all probability Ray was already two to three blocks away from the roominghouse making his escape in the white Mustang by the time the news of the assassination was broadcast at 6:03 p.m. By 6:06 p.m., when the two-block area around the crime scene had been sealed off, Ray could have been in Arkansas. By 6:10 p.m., when the description of the white Mustang was broadcast, Ray could have been halfway to the Mississippi State line.

These time estimates are significant only if Ray did in fact drive to either Arkansas or Mississippi. Based on Ray's testimony to the committee,[171] corroborated in part by the fact that he did abandon the Mustang in Atlanta, Ga., the following morning, it is probable that Ray did drive to the Mississippi State line following the assassination. The route through Mississippi would have been the quickest to Atlanta. The failure of the dispatcher to alert the neighboring States, therefore, may have substantially facilitated Ray's flight from the scene of the assassination.

According to the MPD officer who was in charge of communications at the time of the assassination, it was his negligence that resulted in no APB broadcast and no roadblocks on major arteries.[172] The officer stated that the loop lights had been switched to red to permit the passage through town of emergency vehicles, and emergency radio silence had been maintained following news of the assassination. He stated, however, that a signal Y, calling for an APB and roadblocks, was never broadcast due to the immense volume of traffic and confusion in the aftermath of the assassination. Further, it was not his normal practice to issue an APB to Mississippi because of "a past history of noncooperation from that State."

The committee found the performance of the Memphis Police Department deficient following the assassination in a number of respects. The absence of a contingency plan to seal off the area around the Lorraine immediately was inexcusable, especially in light of the violence that had occured during Dr. King's appearance in Memphis on March 28. Since the MPD was aware of numerous threats to Dr. King, it had good reason to expect trouble in the vicinity of the Lorraine, as the number of tactical units assigned to the area indicated. It would have only been logical, in the view of the committee, to have developed a contingency plan for the use of these tactical units. Similarly, the failure to issue an all points bulletin or to block egress routes from the city was indefensible. Nevertheless, the committee found no evidence that the substandard performance of the Memphis police in the aftermath of the assassination was part of a conspiracy to facilitate the assassination of Dr. King or the escape from Memphis of James Earl Ray. The committee found, instead, that these defects resulted from inadequate supervision, lack of foresight and individual negligence. They did not constitute complicity in the assassination.

3. MISSOURI STATE PENITENTIARY

Tht committee also examined James Earl Ray's escape from the Missouri State Penitentiary, which occurred on April 23, 1967.[175] The possibility of the involvement of prison authorities in the escape had been raised by critics, based on two separate sets of circumstances: (1) The release, shortly after Ray's escape, of a fugitive-wanted poster with incorrect fingerprints; (2) the apparent need for Ray to have secured inside assistance.

The committee sought information from a variety of sources. First, it undertook a complete review of existing prison records, including visitor cards,[176] financial records,[177] and the report of the prison's official investigation into the escape.[178] Second, extensive field interviews were held with key prison officials and former inmate or criminal associates of Ray.[179] Finally, sworn testimony was taken from members of the assassin's immediate family, as well as from Ray himself.[18]

Following the escape, prison officials issued a wanted poster to hundreds of law enforcement agencies throughout the country that had Ray's photograph and physical description on it. The fingerprints on the poster were, however, those of another escaped prisoner,[180] leading to speculation that government authorities had sought to thwart Ray's apprehension and thus facilitate the assassination.

The committee was informed by Harry F. Lauf, the records officer at the prison, that the erroneous poster had been printed by inmates at Moberly Training Center for Men, a medium security institution at Moberly, Mo.[181] When the poster was ready for distribution, Lauf did not check the prints against the original fingerprint card that had been sent to Moberly.[182] The mistake was apparently inadvertent, the result of deadline pressure on Lauf.

The committee then learned that after the mistake was uncovered, immediate instructions were issued to destroy the old posters. By the early summer of 1967, corrected posters had been printed and distributed.[183] Finally, after Ray was positively identified as a suspect in the assassination, an oral report about the incident was made by Lauf to Fred T. Wilkerson, director of the Missouri Department of Corrections.[184]

The evidence before the committee indicated, therefore, that the release of erroneous posters was the result of a regrettable but innocent oversight by prison officials and that efforts made after discovery of the error to rectify it minimized its effect. These considerations, together with the fact that this incident occurred a full year before the assassination, led the committee to find that the mistaken

---

[18]While there were indications that John Ray may have assisted his brother in the escape (sec. II B), the committee limited this phase of its investigation to the question of official complicity.

posters were not part of a conspiracy to assassinate Dr. King.

The method of Ray's escape from the Missouri State Penitentiary was not so easily resolved. Following his arrest in London in June 1968, Ray gave an account of the escape to his attorneys and others that he later admitted was false.[19] It was not until his eighth interview with the committee at Brushy Mountain Penitentiary that he detailed an escape plan that involved concealment in a breadbox while being transported beyond prison walls by the innocent driver of a delivery truck en route to a nearby prison farm.[185] Ray claimed to have planned the escape alone, though he indicated he received assistance from two inmates whom he refused to identify.[20][186]

The breadbox story conformed to conclusions reached by prison officials after their original investigation,[187] and it was more or less corroboraed by committee interviews with prison inmates.[188] Nevertheless, the committee was unable to learn the identity of the inmates who assisted Ray. Specific inmates who worked with Ray in the kitchen were suggested both by informants during the original investigation 189! and by individuals interviewed by the committee.[190] One inmate, Frank Guinan, actually admitted in an unsworn committee interview that he covered Ray with bread, pushed the breadbox to the loading dock and, with the assistance of one other inmate whom he refused to identify, loaded the box on the truck.[191 Guinan, however, later retracted his admission,[192] and Ray has denied knowing him.[193] With the exception of a statement by an inmate[194] whose reliability was challenged by several sources,[195] Guinan's original admission was uncorroborated. The committee, therefore, was reluctant to reach a conclusion on such tenuous evidence. It merely found that Ray escaped from Missouri State Penitentiary in a breadbox with inmate assistance.

The committee also investigated a number of events at the prison that aided Ray in his escape. For example, as a result of an earlier escape attempt when he hid within the prison, officials were still searching for Ray inside the walls

---

[19]Ray told William Bradford Huie, author of "He Slew the Dreamer," that he escaped without assistance from other inmates by scaling the prison wall. (See XII HSCA–MLK hearings, 106–09).

[20]Prison officials speuclated to the committee that the breadbox escape plan was actually formulated by another inmate who had been placed in solitary confinement before he got an opportunity to carry it out. It was further speculated that Ray knew of the plan and decided to try it out while the other inmate was in solitary.

three days after his break.[196] Records indicated that law enforcement agencies were alerted to a "possible escape" after Ray was missed at a 5 p.m. prisoner count on April 23, 1967.[197] Nevertheless, Lt. William R. Turner, the yard officer at the time, told the committee that Ray had just escaped, possibly in a breadbox.[198] Turner said he immediately told his supervisor and alerted the two prison farms that would recieve a breadbox.

Despite some immediate inquiries about the bread deliveries, prison authorities did not learn of the crushed condition of the bread that arrived at Renz Prison Farm until 10 days later, when the manner of Ray's escape was finally determined.[199]

Although it was unable to resolve every inconsistency in the various statements, the committee found that negligence on the part of prison officials, not conspiracy, was an appropriate explanation for Ray's escape.[21] The committee did not find any evidence of official complicity in Ray's escape or in the assassination.

---

[21]The committee noted that as a result of Ray's escape, some prison employees were disciplined for failure to perform their duties properly, although none were dismissed.

E. The Department of Justice and the Federal Bureau of Investigation Performed With Varying Degrees of Competency and Legality in the Fulfillment of Their Duties

Having determined that no agency of Government participated in a conspiracy to assassinate Dr. King, the committee turned its attention to the performance of the Department of Justice and the Federal Bureau of Investigation with respect to the King case. The committee was concerned with the activities of the Department and Bureau before, as well as, after the assassination, since the Bureau had conducted an active campaign to discredit Dr. King and to compromise his standing in society. The results of this phase of the investigation are presented in two parts:

Section E 1 contains an evaluation of the FBI COINTEL program against Dr. King, to determine if it might have had any effect on the assassination and if, consequently, the Bureau or the Department should bear any responsibility for the assassination.

Section E 2 contains an analysis of the performance of the Department and the Bureau in investigating the assassination, in which particular emphasis was placed on the ability of the Bureau to conduct a full and complete investigation in light of its campaign to discredit Dr. King.

1. THE DEPARTMENT OF JUSTICE FAILED TO SUPERVISE ADEQUATELY THE DOMESTIC INTELLIGENCE DIVISION OF THE FEDERAL BUREAU OF INVESTIGATION; IN ADDITION, THE FEDERAL BUREAU OF INVESTIGATION, IN THE DOMESTIC INTELLIGENCE DIVISION'S COINTELPRO CAMPAIGN AGAINST DR. KING, GROSSLY ABUSED AND EXCEEDED ITS LEGAL AUTHORITY AND FAILED TO CONSIDER THE POSSIBILITY THAT ACTIONS THREATENING BODILY HARM TO DR. KING MIGHT BE ENCOURAGED BY THE PROGRAM

An assessment of responsibility for murder is a difficult and complex task, requiring a consideration of a wide range of moral and legal concepts.[1] The extent to which

---

[1] For a discussion of these concepts and the difficulties in assessing responsibility or murder, see the statement of Chairman Stokes on Novem-

law ought to reflect a particular view in the assessment of responsibility and the merits of competing moral philosophies have been the subject of debate for centuries. Society's concepts of moral, as opposed to legal, responsibility, moreover, are frequently at variance. Law can strive, at best, only to reflect a consensus of society's moral values. Consequently, a legal assessment of responsibility may be either narrower or broader than a moral assessment. Further, the extent to which concepts of individual responsibility may be used to assess institutional responsibility is largely unprecedented and therefore not settled.

As it addressed the broad question of the institutional responsibility of the FBI for the assassination of Dr. King, the committee was aware of the complex nature of its undertaking. As noted in section D, the committee found there was no evidence that FBI personnel took intentional action to accomplish or facilitate Dr. King's assassination. It then proceeded to consider a far more difficult aspect of the question of responsibility, one that arose from the FBI campaign to discredit Dr. King and destroy his standing in society.

To resolve this issue, the committee examined both the FBI's security investigation of Dr. King and its subsequent expansion into a COINTELPRO effort against Dr. King and the Southern Christian Leadership Conference.[2] A security investigation—the collection of intelligence on a specified target—is, and was in 1967–68, a legitimate function of the Bureau, when directed at an appropriate individual. COINTELPRO, on the other hand, was never a legitimate FBI function. While it had no fixed definition, it may be described in Dr. King's case as an active covert campaign intended to influence "political choices and social values." (1) As noted by the Senate select committee that investigated COINTELPRO, there is a gray area between "aggressive investigation" and "counterintelligence," and the "line between information collection and harassment can be extremely thin." (2) It must be concluded

---

ber 26, 1978, hearings before the Select Committee on Assassinations, U.S. House of Representatives, 95th Congress, 2d sess. (Washington, D.C., U.S. Government Printing Office, 1979), vol VII, p. 111.

[2] Section II D of this report includes materials generally describing these programs. See also Book III of the Final Report of the Senate Select Committee to Study Governmental Operations With Respect to Intelligence Activities, 94th Congress, 2d sess. (Washington, D.C., U.S. Government Printing Office, 1976), which contains an in-depth review of the FBI's COINTELPRO operations generally, as well as against Dr. King.

that in its COINTELPRO activities, the Bureau grossly abused and exceeded its legal authority.

The committee recognized that Dr. King was a prominent social leader and critic and that his activities and public positions were the subject of considerable debate and controversy that existed apart from the conduct of the FBI. Consequently, it could not be easily determined to what degree the Bureau, in fact, contributed to the climate of controversy that surrounded Dr. King. Nevertheless, it was necessary to review the history of Bureau activities pursuant to the security investigation and COINTELPRO campaign to understand the intensity of anti-King feeling within the FBI and the possible significance of these activities with respect to responsibility for the assassination by the Bureau or the Department of Justice.

Dr. King's developing stature in the civil rights movement became apparent in 1955, as he led a successful effort to eliminate discriminatory seating practices on the buses of Montgomery, Ala.,[3] and, shortly thereafter, with the creation of SCLC.[4] In July 1959, the first of many FBI files was officially opened on Dr. King,[5] although Bureau interest in him was minimal and no data was gathered on his activities for 22 months.[6]

(a) Security investigation and COINTELPRO

The security investigation of SCLC was opened in 1962, based on a suspicion that Dr. King was taking advice from two Communist associates. It was the responsibility at FBI headquarters of the Domestic Intelligence Division, which was supervised by Assistant Director William C. Sullivan.[7] The general function of the Division was to gather intelligence on individuals and organizations considered to be a security threat to the Nation.[8] The investigation of Dr. King and SCLC was handled in the Division by the Internal Security Section.[9] In October 1967, the Racial Intelligence Section was formed within the Division,[10] and the investigations of Dr. King, the SCLC and the civil rights movement in general became its responsibility. The Racial Intelligence Section also carried out the separate COINTELPRO campaign against so-called Black nationalist hate groups and their leaders, including the SCLC (the campaign was formally initiated in August 1967) [11] and Dr. King (formally initiated in March 1968). [12] The Crime Records Division, the

568

Bureau's principal point of contact with Congress and the news media, was the conduit for many of the COINTELPRO initiatives, including derogatory information on Dr. King.[13]

FBI field offices also had an important role in the security investigations as well as COINTELPRO. With respect to the security investigations, Atlanta was designated as the "office of origin," coordinating point for data obtained by all field offices on the SCLC and Dr. King.[14] With respect to COINTELPRO, field offices were asked to submit proposals on ways to implement the program. [15] Virtually all COINTELPRO proposals originated in the field offices and were promptly passed through the Bureau hierarchy for review and authorization.[16]

The Department of Justice played a role in the security investigation, since it was necessary to obtain the Attorney General's approval to tap telephones,[17] but the Department had no role in COINTELPRO. Nevertheless, both the 1977 Justice Department Task Force and the Senate select committee found that the Department failed in its responsibility to supervise the FBI during the development of COINTELPRO operations, and the committee concurred in this judgment.

The position of the FBI toward Dr. King and the SCLC cannot be understood apart from personalities. As noted, Dr. King was a social critic, and FBI Director J. Edgar Hoover was a man who strongly resented criticism of the Bureau from any source. The initial personal interest of Hoover in Dr. King is said to have originated with an article in The Nation in 1959 in which Dr. King commented on the scarcity of Black Federal agents, including FBI agents.[18] This and subsequent criticisms of the FBI by Dr. King were undoubtedly one explanation for Hoover's intense animosity toward the civil rights leader. Examples of the Director's attitude appeared with frequency during the committee's review of FBI files. In February 1962, James Bland, Chief of the Subversive Control Section, sent a memorandum to Assistant Director Sullivan asking whether King should be warned about the suspected Communist background of one of his advisers. A copy of the memo was sent to Hoover who rejected the proposal, writing in the margin, "King is no good anyway.[3][19] In

---

[3]The Bureau passed the information to the Justice Department which, in turn, informed Dr. King of the allegation.

December 1963, Time announced its decision to name Dr. King "Man of the Year." Hoover wrote on a copy of the news release on the decision. "They had to dig deep in the garbage to come up with this one."[20] Hoover's resentment had apparently been compounded by remarks made by Dr. King in 1962 in Albany, Ga., criticizing the Bureau for its failure to pursue aggressively civil rights violations in the South. In the opinion of several FBI agents questioned by the committee, the Albany statement was, from the Director's standpoint, the single most significant reason for the feud,[21] one that came to a public climax in November 1964, when Hoover, in a press briefing, referred to Dr. King as "the most notorious liar" in the country.[22]

In addition to Dr. King's criticism of the FBI, other factors were suggested to the committee to explain the Director's deep-seated hostility. They include "qualities of racism" in Hoover's character;[23] Dr. King's violation of the Director's strict, almost puritanical, standards for behavior by members of the clergy; [24] and Dr. King's philosophy of nonviolence, thought to stand at odds with the Director's personal belief in the ultimate importance of power.[25] In addition, it was suggested to the committee that Hoover, whose opposition to communism was unswerving, was convinced that Dr. King and his movement were susceptible to Communist influence,[26] even though a contrary assessment had been made by FBI experts.

(1) *Hoover's dislike for Dr. King.*—The committee concluded, based on an exhaustive review of FBI files and on the sworn testimony of former FBI and Justice Department officials, that the campaign to discredit Dr. King, up to the time of his death and beyond. [27] continued as long as it did and as intensely as it did only because of Hoover's deep personal dislike for Dr. King. Evidence obtained by the committee indicated that the allegation that Dr. King posed a threat to national security was merely a convenient rationalization used by the Director to justify his personal vendetta against the civil rights leader. For example, in April 1962, the Atlanta "office of origin"[28] submitted to headquarters a report on Dr. King that concluded there was no significant Communist influence being exerted on him. [29] Nevertheless, Hoover ordered that Dr. King's name be added to section A of the reserve in-

dex.[4] [30] And, by October 1962, a full-scale security investigation of Dr. King and the SCLC had begun.[32] The initiation of these investigations, however, cannot be attributed wholly to the personal animosity of Hoover. They also stemmed from a general concern by the FBI about Communist infiltration of the civil rights movement that was prompted by influential people, including Congressmen, who claimed that pending civil rights legislaton was inspired by a Communist conspiracy.

The investigations that followed, on the other hand, revealed there was little basis in fact for this concern.[33] In August 1963, the Domestic Intelligence Division completed a synopsis of the Communist Party's effort to exploit the American Negro.[34] It concluded that while the party had expended enormous effort and resources to influence and control Black Americans, it had been largely unsuccessful.[35] In sworn testimony before the committee, agents from the Domestic Intelligence Division insisted that their conclusion of insignificant infiltration into the civil rights movement reflected their professional judgment then as well as in 1978.[36]

Director Hoover's reaction, reflected in notes appended to the synopsis, was sharply critical:

> This memo reminds me vividly of those I received when Castro took over Cuba. You contended then that Castro and his cohorts were not Communists and not influenced by Communists. Time alone proved you wrong* * *.[37]

Hoover's irritation resulted in a sharp and immediate change in the position of the Domestic Intelligence Division. Reacting to Dr. King's famous "I Have a Dream" address, Sullivan wrote in a memorandum to Assistant to the Director Alan Belmont:

> The Director is correct. We were completely wrong about believing the evidence was not sufficient to determine some years ago that Fidel Castro was not a

---

[4]As described by the Senate Select Committee to Study Governmental Operations With Respect to Intelligence Activities, the index was for people who, the FBI believed, "* * * in a time of national emergency [were] in a position to influence others against the national interest or were likely to furnish material financial aid to subversive elements due to their subversive associations and ideology." [31]

Communist or under Communist influence. In investigating and writing about communism and the American Negro, we had better remember this and profit by the lesson it should teach.

* * * Personally, I believe in the light of King's powerful demogogic speech yesterday he stands head and shoulders over all other Negro leaders put together when it comes to influencing great masses of Negroes. We must mark him now, if we have not done so before, as the most dangerous Negro of the future in this Nation from the standpoint of communism, the Negro, and national security.[38]

By the end of 1963, FBI files reflected a marked difference in the Bureau's approach toward Dr. King and the beginning of a campaign to discredit him. On December 23, 1963, a conference was held in Washington,[39] with members of the Atlanta field office and the headquarters Domestic Intelligence Division in attendance. A memorandum written by Sullivan the following day summarized the results of the meeting:

Recognizing the delicacy of this entire situation because of the prominence of King, the primary purpose of the conference was to explore how best to carry on one investigation to produce the desired results without embarrassment to the Bureau. Included in the discussion was a complete analysis of the avenues of approach aimed at neutralizing King as an effective Negro leader and developing evidence concerning King's continued dependence on Communists, for guidance and direction.[40]

Less than 2 weeks later, the direction of the Bureau's developing course of action became clear. Assistant Director Sullivan authorized a proposal that the FBI consider promoting a new leader for the Black community who would alleviate the confusion expected once Dr. King had been "taken off his pedestal."[41] Hoover attached a note to Sullivan's memo:

I am glad to see that light has finally, though dismally delayed, come to the DID. I struggled for months to get over the fact that the Communists were taking over the racial movement but our experts here couldn't and wouldn't see it.[42]

(1) *Electronic surveillance of Dr. King*—From October 24, 1963, to June 21, 1966,[43] the FBI also engaged in an extensive program of electronic surveillance of Dr. King. The committee found it was conducted in a particularly abusive fashion. FBI agents who monitored the devices, although they were initially instructed to be especially alert for contacts between Dr. King and Communist connections,[44] exercised little discretion in deciding what to overhear and record. Private and personal conversations were recorded, as were conversations between Dr. King and Government officials.[5] In fact, the development of personal information that might be derogatory to Dr. King became a major objective of the surveillance effort.[45] The committee found that the department of Justice shared responsibility for the surveillance, since it was initially authorized by Attorney General Robert F. Kennedy.[6][46]

The nature of the Bureau's campaign against Dr. King is vividly illustrated by one incident. Shortly after Director Hoover's press conference in November 1964, in which he referred to Dr. King as the country's "most notorious liar,"[50] a package was mailed to Dr. King. It contained an anonymous diatribe against the civil rights leader and a copy of an electronic surveillance tape, apparently to lend credence to threats of exposure of derogatory personal information made in the letter.[41] The committee was unable to locate the original letter, but an apparently authentic copy was found in the files of Assistant Director Sullivan. The final paragraph clearly implied that suicide would be a suitable course of action for Dr. King:

---

[5] During this period, there was no statute or regulation requiring "minimization" of the monitoring to insure that only relevant information was overheard, such as is embodied in current law.

[6] While authorization by the Attorney General was required for wiretaps in 1963, microphone surveillance could be initiated by the FBI Director, according to a 1954 Attorney General memorandum. [47] In 1965, the procedure was changed by Nicholas deB. Katzenbach, who replaced Robert F. Kennedy as Attorney General. Katzenbach's order made microphone and wiretap surveillance the responsibility of the Attorney General. [48] Subsequent to the Katzenbach order, according to sworn testimony before the committee, the FBI implemented microphone surveillance in hotel rooms of Dr. King on at least three occasions. [49] While former Attorney General Katzenbach testified before the Senate select committee that he had no specific recollection of the authorizations, the committee found that he had at least after-the-fact knowledge.

573

King, there is only one thing left for you to do. You know what it is. You have just 34 days in which to do (this exact number has been selected for a specific reason, it has definite practical significance). You are done. There is but one way out for you. You better take it before your filthy fraudulent self is bared to the Nation.[52]

In addition to Sullivan's admission of involvement in the scheme in testimony before the Senate select committee.[7] [53] the committee received evidence raising the possibility that the package was delivered to Assistant to the Director Belmont prior to mailing.[55] If this was the case, the committee considered it highly likely that Director Hoover had before-the-fact knowledge of the action.

In the final analysis, the committee was unable to fix personal responsibility for the threatening letter to Dr. King, but it noted that it did reflect the extent of the hostility in the Bureau toward Dr. King.

The FBI campign against Dr. King extended beyond the invasion of his privacy. Efforts were made to interfere with SCLC fundraising and with the awarding of degrees and other honors to Dr. King.[56] Further, an extensive effort was made to smear his name through the dissemination of derogatory information.[57] and attempts were made to create ill feeling between Dr. King and his associates, as well as his wife.[58]

The FBI effort to smear Dr. King by the dissemination of derogatory information was targeted at two general audiences. One was officials of the Government in Washington—congressional leaders, White House personnel, and Federal agency staff members, all of whom were briefed regularly about Dr. King's personal life and the alleged Communist connections and sympathies of his advisers. Lengthy monographs were distributed to Government officials in November 1964.[59] April 1967,[60] and March 1968,[61] and certain key persons were from time to time given personal briefings by the Bureau.[62]

(3) *Manipulation of the media.*—Of far greater signifi-

---

[7]The committee was unable to take testimony from Sullivan, who was killed in a hunting accident in 1977. He testified, however, before the Senate select committee that the project had Hoover's prior knowledge and was, in fact, authorized by the Director. Sullivan said at the time that he personally opposed the idea because it placed future electronic surveillance of Dr. King in jeopardy. [54] The committee noted that at the time of Sullivan's testimony, he had broken with the Director, and his testimony must be viewed accordingly.

cance to the committee, for the purpose of assessing any responsibility of the FBI for the assassination, was the Bureau's program to achieve public awareness of derogatory information about Dr. King. By using friendly media outlets—newspaper and other sources who published material favorable to or supplied by the Bureau—the FBI had potential access to a vast audience.[63] The committee was able to document this COINTELPRO technique from FBI files and from the testimony of Bureau personnel assigned to the Crime Records Division.[64] It was apparent that the FBI's manipulation of the media contributed to a hostile attitude toward Dr. King and what he represented. As an illustration, the committee selected a case that raised difficult and complex questions with respect to the bearing this sort of COINTELPRO activity might have had on the assassination. The committee found the case to be particularly significant, since it occurred in St. Louis, where the committee conducted an extensive conspiracy investigation.[8]

The case involved the relationship between the FBI and the St. Louis Globe-Democrat,[9] as it was uncovered by a rival newspaper, the St. Louis Post-Dispatch. In a series of articles published in 1977, the Post-Dispatch identified the publisher of the Globe-Democrat and a reporter on the paper's staff as individuals who "were looked upon by the St. Louis FBI office as key outlets in the mid-1960's for news the Bureau wanted published. * * *"[65] The Post-Dispatch series was the result of a review of FBI documents the paper had obtained in a Freedom of Information Act request. (The documents were also reviewed by the committee.) The publisher was identified as Richard H. Amberg, who died in 1967, and the reporter as Denny Walsh, who had since left the paper.[66] The name of the publisher of the Globe-Democrat in 1968, G. Duncan Bauman, had been deleted from certain documents the FBI provided to the Post-Dispatch.

The committee obtained copies of internal documents referred to in the Post-Dispatch series, and they revealed the ease with which the Bureau had been able to use the newspaper for its counterintelligence initiatives. For example, a memorandum from the St. Louis special agent-in-

---

[8] See section II B for a detailed discussion of the committee's conspiracy evidence.
[9] See MLK exhibits F-515 to F-522, VII HSCA-MLK hearings, 95, 97, 99, 101, 103, 106, 108, 110 in sequence.

charge to Director Hoover on May 28, 1968.[67] discussed
activities to disrupt "new left" organizations:

> The feeding of well chosen information to the St.
> Louis Globe-Democrat, a local newspaper, whose edi-
> tor and associate editor are extremely friendly to the
> Bureau and the St. Louis Office, has also been utilized
> in the past and it is contemplated that this technique
> might be used to good advantage in connection with
> this program.

Then, on October 18, 1968,[69] the St. Louis office
field received a memorandum from FBI headquarters giving permission to provide a source on the Globe-Democrat with information to disrupt organizing activities by
Students for a Democratic Society at area high schools. A
note appended to the memorandum praised the newspaper
and its staff:

> The St. Louis Globe-Democrat has been especially
> cooperative with the Bureau in the past. Its publisher
> [name deleted] is on the Special Correspondents List.

Denny Walsh, a Globe-Democrat reporter named in the
released FOIA documents, was interviewed by the Post-
Dispatch and by the committee. He verified that the
Globe-Democrat, as well as he personally, had enjoyed a
close working relationship with the FBI.[69]

Knowledge of the presence of a willing news media outlet for the FBI in St. Louis led the committee to scrutinize
carefully a COINTELPRO initiative from FBI headquarters and Globe-Democrat editorial, both of which
preceded the assassination of Dr. King by less than a
week.[10] The editorial addressed a march on Washington that
Dr. King had scheduled for the spring of 1968.

In late 1967, Dr. King had announced plans to lead a
massive march on Washington in the spring of 1968. Al-
ternately called the Washington Spring Project and the

----

[10]Because the committee did not direct its attention to a possible connection between COINTELPRO and evidence of a conspiracy in St. Louis
until the latter part of its investigation, it was not possible to review fully
the relationship of the FBI with the St. Louis Globe-Democrat· or to
assess its possible link to the assassination. Specifically, the committee
was not able to identify each editorial or article whose publication may
have been influenced by the Bureau, determine if the editorial or article
was in fact read by anyone connected with a conspiracy that might have
resulted in Dr. King's death, and assess the effect, if any, of the

Poor People's Campaign, it generated a great deal of interest as well as considerable concern among the hierarchy of the FBI. Following the sanitation workers march in Memphis, led by Dr. King on March 28, 1968, the Bureau decided to seize upon the violence that had erupted as evidence that Dr. King was unable to conduct a peaceful demonstration by a large number of people. The theory behind the strategy was to call into question the peaceful intentions of the Washington Spring Project. On the very day of the ill-fated march, a memorandum was circulated outlining an FBI-authored editorial to be placed with "co-operative news media sources." [11] [70] It took Dr. King to task for getting involved in the Memphis strike and for not being able to control the march, suggesting that Memphis was merely a prelude to what was coming in Washington.[72] The editorial was "handled" that same day. [73]

On March 30, an editorial appeared in the Globe-Democrat,[74] accompanied by a disparaging cartoon of Dr. King. The editorial's similarities to the one outlined in the FBI memorandum were too close, in the view of the committee, to have occurred by chance. The memorandum and the editorial reflected the same basic argument. King called for a strike that he knew would get violent and then King fled. Language in the editorial was virtually plagiarized from the FBI memorandum:

Memphis may only be the prelude to civil strife in our Nation's Capitol [sic].—FBI memorandum, March 28, 1968

Memphis could be only the prelude to a massive bloodbath in the Nation's Capitol [sic] * * *—Globe-Democrat editorial, March 30, 1968

In light of the past relationship between the Bureau and the paper, the committee found that there was sufficient evidence in the editorial itself to conclude that it had

editorial or article. The committee was able to establish, however—by interviews with the publisher of the paper and with former news and editorial page personnel [71]—that (1) there was a close relationship between the Globe-Democrat publisher's office and officials of the FBI, that (2) the paper followed an editorial policy that was generally opposed to Dr. King, and that (3) the paper quite possibly published material about Dr. King at the behest of the Bureau other than that which the committtee considered.

[11] A copy of the March 28, 1968, memorandum is published as MLK exhibit F-521, VII, HSCA-MLK hearings, 108.

been inspired by the FBI memorandum, although the only written documentation of this was the notation, "handled," on the memorandum. Independent testimony to the committee indicated that the normal method the Bureau used to place material with a friendly news source was by telephone.[75] The committee deduced that the placing probably occurred the same day the memorandum was circulated, which would account for its prompt appearance in the Globe-Democrat.[12]

(4) *Analysis of the impact of the FBI-inspired editorial.*—The committee carefully considered the possibility that the FBI's actions were more than defamatory and that they might have placed Dr. King's life in danger by exacerbating anti-King emotions and by seemingly justifying violent action to remove Dr. King from his position of prominence. The committee was not able to determine, however, that James Earl Ray read the Globe-Democrat editorial. Ray testified to the committee that he had been in the habit of purchasing a daily newspaper;[176] the evidence established, however, that he was in Birmingham on March 30, purchasing the rifle he used to assassinate Dr. King, so it is unlikely that he read the Globe-Democrat that day.

Even if Ray had read the editorial, he had, the committee noted, already begun to stalk Dr. King when it was published. Thus, at worst, the editorial might have reinforced a plan that had already been set in motion. On the other hand, the editorial had illustrative significance. If there had been other editorials or articles discrediting Dr. King that had been planted by the Bureau prior to the assassination, their potential significance might have been great. To evaluate this significance, however, would, as noted, require detailing all the COINTELPRO activities in St. Louis, attempting to determine if these activities had come to the attention of Ray or others residing in St. Louis who might have been involved in an assassination conspiracy—John Ray, John Sutherland, or John Kauffmann, as examples—and attempting to assess the impact, if any, of these activities on these individuals.

The committee did obtain evidence that John Ray read and absorbed the editorial. On June 13, 1972, he wrote to

---

[12]Since the March 30 Globe-Democrat was a weekend edition of the paper, the deadline probably would have required telephonic transmission from the FBI.

author George McMillan the following description of Dr. King:

> * * * King was not a saint as these try to picture him. There are millions of Rays in the United States with the same background and beliefs, who know that King not only was a rat but with his beaded eyes and pin ears look like one. A piece in the editorial sections of the St. Louis Globe-Democrat said that King led marches until he got them stir [sic] up, then used a excuse to leave, while the dumb Blacks got their head beat in by police. A week before he was killed [sic], it also said he ran down the alley and jump into a waiting cadiliac [sic].

The letter was written over 4 years after the assassination. It cannot be reliably determined when John Ray first read the editorial—before the assassination or later in prison—though his failure to reflect its content accurately indicates he may noa have had it to refer to when he wrote to McMillan. What is indicated, however, is that the editorial made a significant impression on him.

The committee did not obtain evidence to indicate that any of the other individuals who the committee believes may have been involved in a conspiracy to kill Dr. King read the Globe-Democrat editorial prior to the assassination. The committee was only able to determine, therefore, that the Bureau-inspired editorial was used to rationalize the assassination.

The committee could find no evidence that the Bureau ever specifically considered the possibility that planting derogatory editorials might encourage certain parties to cause bodily harm to Dr. King. In its review of FBI COINTELPRO operations against a wide variety of targets, the Senate committee did note that the dangerous character of some of its COINTELPRO initiatives was, however, recognized by the Bureau. Those techniques that were seen as likely to cause physical, emotional, or economic harm to the target "were scrutinized carefully by headquarters supervisory personnel, in an attempt to balance the 'great good' to be achieved by the proposal against the known or risked harm to the target. If the 'good' was sufficient, the proposal was approved."[78]

The Bureau also recognized that some of their COIN-

TELPRO activities would entail the risk of murder of the target. It realized that falsely labeling someone as an informant in a group that was the target of a COINTELPRO operation always carried the risk that the informant would be killed by the target group.[79] Apparently, the Bureau would not run the risk if it "had information that the [target] group was, at that time actually killing suspected informants."[80]

Apparently, similar caution was not observed in the implementation of COINTELPRO activities against Dr. King. Given the highly charged and emotional atmosphere surrounding Dr. King's activities, the committee concluded that the FBI should have considered the real possibility that its activities might encourage an attack on Dr. King.

While the evidence was insufficient to link COINTELPRO to the assassination, the committee obtained ample evidence to warrant strong condemnation of FBI efforts that were directed against Dr. King and SCLC for the risk they created for Dr. King. The editorial writers at the Globe-Democrat were exercising first amendment freedoms, so their conduct was constitutionally privileged. There was, however, no similar privilege covering the conduct of the FBI. Not only did this conduct contribute to the hostile climate that surrounded Dr. King, it was morally reprehensible, illegal, felonious, and unconstitutional. There is no place in a free society for such governmental conduct. It deserves the strongest condemnation.

2. THE DEPARTMENT OF JUSTICE AND FEDERAL BUREAU OF INVESTIGATION PERFORMED A THOROUGH INVESTIGATION INTO THE RESPONSIBILITY OF JAMES EARL RAY FOR THE ASSASSINATION OF DR. KING, AND CONDUCTED A THOROUGH FUGITIVE INVESTIGATION, BUT FAILED TO INVESTIGATE ADEQUATELY THE POSSIBILITY OF CONSPIRACY IN THE ASSASSINATION; THE FEDERAL BUREAU OF INVESTIGATION MANIFESTED A LACK OF CONCERN FOR CONSTITUTIONAL RIGHTS IN THE MANNER IN WHICH IT CONDUCTED PARTS OF THE INVESTIGATION

The extensive FBI effort against Dr. King in both its security investigation and COINTELPRO operations posed for the committee the additional troubling question of whether the agency had been either willing or able to conduct a thorough and far-reaching criminal investigation of the assassination. It was the committee's task to determine, therefore, whether the FBI had been able to abandon its adversary posture vis-a-vis Dr. King and carry out an aggressive and objective investigation of the person or persons responsible for the murder.[13]

In order to answer this ultimate question, the committee undertook, as its first step, a thorough review of pertinent investigative files of the Department of Justice and Federal Bureau of Investigation. Of primary importance were the files of MURKIN (for Murder-King, the official designation of the Martin Luther King assassination investigation) at both FBI headquarters and the Memphis field office, the office of origin. In addition, the committee reviewed field office reports from 16 FBI districts, including those covering the key cities of Atlanta, Birmingham, New Orleans, St. Louis, Kansas City, Chicago, and Los Angeles. It also looked at Justice Department files on the investigation, a separate department file on Ray's extradition, and the 1977 Justice Department Task Force Report, entitled "Martin Luther King, Jr., Security and Assassination Investigations Report."

The file review was followed by a series of lengthy, in-person interviews with former officials of both the Justice Department and the FBI who played significant roles, either as supervisors or field agents, in the assassination investigation. The interviews were supplemented by the executive session and public hearing testimony of former Attorney General Ramsey Clark; former Assistant Attorney General (for Civil Rights) Stephen Pollak; former Assistant to the Director of the FBI Cartha DeLoach; and Former Memphis Special Agent-in-charge Robert Jensen.

With the exception of J. Edgar Hoover, FBI Director in 1968; Clyde Tolson, FBI Associate Director; and Thomas Robinson, U.S. attorney in Memphis in 1968, all of whom were deceased, the committee was able to interview all individuals whose testimony was considered necessary for a thorough examination of the quality of the performance of the FBI and the Justice Department in the assassination investigation.

(a) The FBI chain of command

In 1968, the FBI was divided into 10 internal divisions. [81] Division Six, the General Investigative Division, head-

---

[19]A more detailed discussion of the investigation conducted by the FBI and the Justice Department appears in a committtee staff report, "An Analysis of the Assassination Investigation of the Department of Justice and Federal Bureau of Investigation," XIII appendix to the HSCA–MLK hearings (hereinafter referred to as Investigation Report).

ed by Assistant Director Alex Rosen, had overall responsibility for investigation of Federal crimes, including civil rights violations. Following Dr. King's assassination, Federal investigative jurisdiction was predicated on a possible violation of 18 U.S.C. 241, the Federal civil rights statute barring conspiracies to interfere with or impede the constitutional rights of an individual.[82] Thus, the General Investigative Division assumed responsibility for the King investigation.

Within the division, the investigation was managed by the Civil Rights Section. A headquarters "case agent" was appointed and information on developments in the investigation passed up through the chain of command to Cartha DeLoach, Assistant to the Director; Clyde Tolson, the Associate Director; and Director Hoover. In a case of such magnitude, major case developments were summarized and passed upward at least once daily.

In the field, the Memphis FBI office, which initiated an investigation shortly after the assassination, was designated "office of origin" and assumed major administrative and coordination functions. While direction of the case was a responsibility of FBI headquarters in Washington—reflecting the national and international scope of the investigation—Memphis received copies of most of the reports from the 57 other domestic offices assigned to the case. In addition, Memphis coordinated and at times initiated investigative leads.

Because the FBI was only one of several component agencies of the Department of Justice, conduct of the MURKIN investigation was ultimately the responsibility of Attorney General Clark and attorneys he assigned to supervise it. The Civil Rights Division was formally responsible for the conduct of the investigation and for any Federal prosecutions that might develop.[83]

Outside of Washington, the Department of Justice was represented by U.S. attorneys, one for each Federal district. Although the actual prosecution of a Federal criminal case is the responsibility of a U.S. attorney, subject only to supervision by the appropriate division of the Justice Department, this was not the practice in civil rights prosecutions in 1968. Political considerations and the need to maintain working relations with local law enforcement agencies often made it awkward for a U.S. attorney to bring Federal civil rights cases against local authorities. At the time, therefore, Federal civil rights investigations and prosecutions were, with very few exceptions, the responsibility of the Civil Rights Division in Washington. [84]

This was the practice in the investigation of the King assassination. The committee's review of investigative files indicated that while the FBI's investigation was carried out by offices throughout the country, local U.S. attorneys in important cities—Atlanta, Memphis, New Orleans, Los Angeles, Chicago, and St. Louis—were excluded from the chain of information and necessarily, therefore, from decision-making.[85]

(b) The fugitive investigation

In light of James Earl Ray's ability to elude authorities for over 2 months subsequent to the assassination of Dr. King, the committee examined the FBI's post-assassination fugitive investigation. The purpose was to determine whether all available resources had been committed to the task of identifying and locating the assassin.

As a first step, the committee pieced together a detailed chronology of the investigation that preceded Ray's apprehension. Dr. King had been shot at 6:01 p.m. on April 4, 1968, at the Lorraine Motel in Memphis, Tenn. Within moments, members of the Memphis Police Department were at the scene. The Memphis field office of the FBI was notified, and Special Agent-in-Charge Robert Jensen contacted Washington headquarters. Jensen recalled that he was put through to DeLoach.[86] who in turn notified Director Hoover.[87]

As the news of the assault on Dr. King was moving through the FBI's command structure, Attorney General Clark was first contacted, he believed, by a Justice Department community relations specialist who was with Dr. King at the time.[88] A short time later, Clark was in telephone contact with DeLoach and thereafter with Hoover. A decision was made, apparently almost automatically, to involve the FBI immediately in the investigation. Later that evening a memorandum was sent from the Justice Department to the FBI ordering "a full investigation" into the possible violation of 18 U.S.C. 241.[89]

The committee's inquiry revealed that the FBI had no specific written guidelines in 1968 for the conduct of an assassination investigation. FBI files as well as committee interviews reflect, however, that the investigation was treat-

583

ed from the beginning as a "major case" or "special" investigation. Additional administrative personnel and agents were assigned to Memphis during the initial stages, including an accountant to maintain nationwide cost figures on the investigation.[90] A 24-hour deadline was imposed on all field offices for checking leads, and a reminder system was set up at headquarters to monitor compliance with the deadlines.[91] On April 7, 1968, an "All SAC" memo was issued from headquarters with instructions similar to those normally issued in "major cases" investigations:

All investigations must be handled under the personal direction of the SAC. Leads are to be afforded immediate, thorough investigative attention. You must exhaust all possibilities from such leads as any one lead could result in the solution of this most important investigation. SAC will be held personally responsible for any failure to promptly and thoroughly handle investigations in this matter.[92]

Finally, in further recognition of the special nature of the MURKIN investigation, the FBI sent an inspector from headquarters to oversee progress in key field offices.[93]

Following these initial administrative steps, there was, according to FBI files, a widespread and extensive effort to identify and apprehend the assassin of Dr. King. Exhaustive field interviews and record checks were performed with every conceivable source of information— banks, telephone companies, audit agencies, and police departments, as well as motor vehicle bureaus, motels and hotels, even dry cleaning establishments, and dancing schools.

Many early investigative breaks resulted from a thorough anaysis by the Bureau of physical evidence, much of which had been found shortly after the assassination in a bundle that had been left in the doorway of Canipe's Amusement Co. on South Main Street, Memphis. Both a pair of binoculars and a .30–06 rifle were traced to their respective places of purchase. The binoculars had been bought in Memphis itself,[94] while the suspected murder weapon was traced to the Aeromarine Supply Co. in Birmingham, Ala.[95] Early ballistics tests on the rifle and the bullet taken from Dr. King's body during the autopsy revealed that while "the bullet could have been fired from the rifle found near the scene," the mutilation of the bullet made it impossible to state "that it was actually fired from this one rifle."[96]

Interviews with clerks at Aeromarine established that the rifle had been purchased on March 30, 1968, by an individual using the name of Harvey Lowmeyer. Lowmeyer was generally described as a "white male, 36 years old, 5 feet, 8 inches tall, 150 to 160 pounds, black or dark brown hair.[97] Finally, in a clear example of both the skill and detail of the Bureau's fugitive investigation, laundry marks found on a pair of undershorts and an undershirt in the bundle were traced to a specific machine model, and ultimately to a particular laundry. Within 1 week of the assassination, the as-yet unidentified suspect's use of the Home Service Laundry in Los Angeles had been established.[98]

Nevertheless, despite the extensive FBI effort, the suspect continued to elude authorities. On April 17, in order to secure an arrest warrant and additional publicity in the fugitive search, the Government filed a complaint with the U.S. Commissioner in Birmingham. It charged Eric S. Galt[14] "and an individual alleged to be his brother" with conspiracy to interfere with the constitutional rights of Martin Luther King, Jr.[99] A fugitive press release was issued with the complaint, and media distribution of the information and accompanying photograph was encouraged.[100]

While the Department of Justice and the FBI were trying to identify "Galt" by issuing a press release asking for public assistance, a fingerprint project was in progress at FBI headquarters. Almost immediatey after the assassination, the Bureau had obtained unidentified latent prints of value from the rifle, binoculars, beer cans, and a copy of the Memphis Commercial Appeal, all of which were found in the bundle thought to have been dropped by the assassin shortly after the murder. An additional latent print was obtained from a map of Mexico discovered in an Atlanta roominghouse used by Galt shortly before the assassination. Comparisons revealed that prints on the Mexico map, the rifle, and binoculars were identical. Apparently made by a left thumb, the print was identi-

---

[14]The suspect's use of the Galt name was established through examination of a registration card at the New Rebel Motel outside of Memphis. He had stayed there the night before the assassination. See "Investigative Report," XII HSCA–MLK hearings, para. 29.

fied as "an ulner loop with 12 ridge counts."[101]

(1) *James Earl Ray identified.*—This and other prints taken from the evidence were compared unsuccessfully with known prints of approximately 400 suspects whose names were drawn from the FBI's single fingerprint file and from outstanding FBI identification orders.[102] Then, a systematic manual search of fingerprints records of fugitives was initiated, concentrating on a group with similar left thumb print characteristics. Shortly after the initiation of this process, and 15 days after the assassination, a positive match was made with the prints of James Earl Ray, a fugitive from Missouri State Penitentiary.[103]

The length of time it took the FBI to match the evidence prints to those of Ray has been the subject of public concern, so the committee closely examined the procedures that were used. The committee found the FBI's performance in the fingerprint check to have been thorough, professional and without defect.[104]

It is apparent from the review of FBI files that the identification of James Earl Ray was the termination point of a major phase of the Bureau's investigation. An inspector from headquarters who had been assigned to coordinate activities in the Memphis and Atlanta field offices was taken off the case;[105] and the Memphis field office was directed to phase out 15 agents and three stenographic clerks who had been assigned to it at the beginning of the investigation.[106]

With the positive identification of Ray, a number of investigative steps were repeated. A new press release was issued, with directions to all field offices to insure "repeated and widespread distribution."[107] Three days later, a directive was sent to all offices reemphasizing the 24-hour lead deadline and directing additional contact with criminal, racial and security informants to determine whether any possessed information on James Earl Ray.

For only the second time in Bureau history, approval was given for a special addition to the Ten Most Wanted List.[108] Short appeals for public assistance in the fugitive investigation were drafted and approved for use on the April 21 and April 28 installments of "The FBI" on television.[109] And within a week of the positive identification, various institutions and officials had offered a total of $150,000 for information leading to the apprehension and conviction of Ray.[110]

Finally, the positive identification prompted additional field investigation at banks, telephone companies, credit agencies, police departments, car rental agencies, motor vehicle departments, dance schools, hotels and motels, laundries, libraries, utility companies, selective service bureaus and labor unions.[111]

Despite the extensive nationwide effort, FBI files indicated a belief within the Bureau that the best chance for success in the fugitive investigation lay with Ray's family. Instructions were sent to the four field offices responsible for areas inhabited by key members of his family:

> Full coverage is to be afforded relatives of subject residing in your respective territories. This will include a spot surveillance of these persons as well as a determination of their associates and individuals making frequent contact with them. You should also obtain all long distance telephone calls from their residences for period April 23, 1967 to the present time. You should make this a continuing project until otherwise advised by the Bureau * * * You should insure that each relative is adequately covered to possibly assist in the subject's location and apprehension.[112]

In the weeks that followed Ray's identification, dozens of interviews with Ray's family members, including his brothers, occurred. A close examination of these interviews indicated, however, that their primary purpose (consistent with the directive quoted above) was to secure information on the whereabouts of the suspect, not to investigate the possibility of family involvement in the assassination.

(2) *Surveillance of Ray family considered.*—On May 9, 1968, the FBI, clearly concerned about its inability to locate Ray,[113] began to consider microphone and technical surveillance (bugs and wiretaps) of John Ray and Carol Pepper, Ray's brother and sister, at their homes and at the Grapevine Tavern, a St. Louis business they jointly owned and operated. The justification used in the authorization request[15] transmitted to the Justice Department on May 13 read as follows:

---

[15]In early 1968, internal Department of Justice procedures required that electronic surveillance, whether by wiretap or bug, be submitted to the Attorney General for approval prior to installation.

These installations could assist in the early apprehension of the subject, which could possibly be instrumental in reducing the stresses and tension placed on our national security subsequent to the death of Martin Luther King, Jr.[114]

The committee, after a thorough consideration of circumstances surrounding the surveillance request, was concerned about several aspects of the surveillance proposal.

First, the national security justification seemed, at best, to have been insubstantial, since the rioting that had been triggered by Dr. King's assassination had subsided. In addition, it is clear that the requested electronic surveillance, if installed, would almost certainly have been judged illegal under 1968 constitutional standards. The purpose, stated explicitly in FBI memorandums, was to surveil the family in hopes of apprehending Ray and not to gather evidence of the commission of a crime by Carol Pepper or John Ray.[115] Moreover, as to Carol Pepper at least, there was no significant evidence in FBI files to indicate her involvement in any criminal activity. Absent a clear threat to national security or probable cause as to the commission of a crime that might have justified an effort to secure a judicial warrant, no constitutional basis existed for the surveillance. Finally, a clear statutory basis for such surveillance did not become law until June 19, 1968.

It is clear that the FBI recognized these legal difficulties. In an internal FBI memorandum analyzing the legality of the proposed surveillance, it is stated:

The worst that could happen [if the proposed electronic surveillance were implemented] * * * is that we illegally learn where the subject is located and thus are able to arrest him on that knowledge * * *. The Court would not allow the prosecution to use as evidence any information obtained through the illegal surveillance but the illegal surveillance would not taint the use of any other evidence obtained either before or after and which was gotten in a legal manner. Nor, to repeat, would the illegality of the arrest alone resulting from whereabouts disclosed by unlawful surveillance, prevent the Court from trying the subject for the offense.[16][116]

---

[16]This memorandum appears in full as MLK exhibit F-502, VII HSCA–MLK hearings, p. 11.

The memorandum continued and warning:

> * * * that since this search and seizure is unconsti-
> tutional as to the Peppers, they have at least a theoreti-
> cal cause of action for damages against those who in-
> stalled the devices by trespass * * *. Moreover, in
> any such case the Government of the United States
> should surely be willing to pick up the tab for any judg-
> ment had against those who installed the micro-
> phones.[117]

The initials of Assistant to the Director DeLoach and
Associate Director Tolson appear on this memorandum.

The committee found that the willingness of the FBI to
proceed with this investigative approach in the face of an
internal legal analysis recognizing its unconstitutional nature reflected an absence of concern for the fundamental
rights of the surveillance targets. In addition, the proposal
was a clear indication either of the Bureau's failure to
consider seriously the possibility of conspiratorial involvement by members of Ray's family, or of its reckless disregard for the damage that this investigative approach could
have done to any later prosecution of Ray's brothers. Assuming, as FBI officials clearly did, the illegality of the
proposed electronic surveillance, any evidence of conspiracy intercepted by the tap would have been inadmissible against individuals with standing to contest that
illegality; in addition, the installation of an illegal tap or
bug would have raised significant taint problems[17] and
seriously jeopardized the ability to use any subsequently
developed evidence in a later conspiracy prosecution.

The problems that could have been created by the
FBI's proposal never materialized. While Attorney General Clark had no recollection of receiving or acting on the
request, it seems clear from the files and from interviews
that the proposal sent to the Justice Department was neither authorized nor implemented. The FBI case agent for
the assassination investigation in St. Louis field office,
which had jurisdiction for the area of the proposed electronic surveillance, told committee investigators he authorized no electronic surveillance in the MURKIN

---

[17] A problem arises when the defendant in a criminal prosecution argues
that evidence is inadmissible against him because it was developed as a
result of, or "through the exploitation of," prior illegal conduct by the
Government. If this conduct can be shown, the evidence is said to be
"tainted" and is inadmissible against the defendant.

investigation. He stated specifically there were no surreptitious entries into the Ray family residences or the Grapevine.[118] In addition, the committee's review of the St. Louis field office files and of the FBI headquarters MURKIN files produced no evidence of implementation of the electronic surveillance.

In a June 11, 1968, memorandum to Attorney General Clark, Director Hoover withdrew the May 13 request for electronic surveillance in light of Ray's apprehension in London.[119]

When questioned in public hearings, former Assistant to the Director DeLoach stated that the opinion of the Division and the attorney who provided the legal analysis of the proposed electronic surveillance was apparently that this investigative step would have been illegal.[120] He also acknowledged that his initials appeared on that memorandum[121] and that he had reviewed the memorandum at the time.[122] When asked by staff counsel to explain this attempt by the FBI to use what was analyzed and recognized by FBI headquarters as unconstitutional and illegal electronic surveillance in the assassination investigation, DeLoach responded:

DeLoach. My only answer * * * is that I did not recall these memoranda. You have given me the opportunity of reviewing them. I recall none of the circumstances surrounding them. The Department of Justice makes the legal determination insofar as the FBI is concerned. The FBI was following an investigative lead through the Department of Justice and the Department of Justice had the responsibility of either accepting it or turning it down in accordance with the rules of the United States as understood by the Attorney General.

Staff Counsel. Would it be fair to conclude from these memos that the FBI in recommending this investigative step was willing to engage in what it recognized as a violation of constitutional rights of the Peppers and perhaps of other people in order to achieve the investigative ends of the proposal?

DeLoach. The conclusion I draw from it is the FBI was very seriously concerned about the national security of the United States by the incident I mentioned previously and the fervent desire to apprehend the man responsible for the assassination of Dr.

King. They followed an investigative lead to the Attorney General, and the Attorney General would make a decision as to whether or not this would be productive.[123]

Efforts to secure precise information on Ray's location from the family did not meet with immediate results. Nevertheless, in a May 9 interview in St. Louis, John Ray reported that James had mentioned an intention to leave the country if he escaped and that he had indicated, on one occasion, admiration for Rhodesian Prime Minister Ian Smith.[124] On May 10, based on the interview as well as on other independent evidence of Ray's interest in African countries,[125] FBI headquarters initiated a passport review in the Washington field office.[126] It was directed initially at the 2,100,000 applications that had been filed since April 1967, the month of Ray's escape from Missouri State Penitentiary. Washington requested Canadian authorities to review Canadian passports records.[127]

(3) *Ray arrested in London*—On June 1, a break occurred when a possible photographic match of Ray turned up in the Canadian passport of George Ramon Sneyd. RCMP officials determined from the Kennedy Travel Bureau in Toronto that "Sneyd" had purchased a Toronto-London-Toronto airlines ticket, with a scheduled departure of May 6, and return on May 21, 1968. Meanwhile the FBI ascertained through fingerprint comparisons that Ray and "Sneyd" were, in fact, the same person.[128] One week later, at 11:11 a.m. on June 8, 1968, Ray was arrested in Heathrow Airport in London.

(c) *The conspiracy investigation*

The conclusion reached by the Justice Department and the FBI following their investigation was that James Earl Ray, acting alone, killed Martin Luther King, Jr. In interviews conducted and testimony taken by the committee, no dissent from this conclusion was voiced.

Director Hoover's views on the question of conspiracy were clearly stated in a memorandum he wrote on June 20, 1968, summarizing a discussion with Attorney General Clark. At one point during the conversation, Hoover said, "* * * in Ray's case, we have not found a single angle that would indicate a conspiracy." Later in the discussion, he added his personal opinion that "he [Ray] acted entirely alone," but then assured the Attorney General that "we are not closing our minds that others might be associated with him and we have to run down every lead." [129]

Clark, in an interview with the committee, indicated his agreement with Hoover's views, adding that the Bureau was probably more inclined to view the assassination in conspiratorial terms than he was. As Clark explained, he believed instinctively that Dr. King's death was the act of an eccentric racist loner. He said he believed that Ray's reference to a brother with respect to the rifle exchange in Birmingham the week before the assassination (a remark that was to provide the factual basis for a Federal conspiracy complaint filed in that city approximately 2 weeks after the assassination) was merely an excuse created by the assassin on the spur of the moment, rather than sound evidence of conspiracy.[130]

Clark characterized the evidence developed during the investigation in the following manner:

> I don't recall any presentation of evidence as distinguished from the circumstances that ever implied direct involvement of another person, and simultaneously I believe I saw an enormous amount of evidence of the direct participation of a single person whose identity was fairly consistently established because I felt I should go on the facts available rather than the circumstances.[131]

Despite the ultimate conclusion of officials in both the Justice Department and the FBI that no conspiracy existed in the assassination, FBI investigative files reflect throughout a consciousness of the possibility of a conspiracy. For example, on April 26, 1968, 3 weeks after the assassination and subsequent to Ray's identification, the FBI documented from a complete review of the King security file some 50 prior threats on Dr. King's life. These threats were set out in investigative leads and transmitted to the appropriate field office for resolution, accompanied by the following instructions:

> The main file on King has been reviewed at the Bureau and leads are being sent out concerning persons involved in prior threats against King. These

leads as well as leads concerning any other suspects developed from any source must be given immediate and thorough handling on a top priority basis. Process has been obtained against James Earl Ray and extensive investigation is continuing to locate Ray and to establish motive of crime. You have been and will be furnished information relating to other possible conspirators. These must all be thoroughly resolved no matter how remote.[132]

Moreover, a review of FBI investigative efforts following Ray's arrest revealed that while there was a significant overall reduction in Bureau expenditures at about this time,[18] a limited number of additional conspiracy leads were still pursued. The major, postarrest effort, and attempt to determine the source of Ray's funds through an intensive reinvestigation of the July 1967 bank robbery in Alton, Ill.,[19] stemmed almost entirely from the Bureau's awareness that Ray's extensive expenditures during 14 months of freedom strongly suggested his association with unidentified individuals.

In addition, FBI files reflected efforts over the months following Ray's arrest: (1) to identify possible criminal associates through rechecking the registrations at the New Rebel Motel in Memphis just before the assassination and at motels, hotels and roominghouses in Birmingham for the time period of the rifle purchase; [133] (2) to investigate the possibility that a Louisiana State policeman was the mysterious Raoul; [134] and (3) to interview Ray himself on the issue of conspiracy. Thus, while officials in both the Justice Department and the FBI were rapidly reaching a unanimous no-conspiracy conclusion, at least a limited amount of conspiracy investigation continued after Ray's arrest.

Despite these efforts, the committee found serious defects in both the method and focus of the FBI's conspiracy investigation.

(1) *The method.*—First, conspiracy leads were at times resolved simply by establishing a potential coconspirator's alibi during the period of March 29 to April 4,

---

[18] See MLK exhibit F–500 (committee diagram of FBI expenditures in the investigation). VII HSCA–MLK hearings, 6.

[19] The committee concluded, after a review of FBI files and an extensive field investigation, that Ray's most likely source of funds during the preassassination fugitive period was, in fact, the Alton bank robbery. See section II B of the final report.

1968, designated by the FBI as the "pertinent period" of the assassination investigation.[135] The inadequacy of this approach is demonstrated by the FBI's own case against Ray, which had produced evidence that his plan to kill Dr. King had begun to take form before March 17, 1968, while he was still a resident of California. The notion that a conspiracy suspect can be absolved by establishing his absence from the scene of a crime or his nonparticipation in an overt act (the rifle purchase) reflects an erroneous view of the law of conspiracy. In 1968, as in 1978, a conspiracy prosecution requires only an agreement and one subsequent overt act by any of the parties in furtherance of that agreement. Proximity to the scene of the crime, while clearly relevant and significant, is not the ultimate issue.

Second, while there was a general canvass of "all racial, criminal and security informants" at various stages of the investigation,[136] FBI files indicate only limited efforts, independent of specific leads, to investigate the possible involvement of extremist organizations such as the White Knights of the Ku Klux Klan of Mississippi or the Minutemen, even though they had demonstrated both a propensity for violence and a clear antagonism toward Dr. King.

For example, the Bureau received evidence of Ray's possible involvement with the United Klans of America when Ray, after his arrest in London, chose Arthur Hanes, Sr., as his defense counsel. Hanes was well known for his defense in 1965 of Klansmen charged with the murder of civil rights worker Viola Liuzzo. In addition, informant information was subsequently received indicating that the UKA might become involved in the funding of Ray's defense. Nevertheless, no concerted effort was made to pursue the conspiratorial implications of this information. Additional steps might have included a cross check of Bureau hate-group indexes against Ray's known or possible associates, or taking of sworn testimony from Klan officials through the use of a grand jury subpena and immunity grants.[20]

Third, FBI and Department of Justice files reflect almost total reliance on field interviews as a means of resolving issues relevant to the overall conspiracy investigation.

[20] See II C for a summary of the committee's investigation of this and several other leads suggesting the involvement of extremist groups in the assassination.

At no time was a grand jury used to supplement the investigation of numerous conspiracy allegations, despite circumstances which the committee believed may have been appropriate for grand jury investigation. Some examples:

Ray's possible association with a Missouri State Penitentiary inmate organization was left essentially unresolved. Extensive field interviews with MSP associates and former associates of Ray confirmed the existence of the group, but "failed to ascertain information concerning the principles or membership or the extent of its network."[137] The use of a grand jury to explore this lead—a logical step following the unsuccessful interview process—was apparently never considered.

Similarly, the FBI's investigation of a CB radio broadcast heard in Memphis shortly after the assassination, thought by some to have been an effort to divert police attention and facilitate the flight of the assassin, was terminated with attention focused on one individual who flatly denied involvement in the incident. Authorities evidently never considered placing this individual before a grand jury for testimony under oath.[21]

Also, the possibility of Ray family involvement in the assassination could have been explored by a grand jury and the judicious use of immunity grants. Nevertheless, the FBI and the Justice Department were satisfied to resolve the issue solely through field investigation.[22] [138]

When questioned concerning the failure to use the grand jury during the assassination investigation, Assistant to the Director DeLoach offered the following opinion concerning its usefulness:

[T]he grand jury would be laborious, inefficient, might perhaps slow down the investigation, when we were looking throughout the world as intensively as we could for James Earl Ray and would be of little usage * * * I think [if] we had established the grand jury investigation during the fugitive investigation, [it] would have taken the time of officials of the Department of Justice, and I doubt very seriously whether it would have been productive, as later investigation has more or less established.[139]

21 See sec. II C for summary of the committee's investigation of the CB broadcast.
22 See sec. II B for summary of committee's investigation of family involvement in the assassination.

* * * the matter of an establishment of a grand
jury is entirely up to the Department of Justice.
Based upon the facts furnished to them by the FBI,
the FBI could not in my opinion, to the best of my
recollection, go to the Department of Justice and say
we want a grand jury. It is not up to the FBI to do
that. We are an investigative agency. We determine the
facts, the Department handles the prosecution, they
determine whether or not a grand jury is to be established.[140]

The committee found DeLoach's remarks well taken.
When asked further, however, why this technique had
not been used following Ray's arrest, "in order to determine whether * * * there might have been associates of
Mr. Ray involved in the assassination," [141] DeLoach
responded that after the Justice Department turned down
an FBI request to use a grand jury subpoena to secure the
notes of author William Bradford Huie, the feeling must
have been that the Justice Department was opposed to the
use of the grand jury generally in the investigation.

I am testifying strictly based on opinion. But I
would certainly think that after a turndown by the
Department of Justice in this one instance, this spread
the philosophy that would have kept the FBI from
making further requests for grand jury investigation.
It would appear the philosophy of the Department of
Justice was there should be no grand jury investigation.[142]

In light of the specific legal grounds for the Department's
decision, however, the committee found DeLoach's explanation for the absence of further FBI proposals for grand
jury work to be inadequate.[23]
Former Attorney General Clark testified there was simply no situation in the investigation which warranted
grand jury investigation:

* * * I do not recall any suggestion that a grand
jury would have utility, any proposal that a certain
person be put before a grand jury. The impression I
had was that we had hundreds, maybe even thousands,

---

[29]A discussion of the proposal to subpena Huie's notes appears in "Investigation Report," XIII, HSCA–MLK hearings.

of FBI agents trying * * * to see whether they could pick up a trace of the guy who led us to believe he might be in hippie areas of different towns, of hundreds of agents looking through millions of passport applications, and things like that. I didn't see a grand jury utility. It never—nothing I ever heard or saw or have seen indicates it would have had any utility. [143]

The committee noted that on June 19, 1968, after several years of uncertainty concerning the legality of electronic surveillance as a criminal investigative tool, Congress passed title III of the Omnibus Crime Control and Safe Streets Acts of 1968. It permitted the use of court-authorized electronic surveillance by law enforcement officers in certain enumerated crimes, including murder.[24] Nevertheless, in signing title III into law, President Johnson announced that the administration's established policy of confining wiretapping to national security cases would continue in force. [144] Ironically, a law which was passed in part because of Dr. King's assassination [145] could not be considered by the FBI during the investigation of that crime.

The committee, in making this observation, did not take a position on the desirability of the use of electronic surveillance generally in society. It merely noted that President Johnson's decision, as implemented by Attorney General Clark, [146] placed one more potentially crucial limitation on the investigation of conspiracy in Dr. King's assassination.

(2) *The focus.*—Of far greater potential significance than the defects that have been noted was the failure of the FBI and the Justice Department to focus a concerted effort on Ray's family, specifically his brothers, during the conspiracy investigation. Absent any extrinsic evidence, family members of the suspected triggerman deserved at least some investigative attention, given the significant amount of direct and circumstantial evidence received by the FBI during the months following the assassination that strongly suggested a great deal more contact among the three brothers than they were willing to admit. The

---

[24] The potential for imaginative investigative efforts provided in this act in murder investigations has been noted in the Report of the National Commission for the Review of Federal and State Laws Relating to Wiretapping and Electronic Surveillance, pp. 150–51 (1976)

failure to pursue this area more aggressively constituted a serious defect in the overall investigative effort.

Because the evidence implicating the brothers has been reviewed previously,[25] no effort will be made to repeat the specifics. It is adequate to say imply that within a relatively short time after Dr. King's assassination, the FBI had collected evidence of possible family involvement from a number of separate sources including:

Reference by James Earl Ray to a brother being involved in the critical preassassination activities, most significantly the purchase of the rifle;

Strong signs of racism exhibited by both John and Jerry Ray;

The probable involvement of John in James' escape from the Missouri State Penitentiary;

The probable involvement of James, John and possibly Jerry in the Alton bank robbery; and

Statements by Jerry indicating his knowledge of a possible $100,000 payoff for the assassination.

Finally, with publication of Huie's Look magazine articles in November 1968 and his book, "He Slew the Dreamer," striking coincidences appeared between the timing of Ray's claimed involvement with Raoul and his preassassination dealings with a brother, raising the strong possibility that Raoul was created to conceal Ray's association with one or both of his brothers.

Clearly this evidence warranted a major and concerted effort by the FBI and the Civil Rights Division of the Justice Department to determine the extent and the nature of Ray's actual preassassination contact with his brothers. In fact, no such concerted effort was made.

It cannot be said that the Bureau ignored the Ray family in its investigation. As has been indicated previously, an intense effort was made to secure assistance and information from various family members during the prearrest fugitive investigation, and during this period the brothers were interviewed on numerous occasions concerning the suspect's location.[26] In fact, at one point the Bureau's preoccupation with the fugitive investigation became so great that a recommendation was made for the use of illegal electronic surveillance on John Larry Ray

---

[25] See section IIB of this report; see also "Investigation Report," XIV HSCA–MLK hearings XII.

[26] The FBI interviewed relatives of James Earl Ray approximately 100 times. Jerry Ray and John Ray were interviewed approximately 20 times each.

and Carol Pepper in an effort to locate the subject. Had such a tactic been implemented, any subsequent conspiracy case against family members could have been seriously jeopardized.

Nevertheless, with the exception of comparisons of the fingerprints[147] and palm prints of the two brothers with unidentified latent prints, an effort to verify Jerry Ray's alibi for April 4, 1968, [148] and the posing of some interview questions arguably connected to a conspiracy investigation, investigative files reflected no significant efforts to determine the extent of their involvement with James in the assassination.

No effort was made, for example, to determine if the 1967–68 travels of either brother coincided with those of Raoul, as Ray related them. Such an effort might have included motel and airline canvases for Ray brother aliases and employment verifications for appropriate periods.

Similarly, no effort was made, other than through direct questioning of the brothers themselves, to establish the alibis of either Jerry or John during the time of the rifle purchase. John's alibi, even for the day of the assassination, went unchecked. The Bureau did cover this ground routinely with other conspiracy suspects. Further, Jerry Ray's statements in June 1968 [27] and again in March 1969, indicating knowledge of a conspiracy were not adequately pursued. He made his March 1969 remarks to Kent Courtney, publisher of the Conservative Journal in Louisiana. He indicated that he would discuss the "conspiracy" with Courtney in a meeting on March 20, 1969. [149] Despite Courtney's apparent willingness to cooperate with the Bureau,[150] no consideration was given to the use of consensual electronic surveillance or of an undercover FBI agent during Jerry's discussion with Courtney. Rather, a decision was made—based on "background data" on Courtney and a consequent fear of Bureau embarrassment—to conduct yet another field interview with Jerry Ray.[151] However, when Jerry Ray refused to be interviewed, Bureau efforts to pursue the lead ceased.

FBI files revealed no efforts to investigate the associates of Ray's brothers, either through direct, saturation interviews, or through the development of an informant apparatus. Thus, Ray's possible connection with a conspiracy

---

[27] See MLK exhibit F–606 (June 11, 1968 FBI interview), VII HSCA-MLK hearings, 457.

599

through one of his brothers was not throughly investigated. Given the criminal nature of many of John's associates, this might well have required the use of a grand jury and immunity grants, investigative tools which might have been useful in the additional areas of John's probable involvement in the MSP escape and in the Alton bank robbery in July 1967. Some of this grand jury and immunity work could have been accomplished without violating a Justice Department policy against compelling testimony of a family member or facing the issue of immunity with either of the brothers.

The committee also sought to evaluate the performance of the FBI in investigating a St. Louis conspiracy involving John Sutherland and John Kauffmann that subsequently came to light.[28] The object was to determine if the information should have been uncovered by the Federal authorities during the original investigation. The findings were as follows:

> There was credible evidence—developed from a police informant in St. Louis in the 1960's, a man who holds a respectable position with a major manufacturing company—that an offer of money for the murder of Dr. King was in fact known in the 1966–68 period. Specifically, it was circulating among individuals who spent considerable time during the period at a motel owned by John Kauffmann.[152]

> Circumstantial evidence also indicated that the offer may have been communicated to a person who did undercover work for several Federal agencies.[29]

> Nevertheless, information about the conspiracy was not developed by the FBI until 1974, and then, apparently due to an agent's error, the information was misfiled and not actively pursued.[30]

Had a more rigorous conspiracy investigation been conducted in 1968, the existence of the St. Louis-based conspiracy might have come to the attention of the Bureau and the Department of Justice at the time when it could have been successfully investigated. The ability of the committee to investigate the St. Louis conspiracy and Ray's possible connection with it was severely hampered by the passage of so much time and the deaths of principals.

---

[28]See section II B.
[29]During executive session testimony before the committee, this witness denied knowledge of the Sutherland/Kauffmann conspiracy. Other evidence received by the committee made it skeptical about this denial.
[30]See II B, *supra*, for discussion of the FBI's misfiling.

(d) Investigative excesses

As was discussed, the FBI's attempt to use electronic surveillance during the fugitive investigation reflected a lack of concern for the constitutional rights of persons targeted by the proposed surveillance. FBI files reflected a similar lack of respect for the constitutional rights of the defendant, James Earl Ray, in two separate incidents following his arrest and return to Tennessee to stand trial for murder.

Prior to his return to the United States, Ray retained Arthur Hanes, Sr., to represent him. Hanes was Ray's primary attorney until November 10, 1968, when Ray replaced him with Percy Foreman.

On September 18, Hanes filed a motion before Judge W. Preston Battle seeking to modify various aspects of his client's conditions of confinement. During an evidentiary hearing on September 30 to determine the facts underlying the motion, testimony was taken on various subjects, including the methods used to monitor Ray's mail. A representative of the Shelby County Sheriff's Department stated that Ray's general mail was read and censored, but he then assured the court that written material passing between Ray and his attorney was perused for security purposes only, and was not read to determine the contents.[153]

Following the hearing, Judge Battle memorialized this procedure in the form of a judicial order, and in a teletype sent from the FBI's Memphis field office to Washington, the essence of the court's ruling was conveyed as follows:

> Judge Battle ruled that written notes exchanged between Ray and his attorney are privileged. However, the Shelby County sheriff or his designated agent has the authority to peruse these notes to determine if there is any attempt to breach security of the jail. These notes should not be perused for the purpose of ascertaining the full contents of the message.[31][154]

Despite the FBI's clear understanding of Judge Battle's order, however, within a month of its issuance, three letters from Ray to Hanes had been intercepted, photocopied,

---

[31]See MLK exhibit F–503, VII HSCA–MLK hearings, 14.

passed to the FBI's Memphis field office and transmitted to FBI headquarters in Washington.[32][155] On one occasion, the covering memorandum sent to Washington directed the reader's attention to particularly interesting parts of the letter:

> Of significance, Ray in his letter to Hanes requests that Mr. Huie not go to any of the addresses in Miami until after the trial. In this connection, Ray also states "that part of the story just covers a few days anyhow and is not too important."[156]

Robert Jensen, SAC in Memphis at the time, conceded in interviews and executive session testimony that his signature or initials were on memoranda transmitting two of the three letters[157] and speculated, although he could not recall definitely, that the source of the letters was Shelby County Sheriff William N. Morris.[158] When interviewed by the committee, Morris did not deny the mail photocopying had occurred, but stated he had no recollection of specific details surrounding the situation.[159] Jensen testified further that he believed the letters were volunteered to him, rather than having been solicited by the Bureau.[160] He had no recollection of informing the State prosecutor or defense counsel of his receipt of the letters,[161] and he did not consider the possibility that receipt of privileged information might taint the prosecution.[162] He explained the situation as follows:

> Where the U.S. Government or the FBI or the Justice Department has an interest in a matter and I am volunteered information relative to the matter, I am afraid that I would accept it, and I think this is what happened in this case.[163]

During his testimony before the committee, Assistant to the Director DeLoach stated that while he had no personal knowledge of the mail interception, he believed the intent of the Memphis office was to peruse the documents for security reasons only,[164] as allowed by the court order.

The committee found DeLoach's explanation com-

---

[32]These three separate letters, and accompanying FBI memoranda, appear as MLK exhibits F-508, F-509 and F-510, VII HSCA-MLK hearings, 81, 83, 86, respectively.

pletely unsatisfactory. First, such an explanation was not offered by Memphis SAC Jensen, who was directly involved in the mail interception. Second, as DeLoach conceded during his testimony, the FBI "had no responsibility * * * for the custody of Ray at the time."[165] Third, if the Memphis office was interested solely in detecting breaches of prison security, there would seem to be no reason to highlight portions of Ray's letters in which he wrote of "addresses in Miami," or in fact to photocopy and transmit the correspondence to FBI headquarters in Washington.

The inherent confidentiality of communications between a defendant and his attorney is a fundamental principle of American jurisprudence. It stems from fundamental individual rights established in the Constitution. The FBI's Memphis office was aware of a specific court order reinforcing the significance of the principle. Even if the FBI did not initiate the mail interception process, its willing and repeated receipt of letters sent by the defendant to his attorney showed a total disregard for Ray's right to privacy during the preparation of his trial defense and encouraged an activity by local officials that was both illegal and unconstitutional. The committee found no justification for such conduct by Federal agents.

On October 31, one month after Judge Battle's order, FBI headquarters, using a carefully worded directive initialed by Associate Director Tolson, Assistant to the Director DeLoach, Assistant Director Rosen and others, instructed the Memphis office as follows:

In view of the above order of W. Preston Battle [referring to Sept. 30, 1968 order], you should not accept any written communication from the sheriff regarding correspondence between Ray and other individuals. If it is not in violation of the court order you may accept information from the sheriff if he volunteers this information and it is on an oral basis only. [166]

With the receipt of this directive, the Bureau's practice of receiving photocopies of Ray's correspondence apparently ceased. There was no evidence in files reviewed by the committee that knowledge of the operation, or of information found in the intercepted mail, spread beyond the Memphis field office and FBI headquarters in Washington.[33]

Another illustration of the Bureau's lack of concern for the constitutional rights of James Earl Ray, as well as insensitivity to legal issues that may have arisen in subsequent trials, occurred after James Earl Ray had entered his guilty plea on March 10, 1969. Immediately following the plea, Assistant Attorney General Jerris Leonard of the Civil Rights Division (who had replaced Stephen Pollak with the change of Presidential administrations in January 1969) instructed the Bureau to consider various approaches to obtain information Ray might possess on conspiracy. Alternatives considered included an immediate interview,[167] an interview at some later date, and testimony under oath before a Federal grand jury. The action was being taken in light of President Nixon's reported plan "to take the position in a future press conference that the Federal Government was continuing to give intensive interest to the possibility of the existence of a conspiracy."[168]

Following some discussion, a decision was made to attempt an immediate interview of Ray. The Memphis field office contacted Shelby County District Attorney Phil N. Canale, Ray's attorney, Percy Foreman,[34] and Harry Avery, Commissioner of the Tennessee Department of Corrections. Foreman approved the interview of his client, [169] and neither Canale nor Avery raised objections.

The interview itself was conducted by Memphis SAC Jensen. Authority for the FBI to conduct the interview was given by D. Robert Owen,[170] Deputy Assistant Attorney General of the Justice Department's Civil Rights Division. In an interview with the committee, Owen recalled no consideration of the possibility of having a Department attorney present during the interview. Director Hoover gave specific instructions that results of the interview be given to him prior to dissemination to the Department.[171]

Jensen's interview with Ray lasted 50 minutes. It cov-

---

[33] A review of the Miami field office MURKIN files, for example, reveals no lead sent out from Washington or Memphis following Ray's mention of "Miami address" in his letter to Hanes.

[34] Ray was taking steps at this time to replace Foreman with court-appointed attorneys to handle an appeal from his guilty plea. No attorney had yet been appointed.

ered a variety of topics, including Ray's dissatisfaction with his attorneys, his plans to reopen his case, Charles Stephens, Charles Stein. "The FBI" television show, fingerprints on the rifle and Inspector Thomas Butler of Scotland Yard. Ray provided no evidence supporting the possibility of a conspiracy.[172]

Ray was not accompanied by an attorney during the interview, nor was he informed specifically of his right to have a lawyer present; his right to terminate the interview at will; his right to remain silent; to have the Government pay for a lawyer if he could not afford one; or the Government's ability to use his statements against him at a later date (*Miranda* rights). In an interview with the committee, Jensen confirmed that he did not advise Ray formally of his *Miranda* rights, explaining that surrounding circumstances, including Ray's extensive criminal record, indicated that he was aware of his rights without formal notification. Moreover, Jensen stated that the interview was not a hostile one, that he had called the guard to terminate the interview when Ray stated he wished to leave, and that he changed the subject matter of the interview when Ray refused to continue along a specific line.[173]

Accepting the accuracy of Jensen's recollection, the committee was disturbed by his failure to consider the implications of interviewing Ray without prior advice of his *Miranda* rights, as well as by the lack of concern for the defendant's constitutional rights as evidenced by this interview procedure. This interview of Ray was the first official effort to gain information on the possibility of conspiracy from the self-confessed assassin. The ability to use any of Ray's statements in a conspiracy case against him would have depended on the Government's ability to survive a motion to suppress the statements that would automatically be filed by a defense counsel.

The committee recognized that many law enforcement officials believed the administration of *Miranda* rights inhibit a person from freely divulging information he may possess. Jensen may well have believed that he would be able to establish a more productive rapport if he omitted the formal warnings. While this argument is not without merit, the committee believed that the fundamental protections designed to be achieved by the administration of *Miranda* warnings required that they be given to Ray in this case, regardless of competing strategic considerations.[174]

(e) Conclusion

The FBI's investigation of Dr. King's assassination exemplified, at times, the best of police work. Efforts first to identify and then to locate and apprehend Ray represented the work of thousands of agents on a national and international scale. In addition, close coordination was required with law enforcement authorities in Mexico, Canada, and Europe. At times the work was meticulous and tedious; ultimately, the fugitive investigation only can be categorized a success.

The committee received testimony indicating that the major effort made by the Bureau in the investigation, apprehension, and prosecution of Ray may well have reflected Director Hoover's concern that failure might be attributed to his well-publicized animosity for Dr. King. In executive session testimony before the committee former Attorney General Ramsey Clark stated:

> I had the strongest, clearest conviction that the FBI would do everything in its power to investigate this case quickly, effectively, and successfully, and it wasn't just logic. It was, I mean, my total being told me that the thing Mr. Hoover really loved most, the Bureau, was on the line here, and that if they couldn't produce here where many would suspect their concern, that their failure would do more damage to them in the minds of the people than any other case they had worked on.[175]

Similar sentiments were voiced by other officials from both the Justice Department and the FBI.[176]

Ironically, this explanation for the best in the investigation may also explain the worst. The disturbing investigative "excesses" detailed above—including the proposal of illegal electronic surveillance, FBI participation in an ongoing process of mail interception at the Shelby County jail, and the failure to administer *Miranda* rights prior to Ray's postguilty plea interview—may well also reflect the importance placed on the case by Director Hoover. While the committee stresses that it had no direct evidence to this effect, it is clear that in all three incidents a priority was placed on investigative breaks with a simultaneous tendency to overlook the constitutional rights of the parties involved. It seemed reasonable to assume that this reflected, at least in part, pressure from above.

III

RECOMMENDATIONS OF THE SELECT COMMITTEE ON ASSASSINATIONS

In 1968, the Commission on the Causes and Prevention of Violence—the Eisenhower Commission—conducted an extensive study which dealt, in part, with assassination. Reports prepared for the Commission concluded that the level of assassination in America was high,[1] particularly in relation to other Western democracies and populous countries.[2] Indeed, nine U.S. Presidents, one in four, have been the targets of assassins (table 1), and four died as a result.[3] In addition, between 1835 and 1968, 81 other public officials or candidates, Federal, State, and local, were assaulted, some fatally.[4]

The Eisenhower Commission did not offer a definition of assassination, although its basic elements were specified in papers prepared for the Commission. Assassination was seen as a murder whose target was a prominent political figure; there was a political motive for the murder; or the murder would have a political impact.[5] The existence of any one of the three elements, it was pointed out, would qualify a murder as an assassination.

The Eisenhower Commission also identified five broad categories of assassination. It noted that not all of them had historical precedents in the United States.[6] The categories were based on objectives:

(1) assassination as a means by which one political elite replaces another without effecting systemic or idealogical change;

(2) assassination whose purpose is to destroy the legitimacy of the ruling elite and to effect systemic or ideological change;

(3) assassination ordered by the ruling elite to counteract political challenge;

    (4) assassination for propaganda purposes—to promote an ideology; and

    (5) assassination to satisfy the pathological needs of abnormal individuals acting under an ideological guise.

The Eisenhower Commission found the typical assassination in the United States to be the act of a deranged, self-appointed savior.[7] In contrast to worldwide patterns, assassination by an organized political group was thought to be rare in this country. Only in the years immediately following the Civil War was assassination undertaken by organized groups to alter government through terror. Further, while the Commission identified as many as 11 public officials who had been targeted for assassination by organized criminal elements, it characterized the victims as low-level officeholders who had either threatened the criminal elements or had been involved with them.[8] The classic form of assassination, therefore, did not generally apply to the United States.

The legitimacy of achieving change by extralegal actions has long been a subject of debate among philosophers and political and legal scholars.[9] Historically, illegitimate authorites have been overthrown by forces acting outside the legal process, with the rationale being natural law, customs, or belief in the primacy of spiritual scriptures. In ancient Greece, for example, it was considered acceptable to murder usurpers. Likewise, medieval Christian thought acceptable assassination of usurpers, but not of oppressive tyrants, although that distinction eventually disappeared. During the Reformation and Counterreformation, the Jesuit theologian Mariana and the Scottish Calvinist Buchanan held assassination of a tyrant to be acceptable under certain circumstances. In recent history, the experience of Nazi Germany—and of this country, as well —in which certain groups have suffered indignities and inequities has served to raise the queston once again. But, generally, arguments for justified assassination have applied only to cases of totalitarian rule, illegitimate leadership, or the unjust suppression of certain groups within a society, although many foremost thinkers accept no justification whatsoever for assassination.

The Eisenhower Commission, nevertheless, asked the question: Had assassination become a part of political life in the United States? It noted that violence seemed interwoven with American history—the fight for independence,

TABLE 1.—ASSASSINATION ATTEMPTS AGAINST PRESIDENTS AND PRESIDENTIAL CANDIDATES

Year	Victim	Assailant and professed or alleged reason	Method of attack and result	Location	Activity of victim at time of attack
1835	Andrew Jackson	Richard Lawrence; declared insane, said Jackson was preventing him from obtaining large sums of money.	Pistol, misfired	Washington, D.C.	Attending funeral service in Capitol rotunda.
1865	Abraham Lincoln	John W. Booth; loyalty to the Confederacy, revenge for defeat, slavery issue.	Pistol, killed	..... do	Attending theatrical performance in Ford Theatre.
1881	James Garfield	Charles Guiteau; disgruntled office-seeker, supporter of opposite faction of Republican Party.	..... do	..... do	Passing through train station to go on vacation.
1901	William McKinley	Leon F. Czolgosz; anarchist ideology.	..... do	Buffalo, N.Y.	Standing in reception line at Pan-American Exposition
1912	Theodore Roosevelt (candidate).	John Schrank; declared insane, had vision that McKinley wanted him to avenge his death.	Pistol, wounded	Milwaukee, Wis.	Leaving hotel to deliver a campaign speech.
1933	Franklin D. Roosevelt (President-elect).	Guiseppe Zangara; hated rulers and capitalists.	Pistol, bullets missed the President.	Miami, Fla.	Leaving after delivering speech in Bayside Park.
1950	Harry S. Truman	Oscar Collazo and Griselio Torresola; Puerto Rican independence.	Automatic weapon, prevented from shooting at President.	Washington, D.C.	Inside Blair House as assassins attempted to break in.
1963	John F. Kennedy	Lee H. Oswald; motive unknown	Rifle, killed	Dallas, Tex.	Taking part in motorcade through Dallas streets.
1968	Robert F. Kennedy (candidate).	Sirhan Sirhan; opposition to U.S. Mideast policy.	Pistol, killed	Los Angeles, Calif.	Leaving primary campaign headquarters through hotel kitchen after delivering speech.

Source: Task Force Report, Assassination and Political Violence (National Commission on the Causes and Prevention of Violence, October 1969).

the Indian wars, slavery and the secession of the South, agrarian reform, the emergence of organized labor, the civil rights movement and conflicts based on religious and ethnic, even political, grounds.[10] The Commission also cited factors present at times of assassinations in other countries,[11] finding them to be increasingly evident in the United States: The publication of extremist rhetoric and vilification of political leaders and Government institutions, rapid socioeconomic change, widespread belief that legitimate demands of Government are not being met, urban guerrilla warfare, social group confrontations, a belief in the efficacy of violence, all leading to a general atmosphere of violence.

Since publication of the Eisenhower Commission's report in 1968, its concern has been underscored by a rash of assassinations or attempted assassinations: Governor George Wallace of Alabama in 1972, President Ford, twice, in 1975, California Congressman Leo Ryan and San Francisco Mayor George Moscone in 1978. These acts of assassination, this committee noted, had a disturbing effect on society that goes beyond their immediate impact, which is the deplorable destruction of human life. These results flow not just from the act of assassination itself, but also from the responses it provokes from citizens and from government. The committee found that assassination is more than a deadly assault:

It is an attack on the foundations of democracy —majority rule, due process of law, consensual decisionmaking, individual rights and liberties;

It undermines the political system by deterring qualified people from seeking public office or exercising leadership;

It produces fear among the citizenry, a "siege mentality," and often leads to the creation of vigilante groups, civil disorder and other counterterrorist activities;

It results in a feeling that the President and other national leaders should be isolated for their protection;

It leads to demands that Government cut short conventional legal processes in bringing assassins to justice and for stronger measures to deal with violence, i.e., increased surveillance, security checks at public facilities, capital punishment and so on;

It exerts pressure on law enforcement agencies that can lead to abuse of authority.

The committee also discovered that assassinations in the United States have seldom achieved the end of causing or preventing change. In fact, in many instances the opposite effect has occurred. Change that an act of assassination was designed to prevent has been hastened, and responsible citizens have been bound closer together in working to achieve objectives for the good of society.[12] The two-party system has been remarkably stable, and the process for the transfer of the Presidency has been effective.

Assassination in the United States has, however, caused serious, destructive upheavals, such as the riots that followed the murder of Dr. Martin Luther King, Jr. Further, the committee recognized that an act of assassination may, in times of strife, result in fundamental change, and a recurrent pattern of such acts might, in time, undermine the social and political systems of the country.

The act of assassination and its threat demand response by both the citizenry and Government. Historically, this response has ranged from the imposition of totalitarian rule to capitulation to the demands of dissidents. In the United States, there has generally been a balanced response. Recognizing that grievances that lead to violence are often legitimate, Government has attempted to eliminate inequitable conditions, but it has also prosecuted those who have circumvented legal processes to achieve change. In addition, the Government has sought legislative and administrative means to prevent recurring violence and to provide more protection for those who are threatened by it.

The committee was acutely aware of the problem of insuring that civil liberties are preserved, while affording adequate protection to the institutions of democratic society and to public figures.[1] It recognized the difficulty in finding a balance between liberty and order. In carrying out its mandate requiring it to address the question of legal and administrative responses to assassination, the committee was mindful of the need to weigh the costs that could accrue to individual privacy, group protest, legitimate dissent, political competition and social change

---

[1]At the request of Chairman Stokes, the American Civil Liberties Union submitted for the committee's record a comprehensive analysis of the committee's recommendations. See, Legislative and Administrative Reform, Select Committee on Assassinations, U.S. House of Representatives, 95th Cong., 2d sess., (Washington, D.C.: U.S. Government Printing Office, 1978), vol. I. p. 148 et seq.

against the benefits of stronger protective measures.

While the committee addressed itself to legal and administrative measures primarily, it was fully cognizant that they can account only partially for the solution to the problem of violence and assassination. It is equally important that society deal with the fundamental problems that underlie violence and that it always adhere to legal responses. As the Eisenhower Commission aptly observed:

> [I]f measures of control were this society's only response to violence, they would in the long run exacerbate the problem. The pyramiding of control measures could turn us into a repressive society, where peace is kept primarily through official coercion rather than through willing obedience to law. That kind of society, where law is more feared than respected, where individual expression and movement are curtailed, is violent, too—and it nurtures within the seeds of its own violent destruction.[13]

The recommendations that follow are addressed to lesiglative and administrative issues as well as the conduct of congressional investigations. They are presented in a logical order that does not reflect relative priorities:

1. LEGISLATIVE RECOMMENDATIONS ON ISSUES INVOLVING THE PROHIBITION, PREVENTION AND PROSECUTION OF ASSASSINATIONS AND FEDERALLY COGNIZABLE HOMICIDES

(a) *Prohibition and prevention*

1. The Judiciary Committee should process for early consideration by the House legislaton that would make the assassination of a Chief of State of any country, or his political equivalent, a Federal offense, if the offender is an American citizen or acts on behalf of an American citizen, or if the offender can be located in the United States.

Evidence received by the committee indicated that the CIA, in conjunction with criminal elements in the United States, plotted the death of foreign leaders.[14] These plots gave rise to widespread speculation that the death of President Kennedy may have been an act taken in retaliation. It was conceded by those involved in the plots that they were without moral justification.[15] Federal law today gives uneven protection to foreign leaders.

While assassination is contrary to executive order,[16] it is criminal only under limited circumstances.[17] Proposed legislaton would make it criminal.[18] Testimony before the committee supported that legislation.[19] The committee has no hesitancy in recommending that legislation be enacted embodying a prohibition against the assassinaton of a foreign leader by those subject to Federal criminal jurisdiction.

2. *The Judiciary Committee should process, for early consideration by the House, comprehensive legislation that would codify, revise and reform the Federal law of homicide, paying special attention to assassinations. The Judiciary Committee should give appropriate attention to the related offenses of conspiracy, attempt, assault, and kidnapping in the context of assassinations. Such legislation should be processed independently of the general proposals for the codification, revision or reform of the Federal criminal law. The Judiciary Committee should address the following issues in considering the legislation:*

(a) *Distinguishing between those persons who should receive the protection of Federal law because of the official positions they occupy and those persons who should receive protection of Federal law only in the performance of their official duties;*

(b) *Extending the protection of Federal law to persons who occupy high judicial and executive positions, including Justices of the Supreme Court and Cabinet officers;*

(c) *The applicability of these laws to private individuals in the exercise of constitutional rights;*

(d) *The penalty to be provided for homicide and the related offenses, including the applicability and the constitutionality of the death penalty;*

(e) *The basic for the exercise of Federal jurisdiction, including domestic and extraterritorial reach;*

(f) *The preemption of State jurisdiction without the necessity of any action on the part of the Attorney General where the President is assassinated;*

(g) *The circumstances under which Federal jurisdiction should preempt State jurisdiction in other cases;*

(h) *The power of Federal investigative agencies to require autopsies to be performed;*

(i) *The ability of Federal investigative agencies*

to secure the assistance of other Federal or State agencies, including the military, other laws notwithstanding;

(i) The authority to offer rewards to apprehend the perpetrators of the crime;

(k) A requirement of forfeiture of the instrumentalities of the crime;

(l) The condemnation of personal or other effects of historical interest;

(m) The advisability of providing, consistent with the first amendment, legal trust devices to hold for the benefit of victims, their families, or the General treasury, the profits realized from books, movie rights, or public appearances by the perpetrator of the crime; and

(n) The applicability of threat and physical zone of protection legislation to persons under the physical protection of Federal investigative or law enforcement agencies.

Federal law prohibiting homicide has grown in response to particular events or circumstances. [20] The process has been piecemeal. On November 22, 1963, there was no general Federal statute that prohibited the assassination of the President.[21] One recommendation of the Warren Commission was that such a statute be enacted.[22] Public Law 89–141, signed on August 28, 1965, enacted 18 U.S.C. 1751, prohibited the killing, kidnapping, conspiracy, assaults or attempt to kill or kidnap the President or Vice President. Similarly, when Senator Robert F. Kennedy was killed in June 1968, there was no general Federal statute that prohibited the assassination of Members of Congress. Public Law 91–644, signed on January 2, 1971, enacted 18 U.S.C. 351, which extended the protection of the Federal criminal law to Members of Congress, paralleling that extended to the President and the Vice President. Next, after an attack on the Israeli Olympic team in Munich, Germany in 1972, Public Law 92–539 was enacted. It extended the protection of Federal criminal law to foreign guests in the United States.

While the committee heard no testimony on issues surrounding the general codification, revision and reform of the Federal criminal code, its study of Federal law of homicide led it to the conclusion that comprehensive legislation in this area is needed. The piecemeal approach should be abandoned. In this connection, the committee identified a number of policy questions which should be resolved in the course of processing the legislation:

(a) Traditionally, the general Federal murder statute applicable to Federal officials has been limited to homicide of designated officials killed "while engaged in the performance of . . . official duties or on account of the performance of . . . official duties. . . ." [23] When 18 U.S.C. 1751 (President and Vice President) and 18 U.S.C. 351 (Members of Congress) were enacted, no similar limitation was placed on their coverage. This reflected the recommendations of the Warren Commission[24] and the Senate Judiciary Committee.[25] While all categories at their outer edges seem arbitrary (even though the policy behind the classification may readily be conceded to be valid), it can be argued that a line ought to be drawn between those who, because of the nature of their office, ought to receive the protection of Federal criminal law without limitation, that is, the President, Vice President, Members of Congress, Supreme Court Justices, Cabinet officers, et cetera, and those who ought to receive such protection only when the threat of homicide is related to their work. Since the committee did not take testimony on where the line should be drawn, it only recommends some category be specifically set forth.

(b) Current Federal law does not extend to high judicial positions or to Cabinet officers the protection of the Federal criminal law, [26] although it is proposed in legislation that has been recently introduced in the Congress. [27] It would seem logical that such protection be so extended.

(c) The assassination of Dr. Martin Luther King, Jr., was not a Federal offense, since he was not a public official whose assassination was covered by Federal law. The basis for an FBI investigation was the theory that Dr. King's right to travel had been abridged under 18 U.S.C. 242,[28] it was described in testimony to the committee as "a pretty tenuous basis for asserting jurisdiction."[29] This illustrates the difficult public policy issues associated with extending protection of Federal criminal law beyond "officials" to "public figures."[30] While a general Federal homicide statute raises the specter of a Federal police agency to enforce it, FBI Director William Webster testified:

616

[A]ll of us have, today, intense sensitivity to people who are injured or killed in the exercise of civil rights or in the assertion of civil rights or in encouraging others to assert legitimate civil rights. It is a special kind of area where we think the Federal Government has such an interest in seeing that constitutional rights are protected * * *.[31]

The committee recognized that there could be homicides that go unpunished, at least to the degree that the Federal Government might wish, because of differing local policies and investigative capabilities. This is the price of a Federal system, since appropriately drafted and specific language is required for a Federal homicide statute to cover private individuals. That coverage cannot be comprehensive and the statute still constitutional. The committee recommends, therefore, that careful attention be given to the reach of Federal criminal laws when new legislation is enacted.

(d) The penalty structure of Federal criminal statutes is not uniform or appropriate. Each statute tends to carry with it its own penalty provision, which may or may not be consistent with similar statutes. The need for a rational, just and equitable penalty structure is manifest.

Discussion of the penalty structure of homicide statutes necessarily raises the delicate issue of capital punishment. [32] The testimony of law enforcement officials before the committee supported it.[33] The committee noted, too, that testimony before it recognized that provisions of current law are most likely constitutionally infirm. [34] The committee, however, conducted no independent study of capital punishment. As a committee, therefore, it had no special expertise with which to jude the merits of the arguments that had been made over the years.

(e) Testimony before the committee addressed the jurisdictional reach of Federal homicide statutes.[35] Traditionally, Federal statutes do not reach overseas, although the question is one of congressional intent and power under international law. In light of evidence before the committee, as noted, of efforts by a U.S. Government agency to assassinate foreign leaders, it would be appropriate to give careful attention to the extraterritorial reach of any comprehensive legislation.

(f) (g) Federal and State criminal laws generally operate side by side, and a Federal criminal statute does

617

not automatically preempt State jurisdiction. But since there was confusion in Dallas following President Kennedy's assassination over who should exercise certain responsibilities (in the absence of a Federal statute), the Warren Commission was led to suggest Federal legislation.[36] Further, Congress placed specific language in 18 U.S.C. 1751(h), the Presidential-Vice Presidential statute, suspending State action until Federal action is terminated, if "Federal investigative or prosecutive jurisdiction is asserted * * *." Similar language appears in 18 U.S.C. 351, the Member of Congress statute. Testimony before the committee raised a number of problems with the language in these statutes. It is not clear, for example, how and by whom Federal action is to be asserted—by a statement of the Attorney General[37] or by actions[38] of the Federal investigative agencies, such as the Secret Service in a Presidential assassination.[39] Questions were also raised about whether Federal action should be optional, [40] and about situations where State law ought to control if the target of the assassin is the President. Because of these questions, the committee recommends careful attention to Federal and State issues in drafting comprehensive new legislation.

(h) Considerable controversy surrounded the autopsy of President Kennedy. Questions arose over the removal of the body from Dallas, over the nature of the autopsy and the manner in which it was performed.

No doubt exists that the President should receive in life the finest medical attention available. Similarly, in death, particularly by unnatural means, the President should receive the best attention by forensic pathologists. Arrangements must also be made to perform forensic autopsies in federally cognizable deaths.

Curiously, no Federal statute explicitly designated who is to perform such autopsies, although authority to perform them in the case of the President's death may be implied from 18 U.S.C. 1751(h). The committee recommends that any question not answered by existing law [41] be cleared up in any new legislation.

(i) When Public Law 89–141, the Presidential-Vice Presidential statute, was enacted in 1964, language was added to it in 18 U.S.C. 1751 (i) that authorizes the use, in the investigations, of the assistance of the "Army, Navy, and Air Force, and statute, rule, or regulation to the contrary notwithstanding." Similar language appears in 18

U.S.C. 351 (g), the Member of Congress statute. In all likelihood,[42] this language was added to these two statutes to set aside the effect of 18 U.S.C. 1385, which makes it a crime to use the military as a "posse comitatus." Nevertheless, questions were raised before the committee as to what extent this language might apply to recently passed legislation restricting law enforcement access to certain kinds of Federal records.[43] Questions were also asked relating to who [44] had to request the assistance and whether it had to be rendered.[45] The committee recommends that attention be given to resolving these questions in the processing of comprehensive new legislation.

(j) When Public Law 89–141, the Presidential-Vice Presidential statute, was enacted in 1965, language was added to it in 18 U.S.C. 1751 (g) authorizing the offer of a reward, not to exceed $100,000, to be paid for information given or services rendered in connecton with a violation of the statute. This provision had the effect of raising from $25,000 the amount authorized for reward in general Federal Criminal matters.[46] The policy question remains whether these amounts adequately reflect the full range of federally cognizable homicides, a question to be resolved in new legislation.

(k) (1) Following the assassination of President Kennedy, two issues arose with reference to the personal property of the alleged assassin.[47] Was any of it subject to forfeiture as the instrumentalities of a crime? Could any of it be condemned as of historical interest? This second question also related to the personal property of the President himself, as well as that of others in some way involved.

Forfeiture proceedings were, in fact, initiated with respect to Lee Harvey Oswald's rifle.[48] They were unsuccessful, since under the law at that time the rifle was not used to commit a Federal offense.[49] A special statute, Public Law 89–318, was passed "for the acquisition and preservation by condemnation of evidence relative to the President's assassination." [50] A variety of personal items have been held to have been validly transferred to the National Archives under the statue.[51]

(m) The assassination of a public official or public figure naturally attracts a great deal of public attention that may be converted into revenue through personal appearances, books, movie rights, etc. Testimony before the committee demonstrated that this is what followed the assassination of Dr. King.[52]

The committee, while it made no special study in this area, noted that legislation had been enacted at the State level to curb what may be fairly described as crass commercialization of macabre situation.[53] Such a provision should be considered in the drafting of any new comprehensive legislation at the Federal level.

(n) The committee heard testimony that it would be advisable to extend the protection of Federal threat legislation[54] and Federal zone of protection statutes[55] to individuals occupying offices other than the President.[56] Mindful that there may be significant differences in the scope of protection required for these other officials, the committee recommends that consideration be given to these suggestions.

3. *The appropriate committees of the House should process for early consideration by the House charter legislation for the Central Intelligence Agency and Federal Bureau of Investigation. The committees should address the following issues in considering the charter legislation:*

> (a) *the proper foreign and domestic intelligence functions of the intelligence and investigative agencies of the United States,*

> (b) *the relationship between the domestic intelligence functions and the interference with the exercise of individual constitutional rights,*

> (c) *the delineation of proper law enforcement functions and techniques including:*

>> (i) *the use of informants and electronic surveillance.*

>> (ii) *guidelines to circumscribe the use of informants or electronic surveillance to gather in be exercising first amendment freedoms, and*

>> (iii) *the proper response of intelligence or investigative agencies where information is developed that an informant has committed a crime.*

> (d) *guidelines to consider the circumstances, if any, when an investigative agency or a component of that agency should be disqualified from taking an active role in an investigation because of an appearance of impropriety growing out of a particular intelligence or investigative action.*

> (e) *definitions of the legislative scope and extent*

of "sources and methods" and the "informant privilege" as a rationale for the executive branch
withholding information in response to congressional
or judicial process or other demand for information.

(f) institutionalizing efforts to coordinate the gathering, sharing, and analysis of intelligence information,

(g) insuring those agencies that primarily gather
intelligence perform their function so as to serve the
needs of other agencies that primarily engage in physical protection, and

(h) implementing mechanisms that would permit
interagency tasking of particular functions.

The committee did not conduct a general inquiry into
the operations of the intelligence or law enforcement
agencies. Nevertheless, its examination of the performance
of the agencies with respect to the deaths of President
Kennedy and Dr. King afforded it a unique perspective
from which to view their operations. In effect, the committee conducted case studies of the FBI and CIA, an experience that led the committee to make a number of
recommendations.

The most important single recommendation the committee can make in this regard is that the proposals for
charter legislation be processed for early consideration by
the House. Law enforcement without law is a contradiction in terms. Those who enforce our law must be able to
look with confidence to a basic charter. Otherwise, their
power will not be legitimate; they will not know their
duties, and they will not know their constraints. All too often the pressure of the moment will dictate their actions.
Just as important, there must be limitations on those who
exercise power to protect those over whom the power is
exercised. Freedom is made possible by power limited by
law. There are a variety of reasons for the abuses of power
uncovered by the committee, particularly the harassment
of Dr. King. One may be clearly identified and must be
remedied: It is the lack of basic charter legislation. In a
society that prides itself on the rule of law, it is remarkable
that so important an area has been left lawless for so long.

(a) Charter legislation must go to the root of the role
that intelligence and law enforcement agencies play in a
free society. It should clearly delineate the difference between the foreign and domestic roles of the agencies. So-

ciety must not permit the morals of war to become the routine policy of domestic agencies. Citizens at home must not be treated as enemies abroad.

(b) Close attention must also be paid to the relation between intelligence functions and first amendment rights. The first amendment seeks to assure those out of power that they can still participate in the shaping of policy. The cry for change must not be misunderstood as a call for violent revolution. Nowhere did the committee find this confusion more clearly demonstrated than in the FBI's efforts to "neutralize" Dr. King in his efforts to secure social and economic justice.

(c) Particular attention, too, must be paid to the proper role in law enforcement of such potentially abusive information-gathering techniques as informants, electronic surveillance, and the infiltration of groups. Abuses or misuses of these techniques characterized the work of the FBI in its investigation of Dr. King. Charter legislation offers a hope of assisting in the effort to control such abuses in the future.

(d) Propriety—and the appearance of propriety—must be the hallmark of the enforcement of law. Power alone is never sufficient to hold the allegiance of a people. Obedience to law is best secured not through a threat of sanctions but through respect for legitimate authority. Appearances, therefore, may sometimes be as important as underlying reality. The processes of justice must not only be just; they must appear to be just.

This issue was sharply delineated by the FBI's investigation not only of Dr. King, but of his assassination. Understandably, many people questioned whether an agency that undertook to discredit Dr. King could be relied upon to seek out his muderer.

Existing guidelines promise that such campaigns to discredit will not occur again.[57] Nevertheless, it is possible to foresee that an individual legitimately under investigation would be an assassination target. To what degree should the agency—or the investigators immediately involved in the investigation—be disqualified from conducting the assassination investigation? It is a difficult issue, one that charter legislation ought to address and, hopefully, resolve.

(e) The intelligence and law enforcement agencies' relationship with Congress must also be spelled out. Individual citizens must be protected against those who would harm our society or violate the laws; they must also be protected against those whose job it is to protect our society and enforce the law. Yet, there is little an individual can do by himself. The courts and the Congress, therefore, play an important role in assuring effective performance and protecting civil liberties. Nevertheless, in order to act, the courts and the Congress must have access to information.

One of the most delicate problems that faced the committee in examining the CIA and the FBI had to do with access to restricted information, some of it classified to protect the national security, some that was confidential to protect the identity of informants. The CIA sought to rely on the National Security Act of 1947, section 102(a) to uphold its position; [58] the Department of Justice cited the informant's privilege.[59] While the committee never conceded that either basis was legally valid to withhold information from Congress, the committee was generally able to negotiate with the agencies the necessary access. On one occasion, the committee voted a subpena for certain materials, but a confrontation was avoided through compromise. Nevertheless, the committee recommends that charter legislation be applied to the security issue so there can be a fixed system for obtaining access and at the same time protecting confidentiality.

(f) (g) (h) Finally, the committee noted that as long as the functions of the various intelligence and law enforcement agencies are separated between agencies and assigned to sections within agencies, there must be institutionalized efforts made to compensate for that separation.[2]

(b) Prosecution

1. The Judiciary Committee should consider the impact of the provisions of law dealing with third-party records, bail and speedy trial as it applies to both the investigation and prosecution of federally cognizable homicides.

Testimony before the committee raised questions about such recent legislation as that dealing with third-party

---

[2]The committee also observed during its examination of the agencies that substantial questions had been raised about the effect of laws such as the Freedom of Information Act and the Privacy Act on the ability of the agencies to obtain necessary information. In addition, the committee noted the substantial costs imposed on the agencies for compliance with the laws.

The committee also recognized the benefits of these laws. They may, for example, deter agencies from keeping files on individuals who are of no records,[60] bail[61] and speedy trial [62] as it might affect the investigation and prosecution of assassination cases or other federally cognizable homicides. Concern was expressed that such legislation might have unforeseen adverse consequences.

The testimony indicated that recent third-party records legislation had made the acquisition of records in the course of investigation "more difficult than in the past." [63] "[I]nformal access" had been largely ended.[64] The effect extended beyond the records covered in the legislation. Other holders of such records are apparently concerned and they are granting access only with "increasing difficulty"[65] because of a fear of "personal liability." [66] To the degree that some recent legislation recognized the special responsibilites of the Secret Service, it was supported.[67]

As for speedy trial legislation, while testimony before the committee was not explicit in its treatment of special problems that might arise in an assassination prosecution, the legislation was thought to be adequate.[68] Nevertheless, it was termed "hastily drawn."[69] and it was observed that the "public would be outraged"[70] if it interfered with the prosecution of an assassin.

While the committee recognizes that it is not possible to draft legislation with all problems in mind, it is possible to review it periodically in terms of special problems, making modifications when they are in order. Nevertheless, the committee agrees with FBI Director William Webster who advised that special rules can raise troublesome issues,[71] and it would be preferable if special cases could be handled without radically altering the system. Declaring "martial law" is not "acceptable;"[72] Webster stated:

> While it is a traumatic experience for anyone to live through the assassination of a President, it ought not to be the predicate for an investigative conduct which in essence is the declaration of martial law. I just simply do not believe that we ought to * * * sus-

legitimate concern to the Government. In addition, the information that these laws have brought to public attention was a significant factor in the creation of this committee.

The committee believed that an assessment of the Freedom of Information and Privacy Acts, to include an analysis of the cost of compliance with them, their effect on the quality and quantity of intelligence information available to the agencies and the benefits achieved by the laws, is warranted.

pend everything that was put in place to protect the rights of citizens.[73]

That such legislation ought to be reviewed, nonetheless, seems appropriate in the opinion of the committee.

2. The Judiciary Committee should examine recently passed special prosecutor legislation to determine if its provisions should be modified to extend them to Presidential assassinations and the circumstances, if any, under which they should be applicable to other federally cognizable homicides.

Recognizing the special problems associated with the investigation of possible improprieties by a President, Vice President and certain other officials, special prosecutor legislation was enacted in 1978.[74] Testimony before the committee considered the wisdom of extending the legislation to Presidential assassinations uniformly and to other federally cognizable homicides on a case-by-case basis. The point most often raised in favor of such legislation was the appearance of impropriety in having the Attorney General, the new President's lawyer, conduct the investigation into the former President's death. [75] Generally, however, the witnesses who appeared before the committee—high Government officials, for the most part—tended to prefer the established system that relies on Federal investigative and prosecutive agencies that are in place, in the absence of specific questions about the suitability of the Attorney General or the Department of Justice.[76]

The committee recommends, nevertheless, as part of comprehensive legislation dealing with Federal homicides, that special prosecutor legislation be carefully considered.

II. ADMINISTRATIVE RECOMMENDATIONS TO THE EXECUTIVE

The Department of Justice should reexamine its contingency plans for the handling of assassinations and federally cognizable homicides in light of the record and findings of the committee. Such an examination should consider the following issues:

    A. Insuring that its response takes full advantage of inter- and intra-agency task forces and the strike force approach to investigations and prosecuions;

    B. Insuring that its response takes full advantage of the advances of science and technology, and determining when it should secure independent panels of scientists to review or perform necessary scientific tasks, or secure qualified independent forensic pathologists to perform a forensic autopsy;

C. Insuring that its fair trial/free press guidelines, consistent with an alleged offender's right to a fair trial, allow that information about the facts and circumstances surrounding an assassination promptly be made public, and promptly be corrected when erroneous information is mistakenly released; and

D. Entering at the current time into negotiatons with representatives of the media to secure voluntary agreements providing that photographs, audio tapes, television tapes and related matters, made in and around the site of assassinations, be made available to the Government by consent immediately following an assassination.

Testimony before the committee indicated that many of the lessons learned in the months after the tragic events in Dallas in 1963 have been incorporated into the contingency plans of the various Federal intelligence and law enforcement agencies. Nevertheless, there is much that can be learned for the future in reviewing the record of the past, particularly with the perspective that the passage of time affords. Four lessons stand out: The need to integrate investigative and prosecutive efforts; to take advantage of the advances of science and technology, particularly in such a fashion as its independence will not only exist, but be seen to exist; to insure that accurate information is immediately given out, consistent with any alleged assassin's right to a fair trial; and to obtain, as soon as possible and with as little difficulty as is possible, as much hard evidence as is possible.

(A) One of the most troubling aspects of the investigations of the deaths of President Kennedy and Dr. King was the failure of Federal agencies to share and use information, and to bring to bear on problems the array of talents, expertise and legal tools available. Even from the point of view that it was not reasonable to do everything, all that could have been done was not done. The need for a task force approach was, according to testimony before the committee, a point well taken.[77] There should also be a requirement for the use of the strike force approach, with particular respect to conspiracy issues not settled by forensics and field interviews.[78] For the future, contingency plans should be written with flexibility in mind. [79]

(B) The most significant new knowledge the committee was able to develop about events in Dallas on November 22, 1963, stemmed from the work of the committee's scientific panels. (In the case of the assassination of Dr. King, to the regret of the committee, there was not as much scientific evidence that could be subjected to scientific analysis and thus cast new light on the assassination.) The lesson for the future, is, therefore, very clear: The potential benefits of science in an investigation must be better realized. The committee noted that science was used to advantage in 1964 and 1968. Nevertheless, its recommendation is designed to insure that the promise of science and technology not be overlooked in the vent of another tragedy.

The committee also found reason to comment on the approach that is contemplated for scientific analysis in the future, particularly in the case of a Presidential assassination. The issue was raised before the committee of the use of nongovernmental experts to achieve not only the greatest degree of expertise, but also the ultimate in property. [80] It was noted, for example, that in its major case operations plan the FBI contemplates using forensic pathologists from the Armed Forces Institute of Pathology. [81] While not wishing to call into question the competency or the integrity of doctors associated with the institute, the committee posed this question: In a society in which liberty has traditionally depended on civilian control of the military, should not efficiency[82] be set aside in favor of symbolism?[83] The committee thought it should.

(C) The handling of public information in Dallas in November 1963 was criticized by the Warren Commission[84] for reasons this committee considered valid. Public comments by officials of the Department of Justice at the time of Dr. King's death also seemed to emanate without careful attention to a set of public information principles. The Department of Justice has guidelines for public information policy in criminal cases,[85] which were being reviewed at the time this committee completed its investigation.[86] But since the impact of such policy pervades all of government, all interested individuals and agencies should participate in the review.[87] It seems important that one objective of this review would be to

627

formulate a procedure for distinguishing between a routine case and one of urgent importance.[88] Beyond that, the committee hopes the Department of Justice's new guidelines will take into account the public information problems that have been exposed by its investigation.

(D) While it is vitally important that the best scientific experts be retained in an assassination investigation, it is equally essential that they be given the best evidentiary materials to examine. This committee demonstrated in its investigation, as did the Warren Commission in the case of the Kennedy assassination, that access to high quality materials is crucial. Thus, the committee sought the best ways to achieve such access. In testimony before the committee, it became clear that the best approach would be to make an immediate effort to negotiate agreements with various news organizations, so that right after an assassination law enforcement agencies can have access to the product of news coverage.[89] These news organizations are understandably concerned with first amendment freedoms. At the same time, law enforcement must have the access. It would be unfortunate if a confrontation occurred over a search warrant or a subpoena. So the time to act is now. Negotiations started at this time would be "very, very useful,"[90] according to testimony before the committee. The process may turn out to be a "long, ongoing dialog which . . . ought to be underway."[91] Because the Department of Justice who testified in this regard in-liberty. Each branch was to check the others. Together, the Department of Justice who testified in this regard indicated the Department would favor discussions with the news media.[92] the committee is hopeful this recommendation will be acted upon forthwith.

III. GENERAL RECOMMENDATIONS FOR CONGRESSIONAL INVESTIGATIONS

The founders of the American system divided the Government into three branches. The purpose of the separation of the branches was not to enhance efficiency but promote liberty. Each branch was to check the others. Together, they would govern the new Nation under the Constitution, realizing, it was hoped, the promise of its peamble.

The balance of power between the executive and legislative branches has always been fluid, although the trend in modern times has been for the executive branch to be dominant. That trend was sharply reversed in 1974, principally because of Congress power to investigate the allegations of wrongdoing by the President. The exercise of the power to investigate, first in the Senate and then in the House, eventually led to the resignation of the President. Ironically, the power that may have done the most to return the Nation to the values of the Constitution in 1974 was not explicitly recognized in the Constitution when it was drafted in 1787.

The investigative authority of Congress is not expressly written into the Constitution, but the precedent for that power is longstanding, both in theory and practice. The British Parliament and the Assemblies of the American colonies frequently exercised it.[93] Political scientists and parliamentarians have long argued that inherent in the power to make laws must be the power to investigate before they are enacted and later to see that they are carried out. In "Consideration on Representative Government," John Stuart Mill wrote that the legislature was best fitted, not for administration or lawmaking, but for the review of the public's business:

> * * * to watch and control the Government; to throw the light of publicity on its acts; to compel a full exposition and justification of all of them which any one considers questionable; to censure them if found condemnable.[94]

In more modern times, Woodrow Wilson propounded a similar viewpoint in "Congressional Government": "Quite as important as legislating is vigilant oversight of administration."[95] He felt that a self-governing people discusses and interrogates its administration. For him, Congress power to inform was as important as its power to legislate. [96] Congress was, he thought, the "eyes and voice" of the Nation. Like the British Parliament, Congress was, in the words of William Pitt the Elder, the "Grand Inquest of the Nation."[97]

The power of Congress to investigate has been challenged a number of times, not only by the executive branch, but also by recalcitrant witnesses who were private citizens and others. The grounds for the challenges have been many, ranging from questions about Congress right to review the executive branch or private organizations and citizens, to doubts about various procedures committees have used in conducting investigations. Since the first congressional investigation in 1792 into the humiliating defeat of General St. Clair by a small band of Indians, in which the House asserted its right to call for persons and papers,[98] the basic power of the Congress to investigate has always been acknowledged. The Supreme Court has always upheld that power, although recognizing that it was subject to certain limitations.

At first, Congress attention focused on government itself. Subsequently, however, the laws became broader. The first instance in which Congress requested that private citizens appear before it and provide documents was in 1827, when the Committee on Manufacturers was considering tariff legislation.[99] Since that time, in areas where business activities or behavior of private individuals are subject to congressional regulation, Congress power to investigate has always been recognized.

The investigative charter of the committee was narrow— to examine the facts and circumstances surrounding the deaths of President Kennedy and Dr. King, and, if necessary, to recommend appropriate measures for the future. Nevertheless, because of the nature of the lives and the deaths of these two great men, the scope of what was pertinent to the mandate of the committee was wide. In a real sense, it encompassed the history of the United States in a turbulent and violent decade. Consequently, the appropriate limitations on the scope of a congressional investigation were ever in the minds of the committee, particularly as that investigation touched on private groups or individuals, raising, however indirectly, questions of their possible connection to the death of either man. How ironic it would have been had the committee, a major concern of which was unlawful Government intrusion into the life of Dr. King, been reckless with the lives of others.

Traditionally, two constitutional limits on the power of congressional inquiry have been raised to circumscribe congressional investigations. Assuming that the subject matter is itself one on which legislation may be enacted and the proper procedural steps have been followed, the first and fifth amendments have been the main shields raised to protect individual liberties, having as a consequence the effect of blocking the inquiry.

The committee looked into the conduct of a variety of

groups whose activities, however personally objectionable, were protected by the first amendment. In all situations, it was possible to conduct the inquiry without subjecting the groups to unnecessary publicity or to invade their privacy beyond that which was essential to a search for the truth. None of the subjects of the investigation felt it necessary to try to block the investigation by contemptuously resisting the committee's processes or questioning.

The committee also looked into the conduct of a variety of individuals whose activities were such that they could legitimately claim this privilege against self-incrimination. While this area of the committee's work is not the subject of a specific recommendation, a comment about it is appropriate.

In 1970, Congress passed legislation changing the character of the immunity it could grant in compelling a witness' testimony over fifth amendment objections.[100] The use immunity concept, reflected in the provisions of the 1970 act,[101] respects comity between State and Federal jurisdictions, limits interference between congressional and executive functions, and does not disrupt administrative remedies of a civil character. For these reasons, the general reluctance that has traditionally accompanied immunity grants by congressional committees is no longer applicable. If the grant is coordinated with the necessary executive officials and the testimony is safeguarded until it is suitable for release, grants of immunity can be made without causing objections. The 1970 act was first used in a more than token fashion in the Watergate hearings in the Senate; it was first used extensively by this committee. Indeed, it constituted a centerpiece in the committee's investigative strategy. The committee found the 1970 act to be a powerful tool in finding the truth. But, while the committee recognized the essential application of the act in future investigations, it cautions that it must be used carefully. The promise of the act in uncovering the truth is only fulfilled by its power to compel reluctant witnesses to speak. A society that ranks individual privacy among its more precious values must recognize that a price is paid for attaining the truth. It may be necessary to pay that price in important matters, such as determining the truth in the deaths of two great leaders. Nevertheless, it ought to be paid only when necessary.

In the course of the investigation, the committee learned

a great deal about congressional investigations and came to certain conclusions about them. There are a variety of issues that ought to be addressed by one or more committees of the House to strengthen and increase the fairness of investigations in the future.

A. The appropriate committees of the House should consider amending the rules of the House to provide for a right to appointive counsel in investigative hearings where a witness is unable to provide counsel from private funds.

A witness before a congressional committee has no general right to counsel, but the rules of the House recognize that witnesses may be accompanied by counsel at investigative hearings to advise them of their constitutional rights. [102] Nevertheless, there is no provision for paying for a counsel in the event a witness is unable to afford one. The committee, in its rules,[103] made an effort to find a solution by arranging with the District of Columbia Bar Association to provide counsel on certain occasions. The arrangement worked well, and the committee believes that an amendment to the rules of the House incorporarting such an arrangement should be considered by the appropriate committees.

B. The appropriate committees of the House should examine the rules of the House governing the conduct of counsel in legislative and investigative hearings and consider delineating guidelines for professional conduct and ethics, including guidelines to deal with conflicts of interest in the representation of multiple witnesses before a committee.

The rules of the House provide that the chairman of a committee may punish breaches of decorum or professional ethics on the part of counsel by exclusion from the hearing. [104] This committee read this rule to deal with the ethical problems of multiple representation. Not all multiple representation presents a conflict of interest. Some conflicts that exist may be cured by full disclosure to the clients and informed consent. Nevertheless, disclosure and consent cannot cure all conflict. Those that touch on the integrity of the factfinding process may not be waived. Consequently, the committee did not follow a blanket rule; it waited until a conflict was ripe on the record. It held a hearing to establish the conflict. It then appropriately disqualified the offending attorney, if disclosure and waiver did not constitute an adequate cure. The standard employed for disqualification was that of professional societies [105] and the courts. [106] Like the Watergate special prosecutor,[107] the committee must express its concern with the conduct of the bar that represented witnesses in its executive sessions. Too often, the lawyers seemed insensitive to their duty to their clients to represent them as individuals and not part of a group. It was necessary for the committee to disqualify more than one attorney to preserve the integrity of the committee's processes. In addition, the committee experienced tactics on the part of several lawyers who represented individuals before the committee that can only be described as efforts to disrupt or obstruct the work of the committee as it labored to determine the truth. There is a need for clearer guidance to investigative committees to deal with these problems. The appropriate committee of the House should look into what, if anything, may be done to assure the integrity of Congress factfinding processes.

C. The Judiciary Committee should examine the adequacy of Federal law as it provides for the production of Federal and State prisoners before legislative or investigative committees under a writ of habaes corpus ad testificandum.

On more than one occasion, the committee heard testimony from witnsses who were incarcerated. Usually, a subpena will guarantee the presence of a witness. Nevertheless, a subpena is unavailing when the witness is incarcerated. Then, a writ of habeas corpus ad testificandum is usually employed. Such writs may be issued by Federal courts under the current law.[108] During its tenure, the Watergate committee obtained 20 such writs.[109] The language of current law, however, does not explicitly grant Federal courts the right to issue such writs in behalf of congressional committees. It is necessary to read the current statute in light of its extensive history to arrive at its proper meaning.[110] The committee was able to secure the writ it sought, but the process was not without difficulty, since the matter of jurisdiction had to be litigated. It would be helpful if clarifying amendments were added to present law if after careful study they are thought essential.

D. The appropriate committees of the House should examine and clarify the applicability to congressional subpoenas of recently enacted legislative restrictions on access to records and other documents.

During the course of its investigation, the committee sought access to or subpoenaed numerous documents. In one instance, the committee's subpoena was challenged. Usually, congressional subpoenas can only be resisted through the contempt process. The speech and debate clause of the Constitution precludes court litigation.[111] Nevertheless, it was argued that by virtue of an act of Congress,[112] the speech and debate clause had been waived. Ultimately, the committee thought it inappropriate to subject those involved to the contempt process, and it submitted the issue to the only court that apparently had jurisdiction, the Probate Court of Shelby County, Tenn. The verdict of the court was favorable to the committee. The committee believed that this result—Congress submitting its processes for review to a State court not of record—was an unintended consequence. The committee, therefore, recommends that the appropriate committee of the House undertake a survey of similar restrictive legislation to determine to what degree it was intended to apply to congressional process. Where necessary, clarifying legislation should be enacted to resolve ambiguous language. If such legislation is to be made applicable to congressional process, provisions should be made for a suitable forum in which to hear pertinent cases.

E. The appropriate committees of the House should consider legislation that would authorize the establishment of a legislative counsel to conduct litigation on behalf of committees of the House incident to the investigative or legislative activities and confer jurisdiction on the U.S District Court for the District of Columbia to hear such lawsuits.

The committee found itself in court on a variety of occasions to secure immunity grants, to enforce its process, and, on occasion, to defend its work or to secure the assistance of the Department of Justice. It was necessary to amend the committee's resolution to authorize these appearances in court.[113] and it was necessary to devote to this litigation resources of the committee that would have been better used if devoted to the investigation. The committee recommends, therefore, that the appropriate committees of the House give careful consideration to the establishment of an office of legal counsel for the House, similar to that established for the Senate.[114] The committee recommends, further, the conferring of appropriate jurisdiction on the District Court of the District of Columbia in such cases.

F. The appropriate committees of the House should consider if rule XI of the House should be amended, so as to restrict the current access by all Members of the House to the classified information in the possession of any committee.

Rule XI(e) (2) of the House provides that committee "records shall be the property of the House and all Members of the House shall have access thereto * * *." Access does not include the right to copy or to use the records, even on the floor on the House; provision for release or access may be regulated by committee rules.[115] The committee adopted special rules governing access to classified documents.[116] Nevertheless, the existence of rule XI posed a sensitive and delicate problem in dealing with governmental agencies from whom the committee sought access or delivery of classified materials. Concern was not expressed with granting access or delivery of material to members of the committee. No problem was raised with disclosure based on a need to know to members of the staff of the committee, each of whom had received an appropriate clearance. Fear was expressed, however, that under rule XI any Member of the House and possibly personal staff members might gain access to the materials. Obviously, the larger the circle of individuals who had access, the greater the danger of intended or inadvertent disclosure. While the committee was able to work around these concerns, it would facilitate cooperation between agencies and committees, given the task of oversight, if the degree of disclosure could be kept within reasonable bounds. Consequently, the committee recommends that appropriate committees of the House carefully study the issue.

IV. RECOMMENDATIONS FOR FURTHER INVESTIGATION

A. The Department of Justice should contract for the examination of a film taken by Charles L. Bronson to determine its significance, if any, to the assassination of President Kennedy.

Toward the end of the committee's investigation, the existence of a film taken by Charles L. Bronson in Dealey Plaza approximately 5 minutes prior to the assassination was brought to the attention of the committee. It was suggested that the movie, an 8-millimeter color film that focused on the area around the sixth floor window of the Texas School Book Depository, showed a figure walking behind the window. The film was forwarded to the committee's photography panel. The panel was unable to discern a figure, and it was unable to say conclusively whether apparent motion behind windows on the fifth and sixth floors was due to film artifacts or real motion.[117] Nevertheless, because the Bronson film was of a quality superior to that of another motion picture film that the panel had subjected to computer processing, the panel recommended that similar work be done on the Bronson film.[118] In light of the recommendations of the panel, the committee recommends to the Department of Justice that it contract for appropriate research to be done to determine what, if any significance, the Bronson film may have to the assassination of the President.

B. The National Institute of Law Enforcement and Criminal Justice of the Department of Justice and the National Science Foundation should make a study of the theory and application of the principles of acoustics to forensic questions, using the materials available in the assassination of President John F. Kennedy as a case study.

It would be difficult to understate the significance of the acoustical analysis done by the committee in its investigation of the death of President Kennedy. As the committee noted, it can be expected that the opportunity and necessity to do similar work will arise in the future. Consequently, it would seem judicious to study the theory and application of the principles of acoustics to forensic issues. The best case study available for such testing is the assassination of President Kennedy, not only for what additional light it might cast on that investigation, but also for the benefit of future investigations. Consequently, the committee recommends that the National Science Foundation and the National Institute of Law Enforcement and Criminal Justice of the Department of Justice undertake appropriate studies and publish the results, so that they may be widely known and used. The committee notes that

636

it would be appropriate for NSF and LEAA to take advantage of the considerable expertise in the private sector and in Federal law enforcement, particularly the FBI, in making the study.

C. The Department of Justice should review the committee's findings and report in the assassinations of President John F. Kennedy and Dr. Martin Luther King, Jr., and after completion of the recommended investigation enumerated in sections A and B, analyze whether further official investigation is warranted in either case. The Department of Justice should report its analysis to the Judiciary Committee.

All the obstacles this committee faced in its investigation of the death of President Kennedy and Dr. King stand in the way of any institution that would continue its work. As even more time has passed since this committee was formed, the trail is colder, and it has been trod upon one more time. The difficulties are formidable, and it may be that little more can be profitably done.

In 1964, it was indicated that the file in the assassination of President Kennedy would remain open, and the same is true in the case of Dr. King's murder. But in light of this committee's investigation, more is required than keeping open files. It would seem only appropriate for the Department of Justice to perform the scientific studies recommended herewith and to analyze the committee's record. Then the Department could assess the wisdom of taking additional steps that might move one or both of these cases toward final resolution.

The choice is not between a full-scale reopening of both investigations and doing nothing, since there are in each case limited areas that lend themselves to further exploration. What the committee found that had not been known before should be applied to a reconsideration by the Justice Department of its original investigations. Whatever the Department decides is the preferable course of action, it should report to the Judiciary Committee, so that its determination may be reviewed by an appropriate congressional body.

IV

SEPARATE REMARKS, VIEWS AND DISSENT OF MEMBERS OF THE COMMITTEE

SEPARATE REMARKS OF HON. CHRISTOPHER J. DODD DISSENTING FROM THE FINAL REPORT OF THE SELECT COMMITTEE ON ASSASSINATIONS

I voted against the adoption of the "Summary of Findings and Recommendations" by the Select Committee on Assassinations. I did so because I could not agree with the committee's first finding which reads,

> Lee Harvey Oswald fired three shots at President John F. Kennedy. The second and third shots he fired struck the President. The third shot he fired killed the President.

On December 29, 1978, I was called upon to decide whether Oswald fired three shots from the Texas School Book Depository. The acoustical evidence showed that the second shot was fired approximately 1.66 seconds after the first shot.[1] The committee had two pieces of evidence available to it that indicated how fast Oswald might have fired his rifle. First, there was a test conducted by the FBI in 1964, using Oswald's rifle, which was a bolt-action rifle

---

[1] The fact that the timing was established by acoustical evidence is discussed below. In addition, it should be noted that originally the experts stated that the time between the first two shots was slightly under 1.6 seconds. II JFK 63. 74 (Barger 1.57 or 1.6). This was the timing I understood as agreed upon by the experts when I cast my dissenting vote. Since then, the experts have further refined their figures by adjusting for the speed at which the sounds were recorded. The experts now believe that the time between the first two shots was approximately 1.66 seconds. V JFK 724 (Blakey memorandum). I use the adjusted figures in these separate remarks.

manufactured by Mannlicher-Carcano. The results showed that this rifle could not be aimed and fired using the telescopic sights in less than 2.25–2.3 seconds.[2] Second, two committee staff members conducted a preliminary test in September, using a Mannlicher-Carcano similar to Oswald's. The results of this test showed that, using the open iron sights, the fastest that the rifle could be fired was somewhere between 1.65 and 1.75 seconds.[3]

On the basis of these tests. I could not conclude that Oswald fired both the first and second shots. The FBI test did not show that it was possible for Oswald to have aimed and fired in 1.66 seconds, and the committee's test was only preliminary.[4] I dissented.

It was the committee's original plan to conduct a final test before voting on the report, and in expressing my concern over this issue in the weeks prior to the vote, I repeatedly requested that a final test be done. Unfortunately, it was not possible to bring together all of the elements required for the final test before the December vote.

On March 29, 1979, a final test was conducted. In this test a Mannlicher-Carcano was repeatedly fired using the open iron sights. This test was conducted by four expert marksmen from the District of Columbia Police Department and two relatively inexperienced committee staff members.[5] None of the expert marksmen were able to aim and fire two consecutive shots within 1.66 seconds. The committee staff members were able to fire two consecutive shots in less than 1.66 seconds by "point" aiming, that is, not aiming through the telescopic or iron sights. These results have not allayed my concern over this issue. When I consider all the available evidence on this problem, I find myself no more near a solution than I was on December 29.

The available evidence, as I see it, presents three options. If the acoustical evidence on this issue is valid, then

---

[2]3 H. 407 (Frazier 2.3); 5 H. 153 (2.25).

[3]There is no direct evidence which would prove how Oswald aimed the rifle. The committee's firearms panel testified that he could have aimed through either the telescopic or open iron sights. 1 JFK 483 (Lutz).

[4]Professor G. Robert Blakey, the committee's chief counsel, stated that the test was "preliminary" when he described it to the committee in public session. II JFK 105–106 (Blakey).

[5]The two committee staff members who participated in this test were the same two members who conducted the preliminary test, Deputy Chief Counsel Gary Cornwell and Chief Counsel G. Robert Blakey.

two shots were fired within 1.66 seconds of one another.[6] This leads to the first two options: either one person fired both shots in 1.66 seconds; or one person fired the first shot, and 1.66 seconds later another person fired the second shot. The third option is that the shots were spaced more than 1.66 seconds apart, allowing ample time for one person to have fired both shots. This third option necessitates a conclusion that the acoustical evidence is invalid on this point. I will discuss these three options in turn.

Option one.—Oswald fired the first two shots within 1.66 seconds of one another.—To believe that this option is correct, one must accept that Oswald was more proficient with a rifle than any of the committee's four expert marksmen or that, like the committee staff members who participated in the test, Oswald "point" aimed and did not take the time necessary to line up his target in the iron sights or the telescopic sight on his rifle. Despite the fact that Oswald may have been more familiar with a Mannlicher-Carcano than any of the committee's expert marksmen, his record as a rifleman makes it hard for me to accept that he was able to fire faster than the experts and still hit both President Kennedy and Governor Connally.

It is even more difficult for me to believe that, having missed with his first shot, as the committee finds, he did not take the time necessary to properly aim his second shot. This becomes almost impossible to believe in that Oswald, by merely pointing the rifle from 165 feet, would have had to hit a target that was moving at 11 miles an hour.[7] It should be noted that the second shot referred to here struck both President Kennedy and Governor Connally. This is the foundation of the single-bullet theory.

There is circumstantial evidence, however, that tends to indicate that Oswald did fire all three shots. Three cartridge cases were found on the sixth floor of the Texas School Book Depository, and ballistics evidence establishes that all three came from Oswald's rifle. In that there is no evidence to suggest that more than three shots came from the Texas School Book Depository, the cartridge cases

---

[6] I readily concede that this analysis is "finely tuned." We are considering differences in tenths of a second. We are using data, moreover, that, while it may be subjected to highly scientific analysis, was not initially gathered by precision instruments. Nevertheless, these are the facts we have to work with.

[7] The test firings in March of this year, as well as the preliminary firings in 1978, were aimed at stationary targets.

support the theory that Oswald fired both the first and second shots.

The cartridge cases are not, however, conclusive proof that Oswald fired both of the first two shots. The ballistics evidence merely shows that the cartridge cases were fired in Oswald's rifle at some point in time; there is no way to tell when they were in the rifle or when the bullets that they encased were fired. In other words, one of the cartridge cases could have been from a bullet fired from Oswald's rifle a day, a week or a month earlier. That cartridge case could then have been ejected from the rifle before firing on November 22, 1963, or in some other way dropped on the floor.

At first glance, it seems easier to believe that the three cartridge cases mean that Oswald fired all three shots than to believe the "ejection" theory. Nevertheless, as this requires me to accept that Oswald fired within 1.66 seconds, the "ejection" theory appears more likely than it does at first glance.

Option two.—An unidentified person fired the first shot, and Oswald fired the second shot 1.66 seconds later.[8]— There is one major problem with this option; there is no other evidence of a second gunman in the Texas School Book Depository, which, according to the acoustical evidence, was the origin of both of the first two shots. This brings me to the first two of my recommendations for further study.

First, a detailed photographic analysis should be made of the Bronson film to determine whether it shows more than one figure in the sixth floor windows of the Texas School Book Depository.[9]   Second, further mathematical calculations should be performed on the data developed by the acoustical experts to determine more precisely the location from which each of the first two shots was fired. The acoustical experts testified that they were able to pinpoint within a few feet the location of the gunman on the grassy knoll. They did so by a series of geometric computations based on the original data developed in the reenactment of the shooting. This more complete analysis was only under-

---

[8]I identify Oswald as firing the second shot, rather than the first, because the second shot appears to be the one that hit the President and Governor Connally, and that bullet matches Oswald's gun. Of course, the unidentified person could have been using Oswald's gun and Oswald his, but that is in the realm of pure speculation.
[9]The committee so recommends. III, IV, A.

taken for the third shot in a sequence of four. If a similarly fine-tuned analysis was conducted for the first two shots, it might be determined whether or not they both came from the same window.

Option three.—Oswald fired both the first two shots and took longer than 1.66 seconds between the shots, giving himself adequate time to properly aim.—On its face, this option seems very attractive; however, it means that the acoustical evidence is invalid, at least on this issue.

The acoustical testimony before the committee is most renowned for the portion of it that indicates that a second gunman fired at the President from the grassy knoll. The validity of this evidence has been widely debated in the short time since it was first presented to the committee and the public, and I suspect that it will remain the subject of debate for years to come.

The acoustical evidence came in two phases. The first time Dr. Barger testified, he indicated the time sequence between the shots but did not state any firm conclusion about the existence of a shot from the grassy knoll.[10] The reaction of the committee and the public was one of frustration with the indefinite conclusions with regard to existence of a shot from the grassy knoll, but the nature of the evidence itself and the expertise of the witness were generally accepted. I do not recall any challenges at that time to an "arcane" science.

The second phase of the acoustics testimony was received quite differently. This time, Barger, Weiss, and Aschkenasy all testified that there was a 95-percent probability that a shot was fired from the grassy Knoll.[11] This time the reaction of the public and committee members was much more skeptical. And rightly so, since this conclusion had much greater significance.

When I first learned of the "new" acoustical evidence and before I heard the testimony, I was very doubtful that it would prove convincing. Nevertheless, after listening to the experts in closed session and going over the data which they presented, I found myself slowly coming to believe that they might be right. Realizing the significance of their conclusion, I determined to withhold belief until I had another chance to question them, this time in open session. I spent a great deal of time preparing myself for the next

[10] II JFK 94, 101 (95 percent 2 shots; 60–70 percent 3 shots; 50 percent 4 shots).
[11] V JFK 556 (Weiss and Aschkenasy): 673–674 (Barger).

round of questioning. I decided that the most useful role I could play would be to act as attorney for the opposition. I would look for the weaknesses in their theory so that I could better judge its strengths, its accuracy. I believe that I succeeded in holding to my plan to be as tough with my questions and as difficult to convince as possible. Yet, after listening to the testimony, I was persuaded.[12]

I remain convinced that the preponderance of the evidence supports the finding of the committee that a gunman fired from the grassy knoll. Yet, I believe that further study of the acoustical evidence is necessary. The acoustical evidence of a gunman on the grassy knoll has enormous significance for our Nation. This by itself makes real the idea of a conspiracy to kill the President. The data upon which the experts base their conclusion should, therefore, be reviewed by other noted experts in this field. If further study would resolve any lingering doubts as to the conclusion, failure to pursue the answers would be inexcusable. On the issue of a President's death we should not deal in shadows of suspected truths when we might have light. In its report, the committee criticizes the Government for its failure in 1963–64 to diligently pursue the truth on the question of conspiracy; our Government should not make the same mistake today.

In addition to the need for continued study of the "grassy knoll shot," further study of the acoustical evidence is necessary to answer the questions surrounding the first two shots. As discussed in option 3 above, the answer may be that the time sequence provided by the acoustical evidence is invalid. This possibility should be explored. Another explanation, discussed in option 2 above, is that the acoustics' time sequence is correct, and that some unidentified gunman fired the first shot while Oswald fired the second. Further work on the acoustics data, as described previously, could conceivable prove the existence of a second gunman in the Texas School Book Depository or elsewhere in the plaza.

Therefore, I recommend that a general review of the acoustical evidence and all other scientific evidence bearing on these questions, be conducted by the National Science Foundation or some other appropriate body.[13] Specifically, I recommend that:

---

[12]I add, too, that I am impressed with the corroboration given to the basic authenticity of the tape and the events it portrays by the other scientific evidence summarized in sec. I B of the committee's report.
[13]The committee so recommends, III, IV, B.

1. A photographic analysis of the Bronson film be conducted.

2. The detailed analysis that was done with regard to the third shot be done with regard to shots one, two, and four.

3. An attempt be made to ascertain the source of the carillon bell which appears on the dictabelt.

4. A thorough review of the tape be conducted in an effort to discover whether shots might have originated from locations other than the grassy knoll and the Texas School Book Depository.

5. An analysis of the various other sounds (for example, the siren) be made to test the tape's authenticity.[14]

I agree with paragraph II. B. on its face which reads,

> The committee believes, on the basis of the circumstantial evidence available to it, that there is a likelihood that James Earl Ray assassinated Dr. Martin Luther King as a result of a conspiracy.

After analyzing all the evidence, particularly the testimony of James Earl Ray, his demeanor and his actions prior to the crime, I am persuaded that he did not act alone in planning the death of Dr. King. Therefore, I agree with the committee's finding in this paragraph.

I cannot, however, agree to all of the underlying commentary. Specifically, I dissent from any and all parts of the King section of the report which identify particular coconspirators. The evidence which the committee musters may suggest the outlines of a conspiracy, but, in my opinion, it falls short. After reviewing all the evidence, I am unable to say with any degree of certainty who conspired with James Earl Ray or under what plan they were acting.

THE COMMITTEE RECOMMENDATIONS

I offer the following comment on paragraph III. B (1) which reads,

---

[14]After the committee's vote on Dec. 29, 1978, the committee received from Robert J. Groden, a photographic consultant to the committee, a series of photos and film frames that purport to show H. B. McLain, the Dallas motorcycle officer, in the place where the acoustics experts said he would be. I note that after his appearance before the committee, Mr. McLain publicly stated that his motorcycle was not the one with the stuck microphone. The material provided by Mr. Groden should be analyzed as the Zapruder film has been, e.g., the frames numbered, the camera speed timed, et cetera. See V JFK 703–721.

The Judiciary Committee should consider the impact of the provisions of law dealing with third-party records, bail and speedy trial as it applies to both the investigation and prosecution of federally cognizable homicides.

COMMENT

The third-party record statutes were enacted to protect an individual's right to privacy in a society which requires that in a variety of situations individuals divulge personal information and place that information in the hands of third parties and institutions. Individuals must put aside their interests in privacy in order to share in many of the benefits of modern society, and to comply with Government regulation of certain activities. With increasingly sophisticated means of maintaining records, the threat of misuse has grown, and in the last decade, the American public has become more aware of the ease with which individual rights of privacy may be violated by the keepers of the files and the seekers of information.

In a series of statutes Congress has acted to protect the right of privacy from undue infringement. These statutes were not enacted in a void; they were drafted to protect privacy rights, but other societal interests were recognized as well. Chief among these interests was the need for adquate law enforcement. Without exception the privacy acts adopted by Congress provide the means for law enforcement agencies to obtain information needed to conduct lawful prosecutions and investigations of criminal conduct.

It may be true, as the testimony before this committee indicated, that informal access to third-party records has ended, that acquisition of records in the course of an investigation is more difficult than in the past, and that holders of third-party records are more reluctant to grant access because of potential civil liability for invasion of privacy. If these results are in fact present, the privacy acts are working to protect those rights which they were intended to protect. "Informal access" is a dangerous tool, and prior to the enactment of the privacy statutes it was grossly abused. The power to acquire records in the course of an "investigation" was so liberally construed that the requirement that there be an ongoing lawful investigation was for practical purposes nonexistent. And the irresponsible manner in which some third-party recordkeepers shared information with others showed little or no recognition of the rights of the individuals involved. Therefore, this affirmative testimony on the "need" to reconsider the privacy acts is unpersuasive and is the same sort of testimony considered by the committees which recommended the adoption of the privacy acts.

The testimony of the witnesses before this committee is most striking for its failure to identify any unique problems that might arise in an assassination case or other federally cognizable homicide case which would justify a recommendation that the privacy acts be reexamined with a special eye to these crimes.

I have carefully examined the Speedy Trial Act and am convinced that its provisions are drawn with adequate breadth to allow ample time for the prosecution to prepare its case in the event of an assassination or other federally cognizable homicide, as well as to allow ample time for the Federal agencies to investigate any such crime. Under the act, in setting a date for trial, the court may consider the unique factors which might be present in the event of an assassination.

The witnesses who testified before this committee, while voicing some general complaints about the act, agreed that in the event of an assassination the act would provide the Government with adequate time to prepare for trial. Responding to general complaints about the Speedy Trial Act is not properly within the scope of this committee's mandate, nor did this committee attempt to take testimony on whether the Speedy Trial Act was in general a good thing. I do not believe that such gratuitous complaints are sufficient basis for recommending that the Speedy Trial Act be reevaluated, especially in light of the fact that witnesses, including the representative of the Department of Justice, found the act adequate to deal with an assassination.

The Federal bail statutes were the subject of limited testimony and consideration by this committee. They were considered only in an effort to determine whether the unconstitutionality of the Federal death penalty, 18 U.S.C. 1111 et seq., would in effect classify Federal homicide as a noncapital crime for purposes of bail. I think it is appropriate for this committee to recommend that the Judiciary Committee examine the bail statutes in considering the Federal death penalty. I do not feel any further recommendation on the bail statutes is warranted.

All of the statutes in this section which the committee recommends be reconsidered are designed with a delicate balance in mind, the balance between individual rights and the state's police power. Disturbing that balance can lead to disastrous results. While individual situations must be considered in striking this balance, without clear and compelling justification new exceptions should not be made and the overall balance should not be shifted. Undoubtedly, assassination is a heinous crime and society demands that the perpetrators of such a crime be brought to justice, but we must not lose sight of other societal values in our eagerness to see justice done. Justice is never served when, in moving toward it, we blindly trample on rights which in calmer moments we earnestly fight to preserve.

CONCLUDING REMARKS

I would like to make some general comments regarding my service on this committee, and in doing so discuss an issue which deserves particular attention.

My service on the House Select Committee on Assassinations was a painful experience. For 2 years my colleagues and I listened to the circumstances surrounding the death of two men: One, an inspired individual who gave this Nation a special understanding of the meaning and importance of freedom; the other, a President who transferred his hope, his ideals, and his youth to a Nation growing old before its time. While they lived the shoulders of a Nation were sturdier, its back was stronger, and its heart a little greater. And although what they gave will remain with this country for all time, with their death we lost forever the glowing promise of their tomorrow.

Thus, my service on the committee was a painful one. But hearing of the conduct that was engaged in by various agencies of our Government in the name of security, in the name of law enforcement, not only added to that pain, but caused me to feel shame and anger in a way in which I can only hope I will never feel again.

The evidence before this committee on some of the activities of the Federal Bureau of Investigation and the Central Intelligence Agency consisted of story after story of abusive practices. The FBI, an arm of our Government, engaged in what was tantamount to a private war against one individual—not a criminal, just a man who spoke out against injustice. The FBI's conduct toward Dr. King not only dishonors that agency, but dishonors each and every one of us.

The CIA, an arm of our Government, locked Mr. Nosenko in a cell, a "vault" for 3 years. For 3 years this agency kept a man in solitary confinement without resort to legal process and under conditions designed to break his mind and his spirit. In addition, the CIA made a number of efforts to kill the leader of a foreign nation and joined forces with organized crime so that they might better accomplish their goal. We must never permit these agencies to dishonor us in like manner again.

This committee heard over and over again from both these agencies that the abuses of the past would never be repeated. Heartening as these assurances are, they are not enough. Now that these abuses have been publicly aired, we have a responsibility to do everything we can to see to it that they are not repeated. Ignorance of the danger can never again be an excuse.

The only means of fulfilling our responsibility to insure that the abuses which occurred in the 1960's do not occur again is to pass legislation restricting the activities in which these agencies may lawfully engage. I, however, am not confident that charter legislation is enough. In addition, I think Congress should consider imposing criminal liability on officers and employees of these agencies who engage in wrongful activities which may now be technically outside the reach of criminal statutes.

These two agencies need the rule of law. The attitude that they were free to function outside or above the law allowed these abuses to occur. There must be no question that Congress intends for these agencies to operate within the law and that the American public demand that they do so. I believe that even today the attitude of being in some way above the law lingers in these agencies. It was apparent in the CIA's choice of a witness to appear before this committee in a public hearing. The CIA sent someone who had an agreement with that agency not to speak about the primary subject of this committee's work, Lee Harvey Oswald.

> Upon what meat doth this, our Caesar, feed,
> That he is grown so great?
> "Julius Caesar." *William Shakespeare.*

Perhaps it is the meat of our indifference. If so, we can afford to be indifferent no longer.

SEPARATE VIEWS OF HONS. SAMUEL L. DEVINE AND ROBERT W. EDGAR

Although seldom achieved, unanimity is often sought in reaching decisions in matters of controversy. Such is the case with the final report of the Select Committee on Assassinations.

Members present in a rather hasty session on December 29, 1978, discussed a draft summary of findings and recommendations. Wording was changed and revised in some portions, and although most members were in agreement with most of the provisions, not all members present totally agreed with all of the findings and/or recommendations.

It is the opinion of the undersigned that Chairman Louis Stokes, members of the select committee, Chief Counsel Robert Blakey and his staff did an outstanding job in an extremely difficult situation. Professionalism dominated the performance of the investigation and hearings, and the congressional mandate has been met with dignity and efficiency, free of political manipulation or personal grandstanding.

The fact all members of the select committee do not totally agree with all of the conclusions should not be construed as any suggestion of dissention or conflict, but merely an indication of a respected legal maxim: "Reasonable minds can reach different conclusions from the same set of facts."

Was there really a conspiracy to assassinate President John F. Kennedy in Dallas? This is the question that many people ask since the U.S. House Select Committee on Assassinations released its preliminary report stating the President "was probably assassinated as a result of a conspiracy."

The report raised nearly as many questions as it answered, and the public understandably wants to know what was the basis for the startling conclusion. The release of the full report offers information on this important point.

How did the committee arrive at its conclusion pointing

to a conspiracy? A premature leak of technical evidence from acoustics experts was overemphasized in the national media, although this evidence was only one facet of a very comprehensive investigation.

As a result, the committee arranged a previously unscheduled public hearing at the 11th hour to clarify the acoustical evidence.

The testimony of acoustical experts was given such weight that most committee members were persuaded that a fourth shot was fired at Kennedy. This shot, actually the third in a sequence of four, apparently came from a "shooter" on the grassy knoll.

Was there actually another "shooter" at another location, and did this person conspire with Lee Harvey Oswald?

Evidence for this view rests on a tape recording made in the dispatcher's radio room of the Dallas Police Department.

An open microphone on a police radio inadvertently recorded the events during the time period immediately before, during, and after the assassination. Experiments with this tape have produced varying conclusions.

Although acoustical study techniques are not new or novel, and were available at the time of the Warren Commission investigation, scientific advances permitted experts to separate noises, distinguishing the sound of a motorcycle from street noises. The acoustical experts believed they could identify gunfire.

The experts concluded there were four shots fired, and one of those did not come from the Texas School Book Depository where Lee Harvey Oswald was.

The experts told the committee they were 95 percent certain—beyong reasonable doubt—there was a second "shooter."

Based on this evidence and testimony, a majority of the select committee concluded there was a "high probability of a conspiracy." This is a conclusion that must be rejected.

First, standing alone, the opinion of acoustics experts that a third shot came from the grassy knoll is simply their opinion. Unless supported by other evidence, it is not sufficient to establish conclusively there was indeed another shot, another shooter, or a conspiracy.

Committee Chairman Louis Stokes, Democrat of Ohio, has said he felt this conclusion was supported by "eye and ear witnesses." Some do not share this view.

The ear witnesses were people in the area to watch the Kennedy motorcade and they disagreed about what they heard.

Less than 12 percent said they heard shots from the grassy knoll. But over 27 percent said the shots came from the Texas School Book Depository.

Another group (17 percent) of ear witnesses believed the shots came from still another building to the rear of the President's limousine.

And nearly 49 percent simply did not know or could not tell.

In short, the ear witnesses disagreed among themselves.

Among the eyewitnesses, there was one who thought he saw a "puff of smoke" in the grassy knoll area. But, a "puff of smoke" is not necessarily evidence there was another shooter, particularly with smokeless power generally used, or indeed a conspiracy.

The acoustics experts are top men in their special field and there is no question as to their integrity or credibility. However, any experienced trial lawyer would apply the same basic legal maxim: "Reasonable minds can reach different conclusions from the same set of facts."

Assuming for the sake of argument there was actually another "shooter," this would simply be circumstantial, not conclusive, evidence of a possible conspiracy.

Apparently, the majority of the select committee dismissed the idea more than one person in the tens of thousands gathered in Dallas that day might have independently desired to kill the President.

There is another reason to doubt the open-microphone evidence. Officer H. B. McLain of the Dallas Police Department was identified by the acoustics experts as being the operator of a motorcycle with an open mike to the left and rear of the President's limousine.

But, apparently the officer himself rejects the assumption, which led to the test and re-enactments. He asks a very simple, but important, question: "If it was my radio on my motorcycle, why did it not record the revving up at high speed plus my siren when we immediately took off for Parkland Hospital?"

The investigation, testimony, and evidence established the facts that Lee Harvey Oswald fired at least three shots from his rifle, from the sixth-floor window of the book depository.

It established the facts that two of these three shots hit

the President, first in the lower neck, upper back, exiting from the front of the throat of the necktie knot.

This bullet, the evidence shows, then struck Gov. John B. Connally, passing through his chest cavity from the rear, then emerging and entering his thigh and right wrist.

Also, the investigation established the fact that the next shot hit the President in the right skull and brain area, resulting in nearly instantaneous death.

There were important results in the investigation of the death of Dr. Martin Luther King, Jr., too.

Here the possibility of a conspiracy is somewhat more plausible because of the direct evidence and testimony involving specific persons with plans or plots to kill King and thousands of dollars being suggested as a payoff.

The committee concluded that James Earl Ray fired the fatal shot, with his rifle, from a roominghouse in Memphis and then escaped.

His apprehension in London and apparent admissions to Inspector Eist of Scotland Yard, together with his decision to plead guilty, assisted the committee to draw this conclusion.

However, evidence of a successful conspiracy to murder King is not conclusive. Plots, plans, and designs to commit murder, separate and apart from the actual murder, do not necessarily amount to a murder conspiracy.

Although some members of the select committee felt a climate was created where the natural consequence of a U.S. Government agency's conduct may ultimately have resulted in the murder of King, the committee found no evidence, direct or indirect, that the FBI had any part in, or engineered, this assassination.

All members did not agree with all findings, conclusions, and recommendations, but they did conscientiously seek answers to murders 10 and 15 years old.

Any further action in these matters should be pursued in the Justice Department, since the select committee has concluded its work.

SAMUEL L. DEVINE.
ROBERT W. EDGAR.

DISSENTING VIEWS BY HON. ROBERT W. EDGAR TO THE FINAL REPORT

An Introduction

It was 10:30 p.m. on Friday, December 29, 1978, when I was faced with one of the most difficult decisions of my congressional career. Chairman Louis Stokes of Ohio challenged those of us on the Select Committee on Assassinations to come to grips with over 2 years of investigative evidence and to decide on what we had found. The mood was somber and sobering, each member weighing months of deliberations. There were a number of important questions to be answered: Did Lee Harvey Oswald act alone, Was it possible for the second shot fired from the Texas Book Depository to pass cleanly through President Kennedy and Governor Connally in near perfect condition? Were there signs of involvement by the Russians, the Cubans, the underworld? What happened in the King case? Did James Earl Ray have help? Who is the mysterious Raoul? How did Ray finance himself during the period from April 23, 1967, when he escaped from the Missouri State Penitentiary until June 8, 1968, when he was captured in England? These and thousands of other important questions had been the subject matter of our committee's efforts.

The select committee came into being in September 1976, in response to a perceived need in the Nation to look again into the deaths of Dr. Martin Luther King and President John F. Kennedy. At that time, it was clear that many people were dissatisfied with the investigations conducted by the Warren Commission and the FBI. The Gallup Poll revealed that over 80 percent of the American people believed that, despite the findings to the contrary, some kind of conspiracy lurked behind both deaths. A host of speculative and often bizarre theories had been promulgated in book and article form, and people calling themselves "assassinologists" had diligently kept alive their pet theories. Thus Congress, responding to continued interest and pressure from the American people for further investigation, established our controversial committee.

Almost immediately, we fell into disfavor. Part of the problem was uncertainty about the leadership of the committee and our task. Congressman Tom Downing from Virginia, the first chairman, served only from October 1976 to early January 1977, when he retired. Then Representative Henry Gonzalez, an outspoken Congressman from Texas, became the chairman, and immediately came into conflict with the equally outspoken new chief counsel, Richard Sprague, from Philadelphia. Congressman Gonzalez and Richard Sprague. spent a good deal of time from January through March struggling over budgets and funding measures. Little time was spent in actual investigations. In March 1977 Representative Gonzalez resigned his chairmanship of the committee; Richard Sprague left shortly thereafter. I took Henry Gonzalez' place as a member of the committee.

Our first priority was to find a new chief counsel. We were able to secure the services, by June 1977, of Professor Robert Blakey of Cornell University, who had extensive experience in the Justice Department as well as some Capitol Hill experience working with the Senate. As a result of these early problems, the actual investigations did not start until July 1977. Mr. Blakey began work by reviewing the staff and making some immediate changes, and by trying to put together a complete investigative plan. We divided our staff into two separate groups: one focused primarily on the death of Dr. King, the other primarily on the death of President Kennedy.

The 12 Members of the House who served on the committee separated into two task forces. The Dr. King task force was led by the Delegate from the District of Columbia, Walter Fauntroy. The task force looking into the death of President Kennedy was led by Congressman Richardson Preyer from North Carolina. In the fall of 1977 we began months of executive session hearings, receiving testimony privately in order to protect the rights of the individuals from whom we heard.

In August 1978, after completing almost a year of executive session testimony, we opened the hearings to public scrutiny. James Earl Ray was brought in for a week of testimony. He and others were cross-examined regarding their involvement in Dr. King's death. In September we had 27 days of hearings into all phases of the death of President Kennedy. In November, 2 days after the congressional elections, the committee reviewed during 17 days of public sessions the events surrounding the death of Dr. Martin Luther King. Finally in December, a month before the committee was scheduled to go out of existence, we began considering in great detail what we had discovered.

The vote that was to be taken on the evening of December 29 followed 2 weeks of extensive review by the committee of some last-minute information that was troubling to all of us. I voted "No" on the committee findings. I voted "No" on that evening after reviewing the evidence and the material very carefully. I voted "No" because I could not accept such a rapid change from the finding that Lee Harvey Oswald acted alone to the new finding that there were two gunmen involved in a conspiracy. The following is a discussion of my reasons for this dissent.

A. Was there a conspiracy?

I agree with the December 13, 1978, first draft of our final report which states on page 64:

> The committee finds that the available scientific evidence is insufficient to find that there was a conspiracy to assassinate President Kennedy.

Up to that moment in the life of the committee, we were prepared to go to the American people with this conclusion. Only after the report of Mark R. Weiss and Ernest Aschkenasy, in the 11th hour of our investigation, was the majority persuaded to vote for two gunmen and a conspiracy. I respectfully dissented.

The use of the term conspiracy does a disservice to the understanding of the American public. As was again noted in our draft report on page 51:

> Supreme Court Justice Oliver Wendell Holmes defined conspiracy as "a partnership in criminal purposes." A conspiracy cannot be said to exist unless evidence is found from which such a partnership may be inferred.

We found no evidence to suggest a conspiracy. We found
655

no gunmen or evidence of a gunman. We found no gun, no shell, no impact of shots from the grassy knoll. We found no entry wounds from the front into any person, including President John Kennedy and Gov. John Connally. We found no bullets or fragments of bullets that did not belong to the Oswald weapon. And we found little, if any, evidence of partnership with Lee Harvey Oswald. Few credible ear-witness accounts back up the marginal findings of our acoustics experts.

According to the committee's own investigation of the statements taken from 178 persons in Dealey Plaza that were available to the Warren Commission, we found the following:

> Forty-nine of them (27.5 percent) believed the shots had come from the Texas School Book Depository; 21 (11.8 percent) believed the shots had come from the grassy knoll; 30 (16.9 percent) believed the shots had originated elsewhere; and 78 (43.8 percent) were unable to tell which direction the shots were fired from. Only four individuals believed shots had originated from both the grassy knoll and the Texas School Book Depository. (P. 32, draft final report of the House Select Committee on Assassinations.)

One of the eyewitnesses referred to in the committee's final report as illustrative of those present in Dealey Plaza on November 22, 1963, who believed a shot came from the grassy knoll was the late S. M. Holland, a signal supervisor for the Union Terminal Railroad. Holland was standing on top of the overpass above Elm Street, looking down on Elm Street. The committee will quote from a deposition by Mr. Holland given to the Warren Commission on April 8, 1964, to substantiate its theory of a fourth shot. For the record, let me share part of S. M. Holland's affidavit taken shortly after the assassination:

> I am signal supervisor for the Union Terminal and I was inspecting signal and switches and stopped to watch the parade. I was standing on top of the triple underpass and the President's car was coming down Elm Street and when they got just about to the arcade I heard what I thought for the moment was a firecracker and he slumped over and I looked

over toward the arcade and trees and saw a puff of smoke come from the trees and I heard three more shots after the first shot but that was the only puff of smoke I saw. I immediately ran around to where I could see behind the arcade and did not see anyone running from there. But the puff of smoke I saw definitely came from behind the arcade through the trees. After the first shot the Secret Service man raised up in the seat with a machinegun and then dropped back down in the seat. And they immediately sped off. Everything is spinning in my head and if I remember anything else later I will come back and tell Bill. (P. 387, "November 22, 1963: You Are the Jury," by David W. Belin, Esquire, affidavit by S. M. Holland.)

Notice the confusion of his account. First, he hears what he believes is a firecracker, then sees a "puff of smoke" coming from the trees, then three more shots. But he sees only one "puff of smoke" after the first shot, not the third. He runs around behind the arcade and sees no one. Notice also the reference to the Secret Service man rising up within the car itself with a machinegun. I doubt that we should place much accuracy on this witness.[1]

I saw little evidence of a conspiracy. I saw a little evidence of a second shooter. And until further study of the acoustics work is undertaken, I will stand by my belief that Lee Harvey Oswald acted as the lone assassin.

B. How accurate is the 95 percent or better probability of the alleged grassy knoll shot?

I agree with the words of Dr. Marvin E. Wolfgang, professor of sociology and law, University of Pennsylvania, in his letter dated January 2, 1979:

I think the works of Barger and of Weiss and Aschkenasy have been exciting from a scientific perspective. I hope their studies will be published in traditional scientific journals where they will receive the usual form of scrutiny. However, I think it is premature and inappropriate for a Federal group,

---

[1]For the comment of the committee on this obeservation, see IB reference No. 155.

like your committee, to make a major policy decision on the basis of their findings.

I also agree with the words of Dr. Francis K. Davis, dean of science, Drexel University, in his letter dated January 8, 1979:

> Lacking something like that [a scientific report] to look at critically, I certainly think that the 95 percent confidence claim is grossly exaggerated, and it would take considerably more scientific evidence to convince me and most other scientists that their conclusions were valid. As it is, I believe that their chi-square probability test indicates a 95 percent probability that certain events on the tape could not occur by chance, but not that there is a 95 percent probability that a shot came from the grassy knoll.

Probabilities are based on history. While the acoustics study is a scientifically derived body of data, there is little precedence as to how to contextualize the acoustics study. Further, the test firings in Dallas, which are the basis for the comparison study, failed to fully utilize all possible shot directions and/or locations. Many, many questions remain, such as:

(1) On what universe of data are the 95 percent probabilities based?

(2) How adequate were their consideration of temperature and temperature gradients in their findings?

(3) Could strong thermal gradients in Dealey Plaza markedly change the direction of sound waves? Even to the point of producing an acoustical mirage?

(4) Was the same analysis done on shots 1, 2 and 4, that was done on apparent shot 3?

(5) Should an echo pattern history be developed by looking at other locales and other positions in Dealey Plaza to establish the uniqueness of the pattern or apparent shot number 3?

(6) How certain are we of the identity of the other sounds on the tape? The bell sound? The sirens?

(7) Are we 95 percent confident that we have the right motorcycle in the right location at the right time?

(8) Could there have been more than one motorcycle police microphone receiving sounds at the same time and making an acoustical collage?

(9) Was the December 13, 1978, report of Anthony J. Pellicano carefully reviewed prior to our December 29, 1978, finding?

(10) Do we know enough to make our judgment on conspiracy accurate?

To the last question, I say no. I call upon the Congress of the United States to immediately request a full and proper restudy of the acoustics project. I suggest that this be the first step toward completing our investigation. This restudy must involve a full review of the work of James E. Barger, Mark R. Weiss, and Ernest Aschkenasy. After more analysis, we may be able to better judge what level of merit we should place on this piece of evidence. As indicated by Dr. Wolfgang:

> That a shot was made from the grassy knoll is not ruled out by any of the acoustical testimony. But neither is it confirmed by the testimony I have read or heard. (Letter to Congressman Edgar, dated January 2, 1979.)

C. Did we rush to a conspiratorial conclusion?

I believe that exhibit "A" will clearly demonstrate a rush to conspiratorial conclusions. You will note three sets of black letter findings. The first in column 1, was presented to the committee for its consideration on Monday, December 18, 1978 (the date of the draft was December 13, 1978). It was on that Monday that we met in executive session to discuss our findings and come to our final conclusions. It was also that Monday when Weiss and Aschkenasy interrupted our session to share their final report. Less than 2 weeks later, on December 29, 1978, we met in public session to review the report finding. That evening at approximately 6 p.m., we began to consider draft No. 2, dated December 29, 1978, and found in column 2 of exhibit "A." The final released document appears in column 3. Note the changes within such a short span of time.

I believe the Members of Congress did not have sufficient time or expertise to ask the tough questions. I believe the committee failed to properly consider how much weight to assign this evidence due to our own limitations of time and familiarity with the science. I believe we rushed to our conclusions and in doing so, overshadowed many important contributions which other aspects of our investigation will have on history. We did a great job up to the last moment, when in our focus on the acoustics, we failed to give proper weight to other findings of the investigation.

In the King case:

D. Should James Earl Ray have been brought back before the committee for questioning in the area of conspiracy?

Yes. One of the major holes left open in the final days of our investigation into the death of Dr. Martin Luther King was our failure to bring James Earl Ray back before our panel in the November public session. Our final report will be filled with important information taken from hours of extensive private sessions with Mr. Ray at Brushy Mountain State Penitentiary in Tennessee. But, in August when he first appeared in public, we had implied strongly to him and his attorney, Mark Lane, that he would be given an additional opportunity to appear in public session to respond to questions in areas such as conspiracy and his activities after the assassination and before his capture in London.

While I believe that James Earl Ray was the assassin of Dr. King, and while I agree that our committee did an extensive investigation into all aspects of the crime, and while I believe that our conclusions would not have been altered by whatever Mr. Ray would have shared in additional public session, I think we failed to give the American public full access to the key actor in what I believe was an assisted effort to kill Dr. King.

E. Where do we go from here?

1. I recommend that the Congress immediately order a full and detailed restudy of the acoustics work, perhaps through the National Science Foundation. Included in this restudy, a panel of scientific experts with knowledge of acoustics should be employed to monitor the methodology used in the study to insure accuracy and determine the level of weight which should be given to this evidence.

2. I recommend an immediate meeting with the Presi-

dent and the Attorney General by all members of our committee to outline in detail our findings.

3. If after restudy, the science of acoustics is confirmed along the lines of Barger, Weiss, and Aschkenasy's report, I recommend the appointment of a special investigator to pursue the leads developed by our committee in the Kennedy case.

4. I recommend that the Justice Department immediately reopen its investigation into the death of Dr. Martin Luther King and focus on the possible St. Louis conspiracy and the possible involvement of others in this death.

5. I recommend that the appropriate committees of Congress which have jurisdiction over science and criminal justice, immediately begin to explore the value of acoustics as a forensic science and possible new tool in the criminal investigation field.

6. I recommend that the Congress weigh carefully the experience of the House Select Committee on Assassinations in order to evaluate the pros and cons of the use of special committees for the purpose of criminal justice investigations. Do we have the tools to fully handle all legal rights?

ACKNOWLEDGMENTS

I would like to acknowledge my appreciation to the following individuals whose sacrifice of time and energies made a significant contribution to this report:

Dr. Francis K. Davis, Dean of Science, Drexel University. College of Science, Philadelphia, Pa. 19104 (215–895–2620).

Dr. Arthur E. Lord, Jr., Professor of Physics, Drexel University, Philadelphia, Pa. 19104

Dr. Marvin E. Wolfgang, Professor of Sociology and Law, University of Pennsylvania, Center for Studies in Criminology and Criminal Law, 3718 Locust Walk CR, Philadelphia, Pa. 19104.

Mr. Shanin Specter, 3417 Warden Drive, Philadelphia, Pa. 19129 (student at Haverford College in Haverford, Pa.).

David W. Belin, Esquire, Belin, Harris, Helmick & Lovrien, 2000 Financial Center, Des Moines, Iowa 50309 (515–243–7100).

Draft, Dec. 13, 1978, final report of the Select Committee on Assassinations, U.S. House of Representatives, 95th Con., 2d sess., vol. 1, findings and recommendations	Draft findings, Dec. 29, 1978, 6 p.m.	Final report of the Select Committee on Assassinations, U.S. House of Representatives, 95th Cong., 2d sess., summary of findings and recommendations, Dec. 29, 1978 (but released on Dec. 30, 1978)
(1)	(2)	(3)

FINDINGS AND RECOMMENDATIONS OF THE SELECT COMMITTEE ON ASSASSINATIONS—TABLE OF FINDINGS

1. Nature and scope of the investigation.
II. Findings of the Select Committee on Assassinations in the Assassination of President John F. Kennedy.
   A. Lee Harvey Oswald was the assassin of President Kennedy

FINDINGS

I. Findings of the Select Committee on Assassinations in the Assassination of President John F. Kennedy.
   A. Lee Harvey Oswald fired 3 shots at President John F. Kennedy. The 2d and 3d shots struck the President. The 3d shot killed the President.

I. Findings of the Select Committee on Assassinations in the Assassination of President John F. Kennedy in Dallas, Tex., Nov. 22, 1963
   A. Lee Harvey Oswald fired 3 shots at President John F. Kennedy. The 2d and 3d shots he fired struck the President. The 3d shot he fired killed the President.

1. President Kennedy was struck by 2 shots fired from behind the President
2. The shots which struck President Kennedy were fired from the 6th floor window of the Texas School Book Depository Building.

1. President Kennedy was struck by 2 rifle shots fired from his rear.
2. The shots that struck President Kennedy from his rear were fired from the 6th floor window of the Texas School Book Depository Building.

1. President Kennedy was struck by 2 rifle shots fired from behind him.
2. The shots that struck President Kennedy from behind him were fired from the 6th floor window of the southeast corner of the Texas School Book Depository Building.

3. Lee Harvey Oswald, on Nov. 22, 1963, shortly before the assassination, had access to and was present on the 6th floor of the Texas School Book Depository Building.
4. Lee Harvey Oswald owned the rifle from which the shots that killed President Kennedy were fired.

3. Lee Harvey Oswald owned the rifle that was used to fire the shots from the 6th floor window of the Texas School Book Depository Building.
4. Lee Harvey Oswald, on Nov. 22, 1963, shortly before the assassination, had access to and was present on the 6th floor of the Texas School Book Depository Building.

3. Lee Harvey Oswald owned the rifle that was used to fire the shots from the 6th floor window of the southeast corner of the Texas School Book Depository Building.
4. Lee Harvey Oswald, shortly before the assassination, had access to and was present on the 6th floor of the Texas School Book Depository Building.

5. Lee Harvey Oswald's other actions are more consistent with a finding that he shot President Kennedy than a
5. Lee Harvey Oswald's other actions tend to support the conclusion that he killed President Kennedy.
5. Lee Harvey Oswald's other actions tend to support the conclusion that he assassinated President Kennedy.

662

Draft, Dec. 13, 1978, final report of the Select Commtitee on Assassinations, U.S. House of Representatives, 95th Cong., 2d sess., vol. I, findings and recommendations	Draft findings, Dec. 29, 1978, 6 p.m.	Final report of the Select Committee on Assassinations, U.S. House of Representatives, 95th Cong., 2d sess., summary of findings and recommendations, Dec. 29, 1978 (but released on Dec. 30, 1978)
(1)	(2)	(3)

finding that he did not shoot the President.		
B. There is insufficient evidence to find that there was a conspiracy to assassinate President Kennedy.	B. Acoustical evidence establishes a high probability that 2 gunmen, acting as part of a conspiracy, fired at President John F. Kennedy; other scientific evidence does not preclude the possibility of 2 gunmen firing at the President, but does negate some specific conspiracy allegations.	B. Scientific acoustical evidence establishes a high probability that 2 gunmen fired at President John F. Kennedy. Other scientific evidence does not preclude the possibility of 2 gunmen firing at the President. Scientific evidence negates some specific conspiracy allegations.
	C. The committee is unable, on the basis of the available evidence, to identify the other gunman or the extent of the conspiracy.	C. The committee believes, on the basis of the evidence available to it, that President John F. Kennedy was probably assassinated as a result of a conspiracy. The committee is unable to identify the other gunman or the extent of the conspiracy.
2. The committee believes, on the basis of the evidence available to it, that the Soviet Government was not involved in the assassination of President Kennedy.	1. The committee believes, on the basis of the available evidence, that the Soviet Government was not involved in the assassination of President Kennedy.	1. The committee believes, on the basis of the evidence available to it, that the Soviet Government was not involved in the assassination of President Kennedy.
3. The committee believes, on the basis of the evidence available to it, that the Cuban Government was not involved in the assassination of President Kennedy.	2. The committee believes, on the basis of the available evidence, that the Cuban Government was not involved in the assassination of President Kennedy.	2. The committee believes, on the basis of the evidence available to it, that the Cuban Government was not involved in the assassination of President Kennedy.
4. The committee believes, on the basis of the evidence available to it, that anti-Castro Cuban organizations were not involved in the assassination of President Kennedy.	3. The committee believes, on the basis of the available evidence, that anti-Castro Cuban groups were not involved in the assassination of President Kennedy.	3. The committee believes, on the basis of the evidence available to it, that anti-Castro Cuban groups, as groups, were not involved in the assassination of President Kennedy, but the available evidence does not preclude the possibility that in-

Draft, Dec. 13, 1978, final report of the Select Committee on Assassinations, U.S. House of Representatives, 95th Cong., 2d sess., vol. 1 findings and recommendations	Draft findings, Dec. 29, 1978, 6 p.m.	Final report of the Select Committee on Assassinations, U.S. House of Representatives, 95th Cong., 2d sess., summary of findings and recommendations, Dec. 29, 1978 (but released on Dec. 30, 1978)
(1)	(2)	(3
		dividual members may have been involved.
5. Organized crime as an institution was not involved in the assassination of President Kennedy. On the basis of the evidence available to it, the committee is not able to determine if individual members of it were involved in the assassination.	4. The committee believes, on the basis of the available evidence, that the national syndicate of organized crime was not involved in the assassination of President Kennedy.	4. The committee believes, on the basis of the evidence available to it, that the national syndicate of organized crime, as a group, was not involved in the assassination of President Kennedy, but the available evidence does not preclude the possibility that individual members may have been included.
6. The Secret Service, Federal Bureau of Investigation and Central Intelligence Agency were not involved in the assassination of President Kennedy.	5. The Secret Service, Federal Bureau of Investigation and Central Intelligence Agency were not involved in the assassination of President Kennedy.	5. The Secret Service, Federal Bureau of Investigation and Central Intelligence Agency were not involved in the assassination of President Kennedy.

DISSENT AND ADDITIONAL REMARKS OF HON. HAROLD
S. SAWYER TO THE FINAL REPORT OF THE SELECT
COMMITTEE ON ASSASSINATIONS

SUMMARY OF FINDINGS AND RECOMMENDATIONS

As filed December 29, 1978

The summary of findings and recommendations of the
Select Committee on Assassinations having been set forth
in summary outline form, this dissent follows the same
form adopting the numerical and alphabetical paragraph
designations of the report, to which a dissent and disagreement is intended to apply.

I disagree with the following designated sections of the
summary report:

Kennedy

(1) Paragraph IB.

(2) Paragraph IC.

(3) That portion of subparagraph IC3 which reads "but
that the available evidence does not preclude the possibility
that individual members may have been involved."

(4) That portion of IC4 where it is stated on the fifth
line "as a group" and its concluding clause "but that the
available evidence does not preclude the possibility that
individual members may have been involved."

(5) That portion of subparagraph ID wherein said subparagraph states (a) "varying degrees of," (b) "President
John F. Kennedy did not receive adequate protection." and
(c) "The investigation into the possibility of conspiracy in
the assassination was inadequate. The conclusions of the
investigations were arrived at in good faith, but presented
in a fashion that was too definitive."

(6) That portion of subparagraph ID1 wherein it states
"The Secret Service was deficient in the performance of its
duties."

(7) Subparagraph ID1 (a).

(8) Subparagraph ID2.

665

(9) Subparagraph ID3(c).

(10) That portion of subparagraph ID5 in that it uses the phrase "varying degrees of."

(11) Paragraph ID5 (b). I agree, however, that information relating to the attempted assassination of Premier Castro which could have been a relevant consideration was withheld from the Warren Commission by the Central Intelligence Agency.

(12) Paragraph ID5 (d).

King

(1) Paragraph IIB.

(2) Paragraph IIE2 insofar as it states "but failed to investigate adequately the possibility of conspiracy in the assassination. The Federal Bureau of Investigation manifested a lack of concern for constitutional rights in the manner in which it conducted parts of the investigation."

RECOMMENDATIONS OF THE SELECT COMMITTEE ON ASSASSINATIONS

(1) Section IV in its entirety.

Attached hereto are additional remarks together with my originally submitted proposed findings and recommendations which I continue to urge.

ADDITIONAL REMARKS

Having dissented from the committee's apparent acceptance of the validity and reliability of the expert acoustical testimony presented to the committee and essentially those other portions of the findings and recommendations flowing directly from such acceptance, I find it incumbent to explain (or perhaps in this context "amplify" would be a more appropriate word) the reasons for my disagreement.

As a threshold premise, it should be noted that I believe it is important that despite the lapse of 15 years and at least two independent investigations, one by the Warren Commission and the other by this committee, which by any investigatory standards were exhaustive, no other evidence or even what might be termed a "scintilla" of evidence has been uncovered which would substantiate a conspiracy or which tends to negate the fact that Oswald operated alone. Those facts, which have been highly exploited by the cult of assassinologists and writers, namely errors and inadequacies in original autopsy testimony, the alleged invalidity of the "single-bullet" theory, the alleged "cropping" of the so-called backyard pictures, and the apparent backward motion of the President's head as shown in the Zapruder film, have been, in my opinion, totally discredited or explained beyond any reasonable doubt by evidence developed by this committee.

There were a number of witnesses present in Dealey Plaza who believed that they heard one or more shots from the direction of the grassy knoll. There were a larger number who believed that all of the shots came from this School Book Depository, and there were others who just did not have an opinion as to the point of origin of the shots. One witness believed he saw a puff of smoke in the area of the grassy knoll. If it is borne in mind that none of these listeners were anticipating a shot and in fact, few if any recognized the initial shot or shots as such, small weight can be given to those beliefs. This weight is further diminished by the echo potentials of Dealey Plaza, being ringed on three sides by tall buildings, and the wide divergence of beliefs expressed by those present. The so-called puff of smoke is in my opinion of little or no evidentiary value in that rifles using modern smokeless powder do not under normal conditions emit visible smoke puffs when fired.

The committee is therefore in a position of being asked on the sole basis of the opinion of three experts, all of whom are presently of the same view and persuasion, to make the momentous decision to disregard everything else and conclude that a second gunman was situated on and fired at the President from the grassy knoll. This I do not find it possible to do.

The tape, or more properly the dictabelt which is the basis of the expert acoustical testimony is now 15 years old, its chain of custody is less than certain and it has been played a wholly indeterminate number of times. To the unaided ear, the dictabelt appears to contain only the noise of a motorcycle, at one point the faint noise of sirens and at another the faint ringing of chimes. Nowhere on it is there any noise or series of noises even suggesting gunfire. No acoustical expert has testified that even his trained ear had detected such. All of the acoustical expert opinions are based upon the tape or print-out of a computer showing three groupings of oscilloscope-like stylus amplitude markings which remain after the filtering out of the motorcycle noise from the dictabelt. The acoustical experts

667

acknowledged that because of the "cutoff point" of a radio transmitter, the full amplitude of loud sounds would not have been transmitted to and recorded on the dictabelt. For this reason, Dr. James E. Barger, the committee's initial acoustical expert was unable to say with either certainty or any degree of conviction whatever, that the bursts of amplitude shown on the computer tape were in fact, either gunshots or even sounds similar to gunshots.

Other difficulties also exist. The transmitter which was stuck on "open" position, the transmissions of which are recorded on the dictabelt, were on Dallas police channel 1, whereas the entire motorcade including of course all of its escorting police, were guarding and transmitting on the specially assigned Dallas police channel 2, so we must make the initial assumption in accepting the validity of the acoustical testimony, that the officer on whose motorcycle the transmitter was located was tuned to the wrong channel. In light of the known possibilities of human error, this would perhaps be acceptable if the transmission in question had occurred in the early stages of the motorcade. The transmission with which we are concerned, however, occurred virtually at its end and therefore one is required not only to accept the occurrence of such human error, but also its tenacious persistence throughout the entire motorcade during which time the officer on whose motorcycle it was located would for some reason have to remain oblivious to the fact that he was not receiving the rather continuous talk on the motorcade channel and also remain oblivious to the fact that he was receiving constant and totally extraneous communications which were continuously being sent over channel 1, the regular Dallas police channel.

The officer who has been identified by the committee staff as the rider of the motorcycle on which the stuck transmitter was located has testified that he was in fact guarding the correct channel, namely channel 2, and denies that he was equipped with the stuck transmitter.

The same officer, together with other police officials located near the Presidential limousine at the time the shots were fired in Dealey Plaza all agree that sirens were activated, and motorcycles and other vehicles were subjected to emergency acceleration within not more than a few seconds following the shots having been fired. No change in the rhythm or intensity of the motorcycle noise appears anywhere on the relevant dictabelt. There is no audible sound even resembling sirens until a full 2 minutes following the last of what is interpreted by the acoustical experts as the shots. When this faint noise of sirens first becomes audible, approximately 2 full minutes following the so-called shots, they seem to be approaching, cresting, and then receding. These several facts would, therefore, be more consistent with the transmitter being situated on a motorcycle located somewhere between Dealey Plaza and Parkland Hospital, which motorcycle would incidently have been properly guarding channel 1.

As stated earlier, the dictabelt also contains the faint sound of chimes. Despite a search by our staff and despite a wide ranging check with others who were familiar with the Dealey Plaza area and environs 15 years ago, no chimes have been discovered or were found to have existed 15 years ago which were audible in Dealey Plaza. On the other hand, they located one set of known chimes which were regularly used and did exist 15 years ago and do now exist in the area between Dealey Plaza and Parkland Hospital.

It is also worthy of note that the police radio monitor or dispatcher within minutes following the shots having been fired in Dealey Plaza, called a squad car on police channel 1 and requested that the car go to an area lying between Dealey Plaza and Parkland Hospital and have a motorcycle officer in that vicinity turn off his transmitter which was stuck in the transmit position on channel 1 and was interfering with central police communications on that channel.

Laying aside the physical and circumstantial items of evidence alluded to above, the testimony of the experts themselves is somewhat disturbing. When Dr. Barger first presented to the committee, in executive session, the computer tape purporting to show three spaced amplitude bursts or groupings, he stated that he did not know whether or not these groupings represented gunshots and explained the problems of the volume cutoff point or limitations of transmitters. He observed that the third or last amplitude grouping on the tape sequence consumed approximately one and one-half again the time span of each of the earlier two which puzzled him, but on which he could not express an opinion whatever as to whether or not it represented the noise of two partially overlapping shots. He stated that to answer this question it would be necessary to locate the position of the motorcycle with the offending transmitter at the time of the shots. He stated that if this could be accomplished, he could then specifically answer the question as to whether this third burst represented one or two shots.

On this basis, the committee authorized Dr. Barger to conduct live firing tests in Dealey Plaza. To accomplish this, live ammunition was fired from a Mannlicher-Carcano rifle from the sixth floor window of the Texas School Book Depository aimed at sandbags which approximated the position of the President at each of the three known shots. A series of microphones with recorders were spaced at intervals along the parade route as it entered and traversed Dealey Plaza.

My next information on the results of these tests was when Dr. Barger, some months later, appeared before the committee in public testimony. He stated then that he thought the amplitude bursts shown on the tape were gunshots (but could not be certain), and he thought there was a "50–50 chance" that the third and last burst was either one or two shots. Dr. Barger testified that through his firing tests he had satisfied himself that he had located the approximate position of the motorcycle; namely, 120 feet behind the President's limousine. I found the uncertainty if his public testimony very disappointing and at variance with what I had understood to be the assurance given by him in executive session. I felt impelled at that time to comment on the record that as a lawyer, I could not even commence a civil suit based on such vague testimony, let alone institute criminal proceedings.

The committee, to my knowledge, received no further information on the acoustical evidence until during the closing weeks of the committee's existence, Dr. Barger reappeared in conjunction with two colleagues from the faculty of Queens College, N.Y.; Dr. Mark Weiss and Dr. Ernest Aschkenasy. Dr. Weiss acted as spokesman for the two and testified that he and his colleagues had accepted as a "given" the motorcycle's location as established by Dr. Barger in his Dealey Plaza test. That such data taken together with the other raw data earlier developed by Dr. Barger was further developed with the use of simple mathematics; namely, algebra and geometry. This exercise evolved from this same data, predicated on which Dr. Barger had been unable to arrive at any firm conclusion, a 95 percent or greater degree of certainty not only that the third amplitude burst constituted two separate noises but that they were in fact two shots, each from a high-power supersonic rifle, and that the first of the two was fired from a point on the grassy knoll from a point determined within plus or minus 10 feet. Dr. Barger then, without reservation, endorsed these conclusions and stated that he concurred in them. All three experts appearing en banc stated in response to a question I asked that we would not be able to find a qualified acoustics expert who would disagree with either their conclusions or the degree of certainty of these conclusions.

In weighing this testimony, laying aside questions of physical or circumstantial evidence alluded to earlier in these remarks, I find it very difficult to accept the fact that a gentleman of Dr. Barger's scientific qualifications would have appeared for public testimony with ample time to review and study the results of his tests in Dealey Plaza without having applied all of the techniques that a qualified acoustics expert would or could apply to all of the various data in his possession; after all, at that time he was under oath giving what was then his final expert opinion on the matter.

In his testimony, Dr. Weiss said that all of his mathematical computations which resulted in his positive conclusions were predicated upon the position of the motorcycle with the stuck transmitter as determined by Dr. Barger in his tests in Dealey Plaza.

Dr. Weiss when asked, however, as to whether all of his conclusions were then dependent upon the accuracy of this given location, stated that unless he were shown an exact replica of Dealey Plaza elsewhere in Dallas that his computations had confirmed or independently verified the correctness of Dr. Barger's motorcycle location.

While I am acquainted with "bootstrap" scientific analytical procedure, it would appear to me that there are far too few, if any, established or verifiable facts in this entire acoustical scenario to permit the use of bootstrap analysis to determine or sufficiently verify a given predicate to permit even reasonable reliability of the conclusions.

As a committee, we were presented with the expert acoustical testimony which I have described by three experts who were all in agreement with each other, one of whom had somewhat inexplicably drastically modified his earlier testimony to conform with that of the other two on the basis of merely an exercise in simple mathematics.

The committee did not have the benefit of either a wholly independent consultant knowledgeable in the science of acoustics or the testimony of a qualified acoustics expert who disagreed with the expert testimony and conclusions which were presented (which despite the statement of the acoustics witness that did appear, I cannot, from long experience, believe are not available or could not easily be found).

Under the foregoing circumstances and giving due weight to both items of physical and circumstantial evidence which I deem to be contradictory to the expert opinions, and what I find to be a less than satisfactory series of presentations by Dr. Barger, and the unpersuasive conclusions of Dr. Weiss and his colleague from Queens College, I do not accept the acoustical testimony and the conclusions flowing from it. Instead, I remain persuaded of the accuracy of my earlier submitted proposed findings of facts and recommendations, a copy of which for reference I attach hereto.

HAROLD S. SAWYER.

CONGRESS OF THE UNITED STATES,
HOUSE OF REPRESENTATIVES,
Washington, D.C., December 6, 1978

To: Hon. Louis Stokes, Chairman, Select Committee on Assassinations.
From: Hon. Harold Sawyer.

I am prepared to vote for the following findings of fact:

Kennedy

1. Lee Harvey Oswald was the lone assassin of President Kennedy, firing three shots from the sixth story window of the School Book Depository. The first shot missed completely. The second shot (the media dubbed "pristine bullet") entered the President's back to the right of his spine and below the shoulder line and emerged at the center base of the neck, the same bullet continued to enter the right back of Governor Connally traversing his chest, shattering one rib and emerging approximately one inch below the right nipple, then shattering his right wrist and coming to rest beneath the skin of his right thigh. This was the bullet found on the stretcher used to transport Governor Connally at the hospital. This so-called single bullet theory has been conclusively established in my opinion by the testimony using still photographs taken at the scene showing the lateral positions and vertical

elevation differential of the President and Governor Connally in the limousine.

It also was established by the neutron analysis of the bullet fragments and the estimates of the velocity of the bullet at various points, including its estimated velocity when it struck Governor Conally's wrist, such velocity being substantially below its impact distortion level and very substantially above the velocity impact required to shatter bone.

The third bullet entered the rear top of the President's head and shattered the entire right hemisphere of the brain and skull and the several pieces of it were found in the limousine. No other shots were fired from any other place. The origin of the shots that struck the President were established conclusively by the reverse projection from the wounds developed by the NASA expert and the characteristics of the wounds, including the beveling in the skull wound, definitely established that both bullets struck from the upper right rear of the President. The Army film taken in 1948 of the goat shooting episodes convincingly reexplained the rearward action of the President's head as seen in the Zapruder film and very convincingly demonstrates that it could not have been caused by the frontal impact of a bullet, and equally convincingly demonstrates that it was caused by the convulsion of upper dorsal musculature receiving false signals from an exploding brain.

2. Oswald acted alone. There is no evidence of any coconspirators. His trip to Mexico and visit to the Cuban and/or Soviet Embassies were not shown to have any significance vis-a-vis the assassination and the so-called "mystery man" photograph was merely the product of compounded mistakes.

3. Oswald was probably stopped by Officer Tippit because of suspicious demeanor and behavior to which an officer such as Tippit would be extremely sensitive. The probabilities are that at the time of his apprehension by Tippit, Oswald was en route to the home of the person identified by the Dallas press as being the Communist defector or informant who through information provided by the FBI, had destroyed the Communist Party in Texas, which story appeared on the same page as the story making reference to the New York lawyer who was defending Communists in New York and who Oswald requested be retained as his attorney immediately following his arrest,

and which page also contained the announcement and description of the President's projected visit to Dallas. The home of this informant was only two short blocks further up the street on which Oswald was proceeding when apprehended by Tippit. The fact that Oswald left his wedding ring in a teacup at the Payne home when he left on the morning of the assassination would be indicative of a total and determined suicidal effort.

4. Oswald's motive was a psychotically proportioned egomania and drive for recognition and importance.

5. As to agency performance, Oswald's presence in Dallas should have been made known to the Secret Service and more effective use should have been made of local police and/or screened volunteers in being present on the floors of such buildings as the School Book Depository and particularly in such areas as the so-called grassy knoll which was a perfect sniper location with ready escape routes.

A further comment on agency performance is in order on the Yuri Nosenko (the KGB defector) episode. The taking into custody of Mr. Nosenko within the State of Virginia without resort to a court and only under the most tenuous color of authority was itself surprising. The then building of a special cell described as a "vault" by the CIA themselves and holding him there in solitary confinement subjected to continuous mental, psychological, and actual physical torture for a period of over 3 years would have been absolutely unbelievable had not the CIA themselves together with its then Director, Richard Helms, fully and in horrible detail admitted it. Mr. Nosenko was paid off with a six-figure cash settlement and apparently a lifetime "consulting" stipend of about $35,000 per year all surreptitiously with taxpayers' funds, as opposed to either killing him or destroying his brain with a drug ministration which were alternatives that were considered. I believe there is a need for the availability of criminal prosecution to prevent this intolerable type conduct by agencies of the U.S. Government.

King

1. James Earl Ray was the lone assassin of Martin Luther King, Jr. He stalked King for a number of days prior to the assassination.

2. James Earl Ray obtained his financing through par-

ticipation by him in a series of bank robberies, the modus operandi of which and his presence at the times and places, are quite circumstantially persuasive. Raoul was a fictitious character, and based on the sequence of numerous meetings, was used as a substitute identity to some degree for one or both of James' two brothers.

3. I do not accept as reliable the testimony of Byers with respect to the $50,000 offer for the killing of King. I feel this story was totally fabricated by Byers and when first used by him, some years after the assassination, was used to "smoke out" the identiy of one of his associates as an FBI informant. It had nothing to do with the assassination.

4. The motivation of James Earl Ray for the assassination was racial hatred and bias reinforced and made respectable in his mind in part by the COINTEL program waged publicly (but covertly as to source) by the FBI against King. This, I believe, reinforced his perception that he would become a national hero with much of the power structure of the country and particularly the South, would serve a nominal length of time, if at all, and could reasonably expect handsome rewards of various kinds and from various sources in the future for his deed.

5. I believe that consciously or subconsciously, Ray deliberately dropped the plastic bag of evidence adjacent to the scene for the purpose of assuring his identification with the commission of the crime.

6. Ray's trips into Mexico involved smuggling and were unrelated to the assassination and he had no other assistance in the planning, execution, or escape from the assassination.

7. The testimony of the young man in executive session who claimed he had been hired to kill James Earl Ray is totally without credibility.

8. Ray's escape from prison was not planned or executed with planning, execution, or escape from the assination.

7. The testimony of the young man in executive session who claimed he had been hired to kill James Earl Ray is totally without credibility.

8. Ray's escape from prison was not planned or executed with the assassination of King in mind.

9. Ray obtained his Canadian passport by stealing the identification of Canadian citizens through a methodology he had probably heard described in prison and with the

675

exercise of no more cunning and ability than the ordinary criminal would be capable of.

10. The failure of the Memphis police to institute roadblocks and other shortcomings of which they have been accused were merely the probable foreseeable fallout of the much greater concern of destructive rioting and general civil disobedience that they were immediately faced with upon news of King's assassination in the city.

11. The behavior of the FBI throughout the extended preassassination period vis-a-vis King was shocking and unbelievable for an agency of the U.S. Government, and I believe it lent its contribution to the twisted perception of James Earl Ray that he would become something of a national or at least a regional hero if he carried out the dictate or inclinations of his racial hatred of King by an assassination.

LEGISLATIVE RECOMMENDATIONS

1. I think any employee of any agency of the United States should be subject to conviction of a felony carrying a maximum term of 5 years and $10,000 fine if acting under the color of the authority of his position, he either orders, carries out, or participates in the carrying out of depriving any person within the United States of their freedom without due process of law.

2. I believe it should be made a Federal crime carrying a 5 year maximum sentence and a $10,000 fine for any member of an agency of the Federal Government to either order, carry out, or participate in the carrying out of any program designed to discredit, humiliate, or harass any person in the United States who is not a fugitive from justice.

REFERENCES

I. FINDINGS IN THE ASSASSINATION OF PRESIDENT JOHN F. KENNEDY

REFERENCES: INTRODUCTION

[1] Arthur M. Schlesinger, Jr., "A Thousand Days: John F. Kennedy in the White House" (Boston: Houghton Mifflin Co., 1965), p. 116 (hereinafter "A Thousand Days").

[2] "World Leaders Voice Sympathy and Shock—A Flame Went Out," The New York Times, Nov. 23, 1963, p. 8.

[3] Nelson Lichtenstein, ed., Political Profiles: The Kennedy Years (New York: Facts on File, Inc., 1976), p. xvi.

[4] See generally, Congressional Research Service, Library of Congress, "History of Presidential Assassinations in the United States Preceding the Assassination of John F. Kennedy," JFK Project No. 7, July 5, 1978, prepared for the committee.

[5] See Congressional Research Service, Library of Congress, "An Analysis of Congressional Investigations into the Lincoln Assassination," Nov. 16, 1978. The U.S. House of Representatives authorized two separate investigations into the assassination of President Abraham Lincoln. In the first, established by resolutions passed on Apr. 9 and Apr. 30, 1866, the House Judiciary Committee was directed to determine whether President Jefferson Davis and other officials of the former Confederate government had been involved in the conspiracy to assassinate Lincoln and other leading Federal officials, including Vice President Andrew Johnson, Secretary of State William Seward and General Ulysses S. Grant. The committee was asked to prove or disprove the involvement of the Confederate officials and to report whether special legislation was needed to bring them to trial if they were conspirators. A special committee was formed, chaired by Representative James Wilson. Its most vigorous member, and the author of the final report, was Representative George S. Boutwell.

The second investigation was authorized by a resolution, passed July 8, 1867, that established a special House committee to make a comprehensive examination of the facts surrounding the assassination and report its findings and recommendations to the House. It was chaired by Representative Benjamin F. Butler.

The committees were established and largely controlled by radical Republicans who had grown increasingly alienated from President Andrew Johnson as a result of his lenient treatment of the defeated South. Republican antipathy culminated in the impeachment trial of President Johnson.

The Boutwell committee reported that Confederate President Jefferson Davis probably took steps to implement proposals to assassinate the President. Boutwell could make no stronger statement against Davis given the lack of substantive evidence tying him to an assassination conspiracy. A hoax perpetrated by a key witness had deprived the committee's majority of its case against Davis, and it was unable to set forth a convincing case against him. Representative Andrew Rogers filed a strongly worded minority report that took issue with the majority conclusion, denouncing the indictment of Davis and other Confederate officials as co-conspirators with Booth.

The Butler committee, in particular the outgrowth of radical Republican reaction to President Johnson's policy of leniency toward the South, attempted to investigate further allegations linking Confederate officials and others in a conspiracy with assassin John Wilkes Booth. The committee interviewed, among others, convicted conspirators Dr. Samuel A. Mudd, Edward Spangler, and Samuel B. Arnold. It appears that after December 1867, the Butler committee took no further action. Butler, however, was one of the most vigorous proponents of Johnson's impeachment during 1867. His involvement and that of other committee members in the impeachment proceedings may in part explain the committee's failure to continue its work.

The Butler committee uncovered little new information on the assassination of President Lincoln and was unable to establish any ink between President Johnson and the conspirators. The body of evidence the Butler committee assembled argued against the charge that has reemerged on occasion since the 1860's that Andrew Johnson was a participant in, or had knowledge of, the conspiracy to assassinate Abraham Lincoln.

[6] See generally, "A Thousand Days"; and Samuel Eliot Morison, Henry Steele Commager and William E. Leuchtenburg, "The Growth of the American Republic" (New York: Oxford University Press, 1977), volume II, chapter XXX (hereinafter "Growth of the American Republic").

[7] Id., "Growth of the American Republic," at p. 762.

[8] "A Thousand Days," p. 635.

[9] Arthur M. Schlesinger, Jr., "Robert Kennedy and His Times" (Boston: Houghton Mifflin Co., 1978), Chapter 13.

[10] Id. at 278.

[11] Id. at 281.

[12] Ibid.

[13] Much of this account of President Kennedy's trip to Texas is based on the testimony of Governor and Mrs. John B. Connally. See testimony of Governor and Mrs. John B. Connally, Sept. 6, 1978, Hearings Before the Select Committee on Assassinations, U.S. House of Representatives, 95th Congress, 2d session (Washington, D.C.: U.S. Government Printing Office, 1979), vol. I, pp. 11–60.

[14] "A Thousand Days," p. 755.

[15] Id. at 98.

REFERENCES: SECTION A

[1] Report of the President's Commission on the Assassination of President Kennedy (Washington, D.C.: U.S. Government Printing Office, 1964), pp. 18–19 (hereinafter Warren Report).

[2] Id. at 86–92.

[3] Ibid.

[4] Deposition of J. Lee Rankin, Aug. 17, 1978, House Select Committee on Assassinations hearing, pp. 75–78 (JFK Document 014027) (for a copy of the deposition, see "The Warren Commission," staff report, Appendix to the Hearings before the Select Committee on Assassinations, U.S. House of Representatives, 95th Congress, 2d Session (Washington, D.C.: U.S. Government Printing Office, 1979), vol. XI (hereinafter WC report,—Appendix to the HSCA–JFK hearings.—)).

[5] Id. at 75.

[6] Ibid.

[7] Testimony of Robert Groden, Sept. 7, 1978, Hearings before the Select Committee on Assassinations, U.S. House of Representatives, 95th Congress, 2d session (Washington, D.C.: U.S. Government Printing Office, 1979), Volume I, p. 99 (hereinafter Groden testimony,—HSCA–JFK hearings,—).

[8] Ibid.

[9] JFK Document 002498.

[10] Report to the President by the Commission on Central Intelligence Activities within the United States (Washington, D.C.: U.S. Government Printing Office, 1975).

[11] I HSCA–JFK hearings, 145.

[12] Testimony of Michael Baden, Sept. 7, 1978, I HSCA–JFK hearings, 185 (hereinafter Baden testimony).

[13] Report of the Forensic Pathology Panel, in "Report on the Medical Evidence and Related Issues Pertaining to the Assassination of President John F. Kennedy," report VII Appendix to the HSCA–JFK hearings (hereinafter forensic pathology report).

[14] Id. at 151ff.

[15] Report of Photographic Evidence Panel, VI Appendix to the HSCA–JFK hearings, para. 512–610 (hereinafter photographic evidence report).

[16] Forensic pathology report, para. 181ff.

[17] Photographic evidence report, para. 512–610.

[18] See JFK Exhibit F–19, I HSCA–JFK hearings, 182, and forensic pathology report, para. 205–235.

[19] Id., forensic pathology report, at 461–557.

[20] Testimony of Larry Sturdivan, Sept. 8, 1978, I HSCA–JFK hearings, 383ff.

[21] Id. at 414–416.

[22] JFK exhibit F–309, I HSCA–JFK hearings, 416.

[23] Forensic pathology report, para. 363–414.

[24] Ibid.

[25] Id. at 415–460.

[26] Ibid.; see also 364–376 and Addendum G.

[27] Ibid.

[28] Compare dissenting views of Dr. Cyril H. Wecht, id. at 558ff.

[29] Warren Report, pp. 97–109.

[30] Id. at 105.

[31] Id. at 97.

[32] Id. at 19.

[33] Testimony of Dr. Vincent P. Guinn, Sept. 8, 1978, I HSCA–JFK hearings, 491ff. (hereinafter Guinn testimony). There are dif-

ferences in the count and weight of the materials examined by the FBI and Dr. Guinn. This is attributable to the character of the FBI tests and to the fact that the Bureau disposed of the samples examined after the tests.

[34] Warren Report, pp. 79–81.

[35] See, e.g., Mark Lane, "Rush to Judgment" (New York: Holt, Rinehart & Winston, 1966), p. 80.

[36] Guinn testimony, p. 533.

[37] Sturdivan testimony, pp. 407–412, 420–424; see also testimony of Dr. Cyril H. Wecht, Sept. 7, 1978, I HSCA–JFK hearings, 350–352 (hereinafter Wecht testimony).

[38] Id., Sturdivan testimony, at 395.

[39] Id., Sturdivan testimony, 407–412, 420–424, and Baden testimony, 298.

[40] JFK exhibit F–331, I HSCA–JFK hearings, 533.

[41] Ibid.

[42] Photographic evidence report, para. 52ff.

[43] Id. at 57–80.

[44] Ibid.

[45] Ibid.

[46] Id. at 156ff.

[47] Id. at 95–103, inter alia.

[48] Testimony of Dr. James Barger, Professor Mark Weiss and Ernest Aschkenasy, Dec. 29, 1978, V HSCA–JFK hearings, 645ff., 555ff., and 556ff. respectively (hereinafter Barger, Weiss, or Aschkenasy testimony).

[49] See momorandum of Chief Counsel G. Robert Blakey, V HSCA–JFK hearings, 723ff.

[50] Report of Dr. William K. Hartmann and Dr. Frank Scott, in the photographic evidence report, para. 92–103.

[51] Warren Report, p. 18.

[52] Ibid., pp. 18–19.

[53] Forensic pathology report, para. 461ff.

[54] Photographic evidence report, para. 110–168.

[55] Testimony of Thomas Canning, Sept. 12, 1978, II HSCA–JFK hearings, 161.

[56] Id. at 161–179.

[57] Id. at 179–191.

[58] Photographic evidence report, para. 127–168.

[59] Ibid.

[60] Id. at 272–287.

[61] Ibid.

[62] Id. at 247–251.

[63] Id. at 257–271.

[64] Id. at 247–251.

[65] See letter of Charles Leontis (JFK document 014205).

[66] JFK documents 014744 and 014833.

[67] Testimony of Luke Mooney, hearings before the President's Commission on the Assassination of President Kennedy (Washington, D.C.: U.S. Government Printing Office, 1964), vol. III, p. 284 (hereinafter Warren Hearings).

[69] Ibid.

[70] Id. at 287.

[71] Testimony of Eugene Boone, III Warren Hearings, 293.

[72] Ibid.

[73] Id. at 294.
[74] Report of the Firearms Panel, VII appendix to the HSCA–JFK hearings, para. 135–146 (hereinafter firearms report); Warren Report, p. 85.
[75] Id., firearms report, at 131–134.
[76] Guinn testimony, p. 533.
[77] Sylvia Meagher, "Accessories After the Fact" (New York: Vantage Books, 1967), pp. 95–100.
[78] See e.g., testimony of Jack D. White, Sept. 14, 1978, II HSCA–JFK hearings, 322ff.
[79] Photographic evidence report, para. 186ff.
[80] Testimony of Calvin S. McCamy and Sgt. Cecil W. Kirk, Sept. 15, 1978, II HSCA–JFK hearings, 425–430 (hereinafter McCamy or Kirk testimony).
[81] Warren Report, pp. 118–121.
[82] Ibid.
[83] Ibid.
[84] Id. at 128–129, 130–131.
[85] Id. at 125–126.
[86] Id. at 122–124.
[87] Id. at 129–137.
[88] Id. at 136.
[89] Meagher, "Accessories After the Fact," pp. 104–105, supra.
[90] Id. at 120–127, 200–209.
[91] JFK Exhibit F–399, IV HSCA–JFK hearings, 255.
[92] Ibid.
[93] Report of Vincent J. Scalice, in the Report on the Subject of the Examination of the Handwriting and Fingerprint Evidence in the Investigation of the Assassination of John F. Kennedy by the Questioned Documents Panel, VIII appendix to the HSCA–JFK hearings, para. 147ff. (hereinafter questioned documents report).
[94] Id. at 27.
[95] I Warren Hearings, 117–118.
[96] Warren Report, pp. 180–181.
[97] Id. at 125–128.
[98] Groden testimony, pp. 124ff.
[99] Photographic evidence report, para. 347ff.
[100] Id. at 366–376.
[101] See, e.g., photographic evidence report, para. 439.
[102] Id. at 377.
[103] Id. at 196, 237.
[104] JFK Exhibits F–396, F–207 and F–208 and related testimony, HSCA–JFK hearings, II–p. 342, II–p. 435 and I–p. 127 respectively.
[105] Photographic evidence report, para. 196.
[106] JFK Exhibits F–183, F–184 and F–312, II–p. 245, II–p. 245 and II–p. 388 HSCA–JFK hearings respectively.
[107] JFK Documents 001198 and 001197.
[108] Photographic evidence report, para. 377.
[109] Questioned documents report, para. 27.
[110] Warren Report, pp. 137ff.
[111] Id. at 143.
[112] Testimony of Roy Truly, March 24, 1964, III Warren Hearings, 215.
[113] See, e.g., testimony of Danny Arce, Bonnie Ray Williams,

Charles Givens, Billy Lovelady and Harold Norman, Warren Report, vol. VI, pp. 363–367, vol. III, pp. 161–184, vol. VI, pp. 345–356, vol. VI, pp. 336–341, and vol. III, p. 186–198, respectively.

[114] Questioned documents report, para. 147ff.

[115] Interview of James Jarmen, Sept. 25, 1977, House Select Committee on Assassinations (JFK Document 003347); testimony James Jarmen, III Warren hearings, 201.

[116] See JFK exhibit F–126 and related Groden testimony, I HSCA–JFK hearings, 107 inter alia.

[117] Warren Report, pp. 147–149.

[118] J. Gary Shaw and Larry R. Harris, Cover-Up (publisher, J. Gary Shaw, Cleburne, Tex., 1976), p. 39.

[119] Photographic evidence report, para. 759ff.

[120] Interview of Billy Lovelady, May 9, 1978, House Select Committee on Assassinations (JFK document 009188).

[121] Testimony of Roy Truly and M. L. Baker, Mar. 24, 1964, and Mar. 25, 1964, III Warren hearings, 212–241, 242–270.

[122] Testimony of Mrs. Robert A. Reid, Mar. 25, 1964, III Warren hearings, 270–281.

[123] The committee is not unaware of arguments to the contrary. See, e.g., P. D. Scott, P. L. Hoch and R. Stetler, eds., The Assassination: Dallas and Beyond (New York: Vintage Books, 1976), pp. 93–100. The committee traveled to Dallas and toured the Texas State Book Depository building. During those visits, the times required to reach the second floor from both the street and the sixth floor were determined. The committee found that the testimony of Truly and Baker does not preclude a finding that Oswald was on the sixth floor at the time the shots were fired.

[124] Warren Report, p. 157.

[125] Id. at 160, 163–165.

[126] Id. at 165.

[127] Id. at 176–180.

[128] Firearms report, para. 198.

[129] See, e.g., JFK Documents 006905, 003533 and 010905.

[130] Warren Report, pp. 650–651.

[131] Interview of Jack Ray Tatum, Feb. 1, 1978, House Select Committee on Assassinations (JFK Document 006905).

[132] Warren Report, pp. 176–180; testimony of James W. Bookhout, VII Warren hearings, 312.

[133] Warren Report, p. 404.

[134] See, e.g., Meagher, Accessories After the Fact, pp. 283–292, supra.

[135] Firearms report, para. 149–150.

[136] Neutron activation analysis report. I HSCA–JFK hearings, 528.

[137] Testimony of Marina Oswald Porter, Sept. 13, 1978, II HSCA–JFK hearings; see also deposition of Marina Oswald Porter, XII appendix to the HSCA–JFK hearings.

[138] Questioned documents report, para. 27.

[139] JFK exhibit F–510, IV HSCA–JFK hearings, 350.

[140] Warren Report, p. 423.

[141] Id. at 375–424.

[142] Id. at 390–394.

[143] Id. at 393.

[144] Id. at 391–392.

[145] Id. at 392.

[146] Id. at 406–412.

[147] JFK exhibit F–178, II HSCA–JFK hearings, 350.

[148] Warren Report, pp. 406–415.

[149] Ibid.

[150] Testimony of Carlos Bringuier, X Warren hearings, 35–36.

[151] JFK staff reports, House Select Committee on Assassinations (classified JFK Documents 014972, 014973, 014974 and 014975).

REFERENCES: SECTION B

[1] Letter from J. Edgar Hoover to J. Lee Rankin, June 10, 1964 (JFK Document 014512).

[2] FBI interview of Samuel Pate, Mar. 10, 1964 (JFK Document 014513).

[3] Letter from L. G. Kersta to J. Lee Rankin, July 17, 1964 (JFK Document 002892).

[4] Outside contact report, Dr. James E. Barger, May 30, 1978, House Select Committee on Assassinations (JFK Document 008926).

[5] "Analysis of Recorded Sounds Relating to the Assassination of President John F. Kennedy," Bolt Beranek and Newman Inc., in "A Study of the Acoustics Evidence Related to the Assassination of President John F. Kennedy," appendix to the hearings before the Select Committee on Assassinations, U.S. House of Representatives, 95th Cong., 2d sess. (Washington, D.C.: U.S. Government Printing Office, 1979), Vol. VIII, sec. 1 (hereinafter BBN report,—appendix to the HSCA–JFK hearings,—).

[6] Id. at sec. 3.

[7] Id. at Foreword.

[8] Testimony of Paul McCaghren, Sept. 11, 1978, hearings before the Select Committee on Assassinations, U.S. House of Representatives, 95th Cong. 2d sess. (Washington, D.C.: U.S. Government Printing Office, 1979), Vol. II, p. 108 (hereinafter McCaghren testimony.—HSCA–JFK hearings,—).

[9] Id. at 109–110.

[10] BBN report, sec. 4.1.

[11] Id. at sec. 3.

[12] Id. at sec. 3.3.

[13] Id. at sec. 4. As explained in sec. 5.3 of the BBN report, the number of sequences tested may be listed at differing points in the committee's record as 4, 5, or 6, depending upon the stage of analysis the acoustical project was at.

[14] Ibid. An additional, less precise screening test was referred to in the hearings on the acoustical project. This screening test was to determine whether the number of impulses in each of the impulse sequences on the Dallas Police Departmnt tape approximated the number of impulses in the expected echo pattern of Dealey Plaza.

[15] Id. at sc. 5.

[16] Ibid.

[17] Ibid.

[18] Id. at sec. 5.1, step 3.

[19] Id. at sec. 5.

[20] Testimony of Prof. Mark Weiss and Ernest Aschkenasy, Dec. 12, 1978, V HSCA–JFK hearings, 556.

[21] BBN report, sec. 5.2(3).

[22] Ibid.

[23] Id. at sec. 5.2(2)

[24] Ibid.

[25] Id. at sec. 5.2(1).

[26] Testimony of Dr. James E. Barger, Dec. 29, 1978, V HSCA–JFK hearings, 649 (hereinafter Barger testimony, Dec. 29, 1978).

[27] BBN report, sec. 5.1, step 3.

[28] Id. at sec. 5.2(1).

[29] Ibid.

[30] Id. at sec. 5.1, step 5.

[31] Id. at sec. 5.1, steps 5 and 6.

[32] Id. at section 5.1, step 6. A technical term for an "invalid match" is a "false alarm"; this term was used during the hearings on the acoustical project and in the BBN report.

[33] Id. at section 5.3.

[34] Ibid.

[35] Ibid.

[36] Id. at section 5.4.

[37] Ibid. During his Sept. 11, 1978, testimony before the committee, before the probability estimate was refined for the BBN report, Barger estimated the probability that this would occur at random as 5 percent. Testimony of Dr. James E. Barger, Sept. 11, 1978, II HSCA–JFK hearings, 67 (hereinafter Barger testimony, Sept. 11, 1978).

[38] BBN report, sec. 5.4.

[39] Ibid.

[40] Id. at sec. 1.4.

[41] Barger testimony, Sept. 11, 1978, p. 94.

[42] BBN report, sec. 1.4.

[43] Ibid.

[44] Ibid.

[45] Weiss and Aschkenasy testimony, p. 556.

[46] Id. at 559.

[47] BBN report, section 1.5.

[48] Weiss and Aschkenasy testimony, p. 566.

[49] An Analysis of Recorded Sounds Relating to the Assassination of President John F. Kennedy, section 14, Professor Mark R. Weiss and Ernest Aschkenasy, in "A Study of the Acoustics Evidence Related to the Assassination of President John F. Kennedy," VIII appendix to the HSCA–JFK hearings (hereinafter Weiss-Aschkenasy report).

[50] Weiss and Aschkenasy testimony, pp. 558–559.

[51] Weiss-Aschkenasy report, section 4.14.

[52] Weiss and Aschkenasy testimony, p. 605.

[53] Id. at 568–569.

[54] Ibid.; Weiss-Aschkenasy report, section 5.3.

[55] Weiss and Aschkenasy testimony, pp. 581–582.

[56] Id. at 556, 605.

[57] BBN report, section 1.5.

[58] Barger testimony, December 29, 1978, p. 684.

[59] Id. at 681.

[60] Weiss and Aschkenasy testimony, p. 586.

[61] Barger testimony, December 29, 1978, p. 681.

[62] Ibid.

[63] Weiss and Aschkenasy testimony, p. 571.

[64] Barger testimony, Dec. 29, 1978, pp. 680–681.

[65] Id. at 681.

[66] Id. at 682.

[67] Interview of H. B. McLain, Sept. 26, 1977, House Select Committee on Assassinations (JFK Document 002378) (hereinafter McLain interview).

[68] Interview of Sergeant Jimmy Wayne Courson, Sept. 26, 1977, House Select Committee on Assassinations (JFK Document 002381) (hereinafter Courson interview).

[69] Capt. P. W. Laurence Exhibit, hearings before the President's Commission on the Assassination of President Kennedy (Washington, D.C.: U.S. Government Printing Office, 1964), volume XX, p. 489 (hereinafter—Warren Hearings,—).

[70] Dallas Cinema Association film (JFK document 005011).

[71] Courson interview.

[72] Dallas Cinema Association film (JFK document 005011).

[73] JFK Exhibits F–668, 669, 670, 671, and 681, V HSCA–JFK hearings, 626, 627, and 628 respectively.

[74] Letter from Robert Groden to Chairman Stokes, V HSCA–JFK hearings, 703.

[75] Testimony of H. B. McLain, Dec. 29, 1978, V HSCA–JFK hearings, 625 (hereinafter McLain testimony).

[76] Id. at 629.

[77] Id. at 630.

[78] Ibid.

[79] Id. at 637.

[80] Id. at 630.

[81] Id. at 635.

[82] Daily assignment sheet for Solo Motors (JFK document 014391), V HSCA–JFK hearings, 721.

[83] Groden letter, p. 704. As detailed on page 702, the committee did not rely on this photographic enhancement because it was completed after the committee's final vote on the findings.

[84] See, e.g., JFK exhibit F–680 (paper submitted by Anthony Pellicano), V HSCA–JFK hearings, 652.

[85] See, e.g., transcript of CBS television interview of H. B. McLain with Eric Enberg, Jan. 4, 1979 (JFK document 014387).

[86] See, e.g., JFK exhibit F–680 (paper submitted by Anthony Pellicano), V HSCA–JFK hearings, 652.

[87] Ibid.

[88] Transcript of November 22, 1963, channel 2 police transmissions (JFK document 006996).

[89] Interview of Gerald D. Henslee, Aug. 12, 1978, House Select Committee on Assassinations (JFK document 013886).

[90] McLain testimony, p. 630.

[91] Transcript of CBS television interview of H. B. McLain with Eric Enberg, Jan. 4, 1979 (JFK document 014387).

[92] Barger testimony, Dec. 29, 1978, pp. 650–651; BBN report, section 5.4.

[93] Weiss and Aschkenasy testimony, p. 592.

[94] McLain testimony, p. 640.

[95] BBN report, section 6.1.

[96] Id. at section 2.1.

[97] See section I A of the Report of the Select Committee on Assassinations: Findings and Recommendations.

[98] Report of the Photographic Evidence Panel, VI Appendix to the HSCA–JFK hearings, paragraphs 64 to 80 (hereinafter photographic evidence report).

[99] BBN report, section 4.1.

[100] Letter from J. Edgar Hoover to J. Lee Rankin, Feb. 3, 1964 (JFK Document 014514).

[101] For a detailed memorandum on the process of synchronizing the tape to the film, see the memorandum of G. Robert Blakey, Feb. 22, 1979, V HSCA–JFK hearings, 723.

[102] Report of the Forensic Pathology Panel, in "Report on the Medical Evidence and Related Issues Pertaining to the Report on the Assassination of President John F. Kennedy," VII Appendix to the HSCA–JFK hearings, pars. 461 to 494 (hereinafter forensic pathology report).

[103] JFK exhibit F–331, section 5 (neutron activation analysis report of Dr. Vincent P. Guinn), I HSCA–JFK hearings, 506.

[104] Ibid.

[105] See section I A 3 of the Report of the Select Committee on Assassinations: Findings and Recommendations.

[106] Dr. Baden acknowledged this extraordinarily remote possibility in discussions with the staff (memorandum of Donald A. Purdy, Dec. 20, 1978, House Select Committee on Assassinations (JFK Document 014996)). He was prepared to respond to questions concerning this theoretical possibility during the Dec. 29, 1978, hearing, but because of the time spent on the acoustical evidence during that hearing, Dr. Baden's scheduled appearance before the committee was canceled. His opinion, and that of the forensic pathology panel, remains that there is no medical evidence that the President was struck by a bullet fired from the grassy knoll.

[107] See Blakey memorandum, Feb. 22, 1979, p. 723.

[108] Photographic evidence report, pars. 182–185.

[109] Testimony of Governor John B. Connally, Sept. 6, 1978, I HSCA–JFK hearings, 42.

[110] Photographic evidence report, par. 68.

[111] Id. at 70.

[112] Id. at 71.

[113] Id. at 72, 74–80.

[114] Forensic pathology report; par. 487.

[115] Photographic evidence report, par. 153.

[116] Id. at 164–166.

[117] Warren Report, p. 117.

[118] Testimony of Robert A. Frazier, hearings before the President's Commission on the Assassination of President John F. Kennedy (Washington, D.C.: U.S. Government Printing Office, 1964), vol. III, pp. 403–412 (hereinafter Frazier testimony,—Warren hearings,—).

[119] Testimony of Monty C. Lutz, Sept. 8, 1978, I HSCA–JFK hearings, 484.

[120] See memorandum of Chief Counsel G. Robert Blakey, printed as an addendum to "A Study of the Acoustics Evidence Related to the Assassination of President John F. Kennedy," VIII Appendix to the HSCA–JFK hearings.

[121] See section I A 3 of the "Report of the Select Committee on Assassinations: Findings and Recommendations."

[123] Photographic evidence report, pars. 90, 98.

[124] Testimony of Dr. William Hartmann, Sept. 11, 1978, II HSCA–JFK hearings, 137.

[125] Photographic evidence report, pars. 10–38, 42.

[126] Id. at 40.

[127] Id. at 41.

[128] Id. at 292.

[129] Id. at 303–04.

[130] Ibid.

[131] Id. at 305.

[132] Id. at 306.

[133] Ibid.; and outside contact report with Bob Hunt, Jan. 15, 1979, House Select Committee on Assassinations (JFK Document 014736).

[134] Photographic evidence report, pars. 321–322.

[135] Id. at 324–327.

[136] Id. at 328–329.

[137] Id. at 328–331.

[138] Ibid.

[139] Id. at 331.

[140] Id. at 297–301.

[141] Id. at 302.

[142] Id. at 307–309.

[143] Id. at 315–317.

[144] Id. at 251.

[145] Id. at 282.

[146] Id. at 283–285.

[147] Id. at 286.

[148] Id. at 287.

[149] Id. at 288.

[150] Ibid.

[151] Id. at 263.

[152] Id. at 265–266.

[153] "Analysis of Earwitness Reports Relating to the Assassination of President Kennedy," prepared by D. M. Green, consultant to Bolt Beranek and Newman Inc., VIII appendix to the HSCA–JFK hearings (hereinafter BBN–Green report).

[154] Ibid.

[155] This possibility was also recognized by the Warren Commission in its discussion of the number of shots that were fired (Warren Report, p. 111). The testimony of Emmett Joseph Hudson may illustrate the difficulty of finding facts based on the recollections of witnesses, especially those who have had the opportunity to read about the events in newspapers or who may have been led to change their testimony by the manner in which they were questioned at the time of the assassination. Hudson was located in front of the stockade fence on the grassy knoll, in a position where he may have been expected to have heard distinctly any shot fired from the knoll. (See JFK exhibit F–129, I, HSCA–JFK hearings, 109). Hudson gave a sworn statement to the Sheriff's Department of Dallas County on November 22, 1963. He said he was in Dealey Plaza, sitting on the steps in front of the stockade fence, facing Elm Street, during the time of the assassination. He heard three shots. They came "from behind and above *me*." (Emphasis added.) (XIX Warren hearings, 481.)

Hudson's testimony would seem to mean "from behind the fence," and his statement has been so understood (J. Thompson, "Six Seconds in Dallas" (Berkeley, Calif.: Berkeley Medallion Books, 1976), appendix A, witness No. 75.

Hudson gave a deposition to the Warren Commission on July 22, 1964; he told counsel the third "shot was coming from above

687

and kind of behind." (VII Warren hearings, 560.) Counsel then asked: "You heard it come from sort of behind *the motorcade* and then above" (Emphasis added.) Hudson answered, "Yes." (Ibid.) Later in the deposition, counsel returned to the question: "But you are quite sure in your own mind that the shots came from the rear *of the President's car* and above it; is that correct?" (Emphasis added.) Id. at 564. Hudson answered, "Yes." (Ibid.) Counsel then continued, "Did you have any idea that they might have come from the Texas School Book Depository building?" (Ibid.) Hudson answered, "Well, it sounded like it was high, you know, from above and kind of behind like—in other words, to the left." (Ibid.) Counsel asked, "And that would have fit in with the Texas School Book Depository, wouldn't it?" (Ibid.) Hudson replied, "Yes." (Ibid.)

Hudson also indicated that he saw the second shot hit the President in the head "a little bit behind the ear and a little bit above the ear" on the right side. (Id. at 560.) According to his testimony, he was lying on the ground facing Elm when the third shot was fired. (Ibid.) He also felt that the first shot was fired shortly after the motorcade had turned off Houston onto Elm at about the first lightpost on Elm on the right (id. at 559); the second—that hit the President in the head—came a little later, near the second lightpost on Elm on the right (id. at 560); and the third occurred at about the steps leading down to Elm Street that he was standing on (id. at 561). According to Hudson, the third shot must have hit the President in the neck. (Ibid.)

If the scientific evidence summarized in the text is correct, Hudson must be wrong in some aspects of his testimony. According to the scientific evidence, the first shot missed, and it was fired shortly after the President's limousine turned onto Elm. The scientific evidence indicated, moreover, that the second shot hit the President in the neck, not the head, when the limousine was between the first and second lightposts; it also indicated the President was hit in the head not by the second, but by the fourth shot, at the point when the limousine was between the third and fourth lightposts, just about where the steps are. According to JFK Exhibit F–129 (I HSCA–JFK hearings, 109), a photograph taken around the moment of the third and fourth shots, Hudson is seen still standing, not lying down as he remembers.

In summary, Hudson was wrong about which shots hit the President in the head and neck, the location of the limousine at each shot and his own body position at the time of the shooting.

It may well be that Hudson's understanding of what happened was influenced by the newspapers after he had given his November statement to the Sheriff's Department. At two points during the July deposition, he indicated in answers that he had read newspapers that said that the President had been hit twice (id. at 561) and that had carried Hudson's pictures in them (id. at 563).

He may also have been led to alter his first statement by the way in which he was questioned by counsel, who gave him an interpretation of his prior statement to the Sheriff's Department and of his own testimony in the deposition that led him to testify in a fashion consistent with what was then generally well known: Oswald had fired three shots from the depository. When Hudson was contacted by the committee, he told his story in words virtually identical to those he had used in his deposition 15 years ago. He added, "Everything I told the Warren Commission was correct." (Outside contact report with Emmett Joseph Hudson, Feb. 3, 1979, House Select Committee on Assassinations (JFK Document 014458).) Hudson, now 71, has heard for years about the controversy about a shot from the knoll; he does not think that one was fired from behind the stockade fence. (Ibid.)

Hudson himself also recognized the other key factor that affects most of the testimony of the witnesses in Dealey Plaza—he noted that "it was just such an exciting time. . . .", Warren hearings, VII, p. 465.

In dissent, Congressman Edgar questions the testimony, quoted in the text, of S. M. Holland. He correctly noted that there are, as in the case of Hudson, differences between what he told the Dallas County Sheriff's Department and the Warren Commission. He also notes that Holland said he saw a machinegun, using it as a basis to call into question Holland's credibility. In fact, Special Agent Ed Hickey had an AR–15, an automatic rifle, in the followup car, and he did have it raised; Holland's testimony about the machinegun, therefore, can be corroborated (XVII Warren hearings, 735). A photograph of the gun is published in "The Torch Is Passed" (A.P. 1964), p. 17.

Congressman Edgar also noted that Holland reported seeing a "puff of smoke" and questioned whether smoke could be seen when "smokeless" powder is used, as it is in modern firearms. As it was explained by the firearms panel, modern weapons do in fact emit smoke when fired (I HSCA–JFK hearings, 485 (Sept. 8, 1978)).

[156] Warren report, p. 110.
[157] Ibid.
[158] Id. at 111.
[159] Id. at 19.
[160] JFK Exhibit 644 (V HSCA–JFK hearings, 504). The committee did not atempt to interview Hargis because of his medical history.
[161] Ibid.
[162] JFK Exhibit 645 (V HSCA–JFK hearings, 508). Newman confirmed to the committee the accuracy of his statement to the Warren Commission. Outside contact report, William Eugene Newman, February 10, 1979, House Select Committee on Assassinations (JFK document 014572).
[163] JFK Exhibit 646 (V HSCA–JFK hearings, 510).
[164] JFK Exhibit 647 (V HSCA–JFK hearings, 519). Landis confirmed to the committee the accuracy of his statement to the Warren Commission. Outside contact report with Paul Landis, February 17, 1979, House Select Committee on Assassinations (JFK document 014571).
[165] Ibid.
[166] JFK Exhibit 648 (V HSCA–JFK hearings, 527). See reference 155, supra.
[167] Ibid.
[168] Ibid.
[169] BBN-Green report, section 4.
[170] Id. at section 5.
[171] Ibid.
[172] Id. at appendix A.
[173] Id. at section 3.1.

[174] Ibid.

[175] "Conspiracy Witnesses in Dealey Plaza," staff report, XII appendix to the HSCA–JFK hearings.

[176] Photographic evidence report, para. 539–560.

[177] Id. at 612–613.

[178] Id. at 617–618.

[179] Id. at 673, 721–731.

[180] Ibid.

[181] During 1963–1964, Crisman was employed at Rainier Union High School in Rainier, Oreg. The committee obtained the affidavits of three teachers at that school, Marva Harris, Norma Chase, and Stanley Peerloom, that Crisman was teaching school in Rainier on November 22, 1963 (JFK document 013925).

[182] Deposition of E. Howard Hunt, Nov. 3, 1978, House Select Committee on Assassinations, pp. 5–10 (JFK document 014506).

[183] See Section I A 3 of the Report of the Select Committee on Assassinations: Findings and Recommendations; photographic evidence report, para. 188–197, 347–511.

[184] M. Eddowes, "The Oswald File" (New York: Clarkson N. Poter, Inc., 1977).

[185] Photographic evidence report, para. 732–748.

[186] Id. at 749–755.

[187] Id. at 756–757.

[188] Id. at 757.

[189] Ibid.

[190] Report on the subject of the examination of the handwriting and fingerprint evidence in the investigation of the assassination of President John F. Kennedy, VIII appendix to the hearings.

REFERENCES: SECTION C

[1] *United States* v. *Kissel*, 218 U.S. 601, 610 (1910).

[2] See Report of the President's Commission on the Assassination of President Kennedy (Washington, D.C.: U.S. Government Printing Office, 1964), chapter VI.

[3] Id. at 245–252.

[4] Id. at 376.

[5] Id. at 374.

[6] Id. at 780.

[7] Id. at 785.

[8] Id. at 333–373.

[9] Id. at 370–371.

REFERENCES: SECTION C 1

[1] See generally Report of the President's Commission on the Assassination of President Kennedy (Washington, D.C.: U.S. Government Printing Office, 1964), pp. 655–658 (hereinafter Warren Report).

[2] Congressional Research Service, Library of Congress, "Soviet-American Relations During the Kennedy Years," June 1, 1978, prepared for the House Select Committee on Assassinations, pp. 2–6 (JFK Document 008899).

[3] Id. at 9.

[4] Ibid.

[5] Warren Report, pp. 21–22, 254–280.

[6] Id. at 255, 374; Commission exhibit (CE) 3138.

[7] Id. at 254–280, and related Commission exhibits; see also testimony of Marina Oswald Porter, Sept. 13, 1978–Sept. 14, 1978, Hearings before the Select Committee on Assassinations, U.S. House of Representatives, 95th Congress, 2d session (Washington, D.C.: U.S. Government Printing Office, 1979), vol. II, pp. 206–319 (hereinafter Porter testimony.—HSCA–JFK hearings,—); see also "Deposition of Marina Oswald Porter," staff report, appendix to the hearings before the Select Committee on Assassinations, U.S. House of Representatives, 95th Congress, 2d session (Washington, D.C.: U.S. Government Printing Office, 1970), vol. XII (hereinafter Porter deposition,—appendix to the HSCA–JFK hearings,—).

[8] Warren report, CE985, 986.

[9] See generally "Oswald in the Soviet Union: An Investigation of Yuri Nosenko," staff report, XII appendix to the HSCA–JFK hearings (hereinafter Nosenko report).

[10] Ibid.

[11] Ibid.

[12] CE 24, 180–198, 294–295, 297–322.

[13] CE 985, 986.

[14] CE 984.

[15] CE 985, 986.

[16] Ibid. (The suspicious nature of the consistently illegible signatures was discussed in a memorandum of Warren Commission Counsel W. David Slawson to J. Lee Rankin, June 4, 1964.)

[17] Nosenko report, sect. 3, 4.

[18] Ibid.

[19] Unpublished classified staff summary of review of CIA files on U.S. defectors to Russia.

[20] Ibid.

[21] Ibid.

[22] Ibid.

[23] Staff report on Yuri Nosenko, Sept. 15, 1978, II HSCA–JFK hearings, 443.

[24] Id. at 449.

[25] Ibid.

[26] Ibid.

[27] Ibid.

[28] Id. at 460–464.

[29] Id. at 464.

[30] See generally Nosenko report, secs. 3, 4, 7.

[31] Undated memorandum of W. David Slawson, Warren Commission counsel (1964), p. 84ff.; executive session testimony of W. David Slawson, Nov. 15, 1977, House Select Committee on Assassinations Exhibit 22 (JFK Document 014668).

[32] Deposition of J. Lee Rankin, Aug. 17, 1978, House Select Committee on Assassinations, pp. 67-68, attachment G, para. 284, in "The Warren Commission," staff report, XI app. to the HSCA–JFK hearings.

[33] See generally Nosenko report.

[34] Id. at sec. 1.

[35] Ibid.

[36] Ibid.

[37] Testimony of John Hart, Sept. 15, 1978, II HSCA–JFK

JFK hearings, 487; see also JFK exhibit F–427, II HSCA–JFK hearings, 536; Nosenko report, sec. 2.

[38] Id., Nosenko report at sec. 3.
[39] Compare Nosenko report, sec. 3, with secs. 4, 7.
[40] See generally Nosenko report, sec. 1.
[41] Ibid.
[42] Ibid.; Porter testimony, p. 206.
[43] JFK document 014873.

REFERENCES: SECTION C 2

[1] "Report on the President's Commission on the Assassination of President Kennedy" (Washington, D.C.: U.S. Government Printing Office, 1964), pp. 658–659 (hereinafter Warren report).
[2] Congressional Research Service, Library of Congress "United States-Cuban Relations, 1959–64: An Analysis," May 1978 (JFK Document 010426), pp. 7–8 (hereinafter "United States-Cuban Relations, 1959–1964").
[3] Id. at 8.
[4] Id. at 9–16.
[5] Id. at 9.
[6] Ibid.
[7] Ibid.
[8] Id. at 10.
[9] Id. at 12.
[10] Ibid.
[11] Id. at 17–25.
[12] Id. at 20.
[13] Id. at 33.
[14] Ibid.
[15] Ibid.
[16] Id. at 35.
[17] Id. at 36.
[18] Id. at 39.
[19] Congressional Research Service, Library of Congress, "A Selected Chronology on Cuba and Castro, March 10, 1952–October 22, 1962," p. 29 (JFK Document 013100).
[20] Id. at 30.
[21] "United States-Cuban Relations, 1959–64," pp. 37ff.
[22] Id. at 45, inter alia.
[23] Id. at 48–49.
[24] Id. at 52.
[25] Id. at 53.
[26] Id. at 54.
[27] Ibid.
[28] Ibid.
[29] Ibid.
[30] Id. at 72–74.
[31] Id. at 70–71.
[32] Id. at 71–72.
[33] Id. at 72.
[34] "Public Papers of the Presidents of the United States: John F. Kennedy" (Washington, D.C.: U.S. Government Printing Office, 1964), pp. 872–877 (JFK document 013574).
[35] Warren report, pp. 406–414.

[36] Id. at 299–311.

[37] Id. at 658–659, 374.

[38] See, e.g., Washington Post article of Mar. 7, 1967 by Drew Pearson and Jack Anderson, "Castro Counter Plot," and Miami Herald article of Mar. 3, 1967 by Jack Anderson, "Did Plot by CIA to Kill Castro Backfire on United States?"

[39] See "Alleged Assassination Plots Involving Foreign Leaders, An Interim Report," Senate Select Committee to Study Governmental Operations With Respect to Intelligence Activities, 94th Cong., 1st sess., Nov. 20, 1975 (Washington, D.C.: U.S. Government Printing Office, 1976) (S. Rept. 94–465) (hereinafter Senate interim report); and "The Investigation of the Assassination of President John F. Kennedy: Performance of the Intelligence Agencies," book V, final report, Senate Select Committee to Study Governmental Operations With Respect to Intelligence Activities, 94th Cong., 2d sess., Apr. 23, 1976 (Washington, D.C.: U.S. Government Printing Office, 1976) (S. Rept. 94–755) (hereinafter book V).

[40] Senate interim report, pp. 71–180.

[41] Id. at 86–90.

[42] Id. at 74–85.

[43] Book V, p. 68.

[44] Ibid.

[45] Ibid.

[46] Ibid.

[47] Ibid.

[48] Id. at 2.

[49] Ibid.

[50] Comments on book V, SSC final report, CIA classified document, August 30, 1977, tab C (hereinafter T.F.R.).

[51] Ibid.

[52] "The Evolution and Implications of the CIA Sponsored Assassination Conspiracies Against Fidel Castro," staff report, app. to the hearings before the Select Committee on Assassinations, 95th Cong., 2d sess. (Washington, D.C.: U.S. Government Printing Office, 1979), vol. X, para. 54 (hereinafter CIA-Castro staff report, —appendix to the HSCA–JFK hearings,—).

[53] CIA-Castro staff report, para. 46.

[54] Book V, pp. 6–7.

[55] T.F.R., p. 10.

[56] Warren report, pp. 308–309.

[57] Book V, pp. 6–7.

[58] T.F.R., tab B.

[59] CIA-Castro staff report, par. 35ff.

[60] See, e.g., T.F.R., tabs B, C,D.

[61] T.F.R., tab B, p. 5.

[62] T.F.R., tab D.

[63] T.F.R., p. 10.

[64] T.F.R., tab B, p. 8.

[65] Ibid.

[66] Ibid.

[67] Ibid.

[68] CIA-Castro staff report, pars. 58–61.

[69] Id. at 63.

[70] Id. at 54.

[71] T.F.R., tab D, p. 4.
[72] Ibid. See also 1967 CIA Inspector General's Report, p. 84 (hereinafter IGR).
[73] Ibid.
[74] T.F.R., tab D, p. 5.
[75] IGR, pp. 89–95.
[76] Id. at 85.
[77] Id. at 86–87.
[78] T.F.R., tab D, p. 11.
[79] Ibid.
[80] Id. at tab D, p. 12.
[81] Id. at 13.
[82] Id. at 16.
[83] IGR, p. 93a.
[84] CIA-Castro staff report, par. 64.
[85] Id. at 65.
[86] Id at 64.
[87] Transcript of conversations and interviews, trip to Cuba, Aug. 25, 1978, House Select Committee on Assassinations (JFK Document 012208).
[88] Ibid. See also interview with President Fidel Castro, reprinted at III HSCA–JFK hearings, 239–240.
[89] Book V, p. 68.
[90] JFK Document 012208, ref. 87 supra.
[91] CIA-Castro staff report, pars. 160–172. See also, generally, pars. 80–201.
[92] Ibid.
[93] Id. at 157–159.
[94] Ibid.
[95] Id. at 157–163.
[96] Ibid. See also pars. 17–22, 30. See also Book V for details on the anti-Castro activities of Maheu, Rosselli, Giancana, etc.
[97] Id., CIA-Castro staff report, 17–19.
[98] Ibid.
[99] Id. at 20.
[100] Id. at 21–22, 30.
[101] Id. at 176–177.
[102] Id. at 23–26, 176–177.
[103] See, e.g., testimony of Ralph Salerno, Sept. 28, 1978, V HSCA–JFK hearings, 468.
[104] See section C 4 and pp. xx of this section, C 2, supra, for details.
[105] See section C 3 for details.
[106] Ibid.
[107] The method of operation was to contact syndicate figures who had contacts in Cuba. See IGR, pp. 16–19.
[108] T.F.R., tab C, p. 2.
[109] Id. at 5.
[110] Senate interim report, p. 104, fn. 1.
[111] CIA classified file review: Robert Maheu, Office of Security file.
[112] T.F.R., tab C, p. 20.
[113] Book V, pp. 60–61.
[114] Ibid.
[115] Ibid.

[116] Unpublished staff report on the Nov. 22, 1963, Cubana flight, House Select Committee on Assassinations, pp. 4–5 (JFK Document 015047).

[117] Ibid.

[118] Ibid.

[119] Book V, pp. 61ff.

[120] Id. at 61–62.

[121] Id. at 62.

[122] Classified staff summary: The Cuban-American, House Select Committee on Assassinations (Ed Lopez), (JFK Document 014858) (hereinafter Cuban-American).

[123] Id. at 2.

[124] Ibid.

[125] Ibid.

[126] Id. at 3.

[127] Id. at 4.

[128] Ibid.

[129] Id. at 5.

[130] Id. at 4.

[131] T.F.R., tab B, p. 16.

[132] Cuban-American, p. 5.

[133] Id. at 6.

[134] Ibid.

[135] Ibid.

[136] Id. at 6–14; see also JFK Document 014519.

[137] Cuban-American, p. 7.

[138] Id. at 7–8.

[138] Id. at 8.

[140] Id. at 9.

[141] Ibid.

[142] Id. at 10.

[143] Ibid.

[144] Id. at 10–11.

[145] T.F.R., tab B, pp. 16–17.

[146] Deposition of Antulio Ramirez Ortiz, Nov. 15, 1978, House Select Committee on Assassinations, pp. 14–16 (JFK Document 013095).

[147] Id. at 16–29.

[148] Antulio Ramirez Ortiz, Castro's Red Hot Hell (unpublished) (JFK Document 005134).

[149] Executive session testimony, Antulio Ramirez Ortiz, Apr. 11, 1978, House Select Committee on Assassinations (JFK Document 014674).

[150] Id. at 26–27.

[151] See JFK Documents 006940, 006975, 007000, 007077, 007078, 007079, 007080, 007132, 007136, 007278, and 007476.

[152] JFK exhibit F–428; III HSCA–JFK hearings, 282.

[153] Ibid.

[154] JFK exhibits F–429B and F–429C, III HSCA–JFK hearings, 196, 197.

[155] Id. at 274.

[156] See, e.g., classified staff summary of Silvia Duran's statements (JFK Document 014862), pp. 9, 12; testimony of Eusebio Azcue, Sept. 18, 1978, III HSCA–JFK hearings, 133; and statements of Silvia Duran, JFK exhibit F–440a, III HSCA–JFK hearings, 6ff.

695

[157] Comments by Chief Counsel G. Robert Blakey, Sept. 19, 1978, III HSCA–JFK hearings, 283.

[158] Ibid.

[159] "Analysis of the Support Provided to the Warren Commission by the Central Intelligence Agency," staff report, XI appendix to the HSCA–JFK hearings (hereinafter CIA performance).

[160] JFK exhibit F–518, IV HSCA–JFK hearings, 181.

[161] Staff summary of Aug. 25, 1978 trip to Cuba, House Select Committee on Assassinations, p. 5 (JFK Document 014859).

[162] Interrogatories of Anna Luisa Calderon Carralero, House Select Committee on Assassinations (JFK Document 014421).

[163] See, generally, JFK Documents 014974 and 014975.

[164] See JFK exhibit F–403, III HSCA–JFK hearings, 300.

[165] Unpublished staff report, Mexico City, House Select Committee on Assassinations, pp. 52–53 (JFK Document 014856).

[166] Interview of Horacio Duran Navarro, June 5, 1978, House Select Committee on Assassinations (JFK Document 011683); interview of Lydia Duran, June 5, 1978, House Select Committee on Assassinations (JFK document 011681); interview of Ruben Duran Navarro, June 6, 1978, House Select Committee on Assassinations (JFK Document 011680); interview of Betty Serratos, June 6, 1978, House Select Committee on Assassinations (JFK Document 014413), inter alia. A summary of the investigative efforts relating to Oswald's trip to Mexico is contained in the classified staff report of Dan Hardway and Ed Lopez (JFK Documents 014974 and 014975).

[167] JFK exhibit F–403, III HSCA–JFK hearings, 300.

[168] See JFK exhibit 440a, III HSCA–JFK hearings, 69 and Azcue testimony, 136.

[169] Id. at 24–25, 112.

[170] Azcue testimony, pp. 135–139.

[171] Id. at 95–96.

[172] Id. at 59.

[173] Unpublished staff report on Elena Garro de Paz, House Select Committee on Assassinations, p. 47 (JFK Document 014856).

[174] Id. at 49–52.

[175] JFK Document 014975, supra, p. 420; Duran statements, III HSCA–JFK hearings, 100.

[176] Id., JFK Document 014975, p. 421; Duran statements, III HSCA–JFK hearings, at 106–107.

[177] Ibid., JFK Document 014975, p. 421; staff summary of Mexico City trip, Aug. 7, 1978, House Select Committee on Assassinations, pp. 3, 7, 8, 10 (JFK Document 012210).

[178] The details of the committee's investigation of Oswald's trip to Mexico City are contained in a 300-page classified staff report, "Lee Harvey Oswald * * * and Mexico City," prepared by HSCA staff Dan Hardway and Ed Lopez (JFK Documents 014974 and 014975).

[179] JFK exhibit F–414, III HSCA–JFK hearings, 399.

[180] JFK exhibit F–419, III HSCA–JFK hearings, 361; memoranda, FBI Miami field office, CD 770.

[181] Testimony of Secret Service Inspector Thomas J. Kelley, Sept. 19, 1978, III HSCA–JFK hearings, 343.

[182] JFK exhibits F–415, 416, 417 and 418, III HSCA–JFK hearings, 401, 425, 433 and 436 respectively.

[183] Narration of Chief Counsel G. Robert Blakey, III HSCA–JFK hearings, 319.

[184] Azcue testimony, pp. 126–178.

[185] JFK exhibit F–429C, III HSCA–JFK hearings, 212–213.

[186] Id. at 214–215.

[187] Id. at 216–217.

[188] Id. at 221ff.

[189] Id. at 222.

[190] See JFK exhibit F–685, III HSCA–JFK hearings, 179, and "United States-Cuban Relations, 1959–1964," p. 72.

[191] JFK exhibit F–429C, supra, pp. 223–224.

[192] Id. at 224–225.

[193] See sec. D 5 of this report.

[194] See sec. D 3 of this report.

[195] "Anti-Castro Organizations and Activists and Lee Harvey Oswald in New Orleans," staff report, X appendix to the HSCA–JFK hearings, para. 109 (hereinafter anti-Castro organizations).

[196] Id. at 110.

[197] Tape of interview with the defector, Dec. 13, 1978, House Select Committee on Assassinations (JFK Document 015049).

[198] T.F.R., Tab B, p. 9.

[199] See executive session testimony of Richard M. Helms, Aug. 9, 1978, House Select Committee on Assassinations, and public session testimony of Richard M. Helms, September 22, 1978, IV HSCA–JFK hearings, for further accounts of Helms' relationship with the Warren Commission. See generally CIA performance, par. 47–68; as explained in sec. D, while Richard Helms and other CIA officials may not have overtly diverted the investigation, this does not mean they fully acknowledged all details to the Warren Commission that might have been pertinent to the investigation.

[200] See generally ref. 191 in sec. C 3 anti-Castro organizations, pars. 205–388.

REFERENCES: SECTION C 3

[1] "Anti-Castro Activists and Organizations and Lee Harvey Oswald in New Orleans," staff report, appendix to the hearings before the Select Committee on Assassinations, U.S. House of Representatives, 95th Cong., 2d Sess. (Washington, D.C.: U.S. Government Printing Office, 1979), vol. X, par. 23 (hereinafter Anti-Castro Cuban report,—appendix to the hearings,—)

[2] Id. at 64–65, 460–463.

[3] Id. at 12.

[4] Id. at 13.

[5] Id. at 15.

[6] Id. at 17ff.

[7] Ibid.

[8] Id. at 18ff.

[9] Id. at 21.

[10] Id. at 23.

[11] See generally Congressional Research Service, Library of Congress, "United States-Cuban Relations, 1959–64: Analysis," May 1978, pp. 17ff. (JFK Document 010426) (hereinafter United States-Cuban Relations).

[12] Id. at 20.

[13] Anti-Castro Cuban report, pars. 25–26.

[14] Id. at 27.

[15] Ibid.

697

[16] Id. at 28.

[17] Id. at 29.

[18] Id. at 28.

[19] Ibid.

[20] Ibid.

[21] Id. at 30.

[22] E. Howard Hunt, "Give Us This Day" (New York: Popular Library), pp. 220–221 (hereinafter Hunt, "Give Us This Day"); see generally Haynes Johnson, "The Bay of Pigs," (New York: W. W. Norton, 1964); and Miami Herald, Dec. 30, 1962.

[23] Ibid.

[24] Ibid.

[25] Hunt, "Give Us This Day," p. 221.

[26] Anti-Castro Cuban report, par. 31.

[27] Id. at 33–42.

[28] Ibid.

[29] Ibid.

[30] Ibid.

[31] Id. at 43.

[32] Id. at 44–45.

[33] "United States-Cuban Relations," pp. 54–55.

[34] Id. at 46–47.

[35] Ibid.

[36] Id. at 48.

[37] Tape recording of a meeting of anti-Castro Cubans in Dallas, Tex., Oct. 1, 1963 (JFK Document 010210).

[38] Ibid.

[39] Ibid.; upon listening to the tape, it is apparent that the statements by Castellanos—"we're waiting for Kennedy" and "we're going to see him * * * to give him the words"—which comes just after Castellanos relates an unsuccessful effort to have a parade or march in downtown Dallas to promote the cause of the anti-Castro Cubans, is only a proposal to demonstrate against President Kennedy during his trip to Dallas. After reviewing the entire tape, the staff concluded that Castellanos' statements were not meant as a threat of physical violence against the President.

[40] Anti-Castro Cuban report, pars. 59ff.

[41] Ibid.

[42] Ibid.

[43] U.S. Secret Service, blank letterhead memorandum, Nov. 27, 1963, Secret Service 2–1–611.0, p. 1 (JFK Document 007601).

[44] Id. at 3.

[45] Ibid.

[46] Ibid.

[47] U.S. Secret Service report, Dec. 3, 1963, file CO–2–34,000, Chicago field office, p. 1; U.S. Secret Service report, Dec. 19, 1963, file No. CO–2–34,104, pp. 1–6; U.S. Secret Service report, Dec. 13, 1963, file No. CO–2–34,030, pp. 1–3.

[48] U.S. Secret Service report, Nov. 27, 1963, file 2–1–611.0, Chicago field office, p. 2 (JFK Document 007601).

[49] U.S. Secret Service report, Dec. 3, 1963, Chicago field office, file CO–2–34,030, p. 4.

[50] The Secret Service continued the investigation despite the FBI's opinion that the group was not involved in illegal activity. U.S. Secret Service report, Dec. 3, 1963, Chicago field office, file CO–2–34,030.

[51] Report of the President's Commission on the Assassination of President Kennedy (Washington, D.C.: U.S. Government Printing Office, 1964), p. ix (hereinafter Warren report).

[52] Deposition of James J. Rowley, Aug. 18, 1978, House Select Committee on Assassinations, pp. 23, 38, 39 (JFK Document 014240).

[53] Id. at 26–29, 38, 39.

[54] U.S. Secret Service report, Dec. 19, 1963, file CO–2–34,104, p. 7.

[55] Letter to James B. Rhoads, Archivist of the United States, from J. Edgar Hoover, FBI, Dec. 28, 1970, Bureau 62–109060–6979. This letter states: "A review of this material indicates it pertained to a matter investigated by the U.S. Secret Service. No investigation was conducted by FBI with respect to the allegations concerning Echevarria."

[56] Anti-Castro Cuban report, pars. 347–348.

[57] See generally material on the Junta del Gobierno de Cuba en el Exilio in the anti-Castro Cuban report, pars. 342–388.

[58] Ibid.

[59] Id. at 351, 365.

[60] See generally Warren report, pp. 321–325.

[61] Anti-Castro Cuban report, pars. 129ff.

[62] Id. at 114.

[63] Id. at 131.

[64] Id. at 181, 131.

[65] Id. at 114.

[66] Id. at 115.

[67] Id. at 142.

[68] Ibid.

[69] Ibid.

[70] Id. at 146.

[71] Id. at 152.

[72] Id. at 129.

[73] Id. at 194, 202, 203.

[74] Id. at 171ff.

[75] Id. at 172–173.

[76] Ibid.

[77] Id. at 181–183.

[78] Id. at 184.

[79] Anti-Castro Cuban report, pars. 173–192.

[80] Id. at 177, 186–192.

[81] Id. at 197.

[82] Ibid.

[83] Ibid.

[84] Id. at 186–190.

[85] Id. at 195.

[86] Id. at 196.

[87] Id. at 198.

[88] Id. at 200–201.

[89] Ibid.

[90] Ibid.

[91] Id. at 64.

[92] Id. at 94ff.

[93] Id. at 95–96.

[94] Id. at 64–65.

[95] Ibid.

[96] Ibid.

[97] Ibid.

[98] Id. at 64.

[99] Ibid.

[100] Ibid.

[101] Id. at 65.

[102] Id. at 93.

[103] Id. at 65.

[104] Ibid.

[105] Id. at 66.

[106] Id. at 67-68.

[107] Letter from J. Lee Rankin to J. Edgar Hoover, July 24, 1964 (JFK Document 002442). Rankin asked Hoover to have the Bureau interview Silvia Odio's sister, Annie Laurie Odio, to investigate this matter further.

[108] Id. at 2.

[109] Memorandum from J. Wesley Liebeler to Howard P. Willens, Warren Commission, Sept. 14, 1964, pp. 4–6 (JFK Document 002539) (hereinafter Liebeler-Willens memorandum).

[110] Warren report, p. 323.

[111] Liebeler-Willens memorandum, p. 5.

[112] Ibid.

[113] Liebeler-Willens memorandum, pp. 4–6.

[114] Id. at 6.

[115] Hearings before the President's Commission on the Assassination of President Kennedy (Washington, D.C.: U.S. Government Printing Office, 1964), volume 26, p. 595 (hereinafter Warren hearings).

[116] Ibid.

[117] Ibid.

[118] Letter from J. Edgar Hoover to J. Lee Rankin, Nov. 9, 1964, Warren Commission exhibit (CE) 1553 (JFK Document 002448).

[119] The report was completed and sent to President Johnson on Sept. 24, 1964 (Warren report, p. v).

[120] Anti-Castro Cuban report, par. 68.

[121] Id. at 71c.

[122] Ibid.

[123] Ibid.

[124] Ibid.

[125] Id. at 68.

[126] Id. at 85ff.

[127] Id. at 85aff.

[128] Id. at 103.

[129] Memorandum to W. David Slawson from Burt W. Griffin, Apr. 16, 1964 (JFK Document 002969). Dr. Einspruch stated that "she is given to exaggeration but that all the basic facts which she provided are true" and that "he had great faith in Miss Odio's story of having met Lee Harvey Oswald."

[130] Memorandum to file from Gaeton Fonzi., June 17, 1978, House Select Committee on Assassinations (JFK Document 009368).

[131] Id. at 1–2.

[132] Anti-Castro Cuban report, pars. 74, 75.

[133] Summary of the testimony of Leon Brown, May 15, 1978, House Select Committee on Assassinations (JFK Document 008343). Leon Brown appeared before the committee on Nov. 16, 1977.

[134] Anti-Castro Cuban report, para. 107–109.

[135] Id. at 109.

[136] Id. at 110.

[137] Ibid.

[138] Ibid.

[139] Warren Report, p. 730.

[140] This evidence consists of statements to the committee and the Warren Commission by Silvia Odio regarding when Oswald allegedly visited her and other statements and evidence establishing Oswald's location at certain times (see Warren Report, pp. 323–24, for more deails). While the committee agreed that Oswald would have had to have traveled by priyate transportation if he had visited Odio on the 25th, 26th or 27th, the committee did not agree with the Warren Commission conclusion that the evidence was "persuasive" that Oswald did not visit Odio at the time she said he did.

[141] Warren Report, p. 377.

[142] Id. at 402–404, 713–725.

[143] Id. at 725.

[144] Id. at 726.

[145] Id. at 728–729.

[146] Id. at 406–412, 728, 729.

[147] Id. at 407.

[148] Ibid.

[149] Anti-Castro Cuban report, para, 220.

[150] Id. at 218.

[151] Ibid.

[152] Warren Report, p. 408.

[153] Id. at 726.

[154] Id. at 727.

[155] Id. at 728.

[156] X Warren hearings, 34–35.

[157] Id. at 37.

[158] Warren Report, p. 728.

[159] Testimony of Carlos Bringuier, April 7, 1964, X Warren hearings, 34–36; deposition of Carlos Bringuier, May 12, 1978, House Select Committee on Assassinations, p. 61 (JFK Document 009084) (hereinafter Bringuier deposition).

[160] Ibid.

[161] Warren Report, p. 729; Bringuier deposition, pp. 61–62.

[162] X Warren hearings, 37.

[163] Ibid.

[164] Warren Report, pp. 728–729.

[165] Ibid.

[166] Id. at 729.

[167] Ibid.

[168] Anti-Castro Cuban report, para. 226–230.

[169] Ibid.

[170] Ibid.

[171] Ibid.

[172] Warren Report, p. 729.

[173] Id. at 39–42.

[174] Ibid.

[175] Ibid.

[176] Id. at 729.

[177] Ibid.

[178] X Warren hearings, 44.

[179] Warren Report, p. 730.

[180] CIA chronology on Lee Harvey Oswald, p. 126 A. & B.

[181] Id. at 120, 126a.

[182] Deposition of Reeves Morgan, Apr. 19, 1978, House Select Committee on Assassinations (JFK Document 008501) (hereinafter Morgan deposition).

[183] Id. at 10–12.

[184] Outside contact report with Frances Fruge, Dec. 19, 1978 (JFK Document 015044).

[185] Bernard Fensterwald, "Coincidence or Conspiracy," 1st ed. (New York: Kensington Publishing Corp., 1977), pp. 297–298, 451–457.

[186] Memorandum from Patricia Orr re Clinton, Feb. 3, 1978, House Select Committee on Assassinations (JFK Document 005003).

[187] Deposition of Henry Earl Palmer, May 17, 1978, House Select Committee on Assassinations, pp. 4, 5 (JFK Document 008499) (hereinafter Palmer deposition).

[188] Deposition of Bobbie Dedon, May 19, 1978, House Select Committee on Assassinations, pp. 4–5 (JFK Document 008498).

[189] Palmer deposition, pp. 10–13.

[190] Id. at 11; affidavit of Corrie Collins, Nov. 7, 1978, House Select Committee on Assassinations, pp. 2–3 (JFK Document 013007).

[191] Ibid.; testimony of John Manchester, Mar. 14, 1978, House Select Committee on Assassinations, p. 12 (JFK Document 008503); deposition of William Dunn, Apr. 18, 1978, House Select Committee on Assassinations, p. 12 (JFK Document 008497)

[192] Anti-Castro Cuban report, para. 448.

[193] Id. at 432.

[194] Id. at 448.

[195] FBI interview of Jack Martin, No. 89–69, Nov. 25, 1963.

[196] Ibid.

[197] Ibid.

[198] Anti-Castro Cuban report, para. 428–438.

[199] Id. at 429ff.

[200] Ibid.

[201] Id. at 439–447.

[202] Anti-Castro Cuban report, para. 441; immunized testimony of Carlos Marcello, Jan, 11, 1978, pp. 58–63.

[203] Id. at 430.

[204] Id. at 431.

[205] Ibid.

[206] Testimony of Guy Banister, Aug. 5, 1963, FAA grievance hearing, p. 840 (JFK Document 014904).

[207] Id. at 218.

[208] Id. at 218ff.

[209] Ibid.

[210] Id. at 224.

[211] Id. at 225.

[212] Id. at 226ff.

[213] Id. at 431.

[214] Ibid.

[215] Id. at 418ff.

[216] Id. at 451; FBI document, interview of G. Wray Gill, Nov. 27, 1963, New Orleans field office, No. 89–69, p. 2.

[217] FBI interview of G. Wray Gill, Nov. 27, 1963, New Orleans field office, file No. 89–69.

[218] Anti-Castro Cuban report, para. 450ff.

[219] FBI interview of David Ferrie, Bureau No. 89–69, Nov. 26, 1963, p. 7.

[220] Ibid.

[221] Id. at 8.

[222] Ibid.

[223] Ibid.

[224] Ibid.

[225] FBI interview of David Ferrie, Bureau No. 89–69, Nov. 27, 1963, pp. 1–2.

[226] FBI interview of David Ferrie, Bureau No. 89–69, Nov. 26, 1963, p. 3.

[227] Ibid.

[228] Ibid.

[229] Id. at 9.

[230] U.S. Secret Service report, New Orleans, Dec. 13, 1963, file CO–2–34,030, p. 5 (JFK Document 003840).

[231] Id. at 1.

[232] Id. at 5.

[233] FBI document, Nov. 25, 1963, New Orleans office, No. 89–69, interview of Jack Martin.

[234] Id. at 5.

[235] Bringuier deposition; deposition of Carlos Quiroga, May 23, 1978, House Select Committee on Assassinations (JFK Document 009394); deposition of Luis Rabel, May 11, 1978, House Select Committee on Assassinations (JFK Document 009080).

[236] Anti-Castro Cuban report, para. 491

[237] Outside contact report with Delphine Roberts, Sept. 1, 1978 (JFK Document 011196).

[238] Anti-Castro Cuban report, para. 503ff.

[239] Id. at 504ff.

[240] Id. at 505.

[241] Ibid.

[242] Ibid.

[243] Deposition of Adrian T. Alba, May 5, 1978, House Select Committee on Assassinations, p. 19 (JFK Document 009964) (hereinafter Alba deposition); see also interview of Jack Mancuso, Jan. 26, 1978, House Select Committee on Assassinations, p. 2 (hereinafter Mancuso interview). Mancuso recognized a photograph of Oswald as someone who frequented his premises, Mancuso's Restaurant.

[244] Alba deposition, p. 52; he remembered that Banister frequented Mancuso's. Mancuso interview; he recognized Banister and Ferrie as persons that frequented his restaurant.

[245] Anti-Castro Cuban report, para. 488.

[246] "The Persecution of Clay Shaw," Look magazine, Aug. 29, 1969.

REFERENCES: SECTION C 4

[1] Report of the President's Commission on the Assassination of President Kennedy (Washington, D.C.: U.S. Government Printing Office, 1964), p. 333 (hereinafter cited as Warren report).

[2] Id. at 333–365.

[3] Id. at 374.
[4] Id. at 357.
[5] Id. at 796–797, 370–371.
[6] Id. at 359–365.
[7] Ibid.
[8] Id. at 369–371, 801–802.
[9] Id. at 370–371, 801.
[10] Id. at 370–371.
[11] Id. at 790.
[12] Ibid.
[13] Id, at 801.
[14] Id. at 373.
[15] "Organized Crime: Staff and Consultant Reports," appendix to the hearings before the Select Committee on Assassinations, U.S. House of Representatives, 95th Congress, 2d Session (Washington, D.C.: U.S. Government Printing ffice, 1979), vol. IX, para. 603–655 (hereinafter HSCA report on organized crime,—appendix to the HSCA–JFK hearings,—).
[16] Ibid.
[17] Ibid.
[18] Ibid.
[19] Warren report, pp. 792–793.
[20] HSCA report on organized crime, para. 620ff.
[21] Ibid.
[22] Ibid.
[23] Warren report, pp. 792–793.
[24] HSCA report on organized crime, para. 620ff.
[25] Id. at 1195–1270.
[26] Id. at 1244–1268.
[27] Ibid.
[28] Ibid.
[29] Id. at 1208–1209.
[30] Id. at 1210ff.
[31] Ibid.
[32] Ibid.
[33] Id. at 1244–1268.
[34] Id. at 829–830.
[35] Id. at 1153–1176.
[36] Id. at 656–793, 1153–1176.
[37] Ibid.
[38] Testimony of Lewis McWillie, Sept. 27, 1978, V HSCA–JFK hearings, 2ff.
[39] Warren report, pp. 801–802.
[40] Id. at vol. XXII, p. 859, Commission Exhibits 1442, 1443.
[41] HSCA staff report on organized crime, para. 665–704.
[42] Id. at 721ff.
[43] Id. at 737–738.
[44] Ibid.
[45] Ibid.
[46] See FBI memorandum Nov. 6, 1959 on Ruby as a PCI, JFK Document 003040; executive session testimony of Charles W. Flynn, Nov. 16, 1977 (JFK Document 014669).
[47] HSCA report on organized crime, pp. 737–738.
[48] Testimony of Jack Ruby, June 7, 1964, V Warren hearings, 202 (hereinafter Ruby testimony).
[49] See HSCA report on organized crime, para. 741.

[50] Ibid.
[51] Ibid.
[52] Ibid.
[53] Id. at 665–676.
[54] Id. at 741ff inter alia.
[55] Ibid.; Ruby testimony, pp. 205–208.
[56] HSCA report on organized crime, para. 678.
[57] Id. at 743ff, 1105–1152.
[58] Ibid.
[59] Warren report, p. 369.
[60] Ibid.
[61] HSCA report on organized crime, para, 1144–1152.
[62] Id. at 663.
[63] "The Evolution and Implications of the CIA-Sponsored Assassination Conspiracies Against Fidel Castro," staff report, X appendix to the HSCA–JFK hearings.
[64] HSCA report on organized crime, para. 685–712, inter alia.[
[65] Id. at 685.
[66] Outside contact report with Judge Burt W. Griffin, Sept. 27, 1978, House Select Committee on Assassinations (JFK Document 015111).
[67] HSCA report on organized crime, para. 710–712, 724–725.
[68] Ibid.
[69] Ibid.
[70] Ibid.
[71] Ibid.
[72] Ibid.
[73] Id. at 695–696, 704.
[74] Ibid.
[75] Ibid.
[76] Ibid.
[77] Id. at 724.
[78] Ibid.
[79] Testimony of Santos Trafficante, Sept. 28, 1978, V HSCA–JFK hearings, 371.
[80] Id. at 370.
[81] Testimony of Ralph Salerno, Sept. 28, 1978, V HSCA–JFK hearings, 430 (hereinafter Salerno testimony).
[82] HSCA report on organized crime, para. 794–830; narration on Ruby telephone calls, Sept. 26, 1976, IV HSCA–JFK hearings, 496–499.
[83] HSCA report on organized crime, para. 1341ff and 794–830.
[84] Id. at 887–907, 794–830.
[85] Ibid.
[86] Ibid.
[87] Ibid.; see also pars. 1153–1176.
[88] Ibid.
[89] Ibid.; see also pars. 1195–1270.
[90] Id. at 829–830.
[91] Id. at 831–864, 794–830; see also, Sept. 26, 1978, IV HSCA–JFK hearings, 496–499.
[92] Id. at 833–834.
[93] Ibid.
[94] Id. at 844–857.
[95] Id. at 863.
[96] Ibid.

[97] Id. at 1356.
[98] Id. at 1358.
[99] Id. at 1359ff.
[100] Ibid.
[101] Id. at 822–823.
[102] Id. at 827–828.
[103] Ibid.
[104] Id. at 818–821.
[105] Ibid.
[106] Ibid.
[107] Id. at 954–958.
[108] Id. at 960–961.
[109] Id. at 958.
[110] Id. at 859.
[111] Id. at 499–602.
[112] Id. at 499–513, 516–522.
[113] Id. at 523ff.
[114] Id. at 525.
[115] Id. at 523–602.
[116] Ibid.
[117] Id. at 526ff.
[118] Id. at 597.
[119] Id. at 523ff. and 581–582.
[120] Ibid.
[121] Ibid.
[122] Ibid.
[123] Ibid.
[124] Ibid.
[125] Id. at 1367.
[126] Id. at 599–600.
[127] Id. at 547–566, 1367, inter alia.
[128] Id. at 583–588.
[129] Id. at 1367.
[130] Id. at 547–566.
[131] Ibid.
[132] Id. at 558–559.
[133] Ibid.
[134] Ruby testimony, pp. 188–189.
[135] Id. at 205.
[136] Id. at 181–213.
[137] Newsweek, March 27, 1967.
[138] Ibid.
[139] Warren report, pp. 336–337; XV Warren hearings, 71–96.
[140] Ibid.
[141] Interview of Burt W. Griffin, Nov. 20, 1978, House Select Committee on Assassinations; statement of Burt W. Griffin, prepared for Seth Kantor, "Who Was Jack Ruby?" (New York: Everest House, 1978), pp. 201–202.
[142] "Report of the Polygraphy Panel on the Subject of the Analysis of Jack Ruby's Polygraph Examination," VIII appendix to the HSCA–JFK hearings (hereinafter polygraphy panel report).
[143] Warren Report, pp. 807–816.
[144] Id., XIV Warren hearings, 584, 598 (testimony of Special Agent Herndon).
[145] Polygraphy panel report.
[146] Ibid.

[147] See, e.g., JFK Document 005089, 007359, 010450, 004770, 007421, and 015112.

[148] Ibid.

[149] Ibid.

[150] Ibid.

[151] Ibid.

[152] Interview of Earl Ruby, Jan, 2, 1979, House Select Committee on Assassinations.

[153] Ibid.

[154] Interview of Irwin S. Weiner, Jan. 2, 1979, House Select Committee on Assassinations.

[155] Salerno testimony, p. 385.

[156] Consultant's report on organized crime (hereinafter Salerno report), in "Organized Crime: Staff and Consultant Reports," para. 14–17.

[157] Salerno testimony, p. 385.

[158] Ibid.

[159] Id. at 386.

[160] Ibid.

[161] See generally Salerno report, para. 30.

[162] Salerno testimony, pp. 386–426, 437–453.

[163] Task Force Report: Organized Crime, 1967, President's Commission on Law Enforcement and Criminal Justice (Washington, D.C.: U.S. Government Printing Office, 1967), pp. 1–3.

[164] Salerno testimony, pp. 434–436.

[165] Salerno report, para. 84.

[166] Id. at 85–115, 154–176.

[167] Salerno testimony, pp. 415–416.

[168] Salerno report, para. 12.

[169] Id. at 13.

[170] Id. at 85, 154–176.

[171] Id. at 248.

[172] Id. at 186–201.

[173] Hearings before the Permanent Subcommittee on Investigations of the Committee on Government Operations, U.S. Senate, 88th Congress, 1st sess., Sept. 25 to Oct. 9, 1963, p. 23.

[174] Salerno report, pars. 186–201.

[175] Ibid.

[176] Id. at 247.

[177] Id. at 186–201.

[178] Ibid.

[179] Ibid.

[180] See generally Salerno testimony, pp. 463–464.

[181] Ibid.

[182] Ibid.

[183] Ibid.

[184] Salerno report, para. 203–224.

[185] Ibid.

[186] Ibid.

[187] Ibid.

[188] Id. at 232–245.

[189] Ibid.

[190] Id. at 225–231.

[191] Ibid.

[192] Id. at 246.

[193] Ibid.

[194] Ibid.
[195] Ibid.
[196] Ibid.
[197] Ibid.
[198] Ibid.
[199] Id. at 247.
[200] Id. at 248.
[201] Ibid.
[202] Ibid.
[203] Ibid.
[204] Ibid.
[205] Id. at 250; for a review of legal issues relating to electronic surveillance programs during that period, see hearings of the National Commission for the Review of Federal and State Laws Relating to Wiretapping and Electronic Surveillance, (Washington, D.C.: U.S. Government Printing Office, 1967), Volume 2, pp. 1637–1646.
[206] Salerno testimony, pp. 428–429.
[207] Id. at 427.
[208] Salerno report, pars, 76, 251ff.
[209] Ibid.
[210] Id. at 118–176.
[211] Id. at 157 (JFK Exhibit F–622, Sept. 28, 1978, V HSCA–JFK hearings, 446).
[212] Id. at 161 (JFK Exhibit F–629, Sept. 28, 1978, V HSCA–JFK hearings, 448).
[213] Id. at 177.
[214] Id. at 118–176.
[215] JFK Exhibit 618, Sept. 28, 1978, V HSCA–JFK hearings, 443.
[216] Cf. Salerno testimony, p. 458.
[217] Ibid.
[218] Id. at 448 (JFK Exhibit F–630).
[219] Ibid.
[220] Id. at 177–178.
[221] See ref. 205, supra, pp. 1596–1636 for a detailed discussion of the nature of conversations recorded by electronic surveillance programs. The Commission provided a detailed overview of the structure, operation, and violent crimes of a well-known La Cosa Nostra family, as disclosed through an electronic surveillance program.
[222] Salerno testimony, p. 454.
[223] Ibid.
[224] Salerno report, para. 166–176.
[225] Ibid.
[226] Id. at 170.
[227] Id. at 169.
[228] Id. at 170.
[229] Id. at 174.
[230] Id. at 178, 247, 294–295.
[231] Id. at 251–285.
[232] Salerno testimony, pp. 454–455.
[233] Ibid.
[234] Salerno report, para. 139–153.
[235] Ibid.

[236] Ibid.
[237] Id. at 262.
[238] Id. at 255–256, 266–269.
[239] Ibid.; see also, para. 135.
[240] Salerno testimony, pp. 454–455.
[241] Salerno report, para. 269.
[242] Salerno testimony, 454–456.
[243] Ibid.
[244] Id. at 31–43, 257–258.
[245] Ibid.
[246] Ibid.
[247] Ibid.
[248] Id. at 252–255.
[249] Arthur M. Schlesinger, Jr., Robert Kennedy and His Times (Boston: Houghton Mifflin Co., 1978), pp. 615–616; interview with former Labor Department official, July 4, 1978, House Select Committee on Assassinations (JFK Document 010423).
[250] Ibid.
[251] "The Warren Commission," staff report, XI Appendix to the HSCA–JFK hearings, para. 277, inter alia.
[252] Id. at 283.
[253] Ibid.; see also para. 284; interview with J. Lee Rankin, Nov. 20, 1978, House Select Committee on Assassinations (JFK Document 013218).
[254] Executive session testimony of Burt W. Griffin, Nov. 17, 1977, House Select Committee on Assassinations, XI Appendix to the HSCA–JFK Hearings para. 283.
[255] Deposition of Courtney Evans, Sept. 6, 1978, House Select Committee on Assassinations (JFK Document 014003).
[256] Ibid.
[257] Ibid.
[258] Interview of Al Staffeld, Aug. 28, 1978, House Select Committee on Assassinations (JFK Document 011096); deposition of Al Staffeld, Sept. 7, 1978 (JFK Document 014929).
[259] Salerno report, para. 173.
[260] Ibid.
[261] Id. at 281–284.
[262] Id. at 288–294, inter alia.
[263] HSCA report on organized crime, para. 300–427.
[264] Id. at 428ff, 817–821.
[265] Id. at 333–369.
[266] Ibid.
[267] Id. at 345; see also, immunized testimony of Carlos Marcello, Jan. 11, 1978, House Select Committee on Assassinations, pp. 37–38, 55–77.
[268] Id. at 431–497; see also, "Anti-Castro Activists and Organizations and Lee Harvey Oswald in New Orleans"; staff report, X Appendix to the HSCA–JFK hearings (hereinafter anti-Castro Cuban report).
[269] HSCA report on organized crime, para. 431–443.
[270] Ibid.
[271] Id. at 442.
[272] Id. at 491–497.
[273] Id. at 431–440; 817–821; see also IV HSCA–JFK hearings, 498.

[274] Id. at 457–490.

[275] Id. at 461; see also, Anti-Castro Cuban report, para. 489–516.

[276] Id. at 464.

[277] Anti-Castro Cuban report, para. 390.

[278] Immunized testimony of Carlos Marcello, House Select Committee on Assassinations, Jan. 11, 1978, pp. 64–65.

[279] Anti-Castro Cuban report, para. 460ff.

[280] Warren Report, p. 292.

[281] Ibid., HSCA report on organized crime, pars. 817–821, 908–923.

[282] Ibid., HSCA report on organized crime; see also interview with Ovid Demaris', Oct. 12, 1978, House Select Committee on Assassinations (JFK Document 012587); FBI interview with Joseph Civello, Jan. 14, 1964, FBI file No. 92–2824–101.

[283] Id., HSCA report on organized crime, at 908–923.

[284] Id. at 370–418.

[285] Ibid.

[286] Ibid.

[287] Id. at 376–389.

[288] Ibid.

[289] Ibid.

[290] Ibid.

[291] Id. at 390–398.

[292] Ibid.

[293] Id. at 331, 416–418.

[294] Id. at 288.

[295] Id. at 338–341.

[296] Interview with Al Staffeld, Aug. 28, 1978, House Select Committee on Assassinations (JFK Document 011096).

[297] HSCA report on organized crime, para. 321–322.

[298] Ibid.

[299] Id. at 284; see also Salerno testimony, p. 381ff.

[300] Salerno testimony, pp. 415, 419.

[301] "The Evolution and Implications of the CIA-Sponsored Assassination Conspiracy Against Fidel Castro," staff report, X appendix to the HSCA–JFK hearings.

[302] Ibid.

[303] Testimony of Santos Trafficante, Sept. 28, 1978, V HSCA–JFK hearings, 357ff.

[304] Id. at 363–364.

[305] HSCA report on organized crime, para. 656–737.

[306] Ibid.; see also para. 1153–1176.

[307] Id. at 721–725, 737–738.

[308] Id. at 741.

[309] Id. at 1054–1104, 1320–1340, 924–970.

[310] Id. at 724–725, inter alia.

[311] Ibid.

[312] JFK Exhibit F–601, interview of José Aleman, Mar. 12, 1977, V HSCA–JFK hearings, 314.

[313] Ibid.

[314] JFK Exhibit F–602, V HSCA–JFK hearings, 311.

[315] JFK Exhibit F–601, see ref. 312, supra.

[316] JFK Exhibit F–602, see ref. 314, supra.

[317] JFK Exhibit F–603, V HSCA–JFK hearings, 317.

[318] Ibid.

[319] Ibid.

[320] Testimony of José Aleman, Sept. 27, 1978, V HSCA–JFK hearings, 301–324.

[321] Testimony of Santos Trafficante, Sept. 28, 1978, V HSCA–JFK hearings, 373–377.

[322] Ibid.

[323] Ibid.

[324] See JFK document 012007.

[325] Salerno report, par. 85–176.

[326] Ibid.

[327] Id. at 288.

[328] Salerno testimony, p. 386.

[329] Ibid.

[330] HSCA staff review of FBI files on Edward G. Partin (JFK document 012218).

[331] Ibid.

[332] Ibid.

[333] Ibid.

[334] Ibid.

[335] Interview of Edward Grady Partin, July 20, 1978, House Select Committee on Assassinations (JFK document 011314) (hereinafter Partin interview).

[336] Ibid.

[337] See ref. 330, supra.

[338] Ibid.

[339] Ibid.

[340] Ibid.

[341] Ibid.

[342] Partin interview: HSCA staff review of FBI files on Edward G. Partin, supra.

[343] Ibid.

[344] Ibid.

[345] Benjamin C. Bradlee, Conversations with Kennedy (New York: Pocket Books, 1976), pp. 125–126.

[346] Ibid.

[347] Interviews of Walter Sheridan, July 10, 1978 and Aug. 24, 1978 (JFK documents 009777 and 010991); interview of former Labor Department official, July 4, 1978 (JFK document 010423).

[348] Ibid.

[349] HSCA report on organized crime, para. 794–831; IV HSCA–JFK hearings, 497–499.

[350] Ibid.; see also, HSCA report on organized crime, para. 887–907.

[351] Id., HSCA report on organized crime at 814–816, 822–828.

[352] Interview with Walter Sheridan, Oct. 26, 1978 (JFK Document 012184).

[353] "The Warren Commission," staff report, XI appendix to the HSCA–JFK hearings, para. 277; HSCA report on organized crime, 794–795.

[354] Memorandum form Warren Commission General Counsel J. Lee Rankin to Deputy Director Richard M. Helms, March 12, 1964, "Jack Ruby, Activities and Associates."

[355] HSCA report on organized crime, para. 1267; interviews with Allen Dorfman, July 14, 1978 and July 19, 1978 (JFK Documents 009918 and 010043.)

[356] House Select Committee on Assassinations staff review of

FBI and Justice Department files on Frank Chavez; interview with Walter Sheridan July 10, 1978, House Select Committee on Assassinations (JFK Document 009777).

[357] Ibid.

[358] Playboy Magazine, December 1975, pp. 83, 96.

REFERENCES: SECTION C 5a

[1] Testimony of John B. Connally, Sept. 6, 1978, hearings before the Select Committee on Assassinations, 95th Congress, 2d session (Washington, D.C.: U.S. Government Printing Office, 1979), vol. I, p. 11 (hereinafter Connally testimony,—HSCA–JFK hearings, –); see "Politics and Presidential Protection: The Motorcade," staff report, appendix to the hearings before the Select Committee on Assassinations, U.S. House of Representatives, 95th Congress, 2d session (Washington, D.C.: U.S. Government Printing Office, 1979), volume XI, par. 12 (hereinafter staff report, The Motorcade),—appendix to the HSCA–JFK hearings,—.

[2] Id., Connally testimony, at 14–18; id., staff report, The Motorcade, at 13.

[3] Id., staff report, The Motorcade, at 4.

[4] Deposition of Jerry Bruno, Aug. 18, 1978, House Select Committee on Assassinations, p. 27 (JFK Document 014025) (hereinafter Bruno deposition); testimony of Kenneth P. O'Donnell, May 18, 1964, hearings before the President's Commission on the Assassination of President Kennedy (Washington, D.C.: U.S. Government Printing Office, 1965), vol. 7, p. 443 (hereinafter O'Donnell testimony,—Warren Hearings,—); see staff report, The Motorcade, par. 4.

[5] Connally testimony, 28; see staff report, The Motorcade, para. 4.

[6] Staff summary of interview of Frank Erwin, July 29, 1978, House Select Committee on Assassinations, p. 10 (JFK Document 010696); see staff report, The Motorcade, para. 4.

[7] See Connally testimony, p. 28.

[8] Bruno deposition, p. 31.

[9] Id. at 39–42; see staff report, The Motorcade, para. 34.

[10] Testimony of Forrest V. Sorrels, May 7, 1964, VII Warren hearings, pp. 334–335 (hereinafter Sorrels testimony). See Bruno deposition, p. 35.

[11] Id., Bruno deposition, at 31–32; Jerry Bruno diary entries, Oct. 31, 1963, p. 7 (JFK Document 011337); O'Donnell testimony, p. 443.

[12] See Connally testimony, p. 51; see also Bruno deposition, p. 49.

[13] Ibid., Bruno deposition, p. 49; see Sorrels testimony, p. 337; see also Connally testimony.

[14] O'Donnell testimony, p. 443; Jerry Bruno diary entries, supra ref. 11, p. 9; interview of Winston G. Lawson, Apr. 21, 1978, House Select Committee on Assassinations, p. 5 (JFK Document 007066); see staff report, The Motorcade, pars. 45–46.

[15] Deposition of Bill Moyers, Aug. 16, 1978, House Select Committee on Assassinations, p. 23 (JFK Document 014018); deposition of Elizabeth F. Harris, Aug. 16, 1978, House Select Committee on Assassinations, p. 14 (JFK Document 013152).

[16] Id., deposition of Elizabeth F. Harris, at 28.

712

[17] Report of the President's Commission on the Assassination of President Kennedy (Washington, D.C.: U.S. Government Printing Office, 1964), p. 2 (hereinafter Warren report).

[18] See staff report, The Motorcade, para. 46, 48, 52, 58.

[19] See e.g., preliminary special Dallas report No. 3 (interview with Lee Harvey Oswald by Captain Will Fritz), Nov. 29, 1963, p. 7 (JFK Document 013921); testimony of Joseph M. Smith, July 23, 1964, VII Warren hearings, 535; testimony of D. V. Harkness, Apr. 9, 1964, VI Warren hearings, 312.

[20] See e.g., testimony of Ronald B. Fischer, Apr. 1, 1964, VI Warren hearings, 196; testimony of Seymour Weitzman, VII Warren hearings, p. 106.

[21] See e.g., J. G. Shaw and L. Harris, "Cover-up—The Government Conspiracy To Conceal the Facts about the Public Execution of John Kennedy" (privately published, 1976), pp. 98–99.

[22] See, e.g., interview of Seymour Weitzman, July 25, 1978, House Select Committee on Assassinations, p. 1 (JFK Document 006646); interview of D. V. Harkness, Feb. 7, 1978, House Select Committee on Assassinations, p. 1 (JFK Document 005884); outside contact report with Ronald Fischer, July 18, 1978, House Select Committee on Assassinations, p. 2 (JFK Document 010560).

[23] Interview of Thomas Lem Johns, Aug. 8, 1978, House Select Committee on Assassinations, pp. 2–3 (JFK Document 010695).

[24] Interview of Forrest V. Sorrels, Mar. 15, 1978, House Select Committee on Assassinations, pp. 4–5 (JFK Document 007062).

[25] See e.g., interview of Seymour Weitzman, July 25, 1978 House Select Committee on Assassinations, p. 1 (JFK Document 006646); interview of D. V. Harkness, Feb. 7, 1978, p. 1, House Select Committee on Assassinations (JFK Document 005884); outside contact report with Ronald Fischer, July 18, 1978, House Select Committee on Assassinations, p. 2 (JFK Document 010560).

[26] CE 768, IV Warren hearings, 320, 322, 346.

[27] Testimony of Joseph M. Smith, VII, Warren hearings, p. 535; see interview of Joseph M. Smith. Feb. 8, 1978, House Select Committee on Assassinations (JFK Document 005886).

[28] Outside contact report with James P. Hosty, Nov. 8, 1977, House Select Committee on Assassinations (JFK Document 006291).

[29] Deposition of Frank Leslie Ellsworth, Jr., July 25, 1978, House Select Committee on Assassinations, pp. 91–92 (JFK Document 010903).

[30] Executive session testimony of Robert E. Jones, Apr. 20, 1978, House Select Committee on Assassinations, pp. 1–25 (JFK Classified Document 014643).

[31] Letter from Department of Defense to House Select Committee on Assassinations, June 22, 1978, p. 6 (JFK Document 009383).

REFERENCES: SECTION C 5b

[1] "Report of the President's Commission on the Assassination of President Kennedy," (Washington, D.C.: U.S. Government Printing Office, 1964), p. 327 (hereinafter Warren report).

[2] See FBI retrieval, preliminary draft of affidavits (JFK Document 011943).

[3] Warren report, p. 327.

[4] R. S. Anson, "They've Killed the President—The Search for

713

the Murders of John F. Kennedy" (New York: Bantam Books, 1975), pp. 42, 48, 154–156, 165–166, 180–189; P. D. Scott, P. L. Hoch, and R. Stetler, eds., "The Assassination: Dallas and Beyond" (New York: Vintage Books, 1976), pp. 466–468.

[5] "The Investigation of the Assassination of President John F. Kennedy: Performance of the Intelligence Agencies," Book V, Final Report of the Select Committee To Study Governmental Operations with Respect to Intelligence Activities, U.S. Senate, 94th Congress, 2d Session (Washington, D.C.: U.S. Government Printing Office, 1976), pp. 95–97 (hereinafter Book V).

[6] Harold Feldman, "Oswald and the FBI," The Nation, Jan. 27, 1964, p. 86; Joseph C. Goulden, "Ruby Posed As TV Camerman's Helper to Get at Oswald," The Philadelphia Inquirer, Dec. 8, 1963, p. 22, col. 1; Lonnie Hudkins, "Oswald Rumored As Informant for U.S.," Houston Post, Jan. 1, 1964, p. 1.

[7] Interview of Alonzo Hudkins, Mar. 15, 1978, House Select Committee on Assassinations (JFK Document 007998).

[8] Ibid.; interview of Joseph Goulden, Mar. 15, 1978, House Select Committee on Assassinations (JFK Document 006452).

[9] Warren report, p. 327.

[10] Warren Commission Document 205.

[11] Executive session testimony of a special agent of the FBI, Nov. 9, 1977, House Select Committee on Assassinations, p. 101 (classified JFK Document 014666).

[12] Id. at 119–128, 137–138.

[13] Id. at 107, 120–121.

[14] Executive session testimony of a special agent of the FBI, Nov. 10, 1977, House Select Committee on Assassinations, pp. 8, 16 (JFK Classified Document 014637).

[15] Id. at 26, 32.

[16] Warren Commission Document 205.

[17] Ibid.

[18] Ibid.; executive session testimony of a special agent of the FBI ref. 14, p. 19.

[19] Id. at 23.

[20] Warren Commission Document 205.

[21] FBI report to the House Select Committee on Assassinations re inquiry concerning pages 696 of FBI Dallas Division report of special agent of the FBI, dated Dec. 23, 1963, July 12, 1978, pp. 9, 16 (JFK Document 010154) (page 696 of Warren Commission Document 205 corresponded with page 25 of the notebook report contained therein).

[22] Ibid.

[23] Id. at 10–11.

[24] Id. at 11–12.

[25] Id. 16–17.

[26] Id. at 18–39.

[27] Hosty deposition, p. 5.

[28] Id. at 7.

[29] Id. at 34

[30] Ibid.

[31] Id. at 34–35.

[32] Ibid.

[33] Id. at 36.

[34] Id. at 37–38.

[35] Commission exhibit 823, hearings of the President's . Com-

mission on the Assassination of President Kennedy (Washington, D.C.: U.S. Government Printing Office, 1964) (hereinafter 17 Warren hearings, 728); vol. 17, CE 824, Warren hearings 736 (exhibit 824); vol. 26, p. 143 (exhibit 2758).

[36] Administrative coversheets to 1962 FBI field report (JFK Document 006032).

[37] Interview of John Fain, June 25, 1978, House Select Committee on Assassinations (JFK Document 009973) (hereinafter Fain interview).

[38] See CE 825 XVII Warren hearings, 741–752.

[39] Fain interview.

[40] Interview of B. Tom Carter, Dec. 6, 1978, House Select Committee on Assassinations (JFK Document 013542).

[41] Fain interview.

[42] Interview of Arnold J. Brown, Dec. 20, 1978, House Select Committee on Assassinations (JFK Document 013922).

[43] Interview of Harry G. Maynor, Mar. 5, 1978, House Select Committee on Assassinations (JFK Document 006901) (hereinafter Maynor interview); see ref. 38 supra.

[44] Interview of Milton Kaack, Dec. 7, 1978, House Select Committee on Assassinations (JFK Document 013674).

[45] CE 826, XVII Warren hearings, 758–762.

[46] Deposition of William S. Walter, Mar. 23, 1978, House Select Committee on Assassinations, pp. 3–6, 55–58 (JFK Document 006847) (hereinafter Walter deposition).

[47] See ref. 38 supra.

[48] Interview of John L. Quigley, Mar. 12, 1978, House Select Committee on Assassinations (JFK Document 009914).

[49] Walter deposition, pp. 7–9.

[50] Ibid.

[51] Id. at 25–26.

[52] Id. at 30–36.

[53] Id., exhibits 85–86.

[54] Id., exhibit 84.

[55] Id. at 38.

[56] Outside contact report with Sharon Covert, Mar. 6, 1978, House Select Committee on Assassinations (JFK Document 006032).

[57] Maynor interview.

[58] Deposition of Orest Pena, June 23, 1978, House Select Committee on Assassinations, p. 5 (JFK Document 010136) (hereinafter Pena deposition).

[59] Id. at pp. 11–13, 16–18.

[60] Id. at 10, 18–20.

[61] Executive session testimony of Warren C. deBrueys, May 31, 1978, House Select Committee on Assassinations, pp. 28–30 (JFK Classified Document 014716).

[62] Id. at 8–9.

[63] Id. at 32–33.

[64] Id. at 68–69.

[65] Pena deposition, pp. 9–10, 12, 15–16, 21–22, 27–28.

[66] Deposition of Adrian Alba, May 5, 1978, House Select Committee on Assassinations, p. 5 (JFK Document 009964) (hereinafter Alba deposition).

[67] Id. at 10–12, 20–30.

[68] Testimony of Adrian Alba, Apr. 6, 1964, X Warren hearings, pp. 219–229.

[69] Alba deposition, pp. 21, 24–25.

[70] Interview of Adrian Alba, Feb. 14, 1978, House Select Committee on Assassinations, pp. 1–2 (JFK Document 005961).

[71] FBI memorandum from Cartha DeLoach to Mr. Mohr, Apr. 30, 1964, House Select Committee on Assassinations (JFK Document 013858).

[72] Interview of Will Hayden Griffin, Mar. 14, 1978, House Select Committee on Assassinations, p. 1 (JFK Document 009916) (hereinafter Griffin interview).

[73] See ref. 38 supra.

[74] Interview of J. Gordon Shanklin, June 26, 1978, House Select Committee on Assassinations, p. 2 (JFK Document 009746) (hereinafter Shanklin interview).

[75] Hosty deposition, pp. 6–9, 34, 54, 61–65.

[76] Ibid.

[77] Id. at 64–65.

[78] Shanklin interview, p. 4.

[79] Interview of Will Hayden Griffin, Dec. 6, 1978, House Select Committee on Assassinations (JFK Document 013543).

[80] Book V.

[81] Id. at 96.

[82] Id. at 97; Hosty deposition, p. 45.

[83] Shanklin interview, book V.

[84] Hosty deposition, pp. 43–50.

[85] Ibid.

REFERENCESS SECTION C 5c

[1] Testimony of John A. McCone, May 14, 1964, hearings before the President's Commission on the Assassination of President Kennedy (Washington, D.C.: U.S. Government Printing Office, 1964), vol. 5, pp. 120–121 (hereinafter Warren hearings).

[2] Testimony of Richard M. Helms, May 14, 1964, hearings before the President's Commission on the Assassination of President Kennedy (Washington, D.C.: U.S. Government Printing Office, 1964), vol. 5, pp. 120–121 (hereinafter Warren hearings).

[3] See, e.g., classified deposition of CIA employee, June 27, 1978, House Select Committee on Assassinations, pp. 29, 32 (JFK Classified Document 014863); classified deposition of CIA employee, May 17, 1978, House Select Committee on Assassinations, pp. 31–34 (JFK Classified Document 014731); classified deposition of CIA employee, Oct. 5, 1978, House Select Committee on Assassinations, p. 156 (JFK Classified Document 014720); but see also classified deposition of CIA employee, June 29, 1978, House Select Committee on Assassinations (JFK Classified Document 014725); and classified deposition of CIA employee, July 18, 1978, House Select Committee on Assassinations, pp. 209–210 (JFK Classified Document 014718).

[4] See letter from Chairman Louis Stokes to Adm. Stansfield Turner, Jan. 27, 1978, House Select Committee on Assassinations (JFK Document 004889).

[5] Letter from Acting Director Frank C. Carlucci to the House Select Committee on Assassinations, Mar. 23, 1978 (JFK Document 006837).

[6] Classified staff summary of interviews with J. Maury and D.

Murphy, June 14, 1978, House Select Committee on Assassinations (JFK Classified Document 014844).

[7] Classified staff summary of interviews with Soviet Russia Division CIA personnel, Dec. 22, 1978, House Select Committee on Assassinations (JFK Document 014845).

[8] Ibid.

[9] Ibid.

[10] Ibid.

[11] Executive session testimony of James Wilcott, Mar. 22, 1978, House Select Committee on Assassinations, pp. 6–8 (JFK Document 014672).

[12] Id. at 11–13.

[13] Ibid.

[14] Id. at 8–12.

[15] Id. at 13–19.

[16] Id. at 38–39.

[17] Id. at 13.

[18] Classified staff summary re the Wilcott allegation, Nov. 1, 1978, House Select Committee on Assassinations, p. 6 (JFK Classified Document 014843).

[19] Ibid.

[20] Id. at 6–7.

[21] Ibid.

[22] Id. at 6.

[23] Id. at 4–7.

[24] Ibid.

[25] Ibid.

[26] Testimony of Richard H. Helms, Sept. 22, 1978, Hearings before the Select Committee on Assassinations (Washington, D.C.: U.S. Government Printing Office, 1979), vol. IV, pp. 185–188 (hereinafter Helms testimony—HSCA–JFK hearings,—); see JFK exhibit F–523, IV HSCA–JFK hearings, 206.

[27] Classified deposition of a CIA employee, June 27, 1978, House Select Committee on Assassinations, p. 5 (JFK Classified Document 014863).

[28] Ibid.

[29] See classified staff summary re opening of Oswald's 201 file, Dec. 15, 1978, House Select Committee on Assassinations (Classified JFK Document 014839); classified deposition of CIA employee, June 27, 1978, House Select Committee on Assassinations, p. 48 (Classified JFK Document 014863).

[30] Helms testimony, pp. 189–191.

[31] CE 910, XVIII Warren hearings, 115.

[32] Classified staff summary re opening of Oswald's 201 file, supra ref. 29, pp. 1–3; see CE 917–918, XVIII Warren hearings, 115–116.

[33] Ibid.; Classified deposition of a CIA employee, July 27, 1978, House Select Committee on Assassinations, p. 48 (JFK Classified Document 014863); Helms testimony, p. 186.

[34] See text accompanying ref. 26, supra.

[35] Classified staff summary re opening of Oswald's 201 file, supra ref. 29, p. 8; CIA classified summary responding to HSCA requests for explanations, Mar. 20, 1979, p. 4226 (JFK Classified Document 015018).

[36] Id. at 14.

[37] Id. at 15.

[38] See CE 931–933, XVIII Warren hearings, 131–135.

[39] See JFK exhibit F–523, IV HSCA–JFK hearings, 206.

[40] Classified staff summary re opening of Oswald's 201 file, supra ref. 29, p. 17; deposition of CIA employee, May 17, 1978, House Select Committee on Assassinations (JFK Classified Document 014731); classified staff interview of CIA employee, Mar. 31, 1978, House Select Committee on Assassinations (JFK Classified Document 000077).

[41] Classified staff summary re opening of Oswald's 201 file, supra ref. 29, p. 19.

[42] Id. at 21.

[43] Id. at pp. 21–23.

[44] See JFK exhibit F–523, IV HSCA–JFK hearings, 406.

[45] See, e.g., classified deposition of a CIA employee, July 17, 1978, House Select Committee on Assassinations, pp. 109–112 (JFK Classified Document 014718).

[46] See, e.g. Helms testimony, pp. 188–189.

[47] Classified staff summary re 201 opening sheet "AG," Dec. 10, 1978, House Select Committee on Assassinations, p. 2 (JFK Classified Document 014836); CIA classified summary responding to HSCA requests for explanations, Mar. 20, 1979 (JFK Classified Document 015018).

[48] Classified deposition of a CIA employee, Oct. 10, 1978, House Select Committee on Assassinations, pp. 15–18 (JFK Classified Document 014717).

[49] Ibid.

[50] Ibid.

[51] JFK exhibit F–523, IV HSCA–JFK hearings, 406.

[52] Classified deposition of a CIA employee, May 17, 1978, House Select Committee on Assassinations, pp. 50–51 (JFK Classified Document 014731).

[53] Classified deposition of a CIA employee, June 27, 1978, House Select Committee on Assassinations, pp. 81–83 (JFK Classified Document 014863).

[54] See JFK exhibit F–524, IV HSCA–JFK hearings, 207.

[55] Ibid.

[56] Ibid.

[57] Classified CIA summary responding to HSCA request for explanations, Mar. 20, 1979, House Select Committee on Assassinations (JFK Classified Document 015018).

[58] Classified deposition of a CIA employee, Oct. 10, 1978, House Select Committee on Assassinations, p. 48 (JFK Classified Document 014717).

[59] Ibid.

[60] Id. at 46–47.

[61] Id. at 45–47.

[62] See JFK exhibit F–522, IV HSCA–JFK hearings, 197; ref. 30 supra.

[63] Helms testimony, p. 189; see "Alleged Assassination Plots Involving Foreign Leaders," an Interim Report of the Select Committee to Study Governmental Operations with Respect to Intelligence Activities, U.S. Senate, 94th Cong., 1st sess. (Washington, D.C.: U.S. Government Printing Office, 1975), p. 83.

[64] Warern Commission Document 871.

[65] Ibid.; see Report to the President by the Commission on

Central Intelligence Activities within the United States (Washington, D.C.: U.S. Government Printing Office, June 1975), pp. 209–210 (hereinafter Rockefeller Commission Report).

[66] Interview of Monica Kramer, Feb. 2, 1978, House Select Committee on Assassinations (JFK Document 005881); interview of Rita Newman, Feb. 2, 1978, House Select Committee on Assassinations (JFK Document 014431).

[67] CIA FOIA Document No. 614–261, p. 1; classified staff summary re Minsk photograph, Nov. 18, 1978, House Select Committee on Assassinations, p. 3 (JFK Classified Document 014840).

[68] Id., Minsk photograph, at 7–12.

[69] Ibid.

[70] Ibid.

[71] Classified staff summary re HT-Lingual program, Dec. 1, 1978, House Select Committee on Assassinations, p. 1 (JFK Classified Document 001438); see letter from George Bush to Subcommittee on Government Information and Operations, Aug. 10, 1976.

[72] Ibid.; see Central Intelligence Exemption in the Privacy Act of 1974, Mar. 15, 1975, June 25, 1975, hearings before a subcommittee of the Committee on Government Operations, 94th Congress, 1st session (Washington, D.C.; U.S. Government Printing Office, 1975), p. 153.

[73] Classified staff summary re HT-Lingual program, supra ref. 71, pp. 12–13.

[74] Classified deposition of a CIA employee, July 20, 1978, House Select Committee on Assassinations, p. 40 (JFK Classified Document 014735).

[75] Classified staff summary re HT-Lingual index cards, Jan. 15, 1979, House Select Committee on Assassinations, p. 1 (JFK Classified Document 014848).

[76] Ibid.

[77] Id. at 1–2.

[78] Ibid.

[79] Ibid.; classified deposition of a CIA employee, July 18, 1978. House Select Committee on Assassination, p. 24 (JFK Classified Document 014718).

[80] Classified deposition of a CIA employee, Oct. 10, 1978, House Select Committee on Assassinations, p. 20 (JFK Classified Document 014717).

[81] Classified staff summary re HT-Lingual index cards, supra ref. 75, pp. 2–3.

[82] Id. at 3; see classified CIA summary responding to HSCA requests for explanations, Mar. 20, 1979, pp. 4218–4219 (JFK Classified Document 015018).

[83] Rockefeller Commission Report, p. 2.

[84] Classified staff summary re HT-Lingual index cards, supra ref. 75, pp. 5–7.

[85] Id. at 6; see classified CIA summary responding to HSCA requests for explanations, Mar. 20, 1979, pp. 4218–4219 (JFK Classified Document 015018).

[86] Ibid.

[87] Ibid.

[88] See ref. 1 supra.

[89] See, e.g., Rockefeller Commission Report, pp. 209–210.

[90] See R. S. Anson, "They've Killed The President—The Search for the Murderers of John F. Kennedy" (New York: Bantam

Books, 1975), pp. 172–173; see, generally, CIA FOIA Document 961–927AG.

[91] See JFK Exhibit F–526, IV HSCA–JFK hearings, 209.

[92] Classified staff summary re CIA Oswald memorandum, Dec. 13, 1978, House Select Committee on Assassinations (JFK Classified Document 014847); classified staff summary re absence of Oswald debriefing by CIA, Jan. 22, 1979, House Select Committee on Assassinations (JFK Classified Document 014841).

[93] Ibid.

[94] Classified staff summary re absence of Oswald debriefing by CIA, supra ref. 92.

[95] Classified staff summary of interviews with Soviet Russia division CIA personnel, supra ref. 7.

[96] Classified staff summary re absence of Oswald debriefing by CIA, supra ref. 92, p. 13.

[97] Id. at 13–14.

[98] Ibid.

[99] Id. at 16; see classified CIA summary responding to HSCA requests for explanations, Mar. 20, 1979, pp. 4196–4198 (JFK Classified Document 015018).

[100] Classified staff summary re absence of Oswald debriefing by CIA, supra ref. 92, pp. 17–23.

[101] See Warren Report, pp. 434–440.

[102] CE908, 910, 917, XVIII Warren hearings, 98, 105, 115.

[103] CE931, XVIII Warren hearings.

[104] CE932, XVIII Warren hearings, 134.

[105] CE971, XVIII Warren hearings, 368.

[106] CE252, XVIII Warren hearings, 706.

[107] CE935, XVIII Warren hearings, 138, and CE909, p. 104.

[108] Ibid.

[109] CE823 and 824, XVII Warren hearings, 729, 736.

[110] Letter from Robert L. Keuch, Department of Justice, to House Select Committee on Assassinations, Mar. 10, 1978 (JFK Document 006235).

[111] Letter from Robert L. Keuch, Department of Justice, to House Select Committee on Assassinations, May 9, 1978 (JFK Document 008241).

[112] CE 2677, XXVI Warren hearings, 32.

[113] Warren Report, p. 258; see also CE946, XVIII Warren hearings, 162.

[114] Interview of Lewis Hopkins, Oct. 25, 1978, House Select Committee on Assassinations (JFK Document 012886).

[115] Ibid.

[116] Ibid.

[117] Letter from J. Lee Rankin to Richard M. Helms, May 25, 1964 (JFK Document 003782); see generally CE2676, XXVI Warren hearings, 32.

[118] Ibid.

[119] Classified staff summary re Oswald's Soviet visa, Dec. 20, 1978, House Select Committee on Assassinations, p. 3 (JFK Classified Document 014742).

[120] Ibid., p. 4.

[121] Ibid., pp. 4–5.

[122] Ibid.

[123] Warren Report, p. 691.

[124] See R. Anson, supra ref. 90, pp. 135–137; Bernard H.

Fensterwald, "Assassination of JFK—By Coincidence or Conspiracy?" (New York: Kensington Publishing Corp., 1977), pp. 566–567; P. D. Scott, P. L. Hoch, R. Stetler, eds., "The Assassinations: Dallas and Beyond" (New York: Vintage Books, 1976) hereinafter "The Assassination").

[125] Deposition of John A. McVickar, May 5, 1978, House Select Committee on Assassinations, pp. 18–19 (JFK Document 008487).

[126] Id. at 3–4, 22.

[127] Executive session testimony of Priscilla Johnson McMillan, Apr. 20, 1978, House Select Committee on Assassinations, pp. 10–17 (JFK Classified Document 014676).

[128] Id. at 16.

[129] Id. at 16–18.

[130] Id. at 8–9, 61–62, 83–89.

[131] Id. (exhibit 95).

[132] Id. at 83–89.

[133] Id. at 31–34.

[134] Classified summary of interviews with Soviet Russia division CIA personnel, supra ref. 7.

[135] Deposition of Richard E. Snyder, June 1, 1978, House Select Committee on Assassinations, pp. 18–19 (JFK Document 009264); CE909, 914 and 919, XVIII Warren hearings, 100–117.

[136] See, e.g., ref. 107 and accompanying text supra.

[137] See, e.g., Bernard H. Fensterwald, supra ref. 112, pp. 221–222; M. Canfield and A. Weberman, "Coup d'Etat in America—The CIA and the Assassination of John F. Kennedy" (New York: The Third Press, 1975), p. 25.

[138] Deposition of Richard S. Snyder, supra ref. 123, pp. 5–7, 11–13.

[139] Id. at 13, 53–54.

[140] Letters from the HSCA to Scott Breckinridge, CIA, June 8, 1978 and July 6, 1978 (JFK Classified Document 014971).

[141] CIA FOIA Document 210–623, CE528.

[142] Classified CIA summary responding to HSCA requests for explanations, Mar. 20, 1979, pp. 4200–4207 (JFK Classified Document 015018).

[143] Outside contact report with William Vance, Jan. 9, 1979, House Select Committee on Assassinations (JFK Document 014140).

[144] Interview with Dennis Flynn, June 16, 1978, House Select Committee on Assassinations (JFK Document 009534).

[145] Interview of Dr. Alexis H. Davison, Jan. 10, 1978, House Select Committee on Assassinations (JFK Document 004686).

[146] CE18, I Warren hearings, 50.

[147] CE994, XVIII Warren hearings, 616.

[148] See, e.g., Bernard H. Fensterwald, supra ref. 112, pp. 219–221.

[149] Davison interview, supra ref. 132; see also interview of Mrs. Hal (Natalia Alekseevna) Davison, Jan. 10, 1978, House Select Committee on Assassinations (JFK Document 004685).

[150] Davison interview, supra ref. 132.

[151] Ibid.

[152] Ibid.

[153] Ibid.

[154] Classified staff summary of interviews with Soviet Russia division CIA personnel, supra ref. 7.

[155] For a detailed discussion of George de Mohrenschildt and his relationship to Oswald, see "George de Mohrenschildt," staff report, appendix to the hearings before the Select Committe on Assassinations, 95th Congress, 2d session (Washington, D.C.: U.S. Government Printing Office, 1979), vol. XII, par. 3 (hereinafter de Mohrenschildt report—appendix to the HSCA–JFK hearings, No.—).

[156] Testimony of George de Mohrenschildt, Apr. 23, 1964, IX Warren hearings, 235.

[157] Ibid.

[158] Ibid.

[159] See, e.g., Bernard H. Fensterwald, supra ref. 112, p. 212–214.

[160] Interview of James W. Moore, Mar. 14, 1978, House Select Committee on Assassinations (JFK Document 014893); see ref. 65 and accompanying text supra.

[161] De Mohrenschildt report, para. 33–34.

[162] Id. at 35–36.

[163] De Mohrenschildt testimony, supra ref. 143, p. 212.

[164] Outside contact report with Roger Gabrielson, CIA, Feb. 28, 1978, House Select Committee on Assassinations (JFK Document 014969).

[165] De Mohrenschildt report, para. 44–45.

[166] Id. at 46–51.

[167] Warren Commission Document 75, p. 588.

[168] Ibid.; deposition of William G. Gaudet, June 15, 1978, House Select Committee on Assassinations, pp. 13, 20 (JFK Document 010347) (hereinafter Gaudet deposition).

[169] Warren Report, pp. 299–311.

[170] Warren Commission Document 75, p. 588.

[171] CE2123, XXIV Warren hearings, 663–691.

[172] Gaudet deposition pp. 7–8.

[173] Id. at 9.

[174] CIA memorandum for Special Assistant to Deputy Director of Operations, subject: William George Gaudet, reference: CIA review staff memorandum 78–0110 dated Jan. 20, 1976 requesting information on William George Gaudet.

[175] Gaudet deposition, pp. 21–22.

[176] Id. at 10–13.

[177] Id. at 11–12.

[178] Id. at 13–14.

[179] See R. Anson, supra ref. 90, pp. 156–159; The Assassinations, supra ref. 112, p. 474.

[180] Folson Exhibit 1, XIX Warren hearings, 665; see also CE 1961, XXIII Warren hearings, 795–796.

[181] Testimony of John E. Donovan, May 5, 1964, VIII Warren hearings, 298.

[182] Outside contact report, file review of Department of Defense files of Robert Royce Augg, Richard Call, Nelson Delgado, John E. Donovan and Zack Stout, Dec. 1, 1978, House Select Committee on Assassinations (JFK Document 013677).

[183] CE 1385, XXII Warren hearings, 705; see also CE 2682, XXVI Warren hearings, 41.

[184] Department of Defense unit diaries, Dec. 5, 1978, House Select Committee on Assassinations (JFK Document 013485).

[185] Id. at 183, 184.

[186] Letter and attachments from Department of Defense to House Select Committee on Assassinations, June 22, 1978, p. 20 (JFK Document 009383).

[187] Folson Exhibit 1, XIX Warren hearings, 658, 704.

[188] Unit diaries, supra ref. 187, pp. 351, 356.

[189] Folsom Exhibit 1, XIX Warren hearings, 668.

[190] Warren report, p. 684.

[191] CE 918, XVIII Warren hearings, 116.

[192] CE 196, XXIII Warren hearings, 797. See also unit diaries, supra ref. 187.

[193] Folsom Exhibit 1, XIX Warren hearings, 724–727.

[194] CE 1114, XXII Warren hearings, 79.

[195] Letter and enclosures from Department of Defense to the House Select Committee on Assassinations, Mar. 28, 1978, p. 2 (JFK Document 006729).

[196] Folsom Exhibit 1, XIX Warren hearings, 723–741.

[197] Id. at 724–727.

[198] Id. at 728–733.

[199] Letter and attachments from American Red Cross to the House Select Committee on Assassinations, Dec. 8, 1978 (JFK Document 013586).

[200] Id. at 23.

[201] Id. at 21–23.

[202] Ibid.

[203] Folsom Exhibit 1, XIX Warren hearings, 740, 743.

[204] Id. at 727.

[205] Id. at 723–727.

[206] Outside contact report with Colonel William A. Cloman, Jr., Aug. 2, 1978, House Select Committee on Assassinations (JFK Document 013595); outside contact report with Lt. Gen. Charles H. Hayes, Dec. 10, 1978, House Select Committee on Assassinations (JFK Document 013593).

[207] Outside contact report with Lt. Col. B. J. Kozak, Aug. 2, 1978, House Select Committee on Assassinations (JFK Document 013594.

[208] Executive session testimony of Col. Robert E. Jones, Apr. 20, 1978, House Select Committee on Assassinations, pp. 18–19, 42 (JFK classified document 014677).

[209] See R. Anson, supra ref. 90, pp. 283–285; P. L. Hoch, "Army Intelligence, A. J. Hidell, and the FBI," Oct. 8, 1977 (JFK Document 002538).

[210] Testimony of Col. Robert E. Jones, supra ref. 211, pp. 6–7.

[211] Id. at 8.

[212] Id. at 8, 11.

[213] Id. at 8–9.

[214] Id. at 19.

[215] Id. at 17.

[216] Id. at 17–18.

[217] Id. at 18–19, 42.

[218] Id. at 20, 42.

[219] Id. at 10, 21.

[220] Id. at 25, 34–37, 49–50.

[221] Id. at 10, 50.

[222] Id. at 20–21, 24.

[223] Id. at 19–20.

[224] Id. at 21.

[225] Id. at 22–24.

[226] Letter and attachments from Department of Defense to the House Select Committee on Assassinations, July 26, 1978, House Select Committee on Assassinations (JFK Document 010247); JFK classified document 000103.

[227] Letter from Department of Defense to the House Select Committee on Assassinations, Sept. 13, 1978, House Select Committee on Assassinations (JFK Document 011964).

[228] Letter and attachments from Department of Defense to the House Select Committee on Assassinations, June 22, 1978, House Select Committee on Assassinations (JFK Document 009383).

[229] Ibid.

[230] Classified staff study: Lee Harvey Oswald, the CIA and Mexico City, Dec. 15, 1978, House Select Committee on Assassinations, pp. 72–81, 124–183 (JFK classified documents 014972–014975).

[231] Ibid. for extensive detail.

[232] Ibid.

REFERENCES: SECTION D 1

[1] Neal, Harry Edward, The Story of the Secret Service (New York: Grosset and Dunlap, 1971), p. 15 (hereinafter Neal, Secret Service).

[2] Id. at 18–19.

[3] Id. at 17.

[4] Id. at 20.

[5] Id. at 22.

[6] Id. at 22–23.

[7] Id. at 23.

[8] Id. at 23–24.

[9] Congressional Research Service, Library of Congress, "The Authority of the Secret Service To Protect the President," Mar. 29, 1978, pp. 1–2 (JFK Document 006845).

[10] Neal, Secret Service, p. 24.

[11] Ibid.

[12] Ibid.

[13] Congressional Research Service, Library of Congress, "Presidential Protection and the Secret Service," Oct. 27, 1976, p. 2 (JFK Document 004157).

[14] Neal, Secret Service, pp. 24–25.

[15] Id. at 25.

[16] Id. at 70.

[17] Id. at 80–82.

[18] Manchester, William, The Death of a President, (New York: Penguin Books, 1977), p. 37 (hereinafter, Manchester, The Death * * *).

[19] Id. at 35, 37, 131.

[20] Id. at 121.

[21] Manchester, The Death * * *.

[22] Letter from Chief of Secret Service James J. Rowley to J. Lee Rankin, General Counsel, Warren Commission, June 9, 1964, p. 2 (contained in JFK Document 012719, title of cover document: U.S. Secret Service—Protective Information Guidelines.

[23] Id. at 2.

[24] Executive session testimony of Robert I. Bouck, Nov. 16,

1977, House Select Committee on Assassinations, pp. 7–33 (JFK Document 014669).

[25] See ref. 22, supra.

[26] See Manchester, "The Death * * *," p. 36. For the extent of the Secret Service's reliance on the Dallas Police Department for manpower, see Lawrence Exhibit, hearings before the President's Commission on the Assassination of President Kennedy (Washington, D.C.: U.S. Government Printing Office, 1964), volume 20, pp. 489–496 (hereinafter—Warren hearings,—). For an assessment of manpower availability in relation to security needs, see testimony of Perdue W. Lawrence, July 24, 1964, VII Warren hearings, 583–584, 585.

[27] U.S. Department of the Treasury Order 173–3, October 29, 1965 (Washington, D.C.: U.S. Government Printing Office, 1965) (JFK Document 014978); see also ref. 24, supra, for Bouck's statements on 1963 PRS procedures for analyzing and disseminating threat data.

[28] Secret Service case files, June 5, 1978 (JFK Document 008894); see also Secret Service file re plot to kidnap Caroline Kennedy, May 10, 1978 (JFK Document 008219).

[29] Report of the President's Commission on the Assassination of President Kennedy (Washington, D.C.: U.S. Government Printing Office, 1964), pp. 463, 465 (hereinafter Warren report).

[30] Id. at 443, 461, 464.

[31] Id. at 445–446, 465.

[32] Id. at 463, 465.

[33] Id. at 447, 466.

[34] Id. at 449.

[35] Id. at 461, 443.

[36] Secret Service files review, Mar. 24, 1978 (JFK Document 006852).

[37] Secret Service case file summaries, June 5, 1978 (JFK Document 008894).

[38] Unpublished staff report on Secret Service files, Oct. 19, 1978, House Select Committee on Assassinations (JFK Document 014588).

[39] Commission Exhibit CE 767, XVII Warren hearings, 593; CE 768, p. 601.

[40] Secret Service final survey report, Dec. 11, 1963, p. 7 (JFK Document 006183).

[41] Secret Service supplemental survey report, Mar. 29, 1963, pp. 1, 2 (JFK Document 014457).

[42] Secret Service supplemental survey report, Nov. 5, 1963, p. 1 (JFK Document 004867).

[43] JFK Exhibit F–450, II HSCA–JFK hearings, 447; Secret Service supplemental report, Dec. 30, 1963, pp. 1–6 (JFK Document 006183); see also Secret Service memoranda of Nov. 12, 1963, and Nov. 14, 1963, Miami field office (JFK Document 008814).

[44] For the article written by the Miami journalist, see Christensen, Dan, "JFK, King: The Dade County Links," in Miami magazine, September 1976, p. 25 (JFK Document 003360). Christensen could not document his assertion therein that a planned motorcade was canceled, other than to say that "many people" believed that a cancellation had taken place; see outside contact report with Dan Christensen, Feb. 2, 1978, House Select Committee on Assassinations (JFK Document 004434). Persons cited by

Christensen as sources for corroboration of his version of the cancellation did not recall that his version was correct; see outside contact report with the Honorable Seymour Gelber, Feb. 2, 1978, House Select Committee on Assassinations (JFK Document 005533); outside contact report with Attorney Richard Gerstein, Feb. 2, 1978, House Select Committee on Assassinations (JFK Document 013458); interview of Miami field office Special Agent Talmadge Bailey, Mar. 1, 1978, House Select Committee on Assassinations, pp. 5–7 (JFK Document 009385); and interview of Miami field office Special Agent Robert J. Jamison, Feb. 28, 1978, House Select Committee on Assassinations, p. 2 (JFK Document 007063).

[45] Secret Service master file on threat subject Thomas Arthur Vallee (JFK Document 009581); Secret Service master file on Joseph A. Milteer (JFK Document 008814).

[46] Interview of Secret Service Special Agent David Grant, Mar. 1, 1978, House Select Committee on Assassinations, p. 1 (JFK Document 005890).

[47] Interview of Presidential Appointments Secretary Pierre Salinger, May 30, 1978, House Select Committee on Assassinations, p. 1 (JFK Document 009690).

[48] Black, Edwin, "The Plot to Kill JFK in Chicago, Nov. 2, 1963," Chicago Independent, November 1975, pp. 7–8 (JFK Document 013589).

[49] Secret Service master file on Thomas Arthur Vallee, memorandum of Nov. 6, 1963, p. 2 (JFK Document 008581).

[50] Interview of 1963 Secret Service Special Agent Edward Tucker, Jan. 19, 1978, House Select Committee on Assassinations, pp. 1–2 (JFK Document 004828).

[51] Interview of Chicago Police Officer Lawrence Coffey, Jan. 28, 1978, House Select Committee on Assassinations, p. 2 (JFK Document 004831).

[52] See attachment to interview of Chicago Police Department, executive assistant to superintendent of police, Richard Brzeck. 18, 1978, House Select Committee on Assassinations, entitled "Arrest Report, Chicago Police Department" (JFK Document 004824).

[53] Secret Service master file on Thomas Arthur Vallee, memorandum of Nov. 6, 1963 by Special Agent Thomas D. Strong, House Select Committee on Assassinations, p. 2 (JFK Document 005881).

[54] Id. at 1.

[55] Id. at 1; see also interview of former Chicago Police Officer Lawrence Coffey, Jan. 17, 1978, House Select Committee on Assassinations, p. 1 (JFK Document 004831).

[56] Interview of former Chicago Police Officer Lawrence Coffey, Jan. 25, 1978, House Select Committee on Assassinations, p. 2 (JFK Document 004831).

[57] See ref. 42 supra.

[58] For indication of receipt by PRS, see deposition of Secret Service Chief James Rowley, Aug. 24, 1978, House Select Committee on Assassinations, Book II, pp. 8, 64 (JFK Document 014026); a report from a field office addressed to the Office of the Chief would be delivered either to PRS or to the Office of the Head of Protective Operations, Ed Wiley. For a copy of the Nov. 6, 1963 memorandum of Chicago field office Special Agent Strong, see ref. 55, supra; it concerned the Service's final preassassination contact with Vallee and

was addressed to the Office of the Chief. For indication of non-receipt by the agents coordinating preparations in Dallas, see testimony of Forrest Sorrels, VII Warren hearings, 338–339; see also interview of SAIC, Dallas Field Office, Forrest V. Sorrels, Mar. 15, 1978, House Select Committee on Assassinations, p. 3 (JFK Document 0070623; and interview of Secret Service Special Agent Winston G. Lawson, Jan. 31, 1978, House Select Committee on Assassinations, p. 4 (JFK Document 007066).

[59] Letter of Nov. 27, 1963 from ASAIC Maurice G. Martineau, Chicago, to Chief, Secret Service, in Secret Service master file on Thomas Arthur Vallee (JFK Document 008581).

[60] Secret Service report, Columbus, Ohio field office, Dec. 2, 1968 p. 2, in Secret Service master file on Thomas Arthur Vallee (JFK Document 008581).

[61] Interview of former Chicago Field Office Special Agent Abraham W. Bolden, Jan. 19, 1978, House Select Committee on Assassinations, pp. 2–6 (JFK Document 004825).

[62] Id. at 3–4.

[63] Id. at 4.

[64] Id. at 3.

[65] Interviews of Chicago field office ASAIC Maurice G. Martineau, Feb. 1, 1978, House Select Committee on Assassinations (JFK Document 008483); and Chicago Special Agent Conrad Cross, Apr. 14, 1978 (JFK Document 009370); James S. Griffiths, Feb. 1, 1978 (JFK Document 005892); Gary McLeod, May 4, 1978 (JFK Document 007995); Robert Motto, Dec. 30, 1977 (JFK Document 008482); Joseph Noonan, Apr. 13, 1978 (JFK Document 009377); J. Lloyd Stocks, Apr. 12, 1978 (JFK Document 009372); and Edward Tucker, Jan. 19, 1978 (JFK Document 004828). House Select Committee on Assassinations staff also interviewed White House Detail Advance Agent David Grant (see ref. 46, supra), who coordinated security preparations in advance of the President's scheduled Nov. 2, 1963 trip to Chicago. None of these agents provided any corroboration of Bolden's version of the Secret Service investigation of an alleged assassination team.

[66] Interview of Special Agent Robert Motto, Dec. 30, 1977, p. 2 (JFK Document 008482).

[67] Interview of former Special Agent Abraham W. Bolden, Jan. 19, 1978, House Select Committee on Assassinations, pp. 1–7 (JFK Document 004825).

[68] Id. at 5.

[69] The Honorable Seymour Gelber, "Diary of a Southern Prosecutor" (unpublished manuscript), pp. 414–415, 427–428 (hereinafter Gelber, Diary); see also the preface of this document, entitled "Summary" (JFK Document 002826).

[70] Interview of former Miami Police Officer Charles H. Sapp, February 25, 1978, House Select Committee on Assassinations, p. 2 (JFK Document 009419); see also interview of former Miami field office SAIC John Marshall, February 2, 1978, House Select Committee on Assassinations, p. 1 (JFK Document 007063); and Secret Service report, Miami field office, November 12, 1963, p. 1 (JFK Document 008814).

[71] Id., Gelber, "Diary," at 426–427.

[72] Interview of former Miami SAIC John Marshall, February 2, 1978, House Select Committee on Assassinations, p. 3 (JFK Document 007063).

[73] Secret Service report, Miami field office, November 12, 1963, p. 2 (JFK Document 008814).

[74] Secret Service report, Miami field office, November 26, 1963, p. 2 (JFK Document 008814).

[75] Ibid.

[76] Ibid.

[77] Id. at 1–2.

[78] Secret Service final survey report, Miami field office, December 30, 1963, p. 7 (JFK Document 006183).

[79] Interview of Special Agent Winston G. Lawson, January 31, 1978, House Select Committee on Assassinations, pp. 4, 9 (JFK Document 007066); see also testimony of Winston G. Lawson, April 23, 1964, IV Warren hearings, 321 (hereinafter Lawson testimony); see also interview of former SAIC, Dallas, Forrest V. Sorrels, March 15, 1978. House Select Committee on Assassinations, p. 3 (JFK Document 007062); and testimony of Forrest V. Sorrels, VII Warren hearings, 338–339.

[80] Gelber, "Diary," p. 433.

[81] See ref. 79, supra, to Winston G. Lawson.

[82] See ref. 24, supra, pp. 32, 58; see also deposition of Thomas Kelley, August 18, 1978, House Select Committee on Assassinations, pp. 5, 54–56, 59–60, 64–65, 71–75 (JFK Document 014586).

[83] Testimony of Forrest V. Sorrels, Apr. 7, 1964, VII Warren hearings, 338.

[84] Manchester, "The Death . . ." p. 121; see also testimony of Kenneth O'Donnell, May 18, 1964, VII Warren hearings, 456.

[85] Warren Report, pp. 447, 448. There is a discrepancy between Dallas Field Office SAIC Forrest V. Sorrels' 1963 protective policy toward traditionally used, publicly known parade routes and the policy of Secret Service Chief Rowley on that subject as set forth on p. 447 of the report. Sorrels testified before the Warren Commission that Main Street in Dallas was always used for parades (VII, Warren hearings, 337), yet Rowley stated to the Commission that, under such circumstances, extra caution was required in inspecting and securing buildings along the route.

[86] Id. at 448.

[87] Lawson testimony, pp. 327, 330.

[88] Warren Report, p. 448, note 173.

[89] Lawson testimony, p. 328; testimony of Perdue W. Lawrence, July 24, 1964, VII Warren hearings, 580; see also statement of Perdue W. Lawrence to House Select Committee on Assassinations, Nov. 4, 1977, pp. 2–3 (JFK Document 003102).

[90] Outside contact report with Mrs. Ina Davidson, Aug. 11, 1978, House Select Committee on Assassinations (JFK Document 010677); see also outside contact report re Ms. Mary Vallee, Mar. 9, 1978, House Select Committee on Assassinations, p. 1 (JFK Document 014490).

[91] Outside contact report with Leonora Reddehase, Apr. 14, 1978, House Select Committee on Assassinations (JFK Document 007494).

[92] One or more representatives from each of the committee staff specialized investigative groups was consulted. None of Milteer's associates was identified by staff members as an associate of Jack Ruby, Lee Harvey Oswald or any of their associates.

[93] Memorandum of conversation between Bernard Fensterwald and Bill Somersett, June 5, 1978, p. 1 (JFK Document 014488).

[94] JFK Exhibit F–124, I HSCA–JFK hearings, 116.

[95] Testimony of Clyde Snow, July 25, 1978, HSCA–JFK hearings, IV 379–382.

[96] Abraham Zapruder film, for example, c. frames 160–313, JFK Exhibits F–211 to F–255, I HSCA–JFK hearings, 71–92; Orville Nix film, for example, JFK Exhibit F–267, I HSCA–JFK hearings, 110, and JFK Document 011265; and James Altgens photograph, JFK Exhibit F–559, IV HSCA–JFK hearings, 372.

[97] U.S. Secret Service School, "Principles of Protection of the President and Foreign Dignitaries" (training manual in outline form) (publisher not stated, 1954), p. 48 on chauffeurs, especially (2) (a); pp. 51–53 on mounting and dismounting moving automobiles; pp. 53–57 on general requirements relating to protection in automobiles, especially p. 55, section (12) on the lead car (JFK Document 006730).

[98] Unpublished staff report on the Secret Service training facility at Beltsville, Md., Sept. 29, 1978, House Select Committee on Assassinations, pp. 1–2 (JFK Document 012888), HSCA staff observed current members of the White House and Vice Presidential details react protectively in a variety of simulated attack situations. The task difficulty, degree of physical danger to the agents during the simulations, and realism of the 1978 training contrasts sharply with the "on-the-job" training which was standard in 1963; see also interview of Winston G. Lawson, Jan. 31, 1978, House Select Committee on Assassinations, p. 2 (JFK Document 007066); and testimony of James J. Rowley, Sept. 19, 1978, III HSCA-JFK hearings, 395.

[99] Testimony of Roy H. Kellerman, Mar. 9, 1964, II Warren Hearings, 104. For the standard applicable in 1963, see U.S. Secret Service School, "Principles of Protection of the President and Foreign Dignitaries" (training manual in outline form) (publisher not stated, 1954), p. 98 at (g). Shielding a protectee with an agent's body during gunfire attacks is described as a "last resort" measure.

[100] Testimony of Secret Service Inspector Thomas Kelley, Sept. 19, 1978, III HSCA–JFK hearings, 328; see also Lawson testimony, p. 321.

[101] Interview of William R. Greer, Feb. 28, 1978, House Select Committee on Assassinations, pp. 2, 8 (JFK Document 014059); see also testimony of Thomas Kelley, Sept. 9, 1978, III HSCA–JFK Hearings, 328.

[102] Interview of William R. Greer, Feb. 28, 1978, House Select Committee on Assassinations, p. 5 (JFK Document 014059); see also U.S. Secret Service, "Principles of Protection of the President and Other Dignitaries" (training manual in outline form) (publisher not stated, 1954), p. 50 at (2) (a): "The Driver of the President's car should be alert for dangers and be able to take instant action when instructed or otherwise made aware of an emergency." (JFK Document 006730).

[103] Report No. 3947, Analysis of Recorded Sounds Relating to the Assassination of President John F. Kennedy, Bolt Beranek and Newman Inc., Appendix to the Hearings before the Select Committee on Assassinations, U.S. House of Representatives, 95th Congress, 2d Session (Washington, D.C.: U.S. Government Printing Office, 1979, vol. VIII (hereinafter BBN report, — appendix to the HSCA–JFK hearings, —).

[104] Testimony of Clinton J. Hill, Mar. 9, 1964, II Warren Hearings, 136–137; see also Lawson testimony, p. 338.

[105] Warren Report, p. 445. The Warren Commission emphasized the lack of adequate definition, within the Secret Service, of the functions and responsibilities of the advance agents who arrive at the Presidential destination days or weeks beforehand in order to coordinate all protective aspects of the Presidential trip. Too much discretion was left to the individual advance agent, whose superiors ordinarily gave him only general instructions and no checklist.

[106] Testimony of Clinton J. Hill, Mar. 9, 1964, II Warren Hearings, 138–140.

[107] Interview of Thomas Lem Johns, Aug. 8, 1978, House Select Committee on Assassinations, pp. 2, 3 (JFK Document 010695).

[108] JFK Exhibit F–559, IV HSCA–JFK hearings, 372, see also statement of Chief Counsel G. Robert Blakey at testimony of James J. Rowley, Sept. 19, 1978, III HSCA–JFK hearings, 397.

[109] Warren Report, p. 450.

[110] Ibid.

[111] Ibid.

[112] Testimony of Thomas J. Kelley, Sept. 1978, III HSCA–JFK hearings, 327, 328.

[113] See refs. 96 and 108, supra.

[114] Testimony of former Secret Service Chief James Rowley, Sept. 19, 1978, III HSCA–JFK Hearings, p. 392.

[115] Letter to ASAIC (Chicago), Maurice G. Martineau to Deputy Chief Paul Paterni, Nov. 27, 1963, p. 1 (JFK Document 007601).

[116] Secret Service memorandum, Chicago Field Office, Dec. 3, 1963, p. 1 (JFK Document 003668).

[117] Id. at 1, 2.

[118] Id. at 1, 2.

[119] Id. at 4.

[120] Id. at 4–5, 6.

[121] Id. at 2, 3, 4, 7.

[122] Id. at 2–3.

[123] Id. at 8 (distribution list, bottom left).

[124] Id. at 3.

[125] Secret Service memorandum, Miami Field Office, Dec. 13, 1963, pp. 1–3 (JFK Document 003842); see also deposition of Edward Tucker, July 18, 1978. House Select Committee on Assassinations, pp. 38–39 (JFK Document 010902).

[126] Secret Service memorandum, Chicago Field Office, Dec. 3, 1963, p. 7 (JFK Document 003668).

[127] Id. at 6. A later phase of the Secret Service's investigation of Paulino Sierra is recorded in Secret Service memorandum, Chicago Field Office, Dec. 19, 1963, p. 5 (JFK Document 008429).

[128] See, generally, "Anti-Castro Organizations and Activities and Lee Harvey Oswald in New Orleans," staff report, X Appendix to the HSCA–JFK hearings, para. 342–388.

[129] Id. at 350.

[130] Id. at 351, 365.

[131] Id. at 376.

[132] Id. at 379.

[133] Secret Service memorandum, Chicago Field Office, Dec. 3, 1963, p. 7 (JFK Document 003668).

[134] Id. at 4.

[135] Letter from J. Edgar Hoover, Director, FBI, to Hon. James

730

B. Rhoads, Dec. 28, 1970, pp. 1–2 (FBI–JFK File 109060, section 1744 at 6979).

[136] Ibid.; see also deposition of Chicago Field Office SA Edward Tucker, Aug. 22, 1978, House Select Committee on Assassinations, pp. 42–43 (JFK Document 010902).

[137] Secret Service memorandum, Chicago Field Office, Dec. 3, 1963, p. 5 (JFK Document 003668).

[138] Secret Service memorandum, Chicago Field Office, Dec. 19, 1963, p. 6 (JFK Document 008429); see also deposition of Joseph Noonan, July 14, 1978, House Select Committee on Assassinations, pp. 21–23 (JFK Document 013260).

[139] Testimony of James Rowley, Sept. 19, 1978, III HSCA–JFK Hearings, 392.

[140] Ibid.

[141] Id. at 329.

[142] Id. at 453.

REFERENCES: SECTION D 2

[1] Staff analysis of FBI file on the investigation of the assassination of President John F. Kennedy, House Select Committee on Assassinations; "The Warren Commission," staff report, XI appendix to the hearings before the Select Committee on Assassinations, U.S. House of Representatives, 95th Congress, 2d session (Washington, D.C.: U.S. Government Printing Office, 1979), vol. XI, par. 4–21, 201–203 (hereinafter W. C. report).

[2] Ibid.

[3] Staff analysis of Warren Commission records, documents, hearings and exhibits, House Select Committee on Assassinations; WC report, para. 1–21.

[4] Testimony of Nicholas deB. Katzenbach, Sept. 21, 1978, hearings before the Select Committee on Assassinations, U.S. House of Representatives, 95th Congress, 2d session (Washington, D.C.: U.S. Government Printing Office, (1979), vol., pp. 644–645.

[5] Ibid.

REFERENCES: SECTION D 3

[1] Congressional Research Service, Library of Congress, "The History of the Federal Bureau of Investigation," prepared for the committee.

[2] Ibid.

[3] Ibid.

[4] Ibid.

[5] Ibid.

[6] Ibid.

[7] Ibid.

[8] Ibid.

[9] Ibid.

[10] Staff analysis of FBI file on the investigation of the assassination of President John F. Kennedy, House Select Committee on Assassinations (hereinafter FBI–JFK assassination file); staff analysis of Warren Commission records, documents, hearing, and exhibits, House Select Committee on Assassinations; "The Warren Commission," staff report, appendix to the hearings before the Select Com-

731

mittee on Assassinations, U.S. House of Representatives, 95th Congress, 2d session (Washington, D.C.: U.S. Government Printing Office, 1979), volume XI, para. 44–70, 113–277 (hereinafter WC report,—appendix to the HSCA–JFK hearings,—).

[11] Ibid.

[12] Ibid., FBI–JFK assassination file; staff analysis of testimony before the Senate Select Committee To Study Governmental Operations With Respect to Intelligence Activities by FBI supervisors of the investigation of the Kennedy assassination, House Select Committee on Assassinations (hereinafter FBI supervisors testimony); WC report, para. 113–277.

[13] FBI–JFK assassination file; testimony of James Malley, September 20, 1978, hearings before the Select Committee on Assassinations, U.S. House of Representatives, 95th Congress, 2d session (Washington, D.C.: U.S. Government Printing Office, 1979), volume III, pp. 462–512 (hereinafter Malley testimony;—HSCA–JFK hearings,—).

[14] Ibid., FBI–JFK assassination file.

[15] Ibid.

[16] Ibid.

[17] Ibid.

[18] FBI supervisors testimony; Malley testimony, pp. 462–512.

[19] Ibid.

[20] Senate Select Committee on Intelligence staff interview with former Assistant FBI Director William C. Sullivan, April 21, 1976; House Government Information and Individual Rights Subcommittee staff interview with former Assistant FBI Director William C. Sullivan, May 2, 1976.

[21] FBI–JFK assassination file; FBI supervisors testimony; Malley testimony, pp. 462–512.

[22] Ibid.

[23] Testimony of former Assistant FBI Director Alex Rosen before the Senate Select Committee To Study Governmental Operations With Respect to Intelligence Operations, April 30, 1976.

[24] Ibid.

[25] FBI–JFK assassination file; FBI supervisors testimony.

[26] Ibid.

[27] Interview of former Assistant FBI Director Courtney Evans, August 24, 1978, House Select Committee on Assassinations; deposition of former Assistant FBI Director Courtney Evans, September 6, 1978, House Select Committee on Assassinations.

[28] Ibid.

[29] FBI–JFK assassination file; FBI supervisors testimony.

[30] Ibid.

[31] Ibid., FBI–JFK assassination file; "The Investigation of the Assassination of President John F. Kennedy: Performance of the Intelligence Agencies," book V, Senate Select Committee To Study Governmental Operations With Respect to Intelligence Activities, 94th Congress, 2d session (Washington, D.C.: U.S. Government Printing Office, 1975), pp. 32–43 (hereinafter book V).

[32] Ibid.

[33] Id. at 6.

[34] FBI–JFK assassination file; WC report, para. 113–227; Malley testimony, pp. 466–476.

[35] Ibid.

[36] Ibid.

[37] Ibid.
[38] Ibid.
[39] FBI–JFK assassination file; WC report, para. 163–205.
[40] Staff analysis of the activities of FBI Special Agent James P. Hosty in connection with the investigation of Lee Harvey Oswald, House Select Committee on Assassinations; deposition of James P. Hosty, August 25, 1978, House Select Committee on Assassinations; book V, pp. 95–97.
[41] Ibid.
[42] Ibid.
[43] Ibid.
[44] Deposition of J. Lee Rankin, Aug. 17, 1978, House Select Committee on Assassinations; for a copy of the deposition, see "The Warren Commission," staff report, XI appendix to the HSCA–JFK hearings, 54.
[45] Testimony of former FBI Inspector James Gale, September 20, 1978, III HSCA–JFK hearings, 513–557; FBI–JFK assassination file; book V, pp. 53–56, 87–93.
[46] Ibid.
[47] Ibid.
[48] Ibid.
[49] FBI–JFK assassination file.
[50] "The Evolution and Implications of CIA-Sponsored Assassination Conspiracies Against Fidel Castro," X appendix to the HSCA–JFK hearings. 80–86.
[51] "B. Carlos Marcello" in "Organized Crime: Staff and Consultant Reports," IX appendix to the HSCA–JFK hearings.
[52] Ibid.

REFERENCES: SECTION D 4

[1] For a detailed history of the CIA and an explanation of the development of its organizational structures, see "Supplementary Detailed Staff Report on Foreign and Military Intelligence," book IV, "Final Report of the Senate Select Committee To Study Governmental Operations With Respect to Intelligence Activities," 94th Congress, 2d session, Senate Rept. No. 94–755 (Washington, D.C.: U.S. Government Printing Office, 1976).
[2] Walter Trohan, "Donovan Proposes Super Spy System for Post War New Deal," Washington Times Herald, Feb. 19, 1945.
[3] Testimony of Allen Dulles, Apr. 25, 1947, hearings before the committee on S. 758, National Defense Establishment (Unification of Armed Services), Senate Committee on Armed Services, 80th Congress, 1st session (Washington, D.C.: U.S. Government Printing Office, 1947), pp. 525–527.
[4] Report to the President by the Commission on Central Intelligence Activities within the United States (Washington, D.C.: U.S. Government Printing Office, June 1975).
[5] Letter from Acting Director Frank C. Carlucci to House Select Committee on Assassinations, Mar. 23, 1978 (JFK Document 096837).
[6] Letter from Chairman Louis Stokes to Admiral Stansfield Turner, DCI, Jan. 27, 1978 (JFK Document 004889).
[7] Classified staff study, "Lee Harvey Oswald, the CIA and Mexico City," Dec. 15, 1978, House Select Committee on Assassinations, pp. 122–150 (JFK Documents 014972–75) (hereinafter "LHO,

the CIA and Mexico City"); see executive session testimony of CIA employee, Apr. 13, 1978, House Select Committee on Assassinations, pp. 103–107 (JFK Classified Document 014739A); see generally deposition of CIA employee, Apr. 28, 1978, p. 33 (JFK Classified Document 014733); deposition of CIA employee, May 16, 1978, House Select Committee on Assassinations, p. 35 (JFK Classified Document 014728); deposition of CIA employee, May 18, 1978, House Select Committee on Assassinations, p. 28 (JFK Classified Document 014730).

[8] "LHO, the CIA and Mexico City," pp. 115–122; see deposition of CIA employee, May 18, 1978, House Select Committee on Assassinations, pp. 33–34 (JFK Classified Document 014730); deposition of CIA employee, Apr. 28, 1978, House Select Committee on Assassinations, pp. 84–89 (JFK Classified Document 014732); deposition of CIA employee, Apr. 28, 1978, House Select Committee on Assassinations, p. 46 (JFK Classified Document 014733).

[9] "LHO, the CIA and Mexico City," pp. 142–143, 160–161; see deposition of CIA employee, Apr. 19, 1978. House Select Committee on Assassinations, p. 29 (JFK Classified Document 014737); deposition of a CIA employee, May 17, 1978, House Select Committee on Assassinations, pp. 78–79 (JFK Classified Document 014731); deposition of a CIA employee, Apr. 28, 1978, House Select Committee on Assassinations (JFK Classified Document 014733); deposition of a CIA employee, May 18, 1978, House Select Committee on Assassinations, p. 37 (JFK Classified Document 014730).

[10] "LHO, the CIA and Mexico City," pp. 124–177.

[11] Report of the President's Commission on the Assassination of President Kennedy (Washington, D.C.: U.S. Government Printing Office, 1964), p. 304 (hereinafter Warren report); see P. D. Scott, P. L. Hoch and R. Stetler, eds., "The Assassination: Dallas and Beyond" (New York: Vintage Books, 1976), p. 452.

[12] "LHO, CIA and Mexico City," p. 137.

[13] Id. at 137–141.

[14] Letterhead memorandum from J. Edgar Hoover, FBI, to James J. Rowley, Secret Service, Nov. 23, 1963 (JFK Classified Document 000169).

[15] FBI materials delivered to the House Select Committee on Assassinations, Nov. 30, 1978 (JFK Classified Document 000169).

[16] Interview of J. Gordon Shanklin, June 26, 1978, House Select Committee on Assassinations (JFK Document 009746).

[17] Interview of John Fain, June 25, 1978, House Select Committee on Assassinations (JFK Document 009973; outside contact report with James P. Hosty, House Select Committee on Assassinations (JFK Document 015035); interview of Arnold J. Brown, Dec. 20, 1978, House Select Committee on Assassinations (JFK Document 013922); interview of B. Tom Carter, Dec. 6, 1978, House Select Committee on Assassinations (JFK Document 013542).

[18] "LHO, the CIA and Mexico City," pp. 180–184.

[19] Testimony of Eusebio Azcue Lopez, Sept. 18, 1978, hearings before the House Select Committee on Assassinations, 95th Congress, 2d Session (Washington, D.C.: U.S. Government Printing Office, 1979), volume III, pp. 127–139 (hereinafter Lopez testimony,— HSCA–JFK hearings,—; see interviews of Eusebio Azcue Lopez, April 1, 1978, Aug. 25, 1978, House Select Committee on Assassinations (JFK Document 007005).

734

[20] JFK Exhibit F–440A, III HSCA–JFK hearings, 25, 69–70, 102–105.

[21] "LHO, the CIA and Mexico City," pp. 206–234.

[22] Id. at 246–247.

[23] Ibid.; see JFK Exhibit F–440A, III HSCA–JFK hearings, 49–50.

[24["LHO, the CIA and Mexico City," pp. 76–78, 240–247.

[25] JFK Exhibit F–438, III HSCA–JKF Hearings, 317–319.

[26] "LHO, the CIA and Mexico City," pp. 93–114.

[27] Ibid.

[28] III HSCA–JFK hearings, 24–25, 112.

[29] Id. at 69–70.

[30] Id. at 33.

[31] Testimony of Alfredo Mirabal Diaz, Sept. 18, 1978, III HSCA–JFK hearings, 173–175.

[32] Lopez testimony, p. 134.

[33] Testimony of Joseph P. McNally, Sept. 25, 1978, IV HSCA–JFK hearings, 352–353.

[34] "LHO, the CIA and Mexico City," pp. 73–79.

[35] Executive session testimony of Richard M. Helms, Aug. 9, 1978, pp. 10, 17–18 (JFK Classified Document 014719); see generally testimony of Richard M. Helms, Sept. 22, 1978, IV HSCA–JFK hearings, 9–12 (hereinafter Helms testimony).

[36] "The Investigation of the Assassination of President John F. Kennedy: Performance of the Intelligence Agencies," Book V, Final Report of the Senate Select Committee To Study Governmental Operations With Respect to Intelligence Activities, 94th Congress, 2d Session (Washington, D.C.: U.S. Government Printing Office, 1976), pp. 67–76 (hereinafter Book V).

[37] "Analysis of the Support Provided to the Warren Commission by the Central Intelligence Agency," Appendix to the Hearings Before the House Select Committee on Assassinations (Washington, D.C.: U.S. Government Printing Office, 1979), volume XI, pars. 3–11 (hereinafter CIA support of Warren Commission,—Appendix to the HSCA–JFK hearings.—).

[38] Id. at 24–28.

[39] Id. at 28–32.

[40] Id. at 40–43.

[41] Id. at 60; see also para. 44–45.

[42] Id. at 49, 57–59.

[43] Id. at 56; Helms testimony, p. 12; see Book V, p. 70.

[44] CIA support of Warren Commission, para. 63; but see Helms testimony, 121–177.

[45] Book V, pp. 6–7.

[46] Id. at 7.

[47] CIA support of Warren Commission, para. 133–162.

[48] Id. at 69–132.

[49] "LHO, the CIA and Mexico City," pp. 178–183.

[50] CIA support of Warren Commission, para. 88–109.

[51] Id. at 107–108.

[52] Id. at 109.

[53] See ref. 12 and accompanying text, supra.

[54] Ibid.

[55] "LHO, the CIA and Mexico City," p. 179; see CIA support of Warren Commission, para. 122–123.

[56] Id. CIA support of Warren Commission, at 127–132.

[57] Id. at 116–117.

[58] Id. at 119.

[59] See ref. 6 and accompanying text, supra.

[60] CIA support of Warren Commission, para. 112–115.

REFERENCES: D 5

[1] "Report of the President's Commission on the Assassination of President Kennedy" (Washington, D.C.: U.S. Government Printing Office, 1964), p. ix (hereinafter Warren report).

[2] Id. at x–xi.

[3] Ibid.

[4] "The Warren Commission," staff report, appendix to the hearings before the Select Committee on Assassinations, U.S. House of Representatives, 95th Congress, 2d session (Washington, D.C.: U.S. Government Printing Office, 1979), volume XI, para. 113–276 (hereinafter WC report,—appendix to the HSCA–JFK hearings.—).

[5] Ibid.

[6] Id. at 113–187.

[7] Id. at 113–276.

[8] Ibid.

[9] Id. at 113–187.

[10] WC report, para. 113–276; staff analysis of Warren Commission records, documents, hearings and exhibits, House Select Committee on Assassinations (hereinafter analysis of Warren Commission records).

[11] WC report, para. 1–112.

[12] Ibid.

[13] Ibid.

[14] Ibid.

[15] WC report, para. 265–277.

[16] Ibid.

[17] Analysis of Warren Commission records, para. 1–112.

[18] Ibid.

[19] Analysis of Warren Commission records; "The Investigation of the Assassination of President John F. Kennedy: Performance of the Intelligence Agencies," Book V, Senate Select Committee To Study Governmental Operations With Respect to Intelligence Activities (Washington, D.C.: U.S. Government Printing Office, 1976) (hereinafter Book V); WC report, para. 1–112.

[20] Id., WC report at 265–277.

[21] Ibid.

[22] Id. at 271.

[23] Id. at 277.

[24] Staff analysis of Warren Commission records; id., WC report, at 1–277.

[25] Ibid.

[26] Testimony of Burt W. Griffin, Sept. 28, 1978, hearings before the Select Committee on Assassinations (Washington, D.C.: U.S. Government Printing Office, 1979), Volume V, p. 478 (hereinafter Griffin testimony,—HSCA–JFK hearings,—).

[27] WC report, para. 44–77; Griffin testimony, p. 478.

[28] Id., Griffin testimony, at 478.

[29] Staff analysis of Warren Commission records.
[30] Ibid.
[31] Warren report, p. 18.
[32] Id. at 24.

II. FINDINGS IN THE ASSASSINATION OF
DR. MARTIN LUTHER KING, JR.

REFERENCES: INTRODUCTION

[1] See generally Congressional Research Service, Library of Congress, "The Civil Rights Movement in the United States: 1955–1970." MLK project No. 1, April 12, 1978, prepared for the House Select Committee on Assassinations.

[2] See generally Congressional Research Service, Library of Congress, "Civil Rights Violence in the United States: 1619–1966," MLK project No. 10, July 7, 1978, prepared for the House Select Committee on Assassinations.

[3] This account of the last month and the last hours of Dr. King's life is, in large part, based on surveys of FBI files and testimony of witnesses, particularly the public testimony of Dr. King's close friend and associate, Dr. Ralph David Abernathy. See testimony of Dr. Ralph D. Abernathy, Aug. 14, 1978, hearings before the Select Committee on Assassinations, U.S. House of Representatives, 95th Congress, 2d session (Washington, D.C.: U.S. Government Printing Office, 1979), volume I, pp. 10–39 (hereinafter Abernathy testimony,—HSCA–MLK hearings,—). See also executive session testimony of Dr. Ralph D. Abernathy, May 23, 1978, House Select Committee on Assassinations (MLK Document 230246); executive session testimony of Rev. Samuel B. Kyles, May 11, 1978, House Select Committee on Assassinations (MLK Document 230247); staff summary of interview with James Lawson, Mar. 15, 1978. House Select Committee on Assassinations (MLK Document 200038); staff summary of interview with Marrell McCollough, Mar. 12, 1978, House Select Committee on Assassinations (MLK Document 200306); and staff summary of interview with Rev. Bernard Lee, May 7, 1977, House Select Committee on Assassinations (MLK Document 090007).

[4] See generally Congressional Research Service, Library of Congress, "Statistics on United States Participation in the Vietnam Conflict," Aug. 15, 1972.

[5] See generally David L. Lewis, King: A Critical Biography (Baltimore: Penguin Books, Inc., 1970), pp. 358-364.

[6] Id. at 358.

[7] Id. at 363.

[8] Carl Greenberg, "Dr. King Asks Johnson Defeat, May Back Another Democrat—Head SCLC Says Both McCarthy and Kennedy Are Competent Men With Good Civil Rights Record," Los Angeles Times, Mar. 17, 1968, p. A3.

[9] Ibid.

[10] See generally Richard N. Billings and John Greenya, Power

to the Public Worker (Washington, D.C.: Robert B. Luce, Inc., 1974), chapter 9, "A Strike for Recognition As a Man," pp. 71–204.

[11] See Thomas BeVier, "King Disappointed in March—He'll Try Again Next Week." Memphis (Tenn.) Commercial Appeal. Mar. 30, 1968, p. A1. According to this article, Dr. King announced at his Mar. 29, 1968, press conference in Memphis that he would return there the following week. He said, "We are going to have a massive nonviolent demonstration . . ." and promised he would not lead a violent march.

REFERENCES: SECTION A

[1] Executive session testimony of Dr. Ralph D. Abernathy, May 23, 1978, House Select Committee on Assassinations, pp. 59–62 (MLK Document 230–246).

[2] Testimony of Dr. Ralph D. Abernathy, Aug. 14, 1978, hearings before the Select Committee on Assassinations, U.S. House of Representatives, 95th Congress, 2d session (Washington, D.C.: U.S. Government Printing Office, 1979), Vol. I, p. 20 (hereinafter Abernathy testimony,—HSCA–MLK hearings,—).

[3] Testimony of Dr. Michael Baden, Aug. 15, 1978, I HSCA–MLK hearings, 48, 49, 54, 62 (hereinafter Baden testimony). See also "Report on the Subject of the Assassination of Dr. Martin Luther King, Jr. by the Forensic Pathology Panel," appendix to the hearings before the Select Committee on Assassinations, U.S. House of Representatives, 95th Congress, 2d session (Washington, D.C.: U.S. Government Printing Office, 1979), XIII, para. 13, 29 (hereinafter autopsy panel report,—appendix to the HSCA–MLK hearings,—).

[4] Id., Baden testimony, at 44, 58; id., autopsy panel report, at 30.

[5] Id., Baden testimony, at 68.

[6] Id. at 60

[7] Id. at 46, 57–59. See also autopsy panel report, at 81.

[8] Id., Baden testimony, at 46, 57; id., autopsy panel report, at 81.

[9] Id., Baden testimony, at 57–58; id., autopsy panel report, at 84.

[10] Id., Baden testimony, at 48, 52, 60; id., autopsy panel report, at 81, 85, 88.

[11] See, e.g., Baden testimony, id. at 59.

[12] See, e.g., testimony of Marrell McCollough, Nov. 20, 1978, VI HSCA–MLK hearings (hereinafter McCollough testimony).

[13] Baden testimony, pp. 47, 59. See also autopsy panel report, p. 128.

[14] Id., Baden testimony, at 59; id., autopsy panel report, at 128.

[15] See generally "Report on the Subject of a Civil Engineering Survey of the Scene of the Assassination of Dr. Martin Luther King, Jr.," XIII appendix to the HSCA–MLK hearings (hereinafter engineering panel report).

[16] See, e.g., McCollough testimony, pp. 418–19.

[17] Engineering panel report, para. 22.

[18] Ibid.

[19] Ibid.

[20] Ibid.

[21] Affidavit of Charles Quitman Stephens, June 13, 1968 (MLK document 080011).

[22] FBI interview of William Anschutz, Apr. 7, 1968 (MLK document 170141).

[23] Designated counsel statement of Charles Q. Stephens, Apr. 14, 1978, House Select Committee on Assassinations (MLK document 210178).

[24] See generally "Charles Q. Stephens: Controversial Eyewitness to the Assassination," staff report, XIV appendix to the HSCA–MLK hearings (hereinafter Stephens staff report).

[25] Interview of Willie Anschutz, July 22, 1977, House Select Committee on Assassinations, pp. 7–8 (MLK document 110009).

[26] McCollough testimony, p. 420.

[27] Interview of Rev. Jesse Jackson by ABC News, Apr. 4, 1968, pp. 4–5 (MLK document 100062). Interview of Ben Branch by the sanitation strike archival project, Aug. 15, 1968, p. 21 (MLK document 010031).

[28] Designated counsel statement of Solomon Jones, Jr. June 23, 1978. House Select Committee on Assassinations (MLK document 270251).

[29] Ibid.

[30] Ibid.

[31] "Report on the Subject of the Examination of Firearm-Related Evidence in the Investigation of Dr. Martin Luther King, Jr. by the Firearms Panel," XIII appendix to the HSCA–MLK hearings, par. 138 (hereinafter firearms panel report).

[32] Testimony of James Earl Ray, Aug. 16, 1978, I HSCA–MLK hearings, 352 (hereinafter Ray testimony, Aug. 16, 1978).

[33] Interview of Donald Wood, Mar. 10, 1977, House Select Committee on Assassinations (MLK document 070038).

[34] MLK exhibit F–35, II HSCA–MLK hearings, 239. See also testimony of James Earl Ray, Aug. 17, 1978, II HSCA–MLK hearings, 40 (hereinafter Ray testimony, Aug. 18, 1978).

[35] Ray testimony, Aug. 17, 1978, pp. 103–104.

[36] Ray testimony, Aug. 16, 1978, p. 352; see also Ray testimony, Aug. 17, 1978, p. 40.

[37] Ray testimony, Aug. 16, 1978, p. 101; see also Ray testimony, Aug. 17, 1978, pp. 61–64.

[38] Ray testimony, Aug. 16, 1978, p. 102.

[39] Interview of Bessie Brewer, Aug. 11, 1977, House Select Committee on Assassinations, pp. 3–4 (MLK Document 120012).

[40] See ref. 23, supra, designated counsel statement of Charles Q. Stephens, pp. 55–57; interview of Bertie Reeves by the Shelby County Public Defender's Office, Feb. 11, 1969 (MLK Document 030115).

[41] Interview of Bernell Finley, July 21, 1977, House Select Committee on Assassinations (MLK Document 110492).

[42] FBI interview of Bernell Finley, Apr. 10, 1968 (MLK Document 170141).

[43] Interview of Guy Warren Canipe, Jr., May 11, 1977, House Select Committee on Assassinations (MLK Document 030156).

[44] FBI interview of Guy Warren Canipe, Jr., Apr. 10, 1968 (MLK Document 170141).

[45] See ref. 43 supra, interview of Canipe.

[46] Interview of Julius Leroy Graham III, Jan. 31, 1978, House Select Committee on Assassinations (MLK Document 300052).

740

[47] Report of laboratory, FBI headquarters to Memphis, Apr. 17, 1968, FBI headquarters Murkin file 44–38861—unrecorded serial.

[48] Ibid. See also Ray testimony, Aug. 16, 1978, p. 92 (where Ray admitted having a radio when he escaped from prison).

[49] See generally "Report on the Subject of Questioned Handwriting Related to the Assassination of Dr. Martin Luther King, Jr.," XIII appendix to the HSCA–MLK hearings (hereinafter handwriting report).

[50] Firearms panel report, para. 108.

[51] Id. at 130.

[52] See FBI interview with Thomas Lau, Apr. 15, 1968, Los Angeles Murkin file 44–1574; FBI interview with Richard Gonzales, Apr. 16, 1968, Los Angeles Murkin file 44–1574.

[53] See MLK exhibit F 25 (interview of James Earl Ray by Dan Rather, Mar. 9, 1977), I HSCA–MLK hearings, 303.

[54] Ray testimony, Aug. 16, 1978, p. 99; see also Ray testimony, Aug. 17, 1978, p. 49.

[55] See MLK exhibit F–52 (change of address card), II HSCA–MLK hearings, pp. 50–51. See also Ray testimony, pp. 49–51.

[56] Ray testimony, Aug. 17, 1978, p. 53.

[57] Id. at 55, 61.

[58] Ray testimony, Aug. 16, 1978, pp. 100, 352.

[59] Id. at 352; see also Ray testimony, Aug. 17, 1978, p. 61.

[60] Ray testimony, Aug. 16, 1978, p. 101. See also Ray testimony, Aug. 17, 1978, pp. 62–63.

[61] See ref. 3, supra executive session testimony of Dr. Ralph D. Abernathy, May 23, 1978, House Select Committee on Assassinations (MLK Document 230246), pp. 51–63.

[62] Ray testimony, Aug. 17, 1978, p. 61.

[64] See stipulation No. 30 of MLK exhibit F–79 (proposed stipulation as to material facts in *State of Tennessee* v. *James Earl Ray*), III HSCA–MLK hearings, 49.

[65] MLK exhibit F–42 (interview of James Garner, Jan. 23, 1978, House Select Committee on Assassinations), II HSCA–MLK hearings, 20. Garner could not recall the date of payment, but stated that it was on Sunday, 1 week from the day Ray registered. Ray registered at Garner's on Mar. 23, 1968.

[66] Ray testimony, Aug. 17, 1978, pp. 64–65.

[67] MLK exhibit F–59 (laundry receipt, Piedmont Laundry), II HSCA–MLK hearings, 65.

[68] Testimony of Annie Estelle Peters, Aug. 18, 1978, III HSCA–MLK hearings, 302–307, 508–512. See also MLK exhibit F–106A (Piedmont Laundry ledger book), III HSCA–MLK hearings, 308ff.

[69] MLK exhibit F–105 (Apr. 1, 1968 articles in Atlanta Journal and Atlanta Constitution), II HSCA–MLK hearings, 96–97.

[70] Ray testimony, Aug. 16, 1978, p. 101.

[71] Id. at 102, 354. See also Ray testimony, Aug. 17, 1978, p. 101.

[72] Executive session testimony of Samuel B. Kyles, May 11, 1978, II HSCA–MLK hearings, 55–56.

[73] See MLK exhibit F–61 (Commercial Appeal), II HSCA–MLK hearings, 100. See also Ray testimony, Aug. 16, 1978, p. 355.

[74] See "Report on the Subject of the Analysis of Fingerprint Evidence Related to the Assassination of Dr. Martin Luther King, Jr.," by the fingerprint panel, XIII Appendix to the HSCA–MLK hearings, para. 14 (hereinafter fingerprint panel report).

[75] See MLK exhibit F–15C (view of Lorraine Motel from

bathroom window at rear of Bessie Brewer's roominghouse), I HSCA–MLK hearings, 81.

[76] Ray testimony, Aug. 17, 1978, p. 101.

[77] See ref. 39, supra, interview of Bessie Brewer.

[78] Ray testimony, Aug. 16, 1978, p. 105.

[79] Interview of Ralph Carpenter, Oct. 7, 1977, House Select Committee on Assassinations, p. 2 (MLK Document 140131).

[80] See MLK exhibit F–15B (photograph of inside of room 5–B), I HSCA–MLK hearings, 80.

[81] Ray testimony, Aug. 16, 1978, pp. 106–107. The general outlines of Ray's testimony are corroborated by extrinsic evidence. First, the FBI located the Mustang in the parking lot of the Capitol Homes housing project in Atlanta. Second, records at Piedmont Laundry show Ray picked up laundry on April 5, 1968. The committee found no records to establish how Ray traveled from Atlanta to Canada; nevertheless, he did check into an apartment in Toronto on April 8, 1968—4 days after the assassination.

[82] Id. at 106; see also Ray testimony, Aug. 17, 1978, pp. 106–107.

[83] Ray testimony, Aug. 17, 1978, pp. 106–107.

[84] Ray testimony, Aug. 16, 1978, p. 106.

[85] Interview of James Earl Ray, March 28, 1977, IX appendix to the HSCA–MLK hearings, 79–80 (hereinafter Ray interview, March 28, 1977).

[86] Id. at 60–84.

[87] Ray testimony, Aug. 16, 1978, pp. 106–107.

[88] Ray interview, March 28, 1977, pp. 92–93.

[89] Id. at 118.

[90] Ray testimony, Aug. 17, 1978, p. 101.

[91] Ray interview, March 28, 1977, pp. 78, 79.

[92] Ray testimony, Aug. 16, 1978, p. 106. See also Ray testimony, Aug. 17, 1978, pp. 106–107.

[93] Ray testimony, Aug. 16, 1978, p. 164.

[94] William Bradford Huie, "He Slew the Dreamer" (New York: DeLacorte Press, Inc., 1968) (hereinafter Huie, "He Slew the Dreamer").

[95] Ray testimony, Aug. 16, 1978, p. 351.

[96] Id. at 164.

[97] Ray testimony, Aug. 17, 1978, p. 108.

[98] Testimony of Coy Dean Cowden, Aug. 18, 1978, III HSCA–MLK hearings, 533.

[99] Ibid.

[100] Testimony of Ernestine Johnson, Aug. 18, 1978, III HSCA–MLK hearings, 547–549.

[101] Testimony of Larce McFall, Aug. 18, 1978, III HSCA–MLK hearings, 552.

[102] Ray testimony, Aug. 16, 1978, p. 356.

[103] William Bradford Huie, "The Story of James Earl Ray and the Plot to Assassinate Martin Luther King." Look, Nov. 12, 1968, p. 104.

[104] Huie, "He Slew the Dreamer," p. 37.

[105] Ray testimony, Aug. 16, 1978, p. 358.

[106] See MLK exhibit F–25, I HSCA–MLK hearings, 235 (interview of James Earl Ray by Dan Rather, Mar. 9, 1977.)

[107] "Playboy Interview: James Earl Ray," Playboy, September 1977, p. 78 (MLK document 230356).

[108] Ray testimony, Aug. 16, 1978, p. 358.

[109] Id. at 94.

[110] Id. at 95.

[111] Ibid.

[112] Id. at 96. It was not clear from Ray's testimony whether Raoul entered Cherpes' boardinghouse or merely left Ray outside.

[113] Id. at 97–98.

[114] Interview of James Earl Ray, May 3, 1977, X app. to the HSCA–MLK hearings, 117 (hereinafter Ray interview, May 3, 1977).

[115] Ray testimony, Aug. 16, 1978, pp. 97–98.

[116] Id. at 99.

[117] See generally Ray testimony, Aug. 16, 1978, p. 100. Ray has told the committee in interviews that he met Raoul at the Starlite the day after a stop in Selma, Ala. A registration card at the Flamingo Motel in Selma establishes that Ray was there at least on the night of Mar. 22, 1968. (See MLK exhibit F–53, II HSCA–MLK hearings, 55.)

[118] Ray testimony, Aug. 16, 1978, p. 100.

[119] Ibid.

[120] Ibid.

[121] See "Compilation of the Statements of James Earl Ray," staff report in III appendix to the HSCA–MLK hearings, p. 218 (ref. 10) (hereinafter staff report on Ray statements).

[122] Ray testimony, Aug. 17, 1978, p. 13.

[123] Ray testimony, Aug. 16, 1978, pp. 101, 102.

[124] Id. at 102.

[125] Ray told the committee in interviews and testimony that he received three separate telephone numbers from Raoul. See, e.g., Ray testimony, Aug. 16, 1978, p. 98. Often, by his story, Ray did not talk directly to Raoul, but rather to a middleman. See, e.g., Ray testimony, Aug. 16, 1978, p. 99.

[126] Staff report on Ray statements, p. 192.

[127] Ray testimony, Aug. 17, 1978, p. 30.

[128] "The 20,000 Words," XII app. to the HSCA–MLK hearings (hereinafter "20,000 Words").

[129] Ibid.

[130] Interview with James Earl Ray, Apr. 29, 1977, X appendix to the HSCA–MLK hearings, 135 (hereinafter Ray interview, Apr. 29, 1977).

[131] Ray testimony, Aug. 16, 1978, p. 100.

[132] Ray interview, Apr. 29, 1977, pp. 135–137.

[133] Ray testimony, Aug. 16, 1978, p. 100.

[134] Ray interview, Apr. 29, 1977, pp. 150–154.

[135] Id. at 144–145.

[136] Ray testimony, Aug. 17, 1978, p. 30.

[137] Affidavit of U. L. Baker, Nov. 15, 1978, House Select Committee on Assassinations (MLK Document 270234) (hereinafter Baker affidavit).

[138] Ray testimony, Aug. 17, 1978, p. 30.

[139] Baker affidavit; interview of Donald F. Wood, Nov. 8, 1977, House Select Committee on Assassinations (MLK Document 150062).

[140] See MLK exhibit F–35 (Aeromarine sales receipt), II HSCA–MLK hearings, 39.

[141] Ray testimony Aug. 17, 1978, p. 40.

[142] Ray interview, May 3, 1977, pp. 67–68.

[143] Interview with James Earl Ray, Sept. 29, 1977, X appendix to the HSCA–MLK hearings, 145.

[144] Ibid.

[145] Fingerprint report, para. 21.

[146] Ray testimony, Aug. 17, 1978, pp. 12–14.

[147] Ibid.

[148] Ray testimony, Aug. 16, 1978, p. 101.

[149] Ibid.

[150] Id. at 101–102.

[151] Ray testimony, Aug 17, 1978, p. 44.

[152] Ray testimony, Aug. 16, 1978, p. 105.

[153] Ibid.

[154] FBI interview of Ralph Carpenter, Apr. 25, 1968 (MLK Document 040055).

[155] Interview with Ralph Carpenter, Oct. 7, 1977, House Select Committee on Assassinations (MLK Document 140131).

[156] See ref. 23, supra, designated counsel statement of Charles Stephens.

[157] Interview of Willie Anschutz, July 7, 1977, House Select Committee on Assassinations (MLK Document 110009).

[158] Testimony of Duncan Ragsdale, Nov. 14, 1978, V HSCA–MLK hearings, 250.

[159] Interview with Wayne Chastain, Oct. 6, 1977, House Select Committee on Assassinations (MLK Document 190167).

[160] See text, infra, at II. D for discussion of the response of the Memphis Police Department immediately following the assassination.

[161] See MLK exhibit F–319 (affidavit of John Jacobs, Nov. 6, 1978), V HSCA–MLK hearings, 434.

[162] See MLK exhibits F–311 (affidavit of Glynn King, Nov. 3, 1978), V HSCA–MLK hearings, 401, and F–312 (affidavit of Tommy Smith, Nov. 3, 1978), V HSCA–MLK hearings, 404.

[163] See MLK exhibit F–312 (affidavit of Tommy Smith, Nov. 3, 1978), V HSCA–MLK hearings 404; F–313 (affidavit of J. D. Music, Nov. 3, 1978), V HSCA–MLK hearings 408; F–314 (affidavit of C. F. Busch, Nov. 7, 1978), V HSCA–MLK hearings, 412; F–315 (affidavit of John Bauer, Nov. 13, 1978), V HSCA–MLK hearings, 417; and F–316 (affidavit of Stephen M. Darlington, Nov. 3, 1978), V HSCA–MLK hearings, 421.

[164] Narration of G. Robert Blakey, V HSCA–MLK hearings, 444.

[165] Interview of Grace E. Walden, July 26, 1977, House Select Committee on Assassinations (MLK Document 120134). See also MLK exhibit F–336, V HSCA–MLK hearings, 581.

[166] MLK exhibit F–340 (interview of Grace Walden by NBC for "Today" show, Aug. 15, 1978), V HSCA–MLK hearings, 622.

[167] Testimony of William L. Srygly, Nov. 14, 1978, V HSCA–MLK hearings, 56–57.

[168] Testimony of Dr. David F. Moore, Nov. 14, 1977, V HSCA–MLK hearings, 102.

[169] Ibid. See also MLK exhibits F–321 (affidavit of James Simpson, Nov. 3, 1978), V HSCA–MLK hearings, 454; F–322 (affidavit of Michael J. Doughtery, Nov. 3, 1978), V HSCA–MLK hearings, 457; F–323 (affidavit of George Willis, Nov. 3, 1978), V HSCA–MLK hearings, 461.

[170] See MLK exhibits F–321 (affidavit of James Simpson, Nov.

3, 1978), V HSCA–MLK hearings 454; F–322 (affidavit of Michael J. Dougherty, Nov. 3, 1978), V HSCA–MLK hearings, 457; F–323 (affidavit of George Willis, Nov. 3, 1978), V HSCA–MLK hearings, 461.

[171] Testimony of Dr. David E. Moore, Nov. 14, 1978, V HSCA–MLK hearings, 110 (hereinafter Moore testimony).

[172] Ibid. See also MLK exhibit F–339 (report of Dr. Roger Peele, M.D.), V HSCA–MLK hearings, 613.

[173] Moore testimony, p. 114.

[174] See MLK exhibit F–327 (affidavit of Dr. Sidney D. Vick, Nov. 7, 1978), V HSCA–MLK hearings, 516.

[175] Ibid.

[176] Testimony of C. Cleveland Drennon, Jr., Nov. 14, 1978 V HSCA–MLK hearings, 138.

[177] Testimony of Dr. James H. Druff, Nov. 14, 1978, V HSCA–MLK hearings, 164–165. See also testimony of Dr. Jack C. Neale, Nov. 14, 1978, V HSAC–MLK hearings, 186–187, and testimony of Dr. Morris Cohen, Nov. 14, 1978, V HSCA–MLK hearings, 219–220.

178] See generally testimony of Drs. Druff, Neale, and Cohen, supra, at ref. 177.

[179] Ibid.

[180] See MLK exhibit F–339 (report of Dr. Roger Peale), V HSCA–MLK hearings, 613.

[181] Transcript of guilty plea proceedings, Shelby County Criminal Court, March. 10, 1969 (MLK Document 010063) (hereinafter transcript of guilty plea proceedings).

[182] Testimony of Phil N. Canale, Nov. 13, 1978, C HSCA–MLK hearings, 132–134 (hereinafter Canale testimony).

[183] Testimony of Hugh Stanton, Jr., Oct. 23, 1974, *Ray* v. *Rose*, p. 223 (MLK Document 010005).

[184] Tennessee Code Annotated Section 39–2405.

[185] Transcript of guilty plea proceedings.

[18] Ibid.

[187] See MLK exhibit F–79 (proposed stipulation as to material facts), III HSCA–MLK hearings, 46. See also MLK Document 110106.

[188] Transcript of guilty plea proceedings.

[189] Letter from James Earl Ray to Judge W. Preston Battle, Mar. 13, 1969 (MLK Document 030102).

[190] Letter from James Earl Ray to Judge W. Preston Battle, Mar. 26, 1969 (MLK Document 030102).

[191] Court ruling on Ray's motion for new trial (MLK Document 030165).

[192] Ibid.

[193] Memorandum decision, *Ray* v. *Rose*, 373 F. Supp. 687 (1973).

[194] *Ray* v. *Rose*, 491 F. 2d 285 (1974).

[195] *Ray* v. *Rose*, 417 U.S. 936 (1974).

[196] Memorandum decision, *Ray* v. *Rose*, 392 F. Supp. 601 (1975).

[197] *Ray* v. *Rose*, 535 F. 2d 966.

[198] Ibid.

[199] *Ray* v. *Rose*, 429 U.S. 1026 (1976).

[200] See generally petitioner's memorandum of points and authorities; memorandum of facts, *Ray* v. *Rose*, Dec. 4, 1972 (MLK Document 110309).

[201] Deposition of James Earl Ray, Nov. 22, 1969, *Ray* v. *Foreman* (MLK Document 030197).

[202] Deposition of Arthur Hanes, Sr., Nov. 7, 1969, *Ray* v. *Foreman*, p. 20–24 (MLK Document 080055). See also Huie-Ray-Hanes contract, July 8, 1968 (MLK Document 110116) hereinafter Hanes deposition).

[203] Id., Hanes deposition, at 5. See also Huie, *He Slew the Dreamer*, p. 186.

[204] Id., Hanes deposition. Id., Hine, *He Slew the Dreamer*, at 193.

[205] See, e.g., interview of Arthur Hanes, Sr., May 9, 1978, House Select Committee on Assassinations (MLK Document 210373).

[206] Deposition of James Earl Ray, No. 22, 1969, *Ray* v. *Foreman* (MLK Document 030197).

[207] Deposition of Percy Foreman, Nov. 11, 1969, *Ray* v. *Foreman*, pp. 11–12 (MLK Document 010050).

[208] Id. at 12–13.

[209] Foreman testimony, pp. 95, 96.

[210] *Ray* v. *Rose*, Feb. 27, 1975, 392 F. Supp. 601 (1975).

[211] Ibid.

[212] Ibid.

[213] Testimony of James Earl Ray, Oct. 29, 1974, *Ray* v. *Rose* (MLK Document 010042).

[214] Foreman testimony, pp. 84–86.

[215] Transcript of court proceedings, Shelby County Criminal Court, Nov. 12, 1968 (MLK Document 010009).

[216] Petitioner's memorandum of points and authorities, *Ray* v. *Rose*, Dec. 4, 1972 (MLK Document 110309).

[217] Interview of Percy Foreman, Apr. 13, 1977, House Select Committee on Assassinations, p. 25 (MLK Document 080006).

[218] Foreman testimony, p. 90.

[219] Deposition of Percy Foreman, Apr. 3, 1974, *Ray* v. *Rose*, pp. 72–82 (MLK Document 020031).

[220] Ibid. See also Foreman testimony, pp. 89–90.

[221] Deposition of Percy Foreman, Apr. 3, 1974, *Ray* v. *Rose*, pp. 44–45 (MLK Document 020031). See also deposition of Percy Foreman, Nov. 11, 1969, *Ray* v. *Foreman*, p. 29 (MLK Document 010050). See also interview of Arthur Hanes, Sr., May 9, 1978, House Select Committee on Assassinations, pp. 7–8 (MLK Document 210373).

[222] Foreman testimony, pp. 89–90. See also deposition of Percy Foreman, Apr. 3, 1974, *Ray* v. *Rose*, pp. 76–78 (MLK Document 020031).

[223] Testimony of Hugh Stanton, Jr., *Ray* vs. *Rose*, Oct. 23, 1974, p. 283 (MLK Document 010005).

[224] Outside contact report with Thomas E. Smith, Dec. 8, 1978, House Select Committee on Assassinations (MLK Document 20079).

[225] Ibid.

[226] Foreman testimony, p. 90.

[227] Shelby County Jail logs, July 19, 1968 through Mar. 10, 1969 (MLK Documents 110160, 110161, 110296, 110325, and 110326).

[228] Testimony of Dr. McCarthy DeMere, Nov. 13, 1978, V HSCA–MLK hearings, 166–167.

[229] Deposition of James Earl Ray, Nov. 22, 1969, *Ray* v. *Foreman*, p. 54 (MLK Document 030168).

[230] Interview of Arthur Hanes, Sr., May 9, 1978, House Select Committee on Assassinations, pp. 7–8 (MLK Document 210373).

[231] See review of prior investigations by Judge McCrae in *Ray* v. *Rose*, 392 F. Supp. 601 (1975), p. 26 (MLK Document 260030); see also Foreman testimony, pp. 89–91; and testimony of Hugh Stanton, Jr., *Ray* v. *Rose*, Oct. 23, 1974, pp. 259–289 (MLK Document 010005); and deposition of William Bradford Huie, Sept. 20, 1974, *Ray* v. *Rose*, pp. 23, 70, 78 (MLK Document 170154).

[232] Testimony of Hugh Stanton, Jr., Oct. 23, 1974, *Ray* v. *Rose*, pp. 259–289 (MLK Document 010005).

[233] Id. at 304.

[234] Id. at 242, 310–311.

[235] Id. at 245.

[236] Habeas corpus testimony of Hugh Stanton, Jr., Oct. 23, 1974, pp. 259–289 (MLK Document 010005).

[237] According to Hugh Stanton, Jr.'s testimony at the habeas corpus proceedings, Foreman had a working knowledge of the case that "amazed" him. It was thorough enough for Foreman to have dictated a 75-page working paper from which the public defender's investigators worked. The record of the habeas corpus proceeding would indicate that although the combined investigation was by no means complete, enough had been learned that Foreman was in a position to make a powerful case for a guilty plea by the time he approached Ray about the possibility. Stanton testimony, *Ray* v. *Rose*, Oct. 3, 1974, p. 259 (MLK Document 010005).

[238] Petitioner's memorandum of fact, *Ray* v. *Rose* (MLK Document 110309).

[239] MLK exhibit F–262, V HSCA–MLK hearings, 91.

[240] MLK exhibit F–78, III HSCA–MLK hearings, 17.

[241] *Ray* v. *Rose*, 535 F. 2d 966 (6th Cir. 1976).

[242] Transcript of guilty plea proceedings.

[243] *State of Missouri* v. *James Earl Ray*, court of the city of St. Louis for criminal cases, circuit court cause 1427–H (MLK Document 280211).

[244] Petitioner's memorandum of facts, *Ray* v. *Rose*, pp. 40–41 (MLK Document 110309).

[245] Testimony of Billy J. Smith, Oct. 22, 1974, *Ray* v. *Rose*, pp. 41–92 (MLK Document 010006), and pp. 103–104 (MLK Document 010007).

[246] Testimony of Dr. McCarthy DeMere, Oct. 23, 1974, *Ray* v. *Rose*, p. 205 (MLK Document 010005).

[247] Interview of Dr. McCarthy DeMere, July 19, 1978, House Select Committee on Assassinations (MLK Document 230381).

[248] Dr. McCarthy DeMere testimony, Nov. 13, 1978, V HSCA–MLK hearings, 161–179.

[249] Ray interview, Sept. 29, 1977, p. 55.

[250] Id. at 54.

[251] Ibid.

[252] Id. at 56.

[253] Petitioner's memorandum of points and authorities, memorandum of facts, *Ray* v. *Rose*, Dec. 4, 1972, pp. 42–43 (MLK Document 110309).

[254] FBI identification record of John Larry Ray, No. 368-725A (MLK Document 240087).

[255] Ray interview, Sept. 29, 1977, pp. 56–57.

[256] Id. at 68.

[257] Id. at 65; see also testimony of James Earl Ray, Oct. 29, 1974, *Ray* v. *Rose*, p. 864 (MLK Document 010039).

[258] Testimony of James Earl Ray, Oct. 29, 1974, *Ray* v. *Rose*, p. 854 (MLK Document 010039).

[259] Ibid.

[260] Ibid.

[261] Missouri court records, *State* v. *Ray*, cause 1427–H (MLK Document 280311); see also testimony of James Earl Ray, Oct. 29, 1974, *Ray* v. *Rose*, *pp.* 916–918 (MLK Document 010042).

REFERENCES: SECTION B

[1] FBI memorandum, Hoover to Tolson, DeLoach, Rosen, Bishop, Sullivan, June 20, 1968: FBI headquarters Murkin file, serial No. 44–38861–4660.

[2] See, e.g., George McMillan, *The Making of an Assassin* (Boston-Toronto: Little, Brown & Co., 1976, 1st ed.).

[3] "Report of the Department of Justice Task Force to Review the FBI Martin Luther King, Jr., Security and Assassination Investigations," Jan. 11, 1977 (Washington, D.C.: U.S. Government Printing Office, 1977), p. 97.

[4] See volume XIII, appendix to the hearings before the Select Committee on Assassinations, U.S. House of Representatives, 95th Cong., 2d sess. (Washington, D.C.: U.S. Government Printing Office, 1979) (hereinafter HSCA–MLK hearings), for the committee's science reports on the King investigation.

[5] See, e.g., ref. 2, supra, pp. 202–209; see also "Dr. Martin Luther King, Jr., Supplemental Studies Pertaining to the Motive of James Earl Ray," staff report, XIII appendix to the HSCA–MLK hearings (hereinafter staff report: Motive).

[6] Staff summary of interview of Leslie Allen Achter, June 9, 1977, House Select Committee on Assassinations (MLK Document 180031); staff summary of interview of Bercia Lee Barbarick, July 12, 1978, House Select Committee on Assassinations (MLK Document 230308); staff summary of interview of Gene Raymond Barnes, November 2, 1977, House Select Committee on Assassinations (MLK Document 150060); staff summary of interview of Julius Maurice Block, August 20, 1978, House Select Committee on Assassinations (MLK Document 260299); staff summary of interview of Frank Boedeker, June 8, 1977, House Select Committee on Assassinations (MLK Document 180036); staff summary of interview of James Thomas Bond, Aug. 1, 1978, House Select Committee on Assassinations (MLK Document 240151); staff summary of interview of James Wilson Brown, July 27, 1978, House Select Committee on Assassinations (MLK Document 240282); staff summary of interview of Floyd Edward Cain, July 13, 1978, House Select Committee on Assassinations (MLK Document 240153); staff summary of interview of Donald Garfield Cox, July 13, 1978, House Select Committee on Assassinations (MLK Document 230309); staff summary of interview of Thomas B. Crews, July 13, 1978, House Select Committee on Assassinations (MLK Document 230307); staff summary of interview of Raymond Louis Curtis, November 30, 1977, House Select Committee on Assassinations (MLK Document 220133); staff summary of interview of Louis Raymond

Dowda, August 22, 1978, House Select Committee on Assassinations (MLK Document 240374); staff summary of interview of George Ben Edmondson, October 31, 1978, House Select Committee on Assassinations (MLK Document 260219); staff summary of interview of Larry Foster, June 9, 1977, House Select Committee on Assassinations (MLK Document 180029).

Staff summary of interview of Ernest "Cadillac" Franklin, June 8, 1977, House Select Committee on Assassinations (MLK Document 100097); staff summary of interview of Benjamin Goodin, former prison civilian chef, June 10, 1977, House Select Committee on Assassinations (MLK Document 100098); staff summary of interview of Joe Hegwood, June 10, 1977, House Select Committee on Assassinations, p. 2 (MLK Document 180032); staff summary of interview of John Kenneth Hurtt, November 10, 1977, House Select Committee on Assassinations (MLK Document 180082); staff summary of interview of Paul Alvin Gail, Jr., Sept. 24, 1978, House Select Committee on Assassinations (MLK Document 300149); staff summary of interview of Eric Lafe Larson, July 14, 1978, House Select Committee on Assassinations (MLK Document 240156); staff summary of interview of Cecil Clayton Lillibridge, November 22, 1977, House Select Committee on Assassinations (MLK Document 170320); staff summary of interview of Joseph J. Maloney, November 10, 1977, House Select Committee on Assassinations (MLK Document 180184); staff summary of interview of Raymond Louis Menard, July 18, 1978, House Select Committee on Assassinations (MLK Document 240157); staff summary of interview of Michael Moore, June 9, 1977, House Select Committee on Assassinations (MLK Document 180033); staff summary of interview of Raymond Patrick, June 9, 1977, House Select Committee on Assassinations, p. 2 (MLK Document 180038); staff summary of interview of Robert L. Powell, November 21, 1977, House Select Committee on Assassinations (MLK Document 170321); staff summary of interview of Jack Romprey, June 9, 1977, House Select Committee on Assassinations (MLK Document 180035); MLK Exhibit F–640 (staff summary of interview of Walter Terry Rife, tee on Assassinations (MLK Document 100094); staff summary of interview of James Stidham, June 10, 1977, House Select Committee on Assassinations (MLK Document 10094); staff summary of interview of Ronald Terry, June 9, 1977, House Select Committee on Assassinations (MLK Document 180037); staff summary of interview of Kenneth Lee Wade, September 4, 1978, House Select Committee on Assassinations (MLK Document 250123).

[7] William Bradford Huie, He Slew the Dreamer (New York: Delacorte Press, 1970, 3d ed.), p. 45.

[8] FBI Document, Mexico City Legat, Non-Prosecutive Summary, p. 14, received from Shelby County, Tenn., Attorney General's office by House Select Committee on Assassinations (MLK Document 040063).

[9] See e.g., ref. 2, supra, pp. 269–270; Gerold Frank, An American Death (Garden City, New York: Doubleday and Co., Inc., 1972, 1st ed.), pp. 304–305.

[10] See MLK Exhibit F–173 (staff interview of Manuela Aquirre-Medrano—aka Irma Morales—June 5, 1978, House Select Committee on Assassinations), IV HSCA–MLK Hearings, 161.

[11] Compare pp. 269–270, ref. 2 supra and pp. 304–305, ref. 9 supra.

[12] Testimony of Alexander Eist, November 9, 1978, IV HSCA–MLK hearings, 21–22 (hereinafter Eist testimony).

[13] See "Dr. Martin Luther King, Jr. Supplemental Studies Pertaining to the Motive of James Earl Ray," staff report, XIII appendix to the HSCA–MLK hearings for a more detailed study of Ray's interest in African countries.

[14] Staff memorandum on phone contact with Dr. David Abrahamson, House Select Committee on Assassinations (MLK Document 300148); staff memorandum on phone contact with Dr. Park Dietz, House Select Committee on Assassinations (MLK Document 300117); staff memorandum on phone contact with Dr. Lawrence Freedman, House Select Committee on Assassinations (MLK Document 300146); staff memorandum on phone contact with Dr. Seymour Halleck, House Select Committee on Assassinations (MLK Document 300144); staff memorandum on phone contact with Dr. Irving Harris, House Select Committee on Assassinations (MLK Document 300145); staff memorandum on Jan. 19, 1978 contact with Dr. Zigmund Lebensohn, House Select Committee on Assassinations (MLK Document 300143); staff memorandum on phone contact with Dr. Irwin Perr, House Select Committee on Assassinations (MLK Document 300142); staff memorandum on phone contact with Dr. Jonas Rappeport, House Select Committee on Assassinations (MLK Document 300141); staff memorandum on phone contact with Dr. David Rothstein, House Select Committee on Assassinations (MLK Document 300140); staff memorandum on phone contact with Dr. Robert Sadoff, House Select Committee on Assassinations (MLK Document 300139); staff memorandum on phone contact with Dr. Andy Watson, House Select Committee on Assassinations (MLK Document 300128).

[15] See pp. 83–84, 91, ref. 7 supra; see also ref. 3, p. 97 (recognizing the possibility that Ray killed Dr. King, in part, out of a "yearning for recognition").

[16] See p. 83, ref. 7 supra.

[17] Id. at 84.

[18] Id. at 91.

[19] Eist testimony, pp. 21–22.

[20] Staff summary of interview of George Ben Edmundson, October 31, 1978, House Select Committee on Assassinations (MLK Document 260219).

[21] Immunized executive session testimony of Marie Martin Levy, April 5, 1978, House Select Committee on Assassinations, pp. 29–34.

[22] See section II D for a detailed examination of the post-assassination activities of the Memphis Police Department.

[23] FBI identification record of James Earl Ray, No. 306 443A.

[24] MLK Exhibit F–642 (St. Louis Post-Dispatch interview) VIII HSCA–MLK hearings, 589.

[25] Testimony of John Ray, December 1, 1978 VIII HSCA–MLK hearings, 119 (hereinafter John Ray testimony).

[26] MLK exhibit F–606 (FBI airtel, June 11, 1968), VII HSCA–MLK hearings, 457.

[27] Ibid.

[28] Testimony of Jerry Ray, November 30, 1978, VII HSCA–MLK hearings, 98–99 (hereinafter Jerry Ray testimony).

[29] Id. at 101.

750

[30] But see James Earl Ray testimony, August 17, 1978, II HSCA–MLK hearings, 489ff (Ray's denial of involvement).

[31] See MLK exhibit F–173 (staff interview of Irma Morales, June 5, 1978, IV HSCA–MLK hearings, 161); see also staff summary of interview of Luis Alberto Garcia, June 2, 1978, House Select Committee on Assassinations (MLK Document 260118); staff summary of interview of Oscar Mendiola, June 3, 1978, House Select Committee on Assassinations (MLK Document 260123); staff summary of interview of Rodimiro Vizcarra de Jesus, June 4, 1978, House Select Committee on Assassinations (MLK Document 260149); staff summary of interview of Manuela Aguirer, June 5, 1978, House Select Committee on Assassinations (MLK Document 250135).

[32] See pp. 109–111, ref. 21 supra; see also immunized execuctive session testimony of Marie Martin Levy, ref. 21, supra, p. 167.

[33] FBI interview of Sharon Rhoades, Apr. 16, 1978, pp. 117–120 (MLK Document 040062); FBI interview of Tomas Lau, Apr. 15, 1968, Los Angeles Murkin Report, pp. 131–133 (MLK Document 040053); staff summary of interview of Sharon Rhoads, Nov. 17, 1977, House Select Committee on Assassinations, p. 2 (MLK Document 160107); staff summary of interview of Tomas Lau, Nov. 14, 1977, House Select Committee on Assassinations, p. 1 (MLK Document 160152).

[34] See immunized executive session testimony of Marie Martin Levy, ref. 21, supra, pp. 143–158; immunized executive session testimony of Charles J. Stein, Apr. 4, 1978, House Select Commitee on Assassinations, pp. 81–95; executive session testimony of Rita Stein, Apr. 6, 1978, House Select Committee on Assassinations, pp. 9–15; see also affidavits for registration for Mimi De Grasse (Marie Martin Levy), Rita Rosas (Rita Stein), Charles J, Stein, Dec. 15, 1967. (MLK Document 160266).

[35] Staff summary of interview with Charles Stein, Jan. 23, 1978–Jan. 26, 1978, House Select Committee on Assassinations (MLK Document 190402).

[36] See, e.g., staff summary of interview of Mickey Medina, Feb. 17, 1978, House Select Committee on Assassinations (MLK Document 190288); staff summary of interview of Felix Valdez, Feb. 14, 1978, House Select Committee on Assassinations (MLK Document 180389); staff summary of interview of Clara Stann, Feb. 15, 1978, House Select Committee on Assassinations (MLK Document 180387); staff summary of interview of Theresa Stone, Feb. 13, 1978, House Select Committee on Assassinations (MLK Document 180386); staff summary of interview of Charles De Carvelho, June 17, 1977, House Select Committee on Assassinations (MLK Document 130079); deposition of Charles De Carvelho, House Select Committee on Assassinations (MLK Document 100261).

REFERENCES: SECTION C

[1] Report of hte Federal Bureau of Investigations, Special Agent William Booth, Feb. 15, 1968; FBI headquarters Vincent DePalma file.
[2] Ibid.
[3] Ibid.

751

[4] FBI airtel from Director to Denver, Feb. 6, 1968, FBI headquarters Vincent DePalma file.

[5] FBI airtel from Springfield to Chicago, Apr. 6, 1968, FBI headquarters Murkin file 44–38841–562.

[6] See, e.g., airtel from SAC, Kansas City, to Director, Apr. 7, 1968, FBI headquarters MURKIN file, 44–38861–171.

[7] See, e.g., FBI airtel from Little Rock to Director, et al., Apr. 10, 1968, FBI headquarters MURKIN file 44–38861–361.

[8] Outside contact report with Dan Senf, May 16, 1978, House Select Committee on Assassinations (MLK Document 210341).

[9] Staff summary of interview with Jerry Milton Brooks, June 26, 1978, House Select Committee on Assassinations (MLK Document 220467).

[10] Interview of Mary Tollerton, May 25, 1978, House Select Committee on Assassinations, p. 4 (MLK Document 220444).

[11] Executive session testimony of Walter Peyson, June 8, 1978, House Select Committee on Assassinations, pp. 81, 89, 108 (hereinafter Peyson testimony).

[12] Executive session testimony of Robert DePugh, June 8, 1978, House Select Committee on Assassinations, pp. 55–56 (hereinafter DePugh testimony).

[13] Peyson testimony, pp. 95–96; id., DePugh testimony, at 52, 67.

[14] Id., Peyson testimony, at 80; id., DePugh testimony, at 54.

[15] FBI airtel from Birmingham to Director, Apr. 15, 1968, FBI headquarters MURKIN file 44–38861–1203.

[16] Ibid.

[17] Ibid.

[18] FBI airtel from Mobile to Director, Aug. 7, 1968, FBI headquarters file 157–9586–616.

[19] Barnes not only refused to comment at that interview but further stated that if he were subpenaed to testify in regard to this matter, he would still decline to give the committee any information; staff summary of interview with Sidney Barnes, May 9, 1978, House Select Committee on Assassinations, pp. 1–2 (MLK Document 210292).

[20] Staff summary of interview of confidential source, Apr. 27, 1978, House Select Committee on Assassinations (MLK Document 210104); staff summary of interview of confidential source, May 18, 1978, House Select Committee on Assassinations, p. 2 (MLK) Document 230010).

[21] See, e.g., staff summary of interview of Admiral John Crommelin, Oct. 26, 1978, House Select Committee on Assassinations (MLK Document 260315).

[22] FBI teletype from Dallas to Director, Memphis, Jackson, Apr. 23, 1968, FBI headquarters MURKIN file 44–38861–1835.

[23] See, generally, FBI headquarters files 157–165—serials 13, 23; FBI headquarters file 157–164—serial 13; Jackson, Miss., Field Office file 157–9586—serial 502.

[24] Staff summary of interview of Myrtis Ruth Hendricks, June 24, 1978, House Select Committee on Assassinations (MLK Document 230041).

[25] Letter from House Select Committee on Assassinations to Attorney General Griffin Bell, July 17, 1978 (MLK Document 310123).

[26] Letter from FBI to House Select Committee on Assassinations, Aug. 14, 1978 (MLK Document 240280).

[27] Telegrams from House Select Committee on Assassinations to Nix, Bowers and McGee, July 7, 1978 (MLK Document 230105).

[28] FBI headquarters MURKIN file 44–38861–497. The Bureau identified the subscribers of the three phone numbers to which the calls from Wisconsin were made: 704–758–2908—Earl Hall Used Cars, Earl Hall, owner, Lenoir, N.C., 101 Molehill Drive; 704–758–4930—Paul Ellison Sanders, Radcliff Rd., Lenoir, N. C., vice president, Sanders Management Co., 704–758–2100—Samuel J. Sanders, Cotrell Hill Road, Lenoir, N.C.

[29] Ibid. The caller allegedly identified himself as "Robert" during the call to 704–754–4930.

[30] Ibid. The caller allegedly had this conversation when speaking to unknown male at 704–758–2100.

[31] See ref. 28, supra.

[32] FBI airtel from Charlotte to Director, June 17, 1968, FBI headquarters MURKIN file 44–38861–4669.

[33] FBI airtel from Milwaukee to Director, June 27, 1968, FBI headquarters MURKIN file 44–38861–4949.

[34] The name George Wilson was used as an alias by this individual in his initial contact with the House Select Committee on Assassinations in January 1977. Although the committee subsequently learned his true identity, the name Wilson will be used throughout to preserve the confidentiality of the source.

[35] Staff memorandum from James Chenoweth to file, January 10, 1977, House Select Committee on Assassinations re: telephone call from George Wilson (MLK document 290050).

[36] FBI letterhead memorandum, July 27, 1969, FBI headquarters file 157–370–66–482.

[37] FBI headquarters file, serial 157–370–4–575.

[38] See FBI airtel from SAC Birmingham to Director, Aug. 20, 1968, FBI headquarters file 157–370–4–640; FBI airtel from SAC Birmingham to Director, Sept. 4, 1968, FBI headquarters file 157–370–4–699; FBI airtel from Birmingham to Director, FBI headquarters MURKIN file 44–38861–4936.

[39] The committee's interest in Ray's choice of Arthur Hanes as his first attorney was based on Hanes' previous defense of the individuals charged with the murder of Viola Liuzzo. These individuals were members of the UKA. It seemed reasonable to assume that Ray's choice of Hanes was influenced by the attorney's reputation resulting from the Liuzzo case; Ray claimed, however, that his only knowledge of Hanes was that he had been mayor of Birmingham. See interview of James Earl Ray, Sept. 29, 1977, XI appendix to the HSCA–MLK hearings, pp. 416–417, 421.

[40] Staff summary of interview with George Wilson, Apr. 27, 1978, House Select Committee on Assassinations (MLK Document 290051).

[41] Executive session testimony of Robert H. Shelton, June 7, 1978, House Select Committee on Assassinations.

[42] Executive session testimony of Melvin A. Sexton, June 6, 1978, House Select Committee on Assassinations.

[43] Executive session testimony of Arthur Hanes, Sr., June 7, 1978, House Select Committee on Assassinations.

[44] Executive session testimony of Furman Dean Williams, June 6, 1978, House Select Committee on Assassinations.

[45] Executive session testimony of James Roberson Jones, June 6, 1978, House Select Committee on Assassinations.

[46] Id. at 20–21; executive session testimony of Furman Dean Williams, June 6, 1978, House Select Committee on Assassinations, pp. 16–17.

[47] Executive session testimony of Arthur Hanes, Sr., June 7, 1978, House Select Committee on Assassinations, pp. 54–56; executive session testimony of Robert H. Shelton, May 26, 1978, House Select Committee on Assassinations, pp. 33–38; executive session testimony of Melvin Sexton, June 6, 1978, House Select Committee on Assassinations, pp. 23–24.

[48] Executive session testimony of Arthur Hanes, Sr., June 7, 1978, House Select Committee on Assassinations, p. 35; executive session testimony of Melvin A. Sexton, June 6, 1978, House Select Committee on Assassinations, pp. 14–29.

[49] Bill Montgomery, "The Mystery of J.B.," Atlanta Journal, Oct. 12, 1977, p. 16–A.; "Atlanta Lawyer to Defend Plot Suspect," Atlanta Journal, May 18, 1961.

[50] FBI report, February 15, 1967, FBI headquarters National States Rights file 105–66233–1867, p. 5; immunized executive session testimony of J. B. Stoner, March 8, 1978, House Select Committee on Assassinations, pp. 6–6 (hereinafter Stoner testimony, March 8, 1978); immunized executive session testimony of Edward R. Fields, March 19, 1978, House Select Committee on Assassinations, p. 200 (hereinafter Fields testimony, March 19, 1978).

NOTE.—While FBI reports, such as the one cited above, and many newspaper reports credit Stoner with being one of the founders of the NSRP, Stoner himself claims he was not involved in the United White Party, the predecessor of the NSRP, nor was he one of the founders of NSRP.

[51] FBI report, July 26, 1964, FBI headquarters J. B. Stoner file 157–97–97.

[52] FBI report, April 8, 1968, FBI headquarters NSRP file 105–66233–2082.

[53] Ibid.

[54] Interview with James Earl Ray, Sept. 29, 1977, XI appendix to the HSCA–MLK hearings, 46–47, 53–54.

[55] "Stoner Is Lawyer for Ray's Brother," Atlanta Constitution, November 3, 1970, p. 15A; news file on John Ray, October 21, 1977 (MLK document 140039); "Ray's Brother Sentenced," New York Times, April 24, 1971 (MLK document 140039).

[56] Immunized executive session testimony of J. B. Stoner, April 19, 1978, House Select Committee on Assassinations, p. 114 (hereinafter Stoner testimony, April 19, 1978); see also "Ray Is Arraigned in Private Session," Atlanta Constitution, July 28, 1970.

[57] FBI report, FBI headquarters J. B. Stoner file 174–425–1; FBI report, FBI headquarters, Christian Anti-Jewish Party file 65–15743, serials 104–195.

[58] David Morrison and Steven Holmes, "Stoner Indicated in Bombing," Atlanta Constitution, Sept. 27, 1977, pp. 1A, 12A.

[59] Interview with Thomas Cook, January 18, 1978, House Select Committee on Assassinations, p. 3 (MLK document 170278).

[60] Immunized executive session testimony of Edward R. Fields,

April 19, 1978, House Select Committee on Assassinations, pp. 184–186 (hereinafter Fields testimony, April 19, 1978).

[61] Indictment in the District Court of the United States for the Northern District of Alabama, Docket No. CR 63–316 (MLK document 290002).

[62] FBI report, prosecutive summary report, March 26, 1964, FBI headquarters J. B. Stoner file 157–1604.

[63] "Rights Party Nominates Atlantan," Atlanta Constitution, Mar. 2, 1964: "States Rights Slate Lists Kasper, Atlantan," Atlanta Journal, Mar. 2, 1964.

[64] Phil Gailey, "J. B. Stoner Studies Foreign Policy," Atlanta Constitution, Nov. 9, 1971.

[65] Bill Montgomery, "Mystery of J. B.," Atlanta Journal, Oct. 12, 1977, p. A1; Ron Casey, "Stoner Says FBI, Jews Are Enemies," Birmingham News, Nov. 28, 1977, pp. 1–6; Ken Willis, "Stoner Funds Under Probe," Atlanta Constitution, Aug. 24, 1973; "Stoner Announces Senate Candidacy," Atlanta Journal, July 6, 1971.

[66] Stoner ran for Governor of Georgia and lost in the primary on Aug. 8, 1978 with only 5.47 percent of the vote, Washington Star, Aug. 9, 1978, pp. A1, A10.

[67] FBI report, June 27, 1968, FBI headquarters NSRP file, 105–66233–2127; see also, Stoner testimony, Apr. 19, 1978, p. 117; interview of James Earl Ray, Sept. 29, 1977, XI appendix to the HSCA-MLK hearings, 46–47, 41–55 (hereinafter Ray interview, Sept. 29, 1977).

[68] Jeff Cohen and Dave Lifton, "A Man He Calls Raoul," New Times, Apr. 1, 1977, p. 32.

NOTE.—Harry Avery, Commissioner of Corrections for the State of Tennessee in March 1969, claimed that in his official position he got to know James Earl Ray and Jerry Ray. Avery claims that while driving Jerry Ray to a meeting, Jerry told him that he (Jerry) was to meet with Stoner and that Stoner had been "our" (implying Jerry's and James' at least) attorney for 2 years before the assassination. The committee was not able to substantiate this claim.

[69] See interview of Harry Avery, Dec. 3, 1976, House Select Committee on Assassinations, p. 12 (MLK document 040007); interview of Harry Avery, June 14, 1977, House Select Committee on Assassinations, p. 29 (MLK document 100051); memorandum to Governor Ellington from W. E. Hopton re: interview of Avery by Hopton, May 20, 1969, pp. 1, 4 (MLK document 200472).

[70] Staff comparison of Stoner and James Earl Ray activities from Apr. 23, 1967 to June 8, 1968, taken from FBI files (MLK document 280212); see also Stoner testimony, Apr. 19, 1978, p. 117; Fields testimony, Apr. 19, 1978, pp. 187–188; also Ray interview, Sept. 29, 1977, pp. 46–47. 51–55.

[71] Letter "To Whom It May Concern From Edward R. Fields, re: James Earl Ray Case, June 14, 1968" (MLK document, 270062).

[72] Ray interview, Sept. 29, 1977, pp. 51–53.

[73] Ray interview, Sept. 29, 1977, pp. 51–53; letter from James Earl Ray to J. B. Stoner, Aug. 9, 1968, re: representation in libel matter (MLK document 110108); "Commotion Vowed in Ray Civil Suits," Atlanta Journal, Mar. 26, 1969.

[74] Ray interview, Sept. 29, 1977, pp. 70–71; "A Retrial for Ray Asked in Memphis by New Lawyers," New York Times, Apr. 8, 1969, p. 14.

[75] Bynum Shaw, "Are You Sure Who Killed Martin Luther King," Esquire magazine, March, 1972, p. 116; Robert Johnson, "James Earl Ray's Chief Defense Lawyer Claims U.S. Government Agents Killed Martin Luther King," National Enquirer, vol. 44, No. 7, Oct. 19, 1969.

[76] Stoner testimony, Mar. 8, 1978, p. 76; immunized executive session testimony of J. B. Stoner, Mar. 9, 1978, House Select Committee on Assassinations, pp. 24–31; Stoner testimony, Apr. 19, 1978, pp. 98–104.

[77] Stoner testimony, Mar. 8, 1978, pp. 137–170.

[78] Ray executed a waiver for Arthur Hanes, Jr., but later tried to withdraw it. See also the following waivers of attorney-client privilege executed by James Earl Ray: Mar. 7, 1977 (MLK document 029005); Nov. 14, 1977 (MLK document 190100); Mar. 27, 1977 (MLK document 070074); May 3, 1977 (MLK document 090004); May 23, 1977 (MLK document 110328); June 22, 1977 (MLK document 130045).

[79] Waiver of attorney-client privilege executed by James Earl Ray, May 23, 1977 (MLK document 110328).

[80] Immunized executive session testimony of J. B. Stoner, Mar. 8, 1978, House Select Committee on Assassinations, pp. 45–49.

[81] Id. at 45.

[82] Id. at 48.

[83] Id. at 46.

[84] Id. at 47–48.

[85] Immunized executive session testimony of J. B. Stoner, Mar. 9, 1978, House Select Committee on Assassinations, pp. 41–42.

[86] Id. at 46, 77; Stoner testimony, Mar. 8, 1978, p. 48.

[87] Interview of Asa Carter, Apr. 6, 1978, House Select Committee on Assassinations, p. 2 (MLK document 200136).

[88] Ibid.

[89] Executive session testimony of William H. Morris, Mar. 10, 1978, House Select Committee on Assassinations, pp. 6–9.

[90] Id. at 33–55.

[91] Id. at 11, 12.

[92] Report on the Federated Ku Klux Klan, Inc., Feb. 20, 1962, FBI headquarters file 157–166–39.

[93] Ibid.

[94] Executive session testimony of William H. Morris, Mar. 10, 1978, House Select Committee on Assassinations, pp. 40–42.

[95] Id. at 12.

[96] Id. at 12–13.

[97] Id. at 12–13.

[98] Id. at 23.

[99] Id. at 27.

[100] Id. at 27, 45.

[101] Memphis Police Department homicide report, supplement No. 85, Apr. 13, 1968 (MLK document 030203).

[102] Id. at 1754–44.

[103] Ibid.

[104] Ibid.

[105] Ibid.

[106] Ibid.

[107] Id. at 1760.

[108] Ibid.

[109] Ibid.; see also staff summary of interview of B. J. Smith,

July 26, 1977, House Select Committee on Assassinations (MLK document 120097); staff summary of interview of W. C. Hughes, Nov. 17, 1977 (MLK document 160044); staff summary of interview of J. H. Jones, Nov. 16, 1977, House Select Committee on Assassinations (MLK document 160045).

[110] Memphis Police Department homicide report, supplement 85, Apr. 13, 1968 (MLK document 030203).

[111] Ibid.

[112] Ibid.

[113] FBI airtel, July 29, 1968, to Director, from SAC Memphis re: CB transmission on Apr. 4, 1968, FBI headquarters MURKIN file 44–38861–5094.

[114] Ibid.

[115] Staff summary of interview of B. J. Smith, July 26, 1977, House Select Committee on Assassinations (MLK document 120097); staff summary of interview of W. C. Hughes, Nov. 17, 1977, House Select Committee on Assassinations (MLK document 160044); and staff summary of interview of J. H. Jones, Nov. 16, 1977, House Select Committee on Assassinations (MLK document 160045).

[116] See road map of Memphis, Tenn. (MLK document 290024).

[117] See Memphis Police Department homicide reports, supplement 85, Apr. 13, 1968 (MLK document 030203); FBI airtel, July 29, 1968, to Director from SAC Memphis re: CB transmission on Apr. 4, 1968, FBI headquarters MURKIN file 44–38861–4095.

[118] See, e.g., staff summary of interviews of Lt. J. D. Hamby, Dec. 6, 1977 (MLK document 140256); Dec. 7, 1977 (MLK document 160260); and Dec. 8, 1977 (MLK document 160261).

[119] Interview of James Raines, Aug. 29, 1977, House Select Committee on Assassinations (MLK document 120095).

[120] Staff summaries of interviews of Carroll S. Carroll on July 27, 1977, House Select Committee on Assassinations (MLK document 120094); Dec. 6, 1977 (MLK document 160253); Dec. 7, 1977 (MLK document 160259); and Dec. 8, 1977 (MLK document 160265). See also working paper, re: Citizen's Band radio broadcast—review of ledgers received from Carroll S. Carroll, May 15, 1978, House Select Committee on Assassinations (MLK document 290028): staff summary of interviews of Capt. J. P. Marby, Dec. 7, 1977 (MLK document 160250); and interview of J. D. Hamby, Dec. 8, 1977, House Select Committee on Assassinations (MLK document 160261).

[121] Staff summary of interview of Neal Talley, Jr., Dec. 1, 1977, House Select Committee on Assassinations (MLK document 160143); staff summary of interview of Jon C. Hellen, Dec. 1, 1977, House Select Committee on Assassinations (MLK document 170046); staff summary of interview of James A. Wallace, Jr., Dec. 7, 1977, House Select Committee on Assassinations (MLK document 160249); staff summary of interview of Michael J. Cimbalo, Dec. 5, 1977, House Select Committee on Assassinations (MLK document 160201); staff summary of interview of Timothy R. Higgins, Dec. 5, 1977, House Select Committee on Assassinations (MLK document 290030); staff summary of interview of Brother Adrian Powers and Brother Stephen O. Malley, Nov. 11, 1977, House Select Committee on Assassinations (MLK document 160142).

[122] Affidavit of Douglas P. Cross, July 8, 1976 (MLK document 290025); affidavit of James Stanton, July 9, 1976 (MLK document 290026); staff summary of interview of Douglas P. Cross,

Dec. 4, 1977, House Select Committee on Assassinations (MLK document 160316); staff summary of interview of James Stanton, Nov. 29, 1977, House Select Committee on Assassinations (MLK document 170044).

[123] FCC report, May 17, 1978 (MLK document 210454); see also outside contact report of Frank Rose, Apr. 12, 1978, House Select Committee on Assassinations (MLK document 210285).

[124] Designated counsel statement of Edward L. Montedonico, Jr., p. 33 (MLK document 290023).

[125] Staff summary of interviews of Robert E. Ferguson, Nov. 16, 1977, House Select Committee on Assassinations (MLK document 160140) and Jan. 10, 1978, House Select Committee on Assassinations (MLK document 290029); see also staff summary of interview of Michael Welting, House Select Committee on Assassinations (MLK document 170336).

[126] Staff summary of interview of Carroll S. Carroll, July 27, 1977, House Select Committee on Assassinations (MLK document 120095); Dec. 6, 1977 (MLK document 160253); Dec. 7, 1977 (MLK document 160259); and Dec. 8, 1977 (MLK document 160265); staff summary of interview of James E. Bethune, Dec. 2, 1977, House Select Committee on Assassinations (MLK document 160167); staff summary of interviews of William H. Austin, Nov. 15, 1977, House Select Committee on Assassinations (MLK document 160046) and (MLK document 170313); staff summary of interviews of Robert H. McCarty, Nov. 15, 1977, House Select Committee on Assassinations (MLK document 160209), and Jan. 19, 1978 (MLK document 170243); interview of Lt. Rufus Wesley Bradshaw, Nov. 8, 1977, House Select Committee on Assassinations (MLK document 170012); interview of Capt. James W. Strauser, Nov. 16, 1977, House Select Committee on Assassinations (MLK document 160041); interview of James Roberts, Dec. 1, 1977, House Select Committee on Assassinations (MLK document 160125); interview of Rhea W. Ferguson, Nov. 29, 1977, House Select Committee on Assassinations (MLK document 160120); staff summary of interview of Cranmer Boyce, Nov. 29, 1977 (MLK document 160123); staff summary of interview of Elmer L. Browning, Nov. 30, 1977, House Select Committee on Assassinations (MLK document 160121); staff summary of interview of L. H. Daniel, Nov. 29, 1977, House Select Committee on Assassinations (MLK document 160122); staff summary of interview of Vaugan Dow, Nov. 30, 1977, House Select Committee on Assassinations (MLK document 160124). See also analytical chart (MLK document 290031).

[127] Outside contact report with Angelo Ditty, May 2, 1978, House Select Committee on Assassinations (MLK document 210038).

[128] FCC report, May 17, 1978 (MLK document 210454).

[129] FBI memorandum, Apr. 20, 1968, FBI headquarters MURKIN file 44–38861–1816.

[130] Ibid.

[131] Ibid.

[132] Ibid.

[133] Notes of author William Sartor (MLK document 010072).

[134] See generally FBI letterhead memorandum, Nov. 21, 1968 (MLK document 040082) with attachments: FBI Memphis office interview of Frank Liberto, Apr. 19, 1968; FBI New Orleans office interview of Anthony Liberto, Apr. 22, 1968; FBI New Orleans

office interview of Mrs. Emma Liberto, Apr. 22, 1968; FBI New Orleans office interview of Vincent Liberto, Apr. 22, 1968; FBI New Orleans office interview of Salvatore Liberto, Apr. 23, 1968; and FBI Memphis office interview of James William Latch, Apr. 19, 1968.

[135] Affidavit of Frank Liberto, June 28, 1978 (MLK document 280063).

[136] See, e.g., staff summary of interview of Vincent Liberto, June 7, 1977, House Select Committee on Assassinations (MLK document 130081); staff summary of interview of Salvatore Liberto, June 7, 1977, House Select Committee on Assassinations (MLK document 130088; staff summary of interview of Ida Mae Verbeek, June 7, 1977, House Select Committee on Assassinations (MLK document 130080).

[137] Staff summary of interview of Ernest Tyler, Apr. 10, 1978, House Select Committee on Assassinations (MLK document 200404); staff summary on interview of Linda Cooper, Apr. 6, 1978, House Select Committee on Assassinations (MLK document 260145); staff summary of interview of Dorothy Conaley, Apr. 5, 1978, House Select Committee on Assassinations (MLK document 260143); staff summary of interview of Mrs. John Walker, Apri. 5, 1978, House Select Committee on Assassinations (MLK document 260142).

[138] Staff summary of interview of James William Latch, Feb. 10, 1978, House Select Committee on assassinations (MLK document 180396); staff summary of interview of Amelia Louis Guasco, Apr. 5, 1978, House Select Committee on Assassinations (MLK document 200426); staff summary of interview of Buddy Mims, May 22, 1978, House Select Committee on Assassinations (MLK document 210545); staff summary of interview of Mary Frances Stampley, Apr. 8, 1978, House Select Committee on Assassinations (MLK document 260144).

[139] Affidavit of Frank Liberto, June 28, 1978 (MLK document 280063).

[140] Staff memorandum to Lehner from Akers and Johnson, Sept. 13, 1977, re: contacts with New Orleans Police Department, House Select Committee on Assassinations, pp. 6–7 (MLK document 290039).

[141] Staff summary of interview of Inspector N. E. Zachary (retired), June 1, 1977, House Select Committee on Assassinations (MLK document 130086).

[142] FBI Memphis Office interviews of John McFerren, Apr. 8, 1968 and Apr. 18, 1968 (MLK document 040082).

[143] Staff summaries of interviews of John McFerren, Mar. 12, 1977, House Select Committee on Assassinations (MLK document 260200); May 10, 1977 (MLK document 090150); and Feb. 9, 1978 (MLK document 190043) see also affidavit of John McFerren, June 22, 1978, House Select Committee on Assassinations (MLK document 220549).

[144] FBI memorandum, Apr. 20, 1968, Director to Attorney General, FBI headquarters MURKIN file, serial 44–38861–1816; see also staff summary of interview of John McFerren, Mar. 12, 1977, House Select Committee on Assassinations (MLK document 260200).

[145] Interview of John McFerren, Mar. 12, 1977, House Select Committee on Assassinations (MLK document 260200).

[146] Ibid.

[147] FBI Memphis Office interview of John Ferren, Apr. 18, 1968 (MLK document 040082).

[148] Notes of author William Sartor (MLK document 110334).

[149] Ibid.

[150] Report of autopsy performed on William Sartor by Hillcrest Baptist Hospital, Waco, Tex. (MLK document 110001).

[151] Manuscript of William Sartor (MLK document 110334).

[152] Ibid.

[153] Ibid.

[154] Ibid.

[155] Staff summary of interview of Sam DiPiazza, May 11, 1978, House Select Committee on Assassinations (MLK document 210503).

[156] Interview of Dr. Lucas DiLeo, Feb. 22, 1978, House Select Committee on Assassinations (MLK document 260205).

[157] Outside contact report with Mr. Acosta, Oct. 23, 1978, House Select Committee on Assassinations (MLK document 260261).

[158] Interview of Charles Stein, Jan. 23, 1968, House Select Committee on Assassinations, p. 17 (MLK document 190402).

[159] Immunized executive session testimony of Carlos Marcello, Jan. 11, 1978, House Select Committee on Assassinations, pp. 27–28.

[160] Deposition of Carlton Pecot, Feb. 15, 1978, House Select Committee on Assassinations (MLK document 190263).

[161] Id. at 16.

[162] FBI memorandum, Nov. 21, 1968, FBI Memphis MURKIN file 44–1987.

[163] FBI teletype, Los Angeles field office to Memphis and New Orleans field offices, Feb. 5, 1969, FBI headquarters Murkin file serial 44–38861–5540.

[164] FBI teletype, New Orleans field office to Director, FBI, Memphis and Los Angeles field offices, Feb. 6, 1969, FBI headquarters MURKIN file, serial 44–38861–5539.

[165] FBI teletype, Los Angeles field office to Memphis and New Orleans field offices, Feb. 5, 1969, FBI headquarters MURKIN file, serial 44–38861–5540.

[166] FBI teletype, New Orleans field office to Director, FBI, Memphis and Los Angeles field offices, Feb. 6, 1969, FBI headquarters MURKIN file, serial 44–38861–5539.

[167] Ibid.

[168] FBI LHM, Los Angeles field office to Director, FBI, Memphis and New Orleans field offices, Feb. 13, 1969, FBI headquarters Murkin file, serial 44–38861–5558.

[169] Civil rights violation—Raoul V. Esquivel, Oct. 8, 1969, FBI file 44–2401.

[170] Louisiana Department of Public Safety, division of State police, attendance and leave records (MLK document 160029); see also deposition of Raoul Esquivel, Jan. 26, 1978, House Select Committee on Assassinations, pp. 7–8 (MLK document 190265).

[171] Interview of James Earl Ray, Nov. 14, 1977, XI appendix to HSCA–JFK Hearings, 159; see also William Bradford Huie, "He Slew the Dreamer" (New York: Delacorte Press, 1970, 1st ed.). p. 37; supplemental deposition of James Earl Ray, *Ray* v. *Foreman*, Nov.

760

22, 1969, pp. 13–14 (MLK document 030316); interview of James Earl Ray, Apr. 14, 1977, IX appendix to the HSCA–MLK hearings, pp. 68, 69, 143.

[172] Notes of George M. Millan, May 30, 1972, interview with Jerry Ray, pp. 3–4 (MLK document 070096).

[173] Id., June 27, 1972 interview with Jerry Ray, at 10.

[174] Ibid.

[175] Id., July 12, 1975 interview with Jerry Ray, at 2.

[176] Id. at 3.

[177] Ibid.

[178] Ibid.

[179] Outside contact report with George McMillan, Dec. 8, 1977, House Select Committee on Assassinations, p. 1 (MLK Document 160168).

[180] Ibid.; see also interview of George McMillan, Mar. 5, 1978, House Select Committee on Assassinations, p. 4 (MLK Document 190554).

[181] Kent Courtney advised that on or about Mar. 20, 1969, he met with Jerry Ray in New Orleans' Lafayette Park. Interview of Kent Courtney, Dec. 12, 1977, House Select Committee on Assassinations, p. 3 (MLK Document 170282). Staff investigators also uncovered a registration card for Jerry Ryan at the Tamanaca Motel in New Orleans for Jan. 20, 1975. Jerry Ray has admittedly used the alias "Jerry Ryan" on numerous occasions. The signature on the registration card is strikingly similar to that of Jerry Ray. See also interview of Lillie Kalon, Dec. 12, 1977, House Select Committee on Assassinations, p. 1 (MLK Document 190111).

[182] Outside contact report with Dave Millesink, Jan. 23, 1978, House Select Committee on Assassinations (MLK Document 170221).

[183] Letter from the FBI to the House Select Committee on Assassinations, Feb. 2, 1978 (MLK Document 180262).

[184] Deposition of Reynard Rochon, Jan. 26, 1978, House Select Committee on Assassinations, p. 17 (MLK Document 190264).

[185] Id. at 6.

[186] Id. at 16.

[187] It was not until Ray's interview with CBS reporter Dan Rather that he first claimed that when he departed from Birmingham he was unaware that the next meeting place with Raoul was to be in Nuevo Laredo, Mexico. Dan Rather interview of James Earl Ray for the CBS program, "Who's Who," Mar. 3, 1977, p. 16 (MLK Document 070077).

[188] Ibid.

[189] Ibid.

[190] Interview of James Earl Ray, Apr. 14, 1977, IX appendix to the HSCA–MLK hearings, pp. 135–138.

[191] Ibid.

[192] Ibid., p. 157; see also interview of James Earl Ray, Sept. 29, 1977, XI appendix to the HSCA–MLK hearings, p. 193.

[193] Interview with James Earl Ray, Apr. 14, 1977, IX appendix to the HSCA–MLK hearings, p. 136; also interview of James Earl Ray, Sept. 29, 1977, XI appendix to the HSCA–MLK hearings, pp. 194–196.

[194] Ibid.

[195] Ibid.

[196] Interview of James Earl Ray, Sept. 29, 1977, XI appendix to the HSCA–MLK hearings, pp. 196–198; also Ray interview, Apr. 14, 1977, IX appendix to the HSCA–MLK hearings, p. 137.

[197] Deposition of Herman A. Thompson, Dec. 9, 1977, House Select Committee on Assassinations, pp. 6, 12 (MLK Document 170001).

[198] Id. at 8.

[199] Id. at 5, 7, 8.

[200] Id. at 16.

[201] Id. at 8, 9.

[202] Id. at 19.

[203] FBI airtel from Buffalo to Director, June 14, 1968, FBI headquarters MURKIN file 44–38861–4541.

[204] Ibid.; FBI memorandum from Rosen to DeLoach, June 14, 1968, FBI headquarters MURKIN file 44–38861–4544.

[205] FBI airtel from New Orleans to Director, no date, FBI headquarters MURKIN file 44–38861–4542.

[206] Ibid.

[207] See staff summaries of interviews of André Salwyn, Feb. 6, 1978 (MLK Document 180162), Mar. 14, 1978 (MLK Document 190482), Mar. 15, 1978 (MLK Document 190481) and Mar. 30, 1978 (MLK Document 200027), House Select Committee on Assassinations.

[208] See staff summaries of interviews of Earl MacRae, Mar. 14, 1978 (MLK Document 190435) and Mar. 16, 1978 (MLK Document 190436), House Select Committee on Assassinations.

[209] RCMP reports supplied by Shelby County district attorney's office, Aug. 31, 1978, pp. 2305–2310 (MLK Document 310108).

[210] Staff memorandum from Wendy S. Collins to Michael C. Eberhardt, Mar. 22, 1978, House Select Committee on Assassinations (MLK Document 310115).

[211] Staff summary of interview of Earl MacRae, Mar. 14, 1978, House Select Committee on Assassinations, p. 3 (MLK Document 190435).

[212] RCMP reports supplied by Shelby County district attorney's office, pp. 2305–2310 (MLK Document 310108).

[213] Outside contact report with André Salwyn, Feb. 6, 1978, House Select Committee on Assassinations, p. 2 (MLK Document 310116).

[214] RCMP reports supplied by Shelby County district attorney's office, pp. 2305–2310 (MLK Document 310108).

[215] Both Joseph Oster and Angelina Lorio, Kimble's former wife, told committee staff that Kimble used counterfeit medical degrees and other fake documents in order to work at a hospital, avoid the draft and secure controlled drugs. Staff summary of interview of Joseph Oster, Apr. 26, 1978, House Select Committee on Assassinations (MLK Document 250282); staff summary of interview of Angelina Lorio, Apr. 30, 1978, House Select Committee on Assassinations, pp. 1–2 (MLK Document 210158). Kimble was arrested on July 26, 1967 for false impersonation of a State policeman, aggravated assault and illegal possession of weapons (see files for Joseph Oster, MLK Document 210233). See also New Orleans FBI field office report, Jan. 12, 1966, Document 157–4403–L; statement of Jules Rico Kimble to New Orleans district attorney, Oct. 10, 1967 (MLK Document 250260).

[216] Staff summary of interview of Joseph Oster, Apr. 26, 1978,

House Select Committee on Assassinations (MLK Document 250282); see also files of Joseph Oster (MLK Document 210233).

[217] Staff summary of interview of Angelina Lorio, Apr. 30, 1978, House Select Committee on Assassinations (MLK Document 210158).

[218] Staff summary of interview of Jules Rico Kimble, May 3, 1978, House Select Committee on Assassinations, p. 2 (MLK Document 210393).

[219] Ibid.

[220] Interview with James Earl Ray by the CBC, 1977, pp. 47–49 (MLK Document 130001).

[221] Rosenson was prosecuted in Federal court for violation of 18 U.S.C. 1407—traveling outside the United States without registering as a convicted felon, *U.S.* v. *Randolph Erwin Rosenson*, Crim. Doc. 38256, filed Jan. 14, 1966, division 6, U.S. District Court, E.D. of Louisiana (MLK Document 140057).

[222] Executive session testimony of Randy Rosenson, Nov. 29, 1977, House Select Committee on Assassinations, p. 26.

[223] Id. at 18–20, 113–115.

[224] Id. at 71, 155–159.

[225] Bank records, Birmingham Trust National Bank (MLK Document 150147).

[226] Executive session testimony of Randy Rosenson, Nov. 29, 1977, House Select Committee on Assassinations, pp. 79–80.

[227] Charles Stein FBI identification sheet (MLK Document 170236); Rosenson FBI identification sheet (MLK Executive Session Exhibit 14).

[228] Outside contact report with George Pittman, Jan. 25, 1978, House Select Committee on Assassinations, p. 2 (MLK Document 170315); see also staff interview of Charles Stein, Mar. 22, 1978, House Select Committee on Assassinations, pp. 1–3 (MLK Document 190402).

[229] Executive session testimony of Randy Rosenson, Apr. 29, 1977, House Select Committee on Assassinations, pp. 29, 31, 42–43, 106, 112, 116, 117, 120, 125, 126.

[230] Staff summary of interview of David Rosen, Oct. 22, 1977, House Select Committee on Assassinations (MLK Document 140270); staff summary of interview of Peggy Rosenson, Oct. 13, 1977, House Select Committee on Assissnations (MLK Document 140266); staff summary of interview of Bill Warner, Oct. 18, 1977 House Select Committee on Assassinations (MLK Document 140280); outside contact report with George Pittman, Jan. 25, 1978, House Select Committee on Assassinations (MLK Document 170315; and outside contact report with John Phillips, Feb. 2, 1978, House Select Committee on Assassinations (MLK Document 180049).

[231] Staff summary of interview of Edna Mathews Lancaster, Sept. 27, 1977, House Select Committee on Assassinations (MLK Document 210560) (hereinafter Lancaster interview, Sept. 27, 1977).

[232] Staff memorandum from Chief Investigator Edward M. Evans to file. Aug. 12, 1977, re Edna Lancaster, pp. 1, 3 (MLK Document 290022).

[233] Id. at 3.

[234] FBI memorandum, May 16, 1968, to SAC Atlanta from SA Joseph G. Shea, FBI headquarters MURKIN file 44–38861–2386.

[235] Ibid.

[236] Staff summary of interview of Charlie Harrison Lancaster,

Sept. 28, 1977, House Select Committee on Assassinations (MLK Document 190164).

[237] Summary of staff interview of Malcom Pittman, Sept. 20, 1977, House Select Committee on Assassinations (MLK Document 190165); staff summary of interview of J. W. McCrickard, Sept. 20, 1977, House Select Committee on Assassinations (MLK Document 190165).

[238] Staff memorandum from Chief Investigator to file, Aug. 12, 1977, House Select Committee on Assassinations (MLK Document 290022).

[239] Interview of Victor Lancaster, Sept. 29, 1977, House Select Committee on Assassinations (MLK Document 190163).

[240] Executive session testimony of Leon Powell, Feb. 9, 1978, House Select Committee on Assassinations.

[241] Id. at 11, 12.

[242] Id. at 14.

[243] Id. at 14, 15.

[244] Id. at 15.

[245] Id. at 6.

[246] Id. at 17.

[247] FBI report, MURKIN file, sec. 86, Serial 44–38861–6069.

[248] Ibid.

[249] Ibid.

[250] FBI memorandum to Gallagher from Peelman, Apr. 2, 1976, FBI headquarters MURKIN file, 44–38861–6115.

[251] Interview, FBI Agent Thomas J. Wilson, Feb. 24, 1978, House Select Committee on Assassinations (MLK Document 190012).

[252] Staff summary of interview of Libby Smith, Apr. 17, 1978, House Select Committee on Assassinations (MLK Document 200346); staff summary of interview of Woodie P. Mobley, Mar. 31, 1978, House Select Committee on Assassinations (MLK Document 200336); staff summary of interview, Diane Brand, Apr. 14, 1978, House Select Committee on Assassinations (MLK Document 200425); staff summary of interview of Clarence Wesley Pitts, Apr. 12, 1978, House Select Committee on Assassinations (MLK Document 200425); staff summary of interview, William L. Smith, Apr. 17, 1978, House Select Committee on Assassinations (MLK Document 200332).

[253] FBI identification sheet, Leon Powell (MLK Document 210494); FBI identification sheet, Claude Powell (MLK Document 210495); obtained from Atlanta Police Department, Jan. 26, 1978.

[254] Executive session testimony of Annie Lois Campos, Feb. 6, 1978, House Select Committee on Assassinations, pp. 6–9; see also staff summary of interview, Annie Lois Campos, Jan. 20, 1978, House Select Committee on Assassinations (MLK Document 180008).

[255] Executive session testimony of Arnold Ray Godfrey, Feb. 6, 1978, House Select Committee on Assassinations, pp. 27–28.

[256] Contempt citation resolution for Claude Powell, Jr. (MLK Document 200480). On Oct. 11, 1978, Claude Powell, Jr., was arraigned and pled guilty to charges of contempt of Congress, On Nov. 21, 1978, Claude Powell Jr., appeared in Atlanta for sentencing, at which time his case was continued until an undetermined date date in December 1978; no final disposition had been made as of that date.

[257] Written statement of Robert Byron Watson, received May 5, 1977 from Atlanta Police Department, p. 2 (MLK Document 090005).

[258] Ibid.

[259] Ibid.

[260] Ibid.

[261] Ibid.

[262] Id. at 3.

[263] Ibid.

[264] Report, Atlanta Police Department, re: Robert Byron Watson, received May 5, 1977, p. 4 of introduction (MLK Document 090006).

[265] Id. at 19.

[266] Id. at 20.

[267] See FBI memorandum, Memphis Field Office, MURKIN file No. 44–1987–777.

[268] Ibid.

[269] See, e.g., taped session of interview and polygraph examination of Robert Byron Watson on July 21, 1971 (MLK Document 150190).

[270] Interview of Robert Byron Watson, Nov. 21, 1977, House Select Committee on Assassinations (MLK Document 150189).

[271] Thomas Bevier, "King Disappointed in March—He'll Try Again Next Week," Memphis Commercial Appeal, Mar. 30, 1968, p. A–1.

[272] Interview of Morris Davis, April 1977, House Select Committee on Assassinations, pp. 2–3 (MLK Document 290052) (hereinafter Davis interview, April 1977); see also interview of David Lifton re: information on Morris Davis provided to Lifton by William Bradford Huie, Mar. 9, 1977, House Select Committee on Assassinations, pp. 1–2 (MLK Document 070035).

[273] Davis interview, April 1977, p. 1.

[274] Newspaper articles received from the Birmingham Police Department, Mar. 17, 1977 (MLK Document 070043).

[275] Davis interview, April 1977, p. 6.

[276] Id. at 2.

[277] Id. at 6.

[278] Id. at 1–2.

[279] Id. at 2.

[280] Ibid.

[281] Id. at 3–4.

[282] Id. at 4.

[283] Id. at 5.

[284] Id. at 6.

[285] Id. at 10.

[286] Executive session testimony of Rev. Ralph D. Abernathy, May 23, 1978, House Select Committee on Assassinations, pp. 118–120.

[287] Staff summary of interview of Fred Shuttlesworth, Mar. 11, 1978, House Select Committee on Assassinations, p. 2 (MLK Document 200026).

[288] Affidavit of Frank Liberto, June 28, 1978, House Select Committee on Assassinations, p. 2 (MLK Document 280063).

[289] Interview of Donald Wood, Mar. 10, 1977, House Select Committee on Assassinations, pp. 1–2 (MLK Document 070038).

[290] Staff memorandum to Robert Lehner from Evans and Gannon re: Gus Prosch/Donald Wood, Mar. 15, 1977, House Select Committee on Assassinations, p. 2 (MLK Document 070159).

[291] Firearms transactions, records and office invoices from Aeromarine Supply Co., A–1, for Dr. Gus Prosch from Jan. 20, 1968 through June 9, 1970 (MLK Document 260141).

[292] Staff notes of interview with Gus Joseph Prosch, Aug. 31, 1978, House Select Committee on Assassinations (MLK Document 290049).

[293] Staff notes of interview with Morris Davis, July 27, 1978, House Select Committee on Assassinations (MLK Document 290048); staff memorandum to Robert Lehner and Edward Evans from Hack and Walker, re: Trip to Birmingham concerning Morris Davis, Oct. 18, 1977, House Select Committee on Assassinations, pp. 2–3 (MLK Document 140121).

[294] Staff notes of interview with Morris Davis, July 27, 1978, House Select Committee on Assassinations, pp. 40–41 (MLK Document 290048).

[295] Staff summary of interview of Walter Maddox, Dec. 6, 1977, House Select Committee on Assassinations (MLK Document 160206).

[296] Ibid.

[297] Ibid.

[298] Outside contact reports with executive offices of Travelodge, Inc., Dec. 5, 1977, Dec. 6, 1977, House Select Committee on Assassinations (MLK Documents 160092, 160094); correspondence from Travelodge to Congressman Stokes, re: report on hotel charges, Dec. 22, 1977 (MLK Document 170009).

[299] Staff summary of interview of Billy Fisher, Jan. 23, 1978, House Select Committee on Assassinations, p. 1 (MLK Document 180334).

[300] Ibid.

[301] Outside contact report with Leroy Roell, Feb. 23, 1978, House Select Committee on Assassinations, p. 1 (MLK Document 220377).

[302] Ibid.

[303] Staff summary of interview of Billy E. Fisher, Jan. 23, 1978, House Select Committee on Assassinations, p. 1 (MLK Document 180334); outside contact report with Leroy Roell, Feb. 23, 1978, House Select Committee on Assassinations, p. 1, (MLK Document 220377).

[304] Executive session testimony of Clifton Baird, Nov. 30, 1977, House Select Committee on Assassinations, pp. 41-42.

[305] Id. at 42–43.

[306] Id. at 42.

[307] Id. at 23–30.

[308] Id. at 46–49; Baird explained to the staff that he had begun taping conversations between himself and other members of the police department as he believed some officers suspected him of the attempted bombing of Officer Brent Hardin's automobile in December 1964. He stated that he recorded Blair's initial offer on Sept. 18, 1965, but later lost the recording.

[309] Executive session testimony of Arlie Blair, Dec. 1, 1977, House Select Committee on Assassinations, pp. 15, 16, 39.

[310] Id. at 5, 20, 28, 29, 30.

[311] Executive session testimony of Clifton Baird, Nov. 30, 1977, House Select Committee on Assassinations, pp. 24–25.

[312] Executive session testimony of James Bibb, Dec. 1, 1977, House Select Committee on Assassinations, pp. 160, 164–165; executive session testimony of Priest Fry, Dec. 1, 1977, House Select Committee on Assassinations, pp. 182–184; executive session testimony of Robert Gregory, Dec. 1, 1977, House Select Committee on Assassinations, p. 197; executive session testimony of Brent Hardin, Dec. 1, 1977, House Select Committee on Assassinations, pp. 106–112, 125, 126; designated counsel statement of Herman Mitchell, Dec. 22, 1977, House Select Committee on Assassinations, pp. 8–10 (MLK Document 190259).

[313] Executive session testimony of William Duncan, Nov. 30, 1977, House Select Committee on Assassinations, pp. 91–108.

[314] Id. at 94.

[315] Id. at 94–108.

[316] Id. at 97, 98, 100–104.

[317] Id. at 111–112.

[318] Id. at 112.

[319] Id. at 109, 110, 111.

[320] Id. at 105–108.

[321] Id. at 94–108.

[322] Interview of William Duncan, Nov. 21, 1977, House Select Committee on Assassinations, pp. 1–4 (MLK Document 160081).

[323] Executive session testimony of William Duncan, Nov. 30, 1977, House Select Committee on Assassinations, p. 104.

[324] Interview of William Duncan, Nov. 27, 1977, House Select Committee on Assassinations, p. 3 (MLK Document 160081).

[325] Executive session testimony of Robert Peters, Dec. 1, 1977, House Select Committee on Assassinations, pp. 149–154; designated counsel statement of Warren L. Walsh, Dec. 22, 1977, House Select Committee on Assassinations, pp. 31–32 (MLK Document 190257); interview of SCA Bernard C. Brown, Nov. 22, 1977, House Select Committee on Assassinations, pp. 1, 2 (MLK Document 160089).

[326] Executive session testimony of Robert Peters, Dec. 1, 1977, House Select Committee on Assassinations, p. 137.

[327] Designated counsel statement of Vernon Austin, Dec. 22, 1977, House Select Committee on Assassinations, pp. 8–9, 14–19 (MLK Document 190258).

[328] Medical records of Clifton Baird, Apr. 25, 1977, six pages (MLK Document 240342); police and medical records of Clifton Baird, Apr. 17, 1977 (MLK Document 240351).

[329] FBI memorandum from W. D. Campbell to Mr. Cochran, June 7, 1977, FBI headquarters MURKIN file 44–38861–6235.

[330] Louisville, Ky., Police Department duty records, Sept. 18, 19, and 20, 1965, for police officers Austin, Baird, Bibb, Blair, Fry, Gregory and Hardin, 33 pages (MLK Document 210239, exhibits C–J).

[331] Executive session testimony of Priest Fry, Dec. 1, 1977, House Select Committee on Assassinations, pp. 187–188; executive session testimony of Robert Gregory, Dec. 1, 1977, House Select Committee on Assassinations, pp. 199–200.

[332] Staff summary of interview of Charles Lee Bell, Oct. 11, 1977, House Select Committee on Assassinations, p. 2 (MLK Document 140082) (hereinafter Bell interview); interview of Charles Lee

Bell, Oct. 17, 1977, House Select Committee on Assassinations (MLK Document 140140) (hereinafter Bell taped interview); statement of Charles Lee Bell to House Select Committee on Assassinations, received Oct. 11, 1977, pp. 19–20 (MLK Document 210221) (hereinafter Bell statement).

[333] Bell taped interview.
[334] Bell statement, pp. 2, 9, 18–20.
[335] Bell taped interview.
[336] Ibid; see also Bell interview, p. 2.
[337] Bell interview, p. 3; Bell statement, pp. 4–23.
[338] Bell interview, p. 3.
[339] Id. at 1–2.
[340] Bell statement, pp. 1–2.
[341] Bell interview; Bell taped interview.
[342] Bell statement.
[343] Interview of A. Wilson Edwards, Dec. 29, 1977, House Select Committee on Assassinations, pp. 1–2 (MLK Document 170077).
[344] Id. at 1–2.
[345] Outside contact report (with Thomas Kitchens), Oct. 30, 1978, House Select Committee on Assassinations (MLK Document 270020).
[346] Ibid.
[347] Outside contact report (with Ella Greathouse, Glen Greathouse and Leroy Greathouse), Oct. 4, 1978, House Select Committee on Assassinations (MLK Document 260032).
[348] Staff summary of interview of Delano E. Walker, Nov. 11, 1977, House Select Committee on Assassinations, p. 1 (MLK Document 170335).
[349] Ibid.
[350] Ibid.
[351] Id. at 3.
[352] Ibid.
[353] Ibid.
[354] Letter from Dr. C. W. Chastain to Warren Hinckle, Ramparts magazine, San Francisco, Calif., June 12, 1968 (MLK Document 290016).
[355] Outside contact report with Dr. C. W. Chastain, Oct. 26, 1977, House Select Committee on Assassinations (MLK Document 290015).
[356] Ibid.
[357] Ibid.
[358] Interview of Delano E. Walker, Nov. 11, 1977, House Select Committee on Assassinations, pp. 1–4 (MLK Document 170335).
[359] Interview of Ruth Ann Walker, No. 11, 1977, House Select Committee on Assassinations, pp. 1–3 (MLK Document 180188).
[360] Interview of Delano E. Walker, Nov. 11, 1977, House Select Committee on Assassinations, p. 2 (MLK Document 170335).
[361] Interview of Ruth Ann Walker, Nov. 11, 1977, House Select Committee on Assassinations, p. 3 (MLK Document 180188).
[362] Id. at 1–2.
[363] Id. at 2; see also interview of Delano E. Walker, Nov. 11, 1977, House Select Committee on Assassinations, p. 2 (MLK Document 170335).

[364] Interview of Ruth Ann Walker, Nov. 11, 1977, House Select Committee on Assassinations, p. 3 (MLK Document 180188).

[365] Somersett died of a heart attack on May 7, 1970. Certificate of death, North Carolina Board of Health, Office of Vital Statistics (MLK Document 110292).

[366] FBI headquarters, Somersett file, vol. 3, FBI memorandum, Miami SAC to Director, Jan. 5, 1962; vol. 3, FBI memorandum, Director to Miami SAC, May 14, 1963; vol. 3, FBI memorandum, Director to Field, Jan. 23, 1964; vol. 1, FBI memorandum, Oct. 22, 1969; vol. 3, FBI airtel, Miami SAC to Director, Oct. 29, 1969; vol. 1, FBI memorandum, SAC Miami to Director, Jan. 8, 1964; see also interview of Judge Seymour Gelber, Mar. 22, 1978, House Select Committee on Assassinations (MLK Document 200085).

[367] Dan Christensen, "King Assassination: FBI Ignored Its Miami Informer," Miami magazine, October 1976, p. 31 (MLK Document 030179).

[368] Id. at 31.

[369] Ibid.; see also FBI documents, supra, ref. 2.

[370] FBI headquarters, Somersett file, vol. 3, FBI memorandum, Rosen to Belmont, Nov. 13, 1961 (recommending discontinuation of Somersett as a racial informant); vol. 3, FBI airtel, SAC Miami to Director, Jan. 5, 1962 (noting that Somersett was no longer a paid informant).

[371] Memorandum report, U.S. Secret Service, Treasury Department, Dec. 5, 1969, file No. CO–2–43,860; memorandum report, U.S. Secret Service, Treasury Department, Mar. 9, 1968, file No. CO–2–43,860.

[372] Memorandum report, U.S. Secret Service, Treasury Department, Dec. 5, 1969, file No. CO–2–43,860.

[373] Deposition of Charles Sapp, Apr. 25, 1978, House Select Committee on Assassinations, pp. 46–47 (MLK Document 210230).

[374] Intra-office memorandum, Miami Police Department, from Lt. Charles H. Sapp to Col. Walter E. Headley, Apr. 25, 1968 (MLK Document 030180).

[375] Deposition of Charles Sapp, Apr. 25, 1978, House Select Committee on Assassinations, pp. 53–55 (MLK Document 210230); see also Dan Christensen, "King Assassination: FBI Ignored Its Miami Informer," Miami magazine, October 1976, p. 31 (MLK Document 030179).

[376] Intra-office memorandum, Miami Police Department, from Lt. Charles H. Sapp to Col. Walter E. Headley, Apr. 7, 1968 (MLK Document 290006).

[377] Ibid.

[378] Ibid.

[379] Interview of Charles Sapp, July 27, 1978. House Select Committee on Assassinations, p. 2 (MLK Document 240021).

[380] Deposition of Everett Kay, Apr. 26, 1978, House Select Committee on Assassinations, pp. 54–60 (MLK Document 210227); deposition of Haywood Swilley, Apr. 26, 1978, House Select Committee on Assassinations, pp. 33–38 (MLK Document 210228); interview of Lockheart Gracey, Mar. 24, 1978, House Select Committee on Assassinations, p. 2 (MLK Document 200084).

[381] See statements of Kay, Swilley, Gracey, supra, ref. 380.

[382] Outside contact report with Paul Long, Feb. 17, 1977, House Select Committee on Assassinations, (MLK Document 110490); outside contact report with Stan Weinbrecht, Mar. 8,

1978, House Select Committee on Assassinations (MLK Document 190206); letter from Stan Weinbrecht to House Select Committee on Assassinations, Apr. 5, 1978 (MLK Document 200063); outside contact report with James E. Smith, May 5, 1978, House Select Committee on Assassinations (MLK Document 210135); outside contact report (with the Library of Congress), Mar. 9, 1978, House Select Committee on Assassinations (MLK Document 190204).

[383] Interview of Otis Humphrey Moore, Mar. 7, 1977, House Select Committee on Assassinations, pp. 7–8 (MLK Document 070031) (hereinafter Moore interview).

[384] Id. at 10.

[385] Id. at 8–9.

[386] Id. at 11, 14.

[387] Id. at 11.

[388] Id. at 11.

[389] Ibid.

[390] Letter from Otis Moore to House Select Committee on Assassinations, with attachments, Feb. 3, 1977 (MLK Document 060004).

[391] Moore interview, pp. 2, 4, 12, 17.

[392] Letters from Wilson F. Colberg and Senator Edward F. Kennedy, dated Mar. 3, 1978 and Nov. 30, 1977, respectively, to House Select Committee on Assassinations (MLK Document 190106).

[393] Ibid.; see also letter from Otis Moore to the House Select Committee on Assassinations, Feb. 3, 1977 (MLK Document 060004).

[394] Letter from Otis Moore to the House Select Committee on Assassinations, Feb. 3, 1977 (MLK Document 060004).

[395] FBI report, Jan. 28, 1977, MURKIN file, Bureau No. 44–38861–6178. It should be noted also that this report refers to a statement by Moore's wife that he was and had been under medical care for a nervous disorder.

[396] Summary of interview of Myron Billett, Dec. 21, 1977, House Select Committee on Assassinations, p. 1 (MLK Document 180065).

[397] Id. at 2.

[398] Ibid.

[399] Ibid.

[400] Id. at 3. See also letter from Myron Billett to House Select Committee on Assassinations, Apr. 9, 1978 (MLK Document 210254).

[401] Ibid., Myron Billett letter.

[402] Interview of Myron Billett, Dec. 2, 1977, House Select Committee on Assassinations, pp. 1–2 (MLK Document 180065). See also request of the House Select Committee on Assassinations to the FBI, dated Jan. 24, 1978 (MLK Document 170274); request of the House Select Committee on Assassinations to CIA and CIA compliance, May 19, 1978 (MLK Document 210423); FBI response to House Select Committee on Assassinations request, Oct. 20, 1978 (MLK Document 260347); outside contact report with J. Aldhizer, Sept. 29, 1978, House Select Committee on Assassinations (MLK Document 260048).

[403] Staff summary of interview of Myron Billett, Dec. 21, 1977, House Select Committee on Assassinations, p. 3 (MLK Document 180065).

[404] Billett's credibility was also undermined by an extensive criminal record, which included convictions for armed robbery, manslaughter, grand larceny, and forgery.

References: Section D

[1] Report of the Department of Justice Task Force to Review the FBI Martin Luther King, Jr. Security and Assassination Investigations, Jan. 11, 1977, p. 141.

[2] MLK Exhibit F–438A (FBI memorandum from William C. Sullivan to A. H. Belmont, Dec. 24, 1963), hearings before the Select Committee on Assassinations, U.S. House of Representatives, 95th Cong., 2d sess. (Washington, D.C.: U.S. Government Printing Office, 1979), vol. VI, p. 156 (hereinafter—HSCA–MLK hearings,—).

[3] MLK Exhibit F–451A (FBI memorandum from Detroit to SAC, Albany, Aug. 25, 1967), VI HSCA–MLK Hearings, 298.

[4] Ibid.

[5] MLK Exhibit F–451B (FBI airtel from Detroit to SAC, Albany, Mar. 4, 1968), VI HSCA–MLK Hearings, 301.

[6] Ibid.

[7] Ibid.

[8] MLK Exhibit F–459 (FBI memorandum from SAC, Memphis to Director, Mar. 14, 1968), VI HSCA–MLK hearings, 522.

[9] Interview of FBI informant, Apr. 4, 1978, House Select Committee on Assassinations (MLK Document 200035).

[10] Testimony of Dr. Ralph Abernathy, Aug. 14, 1978, I HSCA–MLK hearings, 18 (hereinafter Abernathy testimony); see also "King Disappointed in March—He'll Try Again Next Week" Memphis, (Tenn.) Commercial Appeal, Mar. 30, 1968, p. A1.

[11] MLK Exhibit F–451C (FBI memorandum from G. C. Moore, Chief, Racial Intelligence Section, to William C. Sullivan, Assistant Director, Domestic Intelligence Division, Mar. 29, 1968), VI HSCA–MLK hearings, 307.

[12] Abernathy testimony, p. 32.

[13] Chief Counsel's notes, May 17, 1978, Re: FBI's Black organizing project/invaders informant files (MLK Document 300003).

[14] Interview of FBI informant, Nov. 15, 1978, House Select Committee on Assassinations (MLK Document 290041). It should be noted that at the informant's request, the committee has agreed not to disclose his identity in this report.

[15] Ibid.

[16] Testimony of Marrell McCollough, Nov. 20, 1978, VI HSCA–MLK hearings, 417 (hereinafter McCollough testimony).

[17] Testimony of William Lawrence, Nov. 21, 1978, VI HSCA–MLK hearings, 547 (hereinafter Lawrence testimony).

[18] MLK Exhibit F–455 (FBI interview of Marrell McCollough, Apr. 11, 1968), VI HSCA–MLK hearings, 422.

[19] McCollough testimony, p. 433.

[20] See Lawrence testimony, pp. 541, 546–548.

[21] FBI teletype to Director from Memphis, Tenn., Mar. 28, 1968.

[22] Lawrence testimony, p. 547.

[23] MLK Exhibit F–456 (FBI memorandum to Director from

SAC, Memphis, Tenn., Mar. 29, 1968), p. 4, VI HSCA–MLK hearings, 470.

[24] Lawrence testimony, p. 549.

[25] Executive session testimony of Howell Lowe, May 24, 1978, House Select Committee on Assassinations, pp. 11-13.

[26] FBI memorandum from William C. Sullivan to Cartha De-Loach, Mar. 20, 1968, re: MLK's march on Washington, Bureau file No. 157–106670–415.

[27] Executive session testimony of Howell Lowe, ref. 25, supra, pp. 115–118.

[28] See, e.g., Lawrence testimony, Nov. 21, 1978, p. 546.

[29] FBI airtel to Director from SAC Mobile, Mar. 25, 1968, re: racial intelligence, Bureau No. 100–448006–63.

[30] FBI airtel from Director to SAC, Mobile, Ala., Apr. 2, 1968, re: counter-intelligence program—Washington spring project, Bureau No. 100–448006–63.

[31] Letter from G. Robert Blakey to Griffin B. Bell, June 20, 1978, re: Ray associates list (MLK Document 220442).

[32] Letter from Director, FBI, to House Select Committee on Assassinations, Aug. 10, 1978 (MLK Document 240222).

[33] Interview of [name deleted], Oct. 13, 1978, House Select Committee on Assassinations (MLK Document 260219).

[34] Id. at 5.

[35] Id. at 2.

[36] Id. at 3–4.

[37] The seven agents and their 1968 FBI office assignments, as identified from FBI reports, were: Thomas Weaver, Jefferson City, Mo.; Arthur Woods, Springfield, Ill.; Robert Haines, Alton, Ill.; Cletis Bidewell, St. Louis, Mo.; Robert Pevahouse, Des Plaines, Ill.; Mac Oliver, Quincy, Ill.; and Joseph Kissiah, who served as case agent and of the office of origin, Kansas City, Mo. An eighth agent, Rowan Ayers from the Jefferson City, Mo., office of the FBI, was similarly identified but is now deceased. The following MLK documents reflect the interviews of the seven agents listed above: staff summary of interview of Thomas Weaver, July 28, 1978, House Select Committee on Assassinations (MLK Document 250083); staff summary of interview of Arthur Woods, Sept. 1, 1978, House Select Committee on Assassinations (MLK Document 250084); staff summary of interview of Robert Haines, Aug. 29, 1978, House Select Committee on Assassinations (MLK Document 250085); staff summary of interview of Cletis Bidewell, Aug. 31, 1978, House Select Committee on Assassinations (MLK Document 250086); staff summary of interview of Robert Pevahouse, Aug. 28, 1978, House Select Committee on Assassinations (MLK Document 250087); staff summary of interview of Joe Kissiah, July 28, 1978, House Select Committee on Assassinations (MLK Document 250088); and staff summary of interview of Mac Oliver, Sept. 1, 1978, House Select Committee on Assassinations (MLK Document 250082).

[38] Bernard S. Lee, *SCLC* v. *Clarence M. Kelley et al.*, civil action No. 76–1185, U.S. District Court for District of Columbia, memorandum opinion and order, Jan. 31, 1977, pp. 3–4 (MLK Document 270135).

[39] *Lee* v. *Kelley*, motion for the United States to intervene as party defendant, Nov. 10, 1978 (MLK Document 270135).

[40] *Lee* v. *Kelley,* order, Nov. 14, 1978 (MLK Document 270135).

[41] MLK Exhibit F–442A (FBI memorandum from C. D. Brennan to W. C. Sullivan, Assistant Director, Domestic Intelligence Division, Apr. 18, 1968), VI HSCA–MLK Hearings, 181.

[42] Ibid.

[43] FBI memorandum from SAC, Atlanta to file, June 23, 1966, Bureau No. 100–6670E–106.

[44] Letter from the FBI to the Senate Select Committee to Study Governmental Operations with Respect to Intelligence Activities, July 21, 1975.

[45] Testimony of Ramsey Clark, Nov. 28, 1978, VII HSCA–MLK Hearings, 128 (hereinafter Clark testimony).

[46] Id. at 130.

[47] Mark Lane and Dick Gregory, Code Name "Zorro" (New York: Pocket Books, 1978), pp. 151–157 (hereinafter Zorro).

[48] Executive session testimony of Donald H. Smith, Mar. 21, 1978, House Select Committee on Assassinations, pp. 13, 20 (hereinafter Smith executive session testimony).

[49] Testimony of Frank C. Holloman, Nov. 10, 1978, IV HSCA–MLK Hearings, 253 (hereinafter Holloman testimony); interview of James MacDonald, Feb. 23, 1978, House Select Committee on Assassinations, p. 2 (MLK Document 200333).

[50] Compare statement of former Chief of Police Henry Lux that the normal practice was to give Dr. King security (staff interview of Henry Lux, June 22, 1978, House Select Committee on Assassinations, MLK Document 290045) (hereinafter Lux interview), with testimony of Inspector Smith that he did not ever recall providing security for Dr. King previously (Smith executive session testimony, Mar. 21, 1978, p. 12) and statement of Lieutenant Arkin that no previous security was ever provided Dr. Kink because he always said he did not want it (interview of Lieutenant Arkin, Dec. 15, 1976, House Select Committee on Assassinations, p. 11 (MLK Document 040017).

[51] Smith executive session testimony, Mar. 21, 1978, pp. 15–16.

[52] Id. at 19; See also "Civil Disorders; Memphis, Tenn. Feb. 12–Apr. 16, 1968," a report prepared for Frank Holloman, director of fire and police, by Lieutenant Arkin (MLK Document 030198). Portions of this report appear as MLK exhibit F–186, IV HSCA–MLK hearings, 246.

[53] MLK Exhibit F–187 (Apr. 5, 1968, memorandum from Smith to Huston), IV HSCA–MLK hearings, 257.

[54] Ibid.

[55] Ibid.

[56] Smith executive session testimony, Mar. 21, 1978, p. 26.

[57] Id. at 20–27.

[58] Id. at 26–27.

[59] Id. at 27.

[60] Lux interview, p. 3.

[61] Ibid.

[62] Interview of James MacDonald, Feb. 23, 1978, House Select Committee on Assassinations, pp. 2–3, (MLK Document 200333).

[63] Smith executive session testimony, Mar. 21, 1978, p. 28.

[64] Holloman testimony, pp. 263, 264. Holloman stated he was

773

unaware of the withdrawal of the detail until informed of it by the committee in 1978 (Holloman testimony, p. 263). The committee noted that retired Chief of Police Henry Lux said Holloman was not consulted when the decision to withdraw the detail was transmitted by Huston to Smith (Lux interview).

[65] Interview of W. B. Richmond, Mar. 7, 1978, House Select Committee on Assassinations, p. 7 (MLK Document 190430) (hereinafter Richmond interview); testimony of Edward Redditt, Nov. 10, 1978, IV HSCA–MLK hearings, 202 (hereinafter Redditt testimony).

[66] Executive session testimony of Graydon P. Tines, Mar. 21, 1978, House Select Committee on Assassinations, p. 100 (hereinafter Tines executive session testimony).

[67] Executive session testimony of Edward Redditt, Mar. 22, 1978, House Select Committee on Assassinations, p. 24 (hereinafter Redditt executive session testimony).

[68] Id. at 33; Redditt testimony, p. 204; see also MLK exhibit F–229 (MPD internal memorandum, Apr. 4, 1968, from Redditt to Tines), IV HSCA–MLK hearings, 207.

[69] Redditt executive session testimony, p. 34.

[70] Id. at 40.

[71] Id. at 41.

[72] Ibid.

[73] Tines executive session testimony, p. 100.

[74] Memphis Police Department supplementary homicide report, July 22, 1968, p. 1525 (MLK Document 030203).

[75] Richmond interview, pp. 7–9.

[76] Smith executive session testimony, p. 29.

[77] Redditt executive session testimony, p. 25.

[78] MLK exhibit F–229 (MPD internal memorandum, Apr. 4, 1968, from Reddit to Tines), IV HSCA–MLK hearings, 207.

[79] Memphis Police Department memorandum from Tines to Routt, July 17, 1968, re security and surveillance of Dr. Martin Luther King from time he arrived in Memphis on Apr. 3, 1968, until he was assassinated on the evening of Apr. 4, 1968 (MLK executive session exhibit No. 56).

[80] Redditt executive session testimony, p. 26.

[81] Id. at 27–29.

[82] Id. at 24.

[83] Id. at 42.

[84] Tines executive session testimony, p. 102.

[85] Richmond interview, p. 9.

[86] Redditt testimony, pp. 224–225.

[87] Id. at 205, 225.

[88] Id. at 205.

[89] Statement of Edward Redditt given at central police headquarters on Apr. 10, 1968 (MLK executive session exhibit No. 70).

[90] Redditt executive session testimony, pp. 179–180. Portions of this testimony appear at MLK exhibit F–183, IV HSCA–MLK hearings, 211.

[91] Redditt testimony, p. 218.

[92] Id. at 217–218.

[93] Ibid.

[94] Zorro, p. 157.

[95] Redditt executive session testimony, p. 148.

[96] Id. at 150–151.

[97] Richmond interview, p. 20.

[98] Tines executive session testimony, pp. 116–117.

[99] Redditt executive session testimony, p. 152.

[100] Id. at 181, 182.

[101] Redditt testimony, p. 232.

[102] Ibid.

[103] Id. at 233.

[104] Memphis Police Department memorandum from Redditt to Tines, Mar. 8, 1968, re "Threats from Rosetta Miller FC, administrative assistant, U.S. Civil Rights Commission" (MLK executive session exhibit No. 67).

[105] See e.g., MLK exhibit F–229 (memorandum from Redditt to Tines, Apr. 4, 1968 re "Surveillance of Martin Luther King, Jr., and Related Activities"), IV HSCA–MLK hearings, 207.

[106] Tines executive session testimony, p. 108.

[107] Interview of Lieutenant Arkin, Dec. 15, 1976, House Select Committee on Assassinations, p. 23 (MLK Document 040017) (hereinafter Arkin interview).

[108] Tines executive session testimony, p. 108.

[109] Holloman testimony, p. 266.

[110] Arkin interview, p. 23.

[111] Interview of James MacDonald, Feb. 23, 1978. House Select Committee on Assassinations, p. 3 (MLK Document 200333).

[112] Tines executive session testimony, pp. 112–113.

[113] Holloman testimony, p. 267.

[114] Redditt executive session testimony, p. 80.

[115] Redditt testimony, p. 209.

[116] Holloman testimony, p. 267.

[117] Id. at 266.

[118] Outside contact report with Robert Goff, Feb. 4, 1978, House Select Committee on Assassinations (MLK Document 180379).

[119] Holloman testimony, p. 270: MLK exhibit F–189 (MPD memorandum from Tines to MacDonald, Apr. 4, 1968), IV HSCA–MLK hearings, 268.

[120] Holloman testimony, p. 270.

[121] Tines executive session testimony, pp. 110–112.

[122] Arkin interview, p. 21.

[123] Interviews of Phil Manuel, Nov. 23, 1976 and Mar. 18, 1977, House Select Committee on Assassinations (MLK Documents 290044 and 070147).

[124] Deposition of confidential source, Apr. 3, 1978, House Select Committee on Assassinations, pp. 32–38 (MLK Document 280104).

[125] MLK exhibit F–189, IV HSCA–MLK hearings, 268. Although the memorandum discussing Manuel was addressed to MacDonald, MacDonald had no memory of Manuel or any threat Manuel transmitted. MacDonald recalls Redditt's transfer as being the cumulative result of prior threats directed against Redditt and his family. Interview of MacDonald, Feb. 23, 1978, House Select Committee on Assassinations, p. 4 (MLK Document 200333).

[126] MLK exhibit F–190 (Memphis Police Department memorandum from Arkin to Tines, Apr. 4, 1968), IV HSCA–MLK hearings, 269.

[127] Tines executive session testimony, p. 115.

[128] Holloman testimony, Nov. 10, 1978, pp. 270–271.

[129] Statement of Edward Redditt given at central police headquarters on Apr. 10, 1968 (MLK executive session exhibit No. 70), p. 1.

[130] Zorro, pp. 144–150.

[131] Interview of Floyd Newsum, Dec. 13, 1976, House Select Committee on Assassinations, pp. 2–3 (MLK Document 040012) (hereinafter Newsum interview).

[132] Id. at 8.

[133] See Memphis Fire Department strength reports (MLK Document 290040).

[134] Newsum interview, pp. 5–6.

[135] Memphis Fire Department strength reports (MLK Document 290040).

[136] Interview of Norvell E. Wallace, Dec. 17, 1976, House Select Committee on Assassinations, p. 6 (MLK Document 040020).

[137] Memphis Fire Department strength reports (MLK Document 290040).

[138] Tines executive session testimony, p. 118.

[139] Ibid.

[140] Memphis Police Department memorandum, Redditt to Tines, Apr. 4, 1968 (MLK executive session exhibit No. 68), p. 2.

[141] Redditt testimony, pp. 230–231.

[142] Newsum interview, pp. 9, 11.

[143] Id. at 9.

[144] Interview of James O. Barnett, Feb. 23, 1978, House Select Committee on Assassinations, p. 2 (MLK Document 200427).

[145] The estimate, taken from MPD files, includes a MPD undercover officer, Marrell McCollough, who was present at the Lorraine at the time of the assassination, and TACT unit 11, composed of 12 to 16 officers, which was actually located a few yards beyond a mile's radius. It excludes routine ward cars which may have been in the area but for which no records remain in the MPD. The estimate actually reflects the location of most officers at 6:03., when the news of the shooting was broadcast, rather than their locations at 6:01, when Dr. King was shot. See also MLK exhibit F–186 (MPD report from Arkin to Holloman), IV HSCA–MLK hearings, 246.

[146] Holloman testimony, p. 278.

[147] MLK exhibit F–194 (affidavit of Judson Ghormley), IV HSCA–MLK hearings, 285.

[148] Testimony of Marrell McCollough, Nov. 20, 1978, VI HSCA–MLK hearings, 418–419 (hereinafter McCollough testimony).

[149] See e.g., staff interview of P. M. Jowers, July 28, 1977, House Select Committee on Assassinations, p. 4 (MLK Document 120104) and staff interview of Stephen B. Scott, July 29, 1977, House Select Committee on Assassinations, p. 5 (MLK Document 110486).

[150] McCollough testimony, p. 419.

[151] Richmond interview, p. 16.

[152] MLK exhibit F–94 (affidavit of Judson Ghormley), IV HSCA–MLK hearings, 285.

[153] Memphis Police Department supplementary homicide report, supplement No. 27, p. 1 (MLK Document 030203). The sub-

stance of the report, which dealt with the activities of all members of TACT 10, was corroborated in interviews with the staff. See also interview of Emmett Douglas, Aug. 24, 1977, House Select Committee on Assassinations (MLK Document 120112).

[154] Memphis Police Department supplementary homicide report, supplement No. 27, p. 1 (MLK Document 030203). See also MLK Exhibit F–194 (affidavit of Judson Ghormley), IV HSCA–MLK hearings, 285; interview of Barney G. Wright, Aug. 14, 1977, House Select Committee on Assassinations, p. 4 (MLK Document 120018).

[155] Interview of Vernon Dollahite, Aug. 15, 1977, House Select Committee on Assassinations, p. 3 (MLK Document 120101).

[156] MLK exhibit F–194 (affidavit of Judson Ghormley), IV HSCA–MLK hearings, 285.

[157] Interview of Barney G. Wright, Aug. 14, 1977, House Select Committee on Assassinations, p. 4 (MLK Document 120118).

[158] Memphis Police Department supplementary homicide report, supplement No. 27, p. 72 (MLK Document 030203).

[159] Ibid.; interview of Barney G. Wright, Aug. 14, 1977. House Select Committee on Assassinations, pp. 5–8 (MLK Document 120018).

[160] MLK exhibit F–94 (affidavit of Judson Ghormley), IV HSCA–MLK hearings, 285; interview of Vernon Dollahite, Aug. 15, 1977, House Select Committee on Assassinations, pp. 2–3 (MLK Document 120101).

[161] MLK exhibit F–195 (affidavit of Frank Kallaher, with attached transcripts of April 4, 1968, Memphis police radio broadcasts), IV HSCA–MLK hearings, 287.

[162] Ibid.

[163] Ibid.

[164] Ibid.

[165] Ibid.

[166] Ibid; see also affidavit of E. Winslow Chapman, June 7, 1978 (MLK Document 220476).

[167] See, e.g., MLK exhibit F–193 (affidavit of W. O. Crumby), IV HSCA–MLK hearings, 279; see also interview of Clyde S. Bounds, July 29, 1977, House Select Committee on Assassinations (MLK Document 120102) (hereinafter Bounds interview); interview of Stephen B. Scott, July 29, 1977, p. 1, House Select Committee on Assassinations (MLK Document 110486); interview of Henry Lux, June 22, 1978, House Select Committee on Assassinations (MLK Document 290045) (hereinafter Lux interview).

[168] Frank Holloman, former director of fire and safety, stated that after the rioting started, the assassination of Dr. King and the riot situation were "equal priorities." Holloman testimony, p. 322.

[169] See, e.g., Bounds interview; interview of Stephen B. Scott, July 29, 1977, House Select Committee on Assassinations (MLK Document 110486).

[170] MLK exhibit F–195 (affidavit of Frank Kallaher), IV HSCA–MLK hearings, 287.

[171] Testimony of James Earl Ray, August 16, 1978, I HSCA–MLK hearings, 106.

[172] MLK exhibit F–195 (affidavit of Frank Kallaher), IV HSCA–MLK hearings, 287.

[173] Ibid.

[174] Lux interview, p. 4.

[175] During James Earl Ray's incarceration at Missouri State Penitentiary, Jefferson City, Mo., he made two unsuccessful escapes, one in 1961 and the other in 1966. (See James Earl Ray's Missouri State Penitentiary records: Nov. 19, 1961, interoffice communication on attempted escape of Ray; March 13, 1966, interoffice communication on attempted escape of inmate Ray (MLK Document 060018).

[176] Missouri State Penitentiary visitation records (MLK Document 240176).

[177] James Earl Ray's Missouri State Penitentiary records: bank account records from March 22, 1960 to July 14, 1967 (MLK Document 060018).

[178] James Earl Ray's Missouri State Penitentiary records; reports on escape investigations (MLK Document 060018).

[179] See, generally, FBI and House Select Committee on Assassinations interviews with former inmate associates of Ray and Missouri State prison officials, 2 vols., approximately 130 interviews as summarized in MLK Document 280061.

[180] Staff report on contents of Ray's Missouri State Penitentiary records, June 11, 1977, House Select Committee on Assassinations, pp. 8–9 (MLK Document 100038).

[181] Letter from Harry F. Lauf to House Select Committee on Assassinations, June 17, 1977 (MLK Document 100071).

[182] Ibid.

[183] Ibid.

[184] Letter from Harry F. Lauf to House Select Committee on Assassinations, January 26, 1978 (MLK Document 170324).

[185] Interview of James Earl Ray, Dec. 2, 1977, House Select Committee on Assassinations, XI Appendix to the HSCA–MLK Hearings, pp. 8–10.

[186] Ibid.

[187] James Earl Ray's Missouri State Penitentiary records: reports on escape investigation (MLK Document 060018); interview of Major Bernard J. Poiry, June 12, 1977, House Select Committee on Assassinations (MLK Document 180034); interview of Danton Steele, June 12, 1977, House Select Committee on Assassinations (MLK Document 100095); interview of former Warden Harold Rudolfo Swenson, June 7, 1977, House Select Committee on Assassinations (MLK Document 230037).

[188] Staff summary of interview of Raymond Patrick, June 9, 1977, House Select Committee on Assassinations, pp. 1–2 (MLK Document 180038); staff summary of interview of Robert L. Powell, Nov. 21, 1977, House Select Committee on Assassinations, p. 2 (MLK Document 180032); staff summary of interview of Jack Romprey, June 9, 1977, House Select Committee on Assassinations, pp. 1–2 (MLK Document 180035); staff summary of interview of Michael Moore, June 9, 1977, House Select Committee on Assassinations, pp. 1–2 (MLK Document 180033); staff summary of interview of James Stidham, June 10, 1977, House Select Committee on Assassinations, pp. 1–2 (MLK Document 100094); interview of Ernest Franklin, June 8, 1977, House Select Committee on Assassinations, pp. 1–3 (MLK Document 100097); staff summary of Joseph J. Maloney, Nov. 10, 1977, House Select Committee on Assassinations, p. 2 (MLK Document 180184); staff summary of interview of John Kenneth Hurtt, Nov. 10, 1977, House Select Committee on Assassinations, p. 2 (MLK Document 180082); staff summary of interview

of Robert L. Powell, Nov. 21, 1977, House Select Committee on Assassinations, p. 1 (MLK Document 170321).

[189] James Earl Ray's Missouri State Penitentiary records: inter-office communication from Capt. Donald Wyrick, June 19, 1968 (MLK Document 060018); FBI Kansas City 302 S.A. report, June 14, 1968, interview of Danton Steele on May 27, 1968, p. 29 (MLK Document 040058); staff summary of interview of Capt. Danton Steele, June 12, 1977, House Select Committee on Assassinations, p. 2 (MLK Document 100095); staff summary of interview of Maj. Bernard J. Poiry, June 12, 1977, House Select Committee on Assassinations, p. 1 (MLK Document 180034).

[190] Staff summary of interview of James Stidham, June 10, 1977, House Select Committee on Assassinations, pp. 1–2 (MLK Document 100094).

[191] Staff memorandum from Lee and Chenoweth to Lehner re "probable method used to escape from Missouri State Penitentiary," June 24, 1977, House Select Committee on Assassinations, p. 5 (MLK Document 190393).

[192] Staff summary of interview of Frank Guinan, July 13, 1978, House Select Committee on Assassinations, p. 1 (MLK Document 300001).

[193] Interview of James Earl Ray, Dec. 2, 1977, House Select Committee on Assassinations, XII Appendix to the HSCA–MLK hearings, p. 27.

[194] Staff summary of interview of James Stidham, June 10, 1977, House Select Committee on Assassinations, pp. 1–2 (MLK Document 100094).

[195] FBI interview of Donald Garfield Cox, June 5, 1968; reported by S.A. Harold Dobson in St. Louis MURKIN report, June 25, 1968; see also staff summary of interview of Joseph J. Maloney, House Select Committee on Assassinations, p. 3 (MLK Document 180184).

[196] Staff summary of interview of Capt. Danton Steele, June 12, 1977, House Select Committee on Assassinations, p. 1 (MLK Document 100095); staff summary of interview of former Warden Harold Rudolfo Swenson, June 7, 1977, House Select Committee on Assassinations, p. 2 (MLK Document 230037).

[197] James Earl Ray's Missouri State Penitentiary records: inter-office communication, Apr. 23, 1967 re inmate Ray missing at 5 p.m. count; memorandum, Aug. 16, 1967, re escape of Ray (MLK Document 060018).

[198] Outside contact report with Lt. William R. Turner, Oct. 16, 1978, House Select Committee on Assassinations, p. 1 (MLK Document 280090).

[199] James Earl Ray's Missouri State Penitentiary records: inter-office communication, May 4, 1967, re supplement to escape investigation report of May 3, 1967 (MLK Document 160018).

The failure of various prison employees to perform their duties properly resulted in administrative action against them, although none were terminated. Top officials at the prison further concluded it would not be justifiable to take action against any inmates who had helped Ray.

Staff memorandum from Lee and Chenoweth to Lehner re "probable method used to escape from Missouri State Penitentiary," June 24, 1977, House Select Committee on Assassinations, p. 8 (MLK Document 190393).

[1] See final report of Senate Select Committee to Study Governmental Operations with Respect to Intelligence Activities, 94th Congress, 2d session (Washington, D.C.: U.S. Government Printing Office, 1976), book III, p. 4 (hereinafter book III, Senate Intelligence Committee).

[2] Id. at 13.

[3] Testimony of Dr. Ralph Abernathy, Aug. 14, 1978, hearings before the Select Committee on Assassinations, U.S. House of Representatives, 95th Congress, 2d session (Washington, D.C.: U.S. Government Printing Office, 1979), vol. I, p. 12 (hereinafter Abernathy testimony — HSCA–MLK hearings —).

[4] FBI memorandum from Director to Atlanta, Sept. 20, 1947, re: Southern Christian Leadership Conference, Bureau No. 100—438794—X1.

[5] Department of Justice memorandum from Assistant Attorney General Robert Murphy to Assistant Attorney General J. S. Pottinger, Mar. 31, 1976, p. 8 (MLK Document 120023).

[6] Id. at 11.

[7] Testimony of Charles Brennan, Nov. 17, 1978, VI HSCA–MLK hearings, 129 (hereinafter Brennan testimony).

[8] MLK exhibit F–435 (FBI investigative branch organizational chart—circa 1968), VI HSCA–MLK hearings, 83.

[9] Testimony of George C. Moore, Nov. 17, 1978, VI HSCA–MLK hearings, 363 (hereinafter Moore testimony).

[10] Executive session testimony of Charles D. Brennan, June 21, 1978, House Select Committee on Assassinations, p. 7.

[11] MLK exhibit F–451–A (FBI memorandum to SAC, Albany, from Director, Aug. 25, 1967), VI HSCA–MLK hearings, 298.

[12] MLK exhibit F–451–B (FBI airtel to SAC, Albany, from Director, Mar. 4, 1968), VI HSCA–MLK hearings, 301.

[13] Executive session testimony of Thomas E. Bishop, June 21, 1978, House Select Committee on Assassinations, pp. 6–7.

[14] Executive session testimony of Alan G. Sentinella, May 25, 1978, House Select Committee on Assassinations, p. 26.

[15] MLK exhibit F–451–A (FBI memorandum to SAC, Albany, from Director, Aug. 25, 1967, VI HSCA–MLK hearings, 298.

[16] Moore testimony, pp. 366–367.

[17] See refs. 47, 48 and 49, and text, infra, for discussion of Department of Justice authorization procedures for various forms of electronic surveillance.

[18] FBI memorandum from M. A. Jones to Cartha DeLoach, Feb. 7, 1961, re: article in The Nation for Feb. 4, 1961, by Martin Luther King, Jr., unrecorded headquarter serials.

[19] FBI memorandum from Bland to Sullivan, Feb. 3, 1962, FBI headquarters file 100–372450–135.

[20] Washington Capital News Service teletype, Dec. 29, 1963, FBI headquarters file 94–3–4–11–752.

[21] See, for example, executive session testimony of Cartha DeLoach, July 18, 1978, House Select Committee on Assassinations, pp. 12–18, 41–45, and testimony of Arthur Murtagh, Nov. 17, 1978, VI HSCA–MLK hearings, 94–96 (hereinafter Murtagh testimony).

[22] "J. Edgar Hoover and the FBI," Newsweek, Dec. 7, 1964, p. 22.

[23] Testimony of Ramsey Clark, Nov. 28, 1978, VII HSCA–MLK hearings, 74 (hereinafter Clark testimony).

[24] Ibid.

[25] Ibid.

[26] FBI memorandum from F. J. Baumgardner to W. C. Sullivan, Aug. 23, 1963, re: Communist Party, USA Negro question, FBI headquarters file 100–3–116–253X.

[27] See, e.g., FBI memorandum from M. A. Jones to Bishop, Mar. 18, 1969, re: Martin Luther King's birthday, FBI headquarters file 100–06670–3586.

[28] Executive session testimony of Alan G. Sentinella, May 25, 1978, House Select Committee on Assassinations pp. 26–27.

[29] FBI memorandum from Atlanta to Director, Apr. 25, 1962, FBI headquarters file 100–5586, 1–5–16670.

[30] FBI memorandum from Director to Atlanta, May 11, 1962, MLK security file 100–6670–(obliterated).

[31] Book III, Senate Intelligence Committee, p. 87.

[32] FBI memorandum from Director to SAC, Atlanta, Oct. 23, 1962, FBI headquarters file 100–438794–(illegible serial).

[33] Executive session testimony of Alan G. Sentinella, May 25, 1978, House Select Committee on Assassinations, pp. 47–50.

[34] FBI memorandum from Baumgardner to Sullivan, Aug. 23, 1963, re: CPUSA-Negro question, FBI headquarters file 100–3–116–253X.

[35] Ibid.

[36] See, e.g., Brennan testimony, p. 154. See also staff summary of interview with David Ryan, July 13, 1978, House Select Comittee on Assassinations, p. 2 (MLK document 230316).

[37] FBI memorandum from Baumgardner to Sullivan, Aug. 23, 1963, re: CPUSA-Negro question, FBI headquarters file 100–3–116–253X.

[38] FBI memorandum from Sullivan to Belmont, Aug. 30, 1963, re: CPUSA-Negro question, FBI headquarters file 100–3–116–253X.

[39] FBI memorandum from Sullivan to Belmont, Dec. 24, 1963, re.: CPUSA-Negro question, CIRM (illegible serial).

[40] Ibid.

[41] FBI memorandum from Sullivan to Belmont, Jan. 8, 1964, FBI headquarters file 77–56944–19.

[42] Id. at 3.

[43] See MLK Exhibit F–442A (FBI memorandum to Sullivan from Bureau, Apr. 18, 1968, indicating electronic surveillance on Dr. King and SCLC until November 1965), VI HSCA–MLK hearings, 181. See also section II D of this report, refs. 38–44, and text, supra, for discussion of committee review of FBI electronic surveillance materials at National Archives.

[44] Brennan testimony, p. 225.

[45] See FBI memorandum, Mar. 4, 1964, from F. J. Baumgardner to W. C. Sullivan, CPUSA-Negro question (serial illegible).

[46] FBI memorandum from C. A. Evans to Alan Belmont, July 16, 1963, Communist influence in racial matters, FBI headquarters file 166–3–116 (illegible); see also FBI memorandum from C. A. Evans to Alan Belmont, Oct. 10,1963, security matter, unrecorded serial.

[47] Memorandum from U.S. Attorney General Brownell to the Director, FBI, re: microphone surveillance, May 20, 1954.

[48] Book III, Senate Intelligence Committee, p. 123.

[49] See MLK Exhibit F-442A (FBI memorandum to Sullivan from Brennan, Apr. 18, 1968), VI HSCA-MLK hearings, 181.

[50] Testimony of Cartha D. DeLoach, Nov. 27, 1978, VII HSCA-MLK Hearings, 24 (hereinafter DeLoach testimony).

[51] Book III, Senate Intelligence Committee, pp. 158-161.

[52] Id. at 180.

[53] Id. at 159.

[54] Id. at 158-161.

[55] See generally Book III, Senate Intelligence Committee, pp. 158-161. See also deposition of Seymour F. Phillips, Sept. 26, 1978, House Select Committee on Assassinations, p. 13.

[56] See, e.g., MLK exhibit F-446A (FBI memorandum from F. J. Baumgardner to William C. Sullivan, Feb. 1, 1965), VI HSCA-MLK hearings, 254; MLK Exhibit F-446E (FBI memorandum from William C. Sullivan to Alan Belmont, Dec. 12, 1964), VI HSCA-MLK hearings, 261; MLK exhibit F-447A (FBI memorandum from F. J. Baumgardner to William C. Sullivan, Mar. 4, 1964), VI HSCA-MLK hearings, 268; MLK exhibit F-447 (FBI memorandum from F. J. Baumgardner to William C. Sullivan, Dec. 29, 1964).

[57] See, e.g., MLK exhibit F-444A (FBI memorandum from F. J. Baumgardner to William C. Sullivan, Oct. 27, 1966), VI HSCA-MLK hearings, 239; MLK exhibit F-444C (FBI memorandum from F. J. Baumgardner to William C. Sullivan, Nov. 3, 1966), VI HSCA-MLK hearings, 249.

[58] MLK exhibit F-451A (FBI memorandum to SAC, Albany from Director, Aug. 25, 1967), VI HSCA-MLK hearings, 298; MLK exhibit F-451B (FBI airtel to SAC Albany from Director, Mar. 4, 1968), VI HSCA-MLK hearings, 301.

[59] FBI memorandum from William C. Sullivan to A. H. Belmont, Nov. 22, 1964, re: Communism and the Negro movement—a current analysis, FBI headquarters file 100-442569-504.

[60] FBI memorandum from C. D. Brennan to William C. Sullivan, Apr. 10, 1967, re: Communist influence in racial matters (illegible serial).

[61] FBI memorandum, Mar. 11, 1968, from G. C. Moore to William C. Sullivan, Martin Luther King, Jr., security matter, FBI headquarters file 100-106670-3526.

[62] See MLK exhibit F-446 A through G (dissemination to religious leaders, VI HSCA-MLK hearings, 254, 256, 257, 259, 263, 265 respectively; F-447 A through D (interference with awards), IV HSCA-MLK hearings, 268, 270, 272, 275 respectively; F-449 A through E (interference with funding), VI HSCA-MLK hearings, 277, 279, 281, 283, 285 respectively.

[63] See MLK exhibits F-444A through F-444D (dissemination to friendly media sources) VI HSCA-MLK hearings, 239, 247, 249, 251 respectively.

[64] Executive session testimony of Thomas E. Bishop, June 21, 1978, House Select Committee on Assassinations, pp. 25-29.

[65] "FBI Tried to Hide Ties with Globe-Democrat," St. Louis Post-Dispatch. Dec. 1, 1977, p. 1-A.

[66] Ibid.

[67] FBI memorandum from SAC St. Louis to Director, FBI, May 28, 1968, re: COINTELPRO-New Left, FBI headquarters file 100-448698-42.

[68] FBI letter from Director to SAC, St. Louis, Oct. 18, 1968;

re: COINTELPRO-New Left, FBI headquarters file 100–449698–42–7.

[69] Staff summary of interview with Denny Walsh, Mar. 5, 1978, House Select Committee on Assassinations (MLK Document 310096).

[70] See MLK Exhibit F–521, from Moore to Sullivan (FBI memorandum, Mar. 28, 1968), VII HSCA–MLK hearings, 108.

[71] Ibid. See also staff summary of interview with Patrick Buchanan, Mar. 5, 1979, House Select Committee on Assassinations (MLK Document 310095); staff summary of interview with G. Duncan Bauman, Feb. 28, 1979, House Select Committee on Assassinations (MLK Document 300223).

[72] Ibid.

[73] Ibid.

[74] See MLK exhibit F–520 ("The Real Martin Luther King," St. Louis Globe-Democrat, Mar. 30–31, 1968, p. C–2), VII HSCA–MLK hearings, 106.

[75] Executive session testimony of Thomas E. Bishop, June 21, 1978, House Select Committee on Assassinations, pp. 43–44.

[76] See, e.g., testimony of James Earl Ray, Aug. 17, 1978, III HSCA–MLK hearings, 98.

[77] Letter from John L. Ray to George McMillan, May 28, 1972 (MLK Document 290033).

[78] Book III, Senate Intelligence Committee, p. 9.

[79] Id. at 48.

[80] Ibid.

[81] The divisions, in numerical order, were: (1) identification; (2) training; (3) administrative; (4) files and communications; (5) domestic intelligence; (6) general investigative; (7) laboratory; (8) crime records; (9) special investigative; (10) inspection.

[82] The text of 18 U.S.C. section 241 is as follows:

Conspiracy against rights of citizens: If two or more persons conspire to injure, oppress, threaten, or intimidate any citizen in the free exercise or enjoyment of any right or privilege secured to him by the Constitution or laws of the United States, or because of his having so exercised the same; or

If two or more persons go in disguise on the highway, or on the premises of another, with intent to prevent or hinder his free exercise or enjoyment of any right or privilege so secured * * * *

[83] See staff summary of interview with Stephen J. Pollak, June 29, 1978, House Select Committee on Assassinations, p. 2 (MLK Document 250279).

[84] Testimony of Stephen J. Pollak, Nov. 28, 1978, VII HSCA–MLK hearings, 142.

[85] FBI memorandum, Rosen to DeLoach, May 2, 1968, FBI headquarters MURKIN file No. 44–38861–2946.

[86] Executive session testimony of Robert Jensen, July 12, 1978, House Select Committee on Assassinations, p. 14.

[87] Staff summary of interview with Cartha DeLoach, June 26, 1978, House Select Committee on Assassinations, p. 2 (MLK Document 230174).

[88] Clark testimony, p. 11.

[89] Id. at 12. See also memorandum, Stephen J. Pollak to Director, FBI, Apr. 14, 1968, FBI headquarters MURKIN file No. 44–38861–109. Pollak's memorandum read, in its entirety, as follows: "I have been advised by telephone that Dr. Martin Luther King

was this date shot and wounded by an unidentified person or persons in Memphis, Tennessee, where he travelled to lead a demonstration march scheduled for April 8, 1968.

"Please conduct a full investigation into a possible violation of 18 U.S.C. 241 and keep me currently advised of all developments."

[90] See, e.g., staff summary of interview with Robert Jensen, June 20, 1978, House Select Committee on Assassinations, p. 3 (MLK Document 190108).

[91] Staff summary of interview with Richard E. Long, June 2, 1978, House Select Committee on Assassinations, p. 2 (MLK Document 260327).

[92] FBI memorandum, McGowan to Rosen, Apr. 4, 1968; FBI headquarters MURKIN file No. 44–38861–327.

[93] Staff summary of interview with Clem McGowan, June 13, 1978, House Select Committee on Assassinations, pp. 3–4 (MLK Document 220469).

[94] FBI memorandum, Rosen to DeLoach, Apr. 6, 1968, FBI headquarters MURKIN file No. 44–38861–329.

[95] FBI memorandum, Rosen to DeLoach, Apr. 5, 1968, FBI headquarters MURKIN file No. 44–38861–177.

[96] FBI memorandum, Rosen to DeLoach, Apr. 6, 1968, FBI headquarters MURKIN file No. 44–38861–329.

[97] FBI teletype, Director to all continental offices, Apr. 8, 1968, FBI headquarters MURKIN file No. 44–38861–158.

[98] FBI memorandum, Rosen to DeLoach, Apr. 12, 1967, FBI headquarters MURKIN file No. 44–38861–1113.

[99] FBI memorandum, Rosen to DeLoach, Apr. 18, 1968, FBI headquarters MURKIN file No. 44–38861–1367.

[100] FBI teletype, Director to all SAC's, Apr. 18, 1969, FBI headquarters MURKIN file No. 44–38861–1271.

[101] FBI memorandum, C. L. Trotter to Mohr, Sept. 2, 1969, FBI headquarters MURKIN file No. 44–38861–5818.

[102] Ibid.

[103] Ibid.

[104] Much of the public concern is based on the erroneous impression that fingerprint identification is an entirely computerized process. In fact, while computers are of great assistance in many aspects of the comparison process (for example in searching a large number of records for prints of a specific type or characteristic), the actual comparison of a latent print with known set of prints is still done manually.

[105] FBI memorandum, Rosen to DeLoach, Apr. 19, 1968, FBI headquarters MURKIN file No. 44–38861–4046 (insert attached).

[106] FBI memorandum, Rosen to DeLoach, Apr. 19, 1968, FBI headquarters MURKIN file No. 44–38861–1727.

[107] FBI teletype, Director to all SAC's, Apr. 19, 1968, FBI headquarters MURKIN file No. 44–38861–1396.

[108] FBI memorandum, Jones to Bishop, Apr. 19, 1968, FBI headquarters MURKIN file No. 44–38861–1938.

[109] FBI memorandum, Jones to Bishop, Apr. 25, 1968, FBI headquarters MURKIN file No. 44–38861–2584.

[110] See, e.g., FBI teletype, Director to all SAC's, Apr. 27, 1968, FBI Miami Field Office MURKIN file No. 44–1854–614.

[111] See, e.g., FBI headquarters MURKIN file No. 44–38861–2324 (summarizing 1 month's investigation in the Atlanta Field Office).

[112] FBI teletype, Director to SAC's Chicago, Kansas City, St. Louis, Springfield, May 1, 1968, FBI headquarters MURKIN file No. 44-38861-2622.

[113] See, e.g., staff summary of interview with Ramsey Clark, June 21, 1978, House Select Committee on Assassinations, p. 4 (MLK Document 220473).

[114] FBI memorandum, Director to Attorney General, May 13, 1968, FBI headquarters MURKIN file No. 44-38861-3509.

[115] Ibid.

[116] FBI memorandum, J. J. Casper to Mohr, May 10, 1968, FBI headquarters MURKIN file No. 44-38841-3763.

[117] Ibid.

[118] Staff summary of interview with Harold Dobson, June 28, 1978, pp. 2-3 (MLK Document 230396).

[119] FBI memorandum, Director to Attorney General, June 11, 1968, captioned "Electronic Surveillance", FBI headquarters MURKIN file No. 44-38861- (nonrecorded serial).

[120] DeLoach testimony, p. 78.

[121] Ibid.

[121] Id. at 79.

[123] Id. at 81.

[124] FBI interview with John Larry Ray, May 9, 1968, St. Louis Field Office MURKIN file No. 44-775.

[125] See, e.g., memorandum, Rosen to DeLoach, May 10, 1968, FBI headquarters MURKIN file No. 44-38861-3510.

[126] FBI memorandum, Rosen to DeLoach, May 10, 1968, FBI headquarters MURKIN file No. 44-38861-3510.

[127] Correspondence, Director to Ottawa Legat, May 11, 1968, FBI Memphis Field Office MURKIN file No. 44-1987, Sub. L-75.

[128] FBI teletype, Director to SAC's Memphis, Buffalo, and Legat Ottawa, June 5, 1968, FBI headquarters MURKIN file No. 44-38861-4725.

[129] FBI memorandum, Hoover to Tolson, DeLoach, Rosen, Bishop, Sullivan, June 20, 1968, FBI headquarters MURKIN file No. 44-38861-4660, p. 5.

[130] Staff summary of interview with Ramsey Clark, June 21, 1978, p. 3 (MLK Document 220473). See also Clark testimony, pp. 16-19, Ray's statement to the Aeromarine clerk and his purpose in discussing filing the Birmingham complaint charging Ray with conspiracy to interfere with Dr. King's civil rights.

[131] Id. at 18.

[132] FBI teletype, Director to all SAC's, Apr. 26, 1968, FBI headquarters MURKIN file No. 44-38861-2288.

[133] FBI memorandum, McGowan to Rosen, June 18, 1968, FBI headquarters MURKIN file No. 44-38861-4578.

[134] See, e.g., FBI airtel, SAC, Memphis to SAC, New Orleans, Mar. 5, 1969, FBI Memphis Field Office MURKIN file No. 44-1987-Sub. M-423.

[135] See, e.g., FBI teletype, Charlotte to Director, Apr. 29, 1968, FBI headquarters MURKIN file No. 44-38861-2747.

[136] FBI memorandum, Rosen to DeLoach, Aug. 26, 1968, FBI headquarters MURKIN file No. 44-38861-5120.

[137] FBI memorandum, Branigan to Sullivan, June 14, 1968, FBI headquarters MURKIN file No. 44-38861-4682.

[138] The FBI did, on one occasion, request that the Department consider issuing a grand jury subpena as one possible means of

785

securing the notes of the author William Bradford Huie. For a discussion of the Department's response to this proposal, see "An Analysis of the Assassination Invetigation of the Department of Justice and the Federal Bureau of Investigation," staff report, XIII Appendix to the HSCA–MLK hearings.

[139] DeLoach testimony, p. 51.

[140] Id. at 50–51.

[141] Id. at 51.

[142] Id. at 52.

[143] Clark testimony, p. 53.

[144] Article, New York Times, June 20, 1968, p. 23 (incorporating text of President's statement in signing title III into law).

[145] See, e.g., 144 Cong. Record 1629–98 (June 6, 1968, remarks of Pollak).

[146] Clark testimony, Nov. 28, 1978, VII HSCA–MLK hearings, p. 43.

[147] FBI airtel, Director to SAC, Memphis, Aug. 14, 1968, FBI headquarters MURKIN file No. 44–38861–5073.

[148] FBI interview with Mrs. Marguerita Welch, Apr. 24, 1968, FBI Chicago MURKIN file No. 44–1114.

[149] FBI airtel, SAC, New Orleans to Director, Mar. 18, 1969, FBI headquarters MURKIN file No. 44–38861–5661.

[150] Ibid.

[151] FBI airtel, Director to SAC's, New Orleans and Memphis, Mar. 26, 1969, FBI headquarters MURKIN file No. 44–38861–5661.

[151a] Executive session testimony of witness A, Dec. 13, 1978, House Select Committee on Assassinations, pp. 6–8.

[152] Testimony of Capt. Billie J. Smith, evidentiary hearing on defense motion to modify conditions of confinement, Sept. 30, 1978 (MLK Document 110337).

[153] FBI teletype, Memphis to Director, Sept. 30, 1968, FBI headquarters MURKIN file No. 44–38861–5209.

[154] See, e.g., memorandum, SAC, Memphis, to Director, Oct. 11, 1968, and attached communications, FBI headquarters MURKIN file No. 44–38861–5235; memorandum, SAC, Memphis, to Director, Oct. 14, 1968, and attached communications, FBI headquarters MURKIN file No. 44–38861–5242; FBI airtel, SAC, Memphis, to Director, Oct. 24, 1968, and attached communications, FBI headquarters MURKIN file No. 44–38861–5327.

[155] FBI airtel, SAC, Memphis, to Director, Oct. 24, 1968, FBI headquarters MURKIN file No. 44–38861–5327.

[156] See staff summary of interview with Robert Jensen, June 20, 1978 (MLK Document 190108); see also executive session testimony of Robert Jensen, July 12, 1978, House Select Committee on Assassinations, pp. 47–49.

[157] Executive session testimony of Robert Jensen, July 12, 1978, House Select Committee on Assassinations, pp. 50–51.

[158] Staff summary of interview with William Morris, Nov. 21, 1978 (MLK Document 270327).

[159] Executive session testimony of Robert Jensen, July 12, 1978, House Select Committee on Assassinations, p. 51.

[160] Id. at 55.

[161] Ibid.

[162] Id. at 54.

[163] Ibid. at p. 54; Cartha DeLoach had no recollection of any activity in Memphis which might have intruded upon Ray's attorney/

client privilege. (Staff interview with C. DeLoach, June 26, 1978 (MLK Document 230174). Alex Rosen, Assistant Director of the General Investigative Division, did not recall seeing either the Sept. 30, 1968, Memphis airtel detailing Battle's order, or the three letters which followed in apparent contravention of the order. He recognized his initials on the Oct. 31, 1968 headquarters directive to Memphis, but had no independent recollection of the situation that had triggered the directive. Staff interview with Aex Rosen, June 28, 1978 (MLK Document 210237).

Finally, neither Attorney General Clark (executive session testimony of Ramsey Clark, July, 19, 1978, at pp. 89–92) nor Shelby County District Attorney Canale knew of any activity constituting an infringement of Ray's attroney/client privilege.

[164] Ibid.

[165] FBI airtel, Director to SAC, Memphis, Oct. 31, 1968, FBI headquarters MURKIN file No. 44–38861–5310.

[166] FBI memorandum, Rosen to DeLoach, Mar. 11, 1969, p. 1, FBI headquarters MURKIN file No. 44–38861–5612.

[167 Memorandum, Rosen to DeLoach, Mar. 11, 1969, FBI headquarters MURKIN file, serial 44–38861–5612.

[168] FBI airtel, SAC, Houston, to SAC, Memphis, Mar. 12, 1969, FBI Memphis MURKIN file No. 44–1987–Sub. M–447.

[169] FBI memorandum, Rosen to DeLoach, Mar. 12, 1969, FBI headquarters MURKIN file No. 44–38861–5639.

[170] FBI memorandum, Rosen to DeLoach, Mar. 13, 1969, FBI headquarters MURKIN file No. 44–38861–5615.

[171] FBI teletype, Memphis to Director, Mar. 13, 1969, FBI headquarters MURKIN file No. 44–38861–5622.

[172] Staff summary of interview with Robert Jensen, Oct. 8, 1978 (MLK Document 260328).

[173] See, generally, DeLoach testimony, pp. 29–31.

[174] Executive session testimony of Ramsey Clark, July 19, 1978, House Select Committee on Assassinations, p. 63.

[175] See, e.g., staff summary of interview with Wilbur Martindale (former Chief of the Civil Rights Act of 1964 Unit), June 15, 1978 (MLK Document 220471); staff summary of interview with Fred Vinson, Jr. (former Assistant Attorney General of the Criminal Division, Department, Department of Justice), June 30, 1978 (MLK Document 230183); staff summary of interview with Stephen J. Pollak (former Assistant Attorney General of Civil Rights Division, Department of Justice), June 30, 1978 (MLK Document 250279).

III. RECOMMENDATIONS OF THE COMMITTEE

[1] "Assassination and Political Violence," a report to the National Commission on the Causes and Prevention of Violence (Washington, D.C.: U.S. Government Printing Office, 1969), vol. 8, p. 45 (hereafter Assassiation Report).

[2] Id. at 124.

[3] "To Establish Justice, To Insure Domestic Tranquility," final report of the National Commission on the Causes and Prevention of Violence (Washington, D.C.: U.S. Government Printing Office, 1969), p. xxiii (hereinafter Violence Commission Report).

[4] Assassination Report, p. 10.

[5] Id. at 1.

[6] Id. at 2–5.

[7] Violence Commission Report, p. 125.

[8] Assassination Report, p. 11.

[9] See generally Charles H. Whittier, Congressional Research Service, Library of Congress, "Assassination in Theory and Practice: A Historical Survey of the Religious and Philosophical Background of the Doctrine of Tyrannicide," Apr. 12, 1978 (JFK Document 007559).

[10] Violence Commission Report, pp. 2–16.

[11] Id. at 127–28.

[12] See generally R. Rothman, Congresional Research Service, Library of Congress, "The Social and Political Implications of the Assassinations of John F. Kennedy and Martin Luther King, Jr." (MLK Document 260029).

[13] Violence Commission Report, p. xix.

[14] See testimony of Richard M. Helms, Sept. 22, 1978, hearings before the Select Committee on Assassinations, U.S. House of Representatives, 95th Congress, 2d session (Washington, D.C.: U.S. Government Printing Office, 1979), vol. IV, pp. 118–161 (hereinafter Helms testimony, —HSCA–JFK hearings, —); testimony of Santos Trafficante, Jr., Sept. 27, 1978, V HSCA–JFK hearings 357–364.

[15] Id., Helms testimony at 180–81.

[16] Executive Order 12036, sec. 2.305 (Jan. 24, 1978).

[17] As enacted by Public Law 92–539 in 1972, 18 U.S.C. § 1116 extended the protection of Federal law to foreign officials or guests in the United States. Public Law 94–467, enacted in 1976, broadens that protection to include an "internationally protected person," defined to include a Chief of State whenever he was "in a country other than his own." Even though the offender might be subject to Federal criminal jurisdiction, if the assassination occurred in the Chief of State's own country, it would not fall within the scope of the statute.

[18] S. 1437, 15th Congress, 1st session § 1202 (1977).

[19] Testimony of Benjamin R. Civiletti, "Legislative and Ad-

ministrative Reform," hearings before the Select Committee on Assassnations, U.S. House of Representatives, 95th Congress, 2d session (Washington, D.C.: U.S. Government Printing Office, 1979), vol. I, pp. 112–136 (hereinafter Reform).

[20] See generally Murl Larkin, Congressional Research Service, Library of Congress, "Federal Homicide: Public Figures," May 15, 1978 (JFK Document 008417) (hereinafter Larkin).

[21] If the President had been killed as a result of a conspiracy, it would have violated 18 U.S.C. § 372; if the murder had occurred within the special maritime or territorial jurisdiction of the United States, it would have violated 18 U.S.C. §§ 1111(b), 1112(b). Other statutes that might have been involved include 18 U.S.C. §§ 241, 242.

[22] Report of the President's Commission on the Assassination of President Kennedy (Washington, D.C.: U.S. Government Printing Office, 1964), p. 455 (hereinafter Warren Report).

[23] 18 U.S.C. § 1114.

[24] Warren Report, pp. 455–56.

[25] Larkin, pp. 10–11.

[26] See, e.g., 18 U.S.C. § 1114.

[27] S. 1437, 95th Congress, 1st session § 1601 (e) (2) (A) (1977).

[28] Testimony of William Webster, Reform, p. 4.

[29] Id. at 31.

[30] Testimony of Benjamin Civiletti, Reform, pp. 134–35.

[31] Testimony of William Webster, Reform, p. 31.

[32] See Larkin, pp. 15–19.

[33] Testimony of Stuart Knight, Reform, p. 108; testimony of William Webster, Reform, p. 32.

[34] Testimony of Benjamin Civiletti, Reform, p. 128.

[35] Id. at 112, 122, 129–30.

[36] Warren Report, pp. 455–56.

[37] Testimony of Benjamin Civiletti, Reform, p. 126; testimony of William Webster, Reform, p. 25.

[38] Testimony of Stuart Knight, Reform, p. 97.

[39] See also testimony of Stuart Knight, Reform, p. 97; testimony of William Webster, Reform, p. 25.

[40] Testimony of Stuart Knight, Reform, p. 97 (should be presumption of exercise); testimony of Benjamin Civiletti, Reform, p. 132 (should be automatic); testimony of William Webster, Reform, p. 25 (automatic).

[41] Testimony of William Webster, Reform, p. 22; see Kent M. Ronhoude, Congressional Research Service, Library of Congress, "Disposition of the Remains of Victims of Federally Cognizable Homicides," Dec. 18, 1978 (JFK Document 015785).

[42] Testimony of Benjamin Civiletti, Reform, p. 133; testimony of William Webster, Reform, p. 7.

[43] Testimony of William Webster, Reform, p. 28 (concern expressed over possible extension of language).

[44] Testimony of Stuart Knight, Reform, p. 105 (Director of FBI); testimony of William Webster, Reform, p. 25 (Attorney General).

[45] Testimony of Stuart Knight, Reform, p. 106.

[46] 18 U.S.C. § 2509.

[47] See generally Kent M. Ronhoude, Congressional Research Service, Library of Congress, "Government Acquisition of Evidence

Pertaining to the Assassination of President Kennedy and Related Matters," Dec. 11, 1978.

[48] *United States* v. *One 6.5 mm Mannlicher-Carcano Military Rifle*, 250 F. Supp. 410 (N.D. Tex. 1966), *rev'd, King* v *United States*, 364 F. 2d 235 (5th Cir. 1966). See *King* v. *United States*, 292 F. Supp. 767 (D. Colo. 1968).

[49] See 15 U.S.C. 905(b) for the relevant statute then in effect. The relevant statute today is 18 U.S.C. § 924(d).

[50] See *Porter* v. *United States*, 335 F. Supp. 498 (N.D. Tex. 1971) *rev'd, Porter* v. *United States*, 473 F. 2d 1329 (5th 1973) (entitled to realized value related to assassination).

[51] *Nichols* v. *United States*, 325 F. Supp. 130 (D. Kans. 1971), *aff'd* 460 F. 2d 671 (10th Cir. 1972). See testimony of Benjamin Civiletti, Reform, pp. 145–146 (need for general legislation).

[52] Testimony of Percy Foreman, Nov. 13, 1978, V HSCA–MLK hearings, 297–298.

[53] See generally Nancy Lee Jones, Congressional Research Service, Library of Congress, "Constitutional Analysis of a New York Statute Requiring Funds Received by Alleged Criminals for Certain Purposes to be Given to Their Victims," Sept. 8, 1977.

[54] 18 U.S.C. § 871.

[55] 18 U.S.C. § 1752.

[56] Testimony of Stuart Knight, Reform, pp. 96–97.

[57] Testimony of William Webster, Reform, p. 12. On the other hand, testimony before the committee raised questions that these guidelines might be too restrictive. Testimony of Stuart Knight, Reform, pp. 93–94 (too restrictive); testimony of William Webster, Reform, p. 11 (tight, but "one of the assumed risks that we take in a free society"); testimony of Benjamin Civiletti, Reform, pp. 119–120 (quality if not quantity is sufficient).

[58] 50 U.S.C. § 403(d)(3). See *Heine* v. *Raus*, 399 F. 2d 785 (4th ed. 1968).

[59] See VIII J. Wigmore evidence § 237Y (3d ed. 1940).

[60] See, e.g., Right to Financial Privacy Act of 1978.

[61] 18 U.S.C. § 3146.

[62] 18 U.S.C. § 3161.

[63] Testimony of William Webster, Reform, p. 7.

[64] Ibid.

[65] Ibid.

[66] Id. at 18.

[67] Testimony of Stuart Knight, Reform, pp 109–110.

[68] Testimony of William Webster, Reform, p. 37.

[69] Ibid.

[70] Ibid.

[71] Testimony of William Webster, Reform, p. 19.

[72] Id. at 22.

[73] Id. at 28.

[74] 28 U.S.C. 591–98.

[75] See, e.g., the questioning of Chairman Louis Stokes, Reform, pp. 42–43.

[76] Testimony of Stuart Knight, Reform, p. 109; testimony of Benjamin Civiletti, Reform, pp. 131–132; testimony of William Webster, Reform, p. 43; testimony of Frank Carlucci, Reform, p. 87.

[77] Testimony of William Webster, Reform, p. 41.

[78] Id. at 42.

[79] Testimony of Frank Carlucci, Reform, p. 52.

[80] See, e.g., questioning of Chairman Louis Stokes, Reform, p. 23.

[81] Testimony of William Webster, Reform, p. 6.

[82] Testimony of William Webster, Reform, p. 23.

[83] Testimony of Benjamin Civiletti, Reform, p. 131.

[84] Warren report, pp. 231–240.

[85] Testimony of William Webster, Reform, p. 34.

[86] Testimony of Benjamin Civiletti, Reform, p. 139.

[87] Testimony of Stuart Knight, Reform, pp. 106–108.

[88] See e.g., questioning of Congressman Richardson Preyer, Reform, p. 106. Civiletti, Reform, p. 142.

[89] Testimony of William Webster, Reform, p. 35; testimony of Benjamin Civiletti, Reform, p. 142.

[90] Testimony of William Webster, Reform, p. 35.

[91] Ibid.

[92] Testimony of Benjamin Civiletti, Reform, p. 142.

[93] See generally "The Constitution of the United States of America: Analysis and Interpretation," Doc. No. 92–82, 92d Congress, 2d session (Washington, D.C.: U.S. Government Printing Office, 1973), p. 79 (hereinafter Analysis); Arthur S. Schlesinger and Roger Burns, eds., "Congress Investigates: A Documented History 1792–1974" (New York: Chelsea House Publishers, 1975), vol. I, pp. xvii–xviii (hereinafter Investigations).

[94] John Mill, "Considerations on Representative Government," (South Bend, Ind.: Gateway edition, 1962), p. 11.

[95] Woodrow Wilson, "Congressional Government" (Magnolia, Mass.: Peter Smith Publishers, Inc., 1958), p. 303.

[96] Ibid.

[97] Quoted in Investigations, p. xix.

[98] See generally Investigations, pp. 3–101.

[99] Analysis, p. 83.

[100] See 123 Congressional Record H 10256 (daily ed., Aug. 28, 1977) for an extended discussion of the implications of that statute for congressional investigations.

[101] 18 U.S.C. 6001–05.

[102] House rule XI, cl. 2, K(3).

[103] Committee rule 3.7.

[104] House rule XI, cl 2(K) (4).

[105] Code of Professional Responsibility ABA, Canon 5, DR5–105.

[106] See, e.g., *United States* v. *Dolan*, 22 Crim. L. Reprt. (3d Cir. Jan. 23, 1978).

[107] "Watergate Special Prosecution Force Report" 140–41 (1975) (Washington, D.C.: U.S. Government Printing Office, 1975), pp. 140–141.

[108] 28 U.S.C. 2241 (c) (5).

[109] Legal Documents Relating to the Select Committee Hearings, Appendix to the Hearings of the Senate Select Committee on Presidential Campaign Activities, 93d Congress, 1st and 2d sessions (Washington, D.C.: U.S. Government Printing Office, 1974), pp. 2156–2157.

[110] See *Carbo* v. *United States*, 314 U.S. 611 (961).

[111] *Eastland* v. *United States Serviceman's Fund*, 421 U.S. 491 (1975).

[12] The Comprehensive Alcohol Abuse and Alcoholism Preventive Treatment and Rehabilitation Act, 42 U.S.C. 4582.

[113] See 112 Congressional Record H 10255 (daily ed., Sept. 28, 1977).

[114] See S. Rept. No. 95–127, 95th Congress, 2d session 80 (1978).

[115] Constitution, Jefferson's Manual and Rules of the House of Representatives, H. Doc. 94–663, 94th Congress, 2d session 427–28 (Washington, D.C.: U.S. Government Printing Office, 1977).

[116] Rule 13.11, Select Committee on Assassinations.

[117] Letter of C. J. Leontes to Michael Goldsmith, Sept. 11, 1978, House Select Committee on Assassinations (JFK Document 014203).

[118] Ibid.